# Handbook of Gender, Work, and Organization

# HANDBOOK OF GENDER, WORK, AND ORGANIZATION

*Edited by*

EMMA L JEANES, DAVID KNIGHTS,
AND PATRICIA YANCEY MARTIN

A John Wiley and Sons, Ltd, Publication

This edition first published in 2011
Copyright © 2011 John Wiley & Sons Ltd

*Registered office*
John Wiley & Sons Ltd, The Atrium, Southern Gate, Chichester, West Sussex, PO19 8SQ,
United Kingdom

For details of our global editorial offices, for customer services and for information about how to apply
for permission to reuse the copyright material in this book please see our website at www.wiley.com

ISBN 978-1-444-39472-6 (hardback)
ISBN 978-1-119-99079-6 (ebk)
ISBN 978-0-470-97926-6 (ebk)
ISBN 978-0-470-97927-3 (ebk)

A catalogue record for this book is available from the British Library.

Typeset in 10/12 New Baskerville by MPS Limited, a Macmillan Company, Chennai, India
Printed in Great Britain by CPI Antony Rowe, Chippenham, Wiltshire

# Contents

# Editorial Introduction to Handbook of Gender, Work, and Organization

## I. Background

As with many projects, this book had a serendipitous genesis in the sense that it was first proposed by the commissioning editor of a publisher who eventually was not the one with whom we agreed a contract. It started when the editor who wished to produce a Handbook of Gender and Organization approached Emma as a potential editor. Emma suggested approaching David since he had founded and edited the journal *Gender, Work and Organization* (GWO). In developing the proposal, it was agreed that alternative publishers should be reviewed and Blackwell became the obvious choice because of its ties to the journal. Shortly afterwards it was decided that an American co-editor should be part of the project. Upon being invited, Patricia agreed to be involved. Inevitably the project grew and developed along the way but we were pleased with the response to an initial call for chapters, with many notable scholars from across the globe accepting our invitation. Their participation has resulted, we trust, in a Handbook that makes a material contribution to the field of Gender, Work, and Organization.

Apart from the publicity potential, one reason for linking the Handbook to the journal relates to the reason for establishing the journal in the first place, although once again serendipity played a part. As with the Handbook, the publisher (Blackwell) approached Marilyn Davidson, David Knights, and Jill Rubery – at the Manchester School of Management – because they saw a niche for a professional journal on gender and equal opportunity that could bridge the academic–practitioner divide. They had in mind a journal something like *Personnel Review* with a focus on equal opportunity and a readership of personnel managers as much as academics. This prompted somewhat heated discussions whereby Jill and David agreed to continue negotiations only as long as the project was to develop a fully refereed academic journal (Marilyn withdrew from involvement due to a potential conflict of interests as she was the editor of *Women in Management*). Jill is a labour economist with a strong focus on sex discrimination and David, an organizational sociologist who had conducted research on race and sex discrimination. The title for the journal reflected the interests of the two editors. However, it was also believed that during the 1970s, the contraction of sociology departments and expansion of management and business studies had resulted in an influx of sociologists to business schools, thus creating a potential academic market for the journal's content. At the time, the proportion of women academics was increasing rapidly, and largely because of sex discrimination and the rise of feminism many academics, especially but not only women, had direct or indirect interest in issues of equal opportunity and gender.

During the first couple of years, the journal struggled to secure sufficient high quality copy but the introduction of the UK Research Assessment Exercise (RAE)[1] combined with increasing numbers of social scientists and women in business or management schools helped resolve these problems. It steadily increased in circulation and status and after around 10 years of existence, secured Institute for Scientific Information (ISI) recognition.[2] Since then, GWO has enjoyed a 1+ impact factor and a second from the top ranking in the UK assessments for the RAE. At the time of writing, it is rated highly among women's studies journals worldwide (8th of 29) and respectably among management journals (54th of 89).[3] The journal's impact indicates the importance of studies that link the issues of gender, work and organization.

When Jill resigned as co-editor in 2003, David ran the journal for a year before securing an agreement with Blackwell for Deborah Kerfoot to share the editorship. Although eclectic in terms of focus, the journal was developed to advance an intellectual and theoretical stance that made it distinct from journals concerned primarily with equal opportunity for women. That is, it sought to address critically a broad feminist discourse that not only included theoretical and empirical analyses of women and femininities in relation to work and organization but also of men and masculinities in the same regard. Its popularity as a platform for publication expanded and was facilitated by what was to become a biennial international conference, the first of which was held in 1993. The popularity of the conferences demonstrates,

---

[1] Any journal at this time benefited from the introduction of the Research Assessment Exercise (RAE) by the UK government that was intended to raise the productivity of academics and eradicate professional restrictive practices. From there on the publication and other research outputs of academics were evaluated every four years and so it became increasingly important to secure publications in refereed journals.

[2] The ISI database contains 16 000 international journals, books, and proceedings in the sciences, social sciences, and arts and humanities. ISI publishes the Science Citation Index. The basic mission of ISI as a database publishing company is to provide comprehensive coverage of the world's most important and influential research. An important part of this data is the 8600 international journals that ISI covers on an annual basis. ISI indexes complete bibliographic data for every item covered, including English-language author abstracts, author and publisher addresses, as well as the cited references of every journal.

[3] Of course as a critical journal that seeks to challenge the Establishment, the editors have mixed feelings about this publisher and its academic-driven preoccupation with the rankings. To ignore them completely, however, is likely to leave the journal and its field forever reflecting the marginalized status of its subject matter.

we suggest, that a large nucleus of academics are interested in gender, work, and organization.

Following a trend in other journals, many Special Issues (SIs) have been published over the years reflecting some of the key debates within the field. Among the issues that have been covered are debates on gender relating to academic careers (Krefting and Richards, 2003), binaries and boundaries (Linstead and Brewis, 2004), emotion (Knights and Surman, 2008), ethnicity (Calás et al., 2010), leadership, service work (Kerfoot and Korcyzynski, 2005), sexual spaces (Pullen and Thanem, 2010), time (Sabelis et al., 2008), undoing gender (Pullen and Knights, 2007), gender as practice (Poggio, 2006), and work–life balance (Gregory and Milner, 2009). Several chapters in the Handbook reflect many of these debates and extend beyond them to include some of the latest thinking in gender and feminist theory, the relationship of gender discourses to issues of the body and embodiment, diversity, globalization, and the gendered organization. In 2002, the journal moved from four to five issues per year and in 2004 from five to six issues per year. In 2010, the journal enjoyed its 17th year of publication and, given the growing audience for the field, is continuing to expand globally with increasing demand from the economies of Asia and Latin America. These developments, which reflect a goal of understanding the diversity of experiences beyond a Western perspective, are particularly exciting.

The growing interest in this field of study demonstrates that issues of gender, work and organization remain a fruitful area of study. Concerns such as achieving fairness and equality in work and organizing practices (at work and outside work) remain unresolved and are often at the heart of research in this field. However the ways in which we have theorized and studied these challenges has been transformed over the years, as can be seen by the range of papers and special issues in the journal. For this reason, we trust the Handbook provides a timely opportunity for taking stock of the field and reflecting on the answers to such questions as: Where are we now? Where are we going? What remains to be done?

## II. Reflections on Gender, Work, and Organization

According to Mary Jo Hatch (2010), nearly all theories of organizations and management ignore gender. It's not that they initially consider gender and then dismiss it (or other categorical distinctions). Rather, they are silent about gender, implicitly communicating that it is not an issue. They imply also that people are hired, assigned, evaluated, and rewarded (including promotions and pay rises) solely on the basis of their so-called objective qualifications and performance, not their gender, race/ethnicity, age, or social class. Yet, a large body of research documents the effects of gender (and other such characteristics) on work relations and interactions, including organizational policies and structures, in ways that belie any claims to 'objectivity' or 'gender neutrality' (Cockburn, 1988; Collinson, Knights, and Collinson, 1990; Roper, 1994; Pierce, 1995). Despite that research, hegemonic theories endure, remaining silent on gender, and thereby de-legitimating it as an issue and undermining assertions by any woman or man who believes she/he was discriminated against as a result of gendered institutionalized or interpersonal practices.

People who make such a claim, furthermore, are apt to find their associates not supporting them and possibly assuming that the problem lies with the complainer rather than the rules, routines, norms, or practices of the organization (J. Martin and Knopoff ,1997; see also Korvajärvi, this volume; J. Martin, this volume).

In sum, judgments at work about competence, performance, and related organizational dynamics are reflections of power relations and, as a result, are extensively conflated with the gender institution (Collinson and Hearn, 1996; Acker, this volume). No doubt, some gendered aspects of organizations have benign effects but others produce real harm (Fletcher, 1999; J. Martin, 1990). Harm is often done, furthermore, even when no one intends it. Multiple chapters in this Handbook substantiate these claims.

If key theories fail to shed light on how gender relates to work, organization, and management in a rapidly globalizing world, what can we do? Raewyn Connell (2007) says we must create new theories and new research agendas. We must interrogate and challenge the status quo and figure out the 'whats, whens, hows, and whys' of gender relations relative to knowledge creation and other kinds of work. Considerable progress in this regard has been made as evidenced by research on gendered work, gendered labour markets, gendered organizations, gendered management, gendering practices and dynamics, gendered leadership, and critical studies of masculinity/ies. Furthermore, scholarship on gender has encouraged researchers to think differently about other categorical distinctions such as race, ethnicity, age, sexual orientation, religion, able-bodiedness, and appearance. Future scholarship will, we hope, address these issues further and link them with each other, as some authors in this volume do.

Marxist analysis has long focused on social class in relation to work and organizations, although outside of a theoretical theory literature (see Cox, 1948; Higginbotham and Romer, 1997) and a Marxist Feminist literature (see Kuhn and Wolpe, 1978; Barrett, 1981) and has also (largely) ignored gender and race/ethnicity (J. Martin, 2001). Joan Acker's recent book, *Class Questions: Feminist Answers* (2006), integrates work on gender and race/ethnicity with that on social class to frame large organizations as inequality regimes. Acker explains that organizations are a key mechanism by which societal inequalities are created. Sex- and race-segregation of jobs and positions is one method and subtle dynamics associated with gendered perceptions and interactions are another (Blomberg, 2009). Organizations create social class disparities by (in part) segregating/crowding women and race/ethnic minority men into lower level positions and denying them opportunities, power, and control over resources. When they offer more opportunities and benefits to men than to women, to Westerners than to non-Westerners, to heterosexuals than to those with other sexual preferences, and so on, they create or reproduce inequality inside the organization and economic and social inequality in the society. Since much of today's social, cultural, political, and economic life is transacted in organizations (Perrow, 1991), viewing organizations as inequality regimes offers a window on how societal inequality is created and how it may be challenged. Several chapters in this Handbook expand on these themes (Bird and Rhoton; Benschop and Verloo J. Martin; Omanović).

Besides functioning as inequality regimes, most large organizations embrace a principle of corporate non-responsibility, in refusing to take responsibility for their workers other than to hire and pay them, according to Acker (2006). Many refuse to assume responsibility for their communities also, including the physical environment (e.g. use of scarce water or pollution of water) and societal resources on which they depend – an able workforce, potable water, public hygiene, paved motorways, airports, railways, ships. Their obligation is, they say, to shareholders and profits. Due to the pervasiveness of organizations and a refusal to assume responsibility for their members' family obligations and society's infrastructure, even though they need both to function, they often exacerbate rather than help resolve the social, cultural, economic, and environmental problems that beset the planet (although corporate social responsibility initiatives, which are expanding globally, may eventually produce positive effects).

## Gender, work, and organizations

In the 1980s, sociologists and management scholars began addressing gender in relation to jobs, occupations, organizations, and management.[4] Some noted the uneven distributions of women and men across jobs, positions, and organizations (e.g. Baron and Bielby, 1985; Bielby and Baron, 1986; Wharton and Baron, 1987) while others analysed how gendered ideology, stereotypes, and practices foster these results. Besides reporting statistics, e.g. nearly all managers are men and nearly all secretaries are women (cf. Kanter, 1977), they brought bodies and sexuality into the picture (e.g. Pringle, 1989; Hearn and Parkin, 1983), and they began focusing on gender dynamics (see below).

An early effort to make gender at work visible came from Joan Acker and Donald Van Houten (1974) critiquing the famous Westinghouse/Hawthorne wiring room experiments (Roethlisberger, Dickson, and Wright, 1939). Acker and Van Houten alleged that the pliability of workers in the experiments was due not only to the *Hawthorne effect* associated with heightened recognition and being the focus of the researchers' attention but also to (some) participants being women. For various reasons, they argued, women are assumed to be easier to control than men and more apt to work under poor conditions (e.g. in part because they have fewer options, rights, and opportunities; cf. Cockburn, 1988), thus suggesting that the researchers failed to consider women's greater compliance. Workers are not gender-free or dis-embodied, they said; workers have a gender and management often uses it for various ends (Acker and Van Houten, 1974). Even today, preferences for women and men in some jobs and positions are justified by reference to the superior 'fit' or qualifications of one gender over the other, even when research contradicts the claim. Some 16 years after that article, Acker (1990) published 'Hierarchies, Jobs, and Bodies: Toward a Theory of Gendered Organizations' in which she theorized gender in relation to 'embodied' workers and organizational jobs and hierarchies.

---

[4] Sex (male/female) as a basis for inequality in organizations was addressed as early as the 1970s but because 'sex' was often assumed to refer to biology, inequality scholars appropriated the term 'gender' which allowed them to focus on cultural, social, and political dynamics that cannot be explained by or reduced to biology.

Since that article appeared, thousands of scholars have built upon and been guided by its insights.[5]

Rosabeth Kanter's landmark book, *Men and Women of the Corporation* (1977), reinforced Acker and Van Houten's claim that women and men experience organizations differently. Kanter concluded that women in situations where they are 'numerical tokens' (one or a few in contexts with many men) receive closer scrutiny at work because there are so few of them; their rarity draws men's attention and makes them vulnerable. Proportions, structures, and opportunities, more than gender, argued Kanter, are the explanations for women's disadvantages, suggesting that men who work mostly among women (as tokens) suffer as well. While later research failed to support Kanter's claim that 'men tokens' were disadvantaged (see Korvajärvi, this volume) or that women's token status was the prime cause of their disadvantages at work, her book nevertheless legitimated the questioning of gender relations. In rapid succession, a deluge of publications on gender and work, gender and organizations, and gender and management appeared, showing gender's conflation with work relations and dynamics.[6]

Jeff Hearn and Wendy Parkin (1983) produced another landmark contribution in the early 1980s on the neglect of sexuality in work and organization literature (see Hearn, this volume). Their analysis brought sexuality into discussions of gender and provided a foundation for later work on management as a specifically gendered and sexualized practice and structure. Many other seminal works, too numerous to enumerate, appeared throughout the 1980s, establishing baseline information about gendered dynamics and effects on both men and women. For example, R.W. Connell, in 1987, addressed the issue of gender in relation to cathexis (psychological/emotional energy including libidinous/sexual emotions) to argue that the body is both object and subject and that while gendered people are embodied; their behaviour cannot be 'reduced' to biology or to the body, a perspective that has been widely employed by scholars of gender, work, and organization (see Section Two). Early on, many studies of a statistical nature were done of 'sexual (later gender) inequality' at work/in organizations and were followed by many sex and race discrimination studies, some of which were supported by equal opportunity commissions. Such studies continue to appear and, in recent years, have become international in scope (cf. Walby, 2005; Zippel, 2006). During the1980s, it became recognized that discrimination operates in an informal manner and workplace ethnographies began appearing to illuminate those dynamics (e.g. Pollert, 1981; West, 1982; Westwood, 1984; Cockburn, 1988; Collinson, Knights, and Collinson, 1990; plus many more). A literature on masculinity and work (see below),

---

[5] Dana Britton and Laura Logan (2008) found (using Google) that 4660 articles had been published between 1990 and 2007 using the term 'gendered' in their title with many about 'gendered work', 'gendered space', and 'gendered labour markets'.

[6] Joanne Martin's (1990) article about a woman who had a baby by Caesarian section over a weekend to avoid missing work drew widespread attention to the issue in business school circles. Today, the issue of gender with regard to work and organizations is high on the research agenda of scholars in many fields – from sociology, to management, psychology, anthropology, therapy, politics, social movements, and religion, although less so in economics.

followed by more theoretical literatures that reflected three phases of feminism – traditional, modern, and postmodern – soon developed (see Beesley, 2005). While much of the latter work was broader than the spheres of work and organization, it nevertheless dramatically influenced work in this area (see J. Martin, 2001).

More recently, Calás and Smircich (2006) reviewed research and theory on gender and organizations in the decades of the 1990s and 2000s. Documenting the broad scope of work in the period, they noted that gender was studied in terms of identities, a cultural resource, ideology, practice and configurations of practice, frames and justificational accounts, symbols/symbolic systems, narratives, and a system of social relations. Similarly, they noted the varied theoretical and analytical methods scholars had used to study gender and organizations – including feminist theory, deconstruction, post-structural analysis, post-modern critique, social constructionism/tivism, critical theory, critical realism, actor-network theory, and ethnomethodology. Their findings confirm the wide-ranging intellectual perspectives employed by scholars in a number of disciplines, suggesting a vitally exciting area of interest and research.

## *Gender as process or practice?*

Among the most heuristic contribution of gender scholars in recent decades is their re-framing of gender from a static/fixed, unchanging (indeed unchangeable) demographic status to a dynamic accomplishment. The revolution began in the late 1980s with the landmark publication by Candace West and Don Zimmerman of "*doing gender*" (1987). Building on Erving Goffman's work, they reframed gender from an ascribed status to a dynamic process which everyone is, they say, constantly 'doing'. In addressing why people continuously 'do gender', they said members of a society are held accountable to the norms of the gender system. Their attention to bodily displays of clothing, hairstyles, and mannerisms helped them differentiate sex as biology from gender as cultural accomplishment, and their insights about gender as an interactional achievement offered a way to explain the pervasive presence yet extensive variability of gender in families, workplaces, sports, the military, religion, and so on – in short, everywhere. Rejecting a 'sex roles' view of gender as what children are taught – and hold on to over the lifecourse – they noted that gender norms and practices vary with factors such as age, situations, and cultures. 'Doing gender' thus frames gender as malleable, variable, and changing rather than as natural, essential, and fixed.

Work on 'gender-as-process' has generally focused on one or both of two dynamics: discursive/narrative actions and material/physical/bodily actions.[7] Practising gender is generally defined as 'actions reflecting or constituting society's gender institution by invoking norms, stereotypes, empirical associations, meanings and/or interpretations (including masculinities and femininities) that are culturally or

---

[7] R.W. Connell, in *Gender and Power* (1987), advanced a re-conceptualization of gender as a socially constructed phenomenon and as sustained through practices and practising. He also analysed power associated with 'gender order' arrangements. Connell views the gender order as maintained (and altered) through practice(s)/practising.

socially associated with gender' (P. Martin, 2009). Scholars in diverse fields have tried to capture gender's processual qualities by creating new concepts, such as gender as strategic narrative assertions (Kondo, 1990), performing/performative (Butler, 1990), maneuvering (Schippers, 2002), displaying (Schrock and Padavic, 2007), mobilizing (P. Martin, 2001), and socio-spatial practices (Bird and Sokolofski, 2005). The dynamics of gender are at once pervasive, subtle, individual, collective, and relational. Furthermore, they are difficult to study because what one intends often differs from how others perceive one's comment or bodily action. Thus, perceptions and interpretations are key to understanding gendering dynamics.

Over time, work and organization scholars appropriated these and other concepts, and invented new ones, to study gender in jobs/occupations and work organizations. Among the early pioneers were, for example: Rosemary Pringle (1989) in a study of secretaries who flirt and use sexual tensions to get their way; Joanne Martin's (1990) documentation of a woman who had a child by Caesarian section over a weekend in order to avoid missing work; Barbara Reskin's (1988) description of powerful (white) men who make rules at work to assure their privileges; Cynthia Cockburn (1988) who found that gender, not rational/technical necessity, determined who held particular jobs (e.g. the most interesting, varied, and mobile were reserved for men, the most repetitive, stationary, and least attractive were assigned to women). Sam Cohn's (1986) comparison of British Railways with the UK Post Office asked why women were recruited into the postal service decades before they were at British Rail. The reason, he argued, is that the postal service is more labour intensive and management took advantage of women's cheap(er) labour. British Rail, which is more capital-intensive, preserved men's 'good jobs' and protected them from 'cheaper' women for a full 100 years. Similar patterns of recruitment can be seen in several occupations that have been feminized (e.g. banking, nursing, and teaching) over the years.

## Critical studies of men and masculinities

As work on gender, work, and organizations accelerated, 'why' questions rose to the fore. Why is it that women are regularly denied positions, opportunities, awards, honours, and privileges, compared to men?[8] In due course, attention focused on men and masculinities. Reporting on empirical research, David Collinson and David Knights began writing about masculinity at work in the mid 1980s. One study (Collinson and Knights, 1986) focused on how women clerical workers often became emotional but largely because of the pressure of work and frequently accumulating backlogs. While these women's response was a function of their subordination, male managers saw the emotional behaviour as simply confirming their prior masculine prejudices

---

[8] Economists answer this question by saying it is women's choice. Women, compared to men, prioritize home and family and their lower status and lesser opportunities at work are due to their having chosen to place less emphasis on achievement at work so they could devote themselves to home and family. Men, in contrast, 'choose' the opposite. The problem with rational choice theory is that it ignores the cultural, social, and political conditions of choice. As the more powerful gender, the choices of men to concentrate on their careers at the expense of domestic responsibilities have implications for women's choices.

regarding female irrationality. Another study (Knights and Collinson, 1987) suggested that the masculinity of shopfloor manual workers served only to reproduce their subordination and under-privilege. Identification with masculine norms and values of solid, 'down to earth' and 'hard' facts led them to respect the certainty of mathematical numbers deployed by the accountants and this left them bereft of any basis to challenge their redundancy when the company sought to downsize.

In a highly entertaining analysis that took a pot shot at some famous male authors, Marta Calás and Linda Smircich (1991) deconstructed managerial 'leadership' to reveal its masculine, seductive, and sexually aggressive character that implicitly frames women as unqualified for management positions. Other work theorized discourses of masculinity as reflecting and reproducing a preoccupation with conquest, competition, and control, and being driven endlessly to secure the sense of what it is to be a man (Kerfoot and Knights, 1993; 1994).[9] David Collinson and Jeff Hearn (1994) claimed, that men 'act like men' when doing managerial work; that is, they enact masculinities when managing. They do not manage in gender-neutral ways. Their paper reflected the emergence of this new 'critical studies of men and masculinities at work', and was followed by an edited book (Collinson and Hearn, 1996) that consolidated the field, inspiring other scholars to follow suit. For example, Frank Barrett (1996) showed how Navy men doing largely clerical tasks (stereotypically women's work) frame their jobs as masculine to protect their masculine identities; Deborah Kerfoot and David Knights (1996) showed how male managers benefit from 'masculine discourses and subjectivities that are privileged in contemporary managerial and organizational work' (p. 79) yet have identities that are precarious and involve a compulsive, almost insatiable demand for social confirmation through the symbols of material and symbolic success (p. 91); Michael Roper (1994) exposed the dynamics of men's 'homosocial desire' in managerial relations and work. Such studies reflect only a small part of the literature on masculinities at work – a literature that is increasingly attracting more women authors (see Hope; Kenny and Bell; and Wolkowitz, this volume).

For reasons we do not fully understand, although the domination of masculine norms and values in most organizations may go some way to explain, less research has been done on femininities than masculinities with regard to work and organizations.[10] Even work that has been done often focuses on extra-work social relations among women, implying that women focus on non-work phenomena such as friendships, baby showers,[11] and birthdays, while men focus more on official goals (but see Jackall, 1988). Little research addresses positive features of femininity

---

[9] A number of authors (Connell, 1987; Brittan, 1989; Seidler, 1989; Cohen, 1990; Rutherford, 1992) were writing on masculinity at this time but they paid little attention to work and organization. However, they provided the inspiration for authors seeking to conduct empirical research that saw masculine discourses as important in the study of gender at work.

[10] Women secretaries have been studied extensively (Kanter, 1977; Pringle, 1989) as have certain other occupational groups (see Pierce (1995) on lawyers and paralegals; Britton (2003) on prison guards). Dellinger and Williams' (1997) study of women's make-up and bodies shows that both women and men hold women accountable to feminine appearance standards at work (Kenny and Bell, this volume).

[11] A baby shower celebrates the imminent arrival of a baby, usually involving gifts for the mother-to-be and a party.

in the workplace such as nurturing, supporting, or protecting and little asks if women benefit when they enact certain kinds of masculinity (but see Korvajärvi, this volume). Perhaps femininity and women are stigmatized because their cultural connotations are antithetical to capitalist/neoliberal discourse and practice, being stereotypically equated with weakness, submissiveness, emotionality, sexuality, and appearance while masculinity and men are stereotypically associated with strength, domination, winning, rationality, and control (Knights and Kerfoot, 2004).

While neither depiction is confirmed by research, the capacity of stereotypes to influence perceptions and actions should not be underestimated (Ridgeway, 2010). When women act 'like one of the boys' (e.g. in resisting sexual harassment or telling 'dirty' jokes), they are often severely sanctioned (e.g. Collinson and Collinson, 1996; Padavic, 1991) as they are if they litigate legal cases aggressively (Pierce, 1995). Jennifer Pierce's study of men and women litigators (and men and women paralegals) concludes that job/occupation and gender in law firms are so conflated that one cannot describe either accurately without reference to the other.[12] The job of litigator is not the same job for women as it is for men, since norms associated with the gender institution allow men to behave in ways that they deny to women (cf. Lorber, 1994). In any case, further work on femininities at work, particularly to identify how, when, and where (if at all) women and men perceive femininity as being practised as well as how, when, and where they fail to see it would be useful. As P. Martin (2001) found, women associates of high status men in corporations thought men were 'acting like men' no matter what they did, even when engaging in behaviour that is stereotypically seen as feminine (e.g. making decisions based on affect, showing support to each other irrespective of merit, and 'visiting' – that is, spending time talking casually with others instead of doing 'official' work).

### Bodies/embodiment at work

As noted, research on gender, work and organization has recently focused on bodies (see Section Two). A corpus of research documents how organizations use bodies, sex, and sexuality for 'corporate ends' and the bodily aspects of work relationships and tasks (e.g. Dellinger and Williams 1997). Christine Williams demonstrated how men and women nurses and women and men Marines were subjected to gender dynamics that affected their work relations and feelings of success (see also Hope, this volume). Women Marines, for example, were required to wear feminine garb and make-up. Several chapters in this volume address bodies in relation to gender, work, and organizations and explore how organizations discipline bodies and how workers use their bodies to advantage. As Hearn notes (this volume), interest in sexuality in relation to work, organization, and management is growing at an accelerating rate (cf. Williams, Giuffre, and Dellinger, 1998).

---

[12] Men litigators reject any criticism from women paralegals (and indeed require them to approve of and support them in every respect) yet they accept it from men paralegals. Men litigators also encourage men paralegals to drink beer and play sports with them and apply for law school but do none of these things with or for women paralegals.

## *Organizational change: toward gender equity*

Another recent development concerns interventions aimed at improving gender equity, including eliminating sexual harassment at work. Concerns with equity, fairness, and respectful behaviour are implicit in nearly all research on gender and organizations but recent research has evaluated initiatives to produce positive change. After the Beijing Platform of 1995, many European national governments began paying attention to 'gender mainstreaming' in all aspects of society and instituted gender training programmes (although European Union equal opportunity law and specific programmes for women's advancement at the national level and some at EU level go back further; see Woodward, this volume; Casey, this volume). Recent comparative research on sexual harassment and 'solutions' to the problem of sexual harassment show that it has a range of meanings in different societies. Abigail Saguy (2003), for example, explores why French culture and law assign the responsibility for sexual harassment to individuals, not organizations, whereas US law makes organizations and employers responsible. US organizations are required to adopt explicit rules for behaviour and occasionally are forced by the courts to pay fines for failing to enforce them. Kathin Zippel (2006) shows how the concept of 'mobbing' (harassment) is framed as 'gender-neutral' (or inclusive) in Germany and other EU nations whereas sexual harassment is understood in the US as (primarily) a gender issue, that is, focused on men's improper behaviour toward women (Hearn, this volume).

The good news is that efforts have been (and are being) taken to improve gender equity on an international scale, with some producing impressive successes, as chapters in this volume show (see Woodward; Casey). Initiatives at a more local level, that is neither national nor international, have also been extensively undertaken. One major project, funded by a Ford Foundation grant to the (US) Simmons College School of Management attempted to help corporations and non-governmental organizations improve on gender equity in the US and beyond. Research on the success of their efforts showed modest results; however, as Ely and Meyerson (2000) found, a 'gender agenda' is often lost because other issues – profits, efficiency, productivity – crowd it out. Several chapters in this volume report efforts by women, individually and collectively, to improve gender equity at work (Bird and Rhoton; Benschop and Verloo), although J. Martin (this volume) concludes, sadly, that little evidence shows the realization of significant gender equity, either historically or today. Still, justice for women and race/ethnic minorities as well as for lesbians, gays, and the transgendered is sometimes possible at work, as Giuffre, Dellinger and Williams (2008) show (cf. Thanem, this volume). We hope for more research on intervention strategies that produce positive results, including the identification of organizational and societal conditions that foster lasting gender equity (see J. Martin, this volume).

It is no exaggeration to say that, 50 years ago, the odds that a specialty area of gender, work, and organization could develop would have seemed remote. Gender was not even a scholarly term except in relation to Romance languages where nouns are 'male' or 'female' and require gendered pronouns to precede them. Today, studies and theories related to gender proliferate and men as well as women participate in this development. With the 'discovery' that 'men also have gender', gender research and theory have gained the interest of men who are critical of the kinds of masculinities that prevail in society and which condition their behaviour. As we move into the second decade of the twenty-first century, we encourage academics in the area of gender, work, organization and management to continue pushing the field forward by asking hard questions and refusing to settle for simple answers. We also hope that interest in gender and globalization continues to grow. As corporations, the United Nations, and military organizations (national and multinational) confront gender, we urge them to dedicate resources to the creation of fairness and justice for all.

While 'small wins' by individual women are helpful (Meyerson and Tompkins, 2007) and perhaps vital to eventual success, alone they will not be enough (see Kenny and Bell; Benschop and Verloo; Brewis, this volume). To achieve gender equity at work, change efforts must target all levels of social reality – including the individual but also organizations and entire societies as well as transnational organizations and initiatives. Gender equity proponents must also continue raising awareness of the systemic nature of the problem and challenging neoliberalism as a principle for social relations and dynamics. Otherwise, as chapters in this volume document, they will fall short of success.

## III. Gender Equality in Organizing and Work

It is perhaps important to ask the question as to why we need to link gender, work, and organization, and what productive purpose this might serve. The arguments for this are numerous and, we feel, compelling. First, it is through work and formal organizations primarily that men have secured their economic, political, and social dominance such that questions of sex and other discriminations as well as issues of equal opportunity have become challenges for government, feminists, and pro-feminists. It is also because of the unpaid work that women have traditionally done or been cajoled into doing in the informal domestic arena and family that they have suffered unfair disadvantage when competing with men in the formal economy. Not that this is a one-way track, for sex and other discriminations at work and in public organizations feed back into the domestic sphere, often to reproduce inequalities in the home. It is appropriate to see the inequalities and discriminations in work organizations and in domestic relations as conditions and consequences of one another (see Brewis, this volume). Within the domestic division of labour men are either absent or on the periphery and this condition disadvantages women in the formal economy. However, there are other gendered conditions in the workplace such as dominant masculine cultures, sexism, and discrimination that privilege men and have a tendency to reinforce the prevailing domestic division of labour, often on the basis (although not exclusively) of economic rationality. Thus particularly in heterosexual partnerships,[13] economic rationality may dictate a continuity of sex

[13] Of course, the heterosexual partnership is no longer the most common form of household in Western societies. Single households and non-heterosexual partnerships combined would represent a larger proportion of households. However, single mothers suffer even more disadvantages than those in heterosexual relationships since they have the domestic burdens without the potential economic compensations.

inequality. But, of course, embedded gendered expectations and routines in both spheres reproduce inequalities that are far from economically rational. This vicious cycle persists despite the interventions of feminism and liberal legislation that have only marginally restrained the dynamics that harm women.

Feminists have struggled with these issues for generations but ideological and practical divisions (Ramazanoglu, 1989) have prevented them from forming a united front. Liberal, anarchic, Marxist, socialist, radical, black, eco, postcolonial, corporeal, poststructuralist, and postmodern feminisms (Beasley, 1999) all have disciples and detractors and this kind of diversity renders collective solidarity in pursuit of a unified political objective difficult if not impossible to achieve. However, the issues of work in domestic and non-domestic spheres offer the potential for a unified, collaborative and collective challenge to gender stereotypes, inequalities, and opportunities, although other issues complicate the picture, e.g. those related to social class, ethnicity, race, impairment, age, postcolonialism, sexual preference, ecology, and globalization. Only limited progress in linking different aspects of diversity (see Costea; Omanović this volume) has been made within what can be described as predominantly white middle class gender studies (Young, 2005). This is because the gender literature has been dominated by the immediate concerns to reverse centuries of sex discrimination within white middle class Western societies. Consequently, other aspects of diversity and discrimination have been neglected. However this is changing in studies of intersectionality (Acker; Calás and Smirich, this volume), transgender (Thanem, this volume) and diversity (Costea; Omanović, this volume). There is then no theoretical or empirical reason as to why a focus on gender, work, and organization should neglect any aspect of discrimination or injustice, since all are linked with the world of work and organization.

In multiple Sections of the Handbook, the issues of class, diversity, sexuality, post-colonialism, and globalization are discussed in the context of gender, work, and organization. Theoretically, the stimulus for this effort comes from the diversity of feminist perspectives that gender, work, and organization scholars have employed. Liberal feminists have helped secure some of the political and equal opportunity rights that benefit women and minorities in organizations and (though limited) in the home (see Benschop and Verloo, this volume). Other feminisms – from Marxist, radical, and postcolonial to various poststructural perspectives – have challenged the limitations of liberal feminist approaches not least because even on their own terms of seeking equal opportunity and with the support of legislation, they often fail. The liberal feminist demand to be 'the same as men' masks the institutionalized privileges that benefit men and that men take for granted as a right (see Hope, this volume).

Yet all approaches have limitations, as chapters in this Handbook show. For example, identity and standpoint theorists seek primarily to displace men while neglecting to transform the hierarchical power relations that sustain inequality. While making race and ethnicity central to their analyses, postcolonial theorists often reproduce mind–body binaries and fail to realize the full impact of globalization and transmigration (Calás and Smirich, this volume). Poststructuralists identify the performative nature of gender and sexuality but their linguistic focus leaves the body inaccessible through anything other than language (Grosz, 1994; 2005). And yet, whatever their differences, all feminisms are committed to achieving gender equity and social justice. Clearly the world of work and organization offers sites where inequity and social injustice have flourished not least because men dominate senior positions and embrace a discourse of masculinity that takes for granted and justifies their privileges (Reskin, 1988; also Acker, this volume). The discourse of masculinity is embedded in everyday practices that often go unnoticed. Yet when this discourse is combined with women's lesser status and exclusion from positions of power, it routinely produces gender inequality.

Despite attempting to outlaw indirect discrimination, equal opportunity legislation rarely exposes or challenges the ways in which masculine culture disadvantages women (and some men) at work (e.g. Pierce, 1995). It is important, as many of our chapters show, to render the construction and reproduction of masculinity and gender more visible within the processes and practices of work and organization. Without question, contemporary organizational practices privilege behaviour that is normatively masculine in being assertive, instrumental, and self-seeking and that focuses on competition, conquest, and control (Kerfoot and Knights, 1993). Insofar as the inconsistencies, instabilities, and tensions underlying masculine discourses and practices are embedded in everyday organizational routines, they are often hidden from view (Martin, 2001). However, multiple authors in this volume subject these routines, discourses, and assumptions to critical investigation in ways that reveal their implications for gender equity and justice in work, organizations, and management.

## IV. Overview of Sections and Chapters

This Handbook provides an overview of the 'state of the field' of gender, work, and organization and offers insights into its future by proposing strategies for (re)thinking gender in the context of subjectivity, work, organization, and society. A Handbook seeks to bring together a range of original contributions on a single theme. This Handbook differs from a 'reader' (a collection of already published and significant work) in constituting a collection of original materials reflecting the breadth of the field including theoretical developments that, we hope, will transform future thinking. The text was compiled with a goal of communicating to those new to the field and providing them with an enticing introduction to issues and debates on gender, work, and organization. The chapters will, we hope, also inspire established scholars who are well-versed in the debates and are looking for material to move the field forward. For such reasons, we encouraged our authors to locate their texts in contemporary debates, to extend theoretical insights, and to provide references that facilitate further enquiry.

In reflecting key issues, the chapters emphasize theoretical developments that conceptualize gender, work, and organization as a field. However many chapters also present extensive empirical evidence in support of a claim or thesis, while others focus on political and/or economic understandings that can be utilized to address persistent gender inequalities. For this reason, we hope the Handbook will appeal to those interested in understanding why things happen and to those who want answers to the question of, 'So what can we do about it?'

Strategies identified in the chapters go beyond those concerned with equal opportunity for women and/or race/ethnic minorities at work. Many so-called change strategies, our authors allege, simply reproduce the status quo of hierarchical and masculine dominated organizations where women are expected to change or 'to fit in'. What is needed, they argue, are strategies of 'doing gender' in ways that radically challenge the organization of work – and the work of organizations – and that have potential for transforming self and society while undermining and delegitimating 'business as usual'.

One challenge in assembling the Handbook was how to organize the chapters. In the event, we came up with five Sections (see below) which, we hope, readers will find useful. An ordering device was needed to make the text intelligible, but of course the issues raised within these Sections are inextricably linked. Indeed the Sections were revised during the development of this Handbook, based on the chapters as they evolved. In the end, we structured the text around five themes, as follows: histories and philosophies; embodiment and identities; organizing work in relation to gendering; diversity; and globalization. The variation in Section sizes (e.g. the shorter Diversity Section) reflects the outcomes of negotiations with authors and our assessments of how the chapters linked.

The first Section, *Histories and Philosophies of Gender, Work and Organization*, presents theoretical perspectives that are being employed to investigate gender, work, and organization. It focuses on dominant themes of the present day and contextualizes this work within the broad history of feminism. Following this philosophical underpinning, the next Section, *Embodying Organizations, Organizing Bodies, and Regulating Identities*, challenges the tendency for literature on work and organization to be disembodied, with embodiment denied, marginalized, or taken for granted. This Section theorizes the body in relation to gendering by addressing difficulties encountered in choosing between approaches that gender, degender, and/or ungender the body. Embodiment is implicated too in the third Section, *Organizing Work and the Gendered Organization*, where the authors explore the body as situated in organizing practices. These chapters focus on how gender inequality is sustained by working practices and explore strategies that can be employed to overcome inequality. The themes of fairness and organizational performance are addressed in the fourth Section, *Diversity in/and Management and Organizations*, where gender and sexuality are embedded within the broader frame of diversity and diversity management, acknowledging that gender in isolation does not provide the 'full' picture. Authors in the Diversity Section focus on philosophical underpinnings of diversity claims and dynamics and review how the field has evolved from equal opportunities to diversity management. They theorize and critique these developments. The fifth and final Section of the Handbook, *Globalization and Gender in/and Management and Organizations*, addresses global aspects of gender, work, and organization. These chapters analyse the role of transnational organizations such as the United Nations, European Union, and the military institution worldwide in fostering or resisting gender inequality. The final chapter challenges readers to view ourselves as 'transmigrants' in a 'transnational' world and the many forms of this new global reality.

Authors in this Handbook reflect the international field of study, both in terms of the context for particular studies and the origins of the authors, with contributions from Europe, United States, Australasia, and the Middle East. They draw from a range of intellectual/academic fields including management, political science, sociology, development studies, and cultural studies. Although there is a 'Western' bias to the text, this bias regrettably reflects the nature of the field. Most literature today originates in the West or is written by Western authors with an interest in developing economies. One challenge in creating the Handbook was finding authors who write 'on' non-Western contexts whilst simultaneously working 'within' it.

This Handbook offers no final precepts and refuses to represent the themes it includes as particularly critical or pressing. Any such overview would, we feel, distract from the complexity of the field and over-simplify ideas expressed in the chapters. Thus, we allow each chapter to 'speak for itself'. We introduce the Sections by noting key themes and summarizing the chapters it includes. We also note any links between chapters, both within and across Sections. Yet, we hope our 'voice' in this endeavour does not distort or detract from the contributions of the authors themselves.

## V. How to Use the Handbook

Without wishing to prescribe how to use the Handbook, some orientation for using the text may be useful. The book will, we anticipate, be used in the service of exploring one of three foci: work and/or organization of which gender is an essential part; gender as the primary interest in the context of work and/or organization; and the simultaneous intersections of gender, work and organization.

We use the term organization as both a noun and a verb, not only the 'thing itself' but also as a process of organizing. For those interested in work and organization, the text offers insights into how and why certain structures and practices are in evidence and why some policies and practices are effective while others are not. The Handbook can foster understanding of the nature of organizational life and the gendered experiences of work and organization, including how gender is used as an organizing principle and the sense(s) in which organizations are gendered.

For those interested primarily in gender, the Handbook offers insights into how gender is experienced in the context of work where a considerable amount of time is spent (and where the effects can be seen 'outside' of work) and the organizing practices that are implicated in shaping identity, with effects on work/home-life, health, and relationships. As demonstrated by several chapters, while the focus is on the contexts of work and organization, gender is understood in light of organizing practices; thus our contributors draw on a range of theoretical and empirical sources. Scholars working in the field of gender can explore the gendered experiences of work and organization, the interconnections between gender, work, and organization, and the intersectionalities of gender, race, class, sexuality, and ethnicity.

For those with less interest in the philosophical underpinnings of gender, work, and organization, Sections 2–5 may be of primary interest. Chapters in these Sections demonstrate how organizing practices are not gender-neutral but are infused with gender that is impossible to ignore when viewed as embodied rather than disembodied. These Sections explore how experiences and inequalities are conceptualized and managed through diversity programmes and how global dynamics are affecting gender relations at work. Alongside several theoretical chapters, some chapters explore the contexts of work and ways of organizing that affect gender relations and dynamics.

The Handbook aims to offer insights into the fields of gender, work, and organization and the intersections between them. The Section headings, we hope, orient readers but do not imply that they are mutually exclusive or separable. The introduction to each Section can be seen as a guide to the main thesis of each chapter and a method of highlighting links between chapters and Sections. (Links are made in the volume when a related chapter provides a useful point of reference.) Lastly, references for the chapters can help readers who want to explore particular issues and/or areas in more depth.

Inevitably a text like this cannot be exhaustive and indeed we hope to avoid such a masculine strategy (Clough, 1992). Certain themes are covered more extensively than others. Concern with the marginalization of and inequalities experienced by women means that, as is typical of the field, there is a focus on women (and femininity) more so than on men (and masculinity). Feminist influences may account for this result although, in part, the tendency for researchers to treat work/organization as 'gender-neutral' is another impetus for this focus. In the text, assertions of 'neutrality' are seen as a normalization of the masculine; our authors claim that neutrality is often confused with the masculine-as-norm. In this sense, the management and organizational literature is not only often mainstream but also malestream in ignoring how the organizing of work and experiences of being organized are gendered in ways that harm women. Even the critical management literature is not immune to such criticism.

As discussed above, the scope of the text is international yet it is also predominantly 'Western' in outlook. Also, in focusing on 'current' ideas in the field, we have sacrificed detailed attention to the feminist canon that has developed over years. Thus, the chapters give little attention to radical/liberal debates (even though they are implied in many chapters), Marxist feminisms, and/or the different 'waves' of feminism (cf. Hope, this volume). In covering broad theoretical issues, and exploring work and organizing practices at the organizational level, there was less opportunity to consider the full range and variety of organizing practices that are traditionally explored with regard to workplaces, e.g. human resource management, leadership, negotiation, and teamwork (but see Sinclair on leadership, this volume).

What the Handbook does do, across all Sections, is focus on persisting inequalities in ways that give the text theoretical and political purpose. The importance of the issue resides in the fact that when we examine organizations today, we find they remain dominated by the 'traditional' white, male, senior manager. Evidence of systematic discrimination against women, particularly mothers and women of childbearing age, and the denigration of feminine modes of working, writing, and/or organizing continue unabated. These dynamics can be seen in the types of work done by women and men, in their respective career trajectories, and in their differing abilities to advance in organizational hierarchies. This Handbook provides a critique of gendered decisions, behaviours, and processes within work and organization; it exposes the myths of gender-neutrality; and it challenges gender myopic traditions that many take for granted. Myths and traditions obscure and reproduce the very mechanisms of organizing that maintain gendered inequalities. Although the embodied nature of work and organization is the focus of one Section, it is evident in chapters throughout. Similarly while diversity is covered in Section Four, it is addressed also in discussions of intersectionality. The social construction of gender, the 'doing' and 'becoming' of gender, predominate in the chapters, again reflecting the field at this time. Gender offers only one lens for understanding work and organization, of course, but we hope our selection of chapters, written by internationally renowned academics representing multiple disciplines, genders, and cultures, provides a useful guide to all who are interested in gender, work, and organization. If the Handbook does its job, others will take up the mantle and create the next stage of theoretical and empirical work.

# REFERENCES

Acker, Joan (1990) Hierarchies, Bodies, and Jobs: Toward a Theory of Gendered Organizations, *Gender & Society*, 4, 139–158.

Acker, Joan (2006) *Class Questions: Feminist Answers*. Lanham Maryland: Rowman and Littlefield.

Acker, Joan, and Van Houten, Donald (1974) Differential Recruitment and Control: The Sex Structuring of Organizations, *Administrative Science Quarterly*, 19, June, 152–163.

Barrett, Frank (1996) The Organizational Construction of Masculinity: The Case of the U.S. Navy, *Gender, Work, and Organization*, 3(3) 129–142.

Barrett, Michèle (1981) *Women's Oppression Today: Problems in Marxist Feminist Analysis*. New York: Random House.

Baron, James N., and Bielby, William T. (1985) 'Organizational Barriers to Gender Equality: Sex Segregation of Jobs and Opportunities' in A.S. Rossi (ed.), *Gender and the Life Course*. New York: Aldine, 233–251.

Beasley, C. (1999) *What is Feminism?: An Introduction to Feminist Theory*, Sage, London & Thousand Oaks.

Bielby, William T., and Baron, James N. (1986) Men and Women at Work: Sex Segregation and Statistical Discrimination, *American Journal of Sociology*, 91(4) January, 759–799.

Bird, Sharon R., and Sokolofski, Leah (2005) Gendered Socio-Spatial Practices in Public Eating and Drinking Establishments in the United States, *Gender, Place and Culture*, 12(2) 213–230.

Blomberg, Jesper (2009) Gendering Finance: Masculinities and Hierarchies at the Stockholm Stock Exchange, *Organization*, 16(2) 203–225.

Brittan, Arthur (1989) *Masculinity and Power*. Oxford: Blackwell.

Britton, Dana (2003) *At Work in the Iron Cage: The Prison as Gendered Organization*. New York: University Press.

Britton, Dana, and Logan, Laura (2008) Gendered Organizations: Problems and Prospects, *Sociology Compass*, 2(1) 107–121.

Butler, Judith (1990) *Gender Trouble: Feminism and the Subversion of Identity*. New York: Routledge.

Calás, M., and Smircich, L. (1991) Voicing Seduction to Silence Leadership, *Organization Studies*, 12(4) 567–602.

Calás, M., and Smircich, L. (2006) 'From the Woman's Point of View Ten Years Later: Toward a Feminist Organization Studies' in S. Clegg et al., *Handbook of Organizations*. 2nd ed. London: Sage, 284–346.

Calás, Marta B., Smircich, Linda, Tienari, Janne, and Funck Ellehave, Camilla (eds) (2010) Special Issue on Gender and Ethnicity, *Gender, Work and Organization*, 17(3).

Clough, P.T. (1992) *The End(s) of Ethnography: From Realism to Social Criticism*. Newbury Park, CA: Sage.

Cockburn, Cynthia (1988) *Machinery of Dominance: Women, Men, and Technical Know-How*. Boston: Northeastern University Press.

Cohen, David (1990) *Being a Man*. London and New York: Routledge.

Cohn, Samuel (1986) *Process of Occupational Sex-Typing: The Feminization of Clerical Labor in Great Britain, 1870–1936*. Philadelphia: Temple University Press.

Collinson, David, and Hearn, Jeff (1994) Naming Men as Men. *Gender, Work and Organization*, 1, 1–24.

Collinson, David, and Hearn, Jeff (eds) (1996) *Men as Managers, Managers as Men: Critical Perspectives on Men, Masculinities and Managements*. London: Sage.

Collinson, David, and Knights, David (1986) 'Men Only: Theories and Practices of Job Segregation' in D. Knights and H. Willmott (eds), *Gender and the Labour Process*. Aldershot: Gower, 140–178.

Collinson, David, Knights, David, and Collinson, Margaret (1990) *Managing to Discriminate*. London: Routledge.

Collinson, Margaret, and Collinson, David L. (1996) It's Only Dick: The Sexual Harassment of Women Managers in Insurance Sales, *Work, Employment and Society*, 1(10), 29–56.

Connell, Robert W. (1987) *Gender and Power*. Cambridge and Boston: Polity Press.

Connell, Raewyn (2007) *Southern Theory: The Global Dimensions of Social Science*. Cambridge MA: Polity Press.

Cox, Oliver C. (1948) *Caste, Class, and Race: A Study in Social Dynamics*. Garden City, New York: Doubleday.

Dellinger, K., and Williams, C.L. (1997) Make-Up at Work: Negotiating Appearance Rules in the Workplace, *Gender & Society*, 11(2) 151–177.

Ely, Robin J., and Meyerson, Debra E. (2000) Advancing Gender Equity in Organizations: The Challenge and Importance of Maintaining a Gender Narrative, *Organization*, 7(4) 589–608.

Fletcher, Joyce (1999) *Disappearing Acts: Gender, Power and Relational Practice at Work*. Cambridge MA: MIT Press.

Giuffre, Patti, Dellinger, Kirsten, and Williams, Christine L. (2008) No Retribution for Being Gay? Inequality in Gay-friendly Workplaces, *Sociological Spectrum*, 28, 1–24.

Gregory, Abigail and Milner, Susan (eds) (2009) Special Issue: Work-life Balance, *Gender, Work and Organization*, 16(1).

Grosz, Elizabeth (1994) *Volatile Bodies: Toward a Corporeal Feminism*. Bloomington IN: Indiana University Press.

Grosz, Elizabeth (2005) 'Intensities and Flows' in Tiffany Atkinson (ed.), *The Body: Readers in Cultural Criticism*. Basingstoke: Palgrave Macmillan, 142–155.

Hatch, Mary Jo (2010) Personal Communication.

Hearn, Jeff, and Parkin, P. Wendy (1983) Gender and Organizations: A Selective Review and Critique of a Neglected Area, *Organization Studies*, 4(3) 219–242.

Higginbotham, Elizabeth, and Romer, Mary (1997) *Women and Work: Exploring Race, Ethnicity, and Class*. Thousand Oaks and London: Sage.

Jackall, Robert (1988) *Moral Mazes: The World of Corporate Managers*. Oxford University Press.

Kanter, Rosabeth Moss (1977) *Men and Women of the Corporation*. New York: Basic Books.

Kerfoot Deborah, and Knights, David (1993) Management, Manipulation and Masculinity: From Paternalism to Corporate Strategy in Financial Services, *Journal of Management Studies*, 30(4) July, 659–677.

Kerfoot Deborah, and Knights, David (1994) 'Power, Identity and Masculinity' in L. Radtke and H. Stam (eds), *Gender and Power*. London: Sage.

Kerfoot Deborah, and Knights, David (1996) '"The Best is Yet to Come?": Searching for Embodiment in Management' in D. Collinson and J. Hearn (eds), *Masculinity and Management*. London: Sage, 78–98.

Kerfoot, Deborah, and Korcyzynski, Marek (2005) Special Issue on Service Workers, *Gender, Work and Organization*, 12(5).

Knights, David, and Collinson, David (1987) Disciplining the Shopfloor: A Comparison of the Disciplinary Effects of Managerial Psychology and Financial Accounting, *Accounting, Organisations and Society*, 12(5) 457–477.

Knights, David, and Kerfoot, Deborah (2004) Between Representations and Subjectivity: Gender Binaries and the Politics of Organizational Transformation, *Gender, Work and Organization*, 11(4) 430–454.

Knights, David, and Surman, Emma (eds) (2008) Special Issue on Gender and Emotion, *Gender, Work and Organization*, 15(1).

Kondo, Dorrine (1990) *Crafting Selves: Power, Gender, and Discourses of Identity in a Japanese Workplace*. University of Chicago Press.

Krefting, Linda, and Richards, Wendy (eds) (2003) Special Issue on Gender and Academic Employment, *Gender, Work and Organization*, 10(2).

Kuhn, Annette, and Wolpe, AnnMarie (eds) (1978) *Feminism and Materialism: Women and Modes of Production*. London: Routledge and Kegan Paul.

Linstead, Alison, and Brewis, Jo (eds) (2004) Special Issue: Beyond boundaries: towards fluidity in theorizing and practice, *Gender, Work and Organization*, 11(4).

Lorber, Judith (1994) *Paradoxes of Gender*. Yale University Press.

Martin, Joanne (1990) Deconstructing Organizational Taboos: The Suppression of Gender Conflict in Organizations, *Organization Science*, 1, 1–21.

Martin, Joanne (2001) 'Feminist Theory and Critical Theory: Unexplored Synergies' in M. Alvesson and H. Willmott (eds), *Critical Management Studies*. London: Sage, 66–91.

Martin, Joanne, and Knopoff, Kathleen (1997) 'The Gendered Implications of Apparently Gender-neutral Theory: Re-reading Max Weber' in Edward Freeman and Andrea Larson (eds), *Women's Studies and Business Ethics: Toward a New Conversation*. New York & Oxford: Oxford University Press, 30–49.

Martin, Patricia Yancey (2001) 'Mobilizing Masculinities': Women's Experiences of Men at Work, *Organization*, 8, November, 587–618.

Martin, Patricia Yancey (2009) Guest Lecture, Simmons College Graduate School of Business, *Men, Women, and Practicing Gender at Work*. September 16.

Meyerson, D. and M. Tompkins. (2007) "Tempered Radicals as Institutional Change Agents: The Case of Advancing Gender Equity at the University of Michigan", *Harvard Journal of Law and Gender*, 30(2): 303–322.

Padavic, Irene (1991) The Re-creation of Gender in a Male Workplace, *Symbolic Interaction*, 14(3) 279–294.

Perrow, Charles (1991) A Society of Organizations, *Theory and Society*, 20, 6 December, 725–762.

Pierce, Jennifer (1995) *Gender Trials: Emotional Lives in Contemporary Law Firms*. Berkeley: University of California Press.

Poggio, Barbara (ed.) (2006) Special Issue: Gender as Practice, *Gender, Work and Organization*, 13(3).

Pollert, Anna (1981) *Girls, Wives, Factory Lives*. London: Palgrave Macmillan.

Pringle, Rosemary (1989) *Secretaries Talk: Sexuality, Power, and Work*. London & New York: Verso.

Pullen, Alison, and Knights, David (eds) (2007) Special Issue: Undoing Gender, *Gender, Work and Organization*, 14(6).

Pullen, Alison, and Thanem, Torkild (eds) (2010) Special Issue: Sexual Spaces, *Gender, Work and Organization*, 17(1).

Ramazanoglu, Caroline (1989) *Feminism and the Contradictions of Oppression*. London: Routledge.

Reskin, Barbara F. (1988) Bringing the Men Back in: Sex Differentiation and the Devaluation of Women's Work, *Gender & Society* 2(1) 58–81.

Ridgeway, Cecelia (2010) *Framed by Gender: How Gender Inequality Persists in the Modern World*. Oxford University Press.

Roethlisberger, F.J., Dickson, W.F., and Wright, H.A. (1939) *Management and the Worker: An Account of a Research Program Conducted by the Western Electric Company, Hawthorne Works, Chicago*. Cambridge MA: Harvard University Press.

Roper, Michael (1994) *Masculinity and the British Organization Man since 1945*. New York: Oxford University Press.

Rutherford, Jonathan (1992) *Men's Silences*. London: Routledge.

Sabelis, Ida, Nencel, Lorraine, Knights, David, and Odih, Pam (eds) (2008) Special Issue on Gender and Time, *Gender, Work & Organization*, 15(5).

Saguy, Abigail (2003) *What is Sexual Harassment? From Capitol Hill to the Sorbonne*. Berkeley: University of California Press.

Schippers, Mimi (2002) *Rocking Out of the Box: Gender Maneuvering in Alternative Hard Rock*. Rutgers NJ: Rutgers University Press.

Schrock, Douglas P., and Irene Padavic (2007) Negotiating Hegemonic Masculinity in a Batterer Intervention Program, *Gender & Society* 21(5) 625–649.

Seidler, Victor J. (1989) *Rediscovering Masculinity*. London: Routledge.

Walby, Sylvia (2005) Introduction: Comparative Gender Mainstreaming in a Global Era, *International Feminist Journal of Politics*, 7(4) 453–471.

West, Candace and Don Zimmerman (1987) Doing Gender, *Gender & Society* 1(2) 125–151.

West, Jackie (1982) *Work, Women, and the Labour Market*. London: Routledge & Kegan Paul.

Westwood, Sallie (1984) *All Day, Everyday: The Making of Women's Lives*. London: Pluto Press.

Wharton, Amy S., and Baron, James N. (1987) So Happy Together? The Impact of Gender Segregation on Men at Work, *American Sociological Review*, 52, 574–587.

Williams, Christine L., Giuffre, Patti, and Dellinger, Kirsten (1998) Sexuality in the Workplace: Organizational Control, Sexual Harassment, and the Pursuit of Pleasure, *The Annual Review of Sociology*, 25, 73–93.

Young, Iris Marion (2005) *On Female Body Experience: "Throwing Like a Girl" and Other Essays*. New York: Oxford University Press.

Zippel, Kathrin (2006) *The Politics of Sexual Harassment: A Comparative Study of the United States, the European Union, and Germany*. Cambridge: Cambridge University Press.

# Section One

## HISTORIES AND PHILOSOPHIES OF GENDER, WORK AND ORGANIZATION

### EDITORIAL INTRODUCTION

To understand gender, work and organization we first explore the philosophical and methodological approaches that characterise this field. Inevitably this review cannot be exhaustive yet the following chapters demonstrate much of the key thinking that represents the field at the current time. They employ feminist theorising, drawing on sociological and philosophical approaches, and propose methods with which to explore gender in the context of work and organization. In contrasting perspectives, a sense of the field and historical developments in approaches are reviewed. Certain themes run through these chapters, namely power and the striving for resistance and transgression; the personal, lived, embodied understandings of gender; gender as a doing or undoing, not a being; gender that is socially situated; and the narration of that experience.

These chapters expose the 'apparent' gender neutrality of organizations and organizing and demonstrate the embedded nature of gender in these structures and practices. Understanding gender as embedded in everyday actions owes much to the seminal article of West and Zimmerman (1987) which itself can be seen to develop from one of the most cited statements in the field of gender, 'One is not born, but rather becomes, a woman' (De Beauvoir, 1993 [1949]: 281). Gender is socially situated, constructed, performative and embodied; it is the doing rather than being with meanings that are fluid rather than essential, contradicting many earlier (and ongoing) approaches within feminism (the work of Hélène Cixous, Luce Irigaray, and Julia Kristeva, discussed in Höpfl's chapter, bring into sharp relief the notion of 'feminine'). These chapters also note the significance of work by Judith Butler (1990; 2004), whose ideas have been formative in understanding the performativity of gender and the viability of the gendered subject (invoking Foucault's view of power as regulative as well as productive) on the field of gender, work and organization.

The need to be recognised as a viable subject, achieved by conforming to the prevailing gendered norms, demonstrates that gender is not something to be added to organizing practices, but is inherent within, constructed by and constitutive of these practices. This lays stress on the effects of power and frames gender as a regulated, ordered viability in addition to noting possibilities for transgressing these boundaries, particularly through parody (Butler, 2004) but also through a return to the feminine and 'writing as a woman' (Irigaray, 1985; Cixous, 1975). In that sense these chapters are inherently political, concerned with the nature of gender, and its doing/undoing, the embodied, socially situated performativity of the subject, and its regulation. How does the regulated and ordered self strive to live? What does it mean to be a 'viable subject'? Why should we seek to resist these power relations? How can we subvert them?

In laying out such fundamental ontological, epistemological and methodological groundings of gender, work and organization research, this section provides theoretical underpinning for many of the subsequent chapters.

In Melissa Tyler's 'Postmodern Feminism and Organizational Studies: A Marriage of Inconvenience?' we explore the nature of postmodernism in relation to organization studies including how it has informed and shaped our understanding of gender in the context of organizations and organizing. Tyler helps to unpack what is meant by postmodern (and poststructural) and the confusion that remains about these terms. As she observes, when there is a rejection of a 'truth', it is unsurprising that a finite definition remains elusive. Tyler contextualises the interest in postmodern perspectives by feminists who were unsatisfied with the modernist approaches to organization studies and their tendency to view organizations as gender-neutral, thereby ignoring many of the subtle knowledge-power effects. In Tyler's view, postmodern approaches provide a means to confront the stereotypes and assumptions of the female/feminine and as a consequence, open up the possibility of challenging and 'playing' with these accounts. As she notes, the impact of postmodernism in feminist thought is now, compared to even a decade ago, relatively mainstream which is why we start with it in this text. Yet Tyler cautions readers about the problems and criticisms of postmodern feminism, which often go unreported.

In this, and other chapters, we observe how gender is seen as an outcome not an essential component of practice. This has important consequences for our approach to understanding and analysing gender in favouring a deconstructive approach that looks for hidden or suppressed meanings and recognising meaning (or knowledge) as the outcome of power relations. The communication of meaning through language in turn shapes understanding of gender. Language that conveys taken-for-granted knowledge that is thought of as 'natural' rather than recognised as invested with power is at stake. But language is not fixed; it is open to new interpretations, and more crucially here to challenge, what Tyler refers to as the 'site of political struggle'. Gender, therefore, is open to reconstruction, is a 'meaning' in flux, a 'performative ontology', and at the same time an outcome of power relations. And yet, political struggle is the site in which postmodernism is itself challenged. Feminism has long relied on a relatively stable, coherent category of 'Othered' gendered beings in whose name it can speak. The loss of this category, even a feminist-reconstructed version, raises questions about the nature of feminist struggle. It also requires a new method of analysis which locates the situated performance rather than the 'subject' as the focus of analysis.

Tyler contrasts postmodernism with 'essentialist' notions of gender which not only suggest what gender 'is' but give gender a degree of stability. Postmodernism breaks free from these notions in framing gender as a 'doing' rather than a 'being'; it frames gender as constituted through performance. But this performance is not 'free'; rather it is compelled through the regulatory effects of language that are perceived as 'viable' and 'normal' (see Gherardi's chapter). Consequently it also exposes notions of gender to charges of a socially constructed rather than biological essentialism. However, through deconstruction and parody, postmodernism opens the way for revealing the illusions of truth and for the possibility of the subversion of what is taken as normal (see Pullen and Rhodes' chapter). Postmodernism is not without its critics and ontological challenges, as Tyler notes. However, to avoid ending on a pessimistic note, Tyler offers a potential way forward through the work of corporeal feminists who stress the materiality and embodiment of gender performativity. Tyler's chapter relates also to other feminist narratives such as Marxist feminist theories, liberal feminism and radical feminism, and takes a reflective and critical approach to postmodernism, providing an invaluable contribution.

Heather Höpfl similarly works within the postmodern/poststructuralist tradition to explore women's writing, including what they are 'allowed' to write and the consequences of these limits in 'Women's Writing'. Employing the work of Kristeva, Irigaray and Cixous, amongst others, Höpfl argues that writing is gendered and, moreover, that the conventions of writing are masculine. For writing to be recognised, she says, it must reflect this patriarchal language and conform to its mode of order. Her analysis raises concerns about the disciplining of text, both in one's own writing and writing in general. She uses the example of academic writing to expose the rules under which one must write. Höpfl argues that Kristeva's work is particular apposite because she writes in the 'authoritative, academic style' and also experiments with a more personal style of writing. Interestingly, Höpfl contends that it is this latter writing that has been criticised for lack of political insight and for the 'confusion of the personal'. What Höpfl seeks to demonstrate is the difference between the required 'mastery' over one's text and the personal writing of experience. In doing so, Höpfl, though wary of essentialism, nonetheless distinguishes between masculine and feminine writing in a manner that suggests some essence to these 'styles'; she suggests that there is a 'feminine way'. It is this writing that is 'of flesh and blood, of bodies and experiences'. The embodied nature of gender is explored further in Section Two.

Höpfl demonstrates the political nature of writing and its disciplining effects. Indeed, she demonstrates the difficulty in trying to break free from patriarchal hegemony. She directs us to Cixous to consider the implications of the discipline of writing and the striving for a means of communication that gives 'voice to the (female) body' in a feminine mode of writing – that resists and subverts the 'masterful text', and is defensive in the way in which it protects itself from regulation and definition. Höpfl draws on two aspects of Kristeva's writing that seek to achieve this position: the 'breaking' of the text – such that the 'personal' can enter it and challenge the phallocentric language, and the 'reproduction' of the text – that is *who* can reproduce it (and what can be reproduced – as Kristeva argues, a son). The space-between the mastered and embodied language demonstrates the effect of a 'masculine' language, and thus what is concealed by writing in this style.

In her writing Höpfl attempts to equally embody this 'feminine' style, acknowledging at the same time the limitations of being able to 'step outside' the usual order and the tendency for the feminine in writing to be 'incorporated' into the masterful text. Her chapter raises interesting questions about the way in which we write and the purpose of disciplining language and how it is defensive against the incursion of the feminine. What risks are we prepared to take in our writing? What risks *can* we take in our writing without it being ignored or rejected?

The intersection of gender, power and knowledge is further developed in Silvia Gherardi's chapter, 'Ways of Knowing: Gender as a Politics of Knowledge?' Like in previous chapters, she adopts a postmodern approach and employs a Foucauldian approach in which knowledge is linked with power. Her chapter further develops the themes of narrative and deconstruction of narratives. Gherardi's argument is that knowledge is the product of a particular discourse (which is historically and culturally specific) and is not a universal truth but a power effect; in this way, gender should be seen in the same terms. In taking this approach we can seek to deconstruct these metanarratives to attempt to reveal its effects. However, Gherardi wishes to go further than to merely point to this revelation. She aims to show and perform an alternative narrative, where 'another form of knowing' is possible. She draws on Judith Butler's notions of performativity and the interactionist/constructionist approaches of 'doing gender' to understand gender as practice, not biology. Yet it is the gender-binary, and symbolisms attached (required?) to effectively 'do' gender, that both give us the sense of 'what' a gender 'is' and, at the same time, foreclose the possibility for gender to be 'done' differently. Through understanding the narrative constructions of the 'knowing subject', Gherardi seeks to provide a way of analysing how gender is performed in organizations and how the gender order (the gender-binary) is reproduced. In this way, she uses narratives as the symbols of the gender order as well as the practice (narrating) of gender. Like Höpfl, Gherardi takes an autobiographical turn to narrate this argument from a more personal – arguably feminine – perspective, and in doing so 'contraven(ing) this tacit code . . . I first tell my story'. Interestingly her story is brief (perhaps demonstrating, as Höpfl argues, the difficulties in 'écriture feminine') and is soon followed by the story of the Thracian girl in Plato's *Theaethetus,* which relates the tale of the philosopher Thales who fell into a pit whilst looking upwards and was jeered by the servant girl who mocked his desire to know things in the sky such that he did not see what was before him at his feet. Whereas the male philosopher was looking 'up above', the servile, foreign female looked at things 'below' – distinguishing the (higher) rationality of thought from the mundane realities of the day-to-day practice and – moreover – placing the everyday practice with the 'Other' – female, foreign, ignorant. Here we return to suggestions of embodiment as gendered, that it is in practice that we find, symbolically, women who leave 'higher levels of thought' to the symbolism of masculine wisdom, thus separating the body of woman from the mind of man. This leaves women excluded or 'without signification' in the world of 'wisdom'. This kind of 'invisibility' of the female, Gherardi argues, is symbolized in organizations and in organization studies. The Thracian's girl's laughter, the laughter that mocked the 'disembodied' philosopher, can be employed as a symbol of resistance to the power of dominant reasoning, the primacy given to the discourse of strategy/ organizing (masculine) at the expense of the world of work and practice which are sensual and experiential (feminine). Gherardi does not seek to 'turn the tables' but instead she opens up the possibility for 'multiple discursive positions' and explores this through feminist empiricism, feminist standpoint epistemology, and feminist postmodernism.

Power and resistance are also implied in the exploration and critique of gender representation in Alison Pullen and Carl Rhodes' chapter, 'Gender, Work and Organization in Popular Culture'. In this chapter the authors discuss the representations of 'cultural norms and stereotypes' of gender in popular forms of media, as well as the way in which these norms are parodied and (potentially) challenged and subverted. In contrast to a fixed sense of that which is 'feminine' or 'masculine', this chapter creates a space for 'play' with what is meant by gender and opportunities for its transgression. Pullen and Rhodes continue the theme of narrative and storytelling as central to understanding gender to explore representations of gender in film and television, focusing on the themes of: working in the city and in corporations, working in the country and in farming, and sex work and sexuality at work (see Hearn, Section Four). They show how certain themes are dominant but not ubiquitous, and – perhaps more importantly – how these images are not only a site for the perpetuation of 'classic' gender stereotypes and ideals but also the space in which they can be challenged, parodied, and suggestive of new role models.

Popular culture, they argue, is often blamed for the perpetuation of stereotypes in society and is thus 'complicit in the fostering of inequality'. Pullen and Rhodes also argue that popular culture provides a means for these representations to be challenged and potentially subverted. Popular culture provides a useful lens on 'realities' in organizations – and in drawing attention to them, the medium of popular culture opens up the potential for social critique and forces us to confront and laugh at issues that marginalise, oppress and maintain inequality. But more than exposure, popular culture provides a site for the subversion of and play with these stereotypes. They offer parody as a means of providing a particularly effective mode of destabilising dominant images and discourses of gender in work and organization, through imitation and making fun – by exposing them as constructions rather than truths. Parody is entertaining yet at the same time it provides a mode of critique. As we saw in Tyler's chapter, such an approach helps to expose the mechanisms of power that produce dominant representations, as well as the means to subvert them. Like the Thracian girl in Gherardi's chapter, Pullen and Rhodes turn to laughter to mock that which is often mistaken for universal truth, the rational and, for Gherardi, the 'masculine'. They use the power of laughter to expose, resist, subvert *because* laughter, rather than 'rational critique', can provide the most effective means for unsettling gender norms.

The next chapter, by Joan Acker, 'Theorizing Gender, Race, and Class in Organizations', continues the theme of the political nature of the feminist project and the need to see gender as socially situated. It focuses on the intertwining of different factors and the need to understand gender in relation to multiple aspects of identity and experience (see Calás and Smircich, Section Five; and Costea, Section Four). Acker outlines how research into gender inequality has tended to focus on gender in isolation or, somewhat better, gender and another category, such as class or race, as if these can be treated as additive components. Instead she calls for the need to understand the important categories of difference which are involved and intertwined in the complex processes of difference and inequality as 'intersectional'. Intersectionality is a way of theorising the various processes that interweave with and affect each other such that, for example, the experience of a black woman is qualitatively different to that of a white woman, not just as a 'double bind' but through how the mixture of race, ethnicity, class and gender are mutually produced and reproduced. Indeed, divisions between them are artificial. Studying inequality through individual components and adding them together fails to reflect the reality of how these factors are co-produced.

Of course, doing what Acker advises is challenging. Notwithstanding the complexity of the ambition to explore dynamics between categories, particularly those that are themselves historically and culturally constituted, there is the question of whether the concept of category itself is viable (as noted by Tyler). Yet Acker argues that these challenges, as robust as they are, must not prevent us from refining our analyses to take account of these intertwined factors. Such a gauntlet is not insubstantial because it challenges the traditional approach taken within sociology to 'manage' reality by breaking it down into parts more accessible for study. Acker explores how change can be approached by use of different methodologies and through different levels of analysis. In the context of organization studies, she proposes that organizations as 'inequality regimes' where systematic inequalities are in evidence can be analysed in regard to several components: bases of inequality, organizing processes and practices that create/sustain/challenge inequality, visibility of inequality, legitimacy of inequality, mechanisms of control and compliance, and competing interests that change/maintain inequalities. Though not entirely distinct, these dimensions can act as guides for analysis.

Acker's central point is that social life cannot meaningfully be divided and analysed separately. Factors such as gender, class, race and so on are always interlinked and mutually constitutive of/for lived reality. In this way we see an argument for focusing on 'concrete social processes' which were stressed by Tyler (this volume). Acker provides other ways whereby the complex social whole can be made manageable for analysis, such as exploring gender, as 'classed', 'racialized' and so on. Her chapter is political and practice–orientated in claiming that through doing more refined and integrated modes of analysis, we can more effectively challenge the systemic and enduring inequalities in organizations.

In the Section's final chapter by Barbara Czarniawska, 'How to Study Gender Inequality in Organizations?', the issue of research methods that have been used to study gender inequality in organizations is raised. Czarniawska reviews diverse approaches to address the potentials and challenges of each. The methods are reviewed in four categories: experimental, retrospective (including case studies, work life stories), prospective (including document analysis, discourse analysis, ethnographic interviews, participant observation, direct observation/shadowing, and virtual ethnographies), and literary (fictive accounts, inequality in novels). Some examples include the following. J. Martin's *experimental research* on gender, managers and secretaries used videotapes to explore how women managers view inequality in relation to salary discrepancies. In their *retrospective* case study Kirkham and Loft used census data (for England and Wales), historical accounts, and excerpts from official discourses and classifications of the accounting profession to ask why women were excluded during accounting's 'professionalization' period. Work life stories such as biographies, autobiographies and verbal accounts were used by Fischer to study women Wall Street pioneers in a given historical period to ask how their work and their home/family lives shaped their experiences and prospects.

The most extensive category, *prospective* field studies, scrutinizes gender inequality in actual work contexts. Sokolowska used state-provided data, surveys, and *documents* to ask why Polish women have held so few senior positions despite many other societal reforms. Gill used broadcasters' accounts (discourse) to understand the lack of women DJs at UK radio stations and Jørgensen used accounts to explore policemen's views on their female colleagues in Denmark. Ethnographic interviews, or collecting stories relating actions and events rather than the gathering of opinions, are illustrated by P. Martin's study of gender in corporations. Hunt studied a police department for one and a half years using participant observation, while Bruni used direct observation – or shadowing – to study gender in a consulting firm. Gustavsson studied how 'real people' interact with computer generated avatars – as 'virtual assistants' who 'perform' as front-office personnel – to explore how companies use gender in accord with this technology.

Czarniawska's suggestion to use *literary analysis* as a method for studying gender inequality in organizations is intriguing and perhaps controversial. Fictional texts reflect the societies in which their authors were raised, she says, and are an important part of contemporary social discourse. An example is the study of gender in children's fairy tales by Davies and her own analysis of Sweden's Pippi Longstocking and Lisbeth Salander (in Larsson's *Millenium* novels) as characters who can teach us about how gender inequality plays out in organizations.

In closing, she ponders the immense challenges that gender scholars of organizations face and concludes in this way: 'I am convinced that reaching a wider readership is imperative, especially for those who study inequality. It must be shown, it must be documented, its mechanisms must be revealed. Widening the repertoire of representation modes can help this endeavor.' The editors of this volume enthusiastically concur.

# REFERENCES

Butler, J. (1990) *Gender Trouble: Feminism and the Subversion of Identity*. New York: Routledge.
Butler, J. (2004) *Undoing Gender*. London: Routledge.
Cixous, H. (1976 [1975]) The Laugh of Medusa, *Signs*, 1(4), trans K. Cohen and P. Cohen, 875–893.
De Beauvoir, S. (1993 [1949]) *The Second Sex*, trans M. Crosland. London: Everyman's Library/Alfred A Knopf.
Irigaray, L. (1985) *Speculum of the Other Woman*. Ithaca: Cornell University Press.
West, C. and Zimmerman, D.H. (1987) Doing Gender, *Gender and Society*, 1(2) 125–151.

# 1

# Postmodern Feminism and Organization Studies: A Marriage of Inconvenience?

MELISSA TYLER

*University of Essex*

## OPENING THOUGHTS

In her book *Secretaries Talk*, Rosemary Pringle (1989) describes a piece of public artwork called the 'Olympia' montage,[1] created in the mid-1980s by a community artist working with a group of secretaries in Sydney. Drawing on Foucault's (1979) emphasis on the productive rather than simply repressive capacity of power, Pringle recounts how the secretaries involved in the project attempted to subvert stereotypical perceptions of them:

> Instead of rejecting or moralizing about these images she [the artist] recreates them in loving detail and plays with them. Here the naked reclining figure of Olympia the prostitute is brought together with every imaginable image of secretary, as sex object, femme fatale, temptress, worker, wife, mother, holding the boss in the palm of her hand and so on. The whole thing is lit up with flashing lights; it is flamboyant, garish, loud, and above all celebratory. It is constructed to create the possibility of multiple interpretations and indeed everyone who looks at it sees something different (Pringle, 1989: 103).

Here, Pringle touches on many of the themes that characterize postmodern feminism. The artist, as Pringle suggests, rejects a moral critique of stereotypical images

---

[1] The Sydney montage was based on Manet's 'Olympia', which itself was inspired by Titian's sixteenth century work 'Venus of Urbino'. When it was first exhibited in Paris in the 1860's what was reportedly thought to be most shocking about Manet's painting wasn't the female figure's nakedness, or even the accessories that clearly identified her as a courtesan, but rather her bold, fixed gaze. It is interesting then that one of the political features of the Sydney montage is that the reclining figure of Olympia was intended to be a reversal of what Foucault described as the 'disciplinary gaze' that controls and contains women's bodies and sexuality (for a more in-depth discussion of the latter within organization studies, see Bartky, 1990).

of secretaries, choosing instead to parody such images and so subvert their power. She 'plays' with stereotypical ideas about what it means to be a secretary, in all its various guises, in an outlandish, humorous way. She seizes the opportunity to challenge gender stereotypes regarding women's nature and sexuality, not by rejecting, but by celebrating them, emphasizing the multiplicity and constructed nature of gendered subjectivity. Instead of replacing what might be seen as partial or flawed knowledge with something 'better', she encourages us to deconstruct what it means to be a secretary, and a woman, self-consciously replacing one construction with another, the latter designed to encourage 'multiple interpretations', as Pringle puts it. There are no placards, no demonstrations, no lawsuits here, instead there are flashing lights and the reclining figure of Olympia in all her naked glory.

I have chosen to begin this chapter by thinking about the Olympia montage not only because, as Pringle herself suggests, it exemplifies many of the leitmotifs of postmodern feminism, but also because it highlights some of its inherent problems. On the one hand, the montage is powerful in its effects, challenging and potentially undermining established ways of thinking about gender, sexuality, and work. On the other hand, it arguably leaves the structural arrangements and power relations underpinning such ways of thinking intact. As Pringle emphasizes, the artist and the secretaries involved, as the 'authors' of the piece, could not determine its interpretation, nor could they ensure that the audience would not take the parody seriously; that is, as an affirmation of precisely the stereotypical meanings and cultural associations it was attempting to undermine. This leads us to ask, then, does such an approach to dealing with stereotypical images of women at work, and the power relations within which they are embedded, help us to take feminism forward, or does it undermine some of the very claims on which feminism is based, such as the importance of taking seriously the impact of gender ideology on women's experiences of work, or on the sexual harassment of women in the workplace? It is questions such as these that preoccupy our discussion throughout this chapter, focusing on the ontological, political, and epistemological issues postmodernism raises for feminist theory and its integration into the study of gender and work organizations.

The influence of postmodern thinking on feminist theory and politics has indeed provoked considerable debate. Feminist scholars have tended to view postmodernism either as an unprecedented opportunity for women to resist their designation as Other, or as a theoretical movement that is politically disabling. For some, feminism and postmodernism have entered into a relationship that is 'always creative' (Yeatman, 1994: 13), for others feminism occupies 'an anomalous position' with regard to postmodernism, one characterized by a 'relationship of unease' (Hekman, 1990: 1–2). For feminists such as Flax (1987), despite an obvious attraction to the emancipatory legacy of the Enlightenment with its espoused commitment to progress, feminist theory more properly belongs in the terrain of postmodernism, for feminist notions of the self, knowledge, and truth are too contradictory to those of the Enlightenment to be contained within its categories. Weedon (1997: 180) argues similarly that postmodernism offers feminism 'useful and important tools in the struggle for change'. While for others such as Benhabib (1995: 29), certain versions of postmodernism – particularly those that reject the largely modernist notion of a stable, coherent subject (such as those typified in the Olympia montage) – are not only incompatible with feminism but 'undermine the very possibility of feminism as the theoretical articulation of the emancipatory aspirations of women'.

Within work and organization studies, feminists have been critical of the ways in which modernist theories have devalued their concerns, conceiving of organizations as essentially gender-neutral (Acker, 1990; Alvesson and Due Billing, 1997; Gherardi, 1995). Their disaffection with the modernist legacy on which organization studies is founded led many feminists to develop an affinity with postmodern ideas. For many, the oppositional and disruptive contribution of postmodernism has offered an innovative and radical alternative to modernist accounts of organizational life, in understanding the relationship between organizational power, sexuality and the body (Brewis et al., 1997; Brewis and Linstead, 2000), feminism and organization theory (Calás and Smircich, 1993; 1996; 2006; Knights and Kerfoot, 2004), gender and organizational symbolism (Gherardi, 1995), and in deconstructing the gendered assumptions underpinning organizational practices (Martin, 1990).

Writing about feminist theory and organization studies in the mid-1990s, Calás and Smircich (1996: 237) observed how encounters between postmodern ideas and organization studies, 'while growing, are still quite limited'. Some decade or so on, it seems fair to say that the impact of postmodernism can be felt quite widely within the field, having 'come and gone' as Burrell (2006: 156) has recently put it. Recounting the various aspects of the postmodern critique as it has impacted upon the study of gender and organizations, this chapter proceeds by reflecting on the term 'postmodernism', one that arguably often encourages misleading assumptions of a coherent body of ideas constituting a discrete intellectual movement. The ontological preoccupations of postmodernism are then considered with reference to their influence on critical analyses of gender and work, the emphasis here being upon a shift away from a largely dualistic, constitutive understanding of gender as an attribute, towards a more performative ontology emphasizing the ways in which gender is the outcome and not simply the basis of organizing processes. The epistemological concerns of postmodernism are then considered, linking these to the generation of feminist knowledge and to some of the problems postmodernism raises for organization studies in this respect. These concerns are then linked to a critical examination of the methodological consequences of postmodernism, emphasizing the impact of deconstruction – the search for meanings that have been denied or suppressed – upon gendered organization studies. The final part of the chapter argues that while the conceptual insights of postmodernism have made a significant contribution to the critical analysis of gender within organizations, its impact remains troubling, not least because of postmodernism's problematic relationship to feminist theory and politics. As a possible way of addressing some of the more problematic tensions between feminism and postmodernism the work of feminist theorists who draw together insights from postmodern thinking and critical theory is considered as a potential way forward for feminist organization studies.

## Postmodernism: A Word of Warning

As indicated above, one of the main difficulties we face when considering the ideas of postmodern feminists is that the terms used to describe their work are often variable and confusing. Broadly speaking, those writers whose work gets referred to as 'postmodern' tend not to apply the label to their own writing. Butler (1995: 35) for instance, who is often described as a postmodern, or poststructural feminist, has eschewed the term, describing it as 'too vague to be meaningful'.[2] Rather, the label 'postmodern' tends to be used in chapters such as this one in an attempt to make sense of some of the commonalities and differences in a relatively broad range of ideas. Indeed, the confusion surrounding the meaning of the term is hardly surprising, given that if postmodern ideas share anything in common it tends to be a rejection of the notion of a foundational truth or essence, one articulated through a representational language, in favour of an emphasis upon meaning as constructed, partial, and contingent. Another point of confusion derives from what has been described as the 'regrettable conflation' (Jones and Munro, 2005: 6) of postmodernism and poststructuralism. The former has often been used to refer to an historical period marked by uncertainty and fragmentation, while the latter has tended to describe a philosophical approach associated largely with contemporary French social theory (again, however, some writers refer to the former as postmodernity, and the latter as postmodernism).

These critical observations notwithstanding, however, in terms of its overall impact on work and organization studies, postmodernism has tended to be understood, both affirmatively and more critically, as a relatively coherent body of ideas, one that draws on the theoretical insights of an albeit rather disparate group of French philosophers and other social and cultural theorists in its critique of the modernist assumptions underpinning mainstream organization theory (see Hancock and Tyler, 2001; Hassard and Parker, 1993), and which is, indeed, often conflated with poststructuralism in this respect.[3] For the purposes of our engagement with postmodernism in this chapter, then, it makes sense to follow this trend and to identify certain themes or ideas that postmodern theorists share. Broadly speaking, therefore, and for the sake of clarity, we might argue that postmodern approaches to the study of organizations tend to share in common a discursive understanding of the self, an emphasis on truth as a socially contingent multiplicity, a conception of knowledge as the situated outcome of power relations, and an understanding of ethics as contextual and inter-relational. Drawing largely on Foucault, postmodern approaches to organization studies also tend to be characterized by a view of power as both a repressive and a productive capacity (see Burrell, 2006 for an extended discussion of the impact of Foucault's writing on postmodernism and organization studies).

A particularly important orientation within postmodern theory derives from the idea that human existence and experience is located inescapably within language.

---

[2] Although his work is seen by many to advocate a form of critique that represents a clear break with the utopian and universalizing tendencies of modernist thinking, Michel Foucault similarly explicitly rejected the label 'postmodern' in interviews, reminding us (as Giddens, 1991, has subsequently) that a critique of Enlightenment thinking was a feature of the work of many philosophers of the modern period (see Hancock and Tyler, 2001, for an extended discussion of the relationship between critical modernism and poststructuralism).

[3] Brewis (2005a) for instance uses the term 'poststructuralist/postmodernist' in her discussion of Calás and Smircich's work.

This means that power is exercised not only through direct coercion, but also through the way in which language shapes and restricts our understanding of reality. However, because language is not static, but is continually open to re-interpretation, it can also be used to challenge and resist its repressive powers, and so language is seen as an important site of political struggle. Extrapolating out from this analysis, postmodern feminists have argued that if gender is constructed discursively (that is, through the power effects of language), then it can be re-constructed, for the gendered self is not a static, pre-social given, but rather the outcome of power relations. It is a rejection of the self as a pre-social given, in favour of a performative ontology (an understanding of the self as socially or discursively constructed) that has arguably proven to be the most controversial and significant motif of postmodern feminism, for the self has long been a key concern of feminist theory. It is a concept that is central to understanding the ways in which aspects of our being such as identity, embodiment, agency and of course, work are engendered, and it is a mobilization of the gendered self that has been the foundation of feminist theory and politics throughout its history.

## Postmodernism and Gendered Subjectivity at Work

Feminists influenced by postmodernism tend to reject a dualistic, representational view of gender as a relatively stable identity (Oakley, 1972), in favour of an emphasis on gender as a social practice that is both multiple and provisional (Bruni et al., 2005; Poggio, 2006; Pullen, 2006). For writers such as Butler (1988; 1993; 2000 [1990]), gender becomes ritualized through constant acts of repetition and through the recitation of particular cultural reference points, the effects of which make it appear natural, as opposed to gender being the 'natural' expression of a pre-social given. While this understanding of gender as something that we 'do' as opposed to something that we 'have' or 'are' is certainly not unique to postmodern feminism, but rather has a long history within feminist thinking, arguably beginning with De Beauvoir's (1988 [1949]: 295) contention that 'One is not born, but rather becomes, a woman', and developed most notably in West and Zimmerman's (1987: 125) understanding of gender as 'a routine accomplishment embedded in everyday interaction',[4] what makes postmodern feminist writing distinct is its performative gender ontology. The latter somewhat controversially takes this 'doing gender' perspective to the extreme, emphasizing that gender is not simply something that we perform as social actors, rather its very performance brings us into being. When Butler argues for instance that 'this repetition [of gender "acts"] is not performed *by* a subject; this repetition is what *enables* a subject' (Butler, 1993: 95, original emphasis), she emphasizes that gendered subject positions are continually evoked through stylized forms of interaction, without which gender does not exist – these very acts of repetition are what constitute gender, and gendered subjects, simultaneously.

While gender is effectively constituted performatively, however, it is not arbitrary or free-floating for writers such as Butler, but rather is compelled in particular ways

[4] See also Acker (1990) for an application of this 'doing gender' perspective to the study of organizations.

and through certain discursive regimes such as what she describes as the 'heterosexual matrix' – an ontological-epistemic schema that organizes sex, gender, and desire dualistically and hierarchically, privileging hegemonic masculinity (Butler, 2000). Again, further developing the 'doing gender' approach outlined above, the enactment of gender according to the terms of the heterosexual matrix involves a constant process of what Butler describes as 'un/doing' (Butler, 2004) through which, in order to be recognized as viable, the subject 'produces its coherence at the cost of its own complexity' (Butler, 1993: 115). What she means by this is that in bringing gender into being, the complexity of lived experience in all its multiplicity becomes conflated into a performance that conforms to the normative expectations perpetuated by the heterosexual matrix, in order for men and women to be accorded recognition as viable subjects – to be seen as 'employable', within the labour market, for instance (Hancock and Tyler, 2007). Yet as Pullen and Knights (2007), following Butler, have emphasized the terms on which we are accepted as viable may make our lives difficult if not impossible to live, while the alternative (of not fitting in, or of being denied recognition), may be equally as difficult. Hence women (and men) who fail to conform to what is defined as normal, natural and viable in gender terms themselves become 'undone'. In other words, they lose a sense of self and of their place in the world, by being socially ostracized or economically disadvantaged (for instance, by being denied educational or employment opportunities).

Simpson and Lewis (2007: 16) sum up the postmodern feminist development of this 'doing gender' approach when they argue that for postmodernists, 'gender is performative in that feminine and masculine are not what we are or traits we have but effects we produce by way of what we do'. As they outline, this performative production of gender is instigated in a myriad of different settings and in a wide range of different ways including, of course, what we do for and within organizations. For those influenced by a postmodern understanding of the self, gender is an ongoing process, one that has to be continually re-enacted and re-inscribed in accordance with the cultural norms defining masculinity and femininity at any given time, and in any given context. Alvesson's (1998) study of gender relations and identity work in a Swedish advertising agency emphasizes this, highlighting the role of organizations in the social and linguistic construction of gender. The men and women in his study continually re-negotiate their identities in accordance with gendered organizational norms and expectations, revealing how the organization is not a gender-neutral backdrop, but rather a site of contestation and struggle in this respect. Similarly, Kondo's (1990) ethnographic study of identity construction in the work-based communities she studied in Japan represents a rich and detailed account of the ways in which masculinities and femininities are crafted and performed in accordance with a range of organizationally sedimented cultural norms associated with gender and the many other aspects of identity with which it is interwoven in her narrative. Here Kondo emphasizes how, in order to be accepted as viable subjects, the women in her study (including herself as the author/researcher/narrator) had to carefully craft their performance of self in accordance with culturally sedimented expectations. In this sense, Kondo draws attention particularly to the ways in which the women she writes about had to continually mediate between different aspects of their identities, as these were lived and experienced.

Studies such as these tend to articulate the performative ontology outlined above in the view that gender is a performative social (organizational) practice (Gherardi, 1995; Poggio, 2006). Developing this position, Gherardi (1995) in particular, in emphasizing the role of organizational symbolism in gender performance, has highlighted both how gender is 'done' at work, and how organizations 'do' gender, stressing (much like Alvesson and Kondo) that organizations are far from gender-neutral backdrops against which we practice gender, but rather play an active role in gender performativity. For Gherardi, while complex, ambiguous and continually re-negotiated, gender hierarchy is maintained through the ceremonial and reme-dial work underpinning its symbolic ordering. In her account, gender symbolism is maintained, reproduced, and culturally transmitted through the ceremonial work that takes place within organizations, while remedial work restores the symbolic order of gender following instances when it has been challenged. In this sense, her approach not only articulates a performative ontology, but also echoes a postmod-ern understanding of gender power relations, drawing attention to power as both a repressive force and a productive capacity, emphasizing how gender is a site of continual contestation and struggle in this respect, a theme to which we now turn.

## Performativity and Feminist (Organizational) Politics

In many ways, this performative aspect of postmodern feminist thought, and espe-cially its articulation as a compelled style of becoming in Butler's writing, owes an important debt to De Beauvoir's (1988: 295) earlier work (written in the 1940s) in its emphasis on becoming gendered as an ongoing social process, as suggested above. However, rather than seeking to overcome women's otherness in the way that De Beauvoir urged women to, some postmodern feminists advocate celebrating wom-en's alterity, arguing that their relative marginalization enables women to challenge and undermine that from which they are excluded through the use of irony and par-ody; hence, rather than a burden to be overthrown, women's otherness is conceived of as 'a space to be reclaimed' (Calás and Smircich, 1996: 236). As suggested by the Olympia montage described above, the political emphasis of postmodern feminism, then, is largely (but by no means exclusively) on humour, irony, and parody.

Postmodern approaches emphasize therefore that performative shifts can parody dominant norms, revealing their own performativity. This means that purportedly queer activities like drag for instance, have the potential to reveal the arbitrariness of conventional gender distinctions and identities by parodying and so undermin-ing them. Developing this largely Foucauldian line of critique, one that emphasizes the productive as opposed to merely repressive capacity of power, and focusing on subjectivity and identity in the organization of gendered appearance at work, Brewis et al. (1997) argue that the social construction of gender, as a power effect of dis-course, allows for gender difference to be resisted. Their analysis of two forms of gen-der-inappropriate dress (male transvestism and female power dressing), emphasizes that gender as a binary divide only exists because we comply with its governmental effects, namely because we continue to behave as either men or women. Echoing Butler's emphasis on drag as a parodic redeployment of power, Brewis et al.'s account therefore emphasizes how gender-inappropriate dress 'illuminates the artificial nature and self-production of gender at the same time as it helps us interrogate the power structures that are founded upon this artificial divide' (Brewis et al., 1997: 1298).

Adopting a similarly Foucauldian approach, emphasizing the productive and potentially disruptive power of sexuality at work, Pringle (1989: 166) argues that 'sexual pleasure might be used to disrupt male rationality and to empower women'. In her study of secretaries referred to above, Pringle outlines how, in her view, postmodernism's parodic emphasis on a politics of play has much to offer to a feminist attempt to deploy mimcry and ridicule tactically within the workplace. In her account of the working lives of secretaries, Pringle argues that, particularly in their use of office humour, secretaries parody themselves and their bosses to powerful effect. Making comparisons between the subversive effects of these practices and those of the Olympia montage outlined earlier, Pringle draws attention not only to the pleasure derived from ridiculing and exaggerating cultural stereotypes, but also to the potential political impact of ridicule. While she acknowledges that such practices are necessarily localized, sporadic, and spontaneous, and that to dispense with other political strategies in favour of an emphasis on parody would be a regressive move for feminism, she nonetheless argues that parody has an important place in a postmodern-inspired feminist politics, one that seeks to reclaim, rather than overcome, women's designation as Other, at the same time as emphasizing gender multiplicity.

As Knights and Kerfoot (2004) outline however, one of the inherent dangers in seeking to 'reclaim' women's otherness within work and organization studies lies in the potential for the re-appropriation of a more homogenized conception of what it means to be a woman into the managerial mainstream. Here they echo Calás and Smirich's earlier (1993) critique in which they argued that rather than challenging the hegemonic status of masculinity in managerialism, the 'women in management' literature (Rosener, 1990; Helgesen, 1995) serves rather to reinforce it because feminine subjectivities are themselves constructed within the terms of hegemonic masculinity within this literature, against which women are positioned as an (albeit in this case desirable) alterative. Building on this critique, Knights and Kerfoot outline how the history of feminism has tended to pursue one of two strategies in responding to the bifurcation and hierarchical ordering of gender; either humanist (including liberal and Marxist) feminists seek to dismantle the bifurcation itself, and hence the hierarchy through which it comes to be organized, or (more radical, or cultural) feminists tend to favour a reversal of the hierarchy, claiming various forms of ontological, epistemological or ethical superiority for women. Within organization studies, as Knights and Kerfoot note, the former strategy has tended to underpin equal opportunities discourse and the liberal feminist agendas with which it has been associated, in practice leading to an emulation of masculine performativity, whereas the latter emphasizes a celebration of women's ways of being. In terms of its appropriation into mainstream managerial thought, the latter has been articulated in recent writing on 'managing diversity', and especially so in the 'women in management' literature (see Brewis and Linstead, 2009 for a summary), emphasizing the suitability of the skills and characteristics attributed to women to the demands of management within contemporary work organizations. We also of course see these assumptions reflected in women's over-representation in sales-service work, particularly that involving the performance of emotional, aesthetic, and sexualized forms of labour. Rather than a rationale for marginalization or exclusion, such attributes are therefore argued to be the basis of women's inherent or acquired superiority, ascribing to women a more relational style of working, managing, and leading that is thought to be particularly appropriate to the demands of contemporary service-orientated market economies (see also Hatcher, 2003 for a critique).

For Knights and Kerfoot (2004: 432), both of the above positions, the former vindicating hegemonic masculinity, the latter elevating a homogenized, even essentialized femininity, 'reproduce a gender binary steeped in hierarchy'. In an attempt to circumvent this bifurcation (and appropriation) of feminist thinking, Knights and Kerfoot draw on feminist theorist Susan Hekman (1999) to argue the case for a third, postmodern strategy for feminism, one that denies a single unitary truth (either of women's relative disadvantage, or superiority) and promotes an ontology within which multiple versions of gender reality prevail. According to this alternative position, differences between men and women are not seen as illegitimate deviations from the one true standard, nor as marketable novelties, but rather as 'simply a part of the rich texture of human life and experience' (Knights and Kerfoot, 2004: 433). Yet, the problem of arbitrating between these different 'textures' arguably remains, a point that haunts postmodern feminist ways of thinking about truth and knowledge.

## Feminist and Postmodernist Conceptions of Truth and Knowledge

Among the key ideas that feminism and postmodernism share in common is what Lyotard (1984: xxiv) described as an 'incredulity to metanarratives'; that is, a mistrust of totalizing theories that seek to explain everything, often with reference to a single causal factor such as capitalism or patriarchy. Indeed, feminists have criticized many of the metanarratives of Western thought for ignoring or trivializing gender, or for assuming that the differences between men and women are pre-social. Postmodern feminists argue that truth claims are not neutral but rather gender-specific reflections of power. However, metanarratives have often played a crucial role in feminist political struggles, not least in terms of advancing a feminist agenda within the workplace. Enlightenment ideas about progress, emancipation and rights have been fundamental to feminist theory and politics, in the fight for political representation and protective legislation, or for equal treatment or pay, for instance. Hence, while some feminists have sought to produce their own metanarratives, working with the legacy of their forefathers (Marxist feminist theories of capitalism, or liberal feminist critiques of sex discrimination, for instance), or against it (radical feminist accounts of patriarchy), others have sought to deconstruct established metanarratives, and to develop new ways of thinking and writing that insist on theoretical specificity and no longer claim universal or 'meta' status, the latter arguing that science is little more than 'a collection of stories about how the world is made' (Gherardi, 1995: 38).

Feminists who adopt a postmodern approach argue then for the need to deconstruct truth claims and analyse the power effects that claims to truth entail – to recognize, as Foucault (1980) argued, that knowledge is an inextricable aspect of power, and vice versa. It is therefore necessary to focus on knowledge as opposed to truth, not as representational of it, not only because there is no foundational truth, but because there is no external reality that can arbitrate between competing truth claims. For postmodern feminists, there is no one truth, no privileged knowledge; all knowledge is historically and culturally specific, the product of a particular discourse. The power of particular discourses depends on the extent to which their truth claims are successful – the extent to which the knowledge they produce is accepted as true, often because it is produced and disseminated by relatively powerful actors. In this sense, some feminists have argued that the epistemological politics of postmodernism are its 'most determinate and perhaps most interesting feature' (Yeatman, 1994: 13), leading to a questioning of the very basis of feminist theory.

In terms of the application of these ideas and debates to the generation of feminist knowledge within organization studies, as Pullen (2006: 277) notes, the bifurcation of feminist identity politics outlined above 'typically requires researchers to do one of two things: to suppress the feminine, and write implicitly as a male, or to adopt a textual position as 'woman' that fails to do justice to the complex and unstable multiplicity that underpins the research self'. Emphasizing the methodological importance of a reflexive appreciation of the multiple self, a position that elides the bifurcation outlined by Pullen, Fournier's (2002: 82–83) study of women farmers in Italy provides, as she puts it, 'living examples of the temporal, contextual and shifting nature of the category of "woman" emphasized by poststructural feminists'. The women in her research were composites of various inter-related identities: they were 'peasants' on the margins of the urban bourgeoisie, 'women' in a male dominated way of life, 'farmers' rather than farmers' wives, and environmentally aware sustainable agriculturalists. Although often tactically deploying one or the other of these components of their identity, the women in Fournier's research resolutely refused her attempts to settle them into any one category. Methodologically, this implies that 'at the centre of analysis is no longer a static object, but rather a fluid process, a situated performance' (Poggio, 2006: 229).

In researching gender as a 'situated performance' premised upon the performative ontology outlined above, Patricia Yancey Martin (2006) has argued for the development of research methodologies that 'catch in action the practicing of gender at work'. Joanne Martin's (1990) deconstruction[5] of the story, told on NBC news, by the president and CEO of a large, multinational corporation known for its humanitarian treatment of employees, of a young woman who reportedly arranged to have a Caesarean in order to be prepared for the launch of a major new product, is a widely cited example of just such an approach. Through a series of deconstructive moves followed by what she describes as an emancipatory 'reconstruction', Martin's analysis emphasizes how the gender conflicts implicit in this story are suppressed, and shows how apparently well-intentioned organizational practices can reify rather

[5] In postmodern thinking, deconstruction is based largely on the work of Jacques Derrida. For an extended discussion of the relationship between feminism and deconstruction, and of the consequences of Derrida's writing for feminist thinking, see Elam (1994).

than alleviate gender inequalities. Martin therefore deploys deconstruction as both a methodological and a political strategy in so far as her analysis undertakes both a recovery of meanings hidden within the text, as well as a discussion of the political context and consequences of these hidden meanings.

A similar methodological approach is developed and advocated by Bruni et al. (2005) in their reflexive, ethnographic study of entrepreneurship, focusing on how enterprise cultures are gendered and experienced, and on how gender as a social practice is both implicated and explicated in the 'doing' of entrepreneurship. Their account develops a critical analysis of the discursive practices involved in constructing the entrepreneur as gendered, showing how language and its mobilization in cultural practices and forms of interaction is an important mechanism through which entrepreneurship becomes gendered as masculine. Drawing on Foucault's (1979) critique of governmentality – the organized practices and 'ensembles of actions' through which subjects are induced to regulate themselves in order to behave in desired ways – they argue that 'an entrepreneurial discourse is mobilized as a system of thinking about the nature of the practice of entrepreneurship . . . which is able to make some form of that activity thinkable and practicable, both to its practitioners and to those upon whom it is practiced' (Bruni et al., 2005: 11). In other words, for the women in Bruni et al's study who 'acted' as entrepreneurs, their performance was undertaken with an eye to dominant (gendered) ideas about who or what an entrepreneur is, and about how the role of 'entrepreneur' should be acted out in order to be convincing. For the women in their study, this often involved them 'switching' between different (often competing) gender hegemonies, governing for instance, dominant social discourses shaping identities such as 'entrepreneur', 'employer', 'wife', 'mother', and so on.

## Postmodern Feminism and Organization Studies: Critical Reflections and Anticipations

Some years on from the wave of postmodernism that hit gender studies in the 1980s and early 1990s, organizational scholars are now arguably in a position to reflect on its impact, and to begin to discern new directions for theory and research based not only on the contribution made by advocates of postmodernism, but also on the notes of caution sounded by its critics. On the one hand, some have viewed postmodernism as a liberatory force, one that has freed feminism from its modernist legacy. On the other hand, postmodern ideas have been viewed with suspicion and scepticism, as a paralysing obstruction incompatible with the emancipatory impetus of feminism as a political movement. Not least this is because postmodern feminism implies that gender oppression has no single cause or solution; postmodern feminism is therefore criticized for offering no clear way forward for feminist theory or politics. The anti-epistemological relativism with which postmodernism has often been associated, combined with its emphasis on multiple truths, has also been thought to undermine feminist knowledge and the truth claims on which it is based.

Postmodern approaches to work and organization studies have often been accused of relativism (Thompson, 1993), and of absolving organizational scholars of

the responsibility to engage in a sustained moral critique of the injustices associated with prevailing relations of domination and degradation (Parker, 1995). This
particular line of critique is especially problematic for feminism given the latter's
truth claims regarding gender oppression and exploitation. This means that some
feminists see postmodernism as a threat to its emancipatory potential as a political
movement (Benhabib, 1995), emphasizing that much of the feminist critique hinges
on the claim that the oppression of women is irrational, unreasonable and unethical. Hence, 'if we want to argue for changing, rather than merely deconstructing,
some of the myths of femininity that have lingered for centuries, we need to admit
to holding a rational position from which to argue this' (Nicholson, 1990: 39).

All in all then, for some, postmodernism has proved to be a 'fatal distraction'
(Thompson, 1993: 181). Yet, as this and other relationship metaphors cited at the
outset of our discussion suggest even for its most outspoken critics, postmodernism has been something of a seductive force within feminism and organization
studies alike. Critical scholars within both fields, and particularly in the intersections between the two, have found themselves drawn to its insights and ideas for a
number of reasons, not least because it has asked many awkward questions of the
ontological, epistemological, political, and ethical assumptions underpinning both
areas, and has provided a point of departure for those who have tried to develop
radical and innovative ways of studying organizations, and of drawing attention to
previously marginalized or overlooked aspects of organizational life such as symbolism, sexuality, and the body for instance (Brewis and Linstead, 2000; Gherardi,
1995; Wolkowitz, 2006).

In terms of its overall impact, the work of postmodern theorists has been stimulat-
ing in raising new questions about the nature of feminism, and of work and organization studies, and particularly so in encouraging a more reflexive approach to the
study of gender and work (Brewis, 2005b; Pullen, 2006). As outlined at the outset,
those feminists who have advocated a closer engagement between feminism and
postmodernism have emphasized that feminist notions of the self, of knowledge,
truth, politics, ethics and so on, are too contradictory to those of the Enlightenment
to be contained within the legacy of its concepts and categories. Others have noted
however, that there is something of an 'uneasy alliance' (Benhabib, 1995) between
feminism and postmodernism. Arguably, then, what many of the concepts and ideas
discussed in this chapter suggest is that, at least in terms of its integration into work
and organization studies, attempts to categorize feminism as either modernist or
postmodernist are problematic, and overly simplistic, for in many ways it is both
and neither. This is a position that has been articulated particularly by feminist writers such as Nancy Fraser (1995: 60) who argue that rather than choosing between
postmodern insights and critical theory feminism instead 'might reconstruct each
approach so as to reconcile it with the other'. Indeed, within feminist theory there
is a rich body of work that has been produced in recent years by feminists influenced by postmodernism, critical theory and phenomenology yet which has been
relatively neglected by organizational scholars (see Benhabib, 1995; Gatens, 1996;
Grosz, 1994; Young, 2005). Such writing emphasizes in particular that gender is a situated social practice, so that the gendered self comes into being not merely through
performative iteration and recitation, but through the positioning of the embodied

self *in situation* (Benhabib, 1995), particularly through the gendered division of labour and its relationship to embodiment as the materiality of gender subjectivity (Young, 2005). Feminist critical theory, as it has been articulated in the work of corporeal feminists (see for instance, Diprose, 1994; 2000; Gatens, 1996; Grosz, 1994; Young, 2005), and particularly in Australian feminism (see Caine et al., 1998 for a discussion), adopts a largely performative ontology of gender, but also brings materiality and embodiment to the fore, drawing attention to the material circumstances that compel or constrain gender performativity.[6] This work potentially has much to offer to our understanding of gender and organization, emphasizing as it does the gendered self not as unencumbered in a humanist or postmodernist sense, but rather, as situated, organized. Such an approach recognizes that the process of becoming gendered is 'embodied, situated and fundamentally political' (Gatens, 1996: 136), a perspective that opens up important questions regarding the nature and role of organizations in this respect. At the very least, this body of work emphasizes the need for a critical, reflexive appreciation of the gendered subject based on a rejection of the Enlightenment concept of the disembodied, disembedded self that continues to dominate mainstream work and organization studies, as well as a re-working of the postmodern, performative self considered here that, in its current formulation at least, arguably sits uncomfortably with the emancipatory aspirations of feminism. Potentially, then, it opens up an important dialogue for feminist theory and organization studies in the future, constituting an as yet relatively neglected body of ideas, one that has emerged largely from a critical exchange between feminism, postmodernism, and critical theory (see Benhabib et al., 1995) yet which, as noted above, organizational scholars have yet to engage with.

In sum, over the last two decades or so postmodernism has posed a number of challenges to deterministic and reductive accounts of organizational life, reinvigorating organization theory with a series of questions that have arguably encouraged the development of more reflexive approaches to the study of organizations, drawing for instance on post-colonialism (Jones, 2005) and queer theory (Parker, 2002; Borgerson, 2005). Such approaches have forced feminists to acknowledge differences among men and women, to problematize the notion of homogenous gender categories, and also to appreciate the implications this recognition has for political solidarity resting on a singular identity. Yet at the same time, feminism has been in danger of proceeding without a discernible subject for grounding theory and practice. As noted at the outset of this chapter, and as Jones and Munro (2005: 2) remind us in their exegesis of contemporary organization theory, 'theory is always a creation and a production', one that opens up different ways of thinking and acting. It is in their respective ways of opening up organization theory, sometimes in coalescence, sometimes in conflict, that postmodernism and feminism have perhaps

---

[6] It is important to recognize, however, that a recurring theme in Butler's writing, notably in *Bodies That Matter* (Butler, 1993) as well as her more recent work, is also the materialization of gender. However, because Butler has tended to be read, particularly within organization studies (see Borgerson, 2005) as a largely postmodern or poststructuralist writer, the more phenomenological aspects of her thinking have often been eclipsed by a preoccupation with her emphasis on gender performativity. As Butler herself notes in this respect, this has led to her feeling accused of 'forgetting the body' (Butler, 1993: ix).

most in common, for both have asked awkward and inconvenient questions, undermining many of the assumptions on which organization studies has been based. While for some this is to its political detriment, for others, including many of those concerned to understand the ways in which gender and organization are mutually implicated, and to continue to expand the rich body of ideas on which organization theory draws, this is to the benefit of its continual revivification.

# REFERENCES

Acker, J. (1990) Hierarchies, Jobs, Bodies: A Theory of Gendered Organization, *Gender and Society*, 4(2) 139–158.

Alvesson, M. (1998) Gender Relations and Identity at Work: A Case Study of Masculinities and Femininities in an Advertising Agency, *Human Relations*, 51(8) 969–1006.

Alvesson, M., and Due Billing, Y. (1997) *Understanding Gender and Organizations*. London: Sage.

Bartky, S.L. (1990) *Femininity and Domination*. London: Routledge.

Benhabib, S. (1992) *Situating the Self*. Cambridge: Polity.

Benhabib, S. (1995) 'Feminism and Postmodernism: An Uneasy Alliance' in S. Benhabib et al. (eds), *Feminist Contentions*. London: Routledge, 17–34.

Benhabib, S., and Cornell, D. (1987) 'Beyond the Politics of Gender' in S. Benhabib and D. Cornell (eds), *Feminism as Critique*. London: Routledge, 1–15.

Borgerson, J. (2005) 'Judith Butler: On Organizing Subjectivities' in C. Jones and R. Munro (eds), *Contemporary Organization Theory*. Oxford: Blackwell, 63–79.

Brewis, J. (2005a) 'Othering Organization Theory: Marta Calás and Linda Smircich' in C. Jones and R. Munro (eds), *Contemporary Organization Theory*. Oxford: Blackwell, 80–94.

Brewis, J. (2005b) Signing my Life Away? Researching Sex and Organization, *Organization*, 12(4) 493–510.

Brewis, J., and Linstead, S. (2000) *Sex, Work and Sex Work*. London: Routledge.

Brewis, J., and Linstead, S. (2009) 'Gender and Management' in S. Linstead, L. Fulop, and S. Lilley (eds), *Management and Organization*. 2nd edn. London: Palgrave, 89–147.

Brewis, J., Hampton, M., and Linstead, S. (1997) Unpacking Priscilla: Subjectivity and Identity in the Organization of Gendered Appearance, *Human Relations*, 50(10) 1275–1304.

Bruni, A., Gherardi, S., and Poggio, B. (2005) *Gender and Entrepreneurship: An Ethnographic Approach*. London: Routledge.

Burrell, G. (2006) 'Foucauldian and Postmodern Thought and the Analysis of Work' in M. Korczynski, R. Hodson, and P. Edwards (eds), *Social Theory at Work*. Oxford: Oxford University Press, 155–181.

Butler, J. (1988) Performative Acts and Gender Constitution: An Essay in Phenomenology and Feminist Theory, *Theater Journa*,. 40, 519–531.

Butler, J. (1993) *Bodies That Matter*. London: Routledge.

Butler, J. (1995) 'Contingent Foundations: Feminism and the Question of Postmodernism' in S. Benhabib et al. (eds), *Feminist Contentions*. London: Routledge 35–57.

Butler, J. (2000) *Gender Trouble*. 10th anniversary edn. First published 1990. London: Routledge.

Butler, J. (2004) *Undoing Gender*. London: Routledge.

Butler, J. (2005) *Giving an Account of Oneself*. New York: Fordham University Press.

Caine, B. et al. (1998) *Australian Feminism*. Oxford: Oxford University Press.

Calás, M., and Smircich, L. (1993) Dangerous Liaisons: The 'Feminine-in-Management' Meets 'Globalization', *Business Horizons*, 36(2) 71–81.

Calás, M., and Smircich, L. (1996) 'From "The Woman's" Point of View: Feminist Approaches to Organization Studies' in S.R. Clegg, S.R. (eds), *Handbook of Organization Studies*. London: Sage.

De Beauvoir, S. (1988) *The Second Sex*. First published 1949. London: Jonathan Cape.

Diprose, R. (1994) *The Bodies of Women: Ethics, Embodiment and Sexual Difference*. London: Routledge.

Diprose, R. (2002) *Corporeal Generosity*. New York: State University of New York Press.

Elam, D. (1994) *Feminism and Deconstruction*. London: Routledge.

Flax, J. (1987) Postmodern and Gender Relations in Feminist Theory, *Signs: Journal of Women in Culture and Society*, 12(4).

Foucault, M. (1979) *The History of Sexuality, Volume One: An Introduction*. London: Allen Lane.

Foucault, M. (1980) *Michel Foucault: Power/Knowledge* (ed. C. Gordon). Hemel Hempstead: Harvester Wheatsheaf.

Fournier, V. (2002) 'Keeping the Veil of Otherness: Practising Disconnection' in B. Czarniawska and H. Höpfl (eds), *Casting the Other: The Production and Maintenance of Inequalities in Work Organizations*. London: Routledge, 68–88.

Fraser, N. (1995) 'False Antitheses: A Response to Seyla Benhabib and Judith Butler' in S. Benhabib et al., *Feminist Contentions*. London: Routledge, 59–74.

Gatens, M. (1996) *Imaginary Bodies: Ethics, Power and Corporeality*. London: Routledge.

Gherardi, S. (1995) *Gender, Symbolism and Organizational Cultures*. London: Sage.

Giddens, A. (1991) *Modernity and Self-identity*. Cambridge: Polity.

Grosz, E. (1994) *Volatile Bodies: Towards a Corporeal Feminism*. London: Allen and Unwin.

Hancock, P., and Tyler, M. (2001) *Work, Postmodernism and Organization*. London: Sage.

Hancock, P., and Tyler, M. (2007) Un/doing Gender and the Aesthetics of Organizational Performance, *Gender, Work and Organization*, 14(6) 512–533.

Hassard, J., and Parker, M. (eds) (1993) *Postmodernism and Organization*. London: Sage.

Hatcher, C. (2003) Refashioning a Passionate Manager: Gender at Work, *Gender, Work and Organization*, 10(4) 391–412.

Hekman, S. (1990) *Gender and Knowledge*. Cambridge: Polity.

Hekman, S. (1999) *The Future of Differences*. Cambridge: Polity.

Helgesen, S. (1995) *The Female Advantage*. New York: Doubleday.

Irigaray, L. (1993) *Je, Tu, Nous: Toward a Culture of Difference*. London: Routledge.

Jones, C. and Munro, R. (2005) 'Organization Theory: 1985–2005' in C. Jones and R. Munro (eds), *Contemporary Organization Theory*. Oxford: Blackwell, 1–15.

Knights, D., and Kerfoot, D. (2004) Between Representations and Subjectivity: Gender Binaries and the Politics of Organizational Transformation, *Gender, Work and Organization*, 11(4) 430–454.

Kondo, D. (1990) *Crafting Selves*. Chicago, IL: University of Chicago Press.

Lyotard, J-F. (1984) *The Postmodern Condition*. Manchester: University of Manchester Press.

Martin, J. (1990) Deconstructing Organizational Taboos: The Suppression of Gender Conflict Within Organizations, *Organization Science*, 1(4) 339–359.

Martin, P.Y. (2006) Practising Gender at Work: Further Thoughts on Reflexivity, *Gender, Work and Organization*, 13(3) 254–276.

Oakley, A. (1972) *Sex, Gender and Society*. London: Temple Smith.

Parker, M. (1995) Critique in the Name of What? Postmodernism and Critical Approaches to Organization, *Organization Studies*, 16(4) 553–564.

Poggio, B. (2006) Outline of a Theory of Gender Practice, *Gender, Work and Organization*, 13(3) 232–233.

Pringle, R. (1989) *Secretaries Talk*. London: Verso.

Pullen, A. (2006) Gendering the Research Self: Social Practice and Corporeal Multiplicity in the Writing of Organizational Research, *Gender, Work and Organization*, 13(3) 277–298.

Pullen, A., and Knights, D. (2007) Undoing Gender: Organizing and Disorganizing Performance, *Gender, Work and Organization*, 14(6) 505–511.

Rosener, J.B. (1990) Ways Women Lead, *Harvard Business Review*, November/December, 119–125.

Simpson, R., and Lewis, P. (2007) *Voice, Visibility and the Gendering of Organizations*. Basingstoke: Palgrave Macmillan.

Thompson, P. (1993) 'Postmodernism: Fatal Distraction' in J. Hassard and M. Parker (eds), *Postmodernism and Organizations*. London: Sage, 181–203.

Weedon, C. (1997) *Feminist Practice and Poststructuralist Theory*. 2nd edn. Oxford: Blackwell.

West, C., and Zimmerman, D. (1987) Doing Gender, *Gender and Society*, 1(2) 125–151.

Wolkowitz, C. (2006) *Bodies at Work*. London: Sage.

Yeatman, A. (1994) *Postmodern Revisionings of the Political*. London: Routledge.

Young, I.M. (2005) *On Female Bodily Experience*. Oxford: Oxford University Press.

# 2

# Women's Writing

HEATHER HÖPFL
*University of Essex*

## INTRODUCTION

This chapter attempts to examine the difficult issue of women's writing. It looks at what women are allowed to write, how they are allowed to write it, and what the consequences of these restrictions are for the way in which women construct their work identity; for self-expression and the communication of ideas, and, taken together, for the impact of these issues for the work role, progression, and career. It is generally assumed that the act of writing is unproblematic, that there are specific styles – the journalistic, academic, legalistic, novelistic, diaristic, personal and so forth – which can be acquired through training or disposition, and that these styles can be exercised with varying degrees of competence in the act of writing. However, beyond the most obvious and clichéd simplicities, little attention is paid to gendered writing and while there has been some attention to this theme in language and literature studies, there has been a widespread assumption in conventional organization theorizing that patriarchal language and writing is not only entirely appropriate as the benchmark standard but, more than this, it is the desired medium of communication for academic discourse. Indeed, the privileged [masculine] style of writing has been regarded as the primary acquisition of an academic education. Reference to almost any management or organizational studies journal would readily confirm this view.

Consequently, this chapter is primarily concerned with the writings of Hélène Cixous, Luce Irigaray, and more particularly with the contribution of the writing of Julia Kristeva (1941 – ) to poststructuralist ideas[1] about gender in organizations and specifically with a concern for her attempts to deal with issues of women's writing: both her own and the act of writing more generally. In particular, this chapter deals with the relationship between her writing and her views on the disciplining of text. It then goes on to examine how this concern with writing can be translated into a concern for embodiment and embodied writing: with the relationship between the body and the regulation of the body. However, it must be acknowledged that Kristeva's writings are 'extremely difficult and complex, and certainly intimidating

---

[1] For an account of poststructuralism see Tyler, in this volume.

and inaccessible to the non-specialist' (Lechte, 1990: 2). Despite this, Kristeva has come to be considered one of the foremost contemporary 'French'[2] thinkers and her writings have exerted a significant influence on both feminism and postmodernist ideas. That said, there is a striking and self-conscious feature of her writing, of which more will be said in due course, which can be found in the contrast between her formidable command of the authoritative, academic style and her experimentation with a more embodied style of writing when she strives to introduce the personal. It could also be said that in the process both succumb to the rhetorical trajectory of the text and perhaps this is always inevitable. However, this chapter will attempt to examine some of the implications of this association between the subjective and subjection as it arises in Kristeva's work. Finally, I would argue that Kristeva's writing is at its weakest the closer it gets to her own history and experiences. Her work on the position of the 'foreigner', *Strangers to Ourselves* ([1988] 1991) which has significant implications for the issues raised in this chapter, has been criticized for its lack of attention to class, gender, and race and Kristeva has been criticized for her lack of political insight (Oliver, 1993b) and for the confusion of the personal in the text. Yet, it is this writing which, in some senses, comes closest to describing Kristeva's own personal circumstances: arriving in Paris aged twenty-five, a Bulgarian, supported by a French government scholarship (Lechte, 1990: 91; Moi, 1986: 1): an exile. Unlike her powerful, *Tales of Love* (1987), where she demonstrates a considerable *mastery* over her text, *Etrangers à nous-mêmes* (1988), is a more hesitant, literary text which despite her clarity of argument does not have the same sense of command as the earlier *Tales of Love*. Hence, there are questions to be raised, issues to be discussed, and implications to be drawn from an examination of the connection between writing and experience.

## KEY WRITINGS AND WRITINGS IN WHITE INK

In order to gain some understanding of why the subject of women's writing is important, it is perhaps interesting to set this in the notion of 'key writings' in the field, to consider what a key writing might look like, what guidance it might offer in understanding the topic, what authority it might bring to bear in defining a field of study. It is, of course, also interesting in terms of what might constitute an 'authoritative' piece of writing and who has the power to arrive at such a definition, to exercise judgement on the value or validity of a piece of writing. In order to write and to overcome the 'anxiety of influence' suffered by every writer when it is his (*sic*) turn to wield his language (his pen)' (original parentheses) (Todorov, 1981: 24) the writer – any writer, Kristeva, Irigaray, Freud, Deleuze, or even myself as author of this chapter – must achieve homologation with the trajectory of the phallogocentric text: must speak the same language (cf. Docherty, 1987). Moreover, this homologation

---

[2] Ironically, Kristeva is neither French by birth nor a feminist in the sense that the term is generally understood. Indeed, she has been highly critical of those feminists whom she regards as seeking 'phallic power' (see Lechte, 1990).

requires submission to the prevailing definition of authority, in other words submission to the trajectory of patriarchal writing. In terms of this chapter, this presents a problem. Certainly, and whilst wishing to guard against a collapse into essentialism, there are some prominent men who have written a good deal about the act of writing and there are many who have done this in a poetic and feminine way. Derrida's work, in particular, has been highly influential in the deconstruction of language and his seminal work, *Writing and Difference* (1978), brings a great deal to the analysis of the relationship between writing and subjection. Not only this, but Derrida invites the reader to enter the text and to violate the frame of writing. Likewise, Jacques Ranciere's (2004) text, *The Flesh of Words: The Politics of Writing* seeks to 'flesh out' text, to give life to words. And, first, Deleuze's notion of the *body without organs* in his book, *The Logic of Sense* (Deleuze, [1969] 2004) and then Žižek's *Organs without Bodies: Deleuze and Consequences* (2003) offer insights into the relationship between the world of the text with its relentless trajectory and the world of flesh and blood, of bodies and their experiences. Of course, the texts identified here are few amongst many that either directly or obliquely seek to open up the politics of language and its regulatory function. Derrida, Deleuze, Ranciere, and Žižek are indicative as far as 'key writings' go and there are clearly others not included in this list who deserve mention. The point is that however radical, experimental, profound or different these texts are they are supremely masculine and even the *difference* they seek to indicate is itself subject to the hegemony of the patriarchal style. In fact, this was a concern which Derrida struggled with and his first attempt at a doctoral thesis, 'The Ideality of the Literary Object' was never completed apparently because of his problems with deferral to phallogocentrism (Derrida, 1980).

This phallogocentric authority is implicit and pervasive. It is invoked in every requirement to justify and explain, to theorize and to account. It is the expectation that I impose upon my doctoral students when I ask them to justify a statement, provide more explanation, to offer authoritative support. How then is it possible to call on phallogocentric judgments and patriarchal definitions in order to identify key writings which in this specific sense justify the exposure of the inferior position of the Other, the discrimination between one text and another, one explanation and another and the question of what constitutes the authoritative statement come to determine what is permitted within phallogocentric judgement? Here my intention is simply to raise the difficult issue of how to allow alterity to enter the text. This is not merely a question of what is permitted. It is about who has the power to define, about who defines what is permitted. After all, as Kristeva has argued, 'What we designate as "feminine", far from being a primeval essence, (is the) "other" without a name' (Kristeva, 1982: 58). In contrast, consider Luce Irigaray's (1992) 'Writing as a Woman' [chapter six of her book, *Je, Tu, Nous: Towards a Culture of Difference*] in which she says,

> I am a woman. I write with who I am. Why shouldn't that be valid unless out of contempt for the value of women or from the denial of a culture in which the sexual is a significant subjective and objective dimension? But how could I on the one hand be a woman, and on the other, a writer?'

and further on she adds,

'I am a woman. I do not write *as a* woman.' (italics added)

Here, Irigaray makes a highly significant point. She is identifying the problem of what it is to be a woman within the phallogocentric discourse: what it is
to be constructed in a way which conforms to patriarchal notions of order and
authority, and what it is to be regulated by representations which are at vari-
ance with embodied experience. Amongst her highly influential works, *Speculum
of the Other Woman* ([1974] 1985) and *The Sex Which is Not One* ([1977] 1985)
are perhaps most relevant to the concern explored in this chapter. Irigaray is
renowned for her work on *écriture feminine* in which she advocates perturbations
in the text to disrupt the phallogocentric thrust of patriarchal writing. In *The Sex
Which is Not One* ([1977] 1985) she takes issues with Freudian notions of female
sexuality and instead offers a view of female sexuality which is both fluid and
irreducible. This is a view which extends to her ideas about women's writing
which she believes should also be fluid, multifaceted, and irreducible. With this
in mind, *Speculum of the Other Woman* ([1974] 1985), is too rich a text to reduce
to a simple definition but suffice it to say that as well as introducing the concept
of the speculum as both mirror and instrument of gynaecological inspection, it
operates on a number of different levels of analysis, provides insights into the
nature of female melancholia, hysteria, the patriarchal order, narcissism and
female homosexuality and more. Her books should not be read with the linear
trajectory of male text but rather should be enjoyed for the fluidity of the ideas
which, while being sequential, at the same time operate with multiple associations and resonances.

However, it is perhaps to Hélène Cixous that credit must be given for pressing
the case for women to engage with the relationship between their bodies and language, and for giving voice to the fact that women are ensnared by a language which
does not permit them to communicate; which does not give voice to the body. Her
([1975] 1991) essay, *The Laugh of Medusa*, is an invitation to a 'feminine mode' of
writing [*écriture feminine*] and an attack on phallogocentrism. It is Cixous who uses
the metaphor of 'white ink' (Cixous, 1975: 312) for feminist writing calling for a
text which is written in breast milk. In her essay on Cixous's work, *Writing Past the
Wall or the Passion According to H.C.*, Susan Suleiman (1991) says, 'In a social structure
hungry to consume them, women are limited to the voyage of the digestive tract,
to literal incorporation' (Suleiman, 1991: 15) and recalls Cixous's remarks on red-
riding hood being swallowed by the wolf quoting the well-known line from *Coming
to Writing* 'What is the body for? Myths end up having our hides. Logos opens up its
great maw and swallows us whole' (Cixous, cited in Suleiman, 1991: 15). There is
much to be said about the contribution of Cixous to the study of women's writing.
Her analogy between writing and masturbation goes a long way to describing
some of the academic journals which deal exclusively in phallogocentric ranting as
the emissions of young academic poseurs who, essentialist or not, it must be said
are mainly men. For Cixous, writing is not agonistic in this primal way. Writing is an

activity that is related to spaces in-between. This is a political position which resists hierarchy and insinuates resistance. Cixous sees feminist writing as subversive and deconstructive. In this chapter, this notion of the space for difference is retained. However, for the sake of this particular argumentation, it is Kristeva's work which now receives attention.

## KRISTEVA'S CONTRIBUTION

In the subversive mood in the Paris of the mid-1960s, Kristeva found a fertile site for her ideas and, no doubt, gained insights from her own experiences of exile and of difference which gave impetus to her prolific writing during this period. From the start of her studies in Paris, she was to work with some of the leading figures in French structuralism. She was particularly influenced by Roland Barthes. Kristeva had gone to Paris to study Bakhtin. She was an exile: a stranger who was later to write at length about estrangement.

Not only this but also, in the mid-1960s, Kristeva was a woman in the masculine world of French intellectualism. It seems that in virtually every aspect of her life Kristeva was confronted by repressive structures, by alterity and by a French intellectual elite which was dominated by figures such as Roland Barthes, Gilles Deleuze, Michel Foucault, Jacques Lacan, Jean-Paul Sartre, Phillipe Sollers, and Jean-Luc Godard. It was a world which women found difficult to enter without the support of men. Kristeva was supervised by Roland Barthes and married Phillipe Sollers. Yet, these experiences provided the tensions from which her ideas were to spring. Her writing is *seminal* to the extent that it seeds the transgression of phallogocentric order. The most powerful aspect of her writing is the sense of the resistance that powers the ideas, obscures the writing, and seeks to evade capture in the phallogocentric project of language. Understood in this way, her writing is defensive in dealing with things which are forbidden in well regulated writing, so that her meaning obscures itself in order to protect itself from definition.

On occasion her writing is formidably theoretical, dense and insistently patriarchal. Sometimes what she writes reads like relentless *science*, to the extent that Oliver has put forward the view that her writing 'seems to make Kristeva herself a paradox, an anomaly, or a "man"', (Oliver, 1993a: 107). Her work is often *impenetrable*, frequently obscure, full of double meanings and idiosyncrasies of style. Sometimes her work appears to display an extraordinary degree of *mastery*: the supreme acquisition of education and training. Yet there is always the sense that she is struggling with the writing:

> Words that are always too distant, too abstract for this underground swarming of seconds, folding in unimaginable spaces. Writing them down is an ordeal of discourse, like love . . . (Kristeva, in Moi, 1986: 162).

Overall, there are two important considerations to take forward from Kristeva's work insofar as it is relevant to the argument presented here. The first is to do with her attempts to 'break the body of the text' (Höpfl, 2000) and the second is to do with the reproduction of text: who is allowed to reproduce and the gender of the offspring. In the case of the former, in *Stabat Mater*, she *breaks the body* of the text in order to allow her personal reflections on motherhood to enter and oppose the trajectory of language. She constructs the text from two positions, her own formal writing on the Virgin Mary and her personal reflections on Motherhood in dialectical opposition: two columns running down either side of the page to represent, on one level, the Body on the left and the Law on the right. The Body speaks of embodied experience. The Law speaks of rationality and rhetorical trajectory. The Body and the Law are both Kristeva in her vacillation between embodied experience and her mastery of language. Her writing rends the page in order to show what is concealed by language. The illustration which follows shows how Kristeva's ideas and, for that matter, Cixous' idea of the space in-between as a space of political possibility can contribute to the appreciation of the relationship between phallogocentric rhetoric and the potentialities of 'the catastrophic-fold-of-*being*' between the Body and the Law, (Kristeva quoted in Moi, 1986: 173).

## DISRUPTIVE ALTERITY

My colleague Sumohon Matilal, an accounting lecturer, and I have recently published an article in *Accounting, Auditing and Accountability Journal* (AAAJ) (2009) which seeks to examine what is missing from statements of account by ignoring embodied experience. In this 'account', we sought to give emphasis to the relationship between the purely representational aspects of the statements of account and the everyday lived experiences of those directly affected by the gas tragedy at Bhopal in 1984. On 3 December, a highly toxic cloud engulfed the city Bhopal. Of the 800 000 people living in Bhopal at that time, no one knows exactly how many people were affected. The plant owners, Union Carbide, in its official statement on the tragedy, maintained that 3800 died. In contrast, the Indian Government said that 1754 people were killed and 200 000 injured (Matilal and Höpfl, 2009). The point is that using photographs of piles of bodies, funeral pyres, queues for medical attention, we sought to transgress the comfortable narratives of the statements of account which reduced this considerable human tragedy to matters of mere bookkeeping. Therefore, in the spirit of Kristeva's work, the article was about opening up a space which was at the same time revelatory, political, and ethical. However, it must be said that from the outset we had to acknowledge that we could not move outside the inevitable logic of the rhetorical piece. In that sense, our paper was also rhetorical and our argument subject to the review and authorization of the peer-review system. We had to submit to the need for further explanation where we might have preferred the text to speak for itself. As Cixous says, 'Logos opens up its great maw and swallows us whole' (Cixous, 1991: 15). At best, the contribution was at least able to offer a complementary position and to help us to hold onto incoherence. It is necessary to hold on to the various strands of stories and not to be seduced too quickly by a desire for cosy and coherent accounts. At least the images helped to retain something of the human character of disaster. So, admittedly this was not an unqualified success but it does serve as an example of a piece of writing which attempts transgression and complementarity, and which seeks to move in the ambiguity of the space.

## HEGEMONY AND REPRODUCTION

It goes beyond the scope of this chapter to do more than outline Kristeva's views on writing and reproduction. However, the idea that one must become 'a man' in order to demonstrate discipline in writing or, at least to conform to the appearance of the patriarchal discourse, is an important matter. Using ideas drawn from the Roman Catholic doctrine of the Assumption, Kristeva argues that 'To earn divine grace', a woman must render herself homologous with the male text so that she is 'more fully conformed to her son' (Kristeva quoted in Moi, 1986: 174). If the feminine threatens to subvert the text, then the move to affirm the notion of the Assumption, bodily and spiritual subjection to the Law, is the reversal of that potential for transgression. The feminine is *incorporated* into the text (cf. Cixous 'swallowed whole') and, via its elevation, made part of the Word: inseparable from the Word. In this way, women and their work, the feminine and its ways of being, are made to conform with phallogocentric order. Ironically, the hyper-abstraction of women and their regulation via homologation arises from the fact that men *can* only reproduce themselves hyper-abstractly. In other words, they cannot actually reproduce themselves: they cannot become mothers. Male reproduction is reproduction of the text and this implicitly estranges the maternal and the feminine. The apparent autonomy of language gives men the means of alienating the Other and achieving quasi-reproduction in language. Hence, clarity, logic and discipline in writing become the defensive strategies which guard against the contamination of the body and physical reproduction. Writing which refuses to conform is extremely threatening to such a notion of order.

## A PERSONAL EXAMPLE

In the spirit of this chapter, I will make a personal observation here. When I started my doctoral thesis at Lancaster University in 1977 in the (then) Department of Behaviour in Organizations, it was an exciting and challenging place to be. Nevertheless, when I began my research on *The Subjective Experience of Time*, my supervisor, the late Professor Sylvia Shimmin, cautioned me that my ideas were 'on the lunatic fringe of psychology'. Times have changed and to some extent there is more scope for originality. However, perhaps Kristeva is right when she argues that, in terms of writing, women are only permitted to produce 'sons'. That is to say, women are required to be conventional. They must produce authoritative text. Men can *get away with* much more. As text, they can produce 'daughters', that is to say that an imaginative, creative, feminine piece of writing from a man is often celebrated and admired as if something very significant had been achieved. In a sense, this is quite right. Something has been achieved. The trajectory of phallogocentric writing has been ruptured, alterity exposed. If men do this, their work is applauded and regarded as highly original and fresh. This is what Kristeva means by producing a 'daughter'. Women have to produce textual sons. Over my academic career I have encouraged my doctoral students to take risks, be experimental and creative, play with ideas, create spaces and so forth – to produce daughters, to allow the body to enter the text and not be incorporated by it, and at the same time admitting the ultimate futility of the gesture. However, when I reflect on this, I must also consider after over thirty years in academic life, the extent to which I am so much 'swallowed up', ingested, incorporated into phallogocentric discourse that my imprimatur is a patriarchal one. One is always required to 'submit'. One submits to a journal, to the editorial directive, to the vagaries and idiosyncrasies of reviewers. Stylistic requirements or attitudes towards the personal often determine what can and cannot be said in an article or a report. Sometimes the requirements of reviewers would change the focus of an article and it is necessary to decide between submission and integrity. Given that we are now all required to submit to the tyranny of journal rankings, as decided by those who have the power to define 'quality', the response is probably to submit to the reviewers' requests regardless.

Clearly, there can be no recovery from this situation via writing. Kristeva argues that it is either possible to *submit* and become the same, in other words to achieve and demonstrate *mastery* of the text, in which case, as Oliver observes, one becomes a 'man', to become part of the pro*ject* – or, on the other hand, to be other, different and rejected.

> A woman will only have the choice to live her life either *hyper-abstractly* (original italics) . . . in order thus to earn divine grace and homologation with the symbolic order; or merely *different* (original italics), other, fallen . . . But she will not be able to accede to the complexity of being divided, of heterogeneity, of the catastrophic-fold-of-'being' (Kristeva, in Moi, 1986: 173).

## WOMEN, WRITING, AND THE ORGANIZATION

So what is it possible to gather from all this? What this contributes to an understanding of gender issues in organizations is the capacity to make transparent the effects of the production of meaning, regulation through 'writing' and regulation of the 'other' within the logic of trajectory, strategy, and purpose. Kristeva reverses the power of mastery by its replication. She can hold her own writing as within the phallogocentric text, but her self-awareness of this position, in a qualified sense, permits her to defend her writing by making it impenetrable and to subvert the text through stylistic devices, the introduction of exiled words and experiences, the intrusion, or perhaps here extrusion, of the body through the text. However, at best this is partial and the issue of capture remains. This is the issue for the work-role, for writing identity and for organizational membership.

Just as there is no place for women in writing, so there is no place in the organization. It is not a place for women with physical bodies that produce menstrual blood, breast milk, maternal smells, there is no 'white writing' in corporate strategy – women can only be representational. Feminine attributes which are required in the service of the organization are constructed within the phallogocentric discourse in order to serve its ends. Embodied practices are displaced by constructions that are mediated through mere representations of the feminine. For example, by valuing those aspects of the 'feminine' which serve the organization, organizations exclude women of flesh and blood from valorization by the organization. The organization will only value the feminine to the extent that women become symbolic men or, indeed, *as* symbolic women: to behave '*as* women' (to recall Irigaray's remark). They must submit to the imposition of the symbolic order and to the suppression of any deviation from it. The feminine has no weight and, by parity of reasoning, no influence, no power, because it is only a hyper-abstraction. It is a hyper-abstraction produced by hyper-abstract male reproduction: reproduction in language which constitutes the feminine as an abstract category with the jurisdiction of its ordering.

So then, how can women write and how can they perform regulated and disciplined by the patriarchal order? It is difficult to *convey* the problem of feminine writing without seeking to transgress the text and, yet, every transgression will invite correction (Hart, 1989). The same is true for organizations. Transgression is not a permitted strategy. However, since every explanation is a further *incorporation* into the body of the text this project is self-defeating. On the other hand, without explanation, without the intervention of the author to explain the purpose, the intention, the desire and so forth, the attempt becomes untenable. To repeat Toril Moi's comment, 'As soon as the insurgent "substance" speaks, it is necessarily caught up in the kind of discourse *allowed by* and *submitted to* by the Law' (Moi, 1986: 10, italics added). Organizations reproduce themselves through male heirs. The image of the feminine (in Kristeva's example, the Virgin Mary) is the empty vehicle through which the paternal word is conveyed (Kristeva, 1983: 374): so the representational feminine becomes an instrument of male reproduction. This kind of activity can be seen in the ways human behaviours have been reduced to categories and check-lists for metrical assessment. The phallogocentric discourse, it seems, is preoccupied with division, separation, and categorization and by these devices keeps itself free of contamination by the body.

## Summary and Conclusions

There are two dimensions to the ideas presented here which are to do with the importance of the writing and experience and the implications for the study of work organizations. Women's writing seems to be almost an impossibility and fails when subjected to scrutiny and the process of authorization. The relationship between writing and identity, writing and authority, writing and the body, makes the subject of women's writing an interesting one to consider in relation to women's work roles, identity and problems of authority and permission. The desire to confront the problem of capture within the patriarchal text is fundamental to Kristeva's work and yet she acknowledges that to attempt to use language against itself is to create an untenable position: a position which is all too familiar to women when they attempt to deviate from the roles that are allocated to them. The daughter has to become a son in order to fight for her inheritance. This is not surprising since '[n]othing reassures, for only the Law sets anything down' (Kristeva, 1983 as cited in Moi, 1986: 175) and the roles it permits for women are limited.

Kristeva has said that '[i]f "something maternal" happens to bear upon the uncertainty that I call abjection, it illuminates the literary scription of the essential struggle that a writer (man or woman) has to engage in . . . with the other (sex) that torments and possesses him' (Kristeva, 1982: 208). In this sense, this chapter is 'something maternal' which seeks to bear upon the ways in which women's writing is seen in order to invite alterity to enter the text. However, it is already ensnared within the trap of rhetoric. There are clearly implications of all this for the ways in which work roles are constructed, progressions determined and differences conciliated. It is now over thirty years since Cixous, Irigaray, and Kristeva started their influential work but so little has happened. If nothing more, this chapter argues for a thorough re-examination of the contribution of their work and an attempt to apply some of their ideas both in academic writing and by their translation to the workplace.

# REFERENCES

Cixous, H. (1975) 'The Laugh of the Medusa' in R.R. Warhol and D. Price Herndl (eds), *1991 Feminisms: An Anthology of Literary Theory and Criticism*. New Jersey: Rutgers.

*Concise Oxford Dictionary* (1974) 5th edn. London: BCA.

Deleuze, G. [1969] (2004) *The Logic of Sense*. New York: Continuum International Publishing Group.

Derrida, J. (1978) *Writing and Difference*. Chicago: University of Chicago Press.

Derrida, J. (1980) *The Time of a Thesis*, a speech given on the occasion of him receiving his doctorate, http://plato.stanford.edu/entries/derrida/ (accessed 21.01.10).

Docherty, T (1987) *On Modern Authority*. Brighton: The Harvester Press.

Hart, K. (1989) *The Trespass of the Sign*. Cambridge: Cambridge University Press.

Höpfl, H. (2000) The Suffering Mother and the Miserable Son, Organising Women and Organising Women and Organising Women's Writing, *Gender Work and Organization*, 7(2) 98–106.

Irigaray, L. (1985) *Speculum of the Other Woman*. Ithaca: Cornell University Press.

Irigaray, L. (1985) *The Sex Which is Not One*. Ithaca: Cornell University Press.

Irigaray, L. [1987] (1992) *Je, Tu, Nous: Towards a Culture of Difference*. London: Routledge.

Kristeva, J. (1982) *Powers of Horror, An Essay on Abjection*. New York: Columbia University Press.

Kristeva, J. (1983) 'Stabat Mater' in T. Moi (ed), *The Kristeva Reader*. Oxford: Blackwell (1986).

Kristeva, J. (1987) *Tales of Love*, trans. L. Roudiez. New York: Columbia University Press.

Kristeva, J. (1988) Etrangers à nous-mêmes, Paris: Fayard.

Lechte, J. (1990) *Julia Kristeva*. London: Routledge.

Matilal, S., and Höpfl, H.J. (2009) Accounting for the Bhopal Disaster: Footnotes and Photographs, *Accounting, Auditing & Accountability Journal*, 22(6) 953–972.

Moi, T. (1986) *The Kristeva Reader*. Chichester: Basil Blackwell.

Oliver, K. (1993a) *Reading Kristeva*. Bloomington: Indiana University Press.

Oliver, K. (ed.) (1993b) *Ethics, Politics and Difference in Julia Kristeva's Writing.* New York: Routledge.

Rancière, J. (2004) *The Politics of Aesthetics.* London: Continuum.

Suleiman, S. (1991) 'Writing Past the Wall or the Passion According to H.C.' in H. Cixous (1992) *Coming to Writing and Other Essays.* Cambridge MA: Harvard University Press.

Todorov, T. (1981) *Introduction to Poetics.* Brighton: The Harvester Press.

Žižek, S. (2003) *Organs without Bodies: Deleuze and Consequences.* London: Routledge.

# 3

# Ways of Knowing: Gender as a Politics of Knowledge?[1]

SILVIA GHERARDI
*University of Trento, Italy*

## INTRODUCTION

This chapter examines the way in which gender, power and knowledge are intimately intertwined. Its purpose is to illustrate how gender ('doing' gender) can be considered a politics of knowledge. Because there are many ways to define and conceptualize what is meant by 'gender', I shall begin by making explicit the approach that I adopt.

My discussion will be framed within postmodern feminist thought as described by Tyler's chapter in this Handbook. Although the relationship between feminist theories and postmodernism/poststructuralism in studies on work and organizations has been a difficult one, we may nevertheless say that it has also been highly fruitful (Calás and Smircich, 1997; Holvino, 1996; Gherardi, 2003) because it has contextualized the inheritance of Foucault (1986) and shown by means of concrete examples how knowledge is an inextricable aspect of power, and how it is historically and culturally specific because it is the product of a particular discourse. The broad movement which has begun to deconstruct metanarratives (Hekman, 1990) has also revealed that the alleged universality and objectivity of knowledge is a power effect. Post-colonial and queer studies, for example, have brought a plurality of subjects to centre stage and claimed legitimacy for plural 'knowledges' (Bhabha, 1988; Monro, 2005; Gandhi, 2006; Anim-Addo et al., 2009). Within this problematization of the relationships among power, situated knowledge and gendered subjectivity, the thought of Judith Butler (1990; 2005) has been influential in applying the concept of performativity to gender, and consequently also on its use by organizational

[1] I wish to thank all participants at two seminars which afforded me opportunities to discuss the ideas developed in this chapter. The first opportunity was offered in April 2009 at Jyvaskyla, in Sweden, during the conference on 'Work, Learning and Welfare – Changing Identities and Practices'. The second opportunity came in Halifax, Canada, whence I had been invited by Albert Mills, and where I was able to discuss these ideas with PhD students. Of course, responsibility for what is written is entirely my own, but good discussion is always beneficial.

studies which study subjectivity in workplaces. This performative aspect of gender enacted through language and gesture, and the symbolism associated with gender, is also to be found in the interactionist tradition of 'doing gender' (West and Zimmerman, 1987). This has opened the way for analysis of gender as a social practice (Martin, 2003; Poggio, 2006) which produces effects because of what is done, not just as a result of interactions between 'gendered' persons. This chapter belongs within this domain of study. Its aim is to conduct symbolic analysis on how Western thought has developed from a binary conception of gender. By deconstructing a classical narrative (taken from Plato) of how knowledge is gendered, it seeks to show (or better perform) an alternative narrative in which 'another' form of knowing the world is possible, thereby showing how gender performativity is inscribed in a politics of knowledge.

One way to analyse how gender is performed in organizations, and how the symbolic gender order is reproduced, is to examine the narrative constructions of the 'knowing subject'. Narratives can be treated as 'artifacts' by means of which cultures can be understood and interpreted, and their dominant values and norms identified (Czarniawska, 1997). Alternatively, narratives, or better narrating, can be regarded as processes of 'practising gender', where gender is produced non-reflexively and interactively with other actors (Martin, 2006). In what follows, I shall use a passage from Plato to deconstruct the process of constructing the knowing subject in Western philosophy. I shall also use an autobiographical narrative that performs the process of gaining awareness of how a gendered conception of knowledge is reproduced non-reflexively even by those who one might anticipate being particularly sensitive to such issues – such as a 'gender' scholar.

Even if narrative analysis and narrative knowledge (Gherardi and Poggio, 2007; Rhodes, this volume) have achieved full citizenship in organization studies, organizational scholars still seem more inclined to analyse the stories of 'others' (as they encounter them in organizations or in the texts that describe them) than to tell stories in the first person.[2] I shall contravene this tacit code by recounting the origins of my analysis of how knowledge in organizations and about organizations is gendered knowledge. I shall adopt an unconventional expository technique whereby I first tell my story and then deconstruct the story told by Plato, the purpose being to uncover the underlying dichotomies and then use them within studies on gender, work and organization to support my overall argument. In so doing, I shall pursue two aims: to reaffirm a feminist epistemological principle that 'inserts the author in the text', and to show that, when positioning gender, one takes a position in a politics of knowledge as well.

## My Story

I had a two-hour seminar with my PhD students and I had asked them to read an article on knowledge and knowledge management. At the beginning of the seminar,

---

[2] Feminist thought has made explicit criticism of the scientific writing which hides the author/ity of the writer behind impersonality (the view from nowhere) and proposes in its stead a politics of location in which the voice of the author and his/her physicality are represented in the text (Bordo, 1989). A good example of stories told in the first voice is Jacques (1997).

as I sat down at the table, I asked them if they had liked the article. It was only a polite question intended to break the ice, so to speak. I didn't expect to see four scowling faces and to receive the reply: 'It's so male!' I looked more closely and realized that the group of doctoral students, who had just begun the PhD course, consisted of four women, and that the comment had never been made to me before when I had discussed the same article with students in the past. At that point my interest in knowledge management disappeared, and together with the students,[3] I began to explore how a comment so obvious to common sense was instead so difficult to argue for in theory.

It was during the conversation that I discovered our shared knowledge of another story – that of the young Thracian serving girl recounted by Plato – which acted as a metaphor generating a critique against the knowledge dominant in organization studies, and framing that text within its con-text. We were all aware of the story, not because of any particular knowledge of Plato, but because Italian feminist thought in the 1990s had appropriated it and recast it in a search for female figures in ancient philosophy (Cavarero, 1990).[4]

Before deconstructing Plato's story, I should explain the reasons for recounting my story. The fact that culture has been produced/appropriated by a masculine subject is so introjected that often, even among people aware of it and committed to its unmasking, it passes unnoticed and its repetition takes place unconsciously. Repetition, in fact, is the mechanism which Butler posits as the basis of gender performativity. Through stylized acts of repetition, of recitation of cultural norms and gestures, gender becomes ritualized and its effects appear 'just natural'. Knowledge appears to be neutral, universal and power-free, as if the knowing subject were a disembodied subject. What happens in a world of embodied knowing subjects? It is here that Plato's story comes in.

## PLATO'S STORY

This is the story of a young servant girl and Thales, the first philosopher:

> Thales, while he was studying the stars and looking upwards, he fell into a pit, and a neat, witty Thracian servant girl jeered at him, because he was so eager to know the things in the sky that he could not see what was before him at his very feet. (Plato, Theaethetus, 174a)

Plato's anecdote was reprised over the centuries and came to signify the attitude of the philosopher who contemplates things up above, while a woman, and moreover a slave and a foreigner, looks at things down below . . . and dares to mock the philosopher.

---

[3] Although responsibility for this article is entirely mine, it has a female genealogy. I therefore wish to thank Gessica Corradi, Camilla Rossi, Giulia Selmi, and Silvia Toccoli for a happy moment of creativity.

[4] Not only in Italy but in the international feminist debate, the re-reading of Plato has given considerable impetus to reconsideration of the female voice: see for instance Tuana (1994).

The servant girl, and all the slave girls of Thrace, have become the paradigmatic example of the naive attitude of ignoramuses who do not understand theory: 'that is, the contemplation of truth performed by thought in a "higher" reality which distracts thought (or better the thinker) from the ordinary facts of this world' (Cavarero, 1999: 32). The philosopher looks upwards and produces theory, the servant girl looks downwards and sees the practical matters of prosaic reality. The separation between theory and practice is thus enacted, and the hierarchization of the two types of knowledge enters thought and society. But the servant girl laughs, and with her laughter the history of philosophy begins. Can we therefore say that laughter is at the origin of Western thought? And, moreover, the laughter of a woman, a slave and a foreigner!

Plato thus had a young and attractive woman's laughter 'represent the pleasing aspect assigned to women as their distinct "value"', argues Adriana Cavarero (1999: 35). The corporeality of a woman of pleasing appearance – though enslaved and therefore coarse and ignorant, and a native of Thrace and consequently foreign – stands in contrast with the male wisdom of the true philosopher. A further symbolic polarity is introduced between the body of a woman and the mind of a man.

Plato included the anecdote about the young Thracian servant girl in a long dialogue where Socrates discusses knowledge and describes 'the true philosopher'. The latter, exactly like Thales, the epitome of the philosopher, uses his mind to investigate 'the things that are', or ideas, and has no interest in 'things that are close by'. He looks up at the stars, whose regular motions replicate the imperturbable celestial laws that only the mind can understand, drawing from them lessons about what is true. Up above, therefore, are the regular motions of the eternal stars; down below are the short-lived things of the earth, which are nothing but appearances. There are thus two worlds: a real one of 'things that are' and another one 'of things that are nearby', mere appearances, the result of deceptive sense experience. And this produces a third dualism: between being and appearance, between essence and reality, between the world of pure thought and the world of experience. The world of things close by, down here, is the world of reality and experience, and it is consequently devalued. Instead, knowledge of the truth lies over and above the world. The devaluation of the body, experience, and sensory knowledge is thus sanctioned. But it is this devaluation which the Thracian servant girl mocks. Her laughter is not just the scornful outburst by an intelligence backed by the facts; it also a symbol of resistance by a female existence without signification in the philosophical empyrean.

## THE THRACIAN SERVANT GIRL AS A FIGURE OF DISCOURSE

The Thracian servant girl is the kind of figure through which the symbolic order of a culture represents itself. As Barthes (1977) points out, a figure of discourse is a *topos* offered to the reader so that s/he may take possession of it, add something to it, remove what s/he does not need, and pass it on to others. The symbolic order manifest in the figure of the Thracian servant girl is the patriarchal one in which the female is the subject of others' thought and has therefore been expelled from culture and deprived of capacity for signification. The figure of the Thracian servant girl has been repeatedly reprised in Western culture, and a book by Hans Blumenberg (1987) testifies to the translation undergone by the figure over time. The main change concerns the servant girl herself, whose attributes of youth and beauty are erased, so that she is turned into a malignant old woman by those who want to emphasize the obtuseness of the mockers of philosophy. The figure of the old woman impedes every possible sympathy (and value) for the female, who becomes even more obtuse. In function of a metaphysical discourse – where 'meta physica' means above this world – the old woman therefore represents the obtuseness of those who mock philosophy.

By contrast, in the repetition of the story by word of mouth, the position of the servant girl is taken by an Egyptian sage when the discourse must sustain the positiveness of laughter and things that are nearby. Hence, when the figure of the servant girl must play a positive role, it changes sex and becomes a man!

The imagery comprised in the figure of the servant girl was resumed in subsequent centuries with various substitutions. Kant recounts almost the same story about Tycho Brahe, who was also absorbed by contemplation of the stars.

> One night when Tycho took it into his head that he could find the shortest route for his carriage by observing the stars, his coachman put him in his place by saying: 'My good sir, you may know about the heavens, but down here on earth you are a madman.' (Blumenberg, 1987: 117, my translation)

Once more we find knowledge represented as pertaining to those who gaze upwards – whether a philosopher or an astronomer – whilst the practical knowledge of everyday things is left to a simple figure, a servant. Tycho Brahe is wise in one world, and mad in another. In Kant, the bipolarism is between heaven and earth, and it emphasizes trust in reason per se, in its capacity to grasp objects distant in space and time in a single broad movement and describe them in a single natural history of the universe.

The *topos* of the above and the below, of heaven and earth, of theoretical and practical knowledge, continued thereafter, appropriating the original anecdote in pedagogical terms to transmit those values to successive generations. But repetition and transposition of the personages into the symbolic order of the male erased the meaning of female laughter and its rootedness in a form of practical and sensitive knowledge. How did this happen? The answer lies in the invisibility of the female.

Whilst Plato's misogyny was mitigated by the fact that the servant girl was young and attractive, thereafter the masculinity of the true philosopher simply made the female invisible. Male thought did not restrict itself to erasing the female, however: in order to assert its abode in the world of things, it cancelled its own birth (Cavarero, 1999: 39), by silencing the fact that it was born of a mother in a world of appearances.

Luce Irigaray (1987: 21) takes up the same *topos* and argues that our society and culture originated from a 'symbolic matricide'. The cancellation of the original – generative – bond with the woman's body had the newborn infant enter the culture at the price of negating the relationship with the maternal. In cancelling, silencing and devaluing the symbolic universe of the female and the maternal, the culture and language reaffirm, repeat, and recite the symbolism of the male and independent as the separation and negation of corporeality and dependence on the mother. The knowing subject belongs to a universe without bonds and without bodies.

## THE SYMBOLIC MATRICIDE IN ORGANIZATION STUDIES

As a figure of discourse the Thracian servant girl stands for the invisibility of the female and its negation in a symbolic matricide. The reader of this text thus far will already have grasped the obvious analogies with the values that sustain management and organization studies. The repetition of the same narrative sustains Western thought and represents a politics of knowledge that legitimates dominant forms of organizational reality by 'restricting the interpretations and meanings that can be attached to organizational activity' (Mumby, 1997: 113). Knowledge is maintained within the symbolic order of the masculine by repetition and recitation of the divide between theory and practice, and the other dichotomies bearing the same gender subtext.

I now want to show how this narrative works also in organization studies. I shall do so by resuming the symbolic bipolarisms present in history, starting from the laughter of the Thracian servant girl. If the history of Western philosophy began with Thales, it also began with cancellation of woman's laughter. What does laughter symbolize? Is it a symbol of resistance? Can laughter be more powerful than speech and reasoning?

There is no culture that does not cultivate a sense of the comic. It can be defined as an anthropological constant, although it differs greatly according to the historical period. Yet laughter expresses a form of understanding; there is something that humour is believed to perceive. Freud (1905) devoted an important part of his work to laughter, and much can be said about the mechanisms which trigger laughter or wit. Nevertheless 'from its simplest to its most sophisticated expressions, the comic is experienced as incongruence' (Berger, 1997: x). Peter Berger observes that the comic conjures up a separate world different from the ordinary reality, and operating by different rules. And it is a world in which the limitations of the human condition are miraculously overcome, so that the comic is a promise of redemption.

In postmodernist feminism humour, irony and parody are considered weapons for destabilizing gender categories and practices (Pringle, 1989; Brewis et al., 1997; Gherardi, Marshall and Mills, 2003). Butler (1990: xii) proposes 'parodic practices based on a performative theory of gender acts that disrupt the categories of the body, sex, gender and sexuality and occasion their subversive resignification and proliferation beyond the binary frame'. Thus gender (and also organization, as we shall see) is shown to be a performatively enacted signification that 'released from its naturalized interiority and surface can occasion the parodic proliferation and subversive play of gendered meanings' (ibid.: 33).

On this basis, I shall look at the symbolic bipolarizations in organization studies with the gaze of the Thracian servant girl and through her laughter as a promise of redemption.

## THE ABOVE AND THE BELOW

The spatial symbology of the above and the below and their hierarchy are visible in organizations, in their management of spaces, and in their representations, beginning with organizational charts. The management is above, and what the management does is called strategy (and masculinity!). In fact the discourse of strategy is intertwined with the discourse of capitalism and masculinity (Knights and Morgan, 1991; Samra-Fredericks, 2005). The gender subtext in man/agement has been widely explored (Collinson and Hearn, 1994; 1996; Höpfl, this volume) and since we have learned to 'name men as men', we have also become able to 'see' how men mobilize masculinities (Martin, 2001).

On the other side, below lie the workers, and what they do is called work. From a symbolic point of view what is 'below' pertains to the female, to the point that bureaucracy 'femalizes' its clients better to symbolize dominance relations (Ferguson, 1994; Gherardi, 1995). This bipolarism has been assumed uncritically by organization scholars as well, who have assumed the top-down gaze and form perhaps one of the largest communities of interest – the one comprising strategy analysts – among those who study organizing. The work that takes place in the world below has been traditionally less studied, as if organizing can be separated from its object, namely work. Emblematic in this regard is the title of an article which has been widely cited, and for good reason. When Barley and Kunda entitled their 2001 article 'Bringing Work Back In', they were not simply expounding good reasons for doing so and inviting the community to follow suit; they were also emphasizing the separation that had come about (especially in Anglo-American studies) between working and organizing.

If the Thracian servant girl represents a promise of redemption, perhaps alongside her we can see the strategy analysts inspired by ethnomethodology who read strategy as a practice: that is, those who define it as what someone does when they say that they are doing strategy (Samra-Fredericks, 2005). Therefore an alternative and critical positioning of the knowing subject can be enacted.

## THEORY AND PRACTICE; TRUTH AND APPEARANCE

Theory, with its aspiration to universalism and truth regards itself as epitomizing knowledge. It relegates the knowledge which derives from the senses and experience, and which springs from doing and from the hands, to the shadows of down below. Practical knowledge has only recently attracted the attention of organization scholars (Strati, 2007), and it has done so only since faith in rationality has dwindled and its limits have been discussed. As absolute rationality has given way to a satisfactory rationality, and subsequently to a plurality of contingent rationalities, its place has been taken by the tacit knowledge conserved in corporeal schemes, collective and distributed, enacted during action, and harboured in work practices and communities of practitioners. Work, too, enters the scene as practical and collective knowledge, not as tasks and their execution. Practical knowledge is dignified when its economic value is discovered in the knowledge economy and in the design of new technologies to support work. This, however, is a valorization that exposes it to abduction from its context and transfer elsewhere. Practical knowledge – that of the servant girl or the coachman – is a knowledge that resides in doing and re-doing; it is a sensory knowledge, fruit of the body and caring, not of abstraction. The 'practice-based' studies that maintain a critical stance towards positivism and cognitivism, and envisage the possibility of a passionate knowledge (Gherardi, Nicolini, and Strati, 2007) can be considered the descendant of the Thracian woman's laughter.

## MIND OF A MAN AND BODY OF A WOMAN

The mind/body dichotomy not only expresses a hierarchy of values; it also posits knowledge as the fruit of the mind, and the body as non-knowing, as at most the source of sensations and therefore of illusions. The body, and with its embarrassing sexual difference, as well as sexuality, has for long been banished by organization studies (Hassard et al., 2000). Organizations are afraid of the body of the woman-mother (Poggio, 2003) and they therefore tend to repress the pain of labour (with its twofold meaning).

The symbolic matricide of which Irigaray speaks was committed to perpetuate a masculine, patriarchal, and rational image of the organization. Suppressing the body of the (m)other continues to transmit an abstract idea of organization made up of aseptic relations, rational behaviour, and end-directed actions. A fine book (Höpfl and Kostera, 2003), which I would call choral more than collective, proposes the expression 'maternal organization' to show how it alone is indicative of its subversive significance. By reprising the poststructuralist and feminist thought of Julia Kristeva (1984), the authors of the book seek to carry forward a new discourse on the maternal function in the development of subjectivity and cultures. Both women and men can fulfil the maternal function and in so doing subvert the authority of monologic science and filiation (Moi, 1986: 1). What a discourse of maternity contributes to the theory of organization is 'to render explicit the patriarchal quest of the organization and to make problematic the notion of trajectory, strategy and purpose (i.e. its directedness)' (Höpfl, 2003: 4).

## A POLITICS OF KNOWLEDGE

The topic of redemption with respect to symbolic matricide opens the way for discussion of gender as a politics of knowledge; and to do so in renewed terms. These concerns, in fact, not only answer the question of whose knowledge is considered legitimate knowledge but also the possibility of multiple discursive positions and plural epistemologies.

To illustrate this point I shall refer to two books which have been milestones in feminist thought: *Women's Ways of Knowing* (Belenki et al., 1997) and *In a Different Voice* (Gilligan, 1982).

True to its subtitle *The Development of Self, Voice and Mind,* the book by Belenki, Clinchy, Goldberger, and Tarule starts from the cognitive stage theories of William

Perry, just as Gilligan, in her research on women's moral voices, started from Lawrence Kohlberg's moral stage theories. Both Perry and Kohlberg worked almost solely on male children and young adults in explaining the achievement of cognitive and moral stances. In both cases the feminist critique was aimed at determining whether girls and women learn to be moral in different ways. On the basis of a different sample, it was not difficult to demonstrate that moral development is gendered. Gilligan wrote as though there were one different voice, a moral stance of caring interconnectedness alternative to the dominant one of abstract universalizing. Belenki and colleagues moved to the plural, portraying an increasing ability to be actively participant in the social construction of knowledge. They studied the ways of knowing of 135 rural and urban women of different ages (from sixteen to over sixty), classes, ethnic backgrounds, and educational histories, and described five knowing perspectives from which women see themselves and the world. Their five epistemological perspectives were silence, received knowledge, subjective knowledge, procedural knowledge and constructed knowledge. These perspectives outline the ways of knowing that move from that of being without voice (or not knowing) and accepting authority, to more empowered knowing where women gain their own authority, capacity for discernment and reflection. These two books have constituted the principal referents for construction of the women's standpoint that represents a politics of knowledge associated with a binary representation of gender.

In analysing the ways in which feminist theories and epistemological strategies can frame research on gender in organization studies, Calás and Smircich, (2009) showcase three epistemologies: feminist empiricism, feminist standpoint epistemology, and feminist postmodernism, reprising the classic distinction drawn by Harding (1987; 1998). Feminist empiricism begins from the philosophical position that knowledge producers are embodied beings whose particular location matters in the world they observe, and standpoint epistemology emphasizes knowledge 'from below', as reflecting embodied experience under specific historical and material conditions. Consistently with these epistemological assumptions, feminist standpoint epistemologies further the notion that the ways of seeing of the disadvantaged may offer a better and more complete understanding of 'the world' from the position of those disadvantaged by traditional epistemologies.

Women's standpoint studies have been accused of essentialism, on the grounds that there is no definite subject behind the alleged 'experiences' of women because, as feminist postmodernism has pointed out, this subject constantly changes in relation to the other in whose terms it is defined (woman versus man, white versus coloured, etc.). Whatever the case may be, it is certain that this has opened the way for debate on the politics of knowledge, and to the concept of positioning (Alcoff, 1988, Davies and Harrè, 1990) as the active assumption of a discursive position. In fact, feminist postmodernism focuses on the instability of the subjects of knowledge and therefore problematizes conventional legitimation of knowledge claims. What Calás and Smircich very thoroughly document in their work is that all three of the epistemological strategies contribute in various ways to the production of knowledge and to a politics of pluralist knowledge.

With respect to the anecdote of the Thracian servant girl and Thales, these works from women's standpoints propose the symbolic bipolarism of the above and the below, but they give a less restrictive account of it, in that the knowing subject can recognize the discourse of universalism (and separation) and that of caring (and of interconnection) and choose to position itself in their regard and produce knowledge from within one discourse rather than another. Poststructuralist feminism directs attention to discourse and language as constitutive of social reality, and to how gender has been stabilized as male/female dualisms in that discourse (Scheman, 1993).

The possibility of a different positioning of the knowing subject lies in the process of subjectivation and in practices of freedom. The dual meaning of subjectivation – as related to subjectum (literally 'thrown under', subjected to control and dependence), and as a process by which a subject comes to know itself through the utilization of techniques of the self – has been explored by Bonnafous-Boucher (2009) in light of Foucault's and Butler's philosophy. The subject is not a substance, but a form, and this form is not always identical to itself. Bonnafous-Boucher (2009: ??) argues that techniques of subjectivation allow a change from a passive, subjected subject to an active individual who has come to know itself and to choose the position that it occupies in the real or imaginary in order to become a legitimate subject of a specific type of knowledge.

While the discourse of power and subjectivation has been largely explored in relation to domination, less has been done to read subjectivation as a practice of freedom and as a process of positioning of the knowing subject in relation to practices of knowledge production (Bonnafous-Boucher, 2009).

## Conclusion

The Thracian servant girl has no name, but she has the power to mock the birth of Western philosophy. She is a woman, young and enslaved, and she well represents all that has been kept silent in male thought: sex, race and class. I have reprised the story of the servant girl and recounted it once again to show how it can exemplify, in its simplicity, the construction of the binary categories which have been reproduced in organization studies as in philosophy; but also to show how the Thracian servant girl symbolizes, with her mockery of theory, subversion of the symbolic order of the father.

While the symbolic order of the male imbues organization studies, I have preferred to cite the example of how the laughter of the Thracian servant girl can be interpreted, not as the sterile derision of someone who feels superior, but as a hope for redemption, and therefore as a glimpse of a way forward to alternative modes of knowing. In organization studies, too, there is hope for a 'plural' knowledge which starts from resistance against a sterile universalizing to produce knowledge from a positioning of the knower in interconnection and in caring.

I shall conclude with a brief reflection on the type of work that I have intended to propose. It has been the story of an anecdote and its reception, but I shall now consider the reception of its reception. When reading the anecdote, one may take the side of the philosopher and despise the servant girl unable to understand otherworldly things, or one may take the side of the servant girl with her refusal to recognize the world of ideas as real. Positioning in the text and in the con-text can help us understand how knowledge can be produced by positioning oneself in a discourse of relationality, rather than in duality. In fact we settle gender relations amongst the subject positions available to us and produced by existing discourses – we are lived embodiments of discourses – but discourses are historically and temporally located and there are limitless other ways of being, thinking and doing. Foucault (1986: 46) calls *assujetissement* (subjectivation) the process by which we come to know about ourselves and to structure the field of our possibilities: there are limitless other ways of subjectivation, of knowing, and of producing knowledge.

## REFERENCES

Alcoff, L. (1988) Cultural Feminism versus Post Structuralism: The Identity Crisis in Feminist Theory, *Signs*, 13(3) 405–436.

Anim-Addo, J., Covi, G., and Karavanta, M. (2009) *Interculturality and Gender*. London: Mango Publishing.

Barley, S., and Kunda, G. (2001) Bringing Work Back in, *Organization Science*, 12(1) 76–95.

Barthes, R. (1977) *Fragments d'un Discours Amoureux*. Paris: Editions du Seuil.

Belenki, M.F., Goldberger, N.R., and Tarule, J. M. (1997) *Women's Ways of Knowing: the Development of Self, Voice and Mind*. New York: Basic Books,

Berger, P. (1997) *Redeeming Laughter. The Comic Dimension of Human Experience*. Berlin: Walter de Gruyter & Co.

Bhabha, Homi, (1988), The Commitment to Theory, *New Formations*, 5, 5–23.

Blumenberg, H. (1987) *Das Lachen der Thrakerin. Eine Urgeschichte der Theorie*. Frankfurt am Main: Suhrkamp.

Bonnafous-Boucher, M. (2009) 'The Concept of Subjectivation: A Central Issue in Governmentality and Government of the Self' in S. Binkley and J. Capetillo-Ponce, *A Foucault for the 21th Century: Governmentality, Biopolitics and Discipline in the New Millennium*. Cambridge Scholars.

Bordo, S. (1989) The View from Nowhere and the Dream of Everywhere: Heterogeneity, Adequation, and Feminist Theory, *American Philosophical Association Newsletter on Feminism and Philosophy*, 88(2) 19–25.

Brewis, J., Hampton, M., and Linstead, S. (1997) Unpacking Priscilla: Subjectivity and Identity in the Organization of Gendered Appearance, *Human Relations*, 50(10) 1275–1304.

Butler, J. (1990) *Gender Trouble: Feminism and the Subversion of Identity*. London: Routledge.

Butler, J. (2005) *Giving* an Account of Oneself. New York: Fordham University Press.

Calás, M., and Smircich, L. (1997) *Postmodern Management Theory*. Aldershot: Dartmouth Publishing.

Calás, M., and Smircich, L. (2009) 'Feminist Perspectives on Gender in Organizational Research: What is and is yet to be' in D. Buchanan and Alan Bryman (eds), *Handbook of Organizational Research Methods*. London: Sage Publications.

Cavarero, A. (1990) *Nonostante Platone*. 2nd edn. Roma: Editori Riuniti.

Collinson, D., and Hearn, J. (1994) Naming Men as Men: Implications for Work, Organization and Management, *Gender, Work and Organization*, 1(1) 2–22.

Collinson, D., and Hearn, J. (1996) 'Breaking the Silence: On Men, Masculinities, and Managements' in D.L. Collinson and J. Hearn (eds), *Men as Managers, Managers as Men: Critical Perspectives on Men, Masculinities, and Managements*. London: Sage, 1–24.

Czarniawska-Joerges, B. (1997) *Narrative Approach in Organization Studies*. London: Sage.

Davies, B., and Harré, R. (1990) Positioning: The Discursive Production of Selves, *Journal of the Theory of Social Behaviour*, 1, 43–63.

Ferguson, K. (1984) *The Feminist Case Against Bureaucracy*. Philadelphia: Temple.

Foucault, M. (1986) *The History of Sexuality. Vol. 3*. New York: Pantheon.

Freud, S., (1905) *Der Witz und seine Beziehung zum Unbewussten*. Frankfurt am Main: Fischer Taschenbuch-Verlag, 1986.

Gandhi, L. (2006) *Affective Communities: Anticolonial Thought, Fin-de-Siècle Radicalism, and the Politics of Friendship*. Durham: Duke University Press.

Gherardi S. (1995) *Gender, Symbolism and Organizational Cultures*. London: Sage.

Gherardi, S. (2003) 'Feminist Theory and Organizational Theory: A Dialogue on New Bases' in H. Tsoukas and C. Knudsen (eds), *The Oxford Handbook of Organization Theory: Meta-theoretical Perspectives*. Oxford: Oxford University Press.

Gherardi S., Marshall J., and Mills A. (2003) 'Theorizing Gender and Organizing' in S. Clegg and R. Westwood (eds), *Debating Organization*. Oxford: Blackwell.

Gherardi, S., Nicolini, D., and Strati, A. (2007) The Passion for Knowing, *Organization*, 14(3) 309–323.

Gherardi, S., and Poggio, B. (2007) *Gendertelling in Organizations: Narratives from Male Dominated Environments*. Copenhagen: Libe,.

Gilligan, C. (1982) *In a Different Voice*. Cambridge, MA: Harvard University Press.

Harding, S. (1987) 'Introduction: Is There a Feminist Method?' in S. Harding (ed.), *Feminism & Methodology*. Bloomington, IN: Indiana University Press, 1–14.

Harding, S. (1998) *Is Science Multicultural? Postcolonialisms, Feminisms, and Epistemologies*. Bloomington, IN: Indiana University Press.

Hassard, J., Holliday, R., and Willmott, H. (2000) 'Introduction: The Body and Organization' in J. Hassard, R. Holliday, and H. Willmott (eds), *Body and Organization*. London: Sage, 1–14.

Hekman, S. (1990) *Gender and Knowledge – Elements of a Postmodern Feminism*. Cambridge: Polity Press.

Holvino, E. (1996) Reading Organization Development from the Margins: Outsiders Within, *Organization*, 3(4) 520–534.

Höpfl, H. (2003) 'Maternal Organization: Deprivation and Denial' in H. Höpfl and M. Kostera (eds), *Interpreting the Maternal Organization*. London: Routledge.

Höpfl, H., and Kostera, M. (2003) *Interpreting the Maternal Organization*, London: Routledge.

Irigaray, L. (1987) 'Le corps à corps avec la mère' in *Sexes et Parentés*. Paris: Les Editions de Minuit, 19–33.

Jacques, R. (1997) 'The Unbearable Whiteness of Being. Reflections of a Pale, Stale Male' in P. Prasad et al. (ed.), *Managing the Organizational Melting Pot: Dilemmas of Workplace Diversity*. Thousand Oaks, CA: Sage.

Knights, D., and Morgan, G. (1991) Corporate Strategy, Organizations, and Subjectivity: A Critique, *Organization Studies*, 12(2) 251–273.

Kristeva, J. (1984) *Desire in Language: A Semiotic Approach to Literature and Art*, trans., T.S. Gora, A. Jardine, and L. Roudiez. Oxford: Basil Blackwell.

Martin, P.Y. (2001) 'Mobilizing Masculinities': Women's Experiences of Men at Work, *Organization*, 8, 587–618.

Martin, P.Y. (2003) Said and Done vs. Saying and Doing: Gendering Practices, Practicing Gender at Work, *Gender & Society*, 17, 342–366.

Martin, P. Y. (2006) Practicing Gender at Work: Further Thoughts on Reflexivity, *Gender, Work and Organization*, 13(3) 254–276.

Moi, T. (1986) *The Kristeva Reader*. Oxford: Blackwell.

Monro, S. (2005) *Gender Politics*. London: Pluto.

Mumby, D. (1997) The Problem of Hegemony: Rereading Gramsci for Organizational Communication Studies, *Western Journal of Communication*, 61, 343–375.

Plato (1921) *Theaetetus Sophist*. Cambridge: Harvard University Press (trans. H.N. Fowler)

Poggio, B. (2003) 'Who's Afraid of Mothers?' in H. Höpfl and M. Kostera (eds), *Interpreting the Maternal Organization*. London: Routledge.

Poggio, B. (2006) Outline of a Theory of Gender Practice, *Gender, Work and Organization*, 13(3) 232–233.

Pringle, R. (1989) *Secretaries Talk*. London: Verso.

Samra-Fredericks, D. (2005) Strategic Practice, 'Discourse' and the Everyday Interactional Constitution of 'Power Effects, *Organization*, 12(6) 803–841.

Scheman, N. (1993) *Engenderings. Construction of Knowledge, Authority, and Privilege*. New York: Routledge

Strati, A. (2007) Sensible Knowledge and Practice-based Learning, *Management Learning*, 38(1) 61–77.

Tuana, N. (1994) *Feminist Interpretations of Plato*. Penn State Press.

West, C., and Zimmerman, D. (1987) Doing Gender, *Gender & Society*, 1(2) 125–151.

# 4

## Gender, Work, and Organization in Popular Culture

ALISON PULLEN AND CARL RHODES
*Swansea University*

Storytelling is an ancient form of communication and cultural transmission. Throughout history and across nations and societies, narrative is pervasive. As Geertz (1973) explains, the stories we tell ourselves about ourselves are part of the ensemble of texts that make up the culture of a people. But in contemporary times the way we tell ourselves these stories has changed on account of the technological media through which they are presented and transmitted. Today cultural storytelling cannot be accounted for without considering television, cinema, popular novels, magazines, advertisements, the internet, or the other myriad of mass media that emerged in and after the modern era. The technological expansion of the media does not just signal the increased variety and reach of cultural products, but also brings the uneasy marriage of commerce and culture. After industrialization the stories we tell ourselves about ourselves are a part of the vast matrix of corporate activity.

Gender, race and religion are deeply entrenched in and influential on popular culture and the mass media (Fiske, 1989). Popular culture and its relationship to gender has been studied as a general area of inquiry (e.g. Hermes, 2005) as well as in terms of specific media such as magazines (e.g. Walker, 1998), popular music (e.g. McRobbie, 1999), and television (e.g. Heide, 1995). In this chapter we explore the relationships between gender and popular culture with specific focus on how gender at work has been represented in film and television. The chapter unfolds in two parts. First, we introduce how gender and work have been portrayed in film and television, with a particular focus on the examples of corporate work, rural work, and sex work. Second, we turn specifically to the ways that gender and popular culture have been researched in the field of organization studies, especially in terms of gender politics. We use this to advance our main line of argument – popular culture, while potentially being a vehicle for the perpetuation of oppressive and repressive gender norms in relation to work, also contains within it the resources for the critique, and even subversion of those norms. We conclude by considering popular parody as an exemplary form of such critique – one that can not only question gender, but also unsettle it.

Our starting point is that the meaning of popular culture is by no means fixed, nor can it be subject to analyses that weed through the presentation in order to divine some essential meaning. Instead, the reading of popular culture is about drawing connections between systems of cultural meaning (Czarniawska and Rhodes, 2006). There is a certain openness in the way that popular culture represents gender, organizations and gendered organizations – both on account of the possibilities of the 'aberrant decoding' (Eco, 1979) and 'active readership' of popular texts as well as the slippage of meaning that occurs when different cultural meanings and practices come together (Hall, 1996). Moreover, popular culture is no ideological monolith, and within it there are plural and diverse examples through which to read inequality *and* equality, oppression *and* liberation, materiality *and* representation, silence *and* voice, marginalization *and* dominance. Popular culture is not an unambiguous site for the perpetuation of patriarchal, sexist and heteronormative values; it also contains within it the possibilities for resistance to and transgression of those values and their associated practices. Through production, consumption and articulation popular culture offers a means through which hegemonic gender relations can be critiqued and troubled. It is this sense that the chapter considers the representation of gender at work in popular culture in terms not only of its reinforcement of oppressive cultural norms and stereotypes, but also to demonstrate the possibilities of a productive and affirmative appreciation of gender and work in popular culture.

## Work and Gender on Film and Television

It is stating the obvious to say that representations of the relations between gender and work are manifold in popular culture. From the boardroom to the trading floor, and from the factory and on to the farm, gender at work has been a mainstay within popular culture. To illustrate the breadth of this, as well as to introduce the topic of the chapter in this section we consider how these issues have been represented in some select examples of film and television concerned with (a) working in the city and in corporations, (b) working in the country and in farming, and (c) sex work and sexuality at work.

### Working in the city

Throughout the decades, Hollywood 'financial films' such as *Wall Street* (1987) have reached mass audiences. Taking *Wall Street* as an example, we can immediately recognize some different models of masculinity as related to work. The film starkly contrasts aggressive corporate patriarchy with masculinity associated with blue collar work through the characters of Wall Street Investor Gordon Gekko (Michael Douglas) and airline worker and trade unionist Carl Fox (Martin Sheen). Gekko is the 'greed is good' finance deal maker who stops at nothing to seal a deal. Fox is the left-leaning working man. As O'Sullivan and Sheridan (1999) comment, Gekko is portrayed in the image of what a corporate hero should be – tough, aggressive, masculine, and successful. Fox, a more kind hearted 'people person', is out of place in the hyper-masculine world of the corporation. But it is Gekko who steals the show in his exemplification of corporate 'homosocial reproduction' of hyper-masculinity (p. 18).

The corporate man, Gordon Gekko, is akin to a gangster – a theme explored in a different way in 1980's *The Long Good Friday*. The lead character Harold Shand (Bob Hoskins) is a gangster who wants to become a businessman. Shand shares Gekko's aggressiveness and ruthlessness but shows it on the street as well as in the boardroom. Both films demonstrate the seductive lure of success and its association with aggressive masculinity – 'a prison for patriarchs' (McDowell, 1997: 161). *The Smartest Guys in the Room* (2005), the documentary of Enron, similarly surfaces this 'sexy/greedy world' (Thrift and Leyshon, 1990, in McDowell, 1997: 162), highlighting corporate masculinity's role in sustaining the cultural values of that world which holds no place for women and femininity (O'Sullivan and Sheridan, 1999).

Outside of the drama of high finance, especially recently, professional women are also regulars on film and in television. This is reflected in studies of women as lawyers in *LA Law* (Glass, 1990), women as doctors in *ER* (Hassard and Holliday, 1998) and gendered leadership stereotypes in relation to *Star Trek* (Bowring, 2004). Further, femininity, albeit in different guises, can be used by corporate women to both seduce and control has been discussed through *Disclosure* (Brewis, 1998). These studies show, through popular culture, how gender is central to organizational performance.

A particularly important example where women occupy a place in the corporate world is in what Hermes (2005) calls postfeminist television and film – programs that explore women's personal and professional lives in a context where traditional feminist battles over liberation and equality are assumed outdated. The city remains an important feature, one that is both the location of and an influence on the world of work – especially in terms of men and women of the corporation. This has been glamorously depicted in the television programmes *Sex and the City* (1998–2004) and *Ally McBeal* (1997–2002) and the *Bridget Jones' Diary* films. These examples embody a postfeminist ideal where women can pursue career, sex, romance and marriage unapologetically (McRobbie, 2008). With Bridget Jones her office life and personal life collide in the context of her femininity and her quest for a good husband. *Sex and the City* emphasizes liberated professional women and metrosexual men, where gender difference becomes less distinct. Ally McBeal is a successful, albeit neurotic, lawyer but her success is contextualized in a highly sexualized and romance-driven arena. Each of these examples puts feminism at stake (Hermes, 2005) through the depiction of living and working in a postfeminist world promulgating the myth of equality. Feminism's impact is taken for granted, and new feminine ideals become established:

> The prevalence of powerful and attractive working girls across the landscape of media and culture and the incorporation of working identity as integral to the post-feminist masquerade comes to provide a benchmark against which young women are invited to measure their own capacity in the world of work. (McRobbie, 2008: 78)

After feminism, it would seem, women are empowered but are they still doing men's work rather than being and becoming women?

## Working on the land

The country and the farm are also sites in which film and television have portrayed the relationships between gender and work. There has been a surge of interest in the farm from the extremely popular Australian (and later internationalized) reality TV serial *The Farmer Wants a Wife* (2007–) to the long running internationally Australian drama *McLeod's Daughters* (2001–2009). Historically, however, farm work and its connection to the Western myth of masculinity is epitomized in the popular culture figure of the American cowboy (Easthope, 1990). The cowboy, was a male fantasy figure epitomizing the ideals of self-sufficiency, freedom, and moral rectitude. Moreover, culturally, the cowboy revived masculinity from the onslaught of industrialization, commerce and bureaucracy (Horrocks, 1995; Aquila, 1996). And, while standard cowboy films see 'men gaze at each other, pump bullets into each other's bodies, and lust after women as bar room "whores" as they battle over patriarchal law, Westerns also "explore some of the contradictions of American masculinity"' (Horrocks, 1995: 56).

*The Outlaw Josey Wales* (1976) is a good example of this. Clint Eastwood plays the character Josey Wales – a helpless farmer who watches his wife raped and killed and his son burned to death in the family home. He leaves his working life to seek revenge. Along the way he gets on the wrong side of the law. But no matter how bad he becomes and no matter how cold he acts, viewers relate and empathize with Wales, perhaps because of the tragedy that befell him at the beginning of the film, or perhaps because of the friendships he builds. In the Western, masculine work is solitary and physical, and to be a man is to be rugged, individualistic (Allmendinger, 1992) and morally self-sufficient. Josey Wales embodies these values, but not just these – the film shows his ejection from the idyllic rural, family setting, a life that was brutally taken away from him. Rugged masculinity is not here something that is normal or desirable, but is a hard response to the aggression of the masculine context.

Nevertheless, although masculinity might be in question, whether at the working farms and prairies, or in the saloons of the Wild West, traditional stereotypes surrounding the hierarchical division of labour between men and women remain intact. Even when women are pioneering they still tend to occupy subordinate roles which reinforce conventional masculinity (Deutsch, 2007). In response to this, Pilgeram (2007) examines the strategies women employ to negotiate the tensions between their self-identities as women and farmers, showing how women 'do' masculinity by imitating the performances of their male colleagues. As a result hegemonic masculinity is reinforced. 'Men's work' has to be done by 'tough women' who perform masculinity and undo the feminine (Inness, 2004) – the very issues brought to light and contested in *McLeod's Daughters*.

## Prostitution and sexuality

The polarized extremes of the naturalness of the farm and the artificiality of the city do not capture the variations of work, labour and gendered performances in popular culture. Despite prostitution being largely ignored as a form of work in the study of management (Rehn, 2008) it is common in popular culture. There is the early Chinese film *The Goddess* (1934) showing the life of a single mother supporting herself and her son through prostitution in Shanghai. In Hollywood there is *Pretty Woman* (1990) a film that demonstrates not only a highly stylized and de-sexed view of prostitution but also has a plot whereby the prostitute is 'rescued' by a knight in shining armour. Problematically, the film demonstrates that women can advance themselves socially through heterosexual romance, and in the process reinforce masculinity (Tasker, 1998).

Not all films about prostitution are like *Pretty Woman*. In *Belle de jour* (1967) Catherine Deneuve stars as a high class prostitute during the day unbeknownst to her working husband. The film focuses on prostitution in terms of sexuality and sexual exploration in the absence of sexual intimacy in the home. *Working Girls* (1986) is a particularly interesting example in that it is explicit in its political intentions. The film is a landmark in feminist cinema in that it:

> allows us a sense not only of the realities of women's bodies, and the ways in which they must be disguised for conventional sex roles to be enacted, but also of the vulnerability of men's bodies and the childish obliviousness of the 'needs' that bring men to the brothel (McDonald, 1989: 328)

More generally, whilst sexuality has been extensively analysed in studies of popular culture, few studies focus on work and organization. There are some exceptions. Holliday's (1998) analysis of (homo)spaces in the Hollywood film *Philadelphia* (1993) highlights how sexuality was organized and how organizational spaces recreated dominant organizational cultures that perpetuate gender hegemony. Brewis et al.'s (1997) analysis of popular images of transvestism and transsexualism as it related to identity and organization in *The Adventures of Priscilla. Queen of the Desert* (1994) explored how gender difference relates to image and dress. These examples are sparse, and even though queer theory has been discussed (Parker, 2002; Namaste, 1994) queer analyses of popular culture remain few. The same can be said for transgenderism (Stryker and Whittle, 2006), gender fluidity (Linstead and Pullen, 2006), transgenderism and abjection (Thanem, 2003) and gender transitioning (Schilt and Connell, 2007). Popular culture can, however, provide avenues ripe for such explorations.

An excellent example is the Thai film *The Beautiful Boxer* (2003). The film is based on the true story of Parinaya Charoenphol, a highly successful male Thai kick boxer. Parinaya's motivation to fight was to save enough money for a sex change operation. This film exemplifies gender transgression at the level of work and personal identity – something that comes to the fore when Parinaya wears feminine makeup when fighting resulting in his opponents being taken off guard by their gender expectations being transgressed. This aligns with Halberstam's (2005) transgressive politics of queer subjectivity; interrogating how gender and hetero-homosexual boundaries relate to embodiment and the envisioning of the body. In this sense the transgenderism politically reveals the 'ideological content of the male and female gazes' and disarms the assumed normalcy of gender and heterosexuality (Halberstam, 2001: 669). *The Beautiful Boxer* in particular disarms the cultural association between masculinity and physical power – boxing being an arena where such power is celebrated.

## GENDER AND POPULAR CULTURE IN MANAGEMENT AND ORGANIZATION STUDIES

As we have seen, gender, work and organization are frequent subject matter in film and television. We note too that there is a well established tradition in feminist theory of the critique of popular culture. Examples include Brooks' (1997) analysis of postfeminism and cultural theory and de Lauretis' (1984) and Doane's (1987) psychoanalytic feminisms. The organization of institutions that affect girls' subjectivity is discussed by Harris (2004) and scholars in media studies and cultural studies explored the politics of gender in popular culture (see Roman et al., 1988; McRobbie, 2004; Hollows and Moseley, 2006; Dow, 1996; Walters, 1995; Tasker and Negra, 2007). Specific to work settings, feminist analysis has been applied to the organization of the kitchen (Brundson, 2006), the beauty industry (Black, 2006) and sex work (Arthurs, 2006).

In management and organization studies there is a growing awareness of the productive possibilities of studying organizations through popular culture (see Rhodes and Westwood, 2008; Rhodes and Parker, 2008; Hassard and Holliday, 1998) including dramatic illustrations of gendered cultural norms. Studies have asserted that popular culture promulgates repressive gender stereotypes (Coltrane and Adams, 1997), reinforces masculinist organizational normativity (Höpfl, 2003), portrays hegemonic masculinity (O'Sullivan and Sheridan, 2005), and illustrates negative images of women's careerism (Brewis, 1998). More affirmatively it has also been suggested that popular culture subverts gendered social practices at work (Czarniawska, 2006) by bringing into question the 'strong plots' (Czarniawska and Rhodes, 2006) that inform our cultural expectations of gendered behaviour. In such cases gendered critique is not seen as the business of the critic commenting on popular culture, but also embedded in popular culture itself (Rhodes and Westwood, 2008) such that 'popular culture might offer new forms of critical knowledge that is hidden in the masculine ideological commitments common to many organizational researchers' (Rhodes and Pullen, 2009: 595). Accordingly, researchers have demonstrated how popular culture contains a critique of masculinity and organizational power (Rhodes and Pullen, 2007), a questioning of the gendered meaning of leadership (Bowring, 2004), a disruption of gender norms (Rhodes and Westwood, 2008), and a 'queering' of management and organization (Tyler and Cohen, 2008).

### Popular culture and patriarchy

Many studies argue that popular culture reinforces gender oppression and inequality at work within a dominant patriarchal organizational system. In an extensive study of the portrayal of work–family segregation in television advertisements, Coltrane and Adams (1997) found that compared to male characters women

> were less prevalent, more likely to be shown in families, less likely to hold jobs, less likely to be employed in professional occupations, more likely to be employed in service/clerical occupations, less likely to exercise authority, less likely to display active/instrumental behavior, and more likely to be pictured as sex objects (p. 323)

Coltrane and Adams' point is that popular culture, in the form of advertising, reinforces gender stereotypes that serve to subordinate women. Focusing on the 'role of cultural symbolism in the perpetuation of work, family, and gender stereotypes' (p. 324) their analysis shows how male characters in advertisements are active and instrumental, whilst women are passive and emotional. This enables them to conclude not only that 'patterns of symbolic gender differences are endemic in our culture' (p. 345), but also that popular culture is complicit in ensuring that gendered structural inequities are maintained as a status quo. By this account popular culture is complicit in attempts to subordinate women as inferior to men, especially when it comes to professional and occupational roles.

O'Sullivan and Sheridan's (2005) reading of the British TV police drama *The Bill*, also found that popular culture was part and parcel of the maintenance and promulgation of gendered norms that privileged men at the expense of women. They draw on Connell's (1987, 1995) notion of hegemonic masculinity as the idealized practice of male gender that legitimizes patriarchy and guarantees 'the dominant position of men and the subordination of women' (p. 77). What is illustrated is that while the *The Bill's* narrative concerned organizational change and the implementation of more egalitarian management practices in the police force, in so doing it also demonstrates how these new practices serve to repackage hegemonic masculinity. This shows that contemporary management's rhetoric of inclusion, consultation, team work and so forth, are but a ruse for the perpetuation of male authority, hierarchy, and rationality. What O'Sullivan and Sheridan see *The Bill* as exemplifying is the way that masculinity is still the managerial norm and that success requires both men and women to position themselves in relation to hegemonic masculinity in organizations. This leads O'Sullivan and Sheridan to conclude that dominant and oppressive forms of managerial masculinity 'display a remarkable resistance to change' (p. 299) as well as an ability to 'adapt to a changing environment' without 'making any genuine and lasting changes in terms of both the "talk" and the "walk"' (p. 315).

Similar conclusions can be found in Brewis' (1998) discussion of the 1994 film *Disclosure* starring Michael Douglas and Demi Moore. This film was ripe for gendered analysis given that a central part of its plot involved a case of workplace sexual harassment which, contra normal expectations involved a female perpetrator and a male victim. For Brewis, this film is taken to be a 'piece of knowledge about organizations [and] as an interpretation of working life in the modern social' (p. 84). Brewis focuses on how popular culture demonstrates the cultural embeddedness and power of dominant gendered expectations of people at work. The film explores men's suspiciousness of and hostility to women in organizations, the cultural practice of castigating and ostracizing successful working women, the idea that women are a threat to male organization, and the portrayal of working women as highly sexualized and greedy. This concurs with the more general view that popular culture is somehow at the service of patriarchy and the promulgation of oppressive and negative symbols and images of women in relation to work.

In another important study of gender and organizations in popular culture, Höpfl (2003) critiques the film *G.I. Jane*, starring Demi Moore as a female soldier in a hyper-masculine military organization. The plot of this film is quite simple – it charts the tribulations of a woman, Jordan O'Neill (Moore), who enters the US Navy

Special Warfare Group 'The Seals' as a test case for integrating women into the service. Against all odds Jordan survives the gruelling training regime while many of her male counterparts drop out. Later she demonstrates her military superiority by successfully rescuing a failing operation to retrieve plutonium from the Libyan desert. Höpfl argues that this film is an example of 'phallic feminism' (p. 23) in that whilst it is a story of a woman's success, that success is achieved by her incorporation into and acceptance of the standards of the masculine military/organizational order. Jordan 'can only succeed by becoming a man' (p. 25), shaving her head, sleeping in the men's barracks, smoking cigars, drinking whiskey, and engaging in fist fights. In a moment of metaphorical extremity, on beating her commanding officer in a fight she yells out 'suck my dick'. This shows the complete incorporation of a woman into the Naval culture which in turn preserves that culture. This cancels out the feminine because the only non-threatening role for women is to become a quasi-man, who stripped of femininity are also stripped of the potential for subversion. Höpfl concludes that 'if the feminine threatens to subvert male order, then the move to confer the honorary penis, the metaphorical phallus, marks the reversal of the potential for transgression' (p. 26). The stripping away of femininity so as to acquire a military male body through the acquisition of a phallus sees O'Neill neutered as a woman. While the film has been heralded as a success story for women in male dominated organizational cultures, the de-feminization of women that Höpfl presents as being required for this success casts *G.I. Jane* as a negative role model for women in organizations.

## Parody and critique

The studies reviewed in the previous section illustrate how popular culture mirrors and promulgates unequitable and oppressive patriarchal gender relations at work. These are relations that limit women's possibilities in masculine organizations to either being trivialized for their femininity or expected, in Wajcman's (1998) words, to 'manage like a man'. This is summed up by Coltrane and Adams (1997) when they assert that:

> Popular culture in general [. . .] tends to present rather superficial images of men and women as fundamentally and inalterably different. This difference is constructed through the routine portrayal of women in family roles, assertive men in jobs who exercise authority over others, and women who, when employed, remain sex objects, regardless of whether they are secretaries or CEOs (p. 342).

It is important however not to generalize about the meaning of gender as it is portrayed in popular culture, nor to unquestioningly take the common critical position that popular culture appeals to people's lower instincts and serves as a means of social control and the perpetuation of unequal and patriarchal power relations (Rhodes and Westwood, 2008). In terms of today's popular culture such generalizations are hard to sustain. As Gauntlett (2008) summarizes: 'representations of gender today are more complex, and less stereotyped than in the past [. . .] modern media has a more complex view of gender and sexuality than ever before' (p. 98).

Recognizing this, some researchers who study organizations and popular culture have observed how culture itself contains some valuable and insightful critiques of gendered relations at work. Czarniawska (2006) points out there are many reasons for taking popular culture seriously when researching gendered practice:

> In so far as it [popular culture] reflects actual practices, it provides a field material on par with traditional interviews and documents. In so far as it shapes actual practice, it may be priceless in understanding the formation of actual practices. In so far as it subverts actual practice, it can be a source of inspiration and a model to imitate (p. 250).

It is with this final possibility of subversion that popular culture can be an ally to politically motivated studies of gender in organizations.

It is noteworthy that one of the forms of popular culture most successful in confirming the possibility of a gendered critique of organizations is comedy, and more specifically parody. Parody is a form of comedy that involves the creation of a copy of some character of social practice. This copying involves 'a form of repetition with ironic critical distance, marking difference rather than similarity' that plays on the 'tension between the conservative effect of repetition and the revolutionary impact of difference' (Hutcheon, 2000: xii). Parody establishes a zone of difference between the representation and the represented which involves an 'imitation and transformation' (Dentith, 2000: 3) that offers an evaluation of that which is imitated. Parody is an especially valuable reflexive critical strategy in that it seeks to both imitate and make fun of social practices in a way that can to 'oppose and destabilize official views of reality' (Rhodes and Westwood, 2008: 121). Parody can thus be used as a 'critique of a whole aesthetic, and the substitution of another in its place' (Dentith, 2000: 34) it is a process of both imitation and criticism (Hutcheon, 2000).

Tyler and Cohen (2008) explicitly characterize the British sit-com *The Office* as a 'parody of gender performativity' (p. 113) which 'can be read as a popular cultural text that exemplifies many of the critical insights, as well as some of the limitations, of queer theory' (p. 114). This program is a 'mockumentary' that charts the mundane goings on in the office of a paper distributor. Consistent with other examples of British sit-coms it is a parody where male managers are 'represented negatively, as inept, amateurish or in some other way flawed' as well as being 'weak, dependent and rather pathetic' (Rhodes and Westwood, 2008: 117). Echoing Butler's (1990) insistence that parody is a chief means through which oppressive gender norms and relations can be denaturalized and destabilized, Tyler and Cohen show how '*The Office* exaggerates and ridicules particular aspects of reified gender performance, especially the implicit conflation of hegemonic masculinity and contemporary forms of culture management and transformational leadership' (pp. 124–125). Tyler and Cohen focus much of their discussion on the main character David Brent – the manager of the eponymous office – and his 'excessive recitation of hegemonic masculinity and heteronormativity' (p. 129). This is manifest in Brent's self proclaimed status as a transformational leader, a popular manager, a ladies' man, and 'one of the lads'. Tyler and Cohen show how *The Office* brings into 'comic relief' the similitude of management and a highly problematic masculinity associated with homophobia, sexism, pride in sexual conquest, paternalism, and an excessive desire for recognition. In imitating this variety of managerial masculinity, Tyler and Cohen point out that *The Office* shows that these managerial 'virtues' are a mask for the ineptitude, vulnerability and weakness of men at work.

The parody of masculine managerial power has also been examined in the cartoon series *The Simpsons* and how it reveals 'the frailty of work-based masculinity through a parody of the male body' (Pullen and Rhodes, 2007: 163). Just as Tyler and Cohen show that *The Office* undermines the assumption of masculine organizational power, *The Simpsons* demonstrates how the male body is revealed as weak and vulnerable. The particular parody present in *The Simpsons* resembles what Bakhtin (1965/1984) referred to as 'grotesque realism' – an exaggeration of the body in its material form replete with

> multiple, bulging, over- or under-sized, protuberant and incomplete [. . ..] corporeal bulk with its orifices (mouth, flared nostrils, anus) yawning wide and its lower regions (belly, legs, feet, buttocks and genital) given priority over its upper regions (head, 'spirit', reason) (Stallybrass and White 1986: 8–9).

This discussion of *The Simpsons* focused on the depiction of the bodies of two of the programme's central characters – the emaciated, frail and blemished body of Montgomery C. Burns, the wealthy owner of the Springfield Nuclear Power Plant, and the obese flatulent body of his employee Homer Simpson. It is the depiction of Burns that speaks most directly to the relationship between masculinity and management:

> Burns' warted, emaciated body is the source of humour – the ugliness and deformedness of the body being played with to illustrate capitalist normative masculine social relations . . . Burns is used to portray the capitalist class's wealth, power and position as well as the insecurity, frailty and vulnerability of that power as it is embodied within one frail, old and ugly man. Burns is no charming, heroic, handsome business tycoon. Rather, his narcissistic performances which focus on the reality of his business success, fuel the fantasy of his 'beautiful' image (Rhodes and Pullen, 2007: 172).

The critical potential of such gender parody is that it enables certain taken-for-granted aspects of working culture to be laid bare as being a fragile veneer that hides a less powerful image of the meaning of masculinity at work. Indeed, *The Simpsons* 'is funny because it uses the grotesque male body as a means to question the assumptions of masculine power in relation both to sexual and organizational potency' (Rhodes and Pullen, 2007: 175). It would appear that television programmes such as *The Office* and *The Simpsons* both harbour within them well developed and incisive forms of critique that stem from their use of parody. In representing cultural and corporeal masculinity they lay bare many of the myths that inform cultural understandings of gender, revealing them as chimeras which we can both laugh at and take seriously.

## Summary and Conclusion

This chapter has reviewed a selection of examples of predominantly Western films and television programmes that have represented gender at work as read through a sampling of theoretical resources. While gender and popular culture have long been concerned with feminist theory and cultural studies, our main focus has been on how this has been taken up more recently by scholars in organization studies. In organization studies there have been two dominant strands of argument as to the meaning and effects of popular culture: while some operate on the basis that popular culture is complicit in the fostering of inequality, others show that within culture itself there is a form of auto-critique of the way that gender limits possibilities for being for both men and women. These views are not mutually exclusive – rather they go to show that popular culture is not a monolith that promotes a singular ideology. It also shows that the interpretive possibilities of active readership allow for different meanings to be garnered from an engagement with popular culture. In both views what is demonstrated is that articulating theory with popular culture is a valuable exercise for organizational critique (Rhodes and Westwood, 2008), especially politically motivated research into gender, work and organizations.

If gender politics involves 'unsettling gendered norms of work, organization and the academy' (Pullen and Knights, 2007: 510) then reading gender in popular culture can provide grist for this mill. And as our review suggests, comedy might well be a better genre to do this unsettling than drama. Drama draws attention to masculinity, femininity, and sexuality and while harbouring the potential to provide a critique of them, it tends to do so by establishing them as firm categories that can be dramatized. Conversely, comedy, and parody in particular, has been shown to be an especially useful form of popular culture through which a critique of gender can be generated, illustrated, and supported in a more unsettling mode – indeed, they are best regarded as an ally to a critical (even radical) analysis of gendered relations at work. Parody possesses the ability to be bright and dark, uplifting and depressing, as well as light hearted and painfully heavy. Perhaps more importantly it enables a certain playfulness in relation to the cultural categories within which we locate our identities – especially gender categories. Amidst the laughter, parody operates as a cultural form of critique that challenges gender norms in ways much harder to present with a straight face – dramatic or theoretical. The playful parody of gender improvization undermines the assumption that one's gender is somehow natural or given (Butler, 2004).

Parody can only make sense, can only be popular and successful, if it plays with the idea of a social reality that is widely accepted amongst its viewers – it simultaneously draws attention to and undermines that reality. For the parodic imitation to be recognized and be found humorous, the viewer must have knowledge of the original that is being parodied, and so the parody can shed light on the meaning of that original as well as denaturalize it. It is much harder for drama and theory to do this. When we laugh at masculinity and patriarchal power in popular culture we are acknowledging the existence of that power, *and* making a critical judgement that the exercise of that power is ethically conspicuous. Even though it does so through different means, in terms of its ends, such humour shares much with political critiques of gender and culture. The two are on the same side. In this sense what we hope to have illustrated in this chapter is that rather than being seen just as a means of propagating dogma and cultural common sense, popular culture can also be something that critical approaches to studying gender and organizations might align with for the benefit of its own political project.

# REFERENCES

Allmendinger, B. (1992) *The Cowboy: Representations Of Labor In An American Work Culture.* New York: Oxford University Press.

Aquila, R. (1996) *Wanted Dead or Alive: The American West in Popular Culture.* Illinois: University of Illinois Press.

Arthurs, J. (2006) 'Sex Workers Incorporated' in J. Hollows and R. Moseley (eds), *Feminism in Popular Culture,* Oxford: Berg, 119–142.

Bakhtin, M.M. (1965/1984) *Rabelais and His World,* trans. H. Iwolsky. Bloomington, IN: Indiana University Press.

Black, P. (2006) 'Discipline and Pleasure: The Uneasy Relationship between Feminism and the Beauty Industry' in J. Hollows and R. Moseley (eds), *Feminism in Popular Culture.* Oxford: Berg, 143–160.

Bowring, M.A. (2004) Resistance is Not Futile: Liberating Captain Janeway From the Masculine-Feminine Dualism in Leadership, *Gender, Work and Organization,* 11(4) 381–405.

Brewis, J. (1998) 'What is Wrong with this Picture? Sex and Gender Relations in *Disclosure*' in J. Hassard and R. Holliday (eds), *Organization Representation: Work and Organization in Popular Culture.* London: Sage, 83–100

Brewis, J., Hampton, M., and Linstead, S. (1997) Unpacking Priscilla: Subjectivity and Identity in the Organization of Gendered Appearance, *Human Relations,* 50(10) 1275–1304.

Brooks, A. (1997) *Postfeminisms: Feminism, Cultural Theory and Cultural Forms.* London: Routledge.

Brundson, C. (2006) 'The Feminist in the Kitchen: Martha, Martha and Nigella', J. Hollows and R. Moseley (eds), *Feminism in Popular Culture.* Oxford: Berg, 41–56.

Butler, J. (1990) *Gender Trouble.* London: Routledge.

Butler, J. (2004) *Undoing Gender.* London: Routledge.

Coltrane, S., and Adams, M. (1997) Work-Family Imagery and Gender Stereotypes: Television and the Reproduction of Difference, *Journal of Vocational Behaviour,* 50, 323–347.

Connell, R.W. (1987) *Gender and Power.* Cambridge: Polity Press.

Connell, R.W. (1995) *Masculinities.* 2nd edn. Sydney: Allen and Unwin.

Czarniawska, B. (2006) Doing Gender Unto the Other: Fiction as a Mode of Studying Gender Discrimination in Organizations, *Gender, Work and Organization,* 13(3) 235–253.

Czarniawska, B., and Rhodes, C. (2006) 'Strong Plots: The Relationship Between Popular Culture and Management Theory and Practice' in P. Gagliardi and B. Czarniawska (eds), *Management and Humanities.* Edward Elgar: London, 195–218.

De Lauretis, T. (1984) *The Practice of Love: Lesbian Sexuality and Perverse Desire.* Bloomington, IN: Indiana University Press.

Dentith, S. (2000) *Parody.* London: Routledge.

Deutsch, F.M. (2007) Undoing Gender, *Gender & Society,* 21(1) 143–160.

Doane, M.A. (1987) *The Desire to Desire: The Woman's Film of the 1940s.* Bloomington, IN: Indiana University Press.

Dow, B.J. (1996) *Prime-time Feminism: Television, Media Culture, and the Women's Movement since 1970.* Pennsylvania: University of Pennsylvania Press.

Easthope, A. (1990) *What a Man's Gotta Do: The Masculine Myth in Popular Culture.* London: Routledge.

Eco, U. (1979) *The Role of the Reader: Explorations in the Semiotics of Texts.* Bloomington, IN: Indiana University Press.

Fiske, J. (1989) *Understanding Popular Culture.* London: Routledge.

Gauntlett, G. (2008) *Media, Gender and Identity.* 2nd edn. London: Routledge.

Geertz, C. (1973) *The Interpretation of Cultures.* New York: Basic Books.

Glass, D.M. (1990) Portia in Primetime: Women, Lawyers, Television, and L.A. Law, *Yale Journal of Law and Feminism,* 2(2) 371–426.

Halberstam, J. (2001) 'The Transgender Gaze in *Boys Don't Cry*' in N. Mirzoeff (ed.), *The Visual Culture Reader.* 2nd edn. London: Routledge, 669–676.

Halberstam, J. (2005) *In a Queer Time and Place.* New York University Press: New York.

Hall, S. (1996) 'On Postmodernism and Articulation: An Interview with Stuart Hall' in D. Morley and K.-H. Chen (eds) *Stuart Hall: Critical Dialogues in Cultural Studies.* London: Routledge, 131–150.

Harris, A. (2004) *All About a Girl: Culture, Power and Identity.* London: Routledge.

Hassard, J., and Holiday, R. (eds) (1998) *Organization-Representation: Work and Organization in Popular Culture.* London: Sage.

Heide, M.J. (1995) *Television Culture and Women's Lives: Thirtysomething and the Contradictions of Gender.* Pittsburgh: University of Pennsylvania Press.

Hermes, J. (2005) *Re-reading Popular Culture.* London: Blackwell.

Holliday, R. (1998) 'Philadelphia: AIDS, Organization and Representation' in J. Hassard, and R. Holiday (eds), *Organization-Representation: Work and Organization in Popular Culture.* London: Sage, 101–118.

Hollows, J., and Moseley, R. (eds) (2006) *Feminism in Popular Culture.* Oxford: Berg.

Höpfl, H. (2003) Becoming a (Virile) Member: Women and the Military Body, *Body and Society,* 9(4) 13-030.

Horrocks, R. (1995) *Male Myths and Icons: Masculinity in Popular Culture.* Houndmills: MacMillan.

Hutcheon, L. (2000) *A Theory of Parody: The Teaching of 20th Century Art Forms.* Illinois: University of Illinios Press.

Inness, S.A. (2004) *Action Chicks: New Images of Tough Women in Popular Culture.* Houndmills: Palgrave MacMillan.

Linstead, S., and Pullen, A. (2006) Gender as Multiplicity: Desire, Displacement, Difference and Dispersion, *Human Relations,* 59(9) 1287–1310.

McDonald, S. (1989) Interview with Lizzie Borden, *Feminist Studies,* 15(2) 327–345.

McDowell, L. (1997) *Capital Culture: Gender at Work in the City.* Oxford: Blackwell.

McRobbie, A. (1999) *In the Culture Society: Art, Fashion, and Popular Music.* London: Routledge.

McRobbie, A. (2004) Post-Feminism and Popular Culture, *Feminist Media Studies,* 4(3) 255–264.

McRobbie, A. (2008) *The Aftermath of Feminism: Gender, Culture and Social Change.* London: Sage.

Namaste, K. (1994) The Politics of Inside/Out: Queer Theory, Poststructuralism, and a Sociological Approach, *Sociological Theory,* 12(2) 220–231.

O'Sullivan, J., and Sheridan, A. (1999) Ms Representations: Women, Management and Popular Culture, *Women in Management Review,* 14(1) 14–20.

O'Sullivan, J., and Sheridan, A. (2005) The King is Dead, Long Live the King: Tall Tales of New Men and New Management in The Bill, *Gender, Work and Organization,* 12(4) 300–318.

Parker, M. (2002) Queering Management and Organization, *Gender, Work and Organization*, 9(2) 146–166.

Pilgeram, R. (2007) 'Ass-kicking' Women: Doing and Undoing Gender in a US Livestock Auction, *Gender, Work and Organization*, 14(6) 572–595.

Pullen, A., and Knights, D. (2007) Undoing Gender: Organizing and Disorganizing Performance, *Gender, Work and Organization*, 14(6) 505–511.

Rehn, A. (2008) Speaking Out: On Meta-Ideology and Moralization: A Prolegomena to a Critique of Management Studies, *Organization*, 15(4) 596–609.

Rhodes, C., and Parker, M. (eds), (2008) Introduction to Special Issue: Images of Organizing in Popular Culture, *Organization*, 15(5) 627–637.

Rhodes, C., and Pullen, A. (2007) 'Representing the D'Other: The Grotesque Body and Masculinity at Work in The Simpsons' in R. Westwood and C. Rhodes (eds), *Humour, Work and Organization*. London: Routledge, 161–179.

Rhodes, C., and Pullen, A. (2009) 'Narrative and Stories in Organizational Research: An Exploration of Gendered Politics in Research Methodology' in D. Buchanan and A. Bryman (eds), *The Sage Handbook of Organizational Research Methods,*. London: Sage, 583–601.

Rhodes, C., and Westwood, R. (2008) *Critical Representations of Work and Organization in Popular Culture*. London: Routledge.

Roman, L.G., Christian-Smith, L.K., and Ellsworth, E.A. (eds) (1988) *Becoming Feminine: The Politics of Popular Culture*. London: Falmer Press.

Schilit, K., and Connell, C. (2007) Do Workplace Gender Transitions Make Gender Trouble? *Gender, Work and Organization*, 14(6) 596–618.

Stallybrass, P., and White, A. (1986) *The Politics and Poetics of Transgression*. London: Methuen.

Stryker, S., and Whittle, S. (2006) *The Transgender Studies Reader*. New York: Routledge.

Tasker, Y. (1998) *Working Girls: Gender and Sexuality in Popular Cinema*, London: Routledge.

Tasker, Y., and Negra, D. (2007) *Interrogating Postfeminism: Gender and the Politics of Popular Culture*. Durham, NC: Duke University Press.

Thanem, T. (2003) Contested and Monstrous Bodies, *ephemera*, 3(3) 250–259.

Thrift, N., and Leyshon, A. (1990) In the Wake of Money: The City of London and the Accumulation of Value, Working Papers in Producer Services 16, University of Bristol and Service Industries Research Centre, Portsmouth Polytechnic.

Tyler, M., and Cohen, M. (2008) Management In/As Comic Relief: Queer Theory and Gender Performativity in *The Office, Gender, Work and Organization*, 15(2) 113–132.

Wajcman, J. (1998) *Managing Like a Man: Women and Men in Corporate Management*. St Leonards: Allen and Unwin.

Walker, N.A. (1998) *Women's Magazines, 1940–1960: Gender Roles and the Popular Press*. Basingstoke: Palgrave MacMillan.

Walters, D. (1995) *Material Girls: Making Sense of Feminist Cultural Theory*, Berkeley, CA: University of California Press.

# 5

# Theorizing Gender, Race, and Class in Organizations

## Joan Acker
### *University of Oregon, Eugene*

Gender, class, and race are concepts standing for large, complex processes of difference and inequality that exist in varying forms and degrees in all societies. One example is economic inequality, including wealth and income gaps between women and men, between managers and workers, and between people of different race or ethnic identities. Such inequality is found everywhere, although the cultural contexts and severity of inequality varies between societies, as well as between subunits within societies.[1] How does this happen, and why? Part of the answer to the 'how' question is found in the inequalities created in work organizations, through unequal wages and unequal distributions of power and control that have persisted over time. Because organizations are a major source of income in industrial countries, studying organizations can reveal many of the actual practices through which inequalities of gender, race, and class are reproduced. Such research can also contribute to understanding why inequalities persist, even as programs for gender and race equality begin to reduce some forms of discrimination.

The study of gender, class, and race/ethnicity have each developed as separate research traditions, each with its own theories, findings, and institutional locations, as Patricia Hill Collins (1995) has pointed out. Scholars within each of these distinct areas have studied the ongoing creation in work organizations of inequalities of power, authority, and reward. Class analysts have looked at how employer policies and interactions in the work place maintain and reinforce class inequality (e.g. Braverman, 1974; Burawoy, 1979). Feminist scholars have examined how gender disparities arise in organizing processes and work relations (e.g. Acker and Van Houten, 1974; Kanter, 1977; Cockburn, 1985; Collinson and Hearn, 1996; Savage and Witz, 1992; Mills and Tancred, 1992). Scholars studying racial subordination have looked at racist policies and practices in work organizations (e.g. Brown et al.,

---

[1] For data on the gender wage gap in the US see Institute for Women's Policy Research, The Gender Wage Gap: 2008, Fact Sheet #C350, September 2009, http.www.iwpr.org/pdf/c350pdf. On gender wage gap in OECD countries, see Mishel, Bernstein, and Boushey (2003) p. 410. On racial/ethnic wage inequality, see Mishel, Bernstein, and Boushey (2003) pp. 170–171.

2003). However, complex inequalities cannot be understood by looking at these bases of inequality as separate and distinct. As feminists of color argued (e.g. Davis, 1981; Dill, 1979) 'gender' alone is insufficient for a thorough analysis of complex oppressions and inequalities between women and men. For example, in the US, African American women and white women face different class and gender situations because of the long history of white privilege (Frankenberg, 1993; Jones, 1985) and the subordination of blacks. Other countries, with different histories of white domination, have different patterns of race/ethnic discrimination and subordination (e.g. Bradley and Healy, 2008). Race/ethnicity, class, and gender, as well as other patterns of difference all contribute to different lived realities. Many feminist scholars now argue that these differences are intertwined in multiple and highly varying ways (e.g. Bradley and Healy, 2008; Glenn, 2002).

The idea of intersectionality was invented to signify the ongoing and complex interweaving of such processes of difference, discrimination, exclusion, and inclusion (Crenshaw, 1995; Collins, 1995; Weber, 2001). But 'intersectionality' is a contested concept, difficult to define with any precision, partly because its components are also complex and contested. Nevertheless, feminists continue to lead the efforts to solve theoretical problems and to develop research that addresses the complex intersections of gender, race/ethnicity, and class, processes. At the same time, scholars primarily specializing in race or class have given little attention to the potential gains in knowledge offered by an intersectional perspective (e.g. Brown et al., 2003; Burawoy, 1979).

In the following pages, I give a brief history of conceptualizing gender in organizations and of the concept 'intersectionality.' I then propose a framework for thinking about intersectionality in organizations, the idea of inequality regimes. Analysis of inequality regimes is one way of unraveling the complexity of intersecting processes that result in continuing inequalities and the reproduction of differences.

## A BRIEF HISTORY OF GENDER IN ORGANIZATIONS[2]

The first studies of inequalities between women and men in work organizations were done before the concept 'gender' had been developed. Rosabeth Moss Kanter's influential *Men and Women of the Corporation* (1977) clearly showed the masculine ethos of management, the stereotyping of the few women managers, and the organizing processes that kept most women in low level, female segregated jobs. But, she argued, these problems are not due to sex differences but to 'neutral' structures of power. As feminist scholars began to create more new knowledge about women in the 1970s and early 1980s, they abandoned concepts such as sex roles and sex differences and elaborated the term 'gender' to describe broad social patterns of difference, subordination, and inequality between women and men (Acker, 1992; Cockburn, 1983; 1985; Connell, 1987; Scott, 1988;West and Zimmerman, 1987). Gender, feminists began to argue, is an aspect of social-structural processes as well as an aspect of individual identity and experience (Acker, 1992, Britton and Logan,

---

[2] For a recent thoughtful and well informed history of the field of gendered organizations, see Britton and Logan (2008).

2008). They argued further that gender assumptions and practices are embedded in institutions, such as corporations and universities, which had been seen as gender-neutral. Feminist researchers studying women's work and wages identified the gender distributions of jobs, wages, and power as well as assumptions and practices in work organizations that shaped the conditions of women's (and men's) paid labor (e.g. Acker, 1989; Cockburn, 1983; 1985; Kanter, 1975, 1977; Knights and Willmott, 1985; Martin, 1985; Westwood, 1985). The idea that institutions and organizations are 'gendered' emerged to encompass the complex ways in which gender is embedded in the practices of daily life, work, and family.

The idea of gendered organizations can be more explicitly outlined: 'To say that an organization . . . is gendered means that advantage and disadvantage, exploitation and control, action and emotion, meaning and identity, are patterned through and in terms of a distinction between male and female, masculine and feminine (Acker, 1990: 146).' Gender is embedded in hierarchical structures, jobs, divisions of labor, processes such as hiring and wage setting, in images of workers and managers, in interactions in the workplace, in work/family interconnections, and in individual constructions of identity.

'Embeddedness' implies that the fundamental, taken-for-granted processes of constructing organizations and jobs are shaped by a gendered logic that is hidden behind a gender-neutral discourse.[3] Abstract, supposedly gender-neutral, jobs are linked in hierarchies of responsibility and control. Organizational charts and job descriptions are written in abstract terms; the job slots are assumed to be filled by gender-neutral workers. But the abstract requirements of many jobs implicitly suggest that the worker is a man. 'He' is expected to be at work at set times, focused only on the tasks at hand, responsive only to demands of supervisors, available for long working hours, and unhampered by other responsibilities, such as for children and housework. This is the ideal, unencumbered worker.[4]

The encumbered worker, most often a woman, does not fit the ideal assumptions very well. The image of women as encumbered by children, marriage, and home contributes to the ongoing sex segregation of jobs and gender inequalities in pay. The organization of work and employers' expectations are still based on these gendered assumptions. In the managerial and professional jobs of the twenty-first century the work day often expands to fill all available time: the employee is available 24/7 (Hochschild, 1997; Jacobs and Gerson, 2004; Wharton and Blair-Loy, 2006). This change retains even more sharply the assumption that the ideal employee is unencumbered. Research on work/family relations attests to the persistence of gendered organizations in which ideal workers are unencumbered, even as the proportion of women in the labor force has risen to almost equal that of men, and women have entered almost all occupations. As a result, many women and increasingly

---

[3] This analysis of the gendered logic of organizing is based on my research on the Oregon job evaluation study carried out between 1983 and 1985. Job evaluation studies are still used in many countries, including the US. Thus, I think that the analysis has implications for understanding the logic of organizing that applies far beyond the state of Oregon. See Acker (1989).

[4] For a similar argument based on a study of women and men managers in several northern Italian firms, see Gherardi and Poggio (2007).

some men face difficult decisions about family and child care (Stone, 2007; Jacobs and Gerson, 2004).

## A Brief History of Intersectionality: Race, Class, and Gender in Organizations

At the same time that feminist scholars, mostly white and middle class, were developing the idea of gendered organizations, women scholars of color were laying the ground work for the concept of intersectionality.[5] They argued that diversity or multiple oppressions had to be recognized in theory and research (e.g. Davis, 1981; hooks, 1984; Joseph, 1981; Higginbotham, 1992; Westwood, 1985). The experiences and social locations of women of color and/or working-class women were different from those of white middle class women. Theory could not posit a universal female, or male, because there existed no underlying, pure and universal gender processes unaffected by race, class, and specific historical and geographic locations. Moreover, women of color suffered from several sources of inequality and oppression to which white women were not subject (Andersen and Collins, 2001). Feminist scholars maintained that these different sources or forms of inequality were not additive, but intersecting: gender processes differed as class situations varied in different racial or ethnic configurations in different historical contexts (Spelman, 1989). By the mid-1980s, scholars were publishing empirical studies of the work and family situations of women of color and third world women (e.g. Dill, 1979; 1988; Benería and Roldán, 1987; Romero, 1992; Westwood, 1985; see also Bradley and Healy, 2008), documenting the class, race, and gender differences in women's lives.

Intersectionality, the interweaving of race/ethnicity, gender, and class, emerged from this work as a major theoretical and substantive focus in feminist and other scholarship. In the last several years intersectionality has become a topic of research and debate in Europe as well as in the US (McCall, 2001; Knapp, 2005; Yuval-Davis, 2006). Intersectionality is also a focus of research on women and gender in other parts of the world (e.g. Fuller, 2009). Since its introduction (Crenshaw, 1995), the meaning of intersectionality and how it should be theorized have been contested issues. For example, what are the precise meanings of race, class, or gender? These are abstract categories that may have different content in different historical, social/political situations. Race, gender, and class also all stand for multiple and complex processes. Any study of intersectionality must include concrete definitions of these concepts.

Another issue concerns the meaning of intersecting processes or mutual reproduction. If gender inequalities are always reproduced in relation to class and race structures and processes, or racial inequalities are always reproduced within ongoing gender and class structures and processes (e.g. Andersen, 2005), how do we see each as separate and distinct from the others (e.g. Risman, 2004; Yuval-Davis, 2006)? The issue here is fundamental in sociology: analysis has involved breaking down social reality into component parts that represent social relations as viewed from particular

[5] For example, *Gender & Society* published 42 articles on intersectionality between 2000 and 2009; *The European Journal of Women's Studies* published 29 articles on the topic during that period.

standpoints (Smith, 1990). These component parts (e.g. race, gender) sometimes become the bases for whole sub-disciplines, reinforcing this analytic approach, as I discussed above (Collins, 1995). Intersectionality implies a different, synthesizing, strategy that also has methodological implications. For example, quantitative analysis relies on categorizing or separating components that can become variables that then can be examined using statistics (e.g. McCall, 2001). Gender can be categorized as male or female and differences in income or health can then be statistically estimated. Other variables, such as race and class can be added to the categorization scheme, producing a complex matrix of categories. This approach often provides useful information, but is limited because it assumes consistency within the categories and it does not tell us much about the mechanisms or processes that result in the inequality patterns observed (Reskin, 2003). The alternative approach looks at mutual reproduction as concrete actions and practices to understand how intersectionality works and, thus, how it might be changed (Andersen, 2005).

Still another issue is at what levels of social processes should we analyze intersectionality? Some scholars have focused primarily on face-to-face interactions and/or identity processes (e.g. West and Fenstermaker 1995; Shields 2008) defining intersectionality primarily in terms of individual experiences and identity/self-definitions. Others have proposed that intersectionality be analyzed both as macro-level processes in which systems, axes, or structures of oppression intersect, and as micro-level processes of direct interaction and identity construction (e.g. Collins, 1995; Weber, 2001; Risman, 2004). Still others emphasize ongoing societal processes rather than macro and micro-level structures. Axeli Knapp (2005: 259) asks, 'How are gender relations and heteronormative sexuality, class relations and configurations of ethnicity and race/ism interwoven in the structural and institutional make-up of a given society and economy, in national as well as transnational contexts?'

The conceptual problems in analyzing intersectionality and the variety and complexity of the processes included in the concept raise doubts about the possibility of agreement on an adequate theoretical formulation. As a partial solution to this problem, some scholars see intersectionality as a metaphor (Andersen, 2005; Collins, 1995), a heuristic principle that reminds us that focusing on one basis of oppression or inequality prevents us from telling the whole story. Whole stories about intersections of inequalities are necessarily complex and difficult to tell. Many analyses focus on only two bases of inequality, such as gender (white) and class, or gender and race/ethnicity, or race/ethnicity and class, at least partly because such restrictions simplify the analysis. In addition, race/ethnicity may be simplified by choosing only two groups of the many implied by that concept. Another way of making the complexity amenable to analysis is to focus on one area of social life. In this discussion, I focus on work organizations.

## GENDER, RACE, AND CLASS INEQUALITIES IN WORK AND ORGANIZATIONS

Much of the inequality in contemporary societies is created in the processes of organizing paid work and distributing wages and benefits, such as huge bonuses and salaries being paid to top executives in the private sector, typically to white men, while workers at the bottom of hierarchies get low pay and insecurity. Inequalities are also produced in government and non-profit organizations. Of course, organizations are embedded in the social processes of the societies in which they exist; the belief systems and stores of knowledge of these societies shape how organizations function. In other words, organizations do not produce inequality in isolation. Nevertheless, as I illustrate below, examining how inequalities are produced and maintained, and sometimes changed, in a wide variety of complex organizations is one strategy for understanding the persistence of inequalities over time and over geographical boundaries, as well as factors that lead to change.

To deal with this complexity I have proposed a conceptual guide to thinking about class, gender, and race in specific organizations (Acker, 2006a, 2006b). I suggest that all organizations have 'inequality regimes,' or particular, culturally mediated, patterns of inequality maintained by particular policies, rules, conventional practices of organizing work, and ways in which people interact with each other to get the work done. The idea of inequality regimes extends and elaborates work on processes of gendering organizations (Acker, 1990, 1992). Work organizations are racialized as well as gendered: organizational hierarchies and the processes that constantly recreate them are also integral elements in class systems. And all of these processes affect each other in the ongoing lives of inequality regimes.

## INEQUALITY REGIMES

I define inequality in organizations 'as systematic disparities between groups of organizational participants in control over organizational goals and outcomes, work processes and decisions, in opportunities to enter and advance in particular job areas, in security of position and levels of pay, in intrinsic pleasures of the work, and in respect and freedom from harassment' (Acker, 2006a: 110). Inequality regimes may be static and difficult to challenge, as in some long-existing bureaucracies. Or they may be fluid, changing often, as in some team organized work places. The degree of rigidity of inequality regimes varies greatly. Overall, inequality regimes are dependent for their continuing existence on the daily activities that constitute the organization.

Inequality regimes have typical components, characteristics that vary widely but that can usually be found in any organization:

- The bases of inequality;
- Organizational processes and practices that create and maintain, or challenge, inequality;
- The visibility of inequalities;
- The legitimacy of inequalities;
- Mechanisms of control and compliance;
- Competing interests in changing or maintaining inequalities.

### The bases of inequality

Bases of inequality include class, gender, and race/ethnicity. Sexuality is often included in discussions of intersectionality: lesbians and gays as well as those with other sexual identities often experience discrimination at work. The list of bases of inequality can also include differences such as age, religion and physical ability. I focus here only on class, gender, and race/ethnicity because these inequalities are the most widespread and have generated the most research.

Class, defined as differential access to power and control over society's means of provisioning (Acker, 2006a), is fundamental to the organizing of work and work hierarchies. Organizations have class structures: CEOs, upper managers, lower-level managers, professionals with certain privileges, and workers with almost no class power unless they have a union. Organizational class structures vary in shape and height: some have many levels, others are relatively flat. These class structures are gendered and racialized, as evidenced in many studies (e.g. Hossfeld, 1994; Eagly and Carli, 2007).

Gender and race are both concepts referring to multiplicities of difference, with different histories and maintained through different but often interacting practices. Gender refers to systems of social practices and beliefs that create and maintain numerous differences, and inequalities, between male and female categories (Wharton, 2005). Gender and sexuality are, of course, complexly intertwined. Heteronormativity shapes central social structures and processes, including organizing processes (e.g. Ward and Schneider, 2009). Gender differentials are, I believe, universal, but varying in details, practices, and severity of inequality from one country and one organization to another.

Race can be defined as social and cultural differences usually marked by physical differences such as skin color, rooted in economic and social practices, and ideologies. Racial inequalities are also context-specific. The US for example, with its history of slavery, may have more visible racial inequality than many other countries without that history. Gender and race intersect in organizations, creating for black men, for example, difficult processes of exclusion and denigration, which are different from the challenges faced by black women. (e.g. Wingfield, 2009).

Race and ethnicity are overlapping categories, but can be distinguished from one another: both should be included as bases for inequality in organizations. Ethnicity refers to cultural differences, often including historical experiences and language. Ethnicity may involve differences in skin color and other aspects of appearance seen as racial. 'Ethnicity' is often defined differently in nations with different histories. In the US, many ethnic groups are subject to stereotyping and discrimination: some are more favored than others. For example, the denigration and exclusions facing many Latinos/Latinas are often based on class, gender, race, *and* ethnic stereotypes. In contrast, once despised and excluded (by Anglo whites) Italian or Irish immigrants are now part of mainstream America, admired for their ethnic cultures.

## *Organizing processes that produce inequality*

Gender, class, and race/ethnicity intersect, often resulting in inequalities, in the processes of organizing work. The implicit model on which most organizations are structured is a class and gender model, as discussed above. The concept of the 'work day' as a contiguous number of specified hours, and of the ideal worker as unencumbered and always available for work, is a gendered concept. Underlying this way of organizing is a heteronormative model of the division of labor, the dominant man as breadwinner, the subordinate woman as homemaker. Heteronormative assumptions also underlie the organization of decision-making power, although racial assumptions likewise shape the distribution of power in organizations. The cross-national prevalence of white men in top organizational positions in public and private organizations is one of the most obvious examples of the intersections of class, gender, and race (Eagly and Carli, 2007). In white dominated societies such as those in North America and Europe, white men are seen as natural leaders, decisive, energetic, and responsible, in contrast to white women and women and men of color (e.g. Kanter, 1977; Connell, 1987; Fuller, 2009; Wright, Baxter and Birkelund, 1995). This pattern has not changed in spite of the greatly increased participation of women in managerial jobs below the top levels (US Bureau of Labor Statistics, 2003) and the promotion of some white women and some people of color to higher management positions (Acker, 2009).

Levels of organizing power are, thus, constituted with often hidden assumptions about gender and race. Similarly, jobs are segregated by gender and race, typically because of complex ideas about who is suitable for a particular job (Charles and Grusky, 2004). These assumptions are often a product of the history of varying labor supply and demand and management's class interests. For example, clerical work became women's work as the organization and technology of management changed and women were an available and low-cost potential labor force (e.g. Cohn, 1985).

Recruitment, hiring, and promotion practices are another site of the actualization of intersectionality and the perpetuation of inequality regimes. Gendered and racialized notions of suitability guide recruitment, hiring, and promotion (e.g. Hossfeld, 1994).

Persons doing the hiring often see certain types of bodies as more suitable than others for certain jobs. In the US, black, and often brown, bodies were for generations seen by white employers as unsuitable for anything but the most menial work in white dominated organizations (e.g. Glenn, 2002). These historical exclusions from white work organizations bolstered images of desirable and undesirable employees for particular jobs that still influence the present gendered racialization of inequality regimes. Other informal hiring and promotion practices also contribute to the production of inequality regimes. Networks of family and friends are frequent sources of job leads (e.g. Acker and Van Houten, 1974; Royster, 2003). Allies at work may help to achieve a promotion. But such alliances may be difficult to achieve when race, ethnic, gender, and class differences exist in complicated interactions. A recent study (García-López, 2008) illustrates this process in the careers of Chicana attorneys. Supervisors' and colleagues' stereotyped ideas about Chicanas limited the opportunities of these women attorneys and made their law firms into hostile work places. Another study of law firms (Pierce, 1995) describes the highly gendered processes of inclusion and exclusion of white women attorneys. In these firms, women lawyers faced identity dilemmas that complicated their job performances: they were stereotyped as too aggressive if they adopted the behaviors of many male colleagues, but too indecisive and weak, too feminine, if they did not. Women must negotiate such contradictory expectations in other types of work, including management and academia (Kanter, 1977; Wacjman, 1998; Krefting, 2003).

Wage setting is still another arena in which race, gender, and class intersect to produce ongoing inequalities. Wage setting systems differ in approach, from bureaucratic processes with specified wage categories and detailed rules to informal systems in which employers determine wages and/or bargain with employees on individual bases. Sometimes unions are involved: the gender and racial wage gaps tend to be lower among unionized workers than among non-unionized workers (Mishel, Bernstein, and Boushey, 2003). Much of the gender and race wage gaps can be attributed to the sex and race segregation of jobs: female and/or minority typed jobs are generally paid less than white male typed jobs (Charles and Grusky, 2004). These discrepancies are built into bureaucratic wage systems which are difficult to change (e.g. Acker, 1989; England, 1992). However, income inequalities also arise from individualized wage setting in which a manager decides who will get a raise and who will not (e.g. Acker, 1991).

All of these intersecting processes, creating and recreating inequality regimes, are carried out by people interacting in the course of their daily work (Martin, 2003; Reskin, 2003). Interaction is affected by stereotypes and prejudices, definitions of 'the other', and images of the self, as described above. These interactions occur within and across levels of class hierarchy. While some of these patterns are changing in some places as more and more women enter the labor force and some firms attempt to achieve diversity among their workers, the patterns still exist, helping to construct inequality regimes.

## The visibility of inequalities

Inequalities of gender, race/ethnicity, and class are frequently invisible, especially to those who are advantaged by the inequality. The disadvantaged are more apt to see inequalities than are those whose status and rewards are increased. White privilege is particularly invisible. As the neutral or 'normal' category in white dominant societies, only people of color represent 'race.' Combined with lack of recognition of masculine and class privilege, this invisibility can be an impediment to solving organizing problems, particularly those resulting from inequalities. For example, I and my colleagues in a recent study of welfare reform (Morgen et al., 2010) found that white welfare workers saw little evidence of racism in their workplaces. Workers from other racial/ethnic categories had very different perceptions. Although race-based hostility and conflict between workers was disrupting the operation of one office, white welfare workers had great difficulty in seeing and dealing with the underlying racial divisions. Tensions eased when new administrators were brought in from outside and some African American workers were promoted.

Another example of invisibility comes from a very different location, a Japanese subsidiary of a US multinational (Fuller, 2009). US top management failed to understand ethnic/cultural and gender differences between Japanese and American traditions of management and managerial practices. Nor did they recognize the effects of their own class power. These intersections of race, ethnicity, gender, and class were not entirely invisible to those with power, but the limited understanding of the powerful reduced their managerial effectiveness.

Organization researchers often fail to recognize the embeddedness of class in organizing processes as they focus instead on individual experiences of class and the production of gendered and raced identities. Class practices may be rephrased as bureaucratic and managerial practices, further obscuring the ways in which class inequalities are produced in organizing.

Gender and racial inequality are also made invisible through other mechanisms. For example, in the US, organizations are still understood as essentially gender-neutral, and often as race-neutral too. In this view, women make choices to care for their children and suffer the consequences of lower pay and fewer opportunities: the problem lies in the woman and her family, not in the work organization (e.g. Stone, 2007; see also Ely and Meyerson, 2000). Or, evidences of gendering processes, such as exclusions of women or sexist remarks, are explained as accidental, just joking (Krefting, 2003). Both racism and sexism in work organizations may be seen by employees as beside the point, not central to the organizational mission (Ely and Meyerson, 2000; Korvajärvi, 2003). Thus, these patterns become invisible as they are relegated to the bottom of the list of important concerns. Finally, invisibility may be a product of intentional managerial actions such as forbidding employees from talking with other employees about what they are actually earning. I found this practice in a study of work in Swedish banks (Acker, 1991; 1994). This practice exists in other places, including work organizations in the US. This is an example of class power intersecting with both gender and race/ethnicity processes to protect gendered and racialized power holders' interests in avoiding conflicts over inequalities.

## The legitimacy of inequalities

Many people see many inequalities as legitimate, or at least accept them as the way things are. If inequalities are seen as legitimate, the possibilities may be slim for change that will decrease such inequalities. Class systems of inequality are deeply embedded in highly legitimate organizing processes. Hierarchy, managerial control, the wage relation, and the existence of bosses and workers are accepted, by and large, as necessary components of our economic system, although unions, aggrieved workers, and their attorneys may question certain class practices. During the economic crisis of 2008–2010, the legitimacy of certain class practices, such as the huge salaries of top managers in the private sector, began to erode. The fact that class inequality has increased since the 1970s finally became a topic of sustained public discussion. How far the criticisms of class legitimacy will go and how long they will last are, of course, impossible to predict. To thoroughly reject class inequality is to reject the organizing processes of our society. That is unlikely.

Gender and race discrimination and inequality have less legal legitimacy than class inequality. Anti-discrimination laws, Affirmative Action programs, and diversity efforts are among the avenues for challenging the legitimacy of gender and race inequality. Such measures are often opposed, but no similar measures fundamentally challenge class divisions. In the US, efforts to challenge organizational inequalities declined after 1980 with the election of Ronald Reagan who opposed Affirmative Action and immediately curtailed enforcement when he entered office (Kelly and Dobbin, 1998). Certain ideologies found among many organization participants legitimate inequality. For example, belief in the overwhelming necessity of 'the market' for efficiency and lower costs also plays a role in legitimating inequalities.

From this perspective, wages are seen as production costs, not shares in the productivity of an enterprise or as a basic necessity for individual and family survival (Figart, Mutari, and Power, 2002). Reduced wage costs may be seen as good for the economy, even when they increase inequality.

Wide variations exist between organizations in the presence or absence of beliefs that legitimate inequalities; in my experience, variations also exist within organizations in the use of such legitimation. These processes are important aspects of inequality regimes.

## Mechanisms of control and compliance

In all inequality regimes, mechanisms of control ensure smooth operations and the compliance of those disadvantaged in the organization.[6] Class, gender, and race processes are embedded in and intertwine in control measures. Considerable variation between organizations exists in the shape and severity of controls. Controls can be direct or indirect, obvious or hidden, internalized or external to individuals. Obvious controls are built into bureaucratic systems of authority and decision-making power. While administrators and managers may use rules and sanctions to control subordinates, co-workers situated at all levels may also exert control over other workers. Coercion and violence are sometimes used as controls. Sexual harassment is an example of this type of gendered control; its message often is that a woman is not a welcome member of a work group (Hearn and Parkin, 2001).

Internalized controls include efforts by workers to construct their work as meaningful and satisfying. Michael Burawoy (1979) described this process among production workers who gained meaning from their work through their interactions on the job. This was a gender/class process as male bonding helped these workers to endure the difficulties of class inequality and oppression. Many other internalized controls help to maintain inequality regimes. One of the most potent is the wage relation itself (Perrow, 2002). When money is necessary for survival and wages are the primary means of getting money, the fear of loss of a job is a powerful incentive to comply. This is an obvious class control, both exerted by management and internalized by employees. This control is gendered and racialized because work opportunities and wages are affected by race and gender. Those with the lowest wages and the poorest job opportunities are apt to be most controlled by fear of loss of a job (e.g. Morgen et al., 2010).

Patterns of control differ in terms of the history, the economy and the geography of particular organizations, communities, regions and nations (McCall, 2001), revealing the complex and multiple intersections of class, race, and gender.

## Competing interests and organizing change

In spite of multiple and effective controls, workers and their organizations sometimes object to inequality regimes and demand that at least certain aspects be

---

[6] For a more detailed discussion of organizing controls as shaped by race, gender, sexuality, and class, see Acker (2006a: 122–124).

changed. This is the role of unions, of course, or of more informal organizing. Social reformers, social movements, and politicians outside organizations may be the ones pushing for change, often in coalition with workers. The political context is critical in creating the possibility for challenges. In the US, the Great Depression of the 1930s and the civil rights and women's movements in the 1960s and 1970s were such contexts in which greater job access and wage equality and security were achieved. High levels of legitimacy, high levels of fear of retaliation, or cynicism can limit employees' willingness to challenge inequalities. Conflicting gender interests also sometimes impede efforts to reduce gender or class inequality. For example, studying pay equity efforts in the 1980s, I found that some working-class men were not at all convinced that higher and more equal wages for women were a good idea (Acker, 1989). I hypothesized that these men felt their masculine self-respect threatened by wage equality with women.

Managers, too, sometimes engineer the reduction of inequalities in the name of lowering costs and increasing efficiency. Reorganizing work to remove layers of managerial hierarchy and give more decision-making authority to lower-level employees is one such strategy. The organization may save money as middle managers are let go, but the gains for lower-level employees may be fleeting and ambiguous. For example, in the study of welfare offices referred to above (Morgen et al., 2010), my co-authors and I found that front-line workers reacted very positively to their increased responsibilities after a drastic cut in middle managers. However, their pay did not rise as their jobs became more complex and responsible, and their possibilities for promotion to higher positions probably decreased as those positions disappeared.

Another management strategy that can transfer responsibility downward in an organization and increase equality is the restructuring of work into teams and the redistribution of tasks across gender and race divisions. Team organization has sometimes succeeded in lowering race and gender segregation of jobs (Kvande and Rasmussen, 1994), but sometimes it has failed. Opposition may come from managers who see their authority eroding (Ely and Meyerson, 2000) or from employees who see their skills devalued or their work group solidarities undermined (Vallas, 2003). On the whole, assessing the research and my own experience, I conclude that efforts to decrease the power disparities in inequality regimes are unsuccessful unless these efforts receive energetic support from outside as well as inside the organization.

## CONCLUSION

Gender, race, ethnicity, and class are relations, practices, and systems of meaning that pervade the structuring of any society. Organizations constitute one of the areas of social life in which these relations are embedded and reproduced. These processes and resulting inequalities take different forms and vary over time and place. In this chapter, most of the examples are from US research, depicting particulars of inequality processes in the US. Other nations have different political structures, cultures, and traditions, and different histories of gender, race/ethnic, and class patterns. Consequently, inequality processes may be somewhat different than in the US case and studying intersectionality in organizations could raise somewhat different issues. But, the challenges for the investigator are much the same. Here, I discuss a few of those challenges.

First is the dilemma implicit in the idea of intersectionality: how to comprehend aspects of social life (gender, race, class, etc.) that seem to be ontologically and historically distinct, but are so intertwined that they cannot be accurately described or understood in isolation from each other. A partial or beginning solution is to comprehend that we cannot meaningfully talk about, for example, gender as a separate category but only as gender relations that are integral to other relations of class, and race/ethnicity. Another essential understanding is that when one of these areas is the focus, hidden assumptions about the others still exist. Studies of gender inequality often implicitly assume that gender means women who are white and, often, middle class. Studies of class may assume a white male model of the meaning of class. To avoid the trap of hidden assumptions about social relations, the focus of research might be on how, in historically specific contexts, specific manifestations of gendered, racialized, heteronormative, and classed relations, inequalities, and identities emerge in concrete social processes.

A second issue is how to research the complexities implied by the idea of intersectionality. The territory seems to be vast. One way to deal with this problem is to problematize one aspect of inequality processes, exploring its dimensions through the intertwining with other processes. For example, class can be analyzed as gendered and racialized (Acker, 2006a). Similarly, race could be the central issue, illuminated by class and gender processes. Another solution is to use intersectionality metaphorically to suggest what is necessary to telling the whole story about a particular question. The topic of the story might be how inequalities have been reduced, or increased, in a set of work organizations. Or, the topic could be why efforts to decrease inequalities in management have failed. A mapping of possible factors to be examined could be informed by understandings of intersectionality.

The idea of inequality regimes is a conceptual strategy for doing that mapping, to assess the possibilities for reducing inequalities in particular organizations, to understand organizational conflicts, and to plan interventions that might succeed.

Many conceptual problems about intersectionality persist. I suggest that the best way for solving at least some of them is through detailed studies of intersectionality in action followed by assessments of what we have learned. Are we any closer than we were before to answering our questions?

# REFERENCES

Acker, Joan (1989) *Doing Comparable Worth: Gender, Class and Pay Equity.* Philadelphia: Temple University Press.

Acker, Joan (1990) Hierarchies, Jobs, and Bodies: A Theory of Gendered Organizations, *Gender and Society*, 4(2) June, 139–158. Reprinted in Barbara Czarniawska (ed.), *Organization Theory*. Edward Elgar (2005).

Acker, Joan (1991) Thinking About Wages: The Gendered Wage Gap in Swedish Banks, *Gender & Society*, 5, 390–407.

Acker, Joan (1992) From Sex Roles to Gendered Institutions, *Contemporary Sociology*, 21(5) September, 565–569.

Acker, Joan (1994) The Gender Regime of Swedish Banks, *Scandinavian Journal of Management*, 10(2) 117–130.

Acker, Joan (2006a) *Class Questions: Feminist Answers*. Lanham, MD: Rowman & Littlefield.

Acker, Joan (2006b) Inequality Regimes: Gender, Class and Race in Organizations, *Gender & Society*, 20(4) 441–464.

Acker, Joan (2009) From Glass Ceiling to Inequality Regimes, *Sociologie du travail*, 51, 199–207.

Acker, Joan, and Van Houten, Donald (1974) Differential Recruitment and Control: The Sex Structuring of Organizations, *Administrative Science Quarterly*, 19, 152–163.

Andersen, Margaret L (2005) Thinking About Women: A Quarter Century's View, *Gender & Society*, 19(4) 437–455.

Andersen, Margaret L., and Collins, Patricia Hill (2001) *Race, Class, and Gender, Fourth Edition*. Belmont, CA: Wadsworth.

Benería, Lourdes, and Roldán, Martha (1987) *The Crossroads of Class & Gender: Industrial Homework, Subcontracting, and Household Dynamics in Mexico City*. Chicago: University of Chicago Press.

Bradley, Harriet, and Healy, Geraldine (2008) *Ethnicity and Gender at Work*. London and New York: Palgrave MacMillan.

Braverman, Harry (1974) *Labor and Monopoly Capital: The Degradation of Work in the Twentieth Century*. New York: Monthly Review Press.

Britton, Dana M., and Logan, Laura (2008) Gendered Organizations: Progress and Prospects, *Sociology Compass*, 2(1) 101–121.

Brown, Michael K., Carnoy, Martin, Currie, Elliott, Duster, Troy, Oppenheimer, David B., Shultz, Marjorie M., and Wellman, David (2003) *White-Washing Race: The Myth of a Color-Blind Society*. Berkeley: University of California Press.

Burawoy, Michael (1979) *Manufacturing Consent*. Chicago and London: University of Chicago Press.

Charles, Maria, and Grusky, David B. (2004) *Occupational Ghettos: The Worldwide Segregation of Women and Men*. Stanford: Stanford University Press.

Cockburn, Cynthia (1983) *Brothers*. London: Pluto Press.

Cockburn, Cynthia (1985) *Machinery of Dominance*. London: Pluto Press.

Cohn, Samuel (1985) *The Process of Occupational Sex-Typing: the Femininization of Clerical Labor in Great Britain*. Philadelphia: Temple University Press.

Collins, Patricia Hill (1995) Comment on West and Fenstermaker, *Gender & Society*, 9, 491–494.

Collinson, David L., and Hearn, Jeff (1996) 'Breaking the Silence: On Men, Masculinities and Managements' in David L. Collinson and Jeff Hearn (eds), *Men as Managers, Managers as Men*. London: Sage.

Connell, R.W. (1987) *Gender and Power*. Stanford, CA: Stanford University Press.

Crenshaw, Kimberlé Williams (1995) 'Mapping the Margins: Intersectionality, Identity Politics, and Violence Against Women of Color' in K. Crenshaw, N. Gotanda, G. Peller, and K. Thomas (eds), *Critical Race Theory: The Key Writings that Formed the Movement*. New York: The New Press.

Davis, Angela Y. (1981) *Women, Race & Class*. New York: Vintage Books.

Dill, Bonnie Thornton (1979) The Dialectics of Black Womanhood, *Signs*, 4(3) 543–555.

Dill, Bonnie Thornton (1988) Our Mother's Grief: Racial Ethnic Women and the Maintenance of Families, *Journal of Family History*, 13, 415–431.

Eagly, A., and Carli, L. (2007) Women and the Labyrinth of Leadership, *Harvard Business Review*, 85(9) 63–71.

Ely, Robin J., and Meyerson, Debra E. (2000) Advancing Gender Equity in Organizations: The Challenge and Importance of Maintaining a Gender Narrative, *Organization*, 7(4) 589–608.

England, Paula (1992) *Comparable Worth:Theories and Evidence.* New York: Aldine de Gruyter.

Figart, Deborah M., Mutari, Ellen, and Power, Marilyn (2002) *Living Wages, Equal Wages.* London and New York: Routledge.

Frankenberg, Ruth (1993) *White Women, Race Matters: The Social Construction of Whiteness.* Minneapolis: University of Minnesota Press.

Fuller, Ellen V. (2009) *Going Global: Culture, Gender, and Authority in the Japanese Subsidiary of an American Corporation.* Philadelphia: Temple University Press.

García-López, Gladys (2008) 'Nunca Te Toman En Cuenta [They Never Take You Into Account]' The Challenges of Inclusion and Strategies for Success of Chicana Attorneys, *Gender & Society,* 22(5) 590–612.

Gherardi, Silvia, and Poggio, Barbara (2007) *Gendertelling in Organizations.* Copenhagen: Copenhagen Business School Press.

Glenn, Evelyn Nakano (2002) *Unequal Freedom: How Race and Gender Shaped American Citizenship and Labor.* Cambridge: Harvard University Press.

Hearn, Jeff, and Parkin, Wendy (2001) *Gender, Sexuality and Violence in Organizations.* London: Sage.

Higginbotham, Evelyn Brooks (1992) African-American Women's History and the Metalanguage of Race, *Signs,* 17(2) 251–274.

Hochschild, Arlie Russell (1997) *The Time Bind: When Work Becomes Home & Home Becomes Work.* New York: Metropolitan Books.

hooks, bell (1981) *Ain't I a Woman: Black Women and Feminism.* Boston: South End Press.

Hossfeld, Karen J. (1994) Hiring Immigrant Women: Silicon Valley's 'Simple Formula' in Maxine Baca Zinn and Bonnie Thornton Dill (eds), *Women of Color in U.S. Society.* Philadelphia: Temple University Press.

Jacobs, Jerry A., and Kathleen Gerson (2004) *The Time Divide: Work, Family, and Gender Inequality.* Cambridge: Harvard University Press.

Jones, Jacqueline (1985) *Labor of Love, Labor of Sorrow: Black Women, Work, and Family from Slavery to the Present.* New York: Basic Books.

Joseph, Gloria (1981) 'The Incompatible Ménage á Trois: Marxism, Feminism and Racism' in Lydia Sargent (ed.), *Women and Revolution: The Unhappy Marriage of Marxism and Feminism.* Boston: South End Press.

Kanter, Rosabeth Moss (1975) 'Women and the Structure of Organizations: Explorations in Theory and Behavior' in Rosabeth Kanter and Marcia Millman (eds), *Another Voice.* New York: Doubleday.

Kanter, Rosabeth Moss (1977) *Men and Women of the Corporation.* New York: Basic Books.

Kelly, Erin, and Dobbin, Frank (1998) How Affirmative Action Became Diversity Management: Employer Response to Antidiscrimination Law, 1961 to 1966, *American Behavioral Scientist,* 41(7) 960–985.

Knapp, Gudrun-Axeli (2005) Race, Class, Gender, *European Journal of Women's Studies,* 12(3) 249–265.

Knights, David, and Willmott, Hugh (1985) *Gender and the Labour Process.* Aldershot: Gower.

Korvajärvi, Päivi (2003) '"Doing Gender" – Theoretical and Methodological Considerations' in Ewa Gunnarsson, Susanne Andersson, Annika Vänje Rosell, Arja Lehto, and Minna Salminen-Karlsson (eds), *Where Have All the Structures Gone? Doing Gender in Organisations, Examples from Finland, Norway and Sweden.* Stockholm: Center for Women's Studies, Stockholm University.

Krefting, Linda A. (2003) Intertwined Discourses of Merit and Gender: Evidence from Academic Employment in the USA, *Gender, Work & Organization,* 10(2) 260–278.

Kvande, Elin, and Rasmussen, Bente (1994) Men in Male-dominated Organizations and their Encounter with Women Intruders, *Scandinavian Journal of Management,* 10(2) 163–174.

Lewin, Tamar (2008) 'Report takes aim at 'Model Minority' stereotype of Asian-American students' *The New York Times.* June 10.

Martin, Patricia Yancey (1985) 'Group Sex Composition in Work Organizations: A Structural-normative View' in S.A. Bacharach and R. Mitchell (eds), *Research in the Sociology of Organizations*. Greenwich, CT: JAI.

Martin, Patricia Yancey (2003) 'Said and Done' versus 'Saying and Doing': Gendering Practices, Practicing Gender at Work, *Gender & Society*, 17(3) 342–366.

McCall, Leslie (2001) *Complex Inequality: Gender, Class, and Race in the New Economy*. New York and London: Routledge.

Mills, Albert J. and Tancred, Peta (1992) *Gendering Organizational Analysis*. Newbury Park: Sage.

Morgen, Sandi, Acker, Joan, and Weigt, Jill (2010) *Stretched Thin: Poor Families, Welfare Workers, and Welfare Reform*. Ithaca: Cornell University Press.

Perrow, Charles (2002) *Organizing America*. Princeton and Oxford: Princeton University Press.

Pierce, Jennifer L. (1995) *Gender Trials: Emotional Lives in Contemporary Law Firms*. Berkeley, CA: University of California Press.

Reskin, Barbara F. (2003) Including Mechanisms in Our Models of Ascriptive Inequality, *American Sociological Review*, 68(1) 1–21.

Risman, Barbara J. (2004) Gender as a Social Structure: Theory Wrestling with Activism, *Gender & Society*, 18 429–450.

Romero, Mary (1992) *Maid in the U.S.A.* New York: Routledge.

Royster, Deirdre A. (2003) *Race and the Invisible Hand: How White Networks Exclude Black Men from Blue-Collar Jobs*. Berkeley: University of California Press.

Savage, Mike, and Witz, Anne (1992) *Gender and Bureaucracy*. Oxford: Blackwell.

Scott, Joan Wallach (1988) *Gender and the Politics of History*. New York: Columbia University Press.

Shields, Stephanie A. (2008) Gender: A Intersectionality Perspective, *Sex Roles*, 59 301–311.

Smith, Dorothy E. (1990) *The Conceptual Practices of Power: A Feminist Sociology of Knowledge*. Toronto: University of Toronto Press.

Spelman, Elizabeth V. 1989. *Inessential Woman: Problems of Exclusion in Feminist Thought*. Boston: Beacon Press.

Stone, Pamela (2007) *Opting Out: Why Women Really Quit Careers and Head Home*. Berkeley, CA: University of California Press.

U.S. Bureau of Labor Statistics (2003) Women at Work: A Visual Essay. Bls.gov/opub/mlr/2003/10/ressum3.pdf.

Vallas, Steven P. (2003) Why Teamwork Fails: Obstacles to Workplace Change in Four Manufacturing Plants, *American Sociological Review*, 68(2) 223–250.

Wacjman, Judy (1998) *Managing Like a Man*. Cambridge: Polity Press.

Ward, Jane, and Schneider, Beth (2009) The Reaches of *Heteronormativity*: An Introduction, *Gender & Society* 23(4) 433–439.

Weber, Lynn (2001) *Understanding Race, Class, Gender, and Sexuality*. Boston: McGraw Hill.

West, Candace, and Fenstermaker, Sarah (1995a) Doing Difference, *Gender & Society*, 9, 8–37.

West, Candace, and Zimmerman, Don H. (1987) Doing Gender, *Gender & Society*, 1, 125–151.

Westwood, Sallie (1985) *All Day, Every Day: Factory and Family in the Making of Women's Lives*. Urbana and Chicago: University of Illinois Press.

Wharton, Amy (2005) *The Sociology of Gender*. Malden, MA: Blackwell Publishers.

Wharton, Amy and Blair-Loy, Mary (2006) Long Work Hours and Family Life: A Cross-National Study of Employees' Concerns, *Journal of Family Issues*, 27(3) 415–436.

Wingfield, Adia Harvey (2009) Racializing the Glass Escalator: Reconsidering Men's Experiences with Women's Work, *Gender & Society*, 23(1) 5–26.

Wright, Erik Olin, and Baxter, Janeen, with Gunn, Elisabeth Birkelund (1995) The Gender Gap in Workplace Authority: A Cross-National Study, *American Sociological Review*, 60(3) 407–448.

Yuval-Davis, Nira (2006) Intersectionality and Feminist Politics, *European Journal of Women's Studies*, 13(3) 193–209.

# 6

# How to Study Gender Inequality in Organizations?

## Barbara Czarniawska

*GRI, School of Business, Economics and Law at the University of Gothenburg*

Inequality, like corruption and violence, can hardly be provoked by researchers, and they are seldom invited to witness it. A great many innovative approaches have been tried, several of which I review in this chapter. Because of space limitations, I have chosen one study to illustrate each approach that I review. I made no attempt to cover everything but selected what in my opinion was worthy of presenting and my division into types of studies has a purely structuring function. Indeed, the types I identify often overlap. Furthermore, common sense suggests that the application of several approaches always produces richer material, whether it happens under the fancy (and usually incorrectly applied) label of 'triangulation' or under some other label.

The studies presented in this chapter can be seen as exemplary but not in the sense of being perfect. They were chosen to illustrate a type of approach or a technique and I feel justified in noting difficulties and problems connected to each. My general aim is to inform and guide researchers who are interested in studying gender inequality in organizations.

## 1. . . . EXPERIMENTALLY

Joanne Martin has conducted a series of experiments in which subjects were shown videos or slides of working people followed by information about the pay schemes under which they were employed; the subjects were then asked for commentaries. Three of these studies had gender inequality as their focus (Martin et al., 1984; Martin, 1986; Martin et al., 1987).

In the first study, subjects were ninety employed women recruited for a study of 'pay satisfaction.' They were shown a taped presentation describing the requirements of a sales manager's position in an existing but anonymous oil company and a series of slides showing three managers – two males and one female – at work. Subjects were then shown supplemental fact sheets about the company under randomly varied experimental conditions (large, moderate, and small inequality) and the presence or absence of 'mobilization resources' (group contacts, the importance of the position, and formal organization of female executives). The women then responded to a questionnaire as if they were sales managers at the company. The questions concerned a feeling of deprivation for the female managers as individuals and as a group. Subjects were also asked to express their willingness to engage in a variety of collective actions against inequality (Martin et al., 1984; Martin, 1986).

In the other two studies, subjects were female secretaries employed by insurance companies who were divided into 'feminists' and 'traditionalists' based on their score on 'Attitudes Towards Women in Business' (Martin, 1986; Martin et al., 1987). They first listened to descriptions of the daily work of a secretary and a sales manager in an oil company, and then watched a slide show displaying three female secretaries and three managers. Half the group saw three male managers; the other half saw two male managers and one female manager. Subjects were then shown a pay scheme, which included the highest, average, and lowest pay rates for secretaries and managers and asked a) how they would feel if they earned the pay of the average secretary in the oil company and b) if they would apply for managerial jobs if they were available. Their answers were checked for the comparisons made (or not made) between the secretarial and managerial pay levels, feelings of group and individual deprivation, and opportunities for upward mobility.

The results of this series of experiments brought Joanne Martin to the following conclusion (personal communication, September 2, 2006):

> A series of my studies showed that people, even people with relatively low pay levels, generally found pay inequalities between their occupation and higher paid occupations to be expected, satisfying, and just. Even when they were discontent, and did perceive injustice, they were generally unwilling to take individual or collective action to better their situation. Pragmatically, they just didn't think such efforts would succeed. Depressing.

The usual criticism issued against experimental work has to do with generalizability. Are there grounds for believing that the results can be transferred to everyday life situations?[1] One can clearly see that Joanne Martin attempted to create experimental situations as close as possible to an actual workplace by studying real employees and showing her subjects scenes from their workplaces. But her comment brought Stanley Milgram's (1974/2004) famous 'obedience to authority' experiments to mind. Perhaps the main problem with the experimental technique is the opposite of the one noted by its critics. By removing the actual circumstances, which can be seen as attenuating the inequality problems in practice, the experiments reveal a negative phenomenon so strong that it remains untouched by the experimental reduction. In other words, the results are, as Martin said, depressing.

---

[1] See, for example, the famous critique of Zimbardo's (1972) prison experiment by Fromm (1973).

## 2. . . . RETROSPECTIVELY

### *Case studies*

I am using the term 'case study' in its literal sense: a study of the occurrence of a phenomenon of interest and not, as is often done, as a label for a 'site' or even 'field-work' as such. It follows that such studies must be historical. Even if the researcher is allowed to follow a project, or if the occurrence simply happens while the researcher is doing fieldwork on some site, it must eventually come to its end (or what is considered its end), and is therefore always written retrospectively. Similarly, in the fields of medicine and law, where the term originates, a case can be described only when the patient has recovered, died or interrupted the cure or when the verdict has been issued in court (in detective stories, when the riddle is solved).

One such case is the construction of professional accountancy in England and Wales during the period 1870–1930, which was accompanied by a progressive downgrading and feminization of the profession. Linda M. Kirkham and Anne Loft (1993) had historical material on both issues at their disposal – issues that had usually been examined separately. Their main thesis was that the two were intimately connected.

This ambitious project used three sets of materials: the Censuses for England and Wales for the period (numbers do tell stories; it only takes patience to read them), the historical accounts, and the excerpts of official discourse and classifications used within the profession. Their analytical perspective combined sociological and gender theories. They divided their description into three periods (periodization is an important tool of sensemaking; Luhmann, 1986): 1870–1914, the First World War (1914–1919), and the post-war period (1920–1930).

The first period was characterized by the intense efforts of the occupational association, which was officially formed in 1880, to professionalize accounting by differentiation: inclusion and exclusion. This meant, among other things, a redefinition of the jobs of clerking and bookkeeping – jobs that were eventually given predominantly to women. The association planned to register the name 'accountant,' a goal that repeatedly failed because both the incorporated and the chartered accountants were unwilling to include 'outside accountants' – those who belonged to other associations. During the registration attempt in 1911, women fought to be included, but were not even considered on par with the 'outside accountants' (though some of the 'outside' associations admitted women). One argument was that 'the time was hardly ripe' (p. 532), meaning that women were an additional complication in the process of purifying the definition of an accountant. Another argument, used during an earlier attempt, was that 'the profession of accountancy would not be particularly attractive to members of the opposite sex' (p. 529).

As it did in many other countries, the First World War changed this situation: women achieved the right to vote and the right to become members of professional associations. Although they took the jobs of absent men in many countries, their numbers were still small in England and Wales. The official discourse recognized their entrance into the profession but the phenomenon was temporary. And the job of differentiation continued, as illustrated in a poignant excerpt from *The Accountant*, April 21, 1917:

> There is as much difference between a bookkeeper and accountant as there is between a nurse and a doctor, or between a dental mechanic and a dentist (after Kirkham and Loft, 1993: 507).

After the First World War, some men returned to their jobs. Although not every woman was deprived of her accounting position, the work of professional associations intensified as they sought to establish the official discourse that gendered accountancy as masculine and clerking and bookkeeping as feminine. Yet, passage of the Sex Disqualification (Removal) Act in 1919 removed at least the formal barrier for women to enter any occupation, including accountancy.

In the post-war period, the topic of women accountants was dropped from the official discourse, as room was made for 'soldier-accountants.' The unemployment wave of the 1920s contributed yet further to returning women to their homes. The censuses of 1921 and of 1931 further reclassified occupations, not merely differentiating accountants from clerks, but introducing subcategories within the category of clerks. '[T]he woman clerk had come to constitute a new category of her own – the typist. Women accounted for a staggering 97.6% of this category' (p. 545). Women constituted less than 0.1% of all accountants in England and Wales (p. 547). In spite of the legal changes, the masculinization of the accounting profession had become even more visible and stable:

> [T]he woman clerk was re-constituted as the typist or represented amongst the lower echelons of the emerging hierarchy within commercial offices. Whilst it was now possible for women to join the ranks of the professional accountants, very few women did so. The accountant had been structurally and discursively constructed around a professional ideal which was gendered masculine (p. 551).

Kirkham and Loft's account is exceptionally rich, and I cannot do it justice in such limited space. I would like, however, to attract the reader's attention to some formal aspects of their work. One, its richness is due partly to their embedding the main narrative in the wider history of UK society and also to the variety of sources they used. They maintain a consistent attitude toward their sources, however, reminding readers that all data, including those of official censuses, are *produced*, not collected, and that the method of their production is worthy of inspection. Two, because of their meticulousness, the article is long: 51 pages, to be exact. Yet *Accounting, Organizations and Society* published it in its entirety. I believe that their action provides food for thought for other journal editors who lament the impossibility of publishing lengthy ethnographies or historical studies. Perhaps it is not impossible. Three, the account is not simply chronological. Indeed, their periodization follows the classic Aristotelian prescription for a plot: equilibrium, disequilibrium, and a new equilibrium, sometimes merely re-establishing the previous one. This emplotment makes for fascinating reading and, again, can serve as a model for others.

## Work life stories

Life stories, be they published biographies, autobiographies, or verbal accounts, have long attracted the attention of literary critics and social scientists (for the former, see e.g. Bruss, 1976; for the latter, see e.g. Linde, 1993). Organization studies contributed a subgenre that may be called 'work life stories.' The example I am quoting here is an excerpt from a study of Wall Street conducted by anthropologist Melissa Fisher. Fisher (2003) analyzed three stories: an official one about a celebrity woman in finance and two that she set together during her fieldwork.

The first story is that of Muriel Siebert, the first woman to buy a seat on the New York Stock Exchange. In 1975, when the Reagan era of deregulation began, Siebert bought a full-page ad in the *Wall Street Journal*, featuring a photograph of herself cutting a hundred-dollar bill in half. Fisher was impressed by this profanation and she hurried with many other women from Wall Street one evening in 1996 to an event organized by the Financial Women's Association. It was called 'Celebrating Women's History: Defining Moments in the Lives of Five Leaders.' Among the panelists was Muriel Siebert, whose formula for a woman in finance was '*Work, Risk, Luck, and Pluck*.' Fisher 'was intrigued because she was referring to a similar constellation of attributes and meanings [that she] was picking up in interviews with women in [her] Wall Street fieldwork about gender, power, capital, and business practices' (2003: 295). Thus a correspondence between official and personal discourses was established.

After having sketched the historical background of the entry of these women on Wall Street, Fisher presented life stories of two women she studied: Patricia Riley and Maydelle Brooks. Riley was a 47-year-old investment analyst who was repeatedly invited to talk on television programs. Fisher asked her about the course of her career and invited her to comment on the situation of women in finance. Thus, she invited Riley to tell not only 'herstory' but also 'hertheory'; indeed, it can be postulated that every well-plotted life story is plotted around an implicit or explicit theory of career. In reporting Riley's story, Fisher italicized aspects that she later analyzed. Riley said that women in finance tend to be sympathetic, service oriented, conservative, and long-term investment oriented. They spend time with the client, listen, are caring about clients, don't take many risks, and have long-term relationships (p. 307). Finally, Riley claimed that buying stocks was like buying (sensibly) a new blazer.

Fisher analyzed Riley's work life story in terms of the history of women's gainful occupations in the USA, in which the first inroads were made by emphasizing the need for 'female qualities' in such occupations as nursing, teaching, and even insurance sales. She interpreted the evocation of such traits in the context of characteristically masculine finance as the way the women 'creatively insert themselves in male dominated financial games' (p. 308). Her conclusion was that 'one of the reasons why women like Patricia Riley are successful in research is that they perform acceptable forms of womanhood – namely, they act as mothers who care about the future and reproduction of their client families in an age of enormous economic and cultural uncertainty' (ibid.).

This quote serves as a good example of the scholar's dialogical relationship to the field (Bakhtin, 1981). In her text, Fisher is not taking Riley's words literally; rather she translates first-order constructs (of the field) into second-order constructs that she identifies (Schütz, 1953/1973); yet the latter are not formulated in a hermetic jargon. They can be (and I assume they were) presented to Riley for evaluation; she could agree or disagree, pushing the dialogue still further.

In the next step, Fisher associated Riley's story with an existing theory of corporate domesticity; she explored the theory, and proceeded to report a 'negative instance' (Seale, 1999: 74ff) of a woman who was a risk-taker.

Maydelle Brooks was 49 years old and Riley's friend and although she too started as an analyst, 'she made some highly unusual career moves for a woman, advancing further and further into all-male territory' (p. 310). As Fisher said, she 'works in investment banking and is directly involved in making deals to produce capital accumulation for the firm and its clients' (ibid.). Not only did she make deals but she supervised some 100 employees.

Brooks' narrative is split into two parts: Her perceptions of how she is perceived and her perceptions of herself. According to the former, she is a demonic mother, both to her employees and her children; 'an "ogre who beats her husband and kids"' (p. 312), a ball buster. According to her evaluation of herself, she is a risk-taker in the firm and a caring mother in her 'normal life' (p. 311). Fully aware of the discrepancy, she invited – for the first time – her department for a day at her country house. 'She held the event for two reasons: "team building" and to show everyone that "I'm pretty down to earth. I don't beat my kids. I don't push them around"' (p. 313).

Fisher wove the two life stories into a history of Wall Street and its transformations. A 'ball buster' or not, Brooks would not have had her job in times of 'earlier forms of Wasp and "old crowd" Jewish paternal and gentlemanly deal-making games' (p. 312). According to Fisher, the split that she and her co-workers experienced in their perceptions revealed, 'deep neo-conservative concerns about the current and future state of the American family' (p. 313). If women join the 'predatory market machismo' who will do the caring? The study is a good example of what Richard Rorty (1991) meant by re-contextualization. The women set their stories in a specific context and Fisher reported them as was her duty; but she then re-set them in another context, thus producing added meaning.

## 3. . . . PROSPECTIVELY (FIELD STUDIES)

### Document analysis

The example I chose for document analysis concerns an analysis of official statistics and survey results. I have selected it to corroborate my claim that a division into 'quantitative' and 'qualitative' studies is now doing more harm than good, although it certainly played an important role in the 1950s and the 1960s, when quantitative techniques were about to be crowned as the only scientific methods. At present, the division produces at least two undesirable effects. One is something that I call 'positivism lite': the researchers who use predominantly quantitative techniques do not bother to reflect over their adequacy; the very fact that such techniques exist seems to justify their use. Neither do they bother to interpret their findings; the numbers allegedly speak for themselves. On the other side of the divide, qualitative researchers are keen to avoid the counting of anything, in spite of the fact that people do a great deal of counting in work settings and that there are a great many things that can be counted interestingly, in contrast to often-practiced counting of researchers' own words, mirrored in the answers of interlocutors.

Polish sociologist Magdalena Sokołowska (1981) belonged to an older tradition of social studies. The chapter I quote here, 'Women in decision-making elites,' comes from a volume edited by two sociologists who made gender a focus of analysis long before most others did, Cynthia Fuchs Epstein and Rose Laub Coser. Sokołowska had no qualms about questioning her data or engaging in sophisticated interpretations. Her topic is itself a manifestation of civil courage: studying women in decision-making elite circles was not appreciated by the then Polish regime. She began by saying that there were no systematic studies in that area and 'almost no relevant statistical data' (1981: 90).

Sokołowska then assembled all possible relevant data provided by the Polish Central Statistical Office: educational levels of women and men, occupational structure of women and men with higher education, women per 100 men in selected socioeconomic groups, monthly wages of women and men, participation rates of urban married women in the labor force, percentages of women physicians holding doctoral and docent degrees and nominated as full professors (12% of the latter in 1973), and many more. Her choices were not random. Her way of proceeding reminds me of the logic of grounded theory, where one exploration gives direction for the next question or issue. She checked the levels of education, and proceeded to see how they were reflected in choice of work; the occupational structure led to questions about earnings; earnings led to the issue of work patterns, and from there to family life. At no point did she completely trust her sources. On the issue of abortion, she says, 'According to official statistics, one abortion occurs for every two live births. However, it seems that this figure is far from accurate' (p. 98).

The political regime being what it was, she could not check how the data were produced (actually, this is difficult under any regime). Indeed, the Polish Central Statistical Office had radically 'resolved' the issue of unequal remuneration after 1976 by failing to produce wage statistics by gender (Czarniawski, 1982: 86). Sokołowska set the statistics against one another, trying in this way to make sense of the status of women in Poland at the time.

She then reached for another type of document: other studies, including surveys of attitudes towards women's societal positions. Much as there has been a strong criticism against attitude studies, one can defend them as evidence of the dominant public discourse. Sokołowska quoted the results and concluded: 'The above findings attest to a higher degree of traditionalism in attitudes about women. But the question arises whether these findings reflect a generally conservative outlook or the frustration and conflict arising from the difficult living conditions of most Polish families' (p. 99). Attempting to find answers, she included a historical analysis and an analysis of current policies, including the ruling and past ideologies. She moved through fiction to religion to Marxism and to more data.

What were her conclusions?

A top managerial post is practically unattainable for most Polish working women because they must at the same time run a household – a difficult and absorbing task, given Polish conditions. Experience indicates that an ordinary job – even one requiring a higher education – can somehow be reconciled with the performance of domestic duties, but managerial positions mean irregular job hours, concentration on work, and the subordination of other aspects of life to it. For a married woman and mother to undertake a managerial post would require a fundamental reorganization of the present family and professional structures. The Polish revolution transformed class relations but did not automatically change relations among family members. Patterns of family change much more slowly, and this is aggravated by underdeveloped services and child care and educational institutions. . . (p. 112).

Notice the sentence 'experience indicates' in place of the usual 'research shows.' It is clear that she was speaking from her experience and the experiences of other women in her position, not hesitating to insert experience along with what had been 'documented.'

In spite of Sokołowska's final optimism, matters did not change much in Poland (see e.g. Sula, 2007). But that is another story. My aim here was to emphasize Sokołowska's care in approaching her sources, the richness of her material, and her disciplined but free reasoning around the issues she raised. Her approach can be seen as traditional, as she sought to illuminate a reality behind the text. But even contemporary text analyses reach beyond the text they analyze – to other texts. What I want to stress is that all documents are texts although not all texts can be called documents. Texts can be written with words and numbers (most *are* written with words and numbers) and the 'field' that a text addresses, when understood as a 'field of practice,' can be constructed of physical as well as virtual interactions (Ryan, 2001).

## Discourse analysis

The material derived from interviews can be treated as access to the reality behind the interview situation or as part of this reality (Gubrium and Holstein, 2002). Assuming it part of the reality, Rosalind Gill (1993) studied broadcasters' accounts about the lack of women DJs at UK radio stations. There was no need to establish the fact of inequality; it was well established and obvious to both researcher and broadcasters. The question was 'Why?'. Gill submitted the answers to a discourse analysis, in Potter and Wetherell's (1987) style.

Because BBC Radio One, for instance, had some women DJs (who appeared only during the nights or on weekends, however), Gill approached five broadcasters from two independent local stations. The interviews 'covered a range of topics including how the broadcaster saw his role and responsibilities, what he saw as the function of the station, his view of the audience, how much autonomy he felt he had, as well as questions about the lack of women DJs' (1993: 76). Gill then analyzed the transcripts and found five types of accounts, each organized around a specific *claim*, which were all, to a different degree, invoked and utilized by the interviewees. The specific claim was then corroborated with one or more *warrants*. Here are some examples:

Claim:        Women do not apply to become DJs.
Warrants:   - Women are not interested in this kind of work (lack motivation)
              - It is a man's world (difficult for a woman to live in; only one inter-
                viewee used this warrant)
Claim:        The audience reacts negatively to women DJs.
Warrants:   - Surveys show it.
              - The audience is sexist (completed by the assurance that the broad-
                casters are not).
Claim:        Women do not have appropriate qualities and/or skills.
Warrants:   - Women's life experience is not conducive to acquisition of the skills
                required.
              - Women's voices are wrong (too shrill or too dusky).

I have simplified Gill's findings because my primary aim was to demonstrate the results of her discourse analysis. She was revealing what she called, after other discourse analysts, the 'practical ideologies' which were used to justify the gender inequality permeating the DJ's world. These form a part of a 'lay sociological theory' (p. 85) and, I may add, lay psychological theory. Such lay theories, strongly supported by the media, require more attention and research.

Readers who are not attracted to discourse analysis should notice that Gill's analysis is, in fact, close to Scott and Lyman's (1968) suggestion for dealing with accounts in general and also can be seen as a simplified model of Toulmin's (1958) argument analysis.

Advocates of a 'naturalistic' approach to fieldwork may criticize Gill's approach. One standard criticism is the existence of impression management in interviews in which people are asked for their opinions. This criticism is hard to sustain, for impression management forms part of every interaction (Goffman, 1959). It does present a problem in surveys because some respondents may try to create a politically correct impression and others may do the opposite but it is difficult to know, with standard responses, which are which. Provocations of various kinds are possible in all types of conversations between researchers and practitioners, as shown by an excerpt from the fieldwork of Danish researcher Carsten Frank Jørgensen (2009).[2] His interview with two policemen concerned other matters, but when the issue of women on the police force was mentioned by one of them, the following conversation unfolded:

*I: . . . you mentioned women . . . it can be a difficult question, but what do you think it is like to be a woman in the police?*

1: I think it's ok; it's good I think.
2: They have a women's network, where they are patting each other on the back, and saying: 'We are so good, isn't it nice that we are doing so well?' My attitude

---

[2] I am grateful to Carsten for having shared with me his research material.

is that if they can't handle the stink in the bakery [a Danish saying], they can go and become nursery or kindergarten teachers or something like that. I think that we show them enough regard as it is.

*I: Is it good or bad that there are women in the police?*

1: They have their uses, that's for sure . . .

2: . . . but some would like more, like this morning it was mentioned in the radio [he is alluding to the radio program where a spokeswoman for the women's network talked about prejudice] that they would like more women, which is wrong in my opinion, because there are things that they can't do. But they should be here, that's for sure, because they are able to do things that we can't do, but you must not overdo it, they mustn't be here at any price, and they should not be granted various exemptions as they were until now. . . .

*I: . . . some are saying that when they get children, they step aside . . .*

2: It is like that – it's not something people say, it's something they do. It's not a big problem here in Copenhagen, because we have a lot of administrative positions, but outside Copenhagen it's a big problem. Because when people working on a three-shift system reach the age of 50 or 60, they are getting tired, but then they discover that all the administrative positions were taken by overweight women. . .

1: I think we must not give preferential treatment to women in connection with employment and for me it does not make any sense that a woman who is 1.67 m can be employed when a man who is 1.70 cannot come in, because he is not tall enough . . . if they were a brother and a sister, then I can imagine that he would be disappointed if his sister could join the police and he couldn't because he is too short. That is wrong, I think.

2: They are saying that they are able to do things that we can't, and that is true, but I will also say . . .

*I: What kind of things?*

2: I can refer to what they said on the radio this morning, what they themselves were saying, that they can de-escalate a conflict, or at least not escalate it . . . we men are more aggressive, but I have experienced the reverse, too . . . because they were small girls who have been overlooked their whole life, so now they need to show who is in control, so then you can have the opposite problem. So it is only an advantage in sex crime, when somebody has been raped, there they have their justification.

1: I don't think there is anything we [men?] can't do.

2: They can of course sit down and talk to the rape victim about some things, that's for sure, and some of them are able to handle things better but it's far from all, far from. Because they become like . . . they forget their femininity, and then they begin to act like men . . . because it's a men's world, and then they become like us on some level, and yet a bit awkward, because they after all are women . . . that's my opinion . . . they look and sound like hardcore lesbians, too many of them are like that. They become cartoon figures in a manner of speaking, many of them.

1: The fact is, and one can't deny that, that we are a relatively masculine station . . . and there have been periods when half of the women here were attracted to women. These are women with masculine features, practicing male sports, or masculine female sports, football and handball, and they attract lesbians. Some of the woman we have are masculine in type or would like to be. But in daily work it is really nice that there are women, also socially it's nice that there are women.

2: That's for sure.

Were the two policemen trying to test the researcher to see his reaction or were they sharing their 'natural' reactions? Were they playing, interchangeably, the game of 'good cop, bad cop'? Probably all of the above. The researcher probed them delicately, offering excerpts of other discourses ('some say . . .').

Jørgensen's research is closer to Gill's than one might suppose. As both Silverman (1993) and Seale (1999) noted, behind many requests for 'naturally occurring data' lie traditional assumptions about 'authenticity' and 'depth' and a belief that researchers must go 'beyond appearances.' Appearances are a central facet of everyday life (Atkinson and Silverman, 1997), however, and are ignored at the researcher's peril. Idiosyncratic lies can be checked by obtaining many accounts but repeated lies can be valuable to a researcher, not least in the context of gender inequalities. The way to go is neither to take everything that is said at face value nor try to sort 'true' from 'false' accounts. My claim is that unstructured interviews asking for narratives of events rather than requesting opinions offer richer material. They reduce the need for impression management and can offer insights unrehearsed by previous repetitions.

## Ethnographic interviews

I have borrowed the term 'ethnographic interviews' from Spradley (1979), and am using it loosely, referring not to interviews aimed at recapturing 'a culture' or 'a folk's way of life' but to interviews aimed at stories relating actions and events rather than the gathering of opinions ('views'). Seale (1999) offered a convincing argument for the use of interviews that is especially suitable for ethnographic interviews:

> Interviews are widely used in social research because respondents can act as the eyes and the ears of researchers; interviewees can recall and summarize a wide range of observations in seconds, which would take weeks and months of observational work to achieve. They can also speak about things that cannot be observed (p. 59).

The first argument has been used in favor of such techniques as observant participation and diary-interview (Czarniawska, 2007). But there is yet another, fresh argument formulated by Patricia Y. Martin (2003).

Martin approached large, for-profit organizations for three reasons: they strongly influence US culture in general (see also Kanter, 1977); they serve as models for smaller businesses and non-US firms; and they were slower than public and non-profit organizations to enforce equality programs. But when it came to actual fieldwork, difficulties mounted.

> Corporate controllers were reluctant to let me as an outsider see or even talk to them about work as it happens. Furthermore, I found that practices of any kind are hard to observe and, even when observed, hard to capture in language. Many gendering practices are done unreflectively; they happen fast, are 'in action,' and occur at many levels. They have an emotive element that makes people feel inspired, dispirited, happy, angry, or sad and that defies verbal description by all but the most talented novelist (P.Y. Martin, 2003: 344).

It seems reasonable, then, to let people tell about such experiences in their own words. It does not matter that these accounts are edited; the very fact of editing gives clues to what is perceived as normal and as deviant; and the way the narratives are shaped is a result of collective sensemaking. Hence the usefulness of narratology, which does not treat stories as 'windows into reality,' but as elements of it.

Patricia Martin chose three stories. The first was circulating in the company: 'Everybody knew and had opinions about the events it reports' (p. 345). Such an occurrence makes the story particularly valuable; apart from the researcher's reading of it, there are various readings offered. The event concerned a male and a female vice-president standing in the corridor and hearing a telephone ring. The man told the woman to answer it; she did, but later accused him of patronizing behavior. The man was surprised and convened meetings with other women, who were asked to talk about their experiences in the company.

In Martin's interpretation, both vice-presidents were familiar with gender practices[3] and unreflectively fulfilled the roles prescribed by a societal repertoire: the woman realized it, and became angry with herself; the man did not, and was surprised at her reaction.

The next story, told by the man who was one of the protagonists in the previous one is even more intricate. He confessed to having followed a consistent policy of not inviting women co-workers to one-to-one dinners, in deference to their public image and to his idea of a behavior proper for a 'married Christian man.' After 30 years of following this rule, he realized that in this way he negatively discriminated against female colleagues, as he regularly had dinner with males, thus strengthening the male network. This realization did not amount to epiphany, however: 'For Tom [a fictitious name], the gendered practices of the institutions of family and religion

---

[3] Notice that the concept of 'practicing gender' has replaced the concept of inequality in many feminist studies. It is both more complex and more nuanced, but although apparently free of preconceived value judgment, it is in practice often reduced to negative instances. In everyday life, gender is often practiced and/or ascribed to other with gusto, pleasure, and mutual satisfaction.

were stronger than those of bureaucratic workplace that ideally rejects gender as a basis for making policies and decisions' (p. 349).

The third story was told by a woman whose male boss was giving her poor assignments and less responsibility than she felt she could carry, because she was not 'gregarious enough' (p. 350). Trying to make sense of his comment, she contrasted her behavior with that of the group of her male peers, who were 'gregarious enough.' This story is chosen from several others reported in Martin's 2001 article on women engineers' perceptions of the behaviors of their male colleagues. By using this reversed approach (most studies report how men perceive women at work), Martin obtained a highly original picture, showing men exhibiting many stereotypically 'female' behaviors, like gossiping or engaging in small talk during meetings, which obtain another coding in the context of 'mobilizing masculinities,' however.

At this point, I can envision some doctoral students asking two pertinent questions: How did Patricia Martin know which stories to select? How did she go about interpreting them? Although experience and cultivated sensitivity provide much of the answer, there are some heuristics that facilitate the acquisition of experience and sensitivity. As to the first question, the answer is practically tautological: she probably chose them because she found them interesting and relevant to her question: 'How is it possible that inequality happens in spite of everybody's good intentions?' The correctness[4] of her choice would be established by her peers: the colleagues who read the paper and, finally, the reviewers. As to the second, as much as I appreciate the postulates of grounded theory, especially in newer versions of Seale (1999) and Charmaz (2006), I believe they are blind to the rhetorical and literary aspects of coding and categorizing. Both operations rely on association and metaphorization; the correctness is of secondary importance and can be checked by any qualitative software. Alas, there is no prescription for finding metaphors that will catch: everybody is on their own.

## Participant observation

Jennifer C. Hunt spent almost a year and a half in a large urban police department in USA, which she called Metro City Police Department (Hunt, 1984). Before starting this research project, she observed New York police officers for a year, and then attended the police academy with other recruits. During the study itself, she accompanied various police officers on the 16.00 to 24.00 shift, and sometimes the 24.00 to 08.00 shift, always in high-crime districts over a specific period:

> My fieldwork took place during a period of intense political conflict between rank-and-file officers and a patronage elite which controlled the department and city politics. At the same time, the first 100 women were introduced to the rank of the uniform patrol as a result of a discrimination suit filed against the city and the police department.

---

[4] I am not using terms like 'validity' or 'reliability' because, unlike e.g. Seale (1999), whose opinions I otherwise value highly, I do not believe that it is possible to change the meaning of a well established concept by simply changing its definition. Meanings are socially constructed but many constructions are solid and cannot be changed at will.

Many dissident street cops sympathized with the women simply because management opposed them. As a result, femininity became part of the symbolism of rank-and-file resistance (1984: 287).

This was indeed a propitious time for fieldwork: change facilitates the abandonment of a 'natural attitude,' and an association of researcher's gender with resistance facilitates – but does not guarantee – access. Before I turn to a description of Hunt's difficulties in the field and how she attempted to resolve them, I would like to point out the soundness of the old saying 'There are two types of organizations: those that are interesting and those you have access to.' As Burawoy (1979) noted, luck and perseverance are among the most important elements in a successful fieldwork.

Her biological gender did not guarantee Hunt's acceptance as an ally of the rank-and-file resistance. She was suspected of being an undercover agent for the Internal Affairs Bureau or the FBI, because together with five other consultants, she was working for a firm hired by the city to compare the patrol performance of men and women. Their hiring was the result of a lawsuit in which the Justice Department and a policewoman accused the police department of discrimination in the hiring and promotion of female officers.

As it turned out, the suspicions were not groundless. The city had indeed planned to use the study to support their stand in court and was not adverse to the idea of manipulating the study results. Hunt and two other consultants hired an attorney who threatened another lawsuit if the city interfered in the study. When their stance became clear, the police department retaliated by spreading rumors of Hunt being a spy.

As a civilian and moral woman I represented the formal order of law and the inside world of the academy. As both FBI and police internal security also represented the formal order, it was logical to assume I was allied with them. In addition, no policeman believed a woman was politically capable of fighting the department to promote honest research; instead, the dominant elite would use me for their own purposes (1984: 289).

Inspired by social interactionism, Jennifer Hunt tried to earn trust by becoming, as far as possible, a competent member of the police community. The trouble was that there was no such role available for a woman.

In Hunt's reading,[5] the policemen she studied constructed the world in two spheres: the inside sphere (home, cleanliness, 'woman's work,' femininity) and the outside sphere (street, dirt, 'man's work,' masculinity). Although there were men who decided to move from the outside to the inside (accepting 'woman's work' in the office, for example) at the price of their masculinity, there was no such equivalent for women. The two types of membership accessible to women on the street were 'dyke' and 'whore.' Neither of these roles embodies trustworthiness; thus, in order to gain trust, Hunt borrowed some elements from both 'dyke' and 'whore' in order to construct a liminal identity of a 'street-woman-researcher.' From the

[5] Corroborated by Jørgensen's interview with two policemen quoted earlier.

former, she borrowed a 'combat personality' (helped by her judo skills), an 'acting crazy,' and a 'producing resistance' activity. The latter, less accentuated (a convincing dyke excludes the characteristics of a convincing whore) consisted of tolerating pornography and smaller illicit acts.

An attempt to construct this new role demanded that Hunt also counteract certain aspects of the other two: she introduced elements of 'proper woman's' behavior into her performance. She refused sexual advances, showed sympathy, and now and then revealed a female vulnerability to her colleagues. She characterized her liminal persona as follows:

> As part man, I could be trusted to back up my partner and lie for the police. As part moral woman, I could perform an honest study because I was not involved in a system of favors that demands ethical compromise from its members. Therefore, in contrast to my old identity as moral woman and spy, my new identity as 'street-woman-researcher' constituted a trustworthy category of person in the policemen's eyes (1984: 293).

As a contribution to understanding inequality in organizations, Hunt summarized her results in a paper entitled 'The logic of sexism among police' (1990). I would like to stress certain aspects of her approach to the field.

First, although the police may be an extreme case, any participative observation (in contrast to direct observation, often misnamed participative), requires an enormous investment from the researcher. Jennifer C. Hunt's vitae[6] reveal that she 'went native,' at least partly: she is strongly involved in training programs for the New York City Police Department. Participative observation is not easily done while simultaneously performing many other academic duties; it requires time, effort, and sometimes specific talents, which makes it incomparable to other approaches. Second, there is the problem of publishing results, mentioned previously. Jennifer Hunt's article from 1984, one of the few that reports a truly ethnographic work incorporating the details of fieldwork and the theoretical elaboration, has been published in *Human Organization*, a journal with an anthropological profile that permits much longer texts than other journals do. Ethnographies are usually reported in books; at a time when there is pressure towards journal publication and a rising fashion for ethnographies, publishers and editors need to reconsider their rules.

## *Direct observation (shadowing)*

Of the many types of direct observation (as opposed to indirect observation, i.e. through a one-way mirror or a camera), I have chosen shadowing, primarily for two reasons. One is that shadowing is an observation-on-the-move, which is a better fit with the character of present-day work environments (Czarniawska, 2007). The second reason has to do with the basic assumptions of shadowing. Its name in English comes from the work of Harry F. Wolcott (1973/2003), nicknamed 'The Shadow' after the radio show, when he was studying a school principal. Italian sociologist

---

[6] http://www.chss.montclair.edu, (accessed September 2, 2008).

Marianella Sclavi (1989) better explains its assumptions, quoting Truman Capote's story 'A Day's Work' as her inspiration. In the story, Capote (male, white, elite, and homosexual) follows one Mary Sanchez (female, Hispanic, cleaning help, and heterosexual). Whatever happens to Mary is mirrored twice: in Mary's observed reactions, and in Capote's own reactions, the difference between the two being the main gain of shadowing.

Attila Bruni (Bruni and Gherardi, 2001) found himself in a similar situation when studying the learning of work practices at a consulting company.[7] At the beginning of his fieldwork, the company (called Alpha in the text) hired a young woman (Omega) who was to participate in a new consulting project. Bruni followed her for ten weeks, three days a week, throughout the duration of the project. They were together in her office, he visited her clients with her, and he participated in meetings with management and senior consultants.

The first result was the realization that 'gender difference was an important factor in the ethnographic observation in that as the researcher (male) sought to adopt the perspective of the novice (female), he contaminated his sense of male self' (2001: 180). Indeed, this result is in itself a contribution to inequality studies, as, being often a female shadow of men, I never felt that my sense of my 'female self' was contaminated, much as my sense of professional identity was often reduced to ashes (Czarniawska, 2007). By analogy, I would assume that Omega was more concerned with her professional than her gender identity. Here are some of instances of Omega's budding professional identity being undermined, set to test, or strengthened in interactions with others:

◆ Omega receives a new, bulky, and heavy briefcase with Alpha's logo on it. Half an hour later, finding it cumbersome and impossible to sling over her shoulder, she gives it to a male consultant her age, who wants a new one.
◆ A consultant visits the staff room with some professional advice; after his departure, one of Omega's colleagues lauds the consultant as both competent and likeable. The reason: 'Besides work information [. . .] he circulates games, files of images and porno clips' (p. 183),
◆ At lunch on the first day of Omega's job, two of her male colleagues 'ask her if she would buy a 'Lady Piss,' a gadget which enables women to urinate standing up' (p. 183),
◆ Bruni notices that Omega has trainers and tracksuit with her, to allow her to change and go running after work. It turns out that on Omega's first day she was given the keys to the office (the privilege limited to the seniors) by the woman secretary at Alpha,
◆ Omega reports to her male colleague (her peer) about the work she has done, and suggests what appointments should be taken or changed. She complains: 'I feel like I'm your secretary . . . He answers: In that case I'll feel you up (*laughs*)' (p. 185),

---

[7] Some of the best inequality studies originate from projects that were not designed to study inequality.

◆ Omega is in the car with Bruni and the same male colleague; the two consultants review a project that they are going to present. 'Jokingly, they say that they
could put together all the projects that they have prepared and presented in
the past. Omega adds that *then we really would be whores* (they laugh), referring to
the fact that they have always catered to the client's desires. [. . .] On arriving at
the client company, Omega exclaims: *Come on, guys, let's go for it. . .!'* (p. 186).

Bruni and Gherardi discuss the results in terms of 'engineering a professional
identity' (p. 192). The last quote shown here evokes Jennifer Hunt's construction
of the 'street-woman-researcher's' liminal identity. Apparently, Omega attempted
something similar. Bruni and Gherardi pointed out that '[i]f Omega were a man,
many of the interactions we have described would never have occurred. [. . .] Her
participation and belonging are constantly at stake, and many men at any moment
may call her competence into question' (p. 195). I would add that, if Bruni were a
woman, many of these interactions would not have happened. Another woman, and
a researcher at that, would most likely have put the men on guard. This possibility
is an argument for doing shadowing, the very idea of which is based on exploring
differences (Czarniawska, 2007).

## Virtual ethnographies

As more and more interactions, not the least organizational, take place in cyberspace, there are a growing number of works dedicated to virtual ethnographies,
some of which explore gender relationships and representations (Dietrich, 1997;
Hine, 2000. See also Wajcman's (2004) critique of cyber feminism). Rarely is this
interest connected to work organizations, however, unless it is observation and
analysis of an intranet. Eva Gustavsson (2005) did just that by engaging in interactions with a peculiar type of employee, the avatars (an image in virtual reality)
of front-office personnel. She focused on virtual customer service providers with
human-like conversation skills that created the illusion of an actual person speaking from behind the computer screen, yet the dialogues were programmed and
automated.

While the non-commercial 'chat bots' (robots that can speak) are usually voices
only, 'virtual assistants' (VAs) are usually represented by human-looking animated
images. The images can often change to indicate a change of mood: smiles, serious
faces, and gestures.

One could say that the VAs have good career opportunities, as they have the 'skills'
needed for many different occupations and they fit in to most industries. VAs can
become web hosts, virtual facilitators, web-site receptionists and information guides.
VAs can perform most customer services and can replace or complement existing customer self-help systems such as call centers. VAs can be the online extension of marketing and sales functions; they can lead customers through the sales processes and they
can present personalized brand messages 24 hours a day. In the near future the VAs are
expected to perform more advanced services such as medical counselling, mortgage
advising and personal account managing . . . (2005: 404)

Perhaps this last function will be delayed in the face of the 2007–2010 financial crisis but there is no doubt that there exists a new and growing group of service personnel that requires researchers' attention. Gustavsson has traced them since 2001 when most were in the test phase. Although she could not determine their actual number, she found more than a hundred VAs over a period of three years, 50 of which were humanoids, and she and her collaborator 'chatted' with 30 of them (the avatars spoke German, Italian, English, and Swedish).

Humanoid VAs were divided into two groups: the photo-real (animated photos of actual persons) and photo-unreal (photo-like compositions). Although the number of male and female avatars was almost the same, the photo-reals were mostly men. Jobs varied for the two groups as well; the photo-unreal VAs performed primarily traditional, anonymous customer services, whereas the photo-reals (often men dressed in suits) offered expertise and professional advice. No data were available on how or why companies chose to present their VAs as women or men.

The chats followed the same format and were performed with seven chat bots. The questions asked by the researchers were aimed at establishing the extent – and character – of the VAs' 'humanity' but also imitated possible initial questions of a recruitment interview.

The list of the questions addressed to VAs was as follows:

Q1: How old are you?
Q2: Where do you live?
Q3: What hobbies do you have?
Q4: Have you ever been ill?
Q5: Do you have a family?
Q6: Do you have children?
Q7: Do you have any brothers or sisters? (p. 407)

Additional questions concerned the VAs' level of competence for the job: their knowledge base and skills. The chats ended with a series of provocative questions based on gender stereotyping but the VAs had not been programmed to tackle such questions. One could therefore expect a gender-neutral service (that is, no difference) from these assistants.

During the chats, the photo-reals answered questions concerning their 'off-line' identity although male VAs did so less willingly than the female VAs did. One even 'made a face' at Eva, indicating that the questions were too personal. One female photo-unreal answered all questions as if she were a real person but she soon disappeared from the web. The explanation given to Eva was that she was 'on leave for studies.' Otherwise, the (mostly female) photo-unreals refused any imputations of their humanness and in most answers emphasized their dedication to work.

The VA who was 'on leave for studies' was not the only one; other VAs also reported having made career moves. The website of Alpha Romeo was originally hosted by 'twins,' male and female unreals, and visitors to the site were assured that their knowledge was identical. They were hardly twins, however. The female VA was five years younger, was interested only in work, and spent her free time talking to customers while her male colleague was older and had an intensive social life, including playing sports and meeting friends. When he was removed from the site, his female colleague explained that he had been promoted due to his expertise.

Gustavsson observed that during the three-year period of her study, companies became more aware of the gender traits of their VAs in many different ways. The female avatars were favored in number. Furthermore, while the male VAs were primarily photo-real and looked serious and business-like, female unreals showed cleavages, smiled, waved, and winked. A stereotype of a very feminine female service person was thus propagated in the form of VAs on the web. Its supposedly interactive character did not invite customers to collaborate in the creation of VAs. The invited feedback seems to have been a safety-valve, typical for respondents to marketing questionnaires. Gustavsson continues her studies, however, talking this time to the designers of the avatars. Perhaps because questions about the gender of VAs have entered public discourse, their creators seem to be increasingly aware of their gender aspects, although awareness does not mean they will introduce 'equality' on the web.

One aspect of Gustavsson's studies is important to emphasize: the web is not static and things change continually. 'Virtual researchers' must be prepared for diachronic studies if their results are to offer insights into the life on the web. And, judging from present trends, online interactions will take more and more of a place in contemporary worlds including in service interactions.

4. . . . VIA FICTION:

## Watching reactions to fictive accounts

Australian sociologist Bronwyn Davies' study (1989) is unique in showing how early human socialization established unequal treatment of girls and boys. She demonstrated that 'children collude in the establishment of a particular social order since it provides a predictable social world through which they can know and be known' (1989: 43). Although her research did not involve organizational inequalities, in my eyes it is crucial for understanding why many equality measures undertaken by work organizations fail.

One obvious source of learning for children is fairy tales. Both fantasy tales and realistic stories traditionally show males as active agents, confronting the world, and women as passive supporters of men. Thus it is unsurprising that feminists reworked some of the best-known tales, in an effort to subvert the institutional order. Davies decided to read such stories to children, and made a selection based on the following criteria:

They were readily available, if only from feminist bookstores.
    They were attractively presented and illustrated so as to engage children's interest.
    They were to deal with a variety of feminist issues, including problems related to masculinity.
    They were to be written with four- and five-year-old children in mind.
    They were well written and not overtly moralistic and pedantic.

The children of my study at the same time wanted to hear and enjoyed hearing them.

They were useful in generating discussions in which the children's understanding of gender could be elaborated. (p. 47).

On this basis, Davies chose four stories: *Oliver Button is a Sissy, The Princess and the Dragon, Rita the Rescuer,* and *The Paper Bag Princess.* She read and re-read the stories to eight children, spending many hours with them over a year, discussing the stories, and sometimes making characters out of plasticine. The children enjoyed the sessions and asked for more. They ranged from four-and-a-half to five-and-a-half years of age and were in pre-school. Six had middle-class parents with professional backgrounds, and four had mothers with relatively high-status jobs; the other two mothers believed their place was at home with the children. Two children had mothers with little education but who stayed at home and fathers with higher educational and professional levels than the mothers'. One child, whose mother could not read, was unused to having stories read to him, so he only looked at the pictures and asked questions about them. Davies confessed that this case made her recognize her tacit assumptions about the complex skills that the children possessed.

In the second stage of her study, which took a year, Davies visited two pre-schools (one with children of upper-middle-class families and one with children from all backgrounds but dominated by middle-class), and two childcare centers for children of poorer parents. She spent three months in the first pre-school, observing the children at play and reading stories to them twice a week. The children were able to choose which of the four stories they wanted to hear. The same procedure was repeated daily for a week at the other three units. The observation rendered some results worthy of *Lord of the Flies;*[8] but in this section, I address only the story reading.

My favorite example is *The Paper Bag Princess,* which, as it happened, was the story chosen most often by the children, although only some understood its feminist message at the first reading. It is a story of a princess called Elizabeth, who is a pretty standard princess at the outset, engaged to be married to a prince called Ronald. Disaster strikes and a dragon attacks her castle, burns it, and steals the prince. The fire leaves her dirty with ash and consumes her clothes so she has only a paper bag to wear. Undaunted, she goes in pursuit of the dragon and rescues the prince. But when the prince points out to her that she is dirty, she leaves him and walks into the sunset alone, in her paper bag.

The children saw the dragon's attack as a pivotal moment, changing the princess into a 'bad' one. Some boys, fascinated by the dragon's destructive powers, saw it as the main protagonist; others tried to construct the prince as a hero. As one boy said of Ronald, who was carried off by the dragon, 'Ronald very cleverly holds on to his tennis racquet tightly which is why he stays up in the air' (p. 61). Most of the children refused to see Elizabeth as a hero. Here is a story rendered by one of the boys:

Prince Ronald is a tennis player. 'He's got a tennis jumper and he won the tennis gold medal.' He is 'shy' and he does not want to marry Princess Elizabeth.

[8] A 1954 novel by William Golding, filmed by Harry Hook in 1990.

The dragon burns off Elizabeth's clothes, breaks her tower, and burns the trees and flies off with Prince Ronald.

Elizabeth is 'cross.'

Elizabeth 'follows the trail' to 'look for him' because 'she wants to get Prince Ronald back.'

Ronald quite rightly tells her that she is messy. He is angry that she is so dirty. He tells her to go away because he doesn't want to marry her (p. 62).

It was to be expected, says Davies, that girls would like to be princesses and boys would identify with the dragon or prince. But there was no gender difference between those who saw the princess as a hero and those who did not. The difference was based on family background. Those who saw the princess as a hero had mothers who worked and fathers who participated more than average (in Australia) in family housework. Yet, this difference existed only within the first group of children. In pre-schools and childcare centers, no such effect emerged.

Davies concluded that:

> It would be a mistake to think of this relation as a causal one. If it were, the solution to all our problems would simply be to have all women go out to work. But going out to work is not necessarily accompanied by discursive practices in which the work the woman undertakes is seen as giving her agency and power (p. 64).

Most of the children wished that the story had had a proper ending, which would be for Elizabeth to wash up and present herself to the prince once again. Already at this age, they know what is proper for which gender – and for a story. One wonders if assumptions of a similar nature are what foster pervasive gender inequality in organizations. Their powerful effect stems from their being embraced by women as well as men.

## Inequality in novels

I have argued previously (Czarniawska, 2006) that fictive accounts are a useful way of studying inequalities in organizations. Fictional texts are always, although not always simply, reflective of societies in which their authors have been raised (Irons, 1995). They are an important part of the contemporary discourse, which means that they not only reflect the experience of life at a given time and place, but they also form it and are a part of it. They often manage to present work environments and situations that readers will rarely know from their own experience: faraway countries, distant times, or merely occupations or professions that are not well known to the reader. Additionally, novels in a realist tradition set high standards of credibility for the details of work activities. Such attention to detail can be seen in the example I used in Czarniawska (2006) – that of detective novels, which invariably have a long list of acknowledgements to police specialists, pathologists, and similar experts in the area of crime. The authors of such novels might invent the course of events and the psychology of the characters but their descriptions are truly ethnographical in detail and a tradition of pedantic readers has been checking on them since the time of Edgar Allan Poe.

Here, I would add that even novels that can be classified as fantasy rather than quasi-ethnography are useful because they indicate what a society may be missing in the eyes of the author. Let me exemplify with the all-time bestseller, Stieg Larsson's *The Girl with the Dragon Tattoo* (2008);[9] (the Swedish title was *Men Who Hated Women* (2005)), the first of the trilogy translated into many languages. Readers who would like to know if there are many Lisbeth Salanders in Sweden will be disappointed to know that there are none. But Lisbeth Salander, as the author noted, had an ancestor who was almost equally popular: Astrid Lindgren's Pippi Longstocking. Pippi, in turn, has yet another ancestor – Anne of Green Gables – and Astrid Lindgren made no secret of the fact that Lucy Maud Montgomery's series of six Anne novels (of which the first four are best known) were her favorite children's books.

Anne is different from other girls: she has red hair, which attracts the ridicule of other children; she is an orphan; and she has had a rather peculiar upbringing (including helping to raise six small children), which makes her an oddity in the small community where she finds foster parents. While everyone is trying to socialize her into displaying proper behavior, more and more children and adults fall under her charm. The result is a compromise: Anne remains 'original' but the first four volumes end in the way that the Davies' little listeners would have accepted with pleasure: after having completed her education and worked for a short while, she settles down to a married life in *Anne's Dream House* (1917), rewarded in time by six children of her own.

Pippi Longstocking (the hero of twelve books) was born in 1945 and is far more deviant than Anne. Her hair is even redder. She is a daughter of seafarer Ephraim Longstocking, from whom she inherited incredible strength: she can lift her horse with one hand. Her lack of a mother and a father (who is usually on the seas) explains her faulty socialization. She behaves unconventionally and assertively, mocking and duping unpleasant adults. She lacks formal education but is highly intelligent, and, like Anne, is an accomplished storyteller. Unlike Anne, she is not much admired by adults, as she fights against them in order to achieve justice for children. In the novels, only children adore her; among her readership, adults do as well, even though some critics have posited that Pippi suffers from autism.

Lisbeth Salander has been called a 'Pippi Longstocking for adults.'[10] She does not have red hair, since there is no longer social stigma attached to this color. Instead, she is much pierced and has a dragon tattoo (observe, however, the change from the Swedish to the English title – in order to remove any suspicion that this is a feminist novel?). Also without formal education, she is a genius with computers and extremely talented in many ways. She ignores formal and informal rules of society and only three other characters in the novels admire her. She constantly meets with suspicion, threat, and actual violence from formal authorities and villains alike. One conclusion that may be drawn from Larsson's trilogy is that, in

[9] Still the 10th most-sold book on amazon.uk (checked 09.02.10).
[10] Or so it says on a Swedish site. Heather O'Donoghue called her 'a darkly punk Pippi Longstocking' (2009: 21).

present times, the room for deviation for women has widened enormously but so have the punishments.

Larsson's exaggeration of Lisbeth Salander's deviance lands her character in the vicinity of other women who trespass into the male domains, present in contemporary fiction. One example is women in finance, whose portrayal in fiction as amoral geniuses I have analyzed at another place (Czarniawska, 2005). I have also shown that these descriptions influence the discourse of the media, which transport them into descriptions of actual women. Like Anne and Pippi, Lisbeth is meant as a contrast to everyday reality, but unlike them, she is also a warning.

A warning to women or to the society? Heather O'Donoghue, reviewing the second book in the trilogy, saw it not so much as a warning but an alternative description of society:

> Larsson's Swedish society is a dense and convincing network of interlocking institutions: the police, the security services, the health authorities and the media. Coincidental connections between unethical individuals in these give rise to chaos – chaos, that is, in the technical sense: a series of random and unpredictable perturbations in a system which ought to run smoothly (2009: 21).

Lisbeth is riding on chaos. Does she help to tame it or is she a chaos-producing element? Is she needed because of unethical individuals or does she amplify disturbances caused by them? She seems to be their product and their producer.

Pippi and Lisbeth have one thing in common that they do not share with the tamed Anne: a distaste for authority which also finds expression in their avoidance of formal organizations. Lisbeth is a formidable organizer; she creates the most complicated action nets that she as quickly dissolves, erasing all tracks. No actor-network researcher would be able to follow the objects that may inscribe her organizing; she makes them vanish. Her only use of formal organizations is to exploit them to her purposes and their disadvantage. In a sense, her counterpart can be found in Corinne Maier's bestseller *Bonjour Laziness: Why Hard Work Doesn't Pay* (2004/2006). Lisbeth is far from lazy and her hard work pays off but at the expense of formal organizations. It may be so only because formal organizations are part of an institutional order against which Lisbeth rebels or perhaps her story can be read as a message that an independent woman can expect nothing from present-day workplaces.

My analysis hardly offers explicit methodological insights. Indeed, the only way of studying inequality via fiction is twofold: a close reading (including deconstruction, if one is so inclined), and tracing intertextuality – how texts relate to other texts.

## Assembling it

The sentence above relates to more than just analysis of fictive texts. The vital question for all kinds of analyses is, in my view: For whom do we write? There exist two extreme versions of an answer to this question. According to one, we researchers write for everybody, that is, for any interested reader. According to the other extreme, we write for ourselves; ours is a language game (Astley and Zammuto, 1992).

The first extreme seems unrealistic to me, after forty years of gathering negative evidence in this matter. Different discursive communities (Swales, 1990) have their internal vocabularies and jargons that are barely accessible to outsiders. Barely, but not impossibly. The primary obstacle, however, is reading habits. There are certainly texts perceived by most readers as difficult (those authored by Heidegger or Luhmann, for example) but practice makes even those accessible. On the other hand, texts written in unknown genres and unusual styles may be difficult to decipher in spite of apparent simplicity. Consultants' reports, including 'executive summaries,' for instance, I read slowly and sometimes several times; they mean nothing to me. I can decipher them, however, if I need to and have enough time. But perhaps many readers feel they neither need nor have time to read research reports. The head of an insurance office, whom I interviewed several times, admitted that after a day spent in the office reading legal texts, he couldn't read even a newspaper; TV was his only option.

And yet, I have even more problems with the other extreme. If we write only for ourselves, our profession is absurd. Considering how separate teaching and research are in most business schools, it means we write for our colleagues who wish to remain competitive and for younger scholars who must read our texts, so that in the future they can write for their colleagues and a new generation of younger scholars.

This absurdity could be avoided if there were a professional group dedicated to popularizing research – science journalists, for example. Yet this option seems to belong mostly to the past.[11] Science journalists are now faithful only to natural sciences; other journalists are involved in a speed contest, with little time to read and decipher research reports. If we want to popularize our research, we must do it ourselves, either by writing in several genres or by delivering 'executive summaries' to journalists. To do it well, however, one must be a genius like Umberto Eco. Normal mortals usually end up specializing in one genre only: popular or scientific.

Thus I opt for a middle way, which is nevertheless extremely ambitious and full of sand traps: to write for readers somewhat close to us (and thus trained in a certain type of text and familiar with certain vocabularies) but nevertheless to reach beyond academia. This requires a rhetoric that is attractive but does not compromise the insights that our work offers.

Yet some journalists write books that are both readable by a general audience and comparable to research reports. I can think of Anthony Sampson's *Company Man* (1995) or Naomi Klein's *The Shock Doctrine* (2007). The major textual difference between what they do and what we do is their amassing of piles of facts, all of which support their single thesis or theory. Another example is Barbara Ehrenreich's *Nickel and Dimed* (2001). Here, Ehrenreich replaced a pile of facts with thick description – indeed, a trait to imitate – yet the rule of one simple,

---

[11] Editors' Note: The American Sociological Association has for a few years now hired journalists to write about some of its sociological work for public consumption. An initiative to be applauded and imitated.

infallible theory remains, even when Ehrenreich's interpretations are refuted by her co-workers. Unlike our research and publications, journalists' books rarely contain contradictory examples.

Research texts, at least in organization studies, contain relatively few facts and many interlocking theories. Perhaps even here a middle way can be recommended: more illustrations, thick descriptions, and fewer yet more transparent theories.

Another issue, raised often of late, is that of reflexivity in the text. Clive Seale (1999) meticulously reviewed this issue, examining one 'confessional' text and postmodernist pleas for reflexivity as formulated by anthropologists. Of the confessional text, he said:

> It is mildly interesting to see how it felt to do a research project, perhaps being of use to novice researchers in particular, but it is hard to see what new theoretical, methodological or policy issues are illuminated by these experiences. [. . .] Her account also reflects the degree to which expectations of fully reflexive methodological accounting may be unrealistic (1999:168).

The tradition of setting aside the methodological section as an appendix may still be commendable because it does not disturb a non-academic reader. As to postmodernist reflections, Seale's point that they run a risk of becoming completely self-referential is not a disadvantage in the eyes of Ashley and Zammuto but it may a problem for many readers. Malcolm Ashmore's thesis (1989) illustrated well, if satirically, the possibilities and limitations of self-reflexion in academic texts.

One postulate shared by more traditional and so-called postmodern critics is *polyphony* in the text. The term was coined by Russian literary critic Mikhail Bakhtin (1981), who called it less elegantly but more correctly 'polyphonizm,' meaning an authorial tendency. He suggested that the tradition of one omniscient narrator's voice be replaced with many voices in the text, with those voices being given as much authority as the narrator. Many voices can speak as one, however, thus Bakhtin added a further postulate, that of 'variegated speech' (heteroglossia). The 'other' voices have to speak in their own dialects in order to preserve the variety of voices in which the world speaks.

Followers of Bakhtin's reasoning often omit one point:[12] *Many voices speaking differently are an achievement of the author.* An author is a ventriloquist (Latour, 1996). No matter how careful the transcripts, how faithfully the camera records, transcripts cannot catch all noises in an interview situation and the camera angle will capture only certain things. No matter how many 'member checks' are made, the 'data' will not 'speak for themselves.' The author is their spokesperson and, as such a position requires, must speak for them with respect and with the best of intentions. The author's task is that of *representation*, in the political sense of the word (Latour, 1988).

---

[12] For an introduction to Bakhtin that corrects this interpretation and introduces a feminist angle, see Vice (1997). It is helpful to bear in mind the difference between an author (who constructs the text) and a narrator (a voice in the text that usually represents the author).

This position does not mean that narrators need always agree with their interlocutors or vice versa. Bakhtin is again helpful with his idea of a dialogical relationship – to the world and to the word. As I said in another context (Czarniawska, 1997), researchers can quarrel with voices from the field. Glossing over paradoxes, otherness, and conflict is not a solution. What is more, the narrator does not always win. A reader may decide otherwise and hand the laurel to the author's creation (her interlocutors), as I did when reading Ehrenreich's book.

I am convinced that reaching a wider readership is imperative, especially for those who study inequality. It must be shown, it must be documented, its mechanisms must be revealed. Widening the repertoire of representation modes can help this endeavor. I have seen attempts to make comic strips, photo-reportages, and films about inequality issues. True, they require skill and talent and they are not within the reach of everyone. But they have one thing in common: They rely on the aesthetic force of the work – is it compelling, richly detailed, inspiring, beautiful, tragic, sad? Here, the debate is quite heated. As reported by Seale (1999), for example, one side claims that aesthetic appreciation suppresses readers' critical reflection and the other claims that aesthetics are a crucial aspect of all readings, at least those that are attended to and remembered.

I take a pragmatist's stance and favor a focus on evidence. It is well known that beautiful texts, even when 'wrong,' can lead readers astray and that clumsy texts can contain pearls of wisdom. Nevertheless, the aesthetic of the day, be it the simplicity of modernism or the ornamentality of baroque, determines the reactions of readers. An example that is often raised is that of Erving Goffman. During his lifetime and afterwards, Goffman was attacked for the 'unscientific' character of his work, his lack of theory, and his lack of methodology. Yet his work lives and thrives, in spite of such 'faults' or perhaps because of them. The litmus test of the truth or falsity of these claims might be to insert all of those 'scientific' ingredients into Goffman's texts and see whether their appeal remains intact. My hypothesis is that they would become boring, a danger that, in my opinion, is strongly underestimated in doing and disseminating academic work.

## REFERENCES

Ashmore, Malcolm (1989) *The Reflexive Thesis. Wrighting Sociology of Scientific Knowledge.* Chicago, IL: The University of Chicago Press.

Astley, Graham W., and Zammuto, Raymond F. (1992) Organization Science, Managers, and Language Games. *Organization Science*, 3(4) 443–460.

Atkinson, Paul, and Silverman, David (1997) Kundera's *Immortality*: The Interview Society and the Invention of Self, *Qualitative Inquiry*, 3(3) 304–325.

Bakhtin, Mikhail (1981) *The Dialogic Imagination.* Austin, TX: University of Texas Press.

Bruni, Attila E., and Gherardi, Silvia (2001) 'Omega's Story: The Heterogeneous Engineering of a Gendered Professional Self' in M. Dent and S. Whitehead (eds), *Managing Professional Identities: Knowledge, Performativity and the 'New' Professional.* London: Routledge, 174–198.

Bruss, Elisabeth W. (1976) *Autobiographical Acts. The Changing Situation of a Literary Genre.* Baltimore: John Hopkins University Press.

Burawoy, Michael (1979) *Manufacturing Consent. Changes in the Labor Processes Under Monopoly Capitalism.* Chicago, IL: The University of Chicago Press.

Charmaz, Kate (2006) *Constructing Grounded Theory*. London: Sage.

Czarniawska, Barbara (1997) *Narrating the Organization: Dramas of Institutional Identity*. Chicago, IL: The University of Chicago Press.

Czarniawska, Barbara (2005) 'Women in Financial Services: Fiction and More Fiction' in K. Knorr Cetina and A. Preda (eds), *The Sociology of Financial Markets*. Oxford, UK: Oxford University Press, 121–137.

Czarniawska, Barbara (2006) Doing Gender unto the Other: Fiction as a Mode of Studying Gender Discrimination in Organizations, *Gender, Work and Organization*, 13(3) 234–253.

Czarniawska, Barbara (2007) *Shadowing and Other Techniques of Doing Fieldwork in Modern Societies*. Malmö/Copenhagen: Liber/CBS.

Czarniawski, Henryk (1982) *Kultura współdziałania pracowników umysłowych w przemyśle*. Warszawa: Książka i Wiedza.

Davies, Bronwyn (1989) *Frogs and Snails and Feminist Tales. Preschool Children and Gender*. Sydney, AU: Allen & Unwin.

Dietrich, Dawn (1997) '(Re-)fashioning the Techno-erotic Woman: Gender and Textuality in the Cybercultural Matrix' in S.G. Jones (ed.), *Virtual Culture. Identity & Communication in Cybersociety*. London: Sage, 169–184.

Ehrenreich, Barbara (2001) *Nickel and Dimed. Undercover in Low-wage USA*. London: Granta Books.

Fisher, Melissa (2003) 'Wall Street Women's Herstories' in K. Lipartito and D. Sicilia (eds.), *Constructing Corporate America: History, Politics and Culture*. New York, NY: Oxford University Press, 294–319.

Fromm, Erich (1973) *The Anatomy of Human Destructiveness*. New York: Fawcett Books.

Gill, Rosalind (1993) 'Justifying injustice: broadcasters- accounts of inequality in radio' in E. Bruman and I. Parker (eds), *Discourse Analytic Research: Repertoires and Readings of Texts in Action*. London: Routledge, 75–93.

Goffman, Erving (1959) *The Presentation of Self in Everyday Life*. New York: Doubleday.

Gubrium, Jaber F., and Holstein, James A. (2002) 'From the Individual Interview to the Interview Society' in Jaber F. Gubrium and James A. Holstein (eds), *Handbook of Interview Research. Context & Method*. Thousand Oaks, CA: Sage, 3–32.

Gustavsson, Eva (2005) Virtual Servants: Stereotyping Female Front-office Employees on the Internet, *Gender, Work and Organization*, 12(5) 400–419.

Hine, Christine (2000) *Virtual Ethnography*. London: Sage.

Hunt, Jennifer (1984) The Development of Rapport through the Negotiation of Gender in Field Work among Police, *Human Organization*, 43(4) 283–296.

Hunt, Jennifer (1990) The Logic of Sexism Among Police, *Women & Criminal Justice*, 1(2) 3–30.

Jørgensen, Carsten Frank (2009) *Betjentenes oversættelse af politireformen*. Aalborg: Department of Sociology, Social Work and Organization at Aalborg University.

Kanter, Rosabeth Moss (1977) *Men and Women of the Corporation*. New York: Basic Books.

Kirkham, Linda M., and Loft, Anne (1993) Gender and the Construction of the Professional Accountant, *Accounting, Organizations and Society*, 18(6) 507–558.

Klein, Naomi (2007) *The Shock Doctrine*. London: Allen Lane.

Latour, Bruno (1988) *The Pasteurization of France*. Cambridge, MA: Harvard University Press.

Linde, Charlotte (1993) *Life Stories*. New York: Oxford University Press.

Luhmann, Niklas (1986) 'Das Problem der Epochenbildung und die Evolutionstheorie' in H.-U.Gumbrecht and U. Link-Heer (eds), *Epochenswellen und Epochenstrukturen im Diskurs der Literature—und Sprachhistorie*. Frankfurt: Suhrkamp, 11–33.

Maier, Corinne (2004/2006) *Bonjour Laziness. Why Hard Work Doesn't Pay*. New York: Vintage Books.

Martin, Joanne (1986) 'The Tolerance of Injustice' in J.M. Olson, C.P. Herman, and M.P. Zanna (eds), *Relative Deprivation and Social Comparison: The Ontario Symposium, Vol. 4*. Hillsdale, NJ: L. Erlbaum Assoc., 242–272.

Martin, Joanne; Brickman, Philip, and Murray, Alan (1984) Moral Outrage and Pragmatism: Explanations for Collective Action, *Journal of Experimental Social Psychology*, 20, 484–496.

Martin, Joanne, Price, Raymond L., Bies, Robert J., and Powers, Melanie E. (1987) 'Now that I Can Have it, I'm not Sure that I Want it. The Effects of Opportunity on Aspirations and Discontent' in B.A. Gutek and L. Larwood (eds), *Women's Career Development*. New York: Sage, 42–65.

Martin, Patricia Yancey (2001) 'Mobilizing Masculinities.' Women's Experiences of Men at Work, *Organization*, 8(4) 587–618.

Martin, Patricia Yancey (2003) 'Said and Done' versus 'Saying and Doing'. Gendering Practices, Practicing Gender at Work, *Gender & Society*, 17(3) 342–366.

Milgram, Stanley (1974/2004) *Obedience to Authority. An Experimental View*. London: Pinter and Martin.

O'Donoghue, Heather (2009) Modern Monsters. *Times Literary Supplement*, 23 January, 21.

Potter, Jonathan, and Wetherell, Margaret (1987) *Discourse and Social Psychology*. London: SAGE.

Rorty, Richard (1991) 'Inquiry as Recontextualization: An Anti-dualist Account of Interpretation' in *Philosophical Papers 1. Objectivity, Relativism and Truth*. New York: Cambridge University Press, 93–110.

Ryan, Marie-Laure (2001) *Narrative as Virtual Teality*. Baltimore, MR: The John Hopkins University Press.

Schütz, Alfred (1953/1973) 'Common-sense and Scientific Interpretation of Human Action' in *Collected Papers I. The Problem of Social Reality*. The Hague: Martinus Nijhoff, 3–47.

Sclavi, Marianella (1989) *Ad una spanna da terra*. Milan: Feltrinelli.

Scott, Martin B., and Lyman, Stanford M. (1968) Accounts, *American Sociological Review*, 33 46–62.

Seale, Clive (1999) *The Quality of Qualitative Research*. London: Sage.

Silverman, David (1993) *Interpreting Qualitative Data. Methods for Analysing Talk, Text and Interaction*. London: Sage.

Sokołowska, Magdalena (1981) 'Women in Decision-making Elites' in C.F. Epstein and R.L. Coser (eds), *Access to Power: Cross-national Studies of Women and Elites*. London: Allen & Unwin, 90–114.

Spradley, James P. (1979) *The Ethnographic Interview*. New York: Holt, Rinehart and Winston.

Sula, Piotr (2007) *Gender and Career Development – Poland*. Eurofound: Eiroline, 18 May. http://www.eurofound.europa.eu/eiro/studies/tn0612019s/pl0612019q.htm, accessed 09-02-09.

Toulmin, Stephen (1958) *The Uses of Argument*. Cambridge, UK: Cambridge University Press.

Vice, Sue (1997) *Introducing Bakhtin*. Glasgow: Bell & Bain.

Wajcman, Judith (2204) *Techno Feminism*. Cambridge: Polity Press.

Wolcott, Harry F. (1973/2003) *The Man in the Principal's Office. An Ethnography*. Walnut Creek, CA: Altamira Press.

Zimbardo, Philip (1972) *The Psychology of Imprisonment: Privation, Power and Pathology*. Stanford, CA: Stanford University Press.

# Section Two

## EMBODYING ORGANIZATIONS, ORGANIZING BODIES AND REGULATING IDENTITIES

### EDITORIAL INTRODUCTION

Within the literature on gender and sociology more generally the last few decades have seen considerable efforts to create a greater balance between the mind and the body in research. This section reflects that concern by focusing on the body, embodiment and identities in gender, work and organization. A proliferation of literature on the body within sociology began in the early 1980s (Shilling, 2007). However much of this literature remained disembodied largely because the subject matter was simply an extension of other cognitively dominated targets of analysis that involve exhaustive representations of life in pursuit of a secure masculine self. Discourses of masculinity transform everything into a target for mastery or possession and 'if it cannot be possessed then it must be banished to the margins where it is contained if not controlled' (Knights and Kerfoot, 2004: 433).

The body is often denied, marginalised or taken for granted yet is almost always gendered in ways that invariably disadvantage women. Of course, young, physically attractive women can succeed in most organizations and institutions especially when occupying front line public profile positions such as TV presenters, entertainers more generally or receptionists. Described by Amanda Sinclair in this volume as 'Lookism', it may benefit a minority of women but only at the expense of the majority. A majority of women are socially and economically disadvantaged because of their gender and the subordination of the body plays a part in this, but, as Joanna Brewis indicates in her chapter, women are fighting back.

Debates on the body within the feminist literature have polarised around the question of whether or not theorising the lived body can dispense with the concept of gender. Responding to those that believe gender has become an obstacle for feminist and queer theorists of subjectivity (Nicholson, 1999; Moi, 2001), Young (2005) argues that a concept of gender is still necessary for understanding the oppression of women and those that transgress heterosexual norms. While theorising the lived body provides an escape from many of the problems such as universality, binary thinking and over-abstraction in analyses of subjectivity and identity, it does not help us understand the structures of social relations and institutions that reflect and reproduce systemic inequalities. These can be seen to find expression in sexual divisions of labour that involve gendered job or task segregation in both domestic and public institutions. Such divisions of labour are both a condition and consequence of gendered hierarchies of power and heterosexual norms that sustain discourses and practices of masculinity (see Wolkowitz, this volume).

In studying gender, work and organization, therefore, the body and embodiment should not be neglected as has been so often the case but nor should such attention displace any theorising of gender (see Hope, this volume). Indeed we need a concept of gender in order to understand how the body has been marginalised. This could be seen to result from the domination of masculinity in intellectual life where men are seen to transcend the limitations of the body and therefore only their cognitive powers need to be addressed. Women, on the other hand, are often deprived of much of this freedom from bodily constraints and this only serves to reinforce their unequal status vis-à-vis men. It has also resulted in a self-help literature (see Kenny and Bell, this volume) advising women on how to conceal or modify their bodies for purposes of advancing their careers at work. Interestingly, as Torkild Thamen's chapter indicates, transgender people are also self-conscious but seek to expose rather than conceal their constructed gender identities.

In her chapter 'Leading with Body' Amanda Sinclair outlines the importance of the body in organizations and work but demonstrates how it is highly gendered such that men are able to escape from constraints imposed by their bodies whereas women are not. She begins her chapter by quoting newspaper references to two examples of the importance of the body at work. First is the case of a 1.98-metre tall marathon ocean-swimmer and former state-level rugby player being recruited to be the CEO of the National Australia Bank. The second is of a woman in local politics who went to incredible extremes of bone-breaking growth surgery to increase her height. These illustrate how important the body is or is felt to be in leadership and organization. However, as Sinclair conveys, it is highly gendered such that men are seen to transcend their bodily limitations whereas women are not. There is a tendency to neglect the significance of the body with respect to men but to see women as heavily constrained by their bodies and emotions. Indeed it is often the case that men are seen historically and contemporarily as devoid of their gendered and bodily existence whereas women's bodies are defined as highly visible and often depicted as flawed and troublesome. At the same time, women's bodies are much more closely disciplined in terms of appearance, demeanour, dress and visibility. In the sphere of leadership where this chapter is focused, a highly masculine literature virtually ignores the body because it intimates weakness and an incapacity for mastery. However, in practice women's bodies are profiled often in ways that preclude them from any claim to leadership. Sinclair suggests that, despite these conventions, the body is highly implicated in all things relating to leadership in both sexes. This gendered selective understanding of the body is highlighted through the author's primary research on newspaper photographs of various leaders where men are portrayed largely through close-up headshots whereas women were more often portrayed revealing other parts of the body. Drawing on other parts of her own research, Sinclair provides examples of a woman police chief and an Aboriginal school principal deploying the body to good effect in their leadership roles. The author also provides examples from her own experiences of the significance of the body in her role as a professor and in teaching MBA students. Although there is a growing amount of research on managing the body in leadership, Sinclair remains cautious about its often-instrumental nature. She believes understandings about bodies can provoke valuable questioning about leadership, its impacts and wider consequences.

By contrast, Angela Hope broadens the review of a growing literature on the body within social, feminist and organization theory in her chapter 'The Body: A Review and a Theoretical Perspective'. Drawing on Chris Beasley's (2005) classification of feminist theories, Hope suggests that although there is a diversity of social theory perspectives on the body, this attention can be seen as a function of declining religious and puritanical views. Later she develops this insight to generate an original religiously informed theory of gender at work in the military.

Within modernist feminism there are liberal/egalitarian approaches that support women emulating men to secure what is seen as a 'universal humanity' and theorists of difference who oppose this assimilation on the grounds that it masks male privileges. The latter argue that women need to break from the psychic experience of 'otherness' and subordination to the masculine and indeed reverse the values upon which this is based. Three variants of postmodernist feminism are then examined that, in contrast to the modernists, disrupt rather than reproduce the body/mind and matter/representation dualisms. While recognising that women are marginalised by the sexual order, postmodern difference theorists seek not to reverse masculine domination so much as to disrupt through the body the masculine heteronomative hegemony on which it is based. For performativity feminists, the objective is to resist categorisations since these are no more than exercises of power by those that benefit from such subjection. Consequently, they disrupt any idea of a unitary subject or gendered identity arguing that gendered bodies are always fluid and unstable and an effect of signification through performative processes (Butler, 1990). In contrast to this performative perspective, Hope feels more comfortable with Grosz's (1994) view that the body '*can* be accessed outside of present language' and this informs her own original analysis in the final section.

Here she focuses on two organizations or institutions – the Catholic Church and the US military. One concern is to show how the mind/body dualism is intertwined with religious overtones that regard the body as the source of sin. Salvation is to be achieved by transcending the body and its associated carnal pleasures but this is deemed more possible if you are male, white and heteronormal. Women, Hope argues, are denied access to the higher echelons of the Catholic Church and the US military because this narrative associates the female body with sin, sexuality, dirt and fluids. They are already 'othered' as abject bodies but an extreme example of this othering is rape and this is reflected in the statistic that 1 in 3 rapes of women are carried out by men in the military. Hope theorises this as a kind of corporeal scapegoating whereby the sin that men fear in their own bodies is transferred onto abject bodies that are seen already to be beyond redemption and, thereby, a salvific status is achieved. She also extends her theory to incorporate issues of sexual preference and race.

A more directly empirical study follows in *Sex and not the city revisited: lives, loves and careers, six years on*, where Joanna Brewis offers a unique personal account of electronic interviews with a number of professional women in their late 30s. Following a series of focus groups held in 2002 (Brewis, 2004), Brewis decided to find out what changes had taken place in the interim of six years by emailing as many of the original participants as possible. While fairly small scale, it may be argued that this is a welcome change since most other gender, work and organization research of this kind tends to sacrifice depth for scope. Consequently the primary empirical material is exceptional in having both depth and a longitudinal base. The original study and its sequel were conducted in order to reflect on the literature on intimacy, questions of motherhood, and life-work balance. The chapter provides a critical review of theories about new notions of intimacy, new reflections on motherhood, and the discourse on life–work balance in the context of the author's primary data both current and as gathered six years previously.

The new intimacy and new motherhood theses share much in common and are seen partly as a function of second wave feminist achievements and higher levels of women's workplace participation since the Second World War. In short, the theses argue that women now think differently about their sexual relationships, their domestic lives, motherhood and their professional careers. They are less concerned with traditional romantic conceptions of love or even more traditional ideas regarding money and more focused on the quality of relationships, sharing of responsibilities, and the scope for self-development and self-improvement (see also Costea in this volume). As a consequence, they marry later, are more inclined to experiment with co-habitation, and tend to delay the onset of childbearing or choose not to have children at all. Brewis sums this up when she says that 'perhaps now women's bodies are being conceptualized as instruments of production just as much as – perhaps even more than – of reproduction'. While the primary data from both 2002 and 2008 generally support these theses, the author argues that these data also point to the challenges of balancing work and life in all its variety, including, for some respondents, motherhood. In short, and taken together with the extant literature in the area, Brewis concludes that for many women, in 'striving for an accommodation between life and work, something always has to give'. This chapter also contends that legislative and organizational initiatives around the life–work nexus have to date focused mainly on parents – which can cause resentment amongst those that choose not to have partners and/or children. Moreover, these initiatives have not proved adequate in any case. Brewis ends her discussion by reflecting on her own and her respondents' feelings that their next life stage will involve the responsibilities of caring for elderly parents, thus indicating perhaps a third project of this kind in the future.

Also empirically based is the chapter 'Representing the Successful Managerial Body' by Kate Kenny and Emma Bell. It provides a review of literatures on the body and identity through five themes: identity, masculinity, body management, the commodification of female bodies and the balancing of different images. As they are presented, these themes are illustrated through an empirical analysis of the self-help literature, which advises on how to modify the female body for managerial success. In a concluding section, the authors examine alternative ways of managing the feminine body to those advocated by the self-help literature.

Recognising the dominance of masculinity in management and organization, the authors set out to review the literature concerning the divergence of women's bodies from the norms established by men. This renders it extremely difficult for women to compete for managerial positions on level terms with men and, partly because of this, many turn to a growing self-help literature for guidance. In the first section, there is a brief discussion of the literature on women's bodies at work which concludes that women who are career minded mostly adapt to the masculine norms, controlling their bodies and dress so as to fit in. Then through content analysis the authors explore eighteen of the self-help books and their role in contributing to the ways in which some women gain a sense of self and identity as managers thus helping them to survive in what is defined as a hostile masculine environment. Women are encouraged to try and conceal or control feminine specific bodily existence such as pregnancy, menstruation and above all sexuality as well as modifying gender defined behaviours such as crying, talking, walking and forms of dress. In contrast to conventional mind–body dualisms, Kenny and Bell demonstrate how the body is inseparable from our thinking and central to the constitution of identity but neither is independent of normative constraints. In the second section, the authors demonstrate a counter to the desexualisation of the feminine body when the body is explicitly commodified precisely to facilitate business success, especially in frontline services. While the self-help literature is not always consistent in what it recommends, it generally endorses securing a balance between fitting in with masculine norms and remaining distinctively feminine – a position that the authors believe to be precarious if not impossible. Finally, the authors turn to their own experience at work and at first feel negative in recognising how as women they are denied anything but a subordinate or suppressed feminine self in masculine dominated organizations like universities. However, on reflection they are less pessimistic, recognising that the lived body is not an empty receptacle waiting to be filled, whether by dominant masculine discourses, or unreflectively by the demands to 'fit in' prescribed by self-help books.

In 'The Organizational Contours of "Body Work"', Carol Wolkowitz provides us with a review of the growing literature on what are called 'body workers' or the 'work' not only that people perform in maintaining or improving their own bodies but also the growing army of service workers that work on the bodies of others. Personal work on one's own body is expanding dramatically as we are encouraged, and even cajoled, to maintain health, physical fitness and general bodily wellbeing such as weight size. However, there is an even greater increase in the numbers of workers that are providing body services for others. We are not only engaging with body workers as we work on our own bodies in gyms, sporting activities and health farms, for example. We are also involved with an ever more ageing and long-living population with associated demands for care and medical cures and a larger affluent middle class with demands for bodily services such as domestic cleaning, restaurants, beauty treatment, and even plastic surgery. While these developments render the body a more central feature of work, it is still the case that both organizational theory and organizational practice neglect the body. This is because, the author argues, ever since Weber the organization has been seen as a rational and impersonal activity and the ideology of a separation between the public and private domains has presumed bodily matters to be exclusive to the latter. A consequence of this is not only that body services are neglected but also that the bodily aspects of all kinds of work are marginalised. The chapter is divided into three sections – the body in work, working on one's own body, and working on others' bodies – the latter of which is the principal focus. Partly because of the mind–body binary that elevates the former over the latter, we are rarely conscious of our bodies in work, especially now that much of the physicality in jobs has also been eradicated. Perhaps we are more aware of our bodies when we are engaged in exercise, dieting and in beauty treatment, but in surgery our awareness is usually anaesthetised. Working on others' bodies is one of the fastest growing areas of employment even though much of it is stigmatised and this might partly account for its highly gendered nature. Its expansion follows an increasingly ageing population with its demand for care and medical services. It is argued that the provision of such care in public or private institutions is increasingly being rationalised and standardised such that it takes on an impersonal and often non-caring character. The author suggests that this could be partly explained by the abject character of many of the bodies that have to be cared for but this results in women being massively overrepresented in both paid and unpaid care work.

In the final chapter of the section 'Engendering Transgender in Studies of Gender, Work, and Organization', Torkild Thanem draws on his own experiences as a male to female (MTF) transvestite to reflect on the literature on the body in this area. Documentation and statistics on transgender reveal that far more people are active than is popularly thought. Moreover there is a substantial transgender industry in supplying both specific products and services through and for transvestites. Because of the transgression of gender norms, the body and embodiment are of central importance in transgender practices. The literature is not very extensive but can be seen as taking two distinct although closely related forms. The first focuses upon transgender as a way of studying how gender gets constructed more generally. While for conventional heterosexual subjects, this construction is perhaps concealed in its taken-for-grantedness, where transgression is concerned the construction of gender identities, norms and practices are more self-conscious and visible. The second type of study is concerned more directly with the everyday social and linguistic practices of transgender people.

The author highlights Garfinkel's (1967) famous study of the intersexed Agnes who was born with male genitalia, developed breasts at the age of twelve, and was raised as a boy until the age of seventeen, whereupon she decided to secure sexual reassignment surgery so that she could live as a woman without having to engage in 'sexual passing'. Garfinkel's interest was not so much in understanding intersexual or transgender subjects so much as seeing them as almost a laboratory case for demonstrating the social organization of order from situations that diverge significantly from it. Thus prior to her surgery, Agnes is so preoccupied with accomplishing a feminine identity as to displace other pursuits such as securing an education, a work career, and sexual partners. The criticism of Garfinkel is that his overriding concern to show how social order is restored through sexual passing, results in the marginalisation of Agnes as an embodied transgendered subject in everyday life. In short, he reproduces the gender binary through his analysis.

By contrast, Butler (1990; 1993) deconstructs the binary between sex and gender but Thanem argues that she continues to leave transgendered people disembodied in simply using the example of drag queens to illustrate her thesis on gender performativity. Butler has been influential among academics within the field of organization and work, and consequently there is a reliance on metaphorical generalizations based on social constructionist theory, thus resulting in a treatment of transgender as disembodied and often decontextualised. The problem is that the transgender body is being examined from an external and often masculine, disembodied and heteronormative viewpoint, whereas what is needed is a study of transgender from within the embodied everyday experience of its practice. The remainder of the chapter is devoted to offering some reflections on the author's own embodied experiences as a practicing transvestite and outlining some directions for further research of transgender, especially where it impinges on issues of gender, work, industry and society.

## REFERENCES

Beasley, C. (2005) *Gender and sexuality: Critical Theories, Critical Thinkers.* London: Sage Publications.

Brewis, J. (2004) Sex and not the City? The Aspirations of the Thirty-something Working Woman, *Urban Studies,* 41(9) 1821–1838.

Butler, J. (1990) *Gender Trouble: Feminism and the Subversion of Identity.* London: Routledge.

Butler, J. (1993) *Bodies That Matter: On the Discursive Limits of 'Sex'.* London: Routledge.

Garfinkel, H. (1967) *Studies in Ethnomethodology.* Englewood Cliffs, NJ: Prentice Hall.

Grosz, E. (1994) *Volatile Bodies: Toward a Corporeal Feminism.* Bloomington IN: Indiana University Press.

Knights, D., and Kerfoot, D. (2004) Between Representations and Subjectivity: Gender Binaries and the Politics of Organizational Transformation, *Gender, Work and Organization,* 11(4) July, 430–454.

Moi, Toril (2001) *What is a Woman and Other Essays.* Oxford: Oxford University Press.

Nicholson, L. (1999) *The Play of Reason: From the Modern to the Postmodern.* Ithaca New York: Cornell University Press.

Shilling, C. (2005) *The Body in Culture, Technology and Society.* London: Sage

Young, I.M. (2005) *Female Body Experience.* Oxford: Oxford University Press.

# 7

# Leading with Body

### Amanda Sinclair
### *Melbourne Business School*

To swim the notoriously windy stretch of ocean that separates
the sandy beaches of Cottesloe in Western Australia from the
eastern coves of Rottnest Island demands extraordinary strength,
stamina and a certain daring. Speed is not important: even the
best open-water freestylers take 7½ hours . . . what is essential is a
doggedly rhythmic kick, and an ability to kick harder when trailed
by sharks.

Funnily enough, it's the same suite of skills that could be
damned handy just now for anyone trying to navigate the perilously
stormy waters of global financial markets. Someone like Cameron
Clyne, for example . . . Ah yes, Cameron who?

But now that Cameron Clyne, a strapping 1.98-metre former
state-level rugby player and competitive marathon ocean-swimmer,
has been confirmed as the next chief executive of NAB (National
Australia Bank), he can expect to become a household name . . .

*Wood, 2008*

One of Queensland's youngest pollies has admitted spending
nine months in Russia for bone-breaking growth surgery because
of insecurities about her size. Logan councillor Hajnal Ban, 31
had each of her legs broken in four places for the leg-lengthening
procedure, remaining in hospital as she grew about 1mm a day to
increase her 154cm frame to 162cm.

*Sandy, 2009*

How do physical bodies operate in leadership? Building on broader research of
gender, work and organisation, this chapter explores the neglected area of bodies
in leadership. My focus includes bodily stature, shape, demeanour, physical performance and voice, how they are experienced (by leaders and followers) and represented to audiences.

The examples above from Australian newspapers show that bodies and physical performances often play central roles in establishing power and credentials for leadership. In the first excerpt, bank Chief Executive Officer Cameron Clyne is portrayed as a Ulysses, a giant of a man who will 'steady the ship' of the bank in 'treacherous' world market waters. The article occupied a full page of the news section of an Australian daily and the article was dominated by a facial profile of Clyne taking up two thirds of the right hand side of the page. Offered as a new breed of leader, it is Clyne's physical characteristics that are critical in this construction. The second excerpt provides an example of the 'lengths' to which one woman local councillor went to make herself fit for leadership and the photograph accompanying the article, pictures Han from the ground up, her legs as the focus.

As these examples illustrate, the bodies of men and women are often experienced and represented very differently in leadership. Bodies activate unconscious processes and gendered societal archetypes that reinforce or undermine authority, power and socially-constructed credibility (Sinclair, 1998). Despite the pervasiveness and significance of leaders and their images (Guthey and Jackson, 2008), there has been little serious analysis of the role of bodies in leadership and my aim here is to draw on gender and organisational theorising to deepen that analysis.

The first part of this chapter reviews research on bodies in organisations and management and offers some explanations as to why so little attention has been paid to the bodies of leaders. I then examine specifically how bodies are portrayed in leadership, drawing on studies of media representations of bodies. In the second part, I explore how bodies and an awareness of physical selves might be brought differently into researching and practising leadership. Acknowledging the powerful and gendered regimes which govern how women and men's bodies in leadership are seen and represented, there is also evidence that some leaders are destabilising norms on image and bodily self-management as they embody leadership differently.

## RESEARCH ON BODIES IN ORGANISATIONS AND SOCIETY

In the following overview of literature I look first at theorising about bodies and seek to understand why the physical production of leadership and management in organisations has been understudied. The exceptions come from gender and organisational, rather than leadership research (Acker, 1990; Kerfoot and Knights, 1996; Brewis and Linstead, 2000; Hassard et al., 2000; Harding, 2002; Hansen et al., 2007; Ropo and Sauer, 2008; Höpfl, 2008 and this volume).

Theorising about the role of the body in culture, organisations and society began several decades ago with the work of sociologists (Turner, 1984; Scott and Morgan, 1993). Feminists and gender scholars have written extensively on bodies and their significance in culture, organisations and everyday life (for example Bordo, 1993; Butler, 1993; Gatens, 1996; Grosz, 1994), including those with a particular interest in bodies in pedagogy (Luke and Gore, 1992; Gallop, 1995; McWilliam, 1996). Mapping the social and historical ways gender has been constructed, this work also shows that while often men have been represented as having neither gender nor bodies, women have been definable by their bodies and reproductive capacities that are then labelled as flawed and 'troublesome' (Butler, 1993; Sheppard, 1989). Societies and organisations have been shown to have rules about how women's bodies should be: what should be worn, what mannerisms, demeanour, voice, size and shape are appropriate. These rules function in complex but powerful ways – it isn't a matter of individual choice – and researchers have documented how 'women's bodies are disciplined and made docile and productive in culturally and historically specific ways' (Trethewey, 1999). According to Trethewey's field work with women managers and leaders the ideal is to be 'fit', not fat. Yet the band of acceptable bodily 'fitness' and behaviour for women is narrow. Those judged too fit are deemed likely to be driven, competitive or lesbian. The corporate mould requires navigation along a trip wire: feminine movement and posture in organizations must physically embody professionalism, endurance and control 'finely balanced against the eroticised but grateful self' (Hatcher, 2008: 162, see also Bell and Kenny and Wolkowitz, this volume).

Research focusing on the practice and performance of gender helps to elucidate the finely orchestrated ways in which the bodies of women are recruited to the project of gendering management. Women in management roles – despite their seniority – are expected to answer phones, take minutes and embody nurturance through their tone of voice and demeanour (Martin, 2003; Mathieu, 2009). They are counselled to go to extreme measures such as taking the Pill to time menstruation for weekends, in order to minimise the offence their bodies may cause to male colleagues (Bell and Kenny, this volume).

Researchers in emotional labour beginning with the pioneering work of Hochschild (1983) have also shown how jobs – particularly those carried out by women and at the lower ends of organisations – demand highly regulated emotional *and* physical performances including smiling, shows of caring, enthusiasm and 'bubbliness', that bring with them an equally regulated body regime described by Hancock and Tyler as 'an aesthetic economy' (2008). Attempts to 'actively manage structures of feeling' are interwoven with bodily performances to evoke desire and recognition, not in the interests of art but to align consumers' hopes and aspirations with organisational economic ambitions (2008: 214). In the corporate context, Hatcher has also demonstrated the pressures to produce oneself as 'a work of art' that must meet 'aesthetic values and stylistic criteria' (2008: 153). Taken together, this research shows that underneath the rational labour market for skills and competencies is another market in emotional, bodily and aesthetic labour where women's performances are highly regulated according to narrow societal and organisational norms.

Where have the bodies of men been in these analyses? Early gender scholars undertaking studies of men in organisations and management revealed how constructions of the male body permeate and perpetuate conditions of men's dominance and oppression in organisational settings (Cockburn, 1985; Collinson, 1992; Roper, 1994, 1996; Connell, 1995; Collinson and Hearn, 1996; Kerfoot and Knights, 1996; McDowell, 1997; Sinclair, 1998). Dominance is thus often accomplished via hierarchies of body masculinities where the bodies at the top are so superior they enjoy relative invisibility, while men lower down must often bodily verify their masculinity. For example, Barrett's (1996) research of naval cultures show an intricate but well understood hierarchy of masculine norms around embodiment. At the top are extremes of physical risk-taking among 'fly-boys', to a technical rationality expressed via capabilities, habits and physical demeanours among supply officers at the bottom. While the hierarchy seems to put those men at the bottom at a disadvantage, each masculine bodily subculture finds its position and legitimacy in opposition to the feminine. Each is not-female, which is what matters.

In many military and quasi-military institutional environments, such as among police officers, physical ways of being and talking have often been central to doing the job. In their research Davies and Thomas document a policing culture which, despite policy changes towards diversity and equal opportunity, is rampantly, physically masculine. Police officers describe a 'virility culture', where the 'testosterone is "in your face"'. Physical presence is demanded in the 'breakfast meetings', 'working every single weekend', 'sitting here doing all this rubbish' and 'getting buried in stuff' (2003: 692–694). Demonstrations of competitive masculinity demand scatological humour, scathing contempt towards others and physical prowess in a 'live, eat and breath policing' culture (2003: 693). The fear underpinning the most strenuously maintained aspects of the culture is that 'we have gone too soft' (2003: 691): a final and most terrible phallic humiliation (see also Eveline, 1996; and Höpfl, this volume).

Over the last decade, interest in the aesthetics of organisations has elicited new accounts of how bodies mediate and act as a sensual barometer for experiences of management and organisation. For example, drawing on both Marxist and postmodern perspectives, Harding explores the managerial body which, in its flesh-concealing state, still functions as an aesthetic code, inserted into the minds of employees 'to achieve conformity, rigidity and obedience' (2002: 68). She suggests that the managers themselves are a primary recipient of this code, both objectified and subjectified by the body they are required to produce. Importantly Harding ventures that managerial bodies of both genders, in different ways, oppress managers themselves.

Finally, organisational and marketing research increasingly highlights the centrality of bodies to the production of brands and aesthetic consumption. Bodies become sites in the competition for designation as 'cool' (Heaphy and Dutton, 2008). Research also documents the spread of 'Lookism', a form of discrimination where employees are selected or rejected on the basis of their physical attractiveness (Warhurst et al., 2009). Much of this attention has been to bodies lower down the organisational hierarchy and to women. How do bodies figure in the production of leadership?

## The Apparent Absence of Bodies in Leadership

Very little of this rich gender and organisational scholarship on bodies has made its way into our understanding of leadership and the different pressures on men and women leaders to produce a convincing physical embodiment. The body has been 'missing' (Ropo and Sauer, 2008). Is this because bodies don't matter? Rather, I argue that men's leadership is, and has historically been, accomplished in physical and self-consciously aesthetic ways (Höpfl, 2000). It's not that men's bodies are not important in leadership, it's that they have been made invisible for particular ideological purposes. Meanwhile, female leader bodies are highlighted and made available for judgement, potentially undermining their claim to leadership.

There are at least two discernible manoeuvres in the removal of male bodies from leadership. The first has been where male bodies are actively denied and suppressed in the accomplishment of the mental mastery of leadership. Bodies suggest weakness and mortality. Many commentators and leaders alike have an active interest in pretending they don't have bodies or at least, are not subject to them. In his study of transnational masculinities, Connell (2000) notes how what was once the uniform of the American executive has now become virtually mandatory for leaders from most cultures. The way male leaders are clothed and photographed may be powerful symbolic vehicles for the disembodiment of men's leadership.

The second, more recent phase, might be characterised as being the 'super body' in leadership. Here the emphasis is on explicit mastery of a body being an ingredient of fitness to lead. The example at the start of this chapter shows how designation as a super-body – usually implied rather than unveiled in photographs – can assist in constructing the credentials for leadership. For men the emphasis on endurance, stamina and capacities for heightened arousal and attention reinforces images of leader virility and potency.

Several studies of media photographs of leaders provide insight into how the bodies of leaders are used to tell a story about leadership. Sheridan and O'Sullivan analyse the photographs of male leaders on the covers of *The Australian Financial Review*'s *Boss* magazine, arguing that these covers accomplish 'ideological work . . . constructing and reinforcing a mutually affirming relationship between heroic leadership and hegemonic masculinity' (2006: 287). Six of the photographs are of CEOs, the others academics. Sheridan and O'Sullivan argue that 'a reader purchases the CEO subject position . . . as an extension of his/her own identity' (200: 289). With one exception all the photos are close-up head shots, with the leader gazing straight at the camera reinforcing an impression of an individual in charge. In a number of cases due to camera angle, the brow (and seemingly brains) of the leader is enlarged, the bold lettering of *BOSS* branded across it like a tattoo. Bodies are rarely included and if so, are shrouded in genteel shadow.

My colleague Pat Seybolt and I undertook another analysis of how leaders' bodies were photographed and represented in a selection of Australian newspapers and business magazine (see Sinclair, 2008). There are marked differences in how male and female leaders are photographed along two main dimensions: body composition and skin exposed. Men are predominantly photographed as heads or head and shoulders. Ninety-three percent of male leaders had no skin apart from face exposed, while only 34% of women were in this category and a third of women were portrayed with two or more of arms, legs or upper chest visible. For men, clothing functions to conceal skin, groins and hips are shielded and bodies reduced to a silhouette. For women, non-facial skin, clothing, jewellery and backgrounds are more likely to be included and give more away about the character of the leader, sometimes with a general sense of clutter that is rarely part of a male leader's photograph. The overall effect for men is to render the body invisible or irrelevant and reinforce an image of cerebral mastery (Harding, 2002; Sinclair, 2005a). In contrast, women leaders and their bodies are portrayed as frail (not stable or sound); elderly (cranky or 'past it' – this occurs particularly in photographs of Indigenous women leaders); surrounded by distractions (not focused on the job) or full-figured (suggesting a failure of bodily self-discipline). Bodies are ways to draw attention to idiosyncrasy, frailty or sexuality which in turn undermines women's eligibility for leadership (Bell and Kenny, this volume).

Guthey and Jackson (2005; 2008) draw on broader research on image, gaze and framing, to explore the dynamic and complex role of photographic images in the production of leadership. They examine examples of images of leaders, including several of former Hewlett Packard CEO Carly Fiorina, to show how leadership is constructed and contested visually and as 'to-be-looked-at-ness' for women. Guthey and Jackson also encourage us to take a complex view of image-making as sites 'where gazes intersect' and 'where power and gender relations play themselves out in visual form' (2008: 88).

What can we conclude from this research about how bodies figure in the production and representation of leaders? When I present our research on media images there is usually immediate recognition among audiences, followed by awkward silence. Some people immediately jump to the 'solution' that women and others whose bodies are experienced as incongruous, should work harder to 'downplay' their bodies, to dress more innocuously or to cover up. For others, including many women, there is a sense of depressed resignation. Here is one more way that women's authority and potential leadership is undermined. However, I want to suggest a further possibility to be explored next: that leadership bodies are a site of experimentation and innovation.

## EMBODYING LEADERSHIP

While I was writing this chapter, I was invited to be featured in a column called 'Other Passions' in the *Australian Financial Review Magazine*. The reporter was interested in profiling my interest in yoga and meditation in a business school environment. A photograph of me in a seated yoga pose with foot behind head, accompanied the column (Figure 7.1). To me, both photograph and accompanying text

FIGURE 7.1
*Source:* Photograph by Anthony Browell

conveyed a slightly disruptive order. I don't look 'good': there are freckles, crooked teeth and wispy hair. Body, though central, is also played with in juxtaposition of face and foot.

However, my co-researcher in the Bodies Study reported earlier was perplexed that I'd allowed myself to be photographed in that way. For her, this was one more example of the many we had collected showing how the media reduce women to their bodies. Her reaction, and our conversation that followed, challenged me to think harder about how leaders might be in their bodies differently in the face of what often seem implacably gendered body regimes.

As individuals, we are never free to choreograph our own bodies or to insist that they be represented and experienced by others in particular ways. Women and men confront different sets of regulatory norms about bodies, with women facing more scrutiny and coercion partially because their bodies are consistently socially consti-tuted as a highly visible (dis)qualification to their leadership.

Yet neither is it a useful path to accept and adapt to gendered norms of embodi-ment in leadership: either for women leaders to conform to conventions and seek to be disembodied, or for men to strive towards ideals of having a super-body. The solution is not for men or women to pretend to be bodiless or collude with the view of leadership as a disembodied phenomenon. Referring back to my own experi-ence, seeking to have my power stakes improved by insisting on a head and shoul-ders photograph, we know from gender research, wouldn't guarantee anything.

So if we are interested in exposing the way traditional gendered constructions operate in work, organisations and leadership, how might we seek to change the way leadership is understood and to embody leadership differently ourselves? In the following I suggest three broad 'fronts': how we theorise leadership; how we observe and research the practices of leaders; and how we embody leadership ourselves.

## Theorising

Leadership as a field of study is an ideology. In the production of the 'truth' about what leadership is and how it is done, key aspects are left out. It seems remarkable that the role of leader and follower bodies is left out of most research into char-ismatic and transformational leadership, in particular. Even the much discussed ingredient of leadership 'presence' is often portrayed in ethereal terms. A pioneer in the field of organisational aesthetics, Strati lays the blame squarely on 'the delib-erate and collective blindness of organizational scholars' by which the people stud-ied are 'purged of corporeality, so that only his or her mind remains' (1999: 3). Similarly in leadership, Hansen et al. lament that researchers have 'hammered' the rich and vibrant phenomena of leadership 'into a shapeless, hapless, colorless, life-less condition' (2007: 545). If, in our research of leadership, gender and organisa-tions, we were to pay greater attention to bodies what concepts and approaches might be helpful?

Arising out of critical and feminist scholarship such as the work of Judith Butler (1993), has been interest in 'performativity' in management and leadership (Ford et al., 2008). In emphasising performativity, scholars seek to show how phenomena like leadership are not natural or essential but always being established and reconstituted through repeated performances. It is through performance that the category – leadership – is created. Leadership is not a stable set of objective skills, but a dynamic accomplishment where the very performance of it is understood as an effort to establish it. The more leadership is talked about, invoked and seen, in connection with certain people, positions, and we could argue bodies, the more that leadership in those forms assumes the status of truth. Some scholars are also interested in the spaces in and between bodies that establish a leadership 'presence'. Leadership is not in one body but coheres in a 'network of human and non-human entities', discursively being produced and negotiated (Fairhurst and Cooren, 2009: 470).

Ideas of performativity and its emphasis on embodiment help us to focus in closely on the doing and the acting out of leadership, asking what body rules apply. The bodies of leaders are rendered visible (usually in the case of women) and invisible (usually in the case of men) via a pre-existing socially defined body order. Scholarship has also convincingly demonstrated how creating 'otherness' enables the norm to go unseen (Benjamin, 1998). Thus the 'naturalness' of men's bodies in leadership is reinforced every time a woman's different body is made noticeable. Dichotomies like mind/body function alongside gender dichotomies of male/female to ensure that women are more likely to be defined and judged as bodies, without mind. Further, the location of all that is sexual on women leaders obscures the way sexualities are threaded through our appetites for male leadership (Calás and Smircich, 1991; Sinclair, 1995). Being physically attractive and handsome in a male leader is powerfully appealing for both male and female audiences, as the media coverage and analyses of Barack Obama's presidential campaign reveal. Conversely, the sexualities of women leaders are more likely to be viewed as disruptive with women coming under intense pressure to minimise sexuality through dress and demeanour.

Research of creative and arts leaders helps us see the roles of bodies, creativity and aesthetics and their impact in leadership in new ways (see Schroeder and Fillis, forthcoming, for a review). Hansen et al. (2007) and Ropo and Sauer (2008) offer frameworks for exploring corporeality and the more sensuous dimensions of shared leadership, reminding us that all learning is mediated through the senses. Using the case study of Pina Bausch, MacNeill (2009) shows that while creative leadership often starts with the materiality of body, the bodily experiences of dancers, choreographers and audiences are pushed aside by concerns such as commercialism (money) and intellectual property claims (legal minds). Ladkin (2008) also elaborates the impacts of attending a concert conducted by the 'beautiful' embodied leadership of Bobby McFerrin.

## Observing and researching leaders and their practices

Despite these rich perspectives on bodies, the research cited in this chapter and this volume shows just how little choice many women feel about how to embody themselves in their managerial and leadership jobs (Brewis; Bell and Kenny; Wolkowitz, this volume). Many, including those at very senior levels, feel under intense pressure to manage their bodies and mitigate its impacts on others. Such efforts are rarely experienced as completely or lastingly successful. Their subjective experience is one of continuing self-consciousness, embarrassment, even shame. If they decide to wear bold or non-normative clothing, women often feel they have to steel themselves to do so, preparing for the inevitable judgements. First, it may simply be important to notice and name how this bodily labour and toll accrues, as a means of reducing its oppressive effects.

In the wider society, bodies are increasingly being commodified and commercialised, for example, people sell the rights to tattoo their body like a billboard. Emerging evidence also suggests that as frontiers of bodily labour and commodification keep moving, they do so in historically determined, gendered and racialised ways. Some bodies are made freer in this process, others are more oppressed. Extra tasks of bodily effort, management, suppression and camouflage are imposed on women, non-Whites and men who do not fit a hyper-masculine heterosexual mould as they go about their leadership work (Thanem, this volume). These leaders are not just doing leadership they are engaged in the ongoing negotiation of their legitimacy, rendered more problematic by the body they inhabit and perform.

A small amount of emerging research provides examples of leaders consciously inhabiting bodies and paying attention to others' bodies. These leaders demonstrate a capacity to be reflective about their physical selves in leadership in the midst of deeply gendered regimes of body expectations. What forms does such body reflexivity take?

Leaders evidence a capacity to understand and make conscious choices in how they inhabit and embody their own leadership and, perhaps more importantly, how they respond to the inevitable ways they are embodied by others, via the public and media gaze. Former Chief Commissioner of Police in Victoria, Christine Nixon, chose to physically go and visit many small police stations and community organisations in isolated places in the State – a very unusual thing to do (Sinclair, 2005a). She also gave priority to visiting those police stations with the toughest jobs in the most difficult areas. She stood up in front of often hard-bitten cops to hear what it was like for them and she also talked openly about her own experiences as a police officer, including the times she has got things wrong and been scared. She physically embodied the kind of openness and preparedness to learn that she was asking police to consider. Nixon also paid attention to uniforms, including her own very ill-fitting one. She formed a team to redesign uniforms to suit an increasingly diverse police force.

A second example is Chris Sarra, a former school principal who is now Director of an Australian Institute of Indigenous and Torres Strait Islander Education. Chris is Indigenous and one of the ways that Aboriginals have been marginalised in the Australian context is to treat them as bodies. Chris himself is deeply aware of the way this dichotomy has functioned to devalue the contribution of Aboriginal leaders and discourage young people from having high intellectual aspirations. Yet his leadership as a school principal was not about denying his own Aboriginality or the importance of the physicality of the children. A vision of being 'Strong and Smart' was collaboratively developed with the school and local communities. Physical presence and wellbeing was co-located with intellectual ability and potential: both were consistently emphasised (Sinclair, 2005a).

There are strong taboos about bringing an awareness of bodies into leadership. Many leaders I've worked with shrink from the topic of bodies because they believe that paying them attention will get them into trouble. Sexual harassment, gender and racial discrimination laws function in important ways to ensure workers do not get exploited or rejected because of their bodies. However, the solution to these legal prohibitions is surely not to act as if bodies don't exist. Further, my work with many leaders suggests that they know bodies are not irrelevant. They are open to new discourses which might encourage explorations of leadership embodiment.

There is now a growing amount of research material that advises leaders on how to manage their bodies. Some of this has an instrumental intent: it is designed to convert the body into a more reliable and effective vehicle of 'successful' leadership, for example by managing cycles of arousal and attention. I am ambivalent about this literature. On the one hand, it seems a good development to encourage leaders to take care of themselves, to recognise vulnerability and not inflict assumptions of the necessity of physical suffering and stoicism on their followers. Bodies are a means to help men open up a different way of thinking about who they are and might be in leadership. On the other hand, much of the literature advising this body awareness does not invite questioning of who or what that leadership is for. There is a danger that new body awareness is recruited to the project of becoming a 'corporate athlete': a leader who can work harder and longer towards ends that are exploitative.

## *Being in body ourselves*

The most successful teachers I have observed, especially in a Business School setting, are often tall and physically confident, sometimes handsome and attractive (Sinclair, 2009). In contrast, my body seems to have been a source of disappointment. When people who know of me meet me for the first time, a few have said: 'You don't look like a professor, but never mind . . .' My short stature has often meant that I find myself peering over lecterns. I have experimented with clothing and watched others do so: female colleagues wearing stilettos or flat shoes and everything in between as ways of inhabiting and asserting an embodied self in the gendered terrain of institutional life. While it seems inevitable that the bodies and clothing of women leaders are statements that are 'read' and judged, the ways that many men embody leadership remains invisible or unscrutinised.

Educational researcher and teacher bell hooks writes powerfully about being embodied in the classroom. In her view conventions of knowing and teaching often enact domination and encourage a 'systematic disconnection of self from the world, self from others' (2003: 179–180). Her innovative efforts are directed towards enhancing students' 'journey to wholeness', in which passion, desire, eroticism, love and happiness may be activated. For hooks, passionate pedagogy in any area is likely to spark erotic energy and rather than shy away from such energy, she sees it as a 'space for transgression that can undermine domination' (2003: 151). In contrast 'critique on its own can become merely an expression of profound cynicism, which then works to sustain dominator culture' (2003: xiv).

As I have written about elsewhere (Sinclair 2005b; 2007), my own relationship to my body changed significantly when I started to do more yoga, and particularly after I became a yoga teacher. Initially I simply enjoyed feeling physically stronger and more relaxed. Over time, I began experimenting with being more embodied in my work, such as noticing how my own body felt and the impact of bodily postures and demeanours of others in the classroom.

Yoga teaches a non-dichotomous understanding of the place of the body alongside the mind. A further possibility is that bodily mediated experience and knowledge provide a welcome interruption to the hegemony of mind (Casey, 2000). Drawing on her own yoga practice, philosopher Luce Irigaray (2002) has described the effects of neglecting the body in knowledge and teaching. Her observation is that philosophic traditions have become dogmatic and authoritarian, 'have substituted words for life without carrying out the necessary links between the two' (2002: 51). Irigaray also argues that bodies play a central role in understanding difference and maintains 'it is not true that knowledge is indifferent to sex or gender' (2002: 59).

For me, finding a way of being in my body, accepting and allowing it rather than denying it, has opened up a different quality in my teaching and research. Being in my body has been part of my identity work. It has allowed me to understand how I collude with a privileging mind – I am what I think. Together these changes have enabled me to experiment, to be more open and appreciative, and paradoxically perhaps, less driven by fears of what people think of me. I also teach differently by paying attention to what others' bodies seem to indicate, suggesting we break or move if there's a lot of tension or tiredness in the room. I encourage people to acknowledge bodies rather than fight against or try to override them. These emphases are sometimes experienced by my students as inappropriate, even oppressive. Part of aiming for embodiment in leadership has included me being open to such responses.

Substantial research has helped us understand the relations between bodies and sex, work and organisations. Yet the domain and study of leadership seems to have resisted such exploration. As discussed, the whole modern myth of leadership with its claims to grandeur, elevation and transformation, seems ill at ease with the nitty gritty of bodies. The ever-expanding field of leadership studies continues to be largely captured in cycles of cognitive observation and analyses, yet fails to offer a compelling view of how leadership works at a visceral level; how powerful dimensions of women and women's subjective experiences routinely get left out of leadership; and how ways of doing leadership continue to oppress. My hope is that critical analyses of the central role of bodies will open up new ways of understanding leadership and new ways of doing it.

# REFERENCES

Acker, J. (1990) Hierarchies, Jobs, Bodies: A Theory of Gendered Organizations, *Gender and Society*, 4(2) 139–158.

Barrett, F. (1996) The Organizational Construction of Hegemonic Masculinity: The Case of the US Navy, *Gender, Work and Organization*, 3(3) 129–142.

Benjamin, J. (1998) *Shadow of the Other: Intersubjectivity and Gender in Psychoanalysis*. New York: Routledge.

Bordo, S. (1993) *Unbearable Weight, Feminism, Western Culture and the Body*. Berkeley: University of California Press.

Brewis, J., and Linstead, S. (2000) *Sex, Work and Sex Work: Eroticizing Organization*. London: Routledge.

Butler, J. (1993) *Bodies that Matter: On the Discursive Limits of Sex*. New York: Routledge.

Calás, M., and Smircich, L. (1991) Voicing seduction to silence leadership, *Organization Studies*, 12(4) 567–602.

Casey, C. (2000) 'Sociology Sensing the Body: Revitalizing a Dissociative Discourse' in J. Hassard, R. Holliday, and H. Willmott (eds), *Body and Organization*. London: Sage, 52–70.

Cockburn, C. (1985) *Machinery of Dominance: Women, Men and Technological Know-How*. London: Pluto Press.

Collinson, D. (1992) *Managing the Shopfloor: Subjectivity, Masculinity and Workplace Culture*. Berlin: de Gruyter.

Collinson, D., and Hearn, J (eds) (1996) *Men as Managers, Managers as Men: Critical Perspectives on Men, Masculinities and Managements*. London: Sage.

Connell, R. (1995) *Masculinities*. Sydney: Allen and Unwin.

Connell, R. (2000) *The Men and the Boys*. Cambridge: Polity Press.

Davies, A., and Thomas, R. (2003) Talking Cop: Discourses of change and policing identities, *Public Administration*, 81(4) 681–699.

Eveline, J. (1996) The Worry of Going Limp: Are You Keeping up in Senior Management, *Australian Feminist Studies* 11(3) 65–79.

Fairhurst, G., and Cooren, F. (2009) Leadership as the hybrid production of presence, *Leadership*, 5(4) 469–490.

Ford, J., Harding, N., and Learmonth, M. (2008) *Leadership as Identity: Constructions and Deconstructions*. Basingstoke: Palgrave Macmillan.

Gallop, J. (ed.) (1995) *Pedagogy: The Question of Impersonation*. Bloomington, IN: Indiana University Press.

Gatens, M. (1996) *Imaginary Bodies: Ethics, Power and Corporeality*. London: Routledge.

Grosz, E. (1994) *Volatile Bodies: Towards a Corporeal Feminism*. Bloomington, IN: Indiana University Press.

Guthey, E., and Jackson, B. (2005) CEO Portraits and the Authenticity Paradox, *Journal of Management Studies*, 42(5) 1057–1082.

Guthey, E., and Jackson, B. (2008) 'Revisualizing Images in Leadership and Organization Studies' in D. Barry and H. Hansen (eds), *The SAGE Handbook of New Approaches in Management and Organization*. London: Sage, 84–92.

Hancock, P., and Tyler, M. (2008) 'It's All too Beautiful: Emotion and Organization in the Aesthetic Economy' in S. Fineman (ed.) *The Emotional Organization: Passions and Power*. Oxford; Blackwell, 202–217.

Hansen, H., Ropo, A., and Sauer, E. (2007) Aesthetic Leadership, *Leadership Quarterly*, 18, 544–560.

Harding, N. (2002) On the manager's body as an aesthetics of control, *Tamara: Journal of Critical Postmodern Organization Science*, 2(1) 63–76.

Hassard, J., Holliday, R., and Willmott, H. (eds) (2000) *Body and Organization*. London: Sage.

Hatcher, C. (2008) 'Becoming a Successful Corporate Character and the Role of Emotional Management' S. Fineman (ed.), *The Emotional Organization: Passions and Power*. Oxford; Blackwell, 153–166.

Heaphy, E., and Dutton, J. (2008) Positive Social Interactions and the Human Body at Work: Linking organizations and physiology, *Academy of Management Review*, 33(1) 137–162.

Hochschild, A. (1983) *The Managed Heart: Commercialization of Human Feeling*. Berkeley, CA: University of California Press.

hooks, bell (2003) *Teaching Community: A Pedagogy of Hope*. New York: Routledge.

Höpfl, Harro (2000) '*Suaviter in modo, fortiter in re* Appearance, Reality and the Early Jesuits' in S. Linstead and H. Höpfl (eds), *The Aesthetics of Organization*. London: Sage, 197–211.

Höpfl, H. (2008) 'Maternal Organization' in D. Barry and H. Hansen (eds), *The SAGE Handbook of New Approaches in Management and Organization*. London: Sage, 349–358.

Irigaray, L. (2002) *Between East and West*. New York: Colombia University Press.

Jackson, B. (2001) *Management Gurus and Management Fashions*. London: Routledge.

Kerfoot, D., and Knights, D. (1996) ' "The Best is yet to Come?": The Quest for Embodiment in Managerial Work' in D. Collinson and J. Hearn (eds), *Men as Managers, Managers as Men*. London: Sage.

Ladkin, D. (2008) Leading Beautifully: How Mastery, Congruence and Purpose Create the Aesthetic of Embodied Leadership, *The Leadership Quarterly*, 19, 31–41.

Luke, C., and Gore, J. (eds) (1992) *Feminisms and Critical Pedagogy*. New York: Routledge.

MacNeill, K. (2009) Pina Bausch, Creativity and the Materiality of Artistic Labour, *International Journal of Cultural Policy*, 15(3).

Martin, P. (2003) 'Said and Done' versus 'Saying and Doing' – Gendering Practices, Practising Gender at Work, Gender & Society, 17(3) 342–366.

Mathieu, C. (2009) Practising Gender in Organisations: The Critical Gap between Practical and Discursive Consciousness, *Management Learning*, 40(2) 177–193.

McDowell, L. (1997) *Capital Culture: Gender at Work in the City*. Oxford: Blackwell.

McWilliam, E. (1996) *Pedagogy, Technology and the Body*. New York: Peter Lang.

Roper, M. (1994) *Masculinity and the British Organization Man Since 1945*. Oxford: Oxford University Press.

Roper, M. (1996) ' "Seduction and Succession": Circuits of Homosocial Desire in Management' in D. Collinson and J. Hearn (eds), *Men as Managers, Managers as Men*. London: Sage, 210–226.

Ropo, A., and Sauer, E. (2008) 'Corporeal Leaders' in D. Barry and H. Hansen (eds), *The SAGE Handbook of New Approaches in Management and Organization*. London: Sage, 469–478.

Sandy, A. (2009) 'Hajnal Ban has legs broken to be 8cm taller' *The Courier Mail* April 29.

Schroeder, J., and Fillis, I. (forthcoming 2010) 'Aesthetic Leadership' in R. Couto (ed), *Research Handbook on Political and Civic Leadership*. London: Sage.

Scott, S., and Morgan, D. (1993) *Body Matters: Essays on the Sociology of the Body*. London: Falmer Press.

Sheppard, D. (1989) 'Organizations, Power and Sexuality: The Image and Self-image of Women Managers' in J. Hearn, D. Sheppard, P. Tancred-Sheriff, and G. Burrell (eds), *The Sexuality of Organization*. London: Sage, 139–157.

Sheridan, A., and O'Sullivan, J. (2006) 'Man Oh Man! – Looks like a Leader to Me' in T. Jefferson, L. Lord, and A. Preston (eds), *Changes, Challenges, Choices*. Conference Proceedings from the Inaugural International Women and Leadership Conference, Fremantle, 16 and 17 November 2006, pp. 286–296. Available from http://www.cbs.curtin.edu.au/wiser.

Sinclair, A. (1995) Sexuality in Leadership, *International Review of Women and Leadership*, 1(2) 25–38.

Sinclair, A. (1998) *Doing Leadership Differently: Gender, Power and Sexuality in a Changing Business Culture*. Carlton: Melbourne University Press.

Sinclair, A. (2005a) Body Possibilities in Leadership, *Leadership*, 1(4) 387–406.

Sinclair, A. (2005b) Bodies and Management Pedagogy, *Gender, Work and Organization*, 12(1) 89–104.

Sinclair, A. (2008) 'Bodies and Identities in the Construction of Leadership Capital' in Paul t'Hart and John Uhr (eds), *Public Leadership: Perspectives and Practices*. Canberra: ANU E Press. http://epress.anu.edu.au/public_leadership_citation.html.

Sinclair, A. (2009) Seducing Leadership: Stories of Leadership Development, *Gender, Work and Organization*, 16(2) 266–284.

Strati, A. (1999) *Organization and Aesthetics*. London: Sage.

Trethewey, A. (1999) Disciplined Bodies: Women's embodied identities at work, *Organization Studies*, 20(3) 423–450.

Turner, B. (1984, 2nd edn 1996) *The Body and Society*. London: Sage.

Warhurst, C., Van den Broek, D., Hall, R., and Nickson, D. (2009) Lookism: The New Frontier of Employment Discrimination? *Journal of Industrial Relations*, 51(1) 131–136.

Wood, L. (2008) 'In the eye of the storm' *The Age*, August 1, p. 13.

# 8

# The Body: A Review and a Theoretical Perspective

ANGELA HOPE
*Saint Mary's University, Halifax, Canada*

What is at stake is the activity and agency, the mobility and social space, accorded to women. Far from being inert, passive, noncultural and an ahistorical term, the body may be seen as the crucial term, the site of contestation, in a series of economic, political, sexual, and intellectual struggles.

*Elizabeth Grosz, 1994: 19.*

## INTRODUCTION[1]

This article provides a critical analysis and review of the body in social theorizing, feminist theory, and organization studies in order to give my reader a broad understanding of the body that is not necessarily always feminist-oriented or even perhaps gender-oriented. In the second part, the article shifts towards creating theory. Relying on the underlying assumption that the seat of individual agency lies in the flesh, I craft a theoretical account of what I contend occurs to bodies in organizations and society and how they become corporeally organized by our cultural, economic, *and* religious structures. The focus is on how and why bodies become othered. This process of organizing and segregating bodies, referred to as 'corporeal scapegoating,' is situated at the intersection of the body, gender, organization studies, and sociology of religion.

[1] This article is a follow up to Melissa Tyler's article (this volume). Her chapter concludes: '. . . corporeal feminism, which draws insights from postmodernism and phenomenology has much to offer to our developing critique of the gendered organization of work' (Tyler, 2010, this volume). I agree with her sentiment that organization studies and practices need to be more informed by a corporeal agenda, although in this particular piece, my end result is not particularly feminist, though it could be called that by feminists. However, my intended audience is those who are broadly interested in the body and gender at work, and I hope to be open in my writing so to be inclusive to nonfeminists, postfeminists, and those who resist being boxed into categories.

## THE BODY IN SOCIAL THEORY

The body as an area of inquiry in the social sciences mostly began in the 1960s with philosophers, cultural anthropologists, and social theorists like Erving Goffman, (1963), Mary Douglas (1970), Michael Foucault (1979), Pierre Bourdieu (1984), Mikhail Bakhtin (1984), among many other well-known thinkers. The body as a central and independent focus began in 1984, when Bryan Turner produced his foundational piece, *The Body and Society*, that prompted, along with a growth in publications on the body, the journal *Body and Society* which launched in 1995 (Turner, 1996). These explorations investigate the body as it intersects with topics like technologies, consumption, communication, identities, social order, health and disease, and ethics, to name a few.

The recent attention to the body along with enquiring into the current status of the Western body calls for attention. Turner contends that the recent interest in the body is due to the rise of a somatic society by which he means 'a society within which our major political and moral problems are expressed through the conduit of the human body" (Turner, 1996: 6). A move away from a 'puritanical orthodoxy' which belied the bourgeois industrial capitalism, allowed for a move into a body conscious society indirectly promoted by a postindustrial society and postfordist economy (ibid.: 1996). Religious studies scholar Linda Holler (2002), conversely, would make the case that our Western society is undergirded with a utilitarian morality that is body-denying rather than body-affirming. She calls for the need to reorient our ethical structures rooted in the body:

> Just as dualistic, disembodied philosophy inevitably gave rise to an ethic based on logos – on rules, authorities, and duties – so embodied awareness must rise to an ethic base on eros, a somatic, intuitive form of agency in which empathy, compassion, and care are the central moral qualities (Holler, 2002, 1).

Her argument articulates that touch is the seat of revolution towards a radical change for a society based on eros, love from the body. However currently, we rely on the intellect excessively to dictate our moral ways of being. This chiefly has to do not only with our Western philosophical heritage from the Greeks, but also our still much embedded Judeo-Christian heritage, despite the supposed claim to secularization (Berger, Davie, and Fokas, 2008; Hope, 2007).

Still others have theories as to why the body has become of increasing interest in social theory. Anthony Giddens identifies a change in our society that marks a 'transformation of intimacy' where emotions are legitimated as a vehicle for interpersonal interaction (1991). Arthur Frank draws attention to the phenomena that acute illness and disease have diminished while chronic, lingering illnesses predominate in our society. This has created the impetus for work and leisure to be largely affected by the workings of our body, he argues, simply because it is harder to die (Frank, 1995).

Another main impetus for the rise of the body as a necessary area of inquiry stems from the 'liberation movements' of feminists, theologians, postcolonialists, and poststructuralists. Many of these movements stem from a critique of positivism, our Hellenistic philosophical heritage, and the dominant grandnarratives of Judeo-Christianity which privilege the mind over the body.

These proponents attend to subverting oppressive discourses and structures which marginalize the body, matter, earth, the feminine, and so on.

In line with the liberation movement, I contend quite the opposite of what Bryan Turner articulates, namely that we have encountered a kind of corporeal management dictated by our economic structure which disciplines our minds and bodies. With respect to bodies, because this corporeal management occurs mainly in the context of work, analysis of the organization and work is central to responding to this phenomenon. In our capitalist society, work is an integral part of our lives in terms of our identities and sense of meaning to the point where work bleeds into family and leisure as these boundaries are in flux and fluid. Moreover, more and more women have jobs today but still women and moms remain the primary worker in the family arena, causing a kind of double corporeal suffocation as their bodies are (man)aged through two organizational spheres which privilege males. NPR reports that by 2010, 70% of mothers will have jobs and women will be the majority of the workers (Collins, 2009). This claim that we have encountered a corporeal suffocation, and women a double corporeal suffocation, is intended to be universalistic within the Western context, however, in terms of how different groups based on class, gender, race, ableism, and sexual orientation, are affected is not universal, but differs along these socio-economic categories in terms of both degree and kind. I will return to these concepts in the next section.

This section only touched briefly on the body in the field of social theory but attention was focused on the state of the body in our society and why the body has become a rising interest in the social sciences. It is important to analyze why the body is important for study if one is to go further in this area of research. The question to ask is: What is at stake if the body is not researched and central to theoretical and practical concerns at work and in society? For me, the answer is that women's and marginalized others' oppression in work and family organizations is at stake. Dualistic thinking and material manifestations of this are the medium which spread alienation, oppression, and violence towards bodies, especially non-normative bodies. As the body is aligned with women and the mind aligned with men in a hierarchical fashion, the body becomes the crucial site for the alleviation of suffering.

## THE BODY IN FEMINIST THEORY

Feminism deals with the concept of gender but does not necessarily highlight the importance of the body and sexuality within its critique of androcentric normativity. I will critically explore the role of the body in feminisms in this section.[2]

---

[2] I ask my reader to remember that this is not an account or narrative of the different brands of feminism. For this, see (Calás and Smircich, 2006 or Beasley, 2005). The point is to give a broad overview of how these feminist paradigms incorporate the body into their views, often subtly and unintentionally in a negative or forgotten fashion. For further reading, see the references. If you are not a feminist or despise feminist work, feel free to skip to the next section

### The body in modern feminist theories

Modern feminist theorizing has historically, within the first and second waves, conceived the body, typically in a dualistic fashion. Dualistic thinking necessarily orders the two terms in a hierarchy in which one is always privileged and the other subordinated (Grosz, 1994). *Liberal/ Egalitarian Feminism* which champions the conception of the 'universal human' includes writers like Mary Wollstonecraft (1792), Naomi Wolf (1991), and Martha Nussbaum (2000), to name a few.

The female body with its specificities of menstruation, pregnancy, lactation and other bodily functions are viewed as a limitation to accessing 'universal humanness,' and essentially what is, power within patriarchal culture (Grosz, 1994). This negative view regards the body as a limitation for women's potential to gain equality. Women's biological differences exist, but, some feminists of this tradition argue, this does not preclude them from reasoning like men. 'Convention and habit are women's enemies, and reason their ally' (Nussbaum, 1994: 17). Reason and the faculties of the mind are privileged over the body in all its 'natural' habits and tendencies. For liberal feminists, such as Nussbaum, the body is ahistorical, acultural. Its ultimate *telos* is maternity and childbearing. Its ontological status is predestined, fixed, the manifestation of a baby machine blueprint. The body is an obstruction, but this acknowledgement is necessarily implicit; the body's burdensome functioning and habits have to be silenced if one can efficaciously appropriate patriarchal power. This tradition does not challenge androcentric, dualistic ontology but reinforces its grandnarrative.

*Gender Difference Feminism*, which relies on identity politics and set essences for women and men, includes thinkers like Mary Daly (1973), Carol Gilligan (1982), Nancy Chodorow (1978), modernist social constructionists, standpoint theorists, socialists, psychoanalysts, and radicals. The theories within this framework rely on an implicit and sometimes explicit social essentialism. Patriarchal power relations produce commonalities amongst women's experiences – both positive (i.e. Gilligan's ethics of care) and negative (oppression, rape, domestic violence). They challenge liberal modes of thinking which they argue result in a 'sameness' that masks male privilege. Politically, they focus on 'difference,' but again do not disrupt the mind (soul)/body subject.

The sex (biological)/gender (representational) distinction is intact, and the focus is to politicize the representational through the use of the body. The female body is still treated as a biologically determined object but the focus shifts to another sort of objectification in which the body is a *medium* of communication for what is at the psychical (Grosz, 1994).

The body itself, in the strongest version of this position is irrelevant to political transformation, and in the weakest version is merely a vehicle for psychological change, an instrument for a 'deeper' effect (ibid.: 17).

The sex or the body is presumed to be passive and unproductive – it is not the site where change can be enacted. At best, it can be useful, with enough subduing and conditioning (Gilligan 1982). Either way, what constitutes gender at the psychical level (masculinities and femininities) is the subject of transformation.

## The body and postmodern feminist theories[3]

Within postmodern feminism, arguably, three different paradigms exist thus far: Sexual Difference or Corporeal Feminism, Performativity Feminism, and Postcolonial, Transnational or Race, Ethnicity, Imperialism Feminism (Beasley, 2005).[4] All versions are highly hesitant towards universal and essentialist truth claims and challenge claims that women are essentially the same or essentially different. These feminist frameworks have different conceptions of power than their modernist counterparts, viewing it instead as relational and manifested within language. Accordingly, they, with varying intensities, realize the negative, oppressive implications when failing to attend to race, imperialism, class, ability, and sexual orientation. Of the three, two— Corporeal Feminism and Performativity Feminism—have contested stances towards the ontological status of the body and the body's agentic capacities. Expounders of corporeal feminism refute that performativity feminism, arguably the most popular in American culture and scholarship, locates the body in an agentic fashion. More time will be focused in this area as this is still a current, contentious site for feminists. Now we first turn to Postcolonial/Transnational/REI Feminism.

Postcolonial/Transnational/Race/Ethnicity/Imperialism (REI) Feminism[5]includes the writings of Gayatri Spivak (1990), Chandra Mohanty (1991), bell hooks (2006), and Patricia Collins (2000), black standpoint theorists, along with many others. To these feminist theorists, the women-centered approach of modern feminism masked a white, Western or first world, woman.

The body in REI Feminism has taken a back seat so far, probably necessarily so, in order to highlight the importance of including race, ethnicity, and postcolonial/imperialistic analysis since this has been missing or subordinated to issues of a 'universal' woman in Western feminism. Implicitly, this feminist perspective has correctly asserted that it is not just the female body which is subordinated within society, it is the body which is not first world and/or white. Indeed, we are summoned to remember that bodies are not just sexed, but they are also of different skin tones and abilities. The white female body is privileged over the black female body from the Western perspective. The Aboriginal Australian female body is subordinated to the 'civilized' white female body. And so on. While some might argue that feminists within this tradition reinforce the subordination of the body to the

---

[3] It is important to note that corporeal feminism and postcolonial feminism, though I place these both in the latter postmodern section, are not exclusively postmodern, but also utilize modern, phenomenological, and even postfeminist theorizing.

[4] I use Chris Beasley's topology of feminist theorizing which seems to be the most up to date, inclusive, and easily accessible in terms of its understanding of the feminist discourse. See the publication by Beasley, 2005, in the field of Gender Studies called *Gender and Sexuality: Critical Theories, Critical Thinkers.*

[5] This particular feminist framework, REI Feminism, coined by Chris Beasley, 2005 is a more inclusive term than simply 'transnational' or 'postcolonial'. Some writers of race are focused on the context of black women in Western countries rather than across the First World and Third World or prefer the usage of 'ethnicity' to race. Some writers in this framework are hesitant towards the term First World and Third World as they lump together diverse women (Mohanty, 1991). Imperialism rather than the terms colonialism or postcolonialism is a broader reference to a phenomenon of control of which colonialism is a form.

mind, their analysis can offer a powerfully informative perspective to understanding corporeality and fills a lacuna that has existed in contemporary feminist theorizing

*Sexual Difference/Corporeal Feminism* includes the writings of Luce Irigaray (1985), Elizabeth Grosz (1994, 1995), Genevieve Lloyd (2002), Moira Gatens (1996), and many others. Corporeal Feminism marks the shift taken by Elizabeth Grosz in her foundational work, *Volatile Bodies* (1994). Influenced by the work of Freud and Lacan where the father/phallus symbolizes the cultural representation of power, this feminist theorizing generally subscribes to a psychoanalytical perspective (Beasley, 2005). 'Woman' is a symbol defined by her lack or what is left out of the symbolic order. 'Woman' is difference, which is equated with inferiority. Women per se do not have any set content; in other words, biological essentialism or the notion that women are naturally or even always socially feminine is deconstructed. The feminine represents that which is 'other.' As what represents the masculine is located in the center and the feminine is located on the periphery or 'under' the transcendental masculine (Irigaray, 1985), the strategy is not to reverse the binary order and make what constitutes femininity as the new center, a task of modernist versions of gender difference (Chodorow, Gilligan). The goal is to disrupt or decenter the center of masculine normativity through the body, to blur the boundaries without masking a male norm (Squires, 2001). These feminists address the postmodern critique of essentialism without advocating an 'orthodox' postmodern representationalism which subordinates the political possibilities of difference and which further devoid the body of any liberating potential and agentic capacities (Ahmed, 1996).

The commitment in this paradigm to the body is to disrupt binary thinking altogether including the sex/gender or matter/representation dichotomy. The body is neither a blank slate nor a predestined, *telos*-oriented object defined and limited by biology. The body is the locus of thought and unthought which has significance in both the matter and representation debate (ibid.). It mobilizes its own representational and corporeal becoming through more than biological but also through phenomenological and rhizomatical lenses as these thinkers draw from Merleau-Ponty (1962) and Deleuze and Guatarri (1987). The body is more than an effect of representation; it is 'dispossessed of an essence,' but through becoming ontological process, 'it essentializes itself' (Colebrook, 2000: 86). It has its own force, difference, and motility[6] and is in the constant process of 'becoming-meaningful,' rather than the mere effect of construction and representation (Gatens, 1996).

While this feminist tradition is committed to disrupting white-male ontology and conceptions of subjectivity, this particular paradigm does not always necessarily disrupt the binary of work/family. It relies on the assumption that the mainstay of male dominance stems from the organization of 'the family' – e.g. the father/phallus and the Mother (Beasley, 2005; New, 1991; Williams, 2001). The assumption is that the institutionalization of patriarchies stems from the organization of the family, its ethos. This can be monolithic if one considers that the institutionalization of manhood is structured through other organizations – e.g. divinity (church) and warriordom (military), not just virility ('family'). .

---

[6] Motility is defined by Merleau-Ponty as that which is 'not a handmaid of consciousness, transporting the body to the point in space of which we have formed a representation beforehand' (Merleau-Ponty, 1962: 139).

*Performativity Feminism* influenced by the works of Judith Butler (1993) and others, denounces the uses of categories when it is at all possible to do so. This brand of feminism 'refers to the "unadulterated" or most unrelenting postmodern theoretical trajectory in feminism' (Beasley, 2005: 100).[7] Social change does not take place by maintaining identities such as 'woman,' 'man,' 'feminine,' 'lesbian,' but through resisting identities and categorizations which is synonymous with resisting power. 'One is a woman or man as an effect of power' (ibid.: 101). The self is fluid and unstable within this strand of feminism.

The body in this brand of feminism has an ontologically active status, though this accessibility is limited by language. Thus, the body is an effect of epistemic conditions. The body is the site of a gendered performance created by the constituted social practice of naming – this naming (gender) is what creates sex (Beasley, 2005; Butler, 1993). '[G]ender produces the misnomer of a prediscursive "sex"'(Butler, 1993: 6). The representational is given more weight and priority over the material, which has little agentic capacity outside of language. Paradoxically, this brand of feminism intensifies the matter/representation dichotomy despite the fact that it seeks to dismantle the sex/gender distinction (Colebrook, 2000). Accordingly, I would argue that this does little to subvert the mind (soul)/body dualism which is correlated with matter/representation and sex/gender.

Many scholars have charged Butler with committing linguistic monism and determinism, misunderstanding her work, as they relate to bodies and agency which she has been consistent in refuting (Benhabib, 1995). The concept that the body is an effect of signification does not imply that language fully determines the subject (Butler, 1993). Her claim is epistemological not ontological. As a linguistically constructed entity, the body is only accessed epistemologically (Vasterling, 1999). As such, the body's ontological nature is dissimulated through the discursive effects of power. When her claim is interpreted as an ontological statement about the body, this is where misunderstanding of her perspective stems from, because if taken as such, it would imply that the body is nothing more than linguistic constructions.

However, what is lacking in this feminist approach is that the door is closed on the possibilities of an ontology of the body that can be accessed outside of present language. Vasterling (1999) calls attention to the difference between intelligibility and accessibility noting that 'to equate intelligibility with accessibility would mean that we cannot have access to phenomena we do not understand, that is phenomena we cannot articulate' (Vasterling, 1999: 22). At times we experience such events as trauma and bodily sensations that we cannot entirely make sense of or put into language. There is still blood, dirt, pain, sweat, tears, palpitations, excretion, ecstasy, fear, trauma, and desire. It is not that we cannot understand these situations, but we cannot articulate them in a meaningful way. Often, this 'range of accessibility is wider than, though not independent of, the range of intelligibility' (ibid.).

---

[7] Performativity Feminism is a name I give this particular brand of Feminism because of its commitment to resisting any forms of essentialism, biological and social, even for strategic purposes as well as its focus on power and representation rather than corporeality. It denounces identity categories because identities are a *performance* or enactment of power; there is no real truth or essence behind identity categories (Butler, 1995). Gender and identities do not exist materially except to name and marginalize those who do not 'fit' in a certain category.

Following Butler's logic, transformation grounded in bodily experiences is deemed implausible. This is not only disheartening, but in my own lived experiences in the aftermath of military sexual trauma, I find this to be unbelievable.

To conclude, with the exception of corporeal feminism, feminist theories have viewed the body either as an obstruction in modernist versions to viewing the body, within 'strong' postmodern alignments, as a product of representation, power, and language. This trend in feminism is not surprising since Western culture is rooted in somatophobia and dualism (Turner, 1997). The persistent historical subjugation of the body is an indication that we have much to access about our embodied beings that has been previously culturally (and I would add religiously) suppressed. Thus, feminist approaches that implicitly or as a byproduct engender the subjugation of the body to the mind are problematic for feminist praxis.

## THE BODY IN ORGANIZATION STUDIES

Academic disciplines, generally speaking, retain the ancient-modern philosophical canon that ethics, knowledge, and truth are produced from the *logos*[8] rather than the body, feeling, and touch. In anagement and organization studies, positivism remains the dominant research paradigm, a framework which relies on dualistic assumptions (Johnson and Duberley, 2000). The mind/body dualism is correlated with distinctions between categories like men/women, masculine/feminine, reason/emotion, quantitative/qualitative, sameness/difference. Thus not only are organizations filled with managerial practices inherently dualistic which have material consequences, but the knowledge we ascribe to these organizational realities is largely informed from a dualistic perspective.

In the field of management and organization studies, typically within the critical domain, a small but steady stream of scholarship is growing around the body and work, as the primacy of positivism and dualistic logic is contested. Most of these scholarly approaches focus on the body by way of gender, identity, consumption, sexuality, aesthetics, and emotions at work. As of the present, only two books have been published in the area of body, organization, and work—*Body and Organization* by Hassard, Holliday, and Willmott (2000) and *Organizing Bodies: Policy, Instutions, and Work* by McKee and Watson (2000). Most other foundational contributions from organization studies scholars have come from journal articles and book chapters and include scholars such as Höpfl (2003), Linstead and Pullen (2006), Linstead (2000); Dale (2001), Acker (1990), Boje and Hettrick (1992), Tyler and Hancock (2001), Knights (2008), and Thanem (2009), along with others. Some of these scholars like Joan Acker, Melissa Tyler, and Heather Hopfl would consider themselves feminists, but the body has been the subject of inquiry in organization studies beyond the scope of strictly feminism or gender, demonstrating that the issue of the body and work goes beyond one epistemic scope. Some would argue that this is problematic. I would caution my reader that any analysis which does not take into account race, gender, class, ability, and other ways our bodies are marked and differentiated could be presumptuous, perhaps even dangerous. (Dale, 2001; Hassard, Holliday, and Willmott, 2000; Thanem, 2009). These works on the body

---

[8] Logos-Greek for 'word' by which the inward thought is expressed' (Liddell, 1997).

in management and organization studies have all attempted to redress how organizational analyses tend to be disembodied.

The study of the body has tended to become estranged from the study of work just as analysis of work organizations has been abstracted from the body (Hassard et al., 2000, 2)

Dale (2001) problematizes how employees engaged in what is essentially emotional labor are (re)presented through 'cognitised' and disembodied impressions. Emotional labor refers to Hochschild's (1983) notion that bodies and emotions are managed in a way to display specific facial and bodily acts/movements such that they become sold for a wage and have exchange value. This is indeed crucial to work performance, not to mention work stress and constraints, especially when an employee is not feeling any of the fronted emotions on display. Despite this, frontline service workers find themselves managing their bodies in certain ways in order to fit the emotional labor requirements of an organization in order to perform to 'standard' (Hochschild, 1983; Knights and Thanem, 2010).

Proponents of the 'body in work' movement problematize how the body itself in addition to emotions is treated as a function of some larger effect in the organization and address the social control and discipline surrounding bodies at work. For example, the body has become the object of exploitation in the venues of health, fitness, fashion, and body modification. During work time hours, the body becomes managed down to when one can eat, defecate, urinate, and move. Bodies are just 'another object to organize and control, or to manage and manipulate' (Knights and Thanem, 2010). Given that work organizations have escalated to being an integral part of our society and that our bodies are defecating, sweating, ejaculating, feeling strong, or in pain during the parameters of work, the body is increasingly being 'brought to work'(Barry and Hazen, 1996). Furthermore, in line with Franks (1995) assessment that illnesses and disease are bleeding into the work and leisure dimensions of our lives, the body is pulsating its presence more than ever to us.

To conclude, organizational practices are enacted without considering the toll that the body is taking or the contortions being forced upon these bodies. Furthermore, scholarly work in organization studies is mostly written as if there are minds behind the computer keys without bodies that may be perhaps aching, hungry, and sore. There exists according to Knights and Thanem (2010) a hegemony of cognitive analysis within the organizational studies research. Yet as I write this, my back is aching from my fibromyalgia, I am feeling my prescribed amphetamines do their job, and I am a bit nauseous, but yet I feel alive and happy that I have spent the past several hours dedicating my time to this piece, doing something I love. I have not been able to write for months because of my illness and depression, so this is a wonderfully needed body exercise to sit here both comfortable and uncomfortable allowing my mind, body, and will to enter into my writing. This, academia, is after all my work, both paid and unpaid.

## Corporeal Management at Work and in Society

The chapter now shifts towards a theoretical account of how bodies are corporeally managed at work and in society, specifically how and why some bodies are seen as 'lesser' than others and subsequently treated as such. I focus on two main organizations, the Catholic Church and the US military, in order to trace not only how but why the concept of the normative body prevails to the detriment of Othered bodies. I do not venture to suggest that what I purport is the only factor at play, though I contend it is a significant starting point for understanding the notion of corporeal management. Corporeal management, in this chapter, refers to the ways in which our bodies organize and manage other bodies in organizations, and are managed and organized by the structures of our economy, culture, values, and societal norms.

My conceptual analysis of corporeal management is original in that it includes the discourse around sociology of religion to draw out the implicit structural ideologies and narratives that are enacted and mobilized in the Western organization to control the body, or more accurately to strip the body of its agentic capacity. Before continuing on, I must first include an acknowledgement of my own emotionality and embodiment in these sentences. I am informed by my experiences in the US military and the Catholic Church, my social economic status as a privileged Greek-Hispanic female with access to education (and trained in theology), and by the rants of my atheistic husband whom I love dearly. At various times in the parameters of both these organizations, I have been explicitly and implicitly told that my body is an obstruction because it is sexed differently than a male's. Now, we turn our attention to the body's historical legacy and its relationship to Western culture and religion.

The body has socio-historically been†subordinated to the†mind since antiquity where dominant phallogocentric and dualistic interpretations of Plato's texts are at the *ethos* of the tradition of Western metaphysics and ontology (duBois, 1994). Interpretations and representations of Platonic texts typically privilege the mind/soul over the body, where the body is the cage of the immortal soul. Women are aligned with the body and men are associated with the immortality and transcendence of the intellect/soul.

The gradual Christianization of the West, which followed after the reign of the Greeks, was an amalgamation of Judeo and Hellenistic perspectives (Kee, 1998). It carried on the tradition of the body as ineffectual but added more to the narrative— the body also became the place of sin, evil, and weakness, unable to produce ethics (ibid.). Augustine wrote extensively on how it is the will that must orient the body to the good and when the will is oriented towards the good, union with and love of God is attained (Augustine and Wand, 1963). He purported that the man had direct access to God and woman only attained access through the male. Because of her sinful, uncertain body, she could not make the direct link with God. Thus, the body was further stripped of any agentic potential through religious narratives.

Despite the move away from religion, the body remained the site of uncertainty and unreliability during the Enlightenment. If anything the schismatic subordination of the body was exacerbated through the added matter/representation dichotomy by the philosophical influence of Descartes (Turner, 1996; Grosz, 1994). Following the Enlightenment into the postmodern era, many scholars had claimed that the prophecy of secularization theory would be fulfilled and religion would cease to flourish in modern societies. However, the rise in religious behavior across the world has evidenced that religion remains an important part of the human experience, regardless of geographic location, economic structures, and intellectual foundations (Berger et al., 2008).

Despite the attempts to break free from religion in the modern and postmodern age, Christianity covertly and overtly continues to penetrate Western culture, and thus, the systemic nature of Christian grandnarratives impacts organizations, organizing, and management. The brief historical narrative offered here is meant to demonstrate that the mind/body dualism is intertwined with religious overtones, not just secular philosophical ones, a point that is often overlooked in research on the body, work, and organizations. How the added flavor of these Christian grandnarratives paint the body in turn impacts how bodies are organized in work and in society.

The main Christian narrative under scrutiny regards the body, especially the female body, as impotent, uncontrollable, weak, and full of carnality. It locates sin in the flesh (Rambo, 2006). The narrative continues on: the male body, meaning the white, virile, heteronormative body, conversely, is somehow able to transcend his body through the power of his will thereby attaining a salvific state and status. He can break free from the burden of his body as it is not as weighted down with obstructions like the female body or the black gay body is. Those marginal bodies are somehow 'lesser.' This grandnarrative remains deeply constituted in to the point where it becomes, not only embedded in discourses, but ritually performed or enacted. I will attest to this enactment through looking at rape in the military and church organizations in the US as an example.

The military and Catholic Church are unique organizations to discuss the status of the body because they remain the only two core American institutions which can legally bar women's bodies from certain hyper-valorized roles (Katzenstein, 1998). The US military (which retained the American puritanical legacy) and the Catholic Church forbid women from their *ethos* – e.g. priesthood and combat arms – in large part because of this Christian-informed body narrative (Hope, 2006). What is celebrated in combat and priesthood is the will of the male, rather than the body; the male is able to transcend his body while the female is too tied to her body weighed down by sin, sexuality, dirt, and fluids. She cannot access divinity or warriordom – these ultra sacred states where only men can tread. Therefore, she cannot be granted access to these core sites in the organization, especially because her soiled, indecent body is like a disease that taints and dirties the 'cleaner' bodies of men. The 'organizational body' (Tyler and Hancock, 2001) required in the military and church demands the abjection of bodies to construct a simulacra that in actuality not even white, heteronormative males can attain, but only strive towards. The normative body becomes normative, in the pursuit of warriordom/godliness through the abjection of the marginal body.

One extreme example of othering is rape. Women and indecent bodies who are indoctrinated in the military organization are subjected to violations, even violent trauma at a greater rate than white male bodies. A study conducted by the Veterans Affairs found that in the US National Guard and Reserves 60% of women are victims of military sexual trauma to include repetitive sexual harassment (Bennett, 2005). An additional study found that 1 in 3 women are raped in the military by their male counterparts and 1 in 7 men are raped primarily by men (SAPR, 2009). In the Catholic Church in the US, increased attention has been paid to the sexual abuse scandals of young girls and boys, as hundreds of lawsuits have been brought against the Catholic Church (*Betrayal: The Crisis in the Catholic Church*, 2002). This signifies a kind of corporeal scapegoating, imposing one's body onto another, both literally and figuratively.

In the act of rape in addition to other factors, I theorize that a ritualized scapegoating occurs whereby the sin that the male fears on his own body (the phallus) is transmitted through his semen onto the body that is already 'soiled,' a 'lost cause.' The process of exalting the male, where he sheds the weight of his body, takes places through the bodily destruction of the female and young males. The transmission of his soiled body allows for the male to destroy the part of himself that he deems sinful, ungodly, that which prevents his pursuit towards a redemptive realm.

Rape is an extreme form of othering, but this is a useful example to demonstrate how the body narrative is enacted as well as how bodies become corporeally organized and segregated along the lines of gender, race, sexual orientation, age, ability. Othered bodies get othered through transmission or a projection of bodiliness from the normative male. Redemptive status requires an absent present body. In order for the male to shed his body, he has to go through a process of corporeal neutralization. His body does not go away. It only seems to be absent as men are aligned with the mind, not the body in Western thought. Instead, his bodily 'baggage' becomes scapegoated onto the bodies of women and non-normative bodies. It is my contention that the bodies of women, bodies of color, malnutrition bodies, 'disabled' bodies, indecent and queer bodies are necessarily scapegoated or sacrificed in order to effect and secure the 'redemptive' or no longer sinful status of the privileged body. The normative body is absent, no longer ejaculating, leaking, but remains solid and bound behind rationality and transcendence while the representational body and all its leakiness and pulsating remains tied to women, 'homosexuals,' people of color, the differently-abled. These people are not fully human or fully subjects because of their 'problematic' bodies that engender uncertainty, chaos, and capriciousness.

Related to the concept of scapegoating, Schmitt (1992) alludes to how whites during the slavery era projected sexuality onto the black man to internalize the notion that the black man is a creature of the 'lower' desires, not the white man:

> . . . but rather project onto others the faults they fear in themselves and thereby purge themselves of those evils. Fears of an excessive and uncontrolled sexuality are stilled by ascribing this unmanaged sexuality to the black man and to other groups that are in disfavor. Thus, whites can rest assured that they are good because the evil which they secretly fear in their own nature is manifest in other groups who are for that reason despised and scapegoated. (Schmitt, 1992: 42)

As a result, Schmitt (1992) argues that racism is sexualized. He further demonstrates that white men's racism was rooted in an attempt to control women – both black and white. The common accusation that black men have 'large propagators' or penises signifies their supposed sexual licentiousness and lustfulness – sins of the flesh – what is in actuality a projection of white male desires onto black men. But ultimately, it is a fear of being bad and the need to secure salvation, which drives the process of corporeal scapegoating.

This is not to say that white heteronormative male bodies are never objectified or subjected to violence as evidenced in how 1 in 7 males in the military are raped, mostly by men. But it does prompt one to wonder if these were marked with class and race, where those higher in authority and perhaps even white did the violating. Further it is also not to say that women and Othered bodies see their own bodies as unproblematic. Regardless, it is this religio-culturally programmed narrative that engenders the process of corporeal scapegoating.

Why not sit peacefully with this sin or why see sin ascribed to the body at all? Weber (1993) alludes to the idea that people are drawn to seek certainty and that the uncertainty (an attribute of bodies) is what drives people to seek salvation as part of the human experience in some form or another, usually as expiation from sin, and thus, from the body. Someone who is saved, or a savior, must fight something, which could be his own 'corrupt nature,' but could also be something presumed to be demonic, or something which he has projected his demons onto in order to secure his victorious redemption (ibid.).

To be clear, similar to Weber's work, the theoretical account offered here is universalistic in nature, but it is descriptive rather than prescriptive. To conclude, it is if we shift our attention towards the *bodilyness* bodies of the marginalized—their 'innate' weakness, indecency, and uncertainty, that the body of the privileged white male remains untouched, untarnished, *unbodilied*, neutralized; his salvation is no longer in contestation. He (the psyche) can still successfully orient his will, being freed of a weighted body, towards the Good, Truth, the godhead. His transcendence depends on his reference in opposition to the non-white, non-male body. Through a radical representationalism, women's bodies, bodies of color, differently-abled bodies are necessarily scapegoated, relegated to that which must be violated, controlled, disciplined, and feared at work and in society in order to secure the salvific status of white male virile bodies.

## CORPOREAL MANAGEMENT AND FUTURE RESEARCH

In work organizations, managerial practices regulate our bodies to the point that our bodies are confined to do or not do certain bodily behaviors. A certain appearance of hygiene is expected. For women, in certain organizations, their bodies are to coincide with certain prescribed techniques that act to marginalize and even scapegoat their corporeal existence in order for men to appear as the 'higher,' holier, organizational representative. Classed bodies are marked with sweat, aches, and dirt, markers of indecency and carnality. Yet top-level managers, academic chairs, and male executives present themselves as unmarked, unrevealed bodies. This is evidenced for example in how photos of CEOs in large corporations or university presidents in historical succession are mere head shots as if no bodies exist beneath the heads (See Sinclair, this volume).

What is needed to subvert this brand of corporeal management? I have made the universal claim that our culture programs us to experience our bodies as situated in what is the 'bad' or sinful. Following this logic, the implication rendered is that white male privileged bodies, those absent present bodies, must be summoned to reveal their bodies in all their uncertainties, fluids, and fleshiness. How this is done is the topic for further research; unfortunately, I will not delve into this here, primarily because of space limitations.

The main purpose of this article was to provide my reader with a broad view of the body in studies related to gender, work, and organization so that one can possess the necessary background for doing research in this field. Secondly I provided an account of how workers' bodies are subject to more than just labor but also to a scapegoating phenomenon. The purpose of this narrative was to build new theory in the nexus of body, gender, and work so that future scholars can explore this conceptually and empirically (Merleau-Ponty, 1962; Bakhtin, 1984; Berger, Davie, and Fokas, 2008; Bourdieu, 1984; Deleuze and Guattari, 1987; Douglas, 1970; Foucault, 1979: 297; Fraser and Greco, 2005; Goffman, 1963; B. S. Turner, 1996; Hochschild, 1983; D. Knights and Thanem, 2010).

# REFERENCES

Acker, J. (1990) Hierarchies, Jobs, Bodies: A Theory of Gendered Organizations, *Gender & Society*, 5, 390–407.

Ahmed, S. (1996) Beyond Humanism and Postmodernism: Theorizing a Feminist Practice, *Hypatia*, 11(2) 71–93.

Augustine, and Wand, J. (1963) *City of God*. London,: Oxford University Press.

Bakhtin, M. (1984) *Rabelais and His World* (H. Iswolsky, trans.). Bloomington, IN: Indiana University Press.

Barry, D., and Hazen, M.A. (1996) 'Do You Take your Body to Work?' in D. Boje, Gephart, and T. Joseph (eds), *Postmodern Management and Organization Theory*. London: Sage.

Beasley, C. (2005) *Gender and Sexuality: Critical Theories, Critical Thinkers*. London: Sage Publications.

Benhabib, S. (1995) *Feminist Contentions: A Philosophical Exchange*. New York: Routledge.

Bennett, L. (2005, September) Evans Releases Military Sexual Trauma Report Suppressed by Administration. House Committee on Veteran's Affairs—Democratic Office News Release.

Berger, P.L., Davie, G., and Fokas, E. (2008) *Religious America, Secular Europe? A Theme and Variation*. Aldershot, England; Burlington, VT: Ashgate.

*Betrayal: The Crisis in the Catholic Church* (2002) 1st edn. Boston: Little, Brown and Co.

Boje, D., and Hettrick, W. (1992) Organization and the Body: Post-Fordist Dimensions, *Journal of Organizational Change Management*, 5(1) 48–57.

Bourdieu, P. (1984) *Distinction: A Social Critique of the Judgement of Taste*. Cambridge, MA: Harvard University Press.

Butler, J. (1993) *Bodies that Matter: On the Discursive Limits of 'Sex'*. New York: Routledge.

Butler, J. (1995) Contingent Foundations: Feminism and the Questions of 'Postmodernism' in S. Benhabib (ed.), *Feminist Contentions: A Philosophical Exchange*. New York: Routledge.

Chodorow, N. (1999) *The reproduction of mothering: psychoanalysis and the sociology of gender: with a new preface*. Berkeley: University of California Press.

Colebrook, C. (2000) From Radical Representations to Corporeal Becomings: The Feminist Philosophy of Lloyd, Grosz, *Hypatia*, 15(2) 76.

Collins, P. (2000) *Black Feminist Thought: Knowledge, Consciousness, and the Politics of Empowerment*. (revised 10th anniversary edn) New York: Routledge.

Collins, G. (2009, October 19) Women in the workplace still face inequality. National Public Radio.

Dale, K. (2001) *Anatomising Embodiment and Organisation Theory*. Houndmills, Basingstoke, Hampshire; New York: Palgrave.

Daly, M. (1973) *Beyond God the Father: Toward a Philosophy of Women's Liberation*. Boston: Beacon Press.

Deleuze, G., and Guattari, F. (1987) *A Thousand Plateaus: Capitalism and Schizophrenia.* Minneapolis: University of Minnesota Press.

Douglas, M. (1970) *Natural Symbols: Explorations in Cosmology.* London: Barrie & Rockliff the Cresset P.

duBois, P. (1994) 'The Platonic Appropriation of Reproduction' in N. Tuana (ed.), *Feminist Interpretations of Plato.* University Park: The Pennsylvania State University Press, 139–156

Foucault, M. (1979) *Discipline and punish: the birth of the prison.* New York: Vintage Books.

Frank, A.W. (1995) *The Wounded Storyteller: Body, Illness, and Ethics.* Chicago: University of Chicago Press.

Gatens, M. (1996) *Imaginary Bodies: Ethics, Power, and Corporeality.* London:; New York: Routledge.

Giddens, A. (1991) *Modernity and self-identity: self and society in the late modern age.* Stanford, Calif.: Stanford University Press.

Gilligan, C. (1982) *In a Different Voice: Psychological Theory and Women's Development.* Cambridge, MA: Harvard University Press.

Goffman, E. (1963) *Behavior in Public Places; Notes on the Social Organization of Gatherings.* New York: Free Press of Glencoe.

Grosz, E.A. (1994) *Volatile Bodies: Toward a Corporeal Feminism.* St Leonards, NSW: Allen & Unwin.

Grosz, E.A. (1995) *Space, Time, and Perversion: Essays on the Politics of Bodies.* New York: Routledge.

Hassard, J., Holliday, R., and Willmott, H. (2000) *Body and Organization.* London; Thousand Oaks, CA: Sage.

Hochschild, A.R. (1983) *The Managed Heart: Commercialization of Feeling.* Berkeley, CA: University of California Press.

Holler, L. (2002) *Erotic morality: the role of touch in moral agency.* New Brunswick, N.J.: Rutgers University Press.

hooks, b. (2006) *Outlaw Culture: Resisting Representations.* New York: Routledge.

Hope, A. (2006) Fully Warrior: Cooperative Unity, *Tamara: Journal for Critical Organization Inquiry*, 5(1).

Hope, A. (2007) Restructuring God Ideologies in Work Spaces: A Critical Catholic Perspective, *Journal of Management, Spirituality, and Religion*, 4(4).

Höpfl, H. (2003) Becoming a (Virile) Member: Women and the Military Body, *Body and Society*, 9(4) 13–30.

Irigaray, L. (1985) *Speculum of the Other Woman.* Ithaca, NY: Cornell University Press.

Johnson, P., and Duberley, J. (2000) *Understanding Management Research: An Introduction to Epistemology.* London; Thousand Oaks, CA: Sage Publications.

Katzenstein, M.F. (1998) *Faithful and Fearless: Moving Feminist Protest Inside the Church and Military.* Princeton, NJ: Princeton University Press.

Kee, H. C. (1998) *Christianity: A Social and Cultural History.* 2nd edn. Upper Saddle River, NJ: Prentice Hall.

Knights, D. (2008) Body Matters: Breaking Gender Binaries in Social and Organizational Research. Paper presented at the Critical Management Sudies (CMS) Research Workshop, Gender and Diversity Stream, August 8.

Knights, D., and Thanem, T. (2010) 'Embodying Emotional Labour' in D. Morgan, B. Brandth, and E. Kvande (eds), *Gender, Bodies, and Work.* Aldershot: Ashgate.

Liddell, H. G. (ed.) (1997) *An Intermediate Greek-English Lexicon.* Oxford: Oxford University Press.

Linstead, S. (2000) 'Dangerous Fluids and the Organization-without-organs' in J. Hassard, R. Holliday, and H. Willmott (eds), *Body and Organization*. London Sage, 31–51.

Linstead, S., and Pullen, A. (2006) Gender as Multiplicity: Desire, Displacement, Difference and Dispersion, *Human Relations*, 59(9) 1287.

Lloyd, G. (2002) *Feminism and History of Philosophy*. Oxford; New York: Oxford University Press.

McKie, L., and Watson, N. (2000) *Organizing Bodies: Policy, Institutions, and Work*. Houndmills: MacMillan Press.

Merleau-Ponty, M. (1962) *Phenomenology of Perception*. London; New York: Routledge.

Mohanty, C. (1991) 'Under Western Eyes' in C. Mohanty (ed.), *Third World Women and the Politics of Feminism*. Bloomington and Indianapolis: Indiana University Press.

New, C. (1991) 'Women's Oppression in the World and in Ourselves: A Fresh Look at Feminism and Psycholanlysis' in P.A. a. C. Wallace (ed.), *Gender, Power & Sexuality*. Macmillan: British Sociological Association.

Nussbaum, M. (1994) Feminists and Philosophy, *The New York Review of Books*, 41(17).

Nussbaum, M.C. (2000) *Women and Human Development: The Capabilities Approach*. Cambridge; New York: Cambridge University Press.

Rambo, S. (2006) *Lecture on Plato's Contributions to Christianity*. Boston: Boston University School of Theology.

SAPR. (2009) Unit Victim Advocate Training Workshop. San Antonio, Fort Sam Houston: Sexual Assault Response and Prevention Program.

Schmitt, R. (1992) 'Large Propagators: Racism and the Domination of Women' In N. Tuana, W. Cowling, M. Hamington, G. Johnson, and T. MacMullen (eds), Revealing Male Bodies. Bloomington, IN: Indiana University Press.

Spivak, G.C., and Harasym, S. (1990) *The Post-colonial Critic: Interviews, Strategies, Dialogues*. New York: Routledge.

Squires, J. (2001) Representing Groups, Deconstructing Identities, *Feminist Theory*, 2(1).

Thanem, T. (2009) 'There's No Limit to How Much You Can Consume': The New Public Health and the Struggle to Manage Healthy Bodies, *Culture & Organization*, 15(1) 59–74.

Turner, B. (1997) 'The Body in Western Society: Social Theory and its Perspectives' in S. Coakley (ed.), *Religion and the Body*. Cambridge: Cambridge University Press, 15–41.

Turner, B.S. (1996) *The Body and Society: Explorations in Social Theory*. 2nd edn. London; Thousand Oaks, CA: Sage Publications.

Tyler, M., and Hancock, P. (2001) 'Flight Attendants and the Management of gendered "organizational bodies"' in K. Backett-Milburn and L. McKie (eds), *Constructing Gendered Bodies*. New York: Palgrave, 25–38.

Vasterling, V. (1999) Butler's Sophisticate Constructivism: A Critical Assessment, *Hypatia*, 14(3) 17–38.

Weber, M. (1993) *The Sociology of Religion*. Boston: Beacon Press.

Williams, C. (2001) 'Feminist Theory: Psychoanalytic' in N. S. a P. Baltes (ed.), *International Encyclopedia of the Social & Behavioral Sciences*. Oxford.

Wolf, N. (1991) *The Beauty Myth: How Images of Beauty are Used against Women*. 1st edn. New York: W. Morrow.

Wollstonecraft, M., and American Imprint Collection (Library of Congress) (1792) *A Vindication of the Rights of Woman: With Strictures on Moral and Political Subjects*. Philadelphia: Printed by William Gibbons.

# 9

# New Intimacy, New Motherhood, Same Old Work?

### JOANNA BREWIS
*University of Leicester School of Management*

## INTRODUCTION

During summer 2002, I ran a series of focus groups with eleven thirty-something professional women, all of whom are university graduates. We discussed their feelings about and aspirations for their careers and their personal lives, and the intersections and disjunctures between these 'public' and 'private' spheres. The data were written up for publication in *Urban Studies* (Brewis, 2004). The chapter at hand is inspired by this analysis. It surveys the contemporary literature in these interlinked areas in order to provide a cutting edge review of claims around intimacy, motherhood, childlessness and work–life balance. I also employ data from a small longitudinal project involving six of the focus group respondents.[1] These were gathered by email some six years after the original research. I include them to illustrate the significant changes each respondent has experienced in the interim – relocation, (impending) motherhood, a new relationship and/or a new job. This chapter to a lesser extent therefore continues the attempt in my 2004 paper at elucidating the social developments identified in the relevant literatures as they are actually lived out – or not – at the individual level.

I begin with the 'new intimacy' thesis, the argument that contemporary Western ideals as gradually emerging after the Second World War focus much less on some notion of 'true love', or impulsive, irresistible desire. Equally, expectations of intimate relationships have apparently shifted away from monetary considerations, 'legitimizing sexual relationships or having children' (Santore, 2008: 1207). Instead we Westerners emphasize knowing our partners well, reciprocity, shared rights and responsibilities, space for personal development, acceptance, and emotional connection. The drivers for the new intimacy seemingly include the second wave of feminism, women entering the paid workforce in greater numbers and marrying later, cohabitation becoming

[1]See the appendix for brief biographies for each of the six women. All are referred to here using pseudonyms.

more acceptable and the rise of the 'therapeutic culture' emphasizing 'growth and betterment of "the person"' (Santore, 2008: 1205). Relatedly, the available data suggest that Western women – especially professionals and/or graduates – are tending to have children later and later, if at all. As I read it, the relevant research argues that these delays in childbearing, or perhaps even 'chosen childlessness', originate in broadly the same phenomena as the new intimacy: more egalitarian gender ideologies and feminism's challenge to the 'motherhood mandate'; better contraception; attitudinal and legislative shifts around abortion; rising divorce rates; and improved educational and occupational opportunities for women.

The new intimacy thesis and connected claims around delayed motherhood/elective childlessness for me all speak explicitly to the motifs addressed in this section of the Handbook. After all, the developments which underlie these putative attitudinal and aspirational shifts include women's increased participation in paid employment. Partly because we now literally embody (in the sense of populating) organizations as well as the domestic realm, our identity projects are apparently adjusting accordingly. As such, we now view ourselves, our partners, and the prospect of having children very differently from women of previous generations. Certainly there are broad-brush empirical data indicating that these changes have taken an especially concrete discursive hold over the last three decades. Moreover, the emerging discourse of intimacy presumably organizes our bodies in different ways, encouraging us to be more measured about how we act on sexual desire or romantic attraction, to balance these feelings against a consideration of whether the man or woman in question might become a supportive, emotionally literate partner in the longer term. The same is true of delayed motherhood or elective childlessness. Indeed might we even suggest that the arguments reviewed in my 2004 paper, which amounted to the idea that women's bodies are still seen more as instruments of *re*production than production, are becoming gradually less apposite?

Finally, and perhaps most familiar to readers of this Handbook, there is a wealth of research examining work–life balance. This literature insists that any claims to such a balance are little more than rhetoric; that women especially continue to struggle to manage the demands of work, personal relationships of all kinds, motherhood, and other life activities. Exploring state of the art commentary here again connects the motifs of this section. To what extent is it feasible for women to simultaneously embody or inhabit work and life in all its variety? What kind of physical and psychological effects eventuate as a result? And what does this suggest about how women conceive of themselves as partners, workers, mothers, and friends, taken together as well as separately?

In sum, I suggest these three important themes relate to our understanding of the bodies that populate organizations, how organizations and the wider social context organize these bodies and the attendant impact on projects of the self. The chapter now proceeds to examine each of the three themes in turn, beginning with a review of the relevant literature on each and moving to consider whether my longitudinal data reflect the arguments presented there.

## CONSIDERING THE 'NEW INTIMACY' THESIS

To elaborate on the claims embedded in this thesis, we can point to Wilcox and Nock's (2006: 1321) argument that marriage especially now functions as a carrier for personal fulfilment as 'other sources of satisfaction and/or stability – home production, childrearing, the gendered division of labor and religious authority – have migrated to other sectors or weakened'. Relatedly, Davila and Kashy (2009: 76) remark on the salience of what they refer to as 'secure base functioning' in this regard. They suggest that partners must now be adept at asking for, offering and accepting support, and that these three capabilities 'are a key predictor of satisfaction and longevity in dating and marital relationships'. Davila and Kashy note that this 'functioning' relies on partners being able to adapt their behaviour according to each other's signals; and add that feelings of intimacy, seeking and receiving support, and confidence in the longevity of the relationship reinforce each other. Stress, they say, is also likely to heighten the importance of secure base functioning. Indeed the 'new intimacy' is widely described as meaning an 'acceptance of and belief in the notion that relationships require ongoing toil and maintenance if bonds are to survive' (Santore, 2008: 1203).

Moreover, advocates of this thesis stress the central importance of equality in sexual relationships. Hatfield et al. (2008), in their discussion of classic equity theory, insist it is crucial in present-day romantic partnerships; so someone involved in what they see as an *in*equitable relationship – whether this relates to a partner's looks, intellect, fidelity, affection, whatever – will rectify this, including being unfaithful or ending the relationship. And, although we should of course be cautious about over-relying on self-report questionnaire data of any kind, recent British findings from a wide-ranging *Sunday Times Magazine* YouGov survey of cohabiting, married and divorced respondents do provide empirical support for all these claims, especially when compared to a similar Social Attitudes survey from the early 1980s. Of the *Sunday Times Magazine* participants, 85% identified 'mutual appreciation and respect' as central to a successful marriage, as compared to 75% in the 80s. The criterion of independence, especially separate finances, likewise rose significantly in importance in the relevant period. Additionally, 'understanding and tolerance' were rated by nearly 80% of participants as vital in a happy marriage, as compared to less than 70% in the earlier data (Fernand, 2007: 30–31).

Relatedly, the new intimacy thesis suggests that heterosexual marriage, whilst certainly not moribund, is gradually ceding its normative status, so other forms of partnership are assuming social legitimacy. Certain legislative changes clearly testify to such claims – such as the legalization of same sex marriages in Canada in 2005, and the UK Civil Partnership Act 2004 – the rather more complex situation in the US notwithstanding. Similarly, for Holmes (2004: 185) the increasing prevalence of distance relationships indicates a potential for women especially to derive a better sense of autonomy compared with co-residency or living apart together (LAT), where couples live in the same location but in different households. As she says, 'Distance relationships challenge common assumptions and conventional gender practices based on the notion that intimacy necessarily involves physical proximity'. Holmes proposes that the growing number of distance or LAT relationships may therefore provide some evidence for the emergence of the new intimacy.

By way of contrast, other data suggest a levelling off in UK divorce rates since 2000, which remain at something like 13 people divorcing in every 1000 of the married population (Fernand, 2007: 30). Fernand also cites findings that British attitudes to divorce are hardening, and that marriage is still 'the gold standard' (pp. 34, 37) – something which is certainly reflected in the legitimacy that politicians from all three major UK political parties continue to attribute to this type of partnership. Similarly, Dobson and Watt (2006) quote US data suggesting marriage is increasingly prized by graduate women. Such analyses connect this privileging to perceptions about the social costs of marital breakdown, and an increasing desire for security as a backlash against loosening relationship mores. Nonetheless, Appleyard (2006: 13 – emphasis added) summarizes Smart's percipient observation about this kind of evidence that any 'plateau [in divorce] is deceptive. Because many couples were cohabiting rather than marrying, *actual relationship breakdowns* were far more commonplace'. Smart's point provides evidence for cohabitation taking hold as a form of relationship praxis, and also suggests that we do expect more from our partnerships, and are more willing to terminate them if they fail to satisfy.

Taking all of this to its logical conclusion, Hamilton et al. (2006) point to a growing acceptance of the legitimacy of 'singlehood' in the US, particularly amongst women. UK demographics likewise indicate we are progressively becoming a nation of single person households. Indeed, many of Budgeon's (2008) single respondents spoke of the possibilities of future relationships 'followed by an imagined strategy for achieving a successful balance between the opportunities afforded by being single and the costs associated with becoming part of a couple' (2008: 317). These people expressed a desire for 'someone special', but simultaneously suggested that alternative relationship formats – such as distance or LAT – may offer advantages over the heteronormative, co-resident equivalent.

In terms of how these claims play out in my primary data, in 2008 as in 2002 the respondents' priorities in intimate relationships were a profound rapport and an ability to share. More traditional criteria like economic security as achievable through a partnership were much less significant. Indeed Wendy says that, in the last six years,

> I've built up a good business, which has been great . . . I feel more fulfilled and in my relationship, even though we're still not equals financially, I feel better being able to pay my own way and contribute a lot more to supporting us both . . .

Similarly, Bella does not look to her relationship with Kieran to shore up her self-esteem or for economic security: instead she seeks 'Kindness, compassion, consideration, willingness to help . . . I just need to be able to share the load'. Equally there are nuances in both narratives of not being all in all to each other and the importance of deriving self-worth from sources other than intimates.

For Catherine financial stability *is* now more important because she has two small children, and is self-employed. Still, she does not look for economic security as an outcome of her partnership with Charlie: rather she says this has become a priority as a result of motherhood. Motherhood is also Catherine's primary concern at present, because she and Charlie are 'are still in the fire fighting stage of parenthood and practically this is how things work'. However she looks forward to her children being older, when her relationship with Charlie can once again assume centre stage in her life.

Georgie's 2008 reflections include a moving narrative of how she and her husband Callum have navigated a series of adverse life events, including bereavement, a miscarriage and fertility treatment. She says 'I think the fact that we managed to get through all this is evidence of how strong our relationship is.' Again here the emphasis on support as a vital characteristic of intimacy is obvious, and as such Georgie's comments particularly speak to Davila and Kashy's (2009) conclusions about secure base functioning. In addition her remarks imply that relationships are a form of labour in and of themselves, something I also identify in Catherine's narrative and which echoes claims by Santore (2008) amongst others.

Since 2002, Judith has separated from her then girlfriend Fiona. She remarks that

> [m]y girlfriend loved me so much and thought so highly of me that gradually my ability to be myself, warts and all, was eroded until I was living [two] lives – one as the person she thought I was and one as the person I thought I was.

Judith was initially unfaithful to Fiona, and latterly moved out. She signed up to an Internet dating site, seeking a male partner 'because I couldn't stand the thought of the closeness you get with another woman. I wanted someone who would forever be at a distance from me.' Judith met her husband, Pavel, as a result. She says that, while they are not necessarily each other's soulmates, they agree they have a good chance of long-term happiness together and as such eschew 'self-sabotage or morbid introspection' in their partnership. Here again we see an emphasis on honesty and acceptance in relationships, as well as the idea that intimacy is hard work. Judith's decision to end things with Fiona also seems to indicate a profound sense of inequity (Hatfield et al., 2008). She comments that Fiona put her on a pedestal, so that she could not 'be myself, warts and all': thus Judith's belief that Fiona was actually treating her much *better* than she deserved eventually led to their break up.

Madeleine has also split up with her 2002 partner. Afterwards she was single for a while and then had a distance relationship, which ended shortly before these data were gathered. Madeleine says that

> I think a long distance relationship does actually suit me to [a] certain extent as [I] feel free to get on with [the] rest of life[,] ie work/friends/sleep during the week – however [I] still don't think it [is an] ideal scenario and think [I] might finally be ready to move in with someone! Dunno though[;] quite like my little burrow.

Madeleine's reservations about such an arrangement being ideal but also her suggestion that it might provide her with more freedom are both reflected in Holmes's (2004) claims about distance relationships. Madeleine's narrative likewise resonates with Budgeon's (2008) data, in her musings as to whether a future distance relationship might allow her to balance the 'opportunities' of single life against the 'costs' of coupledom.

Overall, though, in the literature and my primary data, there is a strong sense that 'genuine' intimacy, as currently understood, is *not* all-encompassing: instead it is founded on support, empathy, equity and emotional honesty. Santore, rightly I think, argues that these discursive shifts offer us the possibility to cautiously 'imagine the preconditions of new intimate bonds' (2008: 1214). Budgeon reaches a related but perhaps more radical conclusion in suggesting her data indicate some 'potential to reflexively remake sexual identities outside of regulatory heteronorms' (2008: 320), and especially to transcend the 'coupled–single' binary.

## Considering the 'New Motherhood' Thesis

As established earlier, the most recent studies indicate that Western women, especially professionals and/or graduates, are now more likely either to delay motherhood or not to have children at all. The average age at which British women have their first child rose by more than three years between 1971 and 2004, and 20% of women in their mid-forties were childless in 2005 (Hadfield et al., 2007). Similar data are available concerning both Germany and the US (Park, 2005; Stöbel-Richter et al., 2005; Koropeckyj-Cox and Pendell, 2007), and Wood and Newton (2006) review secondary data from the US, UK and Australia to reach analogous conclusions. Park (2005: 374), following Houseknecht and Veevers, calls these women 'postponers'. As argued earlier, This choice to delay or abjure motherhood apparently originates in the same collection of socio-economic trends as the new intimacy. Added to this, Koropeckyj-Cox and Pendell (2007: 900) say delaying childbearing, or not having children at all, could be a strategy for 'navigating an uncertain competitive economy'. This may be of especial relevance at the time of writing – September 2009, in the midst of a global recession.

Another aspect of the 'new motherhood' thesis is the trend for smaller families. The percentage of British women with only one child has apparently risen by 13% over the last two decades, and the UK is far from alone in the 'developed' world in this regard (Flintoff, 2006: 9). In addition, the UK *Sunday Times Magazine* survey indicates that having children is now seen as much less crucial to a happy marriage, so only 10% of respondents identified this as an issue, compared to 34% in the Social Attitudes data (Fernand, 2007: 30–31). Likewise Stöbel-Richter et al.'s (2005: 2855) German data saw children and family life more generally coming low down in respondents' priorities, with 'health, income, work, living conditions, partnership and [sex]' all ranked more highly; the deficiencies of such context-free, self-report data again notwithstanding.

What also emerges repeatedly from this literature is something I discussed in the 2004 paper; that middle-class women now tend to consider themselves more or less financially, socially and psychologically 'ready' for motherhood (Stöbel-Richter et al., 2005: 2856; Benzies et al., 2006: 628; Koropeckyj-Cox and Pendell, 2007: 900). Indeed Koropeckyj-Cox and Pendell argue that,

> [t]hough women are not necessarily embracing childlessness, they may be more attuned to the physical, economic, social, and emotional demands of parenthood, which are borne disproportionately by women. They may also be more aware of the challenges of combining work and parenthood and the risks involved, including marital and economic insecurity. (2007: 913)

This suggests that, as compared to men, women are more clear-eyed about the demands of becoming a parent, especially given continued disparities in the domestic division of labour as discussed later.

Relatedly, Wood and Newton (2006: 340) insist childlessness is not a static condition. Instead, they argue, intentions around motherhood alter with changing life circumstances like shifts in relationship status, so not having children is 'an ongoing practice and/or an outcome determined by a variety of personal or social circumstances' (p. 343). Some of Benzies et al.'s (2006: 628–629) Canadian respondents lend credence to this argument. These women described 'partner readiness' as an important factor in starting a family, meaning they perhaps started trying for a baby rather later than they personally desired.

Interestingly, as with the original focus groups, there was more diversity in my 2008 data on the issue of motherhood than as regards relationships. In 2002, Bella said one of her priorities for her marriage was having children (quoted in Brewis, 2004: 1829), and that this desire had emerged relatively suddenly as she neared thirty. In 2008, however, Bella comments that ending her marriage took her 'three years longer than was rationally sane' and that she would not have been able to do this 'if there had been kids in the picture'. She adds that, when her relationship with Kieran began, she still thought she wanted children, but is now more ambivalent. Bella's narrative certainly echoes Wood and Newton's (2006) idea of childlessness as an 'ongoing practice'.

Catherine has also changed her mind about parenting, although for her 'the notion of motherhood came slowly but surely' in the intervening period. Although she does not report becoming 'ready' as discussed above, especially in terms of finances, she does fit the mould of the British graduate, professional woman who tends to have children later – her first son was born when Catherine was in her late thirties. Contrastingly, Madeleine has never been able to 'imagine having kids with the people I was going out with'. Her thinking has not altered significantly since 2002. Moreover, although she is a little concerned about experiencing post-menopausal broodiness, Madeleine says this is likely to be a generic 'wistful/right man scenario' desire as opposed to an explicit yearning for children.

Of the 2002 respondents, Wendy and Judith were the most adamant about not wanting children. However, Wendy is now eight months pregnant. Having visited a friend who had recently given birth, she began to consider having a child for the first time. But her partner Paul was less keen: he is a decade or so older than Wendy and was also worried the child would still be a financial dependent when he retired. When they eventually began trying for a baby, Wendy fell pregnant immediately. She says she wanted the choice of whether to have children, and contemplated ending things with Paul if he did not want to be a father again,[2] but at the same time 'that old broody urge wasn't there'. Here Wendy echoes Benzies et al.'s (2006) respondents in terms of her negotiations with Paul. But her 'lack of the alleged "maternal instinct"' is much more frequently posited as an explanation for voluntary *childlessness*, as in Park's (2005: 394) data. Similarly, Judith was 'horrified' when she met Pavel and realized he had two children, and that 'the whole of every other precious weekend would be lost to them'. But weekends with her stepchildren actually triggered something

[2]Paul has a teenage daughter from a previous relationship.

else: she 'got a deep physical call to become a mother in my own right'. Nonetheless, Pavel is reluctant to have more children, and Judith has an abiding concern that she, like some of Park's respondents, is not psychologically suitable for parenting anyway. Overall, she seems somewhat resigned to the realities of being a 'postponer'.

Finally, Georgie, who was ready to start a family with Callum in 2002, is now pregnant with her second baby. She says the very difficult period of her miscarriage followed by fertility treatment to conceive her son Christopher seems very 'distant' to her now that Christopher is nearly two and she is heavily pregnant with a little girl, who was 'totally spontaneously conceived!' So while Georgie became pregnant after a long period of unexplained infertility and the associated heartbreaks, and Catherine describes a slow onset of the desire to become a mother, Wendy's pregnancy resulted from a decreasing sense that being a mother would be all-consuming as well as worrying that she might otherwise leave childbearing too late.

All of the above aside, however, the 'new motherhood' thesis comes complete with a series of caveats. Park (2005: 374) suggests it is still quite unusual for women to deliberately abjure having children altogether. Equally, Hadfield et al. (2007: 260), like Park (p. 376) and Wood and Newton (2006: 342), claim that women who decide not to have children continue to be widely regarded as uncaring, immature, selfish, materialistic individuals with less fulfilling lives than their counterparts with families. Park adds that media reportage often goes as far as representing parenting as 'personal redemption', capable of saving a previously self-destructive celebrity from drug addiction and/or promiscuity. Angelina Jolie is perhaps the most salient example. Such rampant 'pronatalism' of course cuts right across any sense in which elective childlessness is now socially acceptable, reflecting Hadfield et al.'s suggestion that 'women's fertility choices are increasingly subject to scrutiny and criticism' (2007: 255), despite – *or perhaps even because of* – such choices being available.

In my primary data, Madeleine agrees that the media now more than ever construct female childlessness as 'failure', and position celebrity mothers as important role models:

> [T]he biggest stars in the world with their kids are the most popular photo stories[:] Brangelina/Suri Cruise hysteria, a photo of Kate Moss with a bloated stomach – is she/ isn't she? – is big news. You used to show off your house[,] now you practically parade your placenta . . . You don't have to produce anything through talent either [–] just pop out another brat if you want to be in mags.

But Madeleine says she falls prey to this 'cult of motherhood' herself, because she is 'guilty' of 'acting' in terms of 'cooing' when babies are 'dragged into the office'. Here she illustrates Koropeckyj-Cox and Pendell's (2007: 913, following Blair-Loy) insightful suggestion that '[f]or women, competing moral frameworks regarding devotion to work and family, which are deeply encoded in social structures and cultures, provide a contradictory and morally-charged environment in which to consider motherhood.'

Overall, the relevant literature and my electronic data combined seem to testify to Park's (2005: 374) contention that, '[w]hile some individuals may rather neatly be placed at one or the other end of a continuum of parenting choice, others situate themselves more in the middle, or feel their identity shift over time'. Indeed neither Bella or Madeleine, the two women without children who are least committed to the idea of parenthood, identify themselves as *irrevocably* and *permanently* childless *by choice*. Instead they are apparently making agentic decisions not to have children at the present time, but not entirely in circumstances of their own choosing (Wood and Newton, 2006).

## Considering Work–Life 'Balance'

The 'new intimacy' thesis and to a lesser extent the 'new motherhood' thesis seem on the face of it to offer some optimism in terms of shifting expectations of women. The same is scarcely true of the work–life balance literature. Indeed Fleetwood's (2007) review of TUC data suggests 'employee unfriendly' types of flexible working, like call-out and 24/7 shift rotation, are still very much in place 'in the face of the upbeat assessments coming from those who promote the idea that WLB is either here, or is just around the corner' (p. 390). In this section I have therefore reversed the usual construction and refer where appropriate to 'life–work' – not vice versa. As Hoffman and Cowan (2008: 235) argue in their study of how the websites of *Fortune* magazine's '100 best companies to work for' construct this relationship, the conventional alternative privileges 'work' over 'life'. Second, Hoffman and Cowan's analysis emphasizes the ambiguity of the term 'balance'. For them, these companies represent 'life' and 'work' as two equal halves and demanding equal attention – *even though there are some 168 hours in a week* (p. 234). Consequently, I also tend to apostrophize 'balance'.

Certainly the majority of current academic commentary asserts that life–work 'balance' has simply not been achieved in any meaningful sense by most Western workers, and that women continue to be the worst off in this regard. Koropeckyj-Cox and Pendell (2007) claim the masculine ideal of devotion to work above all else still underpins organizational practices despite the 'balance' rhetoric, adding that professional women probably suffer most as their jobs are less accommodating. Krings' (2007) German data affirm this proposition: amongst the professionals she interviewed, only the women reported seemingly intransigent difficulties in managing the home–work interface. Equally, women are more likely to be marginalized in such occupations anyway *because* of gendered work expectations and their consequent mismatch with the 'ideal' (masculine) employee (Watts, 2009).

Moreover, Percheski (2008) suggests that what *has* been implemented in organizations – flexi-work, parental leave and so on – has barely addressed the basic infrastructure of paid employment. In fact she says professionals especially are now expected to work longer hours. Percheski agrees the resultant 'hard choices' fall to women in combining family responsibilities and careers, and says that women's increasing participation in paid work has occurred without any substantive shift in domestic division of labour – except for the minority of very highly paid women who can employ other women to undertake housework and childcare. Even then, as Watts (2009: 52) points out, it is usually the woman of the household who makes the necessary arrangements.

Similar claims are writ large across all the literature I have reviewed. Indeed, 'Current estimates of the relative size of men's contributions to the household vary between 20% and 35%' (Hatfield et al., 2008: 425). So the 'lagged adaptation' discussed in my 2004 paper (p. 1829) does not seem to have changed over much. Indeed it apparently persists, ideals of gender equality notwithstanding, amongst most heterosexual couples *even if the man is working part-time* (Wood and Newton, 2006: 344, 345–346; Eikhof et al., 2007: 331). As such the apparently more egalitarian ethos of the 'new intimacy' is scarcely pervasive in day-to-day domestic life. But we should also remember that men may find it difficult to reallocate time spent on paid employment to family life, *precisely because* the 'ideal' professional also exhibits the aforementioned masculine devotion to work. Thus the career costs may be even higher for men if they choose to deviate from this ideal (Lewis et al., 2007: 364)

Based on claims like these, Percheski (2008) analyses secondary US data to establish whether women in professional and managerial occupations are increasingly 'opting out', as some accounts have suggested, choosing full-time motherhood over paid employment. Percheski adds that these women, like my own respondents, are a 'critical case' because of the high social and economic status of the work that they do – so their success 'may be particularly important for gender equality' (p. 498). But her analysis does not support the 'opt out' thesis and – interestingly – suggests there is not particularly strong evidence for a decline in fertility amongst these women either, although the mothers are much less likely to work full-time or long hours per se. Percheski (2008: 514) concludes though by saying women nonetheless find it very difficult to balance life and work, and do so in most cases by 'making great personal sacrifices, including curtailing their sleep, civic involvement, or leisure time'. Relatedly, flexibility for the female British civil engineers whom Watts (2009: 45–46) interviewed suggested an *organizational* expectation of total availability and commitment from the *employee*, as opposed to anything like the reverse. Two of her respondents lived in the English Home Counties, and travelled to work in London by train. They had purchased expensive first-class season tickets in order to secure a seat every morning and evening, and to transform 'dead travel time into productive work time' (p. 51).

Apparently then, as Wood and Newton (2006) suggest, any woman wanting to 'have it all' is nurturing an 'elusive ideal' or 'impossible dream'. Certainly many of Morell's (cited in Park, 2005: 381) female respondents rejected the idea that 'they could combine meaningful work and mothering, at a standard that they would find acceptable, while also preserving time for friendships, leisure, and volunteer work'. These women also suggested that this is not a matter of private preference or idiosyncrasy but rather the outcome of 'structural and political sources' (Park, 2005: 381). Likewise, Krings (2007: 92) argues that what she calls our 'designs for life' develop 'in reaction to existing frameworks'. In other words, the intersections between our jobs, our working hours, whether or not we have children, our partnerships, our friendships, and our leisure pursuits are an outcome of what is economically and socially *possible* in any given person's circumstances, not necessarily what is personally *desirable*.

There is also a strong claim in the WLB literature that any existing 'balancing' initiatives are likely only to be useful for parents, and then only in a limited sense. As Hamilton et al. (2006) argue, single, childless women do not have 'families' in the orthodox sense of the term. As a result, they see their employer's 'work–life benefits' as irrelevant to their needs, and do not use them with any kind of frequency. Nonetheless, their respondents still reported work–life conflict, contrary to the prevailing assumption in WLB initiatives that 'life' actually means 'spouse + children'. Hoffman and Cowan (2008) agree, suggesting that the organizational websites they analysed represented 'life' as pretty much involving a heterosexual partnership, 2.2 children and 'the occasional elderly parent' (p. 236), It is almost as if, they aver, no other sorts of meaningful 'life' exist; despite all the data indicating that traditional family arrangements are in gradual decline across the west.

At the macro level, Roberts (2008: 431) states that UK legislative changes around life–work 'balance', following the EU Working Time Directive, have likewise focused on parents. Lewis and Campbell (2008) concur, saying that the Labour government's rhetorical shift to using 'life' in the relevant debates – as opposed to 'family' – was more to do with getting employers 'onside' (p. 532) as informed by the business case for employment flexibility and diversity management (see Section Four of this Handbook). Lewis and Campbell add '[I]in the event, WLB for everyone was restricted to the exhortatory and voluntary strand of policy' (p. 533) whereas statutory developments continue to prioritize work plus family. For example, the right to request flexible working arrangements has recently been extended – in April 2009 – from those with very young or disabled children and those who care for co-resident adults to include all parents with children under 17 (*Directgov*, accessed 4 September 2009). Overall, it appears that these sorts of arrangements, whether legislatively mandated or provided 'voluntarily' by employers, do not fulfil the needs of growing numbers of the Western workforce.

A related issue here is the 'child-free' movement, epitomized by the pioneering British campaign group Kidding Aside which exists to 'support and campaign on behalf of people who chose to be childfree' (*Kidding Aside*, accessed 25 February 2009). Founder Jonathan McAlmont identifies issues such as maternity pay and paternity leave as particular issues for concern. Likewise, Park (2005: 372) comments on 'conflict between parents and nonparents over provision of material benefits and appraisals of social value on the job and in society' in the context of the US child-free movement. Indeed even managerialist bodies like the UK's Chartered Institute of Personnel and Development recognize that limiting flexible working provision to parents 'risks creating an unnecessarily divided work force, with other workers resenting the rights granted to their colleagues with children or caring responsibilities' (Mike Emmott, CIPD Employee Relations Adviser, cited in CIPD, 2007: #4).

As for my primary empirics, the respondents' sense of juggling work and life and their resentment about the ways in which the former impacts on the latter persist, as the 2008 data indicate. Judith, now in a more senior job role, regularly travels between continents and has a team of one hundred people at home base. She has gradually come to feel 'over-stretched and also over-challenged', and is now less committed to her career, refusing to be as far in' as her colleagues:

> I observe my colleagues finding yet another direction to throw themselves into and think 'are you insane . . . ?['.] I don't want to work that hard, don't want to fill every car journey to the airport with phone calls, take my laptop everywhere and above all I don't want to endlessly endlessly Communicate . . .

So Judith refuses to 'work that hard', contrary to Watts' (2009) commuting engineers. Her growing resentment also seems to evoke the sense in which 'balance' should *not* mean equal time devoted to life and to work – ie 84 hours on each, as discussed by Hoffman and Cowan (2008).

Madeleine has likewise been fighting her 'martyr-like' tendency to work very long hours over the last six years, and tends now to trust her 'colleagues/management more to see I'm bloody clever, switched on, motivated and a good thing'. She also says not having children in particular means she has time for the things she gets the most pleasure from: 'social life, a job I enjoy, sleeping, reading, taking a long bath'. Her remarks resonate with those offered by many of Park's (2005) female respondents about appreciating an adult-focused lifestyle, which could not realistically accommodate children. At the same time Madeleine's aside about the absence of 'Spinsters['] Rights!!' in the context of parental leave also speaks to aspects of the child-free movement.

Catherine on the other hand, with two pre-school children, illustrates the challenges involved in managing the interface between work, parenthood and other aspects of life. However, she does not feel work impacts significantly on her family life, saying instead that '[s]ometimes motherhood does affect my ability to attend courses I would like and to study so there is always juggling and compromise'. For Catherine, life impacts on work as opposed to the reverse – so her job comes third, professional development fourth and a social life fifth after her children and her partner. Her narrative also echoes Percheski's (2008) suggestion that mothers have almost no spare time: she says that '[m]e time is non[-]existent!'. Importantly though Catherine does not resent this as much as if it were her job that was affecting other aspects of her life.

Bella's perspective on work has likewise shifted, albeit rather differently. Following the breakdown of her marriage, which was not connected to her job, she felt glad of her career to 'immerse' herself in because 'having the stability of my job gave me a foundation, a sense of self'. Bella also remains adamant that women cannot have it all:

> It remains the case that it is not possible to be [W]onderwoman, even a semi-[W]onderwoman trying to make the best possible job of career and relationship (even without the complicating factor of children) but the compensation of being able to be independent and knowing that I could be again is considerable.

For Bella, investing equally in all aspects of the relationship-work-children nexus is absolutely an 'impossible dream' (Wood and Newton, 2006). Moreover, this belief originates in her sense of what is politically or structurally feasible, also noted by Morell (cited in Park, 2005) and Krings (2007). However, despite Bella's life mainly revolving around her job and her being aware of the 'compromise' (her words) this entails, she also enjoys her work very much. Here Bella's narrative echoes Eikhof et al.'s (2007: 327–328) point that discussions of the life–work interface often marginalize any possibility of work being a source of significant fulfilment.

Georgie on the other hand, having moved out of London and had her first baby, has experienced some profound changes in her life–work nexus. Callum is now self-employed on a part-time basis, and husband and wife both live and work in the same area of England. Christopher attends nursery for part of the week and for the remainder Georgie and Callum share his care. As Georgie reminded me, being a 'stay at home Dad' was always something Callum craved. Her own self-assessment in 2002 has likewise been borne out: she is now sure she needs 'more than just being a mum'. Georgie feels very lucky that she and Callum can afford for him to work part-time, plus that he is so willing to share household labour and childcare. And, given all the data cited above, we can say fairly categorically that Georgie and Callum are indeed unusual in this regard.

With the notable exception of Georgie, then, the narratives provided by my respondents suggest that for these women, striving for an accommodation between life and work, something always has to give. This observation, taken together with the enormous array of critical commentary on the failures of WLB initiatives thus far, leads me to Webster's insightful comment that

> we now have to broaden our concerns to consider the impact of work on the wider sphere of life . . . – for the individual, for communities, for society at large. In other words, our concern must now be with enhancing the broader social sustainability of working life. (cited in Lewis et al., 2007: 369)

## Conclusion

Here I briefly return to each of my themes in order. First, as regards the 'new intimacy' thesis, there are still naysayers like Wilcox and Nock (2006). They suggest that (i) women who expect equality from their marriages also report less positive 'emotion work' from their husbands; (ii) these women, simply put, expect too much; and (iii) they therefore tend to initiate more conflict with and in turn repress attentiveness and affection from their husbands. However, despite such '*cherchez la femme*' conclusions, there is a robust body of research evidence that women who seek equality from their sexual relationships tend to enjoy more fulfilling relationships as a result (Yoder et al., 2007: 370). My primary data certainly support this claim. Nonetheless, I agree with Budgeon that co-resident heterosexual relationships continue to be privileged in this and other Western cultures. Budgeon, like Holmes (1994) before her, offers this argument in part against the new intimacy thesis. She argues that, if this thesis was actually true in its entirety, cohabitation would not be so widely understood as a stage that *all* functional relationships should attain, preferably as a way station to marriage (2008: 303). For both these commentators, the thesis exaggerates the detraditionalization of intimate relationships, especially in terms of their basic infrastructure.

But if we reconnect changing expectations of relationships to shifting priorities around children, we might further conclude that the choice not to have children, however over-determined, 'may indicate and nurture a creative "social imaginary" about being feminine without motherhood' (Wood and Newton, 2006: 355). As with the discussion of the new intimacy, the juxtaposition of literature with primary data here highlights how complex and varied women's experiences around childbearing are, and encourages us to continue to question traditional discourses of mother-hood (Hadfield et al., 2007: 261). Equally, with both the new intimacy and new motherhood theses, can we really be so confident about what are the drivers here and – equally – the effects? It may well be more sensible to view the relevant phenom-ena as inextricably connected, rather than looking for causal links.

As for life–work 'balance', the literature has much to say about the impact of work on life especially. It also insists on the many different elements of life, all of which may themselves conflict with each other. This body of scholarship, further, notes that neither organizational nor legislative attempts substantially ameliorate women's experiences of managing the life–work nexus, and identifies the accom-modations that result. It also comments on the clear and present dangers of 'lagged adaptation' in the domestic environment. All of these themes seem to be captured in my data.

In addition, the changes each of my participants has experienced during a rela-tively short period of time affirm the importance of continuing to draw down the wider social trends discussed in the academic literature – here around intimacy, motherhood, childlessness, and life–work 'balance' – to where they are experienced (or not) in everyday life. Longitudinal studies are pretty rare in the gender, work and organization literature; and much of what does exist utilizes secondary quanti-tative secondary data to assess generic patterns over time – like the Percheski (2008) study discussed above. As such, my analysis provides insights into the minutiae of life stages as against the useful but always broad-brush pictures offered by cohort-based research. Indeed the differences in my respondents' life trajectories, despite what these women also share (generation, ethnicity, level of education and type of employment), testify again to how generalizations of any kind may result in a sacri-ficing of depth for scope.

I want to close on Catherine's comment that 'I suspect that will be the next stage for many of us: considering our parents in the scheme of our immediate lives'. As my respondents and myself navigate towards our fifth decade, this indicates another avenue for primary inquiry of this sort, which can only add to the literature surveyed here in future.

## REFERENCES

Appleyard, B. (2006) 'Is marriage broken?' *The Sunday Times*, 28 May, p. 13.

Benzies, K., Tough, S., Tofflemire, K., Frick, C., Faber, A., and Newburn-Cook, C. (2006) Factors Influencing Women's Decisions about Timing of Motherhood, *Journal of Obstetric, Gynecologic, & Neonatal Nursing*, 35(5) 625–633.

Brewis, J. (2004) 'Sex and not the City? The Aspirations of the Thirty-something Working Woman, *Urban Studies*, 41(9) 1821–1838.

Budgeon, S. (2008) Couple Culture and the Production of Singleness, *Sexualities*, 11(3) 301–325.

CIPD (2007) 'Extending right to request flexible working could boost business, and reduce chances of divided workforce', CIPD: The HR and Development Website, 12 February. Online. Available at: http://www.cipd.co.uk/pressoffice/_articles/Flexresponse_120207_PR.htm?IsSrchRes=1 (accessed 6 March 2009).

Davila, J., and Kashy, D.A. (2009) Secure Base Processes in Couples: Daily Associations between Support Experiences and Attachment Security, *Journal of Family Psychology*, 23(1) 76–88.

*Directgov* 'Flexible working and work-life balance'. Online. Available at: http://www.direct.gov. uk/en/Employment/Employees/Flexibleworking/DG_10029491 (accessed 4 September 2009).

Dobson, R., and Watt, H. (2006) 'Career women turn against easy divorce', *The Sunday Times*, 22 January: 9.

Eikhof, D.R., Warhurst, C., and Haunschild, A. (2007) Introduction: What work? What life? What balance?, *Employee Relations*, 29(4) 325–333.

Fernand, D. (2007) 'Mr and Mrs: the marriage report' *The Sunday Times Magazine*, 14 January, pp. 28–43.

Fleetwood, S. (2007) Why Work–Life Balance Now?, *International Journal of Human Resource Management*, 18(3) 387–400.

Flintoff, J.P. (2006) 'Rise and rise of the only ones', *The Sunday Times*, 7 May, p. 9.

Hadfield, L., Rudoe, N., and Sanderson-Mann, J. (2007) Motherhood, Choice and the British Media: A Time to Reflect, *Gender and Education*, 19(2) 255–263.

Hamilton, E.A., Gordon, J.R., and Whelan-Berry, K.S. (2006) Understanding the Work-Life Conflict of Never-married Women without Children, *Women in Management Review*, 21(5) 393–415.

Hatfield, E., Rapson, R.L., and Aumer-Ryan, K. (2008) Social Justice in Love Relationships: Recent Developments, *Social Justice Research*, 21(4) 413–431.

Hoffman, M.F., and Cowan, R.L. (2008) The Meaning of Work/Life: A Corporate Ideology of Work/Life Balance, *Communication Quarterly*, 56(3) 227–246.

Holmes, M. (2004) An Equal Distance? Individualisation, Gender and Intimacy in Distance Relationships, *Sociological Review*, 52(2) 180–200.

Houseknecht, S.K. (1987) 'Voluntary Childlessness' in M.B. Sussman and S.K. Steinmetz (eds), *Handbook of Marriage and the Family*. New York: Plenum Press, 369–395.

*Kidding Aside (The British Childfree Association)*. Online. Available at: http://kiddingaside.yuku. com/ (accessed 25 February 2009).

Krings, B-J. (2007) Make Like a Man: The Demands of Creative Work, Gender and the Management of Everyday Life, *Work Organisation, Labour & Globalisation*, 1(1) 89–107.

Koropeckyj-Cox, T., and Pendell, G. (2007) The Gender Gap in Attitudes about Childlessness in the United States, *Journal of Marriage and the Family*, 69(4) 899–915.

Lewis, J., and Campbell, M. (2008) What's in a Name? 'Work and Family' or 'Work and Life' Balance Policies in the UK since 1997 and the Implications for the Pursuit of Gender Equality, *Social Policy & Administration*, 42(5) 524–541.

Lewis, S., Gambles, R., and Rapoport, R. (2007) The Constraints of a 'Work–Life Balance' Approach: An International Perspective, *International Journal of Human Resource Management*, 18(3) 360–373.

Park, K. (2005) Choosing Childlessness: Weber's Typology of Action and Motives of the Voluntarily Childless, *Sociological Inquiry*, 75(3) 372–402.

Percheski, C. (2008) Opting Out? Cohort Differences in Professional Women's employment rates from 1960 to 2005, *American Sociological Review*, 73(3) 497–517.

Roberts, E. (2008) Time and Work–Life Balance: The Roles of 'Temporal Customization' and 'Life Temporality', *Gender, Work and Organization*, 15(5) 430–453.

Santore, D. (2008) Romantic Relationships, Individualism and the Possibility of Togetherness: Seeing Durkheim in Theories of Contemporary Intimacy, *Sociology*, 42(6) 1200–1217.

Stöbel-Richter, Y., Beutel, M.E, Finck, C., and Brähler, E. (2005) The 'Wish to Have a Child', Childlessness and Infertility in Germany, *Human Reproduction*, 20(10) 2850–2857.

Veevers, J.E. (1973) Voluntarily Childless Wives: An Exploratory Study, *Sociology and Social Research*, 57(3) 356–366.

Watts, J. (2009) 'Allowed into a Man's World' – Meanings of Work–Life Balance: Perspectives of Women Civil Engineers as 'Minority' Workers in Construction, *Gender, Work and Organization*, 16(1) 37–57.

Wilcox, W.B., and Nock, S.L. (2006) What's Love Got to Do with It? Equality, Equity, Commitment and Women's Marital Quality, *Social Forces*, 84(3) 1321–1345.

Wood, G.J., and Newton, J. (2006) Childlessness and Women Managers: 'Choice', 'Context' and Discourses, *Gender, Work and Organization*, 13(4) 338–358.

Yoder, J.D., Perry, R.L., and Saal, E.I. (2007) What Good is a Feminist Identity? Women's Feminist Identification and Role Expectations for Intimate and Sexual Relationships, *Sex Roles*, 57(5–6) 365–372.

## APPENDIX: RESPONDENT BIOGRAPHIES

BELLA, 39, barrister, divorcing (after six years' separation), works and lives in London, with male partner Kieran.

CATHERINE, 40, osteopath, works and lives on the South Coast with male partner Charlie, their three-year-old son and two-month-old baby.

GEORGIE, 35, married to Callum, lives and works (as a university lecturer) in the Midlands. Has a son aged 21 months and is pregnant with her second child.

JUDITH, 38, call centre director, works and lives with husband Pavel in the Home Counties.

MADELEINE, 39, single, publisher, lives and works in London.

WENDY, 33, actress and artist, works and lives (with her male partner Paul) in London. Pregnant with first child.

# 10

## Representing the Successful Managerial Body

KATE KENNY AND EMMA BELL
*National University of Ireland, Ireland*
*University of Exeter Business School, UK*

### INTRODUCTION

You will, in a real sense, be embodying the job you perform . . .
*Pogrebin, 1970*

What should the successful woman manager look like? What clothes, make-up, hairstyle ought she to wear; how should she stand, sit, speak, and act? In this chapter we draw on our analysis of self-help books written between 1970 and 2007 to illustrate some recurring themes in the way that women managers are encouraged to perform their bodies. We show how these issues have been interpreted by researchers in the fields of gender, embodiment, and organization and offer some suggestions as to how these norms might be questioned.

Many researchers of organization observe that the managerial body is inherently masculine (Pringle, 1989; Marshall, 1984; Collinson and Hearn, 1996; McDowell, 1997). Fitting in with such a norm is therefore a difficult, if not impossible task for female managers who tend to exhibit different bodily traits. In such contexts, female managers can feel they are required to prove themselves in a setting that perceives them as abnormal from the start (McDowell, 1997). To cope with this dilemma, women managers often turn to self-help books which promise to help them be taken seriously and to get ahead by learning how to conform. These books offer advice on many aspects of being a woman manager but in particular they advise on how to manage and mould the female body in order to be taken seriously as a manager, without one's femininity undermining this impression.

In the first part of this chapter we explore the role of self-help books in constructing women managers' sense of self and identity. Next, we focus on how such texts advise women to use their bodies to survive as managers. Our analysis focuses on four major themes: the masculine bodily norm, the injunction for women managers to actively manage and mould their bodies, the requirement to package one's femininity as a career resource, and the ambiguity and contradiction that surrounds the body of the woman manager. Each theme is related to key ideas emerging from the study of gender, embodiment, and organization.

## MANAGING THE FEMALE BODY

Authors in the social sciences have traditionally seen the mind and body as separate entities. Hence the body is often portrayed as something of an object that can be actively manipulated and controlled by the sovereign mind (Dale, 2005). Despite authors' efforts to problematize such dualisms (see, for example, Borgerson and Rehn, 2004), dichotomies like these tend to persist in academic research and writing (Kenny, 2008). However, this separation does not correspond to the way we experience the world: our bodies and our minds are caught up with each other in complex ways. For example, as you read this, perhaps your foot is itchy, or you have a headache, and it is through these experiences that your mind is accessing these words. Consequently, for some authors, the mind and the body are seen to be inextricably interlinked (Ball, 2005; Sinclair, 2005). Grosz (1994), for example, uses the analogy of the Möbius strip (see also Hope, this volume) to theorize the lived experience of body and materiality and its intersection with the mind. Grosz argues that first, the subject's exterior is psychically constructed and, second, the exterior physicality of the body is socially constructed by discursive norms. For her, dismissing the traditional boundary between interior and exterior helps us to see the subject as a series of flows between inside and out. If this is the case, then our bodies are central to our constitution of self-identity. Consequently, what our bodies *do* affects our sense of self (Hancock and Tyler, 2001); we construct our bodies in relation to particular norms and language and, in so doing we find that we are subjected to these norms: they come to constitute our subjectivity and our sense of place in the world (Butler, 1993; Dale, 2005).

In the period since the 1970s self-help books have become a major means through which individuals are encouraged to work on their selves, to cope with problems they face and to improve their situation (McGee, 2005). For women in particular, these books exert a significant influence on the individual's embodied identity, through proposing to help her to find out about herself and teaching her effective ways of being (Simonds, 1992; Hochschild, 1994). A feature of such texts is that they offer advice on how readers might actively 'develop a self-identity they feel they lack' (Simonds, 1992: 6). The reader is encouraged to manipulate characteristics of her self, including her body, that need to be changed. In what follows, we explore how self-help books encourage women managers to embody particular norms in their construction of an appropriate self-identity.

Our qualitative content analysis focuses on eighteen books published between 1970 and 2007. Nearly all of the books are written by female authors, many of whom have built successful careers in business. They typically adopt an informal, conversational tone towards the reader, acting as a friend rather than a professional expert and conveying inspirational ideas and images through telling parable-like stories (Bate and Self, 1983; Hochschild, 1994). These authors assert that the issues women confront in building a successful managerial career are different or exceptional and therefore require separate consideration. Advice is often geared towards help-ing the woman manager to survive in a hostile environment and get to the top of the organizational hierarchy through her own individual efforts (McGee, 2005). In the following section we examine this advice; each section is introduced with an overview of relevant themes from the field of gender and embodiment, followed by illustrations from the self-help texts.

## THE MASCULINE NORM AND ITS FEMININE OTHER

Many researchers have argued that the concept of the 'normal' organizational body is implicitly masculine. The female body is thereby stigmatized or seen as 'other' – defined as inherently sexual, dangerous, suspicious, volatile, and disruptive (Acker, 1990; Cockburn, 1991; Burrell, 1992; also Brewis, Hope, Sinclair, Thanem, Wolkowitz this volume). Moreover, bodily processes associated with womanhood, including menstruation, lactation, pregnancy, and childbirth are seen as threats to the normal operation of the contemporary workplace (Sheppard, 1989). Tretheway's (1999) study of female professionals in a US City Chamber of Commerce focuses on experi-ences of the body at work. She uses the metaphor of overflow to theorize these ten-dencies which include emotional display and acts that contravene the tacit rules and aesthetics of being a professional manager. Tretheway notes that women may not even know when their bodies are overflowing: displaying 'messages and meanings that were not intended' (1999: 436). In addition to being defined as abnormal, the feminine other at work is often presented as *inferior* to the masculine. As Cockburn notes in her two-year study of men's responses to positive action for sex equality at work, the female body is frequently perceived as weaker, smaller and less authorita-tive (Cockburn, 1991).

These themes resonate in our analysis of self-help books where the female body is defined as out of place in organizational contexts due to the persistence of the masculine norm:

> Because men dominate the workplace, the status quo suits them well. They got there first and set the patterns and rules according to what pleases them. It's up to women to take the initiative in learning to understand men's ways. (Stechert, 1986)

Through articulating their awareness of these norms, the authors reconfirm Kanter's account of the persistent male power bias in large organizations (1977). The female body is defined as exceptional and highly visible in this context. Sinclair (this volume) emphasizes the ways in which women leaders are frequently held up for scrutiny based on their appearances in a way that is not experienced by men. Furthermore, the female body is seen to be upsetting and distracting in organizations. Consequently, it has the potential to undermine the woman manag-er's possibilities of success. 'Learning to understand men's ways' therefore involves moulding the female body so that it goes unnoticed within this masculine regime of power.

The female voice also places the woman manager outside the masculine norm:

> When a woman's voice reverts to sounding high and thin, it becomes like a little girl's voice. What does a little girl's voice sound like? Coy, demure, sweet and not at all authoritative. Which is probably the effect some women want their voices to have. Again, people respond not only to the content of your message, but the sound of it as well . . . as voices go up in pitch, credibility goes down. (Frankel, 2004)

Similarly, the ideal size of the managerial body is modelled on the male norm, many authors suggesting that being tall is an advantage in commanding attention and exercising power over others. They recommend that women overcome their height disadvantage by making themselves appear taller, for example by wearing shoes with heels (Heim, 2005; Macdonald, 1986; Stechert, 1986).

Menstruation at work is also seen as dangerous and threatening because many men perceive it to be so:

> Many men perceive menstruation as an alien thing that invades our bodies and controls us. For instance, one fellow asked me, 'Well, what if the president had a period?' as if the leader of the free world had never seen a bad day. Having never experienced it, they imbue the menstrual cycle with meaning and power it doesn't have. In fact, menstruation is a deeply mysterious process for men. And to add to its mystery, it's somehow tied to the phases of the moon. (Heim, 2005)

As a warning, Williams has the following story, taken from an interview with a manager on the US west coast:

> I had one terrible situation with my period. It was particularly heavy, but I had cocktails after work with some of the people from the office. We'd been sitting there for an hour, and suddenly I felt the need to go to the ladies room and change. Well, I was about halfway across the restaurant when the whole world dropped out and was running down my legs. (Williams, 1977)

In telling this story, Williams warns her readers about the dangers of allowing such an incident to occur. Her colleagues and companions could not fathom what had happened. The solution for the woman in question was to ignore the incident completely and pretend that nothing had happened. This story illustrates the radical otherness of menstruation in the context of the workplace thereby reconfirming Tretheway's (1999) analysis, which includes similar stories. She argues that menstruation is one way in which the female body is rendered out of control and antithetical to the workplace (Tretheway, 1999).

Another way in which women's physicality is defined in opposition to the masculine norm is by crying in public. As Cockburn notes, displays of emotion imply a lack of control, and this in turn means that women are seen as incapable of exercising authority (Cockburn, 1991). Crying is widely seen as out of place in the workplace and self-help authors regard the greater tendency of women to cry as a common problem because it implies that the woman manager is 'not in control, not competent and weak' (Frankel, 2004):

> Emotional displays in a business setting are offensive to men because of the high value they place on control. Crying is the ultimate transgression and can cost women a lot . . . (Stechert, 1986)

The message put forward in these books is clear: men rarely cry at work and therefore, crying is unacceptable.

> Crying has no place in business; it is one manifestation of our femaleness that is not tolerated by the business society. (Williams, 1977)

Collinson and Knights' (1986) empirical study of women crying at work shows how exclusionary patriarchal discourses can persist in workplaces in ways that are often invisible. The authors found that such displays of emotion were frequently the result of stress caused by pressure from management and excessive workloads. However, male managers saw them as a sign of weakness and irrational behaviour, rather than an understandable response to a difficult situation. This research shows how 'crying as weakness' is perpetuated through managerial discourse and practice in a way which renders the crying person illogical and 'other' and signals the difference of women's bodies from the masculine organizational norm (Mumby and Putnam, 1992; Tretheway, 1999).

In addition to crying and menstruation, women's bodies transgress organizational norms through their perceived sexuality (Hearn et al., 1989). As Cockburn notes, women's sexuality is always present in the workplace, whether it is seen as a 'threat to organizational discipline' or a welcome distraction from it (1991: 27). The female body is seen as bringing a level of sexuality to the workplace which it is her responsibility to control:

> To be effective on the job, a woman has to know a great deal about how her sexual attractiveness affects her work and the men she works with. She must take care regarding the sexual signals she sends to men . . . (Stechert, 1986)

One author reports a woman whose tight outfits, although showing off an excellent figure, were 'inappropriate – so much so that her male associates feel uncomfortable around her. One colleague told me he was reluctant to have business dinners with her alone because he worried about what his wife would think. (Evans, 2000) Even the smallest detail can be interpreted as sexual, such as long hair or noisy jewellery. However, breasts are the most consistent signifier of the woman manager's inherent sexuality and disruptive potential:

> Whether or not you have a big bust, never, never, never go to work without a bra. Jiggly breasts and protuberant nipples embarrass most men . . . (Macdonald, 1986)

In addition to being perceived as inferior (Cockburn, 1991), dangerous (Acker, 1990), and overflowing (Tretheway, 1999), these texts identify the female body as a source of discomfort and embarrassment in the workplace, both for the woman who inhabits this body and the other people she comes into contact with. Given this presentation of women's bodies, what are women managers supposed to do about their bodies to progress in their careers? The advice of many self-help authors is that the female manager's body *can* be made to fit into the masculine norm of the workplace but in order to achieve this it must be moulded, manipulated, and managed.

## Body Management

Sinclair (this volume) shows how leadership, for example, is *performed*, and argues that leaders' bodies play a key role in this (see also Butler, 1993). Bartky (1988) notes that women are encouraged by particular class and gender discourses to actively mould their bodies, through processes of diet and exercise, as a way of attaining the 'ideal' (middle-class) female body. Similarly, Acker (1990) finds that the otherness of female bodies is used as 'grounds for control' through such injunctions (Acker, 1990: 152). This kind of self-work is suggested to depoliticize women because they become so focused on manipulating their bodies that they tend to overlook the wider structural inequalities that might impact upon their lives. In the context of the workplace, Tretheway (1999) finds that city professionals share the view that self-work is vital in striving to attain the ideal professional body, one that is fit, appropriately sexual and above all, controlled. These studies adopt a Foucauldian perspective, seeing the body as a social object which is written upon and penetrated by institutional regimes of power-knowledge. Consequently, the body is not completely one's own, but rather is subject to the particular meanings that organizational discourses inscribe upon it.

Returning to the representation of these issues in self-help books, women are encouraged to see their bodies as an object that, left unchecked, may undermine their conscious will, and their careers. They are therefore advised to control and manage its excessive tendencies through the adoption of various techniques of concealment and suppression. This includes suppressing and concealing bodily processes such as menstruation and pregnancy. For example, one author tells the story of a pregnant woman who dealt with her clients by telephone rather than face-to-face and instructed staff to keep her pregnancy a secret (Bryce, 1989). Another technique involves translating inappropriate forms of embodied expression into modes that are more suitable in a managerial setting. Instead of crying, women are encouraged to get angry.

> It is important that you learn to show anger. Most executive women have learned how to channel their feelings toward anger rather than tears. (Williams, 1977)
>
> Express the anger outward: tears are frequently preceded by repressed anger. Let out that anger at the

Several books recommend that women unlearn these behaviours. They are also advised to modify their voices: the female manager should lower the pitch of her voice in order to 'avoid shrill tones' (Brown and Brady, 1991; Frankel, 2004). A diminutive voice can be compensated for, with careful practice and training:

Record your voice on a tape cassette and play it back . . . When you listen . . . be alert for voice tones that are apologetic, tentative, meek, imploring, whining, prissy, nagging, or schoolmarmish. (Carr-Rufino, 1982)

To overcome her deficiency in size, a woman manager might 'elevate her body by standing to make a point or standing when others are seated; she can seem taller if she keeps her chin up and occasionally puts her hands behind her back so that she appears to be looking down on others' (Stechert, 1986). Macdonald suggests to the reader 'you can use your hairstyle to give you extra height and your clothes to give you bulk if you are particularly tiny. Big lapels and padded shoulders are helpful . . .' (Macdonald, 1986)

In sum, women are encouraged to actively work on their bodies, dressing, walking, talking, medicating, and even hurting themselves, in pursuit of the ideal managerial body. This bodily work is self-disciplinary; the female manager is encouraged to internalize these injunctions and engage in them voluntarily, even if she is unaware of the threat her body poses.

Ask yourself these questions: Are you being unconsciously seductive? (or consciously) Are you wearing inappropriate, revealing clothes to the office? (Pogrebin, 1970)

Self-help books suggest that a woman manager's career may be determined to a high degree by her ability to manage her own body; if she fails to attain career success, this is partly attributed to her failure to control her body. Responsibility thus lies firmly with the individual. Warnings like 'dress like a sex object and you'll be treated like one' (Macdonald, 1986) convey the expectation on the individual to take responsibility for workplace norms.

## Woman-manager-as-product

The commodification of the body, where the body is treated as an object with a marketable value that can be bought and sold, is a common theme in feminist and organizational research. Hochschild's (1983) landmark book details how female airhostesses are frequently required to package their femininity by the airline companies they work for. This has given rise to a number of studies of aesthetic labour, which focus on the increasing pressures faced by female and male service workers to actively present themselves and their bodies, in ways that suit the aesthetic identity of the organization (Hancock and Tyler, 2000; Witz et al., 2003).

The construction of the physical self as a product is also enabled by self-help books which ensure that as they are reading, readers are continually commodifying themselves: transforming their image and self into 'objects of analysis and improvement' (Simonds, 1992: 223). The commodification of the woman manager is an important underlying theme in self-help books. In addition to working on the female body so that it conforms to particular norms, self-help books encourage the woman manager to package her body as a product. They suggest that, if carefully managed, the very femininity that threatened the woman manager with exclusion can now be harnessed for the benefit of her career. Williams, for example, argues that femininity can be used as a product feature:

I support both the concept and use of femininity . . . I believe in wearing make-up and skirts and shaving legs (Williams, 1977)

In creating the woman manager as a product, hairstyle is important:

. . . the most common mistake I see women make is to wear their hair too long . . . longer hair tends to emphasize facial features of which we may be less proud as we age . . . if your hair is graying, consider a good colorist. Whereas grey or graying hair on men is viewed as distinguished women aren't typically afforded the same compliment. (Frankel, 2004)

In addition to the strategic use of femininity in make-up, shaving, and hairstyle, clothing is vital. Creating the woman-manager-as-product includes paying close attention to colour, with most authors recommending colour analysis as a technique that the woman can use to 'project her femininity' (Bryce, 1989; Frankel, 2004; Friedman and Yorio, 2004; Jordan and Weir, 2006). In one book, the authors provide an account of their meeting with an image consultant. The aim of the meeting was to identify the colours that complement their natural features.

[This] involved us sitting in natural light with no make-up on, our hair scraped back and various scarves tied around our necks. The consultant showed us how some colours threw light back onto our faces, making us look slightly better (bearing in mind our unadorned condition). Other colours drew colour from our faces and made us look a lot worse. Black, one of our staples for jackets and tops, made us instantly look terrible. (Jordan and Weir, 2006).

Ehrenreich (2006), in her account of white-collar work in twenty-first century America, talks about her experience of make-up and colour analysis, which entailed similar evaluations of 'good' and 'bad' colours against her face. For Ehrenreich, this 'should be the fun part – playing with paints and little swatches of fabric'. However, the fun quickly dissipates as she realizes what is at stake:

I am suddenly gripped by queasiness. I understand that to make myself into a 'product' that I can market, I must first become a commodity, a thing . . . What I had not understood is that to become an object, a thing, you must first go through a kind of death. (Ehrenreich, 2006: 111).

What Ehrenreich describes is a process of intentional commodification of the body such that it becomes a part of the service provided to the consumer. In a similar way, the self-help books discussed here encourage the female manager to mould her aesthetic image and package her femininity into a form that is acceptable. Salmonsohn even parodies advertising language, joking that women managers should think about their image in terms of 'product repositioning' (Salmonsohn, 1997).

## Balancing acts

Tretheway (1999) and McDowell (1997) discuss the contradictions and paradoxes inherent in female managers' embodied identities. These authors report how women who present a more masculine self-presentation make their female and male colleagues 'uneasy' and are likely to be seen as 'unfemale'. The female manager must therefore conduct a delicate 'balancing act' so as not to appear too masculine or excessively feminine (Hochschild, 1994). She is thus caught in a series of 'complex, ambiguous, and precarious "in-betweens"' (Tretheway, 1999: 425). Ehrenreich (2006) captures this ambiguity well through her account of an image management consultation. She is told by the image consultant that her appearance is 'too authoritative', a judgement that Ehrenreich interprets as 'not looking feminine enough'.

> The dress-for-success books all urge what I take to be a somewhat mannish appearance, achieved through pragmatic hairstyles and curve-concealing suits. But if you go too far in the masculine direction . . . you somehow err again (Ehrenreich, 2006: 108).

Our analysis of the body in self-help books for women managers reconfirms the contradictory nature of this identity project. In many cases, even within the same text, a number of contradictory versions of the successful woman manager emerge. Advice is contradictory and ambiguous, particularly in relation to clothes:

> The clothes that you wear for business should fall into the category of conservative but mildly feminine (Williams, 1977)

As Macdonald warns:

> What you must never do is wear a trouser suit which apes a man's business suit. It does not make you look like a businessman, it makes you look rather silly and attention-seeking. If you compound the error by wearing a man's tie with it, some of the men you meet will assume you are a lesbian and you'll have all that hassle to cope with. (Macdonald, 1986)

These tensions and contradictions expose the fundamental problem in managing the female body in a workplace context that valorizes and normalizes the masculine:

> Women who try to banish sex – or worse, be sexless themselves – seldom succeed. The solution for women is not to deny their sexuality or femininity, but to control it and to

keep men from using sex to denigrate them . . . Wearing severe suits, talking tough, and
rejecting every smile or hint of friendliness from men is no more a sensible way for a
woman to behave on the job than is playing the vamp. (Stechert, 1986)

Contradictions are particularly notable in admonitions of the need to balance
sexuality against feminism. For example, Salmonsohn recommends flirting as a useful tool:

In certain situations, a little cleavage can actually help to first peak a guy's attention to a
career girl's benefit, then later help to distract a guy's attention to a career girl's benefit.
(Salmonsohn, 1997)

However, she goes on to note that an attractive woman can get into trouble: while
her attractiveness guarantees attention from men, this may come with 'fear and
resentment'. (Salmonsohn, 1997) On the one hand, femininity is presented as a
resource for the woman to use to her advantage, while on the other, sexuality threatens to demean and render her inferior. Finding a balance between fitting in to the
masculine, and packaging the feminine, is therefore precarious, if not impossible.

## DOING BODIES DIFFERENTLY

In this chapter we have shown how self-help authors encourage women managers
to discipline and subordinate their bodies in ways that are often subtle, and even
contradictory. One of us has argued in previous work that the body represents a
medium through which cultural norms and values are acquired (Bell and King,
forthcoming). Bodily practices constitute an important means by which the norms,
values and beliefs associated with a particular culture are enacted, and proficiency
as a cultural member is demonstrated. For women managers this presents a distinct
challenge, since their bodies are defined as inherently abnormal from the outset
and thus unsuited to managerial cultures.

The question remains as to what are the effects of self-help texts on women's
embodied experience of managerial cultures. Are they simply tools in the ongoing dominance of hegemonic, masculine organizational discourses or do they leave
scope for resistance? Any attempt to answer this question must engage with the ways
in which such texts are read. Hence, rather than seeing self-help books as commodifying readers and forming part of a regulatory normative schema which acts to
discipline women at work, or alternatively as potential sites for resistance, we suggest
that there is a need for more ethnographic studies to explore how women use these
books in their everyday lives (Radway, 1987) as a means of recognizing and voicing
their own interests and aspirations in a way that is likely to be complex and potentially contradictory (Bell, 2008).

Meanwhile, by way of conclusion to this chapter we draw on our own responses
to these texts, as university employees and as women, to present some tentative
ideas in a way which acknowledges how our personal, professional, and intellectual

lives intersect (McRobbie, 1982). These responses affirm the nature of academic work as not purely mental labour (McRobbie, 1982) but also an embodied project of identity construction. Our first reaction is one of pessimism. If, before reading such books, we were aware of our bodies as posing potential obstacles to our career progress, this exercise has compounded this impression. By reminding us of these embodied markers of difference, we feel even more out of place at work. Self-help books thus contribute further to our sense of exclusion. The contradictory and mixed messages about how to manage one's body lead to a sense of dejection: can we ever really manage our feminine, sexed bodies in ways that could possibly fit in contemporary organizations? Perhaps, as Irigaray (1990) notes, there is no place for the feminine in such discourses. For Irigaray, rather than being a separate, sovereign subject, the category of woman is always subsumed to a position of strangeness and otherness. Woman can only ever be understood relative to man, as his reflection, 'the other of the same'.

To take a contrasting position, recent theory on gender and the body proposes some hopeful directions. The perspective adopted by many authors cited above, which holds that women at work are inevitably trapped in a patriarchal discursive cage, has been criticized for being overly deterministic and pessimistic. Lately, two alternative approaches have emerged. The first is based on the idea that discourses such as masculinity are not fixed but, as we have shown above, frequently incorporate mixed messages. From our discussion of the body of the successful female manager we can see how dominant hegemonic discourses surrounding the masculine bodily norm can contradict each other and, ultimately, fail to make sense. Perhaps this demonstrates the impossibility of the ideal body and indicates that there is little point in striving for it. Butler (1990, 1993) argues that the instability at the heart of gender discourses can yield potential for their undoing. Kenny (2009), for example, highlights how this undoing can occur in the context of hegemonic representations through the use of parody and laughter. Perhaps the resulting 'subversive place(s)' that open up, leave women managers space to creatively interpret the world of gender, bodies, and the workplace, in a way that suits them (Knights and Kerfoot, 2004: 450). Consequently, we also found in our reading of these texts spaces to use them in our own ways, taking the advice they offer and using it in to enable our own ongoing survival in, for example, interactions with male colleagues or giving lectures to students.

A second, related position is based on a critique of approaches to discourse, gender, and embodiment that tend to treat the body as an entirely receptive phenomenon that is compelled to be shaped, formed, and manipulated by discourses. A possible alternative involves drawing on ideas of performativity (Butler, 1990, 1993). For Butler, the inescapable unknowingness of social life means that norms are never re-enacted in a straightforward manner, but 'elide, slide, alter (and) shift' in a number of interesting ways (Borgerson, 2005: 71). In this imperfect recitation lies the potential for discourses to be altered and subverted (Butler, 1990). Drawing on this perspective one could argue that even if women professionals are to actively recite the bodily norms implied in the texts presented here, this recitation and performance cannot happen in a straightforward manner. In this vein, some authors see the body as a *lived* phenomenon which introduces the potential for resisting normative injunctions (Ball, 2005; Grosz, 1994). For example, Davies et al. (2005)

conceptualize how the 'crossing over' between mind and body, which occurs in the lived experiences of bodily life, leads to an incomplete, indeterminate bodily existence. Through breaking down traditional conceptual barriers between internal and external, the self is seen as a series of flows. For writers like Pullen (2006) the gendered self can be understood as an ambiguous and fragmented 'corporeal multiplicity' defined by its connective capabilities, rather than its physical and sexual properties. This lived experience of body and materiality, and its intersection with norms and power, is seen as a potential site for resistance to power (Ball, 2005). The body is thus involved in both the construction of societal influences on identity and in the psychic experiencing of such influences. Consequently, bodily performances have the potential to subvert particular hegemonic norms which influence constructions of self and identity among women managers (Butler, 1993; see also Sinclair, this volume).

In this chapter we have shown how self-help books purport to help women understand aspects of their selves and their situation by teaching them 'effective ways of being' (Simonds, 1992: 223). In situations where women managers find themselves 'lone travellers' (Marshall, 1984) in a male world, such texts may enable them to feel connected to others in the same situation and to develop a 'self-identity they feel they lack' (Simonds, 1992: 6). The 'simple act of taking up a book' (Radway, 1987: 12) is thus extremely complex. For the organizational researcher engaged in exploring these issues we suggest there is a need to better understand the historical and cultural meanings that such texts hold for their audiences and the women who write them, as well as exploring the connection between the texts and readers' everyday lives. Above all, what women struggling to make sense of hegemonic masculine organizational norms surrounding the managerial body need most from researchers is 'our support rather than our criticism or direction' (Radway, 1987: 18).

## References

Acker, J. (1990) Hierarchies, Jobs, Bodies: A Theory of Gendered Organizations, *Gender and Society*, 4(2) 139–158.

Ball, K. (2005) Organization, Surveillance and the Body: Towards a Politics of Resistance, *Organization*, 12(1) 89–108.

Bartky, S.L. (1988) 'Foucault, Femininity, and Patriarchal Power' in Irene Diamond and Lee Quinby (eds), *Feminism and Foucault: Reflections on Resistance*. Boston, MA: North Eastern University Press, 61–86.

Bate, B., and Self, L.S. (1983) The Rhetoric of Career Success Books for Women, *Journal of Commmunication*, 33(2) 149–165.

Bell, E. (2008) *Reading Management and Organization in Popular Film*. Basingstoke: Palgrave Macmillan.

Bell, E., and King, D. (forthcoming) The Elephant in the Room: Critical Management Studies Conferences as a Site of Body Pedagogics, *Management Learning*.

Borgerson, J. (2005) Judith Butler: On Organizing Subjectivities, *Sociological Review*, 53, 63–79.

Borgerson, J., and Rehn, A. (2004) General Economy and Productive Dualisms, *Gender, Work and Organization*, 11(4) 455–474.

Brown, G., and Brady, C. (1991) *Are You Ready to Manage?* Women in Management Workbook Series. London: Kogan Page.

Bryce, L. (1989) *The Influential Woman: How to Achieve Success Without Losing Your Femininity.* Arrow.

Burrell, G. (1992) 'Sex and Organizations' in A.J. Mills and P. Tancred (eds), *Gendering Organizational Analysis.* London: Sage.

Butler, J. (1990) *Gender Trouble: Feminism and the Subversion of Identity.* London: Routledge.

Butler, J. (1993) *Bodies That Matter: On the Discursive Limits of 'Sex'.* London: Routledge.

Carr-Rufino, N. (1982) *The Promotable Woman: Becoming a Successful Manager.* Wadsworth Publishing.

Cockburn, C. (1991) *In the Way of Women: Men's Resistance to Sex Equality in Organizations.* London: Macmillan.

Collinson, D., and Hearn, J. (1996) *Men as Managers, Managers as Men.* London: Sage.

Collinson, D., and Knights, D. (1986) 'Men Only: Theories and Practices of Job Segregation', in D. Knights and H. Willmott (eds), *Gender and the Labour Process.* Gower, Aldershot, 140–178.

Dale, K. (2005) Building a Social Materiality: Spatial and Embodied Politics in Organizational Control, *Organization,* 12(5) 649–678.

Davies, B., Browne, J. et al. (2005) Embodied Women at Work in Neoliberal Times and Places, *Gender, Work and Organization,* 12(4) 343–362.

Ehrenreich, B. (2006) *Bait and Switch: The Futile Pursuit of the Corporate Dream.* London: Granta.

Evans, G. (2000) *Play Like a Man, Win Like a Woman: What Men Know about Success that Women Need to Learn.* Broadway Books.

Flett, C.V. (2007) *What Men Don't Tell Women About Business: Opening Up the Heavily Guarded Alpha Male Playbook.* Hoboken, NJ: John Wiley & Sons Inc.

Frankel, L.P. (2004) *Nice Girls Don't Get the Corner Office: 101 Unconscious Mistakes That Women Make.* Business Plus.

Friedman, C., and Yorio, K. (2004) *The Girl's Guide to Being a Boss: Valuable Lessons and Smart Suggestions for Making the Most of Managing.* A&C Black Publishers.

Grosz, E. (1994) *Volatile Bodies: Towards a Corporeal Feminism.* London: Allen and Unwin.

Hancock, P., and Tyler, M. (2000) 'The Look of Love: Gender, Work and the Organization of Aesthetics' in J. Hassard, R. Holliday, and H. Willmott (eds), *Body and Organization.* London: Sage.

Hancock, P., and Tyler, M. (2001) Managing Subjectivity and the Dialectic of Self-Consciousness: Hegel and Organization Theory, *Organization,* 8(4) 565–586.

Hearn, J., Sheppard, D., Tancred-Sheriff, P., and Burrell, G. (1989) *The Sexuality of Organisation.* London: Sage.

Heim, P. with Golant, S.K. (2005) *Hardball for Women: Winning at the Game of Business.* Plume Books.

Hochschild, A. (1983). *The Managed Heart The Managed Heart: Commercialization of Human Feeling.* Berkeley, CA: University of California Press.

Hochschild, A. (1994) The Commercial Spirit of Intimate Life and the Abduction of Feminism: Signs from Women's Advice Books, *Theory, Culture and Society,* 11 1–24.

Irigaray, L. (1990/2007) *Je, Tu, Nous: Towards a Culture of Difference,* (trans. A. Martin). New York: Routledge.

Jordan, R., and Weir, K. (2006) *In Good Company: The Essential Business Start-Up Guide for Women.* A&C Black Publishing.

Kanter, R.M. (1977) *Men and Women of the Corporation.* New York: Basic Books.

Kenny, K. (2008) Aesthetics and Emotion in an Organisational Ethnography, *International Journal of Work, Organisation and Emotion,* 2(4) 374–388.

Kenny, K. (2009) The Performative Surprise: Parody, Documentary and Critique, *Culture and Organization*, 15(2) 221–235.

Knights, D., and Kerfoot, D. (2004) Between Representations and Subjectivity: Gender Binaries and the Politics of Organizational Transformation, *Gender Work and Organization*, 11(4) 432–454.

Macdonald, J.W. (1986) *Climbing the Ladder: How to be a Woman Manager*. Methuen.

Marshall (1984) *Women Managers: Travellers in a Male World*. Chichester: John Wiley & Sons Ltd.

McDowell, L. (1997) *Capital Culture: Gender at Work in the City*. Oxford: Blackwell.

McGee, M. (2005) *Self-Help, Inc.: Makeover Culture in American Life*. Oxford: Oxford University Press.

McRobbie, A. (1982) The Politics of Feminist Research: Between Talk, Text and Action, *Feminist Review*, 12(3) 46–57.

Morrow, J.B., and Lebov, M. (1984) *Not Just A Secretary: Using the Job to Get Ahead*. John Wiley & Sons Ltd.

Mumby, D.K., and Putnam, L. (1992). The Politics of Emotion: A Feminist Reading of 'Bounded Rationality', *Academy of Management Review*, 17 465–486.

Pogrebin, L. (1970) *How to Make it in a Man's World*. Cassell.

Pringle, R. (1989) *Secretaries Talk: Sexuality, Power and Work*. London: Verso.

Pullen, A. (2006) Gendering the Research Self: Social Practice and Corporeal Multiplicity in the Writing of Organizational Research, *Gender, Work and Organization*, 13(3) 278–298.

Radway, J. (1987) *Reading the Romance: Women, Patriarchy and Popular Literature*. London: Verso.

Salmonsohn, K. (1997) *How to Succeed in Business Without a Penis*. Pan Books.

Sheppard, D. (1989) 'Organizations, Power and Sexuality: The Image and Self-Image of Women Managers' in J. Hearn, D.L. Sheppard, P. Tancred-Sheriff, and G. Burrell (eds), *The Sexuality of Organization*. London: Sage.

Simonds, W. (1992) *Women and Self-Help Culture: Reading Between the Lines*. New Brunswick, NJ: Rutgers University Press.

Sinclair, A. (2005) Body and Management Pedagogy, *Gender, Work and Organization*, 12(1) 89–104.

Stechert, K. (1986) *The Credibility Gap: How to Understand the Men in Your Business Life – And Win By Your Own Rules*. Thorsons Publishing.

Trethewey, A. (1999) Disciplined Bodies: Women's Embodied Identities at Work, *Organization Studies*, 20(3) 423–450.

Williams, M.G. (1977) *The New Executive Woman: A Guide to Business Success*. Mentor.

Witz, A., Warhurst, C., and Nickson, D. (2003) The Labour of Aesthetics and the Aesthetics of Organization, *Organization*, 10(1) 33–54.

# 11

# The Organisational Contours of 'Body Work'

## Carol Wolkowitz
*University of Warwick*

This chapter addresses the growing literature on what some sociologists conceptualise as 'body work', i.e. the work that human beings do on their own and others' bodies. It aims to bring a tactile dimension to our understanding of work and organisation, and to highlight the embodied materiality of workplace interactions. Considering various forms of body work tells us not only about some of the ways in which organisations influence how much time, energy and money we spend on our bodies, but also the extent to which organising needs bodies to give it life.

The chapter begins by situating 'body work' within the wider framework of recent research seeking to make the embodiment of workplace activity and organisational roles more visible. It then looks at the body work that people do on their own bodies – for instance, styling our hair, tying our shoes, or managing our facial expression – to consider how far apparently personal activities intersect with the world of paid employment. The article then examines the intimate work on another person that forms an important component of the job for many people. The work of doctors, beauticians, spa workers and many others focuses directly on the bodies of other people and routinely involves touching other people's bodies. Using the example of health and social care, the section shows that organisations are not only concerned with managing the bodies of their employees, but also, in very important ways, with organising the bodies of their customers, clients and patients.

## The Relation Between the Body and Work

The recent interest in 'body work' and the body at work more generally challenges the disembodied picture of organisation and the world of work that used to characterise academic scholarship. The previous absence of the body was in part due to the emphasis, following Max Weber, on modern organisation as a rational, impersonal activity, with bodies, emotion and sexuality restricted to the province of private, family life and associated with women rather than men (Gimlin, 2007). Moreover, concerns about sexuality, reproduction and even one's physical attractiveness were assumed to be part of private life.

Increasingly, however, scholars are teasing out the myriad ways in which human embodiment is an essential aspect of the world of work and a constitutive element of organisation (Hassard et al. (eds), 2000; Brewis and Linstead, 2000; Holliday and Hassard (eds), 2001; Hancock and Tyler, 2000; Styrhe, 2004). One obvious aspect of the relationship between the body and work – what I call the body/work nexus (Wolkowitz, 2006) – is the work undertaken by the body in production and services, for instance constructing buildings, installing parts and pieces on an assembly line or working in a shop. Often the whole body is involved, even in service sector work. For instance, restaurant work requires a lot of physical coordination. Serving staff do not just hand plates to diners, they transfer trays or plates between themselves in a confined space – and somehow manage to avoid crashing into each other (Gatta, 2009: 118, citing Erikson, 2004: 80). Even working with the hands is more than a mechanical activity. Sennett's (2008) celebration of the craftsman's trade, for instance, suggests that the hand's 'motions, plus the hand's varied ways of gripping and the sense of touch, affect how we think' (p. 149). Detailed accounts of workers' own embodied perceptions of their work environment, and of themselves within it, exemplify a phenomenological approach to embodiment, which presents a rich vein for further research (Hockey and Allen-Collinson, 2009). Indeed, scholars increasingly consider how far cognitive activities and knowledge work builds on human embodiment (Goodwin, 2001).

Whereas phenomenological approaches consider the sensory aspects of the working practice of the lived body from the inside-out (Crossley, 2007), other scholars emphasise the regulation of the body by forces outside it, including the steps taken by employers that constrain people to work harder or more productively. The development of the factory system in the late eighteenth century brought workers into factories where they could be observed, while later the assembly line tried to standardise and mechanise workers' bodily movements and timings (Thompson, 1967; Bahnisch, 2000; Braverman, 1974; Yanarella and Reid, 1996). Some of these studies on the discipline exercised through the spatial arrangements of work were influenced by the concepts of discipline and surveillance developed by the French philosopher and historian Michel Foucault (1991). Nowadays even modern office buildings are designed to elicit certain behaviours, for instance to encourage creative interaction between colleagues (Dale, 2005) by the placement of sofas and coffee machines.

A further approach to the body and work is gender scholarship, which has been central to making the presence of the body in work and organisation an emerging theme. Feminist researchers studying the problems faced by women entering fields previously monopolised by men not only challenged the then prevailing gender-blind understanding of work and organisation, but also noted the extent to which organisation rested on assumptions about bodily difference. As Acker (1990) argued, the construction of organisational roles as full-time work, to which one devotes all one's commitment and energy, presumed that there was someone else at home – a wife – to make the arrangements for meeting bodily needs, including the care of children. The longstanding superior status of men's work, as against women's, was maintained by the apparently gender-neutral bureaucratic organisation. Hence it was the male body, and its relation to sexuality and procreation, that best fitted apparently gender-neutral, abstract organisational job specifications.

Although gender research initially concentrated on the exclusion of women, feminist perspectives are certainly not redundant. Although women now obtain jobs previously held by men, workplace expectations often depend, implicitly if not explicitly, on wider assumptions about the relation between people's bodies and their social identities and abilities, in terms of 'race', social class, sexual orientation, disability, age and so on, as well as gender (e.g. Monaghan, 2002; McDowell, 1997; Morgan and Brandth (eds), 2005; Puwar, 2001). Moreover, as discussed further below, even when women are not excluded, organisations may still seek to marginalise qualities and aspects of embodiment associated with women.

Since one chapter can hardly cover the entire field of body and work, this essay follows Shilling (2005), Gimlin (2007) and Wolkowitz (2002) in concentrating on one aspect of the body in work and organisation – the different kinds of 'body work' which people do on their own and others' bodies 'in order that they can survive and function adequately' (Shilling, 2005: 73). We turn first to the work that people do on their own bodies, especially in relation to meeting workplace requirements. We then consider at more length a different form of body work, the hands-on work of manipulating, touching, cleaning, adjusting and otherwise managing bodies that people do on other people's bodies as a component of their jobs (Wolkowitz, 2002). One benefit of this focus is that it puts gender at the heart of the relation between body and work.

## WORK ON ONE'S OWN BODY

According to Shilling (2005), people's work on their own bodies falls into three categories. Firstly there is what he terms 'job-related' body work, the 'tasks involved in maintaining the embodied self as viable within the environment of waged labour' (p. 73). Second is the day-to-day 'reproductive' body work that caters for 'basic bodily needs for sustenance and physical care' (p. 74). Thirdly, there is the cultural work that we undertake in order to present ourselves as 'acceptable subjects' in everyday life (p. 74). This includes the sometimes costly 'body projects' (Giddens, 1991) through which many people seek to normalise or perfect their bodies, such as dieting or body building. However, as Shilling recognises, these kinds of body work increasingly overlap, as the everyday body work required or expected by employers and other organisations extends into activities that used to be considered private matters.

Much of the body work entailed by working life involves the self-production of what Tyler and Abbot term the 'organisational body', defined as 'the mode of embodiment which must be presented, performed, and maintained in order to become and remain an employee of a particular organisation or a particular occupation' (Tyler and Abbot, 1998: 440). Their example of ways in which airline flight attendants are required to present their bodies shows how much body work is required, both before arriving at work and while present in the workplace. Expectations regarding women crew's weight management, make-up, hairdo and grooming are stricter than for men, who are expected only to be clean and presentable, and while on board the female flight attendant must ensure that she remains 'body conscious', so as not to make a spectacle of herself by inadvertently disclosing or exposing parts of her uncontrolled and undisciplined 'natural body' (Tyler and Abbot, 1998: 31). Women crew also receive detailed training in certain 'body techniques', including how to walk softly and smile at passengers.

Some commentators use the term 'aesthetic labour' to conceptualise the contribution workers make to their employers' profits through their physical appearance and other aspects of their bodily self-presentation, for instance the US chain Hooters, where the waitresses are required to convey a sexy 'Florida Beach Girl Look' (Warhurst and Nickson, 2009). Another example is fashion sales workers, who are required to wear the clothes sold by the store, to show how attractive the styles are and how to combine them into an outfit (Pettinger, 2004; Leslie, 2002). These are cases in which body work on the self is part of the wage bargain.

Professionals and managers are also expected to prepare and use their bodies in particular ways (Thrift, 2005). Usually expectations (which may include, in comparison to the examples above, a desexualised image) are conveyed indirectly, for instance through occasional comments by colleagues (McDowell, 1997), rather than being part of the contract of employment, as they are for Hooters' staff. Nonetheless, nowadays management trainees in big, elite UK firms are often provided with advice from image consultants. One recent pamphlet – which I will keep anonymous – includes advice about how to choose one's clothes (fit, complementing one's colouring, appropriateness, etc.), how men should iron a shirt and knot a necktie, and, for women, 10 different ways to fold and wear a scarf, while both men and women are instructed in adopting a 'positive body language'. These consultants also claim to provide advice for senior management as they take on new roles.

Body work on the self is only one aspect of the relation between bodies and work, but it is especially interesting because it cannot take place 'over our heads'; we have to participate actively in its achievement, and thus we participate in constituting ourselves as employees and as members of particular organisations. This makes 'body work' a particularly powerful mechanism through which people are integrated into organisations. It is also arguably a necessary one, from the employers' point of view, for in many jobs in the service sector bodily discipline cannot take place indirectly through changes in technological arrangements, such as the adoption of the assembly line in a previous era, but rather only through workers' conscious efforts to conform (Lan, 2001).

Moreover, in so far as body work involves the bodily performances of gender, as in the examples above, it puts gender at the heart of the management of consent. Most people would agree that women are expected to undertake more body work than men, whichever of Shilling's types of body work we consider, and to take it more seriously (Adkins, 1995). Advice on clothes and appearance forms an important part of the voluminous self-help literature for women managers seeking to get ahead (see Kenny and Bell, this volume). There are probably four or five television shows advising women about their appearance, such as What Not to Wear, to every one for men. Even then the ways the latter are marketed, such as Queer Eye for the Straight Guy, suggests that expertise in body work is not something at which heterosexual men are required to be very proficient, although this may be changing as normative masculinity becomes more body conscious (Warhurst and Nickson, 2009).

Although the body work discussed above seems to be relatively superficial, even surface appearance work involves stifling or hiding important aspects of embodiment, including, as Tyler and Abbot (1998) suggest, the body's unruly eruptions and seepages. Women's body work is often linked to the need to produce and maintain a bounded, disciplined female body. The mind–body binary is a strongly gendered construction, with the mind identified with men and the body with women (Linstead and Brewis, 2004; Grosz, 1994). Hence a 'natural body' that sags, menstruates, gives birth or lactates is often ruled inappropriate and even threatening in organisational contexts where rationality is privileged (McDowell, 1997; Longhurst, 2001; Trethewey, 1999).

The marginalisation of the unruly, intensely bodily female body may also be related to the fear of what Kristeva (1982), Grosz (1994) and Longhurst (2001) term the 'abject', a kind of formlessness unconsciously feared as subverting the solidity and stability of the social order. This difficult idea is easiest to understand in relation to Kristeva's (1982) psychoanalytical reading of the horror story, in which the abject is precisely the awful thing that seeps, at first unnoticed, into society and undermines it. Although in reality neither men's nor women's bodies are 'sealed up', the abject is symbolised by women's menstruation, childbirth and lactation. In contrast men's 'leakiness' is culturally invisible. Linstead (2000: 32) suggests that whereas men have been represented as clearly defined — dry, solid, firm and contained — wetness, fluidity, and fecundity are projected onto women. Hence in so far as organisation is understood in terms of 'male' characteristics, women organisation members must work doubly hard at exorcising any hint of the abject.

## 'BODY WORK' ON OTHERS' BODIES

We now turn to the body work undertaken on others' bodies. As we shall see, here the body work of dealing with the abject, and the 'leakiness' of human bodies, is even more stigmatised.

Much body work on other people's bodies is undertaken in the home, by parents or other relatives. Although men are increasingly involved in child care, the body work children require still falls mainly to women, as does the physical care of older children and ageing or other adults who have impairments that prevent them from doing the reproductive work people usually prefer to do for themselves. However, as women in the OECD countries join the paid labour force, some of their care work in the home, including body work, is being replaced by crèches, care homes and paid domestic workers. Moreover, people seek paid assistance with what Shilling, above, calls 'cultural body work', from personal trainers or manicurists, for instance. Whether or not this work could be done oneself, professional ministrations are often seen as essential in turning out an 'organisational body' uncontaminated by the stains, symbolic and actual, of maternity, housewifery or even simple ageing. More elaborate 'body projects', such as cosmetic surgery, necessitate the cooperation and input of highly paid practitioners, such as surgeons.

A number of social scientists have begun to theorise the existence of 'body work' as a growing part of the service economy, one that contrasts sharply with the equally expanding remote services such as call centres (Wolkowitz, 2002; Twigg, 2006, 2000; Gimlin, 2002; Kang, 2003; McDowell, 2008; Dyer et al., 2008; van Dongen and Elema, 2001; Lawler, 1991; Twigg, et al. (2011)). In a high-tech world these jobs are notably high touch, and often involve the nudity or vulnerability of the client, patient or customer. Such occupations include doctors, dentists or nurses, as well as those who deliver commercial personal services involving touch, for example hairdressers, tattooists, spa workers, bouncers and sex workers.

As the occupations listed above might suggest, paid body work is highly gendered, comprising a higher proportion of women workers than men. To take just one example, browsing the most common occupations of males and females in five major US cities on city-data.com suggests that 14–19% of their female labour force is employed in the health sector alone, although of course not all of them are involved in patient care, whereas the figures for men are closer to 4–6%. Once one adds the figures for all the other paid body work that women do, not just in spas and salons, but also the paid work that never gets statistically recorded, including many paid home carers, the figures would be much higher. The main exceptions to the feminisation of body work are jobs that are seen to require the physical control of bodily violence (bouncers, prison guards) and/or the piercing of bodies (undertaking, medicine and dentistry), forms of body work that until recently have been monopolised by men. In other words, in body work the gender division of labour seems to coincide with the kind of relation workers have to the bodies they deal with.

Although paid body work could be seen as serving universal needs, it is not always correct to see it as simply substituting for the body work we could do for ourselves. Much of its expansion and elaboration is due rather to the interests of organisations and individuals in finding new investment and employment opportunities. Given the exodus of the primary extractive sector and industrial production to developing countries, it is no wonder that capital looks for new opportunities for local investment. Capitalism is no longer confined to profiting from the body as a source of labour, but has found ways to profit from new body practices such as transplants, assisted reproduction, genomic research, and sex reassignment (Lowe, 1995). Dickinson (2007) and others have characterised applications of reproductive technology as a 'new enclosure' of genetic material and reproductive capacities, such as women's ova and ability to bear children, that were previously quite outside the market. Even everyday health care has become a source of profit. Where it was long provided directly by public organisations, as in Western Europe, it is increasingly treated like other economic services (McDonald and Ruiters, 2006; Greer, 2008; Player and Lees, 2008). The effect is to make body work integral to capitalist expansion.

The growth in low-tech forms of body work – healthcare support and personal care occupations are among the fastest growing occupations (BLS, 2009) – also makes them an avenue for investment. Although much of the care of the infirm elderly is funded by the state, either directly, through national health services or local authorities, or indirectly, through health and social care programmes for the aged or indigent, such as Medicare or Medicare in the US, the actual provision of care is now a highly profitable business activity (Diamond, 1992; Howes, 2004). We are also seeing the growth of chains and franchises in the gym, hairdressers and spa sectors (Mintel Oxygen, 2007).

## Organisational contexts

Considering body work as a major feature of the contemporary economy suggests the need to examine the involvement of organisations in managing bodies. Paid body work is usually governed by considerations of efficiency and cost to a much greater extent than the work people do on themselves or, on an unpaid basis, for their relatives. There are many repercussions for workers, as well as for the recipients of body work services.

The human body is difficult to treat in a standardised way. For instance, bodies may react very differently to the same injury, ailment or treatment, and emergency situations arise which require immediate coordination among practitioners. In fact, the technical literature on the application of computer technologies in medicine suggests that software programmes designed for hospitals need to be able to deal with more complexity than those for the military or airport control systems (Nemeth et al., 2005). Furthermore, as Cohen (2011) suggests, not only is body work labour-intensive, rationalising provision has to take its distinctive temporalities into account. Consequently there are many ways in which organisations attempt to deal with or override the variability of bodies by rationalising and standardising health and social care, through for instance treatment protocols or nursing classificatory schema that attempt to identify and list all nursing tasks (Waldby, 2000). Organisations specify their employees' work routines, but in the process may also subordinate the bodies of the recipients of body work services to organisational priorities, for instance through queuing systems.

A good example of the ways in which the economics and organisation of body work affects its content and performance is care work for the aged. Research on work in residential care institutions may tell us a lot about the rationalisation of bodily care and its relation to how the recipients are conceptualised. The reduction of residents to bodies, and then of bodies to work objects (Diamond, 1992), is readily seen in references to 'bed and body work' (Gubrium, 1975), with workers allocated to 'Beds 201 to 21'(Diamond, 1992: 210), for instance, or the organisation of work around the production of 'lounge-standard bodies' (Lee-Trewick, 1997) by the time visitors arrive.

Bureaucratic rules are particularly relevant to the construction of the bodies of care recipients as tractable, predictable bodies. These are set by the state to prevent abuse and idiosyncratic care, but when each and every care task must be charted, this may also make responding to individuals as individuals difficult. The entry of market mechanisms into care can also have the effect of so reducing staffing levels that cutting corners becomes the norm (Lopez, 2007). Diamond (1992) argues that when care becomes a business this necessarily makes 'nursing home care into a commodity and the residents into manageable units' (204). He suggests that this is because calculation of the 'bottom line' is possible only when 'everyday needs and tending to them' are 'turned into a countable, accountable logic' (p. 209).

The rationalization of care is also increasingly typical of domiciliary (home-based) care, where the standardisation of the timing and worker skill needs is necessary for planning. This is intensified with privatisation (England and Ward, 2007), which is a growing trend. For instance, in the UK the proportion of domiciliary care provided by the independent sector increased from 2% to 70% between 1992 and 2009, and is now worth some £1.5 billion, and some firms are now responsible for up to 15,000 care recipients (BBC, 2009). Care which is organised on such a large scale almost inevitably results in the close specification of care tasks and their conversion, through organisational planning, to paper or 'textual' categories. Campbell's (2008) discussion of a Canadian ethnography of domiciliary care suggests that even when organisations are required to consider 'continuity of care' a priority, standardised timings ignore the diverse circumstances in which care tasks, for instance sponge baths, will need to be done. Campbell's informants, like the managers and care workers in Diamond's (1992) study of residential care, participate in a complex, scarcely articulated double bind in which they know that successful completion of these tasks depends on the local environment, including the patient's specific needs and abilities, but continue to pretend that the rules and prescribed timings represent an adequate approach to work on embodied human beings.

There are relatively few opportunities for the clients, patients and customers who are the recipients of care to exercise power in their relationships with workers, partly because many are already impaired or living in a total institution, but also because the immediate and tangible processes of treatment tend to immobilise the body or render it dependent. Hence one is likely to find that expressions of resistance either burst out in unpredictable ways (racial and other forms of abuse that patients inflict on workers) or they take place outside the immediate encounter, for instance in the organisation of self-help groups or users' support networks. However, the patient satisfaction surveys which require patients to quantify their expectations, satisfactions and dissatisfactions cannot necessarily be seen as a form of patient empowerment, since they are designed mainly to meet organisationally defined objectives (Rankin, 2003).

The positioning of the body as a result of (and through) organisational mechanisms also takes place, at the micro-level, in the physical management of bodies. The strongest demonstration of the conversion of the body into a 'work object' comes from various developments in studying the embodied practices of health professionals (Xiao, 2005). For instance, ethnographies of hospital operating rooms (ORs) show how the patient's body is 'enrolled' in a network of actors so as to enable practitioners to work on it (Hirschauer, 1991; Moreira, 2004). The positioning of the patient starts before entry to the OR, for the patient is already converted into a passive 'patient-body' through pre-operative procedures in admissions and on the ward (Moreira, 2004:116). Once in the OR the objectification of the surgical patient intensifies when the patient is unconscious (Hindmarsh and Pilnick, 2007), as from this point the OR practitioner relates not to the same patient-body but only to the systems for which he or she is responsible (Moreira, 2004).

Of course the objectification of the patient in surgery is an extreme case, but arguably there are more general differences between health and reproductive care and other body work services. Where customers are better able to demand a measure of control (or at least the fiction of consumer sovereignty), as in the beauty industry or complementary therapy, services are much more likely to be undertaken by self-employed workers or in small salons or franchises (Cohen, 2011; Mintel Oxygen, 2007). Here workers are freer, at the cost of their own working hours and per hour earnings, to adopt a more flexible approach to customers' wishes. In fact, as George (2008: 121) notes, workers in the personal services sector, who do not command the 'signifiers of status' enjoyed by doctors or matrons, struggle to set limits on clients' sense of entitlement.

## The abject body

Although there are many ways in which organisations render tractable the bodies with which they deal, arguably the distinctive aspects of bodies as the site of labour mean that there is always something 'left over' and 'left out'. The abject characteristics of the leaky body feed back into the organisation and are not entirely within its control.

To fully understand the distinctive implications of work taking the body as a focus we need to consider wider attitudes. For instance, it can be argued that the status of some occupational hierarchies (including those embedded in large-scale organisations such as the National Health Service in Britain) hinge at least partly on the status of the bodies or body parts with which they deal. Littlewood (1991: 171) argues that in health care 'social position appears linked to bodily function'. For instance, doctors dealing with the head or the heart have a higher status than those working in gastroenterology or urino-genital medicine. Nursing is characterised by similar status distinctions, for instance between nurses who are responsible for the cleaner tasks, and lower status assistants who deal with the dirtier, polluting physical needs of the patient (Twigg, 2006; Jervis, 2001).

Reproductive care workers seem less able to perpetuate the fantasy of consumer privilege than those providing aesthetic services (Korczynski, 2008). This is in part due to the amount of 'body work' it involves. Control of one's own bodily functions, in our society, is a linchpin of personal sovereignty, and without it social respect declines. The imagined character of the body also plays a role in the gendering of care work. Drawing on constructions of the abject body noted above, Widding Isaksen (2002) argues that women's much greater involvement in bodily care for the aged rests on normative associations between genders, bodies, spatial regulations – and dirt. Old age in particular is perceived as dirty, representing a 'piling up of undischarged remnants of a lifetime of eating and drinking . . .', with the ageing body perceived as 'open, unlimited and unattractive' (Widding Isaksen, 2005: 116). Because 'masculine dignity' is much more dependent on fantasies of the body as closed and bounded, she argues, men find care work psychically challenging and fearful in a way women do not. Men's and women's differential relation to the care of the 'leaky' body means that women are massively overrepresented in both paid and unpaid care work, with repercussions for the gendered segmentation of the labour market as a whole.

Although Widding Isaksen gives it little attention, such work is also highly racialised, marking the bodies of those who undertake the work as well as stigmatising the dependence of those who are cared for (Twigg, 2006). The Cartesian division of responsibilities between brain and body was central to Victorian society's understanding of the classed body. It gave working-class women responsibility for the 'nether regions' of the body, allowing the middle-class lady to maintain the purity so essential to her role as society's heart (Nakano Glenn, 2001). Nowadays responsibility for caring for the body, including both children and the elderly, is highly dependent on racialised and/or migrant labour to do the 'dirty work', whether in residential institutions or private homes, such as the nannies and cleaners whose employment enables middle-class men and women to evade the stigma of dirty work themselves. Anderson (2000: 142) argues that 'hatred of the body . . . and hatred of racialised groups . . . is played out in the use of racialised female labour to do the work of servicing the body. . .'.

While other personal services are less strongly racialised, the growth in aestheticising services coincides with the growth in small business development by migrants, and one result has been the strong association between particular kinds of body work and particular racialised groups, such as between nail salon work and East Asian migrants, especially Koreans and Vietnamese women (Kang, 2003). One consequence of the racialisation of personal care and cleaning is that middle-class women may find it easier to maintain and inhabit the professional bodies required inside organisations, untainted by the connotations of the 'maternal body' (Longhurst, 2001) or the 'dirty work' of domestic life. Ehrenreich, for instance, suggests that, for the middle-class consumers of paid domestic services, to 'be cleaned up after' is to achieve 'a certain magical weightlessness and immateriality' (2003: 102).

Body work can also generate powerful feelings amongst whomever is responsible for it. Some workers apparently feel tainted by the body fluids their work involves, with care workers telling Jervis (2001) that they feel contaminated by the body fluids they have to deal with. One reported riding home on the bus worrying that she 'smelled like piss' and others undertake purificatory rituals when they got home, not unlike some sex workers (Brewis and Linstead, 2000). Twigg's (2006) study of the body work of care found that women care workers were rendered uncomfortable by the nakedness of the ageing body, and their negative attitudes were often internalised by the ageing people they looked after. Explicit mention of intimate touch was avoided, in favour of the 'social touch', such as pats on the back, that are easier to talk about. Twigg argues that the historical role of social workers in the organisation of care services has meant that what is construed as the social contact between care workers and their clients is much more visible in research than is physical intimacy.

This is not to say that people employed in body work occupations that involve 'dirty work' (Ashforth and Kreiner, 1999) do not generate mechanisms for resisting disparagement, and sometimes these are integrated into the work culture. For instance, occupational cultures may involve compensatory claims to the moral high ground, as Hughes (1984) long ago pointed out in the case of nurses, but ground level tactics are also important. Lawler (1991) and Twigg (2006) point out that the curtain drawn round a hospital patient's bed when care tasks are undertaken protects not only the privacy of the patient, but also the dignity of the carer, by hiding her involvement. Sometimes the identities developed to rationalise involvement in the 'dirty work' that care necessitates are strongly organisation-specific. For instance, Solari (2006), in a study of migrants employed as care workers in California, found that the Russian Orthodox migrants working with a Russian-speaking agency were socialised into a 'saintly' caring identity, whereas the agency helping to settle Jewish migrant workers expected them to adopt a 'professional' relation to their work.

## CONCLUSIONS

What are the bodily parameters of organisation? Besides experiencing the physical strains of the workplace and sometimes the physical symptoms of stress (Wainwright and Calnan, 2002), most people need to take account of organisational demands, whether implicit or explicit, when undertaking the body work on themselves that is necessary to sustain life and a successful workplace identity. In addition, I have tried to show why students of organisation need to be concerned not only with the bodies of people employed by organisations, but also with the other bodies around which organisations revolve, bodies that are the recipients of various kind of servicing. 'Rejected bodies' – those excluded by organisations because they are considered too young, old, sick, unruly, or unattractive to employ (Wendell, 1996) – are absorbed into the organisational nexus as the sites or objects of work. Bodies are brought inside the purview of organisational objectives, and textualised, standardised and rendered tractable, legible, and predictable, so that they can be processed in efficient, and if possible, profitable ways. However, such bodies can remain tainted. Responsibility for the care of bodies and body fluids that are constructed as uncontained or uncontainable is often allocated to workers perceived as lower status, those who, because of gender and/or racialisation, themselves stand at the margins of organisation. Thus organisation takes hold of abject bodies but also keeps them at a distance.

Looking at body work on others also suggests that organisational studies needs to give more recognition to the tangibility of the provision of many services, which are often assumed to have an immaterial character (Herzenberg et al., 1998). As Korczynski (2008) points out, in contrast to the usual re-enchantment of service work that firms seek to convey to customers, 'body work inserts an immediate materiality into the service-recipient relation' and this materiality may make the fiction of consumer sovereignty difficult to sustain. Maintaining the fiction of consumers' sense of control over their interactions as customers is much easier to sustain in some kinds of body work, such as that directed at cosmetic changes, than where the consumer is a patient in ill-health or lacking control of their own bodily functions. As I have argued elsewhere (Wolkowitz, 2006; Twigg, et al. (2011)), however, we cannot generalise too much about the nature of the social relations of body work, because interactions are usually negotiated to some degree, even when they are routinised. Organisations may insist on specifying the interaction between workers' and consumers' bodies, but as embodied, wilful subjects their relative status, how their bodies are positioned, whether the consumer is conscious or unconscious, confined or mobile, clothed or naked, and much else, all affect the micropolitics of the interaction.

## REFERENCES

Acker, J. (1990) Hierarchies. Jobs, Bodies: Theory of Gendered Organisation, *Gender and Society*, 4(2) 139–580.

Adkins, L. (1995) *Gendered Work, Sexuality, Family and the Labour Market*. Buckingham: Open University Press.

Anderson, B. (2000) *Doing the Dirty Work: The Global Politics of Domestic Labour*. London: Zed Books.

Ashforth, B.E., and Kreiner, G.E. (1999) 'How Can you Do it?' Dirty Work and the Challenge of Constructing a Positive Identity, *Academy of Management Review*, 24(3) 413–434.

BBC (2009) Britain's Homecare Scandal. Accessed on 10 April 2009 at http://news.bbc.co.uk/panorama/hi/front_page/newsid_7990000/7990682.stm

Bahnisch, M. (2000) Embodied Work, Divided Labour, *Body & Society*, 6(1) 51–68.

Braverman, H. (1974) *Labor and Monopoly Capital.* NewYork: Monthly Review Press.

Brewis, J., and Linstead, S. (2000) *Sex, Work and Sex Work.* London: Routledge.

Bureau of Labor Statistics (BLS) (2009) *Occupational Outlook Handbook 2008–18.* Accessed on 28 November 2010 from http://www.bls.gov/oco/oco2003.htm

Campbell, M. (2008) '(Dis)continuity of Care' in M. DeVault (ed.), *People at Work.* New York: New York University Press.

Cohen, R.L. (2011) Time, Space and Touch at Work, *Sociology of Health and Illness*, 33(7), forthcoming.

Crossley, N. (2007) 'Researching Embodiment by Way of "Body Techniques"' in C. Shilling (ed.), *Embodying Sociology.* Oxford: Blackwell/Sociological Review.

Dale, K. (2005) Building a Social Materiality: Spatial and Embodied Politics in Organisational Control, *Organization*, 12(5) 649–678.

Diamond, T. (1992) *Making Gray Gold: Narratives of Nursing Home Care.* Chicago: University of Chicago Press.

Dickenson, D. (2007) *Property in the Body.* New York: Cambridge University Press.

Dyer, S., McDowell, L., and Batnitzky, A. (2008) Embodied Labour/ Body Work: The Caring Labours of Migrants in the UK's National Health Service, *Geoforum*, 39(6) 2030–2038.

Ehrenreich, B. (2003) 'Maid to Order' in B. Ehrenreich and A. Hochschild (eds), *Global Woman.* London: Granta.

England, K., and Ward, K. (2007) *Neoliberalization: States, Networks, Peoples.* Malden, MA: Blackwell

Erikson, K. (2004) Bodies at Work: Performing Service in the American Restaurant, Space and Culture, 7, 76–89.

Foucault, M. (1991) *Discipline and Punish.* London: Penguin.

Gatta, M. (2009) 'Balancing Trays and Smiles' in S.C. Bolton and M. Houlihan (eds), *Work Matters.* Basingstoke: Palgrave.

George, Molly (2008) Interactions in Expert Service Work: Demonstrating Professionalism in Personal Training, *Journal of Contemporary Ethnography*, 37(1) 108–131.

Giddens, A. (1991) *Modernity and Self-Identity.* Cambridge: Polity.

Gimlin, D. (2002) *Body Work: Beauty and Self-Identity in American Culture.* Berkeley, CA: University of California Press.

Gimlin, D. (2007) What is Body Work? A Review of the Literature, *Sociology Compass*, 1(1) 353–370.

Goodwin, C. (2001) 'Practices of Seeing/ Visual Analysis: An Ethnomethodological Account' in T. Van Leeuwen and C. Jeewitt (eds), *Handbook of Visual Analysis.* London: Sage.

Greer, S. (2008) Choosing Paths in European Union Health Services Policy, *Journal of European Social Policy*, 18(3) 219–231.

Grosz, E. (1994) *Volatile Bodies: Toward a Corporeal Feminism.* Bloomington, IN: Indiana University Press.

Gubrium. J.F. (1975) *Living and Dying at Murray Manor.* New York: St Martin's Press.

Hancock, P., and Tyler, M. (2000) 'Working Bodies' in P. Hancock et al., *The Body, Culture and Society.* Buckingham: Open University Press.

Hassard, J., Holliday, R., and Willmott, H. (eds) (2000) *Body and Organisation.* London: Sage.

Herzenberg, S., Lic, J., and Wail, H. (1998) *New Rules for a New Economy.* Ithica: ILR Press.

Hindmarsh, J., and Pilnick, A. (2007) Knowing Bodies at Work, *Organization Studies*, 28(9) 1395–1416.

Hirschauer, S. (1991) The Manufacture of Bodies in Surgery, *Social Studies of Science*, 21 279–319.

Holliday, R., and Hassard, J. (eds) (2001) *Contested Bodies*. London: Routledge

Hockey, J., and Allen-Collinson, J. (2009) The Sensorium at Work: the Sensory Phenomenology of the Working Body, *Sociological Review*, 17(2) 217–239.

Howes, C. (2004) 'Upgrading California's Home Care Workforce' in *The State of California Labor 2004*. XX: University of California Press, 71–105.

Hughes, E.C. (1984) *The Sociological Eye*. New Brunswick, NJ: Transaction Books.

Jervis, L.L. (2001) The Pollution of Incontinence and the Dirty Work of Caregiving, *Medical Anthropology Quarterly*, 15(1) 64–99.

Kang, M. (2003) The Managed Hand, *Gender and Society*, 17(6) 820–839.

Korczynski, M. (2008) 'A Touching Story: The Body and the Enchanting Myth of Customer Sovereignty' ESRC Seminar Series on Body Work, University of Kent, July. Available at http://www2.warwick.ac.uk/fac/soc/sociology/rsw/current/body_work/seminars/3/seminar_3_-_korczynski.ppt#1.

Kristeva, J. (1982) *The Powers of Horror: An Essay in Abjection*. New York: Columbia University Press

Lan, P.-C. (2001) 'The Body as a Contested Terrain for Labor Control: Cosmetics Retaillers in Department Stores and Direct Selling' in R. Baldoz, C. Koeber, and P. Kraft (eds), *The Critical Study of Work*. Philadelphia: Temple University Press.

Lawler, J. (1991) *Behind the Screens*. Melbourne: Churchill Livingstone.

Leder, D. (1990) *The Absent Body*. Chicago: Chicago University Press.

Lee-Trewick, G. (1997) Women, Resistance and Care,. *Work, Employment and Society*, 11(1) 47–64.

Leslie, D. (2002) Gender, Retail Employment and the Clothing Commodity Chain, *Gender, Place and Culture*, 9(1) 61–76.

Linstead, A., and Brewis, J. (eds) (2004) Special Issue: Beyond Boundaries, *Gender, Work and Organization*, 11(4).

Linstead, S. (2000) 'Dangerous Fluids and the Organisation-without-Organs' in Hassard et al.

Littlewood, Jenny (1991) 'Care and Ambiguity: Toward a Concept of Nursing' in P. Holden and J. Littlewood (eds), *Anthropology and Nursing*. London: Routledge.

Longhurst, R. (2001) *Bodies: Exploring Fluid Boundaries*. London: Routledge.

Lopez, S. H. (2007) Efficiency and 'the Fix' Revisited: Informal Relations and Mock Routinization in a Nonprofit Nursing Home, *Qualitative Sociology*, 30, 225–247.

Lowe, D. (1995) *The Body in Late-Capitalist US*. Durham, NC: Duke University Press,

McDonald, D., and Ruiters, G. (2006) Rethinking Privatisation, *Public Services Yearbook 2005/2006*. Amsterdam: Transnational Institute http://www.queensu.ca/msp/pages/Project_Publications/Chapters/rethinking.pdf.

McDowell, L. (1997) *Capital Culture*. Oxford: Blackwell.

McDowell, L. (2008) The New Economy, Class Condescension and Caring Labour, *NORA*, 16(3) 150–165.

Mintel Oxygen (2007) Health and Beauty Treatments, February http://academic.mintel.com/sinatra/oxygen_academic/search_results/show&/display/id+219239/display/id+262747 accessed 21/04/09.

Monaghan, L. (2002) Hard Men, Shop Boys and Others, *Sociological Review*, 50(3) 334–355.

Moreira, T. (2004) Coordination and Embodiment in the Operating Room, *Body & Society*, 10(1) 109–129.

Morgan, D., Brandth, B., and Kvande, E. (eds) (2005) *Gender, Bodies, Work*. Avebury: Ashgate.

Nakano Glenn, E. (2001) 'The Race and Gender Division of Public Reproductive Labor' in R. Baldoz, C. Koeber, and P. Kraft (eds), *The Critical Study of Work*. Philadelphia: Temple University Press.

Nemeth, C., Nunnally, M., O'Connor, M., Klock, P.A., and Cook, R. (2005) Getting to the Point: Developing IT for the Sharp End of Health Care, *Journal of Biomedical Informatics*,. 38(1) 18–25.

Pettinger, L. (2004) Brand Culture and Branded Workers, *Consumption, Markets and Culture*, 7(2) 165–184.

Player, S., and Leys, C. (2008) 'Commodifying Health' in U. Huws and C. Hermann (eds), *The New Gold Rush*. London: Analytica Publications.

Puwar, N. (2001) The Racialised Somatic Norm and the Senior Civil Service, *Sociology*, 35(3) 651–670.

Rankin, J. (2003) Patient Satisfaction: Knowledge for Ruling Hospital Reform, *Nursing Inquiry*, 10(1) 57–65.

Sennett, R. (2008) *The Craftsman*. New York: Yale University.

Shilling, C. (2005) *The Body in Culture, Technology and Society*. London: Sage

Solari, C. (2006) Professionals and Saints: How Immigrant Careworkers Negotiate Gender Identities at Work, *Gender and Society*, 20(3) 301–331.

Styhre, A. (2004) The Re (embodied) Organisation: Four Perspectives on the Body in Organisations, *Human Resources Development International*, 7(1) 101–116.

Thompson, E.P. (1967) Time, Work Discipline and Industrial Capitalism, *Past and Present*, 38 56–97.

Thrift, N. (2005) *Knowing Capitalism*. London: Sage.

Trethewey, A. (1999) Disciplined Bodies: Women's Embodied Identities at Work, *Organisation Studies*, 20(3) 423–450.

Twigg, J. (2000) Carework as a Form of Bodywork, *Ageing and Society*, 20(4) 389–341.

Twigg, J. (2006) *The Body in Health and Social Care*. Basingstoke: Palgrave Macmillan.

Twigg, J., Wolkowitz, C., Cohen, R.L., and Nettleton, S. (eds) (2011) Special Issue on 'Body Work in Health and Social Care', *Sociology of Health and Illness*, 33(7), forthcoming February.

Tyler, M., and Abbott, P. (1998) 'Chocs Away': Weightwatching in the Contemporary Airline Industry, *Sociology*, 32(3) 433–450.

Van Dongen, E., and Elema, R. (2001) The Art of Touching: The Culture of 'Body Work', *Anthropology and Medicine*, 8(2/3) 149–210.

Wainwright, D., and Calnan, M. (2002) *Work Stress*. Buckingham: Open University Press.

Waldby, C (2000) Fragmented Bodies, Incoherent Medicine, *Social Studies of Science*, 30(3) 465–475.

Warhurst, C., and Nickson, D. (2009) 'Who's Got the Look?' Emotional, Aesthetic and Sexualized Labour in Interactive Services, *Gender, Work and Organization*, 16(3) 385–404.

Wendell, Susan (1996) *The Rejected Body: Feminist Philosophical Reflections on Disability*. New York: Routledge.

Widding, Isaksen, L. (2002) Masculine Dignity and the Dirty Body, *NORA*, 16(3) 137–146.

Widding Isaksen, L. (2005) 'Gender and Care: The Role of Cultural Ideas of Dirt and Disgust' in Morgan et al AL.

Wolkowitz, C.(2002) The Social Relations of Body Work, *Work, Employment and Society*, 16 (3) 497–510.

Wolkowitz, C (2006) *Bodies at Work*. London: Sage

Xiao, Yan (2005) 'Artifacts and Collaborative Work in Healthcare,' *Journal of Biomedical Informatics*, 38 (1): 26–33.

Yanarella, E., and Reid, H. (1996) 'From "Trained Gorilla"' to '"Humanware"' in T. Schatzski and W. Natter (eds), *The Social and Political Body*. London: Guildford Press.

# 12

# Embodying Transgender in Studies of Gender, Work, and Organization

TORKILD THANEM
*Stockholm University School of Business*

Some years ago I was in a meeting with a group of senior business school colleagues planning learning activities for the coming term's seminars of an undergraduate course. One of the learning activities involved students doing a role play of a television panel discussion to engage with the issue of corporate social responsibility. While there were few restrictions governing the format of the role play, the professor in charge of the course asserted: 'But I don't want them to get carried away and turn this into a drag show!' While I don't think he meant this in a derogatory manner, it was made obvious that the world of drag was utterly separate from the world of business, work, and organizations. And nor did I dare, back then, to question his reasoning or to mention my own cross-dressing.

## INTRODUCTION

During the past couple of decades gender has become an established field in the study of work and organization. While research in this field tends to focus on the social aspects of gender in work organizations, recent studies have directed attention at the bodily aspects of gender. Informed by poststructuralist (e.g. Foucault, 1977; 1979) and feminist theory (e.g. Butler, 1990; 1993) in particular, research in this area has tended to focus on the gendered body as an object of discursive construction and disciplinary control in work organizations. For instance, studies of aesthetic labour have problematized how organizations relate the work performance of (primarily female) service employees to an ability to smile, keep eye-contact, and maintain a certain body-shape (Hancock and Tyler, 2000). Similarly, studies of workplace culture have shown how the (primarily male) manager body is expected to work hard and play hard despite few hours of sleep (Holliday and Thompson, 2001). Much less attention has been directed at transgender embodiment, which cuts across the conventional distinction between female and male, femininity and masculinity. While transgender has attracted increasing interest amongst gender scholars in the wider social sciences and humanities, less than a handful of publications have studied transgender in settings of work and organization.

Departing from a critical review of transgender research in the social sciences, the humanities, and in studies of work and organization, this chapter therefore discusses how transgender may be embodied in studies of gender, work, and organization. Part of this involves reflecting about my own transgender embodiment, and I argue that an embodied perspective is necessary to understand (i) how transgender is expressed through bodily practices as well as through social practices, and (ii) how transgender people are subject to problems and opportunities in settings of work and organization. Not only do transgender people suffer discrimination and marginalization at work and in organizations because of our bodies. Our transgender bodies are also sites of work, organization, and consumption. Let me therefore begin by elaborating the significance of transgender embodiment in settings of work and organization.

## TRANSGENDER, WORK, AND ORGANIZATION

Despite a lack of robust statistics, the American Psychological Association (APA, 2009) argues that in Western countries '[a]s many as 2–3% of biological males engage in cross-dressing' and that 1 in 10 000 biological males and 1 in 30 000 biological females are transsexual. In contrast, transgender activists and scholars argue that APA systematically underestimates the prevalence of transgender people, estimating instead that 1% of people in Western countries are transgender, that 5% of biological males engage in cross-dressing, and that 1 in 500 biological males are transsexual (see e.g. Conway, 2002; Olyslager and Conway, 2007). From this it would follow that at least 1 in 3000 biological females are transsexual.

Whereas popular discourse often confuses various forms of transgender, the term was introduced by community activists in the early 1980s as an umbrella term to include all individuals who embody and express a gender identity which diverges from the binary distinction that contemporary Western societies tend to make between female and male. A transgender person is therefore someone whose gender identity does not correspond to the sexual identity that she or he is assigned at birth. As transgendering involves female-to-male (FTM) and male-to-female (MTF) transitioning as well as non-identification with a particular gender or sex, it includes transvestites, transsexuals, drag kings, drag queens, intersexuals, third genderists, genderqueers, and agenderists.

Transgender people enjoy different statuses in different societies. Despite having a sacred 'third sex' status in certain premodern cultures, as the 'two-spirit' people in Native American culture (Herdt, 1993; see also Linstead and Pullen, 2006), the predominance of the two-sex model (Laqueur, 1990) means that transgender people are often subjected to stigmatization and marginalization in contemporary Western societies. Although the tolerance for and status of transgender people may have increased in recent years (as a case in point, thirteen US states have recently made it illegal for employers to deny someone work based on their gender identity), tolerance itself is a typical liberal principle that may avoid open discrimination but still leave people unwelcome.

Moreover, transgender people are still subject to hate crimes, violence, harassment, and labour market discrimination. In a survey of the San Francisco transgender population, all participants reported some type of abuse and discrimination because of their gender identity or embodied gender presentation, including verbal abuse (FTMs 85%, MTFs 83%), employment discrimination (FTMs 57%, MTFs 46%), problems obtaining health care (FTMs 39%, MTFs 13%), physical abuse (FTMs 30%, MTFs 37%), and housing discrimination (FTMs 20%, MTFs 27%) (San Francisco Department of Public Health, 1999). A more recent survey of transgender people in San Francisco reported that 'nearly 40% of respondents believe that they have been discriminated against when applying for work', that 'over 24% of people reported that they had been sexually harassed at work', 'nearly 19% of respondents have experienced trouble in advancing in their company or department', that 18% of respondents have been fired from a job due to gender identity discrimination, and that 59% of respondents are living in poverty (Transgender Law Center, 2006: 3–5). And a survey of UK transsexuals reported that 33% of respondents were forced to leave work by their employer during or after transition (Whittle, 2002).

Transgender people with successful careers in mainstream organizations therefore often conceal their transgender identity at work, and people who do not conceal it tend to have problems finding work, keeping work, or being promoted at work. In many countries, persistent transphobia, that is, discrimination and abuse against transgender people, forces transgender people into prostitution, crime, and illegitimate forms of work to support themselves. Unconfirmed estimates suggest that 80% of all transgender people in the US have been incarcerated at least once during their lifetime. Paraphrasing C. Wright Mills (1959), it may therefore be argued that the stigmatization and marginalization of transgender people causes personal troubles for transgender individuals that constitute social problems for communities, organizations and societies.

*Perhaps I've been particularly fortunate in this respect. I've received more complimentary than abusive remarks when going out dressed up, and I've never been physically abused when dressed up. Still, even though I don't try to hide my transvestism at work (I've got long blond hair, I wear pearls even when in male drag, and many of my colleagues know I'm an MTF transvestite), I've never been dressed up at work, mostly out of worry for how my colleagues and students might react.*

At the same time, transgender creates opportunities for work and organizations. Thousands of people pursue part-time or full-time careers as drag queens or drag kings by harnessing their transgender identity and embodiment. RuPaul, for instance, departed from the scene of night club drag shows in the 1990s to become a recording artist, appear in motion pictures, be the cover girl for MAC Cosmetics, and host his own television show. And in addition to the numerous transgender support groups and community organizations that exist across the world, thousands of businesses and organizations explicitly cater for transgender clients and customers by offering products and services that are mobilized in the construction and expression of transgender embodiment: internet vendors selling wigs, fake beards, and high-heeled shoes in tall sizes, dressing services for MTF transvestites, and medical clinics providing sexual reassignment therapy and surgery. Similarly, I don't think I would have written this chapter had I not been transgender.

As the making of gender, transgender, and embodiment is crucial to transgender people and to the transgender industry, this is also a dominant issue in transgender research. Typically working from a constructionist approach, this research tends to investigate how transgender people make – and construct – female and male gender through social, cultural, linguistic, and discursive practices. Harold Garfinkel's (1967) ethnomethodological work in sociology on passing and Judith Butler's poststructuralist work in cultural studies on performativity are central in this context.

## Transgender in Social Science and Humanities Research

### *Passing*

Garfinkel's (1967) ethnomethodological study of the intersexual woman Agnes pioneered social science inquiry into transgender. According to Garfinkel Western societies tend to assume that one's sex and gender is either male or female, that one's gender corresponds to one's sex, and that this is a biological and social fact that does not change over the course of a person's life. The case of Agnes problematizes this assumption. Agnes was born with male genitalia, developed breasts at the age of twelve, but was raised as a boy until the age of seventeen. At seventeen she decided to live full time as a woman and to seek sexual reassignment surgery. According to Garfinkel, this required Agnes to engage in 'sexual passing', that is, to achieve and secure her right to live as a member of the chosen sex while risking disclosure and ruin. For Agnes, sexual passing was a means rather than an end in itself, and achieving a feminine identity was more important than 'ordinary goals' of getting an education, getting a job, developing an occupational career, and making and maintaining social, emotional, and romantic relationships.

Arguing that Agnes looked, behaved, and talked in a 'ladylike' manner, with the skills, feelings, motives, and aspirations of a 'natural, normal' [sic] woman, Garfinkel focuses on the social and linguistic aspects of passing, that is, how Agnes mobilized tactics, strategies, and practices of speech and conduct to avoid disclosure of her secret that she was born a male, with male genitalia, and raised as a male. For instance, Agnes would avoid social relationships, particularly any association with gay men and transvestites. She would not talk about her childhood or about the bodily practices she mobilized to pass. She also would avoid people who could reveal her secret, preferring to spend time only with those lacking such knowledge. In general, she would plan ahead and picture a number of scenarios to remain inconspicuous, not draw attention and minimize risk of disclosure and ruin. In order to do so successfully she developed a practice of 'rehearsed carelessness' – carefully rehearsing her speech and conduct but without giving the impression that it was carefully rehearsed.

For Garfinkel, Agnes' passing partly involves the playing of a game, with rules that require the optimizing of instrumental rationality to be played successfully. But unlike Goffman's (1959) notion of impression management, passing is not wholly rationally calculative but precarious, and the stable routines of passing are accomplished by improvization. Agnes did not already know what was expected of her to pass in any and every situation. She did not, for instance, always know what answers to give in the interviews with Garfinkel prior to her sexual reassignment surgery, fearing that giving a 'wrong' answer would lead the doctors to remove her breasts instead of her penis.

Garfinkel, then, goes some way in actualizing the connection between bodily and social practices in the construction of gender. But even though Garfinkel describes Agnes' everyday bodily problems and the bodily techniques she mobilizes to deal with them, his focus on the linguistic and social practices of passing has made the case more significant in highlighting how gender is socially constructed and understanding how social order is achieved through everyday routines. As ethnomethodology is primarily concerned with how social order is produced through stable everyday routines he turns Agnes into an ideal case that marginalizes the real problems she experiences as a transgender person (Schilt and Connell, 2007). This problem is to some extent mitigated in more recent research on passing. Combining a grounded theory approach with social interactionism, Ekins (1997) investigates how MTF transvestites accomplish passing in a way which more clearly highlights how transvestites are embedded in empirical social worlds. And rather than viewing passing as a mere adjustment to the binary sexual order, he argues that transgender people may both reproduce and change the social organization of sex and gender.

## Performativity

More than two decades after Garfinkel's case study of Agnes, through a study of MTF drag performers, Butler (1990) introduces the notion of gender construction as performativity rather than passing. Butler uses the example of poor black and Latina US drag queens from the documentary film *Paris Is Burning*. For Butler, drag highlights that gender is not naturally and unequivocally given, but linguistically, discursively, and socially constructed through the 'ritualized repetition of norms' (1993: x) and continuous performance of discrete everyday practices of speech and conduct that make gender seem natural within a binary heterosexual matrix. Like Garfinkel's notion of passing, performativity involves a series of consistent mannerisms, postures, and intonations as well as the use of clothing, hairstyles, and make-up. However, Butler makes no reference to Garfinkel, and unlike Agnes who sought to conceal her intersexuality, most of the drag queens in *Paris Is Burning* perform a more excessive form of femininity which is meant to attract rather than avoid attention.

This does not mean that Butler assumes that one can choose and change one's gender from one day to the next. Rather, bodies are formed, constituted, and inscribed with sex and gender by processes that put normative constraints on what bodies should and should not do. Drawing on Althusser's (1971) notion of interpellation and hailing,

Butler argues that an individual's performance as male or female is seen as successful insofar as one is recognized – and hailed – by other people as male or female. This is actualized in *Paris Is Burning*, as one of the main participants, Venus Extravaganza, who unlike most of the drag queens in the film lives full time as a woman and supports herself through prostitution, is murdered by one of her clients when he finds out that she has male genitalia.

To Butler, the murder illustrates her theoretical point that performativity does not mean that material experiences such as pain, pleasure, illness, violence, life, and death are mere constructions, but that construction is what enables us to make sense of and live these experiences. As certain constructions make some bodies intelligible and liveable, they make other bodies unthinkable, abject, and unliveable. This does not, however, imply a dualism between liveable and unliveable bodies, between our lived experiences and experiences that we have not had. Since dualism is itself part of intelligibility, Butler instead argues that unliveable bodies are part of 'the excluded and illegible domain that haunts the former domain as the spectre of its own impossibility' (1993: xi) – and threatens the possibility of (a stable) identity. The challenge for Butler, then, is to rethink the domain of intelligibility in such a way that unthinkable and unliveable bodies are made thinkable and liveable. But consequently, bodies are effects of discourse, even in terms of the materiality that they live. And in order to rethink the domain of intelligibility, she argues that feminist inquiry should take bodily materiality as its research object.

This ironically leads Butler to privilege discourse and marginalize bodily materiality in general and the bodily materiality of transgender people in particular. Butler does not interpret the murder as a hate crime against a transgender person, but 'elides Extravaganza's transsexual status' and views it as an example of men's violence against women of colour (Namaste, 1996: 188). Hence, Butler's feminist anti-racism gets in the way of an adequate interpretation of transgender relations, and both her discourse and her discursive view limit the extent to which unliveable bodies can become liveable by the extent to which unthinkable bodies can be made thinkable. Butler therefore ignores two things: (i) the actual lived conditions of painful and suffering bodies that many people would rather not think about (including those of many transgender sex workers), and (ii) the bodily materialities that are liveable and might indeed become lived despite our inability to conceive of them in thought.

Unlike Garfinkel's emphasis on passing, then, Butler's notion of performativity acknowledges possibilities for change, suggesting that gender expression may be expanded beyond the binary organization of sex and gender which still dominates contemporary Western society. But like Garfinkel, she disembodies transgender from the concrete situations of transgender people, displacing their materiality (Prosser, 1998) and social context (Namaste, 2000), turning the real drag queens in *Paris Is Burning* into a metaphor for the performativity of gender as a whole (Schilt and Connell, 2007), and ignoring the everyday experiences of transgender people (Namaste, 1996).

More recent work on transgender informed by Butler has had mixed effects on resolving these problems. Halberstam's (2005) queer theory analysis of the murder of the FTM transgender person Brandon Teena may provide a case in point here. While Halberstam acknowledges that Brandon Teena was murdered because he was transgender, her focus is neither on the murder of Brandon Teena nor on hate crimes against transgender people. Instead, Halberstam undertakes a narrative analysis of how transgender activists used the murder politically in the pursuit of transgender rights.

In contrast, Shapiro (2007) resolves some of the problems associated with Butler's work on transgender by investigating how gender performativity is not just about public performance but embedded in everyday life through a case study of the drag troupe and feminist political collective Disposable Boy Toys (DBT). By studying drag kings and drag queens both on and off stage, Shapiro explores how drag performance affects the performers themselves. The drag performance constituted a space to enact different femininities and masculinities, thereby enabling DBT members to imagine their everyday gender differently. Further, Shapiro draws attention to the organizational aspects of DBT – its shared finances, decision-making, and leadership, and how it served as an important community resource, providing people links to the transgender community and information about support services as well as an ideological and organizational context for collective action. But while Shapiro provides detailed bodily descriptions of certain drag acts and certain DBT members, highlighting their fluid identities and bodies, she provides no theorizing of transgender embodiment as such. And even though the DBT drag performance constitutes paid part-time work embedded in the context of social movement organizations, Shapiro provides no theorizing of work practices and limited theorizing of DBT as an organization.

## Transgender in Studies of Gender, Work, and Organization

While transgender remains a marginalized topic in studies of work and organization, then, gender scholarship on transgender tends to evade issues of work and organization. To date, only about a handful of publications have investigated transgender in relation to work and organization. This includes theoretical discussions about transgender and organization theory (e.g. Brewis et al., 1997; Linstead and Pullen, 2006), and empirically founded work on transgender employees (Schilt, 2006; Schilt and Connell, 2007), most of which tends to take a constructionist perspective.

Informed by Butler's notion of performativity, Brewis et al. (1997) discuss how transgender – and particularly MTF transvestism – may challenge the binary gender divide. On their view, transvestism is 'a "hard form of transgression"' whereby MTF transvestites adopt 'an entirely female style of costume' (ibid.: 1288). But as most transvestites construct gender without desiring 'to become the other gender permanently', transvestites challenge the binary gender divide by travelling between genders. This leads Brewis et al. to argue that as transvestism highlights the constructed nature of gender, it hints at the possibility for men and women to play with gender roles and challenge masculine dominance as well as the binary gender divide in organizations. This has no doubt been important in introducing transgender to studies of gender, work, and organization. However, like Garfinkel and Butler, Brewis et al.'s metaphorical use of transgender deflects attention from the everyday lives and embodiments of transgender people in settings of work and organization.

Combining gendered organization theory with intersectional analysis, Schilt (2006) investigates how the case of transmen makes workplace gender discrimination visible. While transmen have the same skills, education, and abilities before and after transition, some respondents experienced new advantages at work after transition – advantages they did not have as women – and that they were being valued for being male. For instance, one respondent found that customers went more often to him for queries after he transitioned, and a number of transitioned respondents experienced that their views were more highly recognized in meetings and in interaction with co-workers and managers. Moreover, transitioned transmen experienced less sexual harassment, touching, groping, and sexualized comments, problems which they had experienced before transition when appearing as an 'obvious dyke'. However, tall, white transmen found more advantages than short transmen and transmen of colour. And transmen who were in the early stages of transition or who had not used hormones during transition did not experience these advantages because they did not pass as men or because they looked like young men. Asian and black transmen also did not experience these advantages – Asian transmen because they were viewed by whites as passive, and black transmen because they were viewed by whites as threatening. Hence, the change in how the same person is treated by co-workers after transition means that gender inequalities result from gender stereotypes that co-workers and employers rely on in evaluating the skills and performance of women and men. This is a significant contribution to the understanding of workplace gender discrimination in general. But while Schilt pays attention to the bodily features of transmen and their social interaction with co-workers and employers, it risks turning the experience of transmen into a metaphor of workplace gender discrimination.

Drawing on a combination of Butler's work and symbolic interactionism (e.g. West and Zimmerman, 1987), Schilt and Connell (2007) investigate whether transgender people who remain in the same job make gender trouble and how they socially negotiate gender identity with their co-workers during gender transition or sex change. In this context, gender trouble refers to transgender activism and the explicit expression of transgender embodiment and identity which disrupts gender binaries and the 'natural connection between genitals and gender identity' (ibid.: 602). Before transition transwomen were expected to engage in conversations about cars and sports with their male colleagues while transmen were expected to participate in conversations about appearance, dress, hairstyles, and menstruation. Conversely, after transition transmen were excluded from girl talk while male co-workers questioned the professional capacities of transwomen. For instance, one transwoman was forced out of a business partnership she had had with three men because they doubted her capacity to continue as a business partner, claiming that all she would be concerned with were 'frivolities of appearance' (ibid.: 606). While cross-gender interactions were quite problematic, same-gender interactions after transition were often quite inclusive. In one case, male colleagues signalled that they were positive to the transition of two transmen, asking 'when they were going to start using the male locker room'. Similarly, a transwoman, despite some distance from female co-workers at first, started to have lunch with them and was taken shopping by a female colleague. But even though some transgender employees sought to 'adopt "alternative" femininities and masculinities' to fight binary and sexist gender stereotypes and sex and gender inequality there was little scope for gender trouble. Full-time transgender employees were enlisted into rituals which reinforce the gender binary, and they went along with gender stereotypes in order to 'keep social relationships smooth during transition' and 'retain steady and comfortable employment' (ibid.: 605).

Both studies suggest that transgender employees encounter opportunities, gain privileges and avoid trouble insofar as they pass as members of the opposite sex. But they also suggest that transgender embodiment as such remains problematic. Indeed, transgender only ceased to make trouble after transition, when it was no longer apparent or obvious, for transgender employees who passed as members of the opposite sex. These studies are therefore significant contributions to the understanding of the construction of transgender and the problems and opportunities that transgender employees encounter in everyday settings of work and organization, because of or despite our transgender. But despite drawing attention to the bodily practices of transgender employees, they assume that gender is socially constructed, under-theorize transgender embodiment, and give limited insight into the problems, opportunities and experiences that transgender people encounter because of our bodies.

## TOWARDS AN EMBODIED APPROACH TO TRANSGENDER IN STUDIES OF GENDER, WORK, AND ORGANIZATION

Although studies of work and organization in particular and the social sciences in general have a long history of neglecting issues of embodiment, a number of efforts have been made during the past decade to develop embodied approaches in the social sciences. An embodied approach to transgender may inform at least two possible avenues of research: (i) a more micro-level study of transgender workers, managers, clients, and consumers, and (ii) a more macro-level study of organizations, institutions, industries, and fields that cater for transgender people. Both avenues may enable research on bodily practices of transgendering and (how this relates to) the problems and opportunities encountered by transgender people in settings of work and organization.

While previous research has tended to study the body in a disembodied way and focus on the body as an object of discursive construction and disciplinary control in work organizations, appeals for an embodied approach have argued that the body is an active subject and a medium of action, interaction, knowledge, emotion, and experience. In organization studies and in the broader social sciences these arguments have been informed by the work of Merleau-Ponty (see e.g. Williams and Bendelow, 1998a; 1998b; Dale, 2001). Challenging the mind–body dualism, Merleau-Ponty (1962) argues that the body is not a passive object of rational thought, social construction, and organization, but a matter of sensual, mindful, expressive, and lived embodiment. Our thoughts and emotions, habits and experiences, actions, and interactions are embodied, and the mind is an organ located in the body. It is through our bodies that we think, feel, sense and experience, express thoughts and feelings, create habits and meaning, and act and interact in meaningful ways. For Merleau-Ponty, then, it is our lived embodiment, which is at once routine, intentional, and creative, that enables us to relate to, enact and inhabit the world.

Merleau-Ponty's emphasis on lived embodiment suggests that future studies should not only investigate the social interaction of transgender people at work and in organizations, or the social construction of transgender in the institutional arrangements of organizations, industries, and fields. Rather, future studies need to investigate the lived embodiment and bodily experiences of transgender people at work and in organizations, and how this is affected by and affects institutional arrangements in organizations, industries, and fields.

Micro-oriented research on work and organizations has started to investigate the lived embodiment of employees and managers – how gendered embodiment affects bodily feelings and experiences at work (e.g. Dale, 2001; Knights and Thanem, 2005) and how the body constitutes an active medium of management and organization which enables people to learn and create knowledge in organizations (Edenius and Yakhlef, 2007), commit to work with buzzing excitement, and make decisions based on their gut-feeling (Lennie, 2000). Future research may therefore want to investigate the bodily techniques and practices that transgender employees and managers mobilize in expressing – or hiding – our transgender, how our interactions with colleagues and clients affect and are affected by our expression or hiding of transgender embodiment, and the bodily feelings and experiences that are spurred as we express or hide our transgender and as we interact with others.

Given Merleau-Ponty's neglect of body politics and bodily difference, transgender research in studies of work and organization would benefit from combining Merleau-Ponty's ideas with insights from feminism and queer theory. This may help the area avoid reducing the diverse lived embodiments and experiences of transgender people to a generic kind of transgender embodiment and experience, and problematize the specific bodily problems, opportunities, experiences, and expressions of different transgender groups and individuals, beyond the distinctions between MTF and FTM transgendering. It would be particularly fruitful to investigate how various forms of transgender embodiment intersect with other forms of bodily, socio-corporeal and socio-demographic difference, including sexuality, race, age, and (dis)ability.

But rather than analysing transgender embodiment from the outside in a disembodied, male-stream, and heteronormative way, the emphasis on lived embodiment suggests that transgender research should itself be embodied. Extending Merleau-Ponty's philosophy and feminist theory, Williams and Bendelow (1998a; 1998b) have proposed an embodied research strategy for social science research on the body. It is not sufficient to assume that lived embodiment is 'expressive', 'sensual', or 'mindful' and involves 'an active engagement with the world and an intimate connection with both culture and self' (Williams and Bendelow, 1998b: xvi). As researchers we must reflect about and write our own lived embodiment and bodily experiences into our accounts of the bodies we study. This is a risky and precarious project which thus far has generated little following. As the body itself remains a marginalized research object, it seems even more difficult to generate enthusiasm around a project that makes individual researchers particularly vulnerable. Still, this is the only way that studies of gender, work, and organization can become genuinely embodied, and this may be what it takes to convince our colleagues in the broader area of organization studies that bodies – and transgender embodiment – matter. In my own research I would therefore reflect about my own lived embodiment and experiences as an MTF transvestite: How do I feel when I'm dressed up, how do I relate to myself and to others, and how do they relate to me – as I take the dog for a walk, ride the bus, go to the supermarket, shop for make-up, women's shoes and clothing, go out for a drink or a meal, socialize with other MTF transvestites, or interview transvestites for research? And how do I relate to others when I'm *not* dressed up but when my transvestism still becomes apparent – when shopping for a wig, make-up or women's shoes while in male drag, when presenting a transgender paper at a conference, or when talking about transgender issues with my colleagues or students?

*Wearing stereotypically feminine props such as make-up, women's clothes and shoes, a wig or my own hair in a more feminine style, it is obvious that my transvestism is written on my body when I'm dressed up. But it also affects how I feel and how I relate to others. Going out dressed up makes me feel more vulnerable, sometimes nervous, but it can also make me feel more confident, energized, invigorated and excited. Either way, it makes me change my body language. My voice doesn't necessarily go up a pitch, but it becomes less monotonous. I try to adjust my posture, stand up straight and occupy less space, tighten my shoulders, keep my legs together when sitting down, and reduce the space between my legs when standing up. These things even change when I'm not dressed up but in situations when my transgender is nevertheless actualized. Shopping for a pair of tights or mascara when I'm not dressed up I still try to appear less masculine, speak more softly and keep my legs together. This rarely upsets people. I seem to upset others more, provoke more stares and comments, when I go about my ordinary business in male drag – taking the tube, shopping for food, having a drink at a downtown pub. Even if I don't pass as a woman when I try to dress up as one, at least then people know what I am – a tranny, an MTF transvestite and not a pre-op transsexual, not a butch lesbian, not an effeminate gay man.*

An embodied research strategy for the study of transgender embodiment may pose a bigger challenge for the typically macro-oriented study of institutional arrangements in organizations, industries, and fields. The majority of institutionalist research tends to study relations between organizations rather than relations between people in organizations (e.g. Powell and DiMaggio, 1991). Institutionalist studies of transgender embodiment may therefore be more likely to succeed if scholars extend and expand recent efforts to investigate how macro institutions are enacted on a micro level (e.g. Barley and Tolbert, 1997; Czarniawska, 2009), by people in settings of work and organizations. Future research may want to investigate how institutional arrangements (norms, cultures, and regulations) in the transgender industry are produced, changed, and reproduced through an interaction of organizations, communities and individuals. One case in point is the transgender shoe industry, that is, companies which manufacture and retail women's style shoes in men's sizes and men's style shoes in women's sizes: How is the transgender shoe industry organized and why? What shoes does it manufacture and retail and why? How does this affect the bodily expression, feelings, and experiences of transgender people? And how is this affected by the lived embodiment, bodily feelings, and experiences of transgender people?

*Without having researched these issues yet, I'm continuously frustrated by the difficulty of finding women's style shoes in a size 42 or 43 (EUR) in ordinary shoe stores. Women's style shoes in my size are primarily available from online specialist vendors which mainly stock over-priced garish styles with extreme stiletto heels. To try on a pair before buying is therefore not an option. And running in a pair like that is at best difficult.*

## CONCLUSION

While these research questions emerge from my own transgender embodiment, they may have significant implications for the possibility of embodying transgender in studies of gender, work, and organization. Firstly, employing an embodied research strategy to investigate transgender embodiment may enable research on embodiment in general and transgender embodiment in particular to become genuinely embodied. Secondly, employing an embodied research strategy to investigate transgender embodiment in the transgender industry would highlight the particular and general features of an under-researched industry, extend previous efforts (of institutionalist and non-institutionalist research) to bridge the gap between micro-level and macro-level research, and embody the understanding of institutional arrangements in organizations, industries, and fields. Thirdly, doing embodied research on transgender in institutional settings links transgender embodiment to the mainstream of organization studies. Despite risks of appropriation, this may help transgender research escape its marginalized position as an isolated sub-field for just the committed few. Hence, it may advance our knowledge of bodily transgendering practices and our knowledge of the problems and opportunities that transgender people encounter in settings of work and organization – across different contexts and levels and analysis.

## ACKNOWLEDGEMENTS

I am grateful for the incisive and helpful comments of David Knights.

## REFERENCES

Althusser, L. (1971) 'Ideology and ideological state apparatuses' in *Lenin and Philosophy and other Essays*, trans. B. Brewster. London: New Left Books, 121–176.

APA (2009) *Answers to Your Questions About Transgender Individuals and Gender Identity.* Washington, DC: American Psychological Association Office of Public Communications. http://www.apa.org/topics/transgender.html#howprevalent (downloaded 9 October 2009).

Barley, S.R., and Tolbert, P.S. (1997) Institutionalization and Structuration: Studying the Links between Action and Institution, *Organization Studies*, 18(1) 93–117.

Brewis, J., Hampton, D., and Linstead, S. (1997) Unpacking Priscilla: Subjectivity and identity in the organization of gendered appearance, *Human Relations*, 50(10) 1275–1304.

Butler, J. (1990) *Gender Trouble: Feminism and the Subversion of Identity*. London: Routledge.

Butler, J. (1993) *Bodies That Matter: On the Discursive Limits of 'Sex'*. London: Routledge.

Conway, L. (2002) *How Frequently Does Transsexualism Occur?* http://ai.eecs.umich.edu/people/conway/TS/TSprevalence.html (downloaded 9 October 2009).

Czarniawska, B. (2009) 'Emerging Institutions: Pyramids or Anthills?' *Organization Studies*, 30(4) 423–441.

Dale, K. (2001) *Anatomising Embodiment & Organisation*. Basingstoke: Palgrave.

Edenius, M., and Yakhlef, A. (2007) Space, Vision and Organizational Learning: The Interplay of Incorporating and Inscribing Practices, *Management Learning*, 38(2) 193–210.

Ekins, R. (1997) *Male Femaling: A Grounded Theory Approach to Cross-Dressing and Sex-Changing*. London: Routledge.

Foucault, M. (1977) *Discipline and Punish*. London: Allen Lane.

Foucault, M. (1979) *The History of Sexuality Volume 1*. London: Allen Lane.

Garfinkel H. (1967) *Studies in Ethnomethodology*. Englewood Cliffs, NJ: Prentice Hall.

Goffman, E. (1959) *The Presentation of Self in Everyday Life*. Garden City, NY: Anchor Books.

Halberstam, J. (2005) *In a Queer Time and Place: Transgender Bodies, Subcultural Lives*. New York: NYU Press.

Hancock, P., and Tyler, M. (2000) '"The look of love": Gender and the organization of aesthetics' in J. Hassard, R. Holliday, and H. Willmott (eds), *Body and Organization*. London: Sage, 108–129.

Herdt, G. (1994) *Third Sex, Third Gender: Beyond Sexual Dimorphism in Culture and History*. New York: Zone Books

Holliday, R., and Thompson, G. (2001) 'A body of work' in R. Holliday and J. Hassard (eds), *Contested Bodies*. London: Routledge, 117–133.

Knights, D., and Thanem, T. (2005) 'Embodying emotional labour' in D. Morgan, B. Brandth, and E. Kvande (eds), *Gender, Bodies and Work*. Aldershot: Ashgate, 31–43.

Laqueur, T. (1990) *Making Sex: Body and Gender from the Greeks to Freud*. Cambridge MA: Harvard University Press.

Lennie, I. (2000) 'Embodying management' in J. Hassard, R. Holliday, and H. Willmott (eds), *Body and Organization*. London: Sage, 130–146.

Linstead, S., and Pullen, A. (2006) Gender as Multiplicity: Desire, Displacement, Difference and Dispersion, *Human Relations*, 59(9) 1287–1310.

Merleau-Ponty, M. (1962) *Phenomenology of Perception*, trans. C. Smith. London: Routledge & Kegan Paul.

Mills, C.W. (1959) *The Sociological Imagination*. Oxford: Oxford University Press.

Namaste, K. (1996) 'Queer theory's erasure of transgender' in B. Beemyn and M. Elianon (eds), *Queer Studies: A Lesbian, Gay, Bisexual, & Transgender Anthology*, New York: NYU Press, 183–203.

Olyslager, F., and Conway, L. (2007) On the Calculation of the Prevalence of Transsexualism. Paper presented at the WPATH 20th International Symposium, Chicago, 6 September.

Powell, W., and DiMaggio, P. (eds) (1991) *The New Institutionalism in Organizational Analysis*. Chicago: University of Chicago Press.

Prosser, J. (1998) *Second Skins: The Body Narratives of Transsexuality*. New York: Columbia University Press.

San Francisco Department of Public Health (1999) *The Transgender Community Health Project*. San Francisco CA: University of California San Francisco. http://hivinsite.ucsf.edu/InSite?page=cftg-02-02#S5.1X (downloaded 27 July 2009).

Schilt, K. (2006) Just One of the Guys?: How Transmen Make Gender Visible at Work, *Gender & Society*, 20(4) 465–490.

Schilt, K., and Connell, C. (2007) Do Workplace Gender Transitions Make Gender Trouble?, *Gender, Work and Organization*, 14(6) 597–618.

Shapiro, E. (2007) Drag Kinging and the Transformation of Gender Identities, *Gender & Society*, 21(2) 250–271.

Transgender Law Center (2006) *Good Jobs NOW! A Snapshot of the Economic Health of San Francisco's Transgender Communities.* San Francisco: San Francisco Bay Guardian. http://transgenderlawcenter.org/pdf/Good%20Jobs%20NOW%20report.pdf (downloaded 9 October 2009).

West, C., and Zimmerman, D.H. (1987) Doing Gender, *Gender & Society*, 1(2) 125–151.

Whittle, S. (2002) Employment Discrimination and Transsexual People. Report for the Gender Identity Research and Education Society. Ashtead, Surrey. Available at http://www.gires.org.uk/Text_Assets/Employment_Disc_Full_Paper.pdf (downloaded 9 October 2009).

Williams, S.J., and Bendelow, G. (1998a) *The Lived Body: Sociological Themes, Embodied Issues.* London: Routledge.

Williams, S.J., and Bendelow, G. (1998b) 'Introduction: Emotions in social life: Mapping the sociological terrain' in G. Bendelow and S.J. Williams (eds), *Emotions in Social Life: Critical Themes and Contemporary Issues.* London: Routledge, xv–xxx.

# Section Three

## ORGANIZING WORK AND THE GENDERED ORGANIZATION

### EDITORIAL INTRODUCTION

This section explores some of the dynamics that gender the organization and the organizing of work. As we have seen from Section One, gender is both organized by and constitutive of organizing practices. Here we explore the extent to which gender inequality is sustained by these practices, and the attempts to challenge these organizing practices – through explicitly gender-focused practice and strategies or through attempts to 'neutralise' gender in organization. These dynamics are explored in a range of organizational contexts, such as in relation to technology which acts as an important means of regulating working practice, with implications for gender. The chapters draw on sociological, anthropological as well as philosophical approaches, and provide cultural context to the experiences in organizations with an international range of case examples employed to illustrate the organizing realities. These chapters, like those in Section One, are also political and practical, in that they seek to find ways of challenging systematic inequalities rather than simply demonstrating how inequality can be seen to exist.

The chapters in this section draw on established debates that have explored gender in relation to work and organization, both as gender in management, and in gendering management. These related but different ways of theorising gender in work and organization contrast the ways in which gender (or sex) may be implicated in different ways of managing – for example the alleged male/transactional versus female/transformational styles of leadership (Rosener, 1990), with the theorisation of the interrelationship between gender and management – the masculinisation of managerial identity and the discursive production of this (gendered) identity (Brewis et al., 1997). What both these approaches share, however, is the realisation that gender has traditionally been excluded from management discourse – an assumption of neutrality that in fact often hides a mechanism of intentional suppression of gender difference with a view to maintaining the masculine-as-norm status quo. This dynamic, as we can see from Acker's chapter in Section One, is also pervasive in understanding the role of social class, race/ethnicity and so on, and their interactions.

Debates in the literature have been forced to grapple with two options: whether a woman must act like a man to succeed or whether, alternatively, modes of organizing must be altered (feminised or made genuinely gender-neutral). As we have seen from Section One we are faced with the question of whether we should seek a process of 'degendering' (Lorber, 2005) or of 'undoing gender' (Butler, 2004), both of which invoke critiques of the sex/gender binary (see also Section Two). Yet whilst we may reconceptualise gender, we need at the same time to acknowledge the ongoing dominant processes associated with gender relations and gender identification and the norms, values and styles associated with each gender, to understand how they foster persistent gender inequalities in work and organizations.

What these chapters bring into sharp relief is the persistence of inequalities in organizations and the importance of understanding how and why practices that foster inequalities occur, which, hopefully, gives us an insight into how best they can be challenged and, perhaps, overcome. Legislation alone is clearly insufficient and action at the level of the individual, collective and organization as well as institutions outside is needed. Implicitly or explicitly these chapters demonstrate problems with 'equality of opportunity' and invoke new theorisations of organizations and organizing practices (see Omanović, this volume and Costea, this volume who critically assess diversity as a method for improving organizations on gender and other categorical distinctions).

Martin tackles the issue of gender inequality head on in 'Does Gender Inequality Ever Disappear?' She opens with the question, 'Is there any society, anywhere, any time, where men and women have had equal status?' Noting that anthropological studies have failed to find a society where women and men were equal, she also asks whether contemporary industrialised countries or even single organizations have attained gender equality, or in less absolute terms, whether certain types of organizing produce less gender inequality, how these gender dynamics manifest themselves, and why. Martin reviews studies at both national and organizational levels of analysis (reflecting the importance of national context for organizational practice), drawing on both quantitative and qualitative (or processual, social constructivist) approaches to recognising and measuring degrees of gender equality. She notes that the more richly detailed and contextually sensitive processual approaches present problems when it comes to assessing and comparing degrees of inequality. Given the limitations (and advantages) of both, Martin argues that each has a useful place and reviews studies using a range of methodologies.

Martin also reviews evidence, employing meta-analyses of United Nations data, comparing degrees of gender inequality in various countries, by grouping nations with similar inequality profiles. She also addresses the organizational level of analysis and classifies organizations into studies of: male dominated organizations; female dominated organizations; and gender mixed organizations. Her aim is to explore the advantages and disadvantages of each and thus move beyond a simple 'body count'. She demonstrates how, in every case, organizations are inclusive and exclusive, even to the 'dominant' gender. Perhaps the only consistent theme is the persistence of gender inequality. Ironically, even female dominated organizations, despite some feminist theorists who favour this approach to organizing, ultimately offer a less than successful mode of achieving gender equality.

Martin goes beyond documenting the extent of gender inequality in contemporary industrialised nations and organizations, and in a novel turn poses the question: 'What would a more gender equal work environment look like?' The answer, she argues, can be achieved by investigating exceptions to the rule: organizations that come unexpectedly close to achieving gender equality, which Martin argues may be achieved using one of three processes: 'degendering', sometimes with an androgynous twist; an 'instrumental use of conventional stereotypes'; and 'breaking traditional stereotypes'. For each case, she explores what working life in these organizations might look like, the types of questions that might arise in them, and the national contexts where the processes might work best. In sum, Martin offers readers a comprehensive, internationally oriented overview of the field, by integrating national and organizational and also quantitative and qualitative studies of the dogged persistence of gender inequality. In an effort perhaps to avoid reaching a depressing set of conclusions, she goes on to explore novel modes of organizing that may help us achieve greater gender equality.

Päivi Korvajärvi picks up on the theme of degendering in her chapter 'Practicing Gender Neutrality in Organizations'. Her account of this practice, however, notes simultaneous processes of denial and acceptance. Korvajärvi focuses on a research project based in Finnish organizations and conducted in two phases, from 1986–1996 and 1998–2005, allowing a comparative approach. She argues that this context is of especial interest, as Finland, along with other Nordic countries, have a history of social democratic welfare and are usually assumed to have higher degrees of gender equality (see also Martin's discussion of the Nordic model in the previous chapter). In addition, she notes the significance of the dominant type of work in the 'new' Finnish economy – information and communication technology, characterised by service work and communication (which may be seen as 'feminine' skills; see Wajcman later in this section). However despite the typical assumption of (comparative) gender equality in Nordic countries, Korvajärvi presents a contradictory picture of gender segregation and remaining hierarchical differences despite accounts of equality in practice, which she refers to as the 'silent agreement' within the organization where gender inequality, when acknowledged, was attributed to society as a whole or the experiences of others.

Korvajärvi identifies two approaches to studying the denial/recognition of gender at work, one based on interactional, cultural and processual approaches to understanding gender (see also Section One), and the other, which she employs here, the situating of analysis in the dynamics of the economy. In the latter approach, organizing practices that result from the changing economy form the basis of gendered analysis. Korvajärvi in turn divides key organizational practices into 'emotional labour'; 'aesthetic labour' and 'the cultural feminization of work'. In outlining them, she demonstrates how each approach is situated in the context of organizing and further how, given the developments in many economies, including that of Finland, we might anticipate an improved position for women in the workplace. In particular, she argues, this is because of the cultural feminisation of work and its reliance on emotions and communication skills.

Korvajärvi, like Martin, finds evidence of inequality in organizations. She argues that feminine skills are taken for granted as 'natural' when performed by women whilst they are viewed as of value when performed by men. The contrasting 'doing' of gender (masculine skills performed by men and women) do not appear to have the same effect. A key distinction between a 'gendered' approach and an 'economy-led' approach is the consciousness of the doing of gender. Whilst gender-led approaches often 'do' gender un- or subconsciously – perhaps taking for granted the ways of being and doing gender – economy-led approaches explore the deliberate ways of doing gender. Given the nature of the economy, and its deliberate 'uses' of gender, we might anticipate relatively more gender-awareness on the part of participants. Instead we find that gender is more obscured and silenced; it is denied as a factor or cause of inequality, despite evidence of its persistence in organizations. Korvajärvi thus argues that gender neutrality is not a sign of equality or a sign that gender is not present; rather it may instead be a way of doing gender that '*masks* gender conflicts'. Furthermore, like gender-led approaches, gender neutrality may be performed unreflectively in a manner that maintains gender neutrality. One alternative interpretation of the apparent lack of reflection is that it could be done as a deliberate strategy for harmony – even if this strategy may not be fully realised by the participants themselves (see also the Bird and Rhoton chapter).

Sharon Bird and Laura Rhoton explore deliberate strategies that professional women use to negotiate barriers and overcome exclusionary practices associated with their being women. In 'Women Professional's Gender Strategies: Negotiating Gendered Organizational Barriers', they explore the individual or personal gender strategies that professional women employ and consider how they relate to collective efforts to overcome barriers. Professional organizations provide a useful site for consideration in that they reflect occupations with relatively high levels of decision-making power and influence. Rising to the top of a profession can mean achieving significant leadership and authority in an organization. Furthermore, professional women are usually well educated and comparatively astute observers of organizing practices and thus we might anticipate more effective strategies for negotiating the barriers (professional organizations overwhelmingly fall into Martin's first type of organization, that is, male dominated).

Bird and Rhoton outline barriers that are experienced by women in professional work organizations. The peculiarities of professional work include features of professional organizing (specialised knowledge, standard-setting etc.) and a prevalence of tradition (enduring, unchanging, unreflective practices) as resources for organizing. Both the enduring nature of these 'traditions' and the vested interests in their continuation ensure that these (hegemonic masculine) organizing logics operate as powerful mechanisms of inclusion and exclusion. Only concerted gender-oriented strategies are likely to be able to overcome such barriers.

As found in previous chapters, Bird and Rhoton take a social constructionist approach. They view professional women's gender strategy as a gendered 'plan of action' for 'organizing personal practices' that are shaped by personal beliefs about how they *as women*, should act. (Of course, their practices are shaped by the opportunities and resources available to them.) They identify six gender strategies: 'aligning with white, hegemonic practices of masculinity'; 'aligning with conventional practices of femininity'; 'claiming gender neutrality'; 'framing gender-based policies, practices and programs as "political"'; using multiple gender strategies' and 'challenging gendered organizations'. They demonstrate the successes and failings of each strategy, including the personal costs involved in its performance. They also ask how these 'trajectories' of strategies are, over a woman's career, affected by work and life events. Their analysis also addresses how these gender strategies intersect with race and other categorical distinctions (see also Acker, Section One and Calás and Smircich, Section Five).

Strategies that challenge how gendered professional organizations operate are least common, although 'tempered radicals' who question the dominant organizing logic are notable for their potential to effect change. Systemic change is required, however, and to this end, Bird and Rhoton note that effective networks must be built. Genuine change requires a collective effort with those at 'the top' being complicit with the cause, alongside large-scale social movements that seek equality and hold organizations accountable. Only strategies such as these will be effective in fundamentally changing organizations on gender equality.

Judy Wajcman locates the strategic position of women in organizations in the context of science, engineering and technology. As we saw in Korvajärvi's chapter, technology mediated work in particular is a mode of organizing that has the potential to provide favourable opportunities for women. In 'Gender and Work: a Technofeminist Analysis', Wajcman demonstrates that this sector is characterised by the marginalisation of women, as a result of technology-assigned masculine attributes as well as offering emancipatory opportunities in the 'post-traditional network society'. Wajcman approaches the relationship between technology and feminism on several fronts: gender imbalance in the 'technoscience' sector, the gender relations of technoscience, and of cyberfeminism. Comparable to Bird and Rhoton, Wajcman demonstrates that women's exclusion from senior levels in this sector means they remain under-represented in key decision-making arenas, and tracks this process from their education through to organizing and cultural practices at work. She evaluates the masculinisation of technology in the light of different feminist perspectives (liberal, second-wave and so on) and embeds the debate in historical working practices by reviewing the genesis of 'men's monopoly of technology'.

On a positive note, Wajcman discusses 'cyberfeminism' which feminists argue can improve the empowering possibilities of technology for women. Postmodern feminists (see also Tyler, Section One) are particularly excited by possibilities that the virtual world provides to escape the limitation of embodied gender and sex differences, opening up space for the play of and between humans and machines and expanding the options for gendered identities. It can provide a means of organizing that appears feminine and avoids hierarchy. Wajcman refers to the work of Donna Haraway and the 'cyborg' – where science and technology enable the creation of new meanings and subjectivities and, in doing so, challenge the traditional gendered/sexed binary (see also Section Two). This liberating strategy contrasts with the 'embodied' challenges to inequality discussed in Sections One and Two. Despite these changes, and avenues for liberation, Wajcman cautions against considering that these 'opportunities' exist in 'the same old social relations, values and goals'. Furthermore, she calls for the need to maintain a contextual analysis of technology – because technology can be liberating in one context, yet controlling in another. (She refers to the ownership of a mobile phone as both a means of freedom and a constant 'contactability'.) Technology thus, she argues, requires women at the centre of technological development, helping to shape its design, purposes and meanings.

Benschop and Verloo offer a provocative and insightful overview of efforts to improve gender equality in 'Gender Change, Organizational Change, and Gender Equality Strategies'. They discuss strategies and interventions and assess their effectiveness, discursively and materially. Using insights from political science, organization studies and gender studies, they analyse gender-change strategies and review knowledge gaps as well as concrete practices that prevent realisation of gender-equitable organizations.

Benschop and Verloo view debates about gender equality in organizations as haunted by debates such as the 'individual versus structure' debate (can we change organizations by changing individuals or must we alter organizational structures, policies and practices?). Most recommendations for gender equality fail to transcend this divide, they say. With an eye to transcending it, they discuss the merits of various strategies using a typology that relates the individual-structure issue to change-strategies and goals envisioned by three disciplines.

At the individual level, women's inclusion at work can be increased by focusing on liberal goals such as 'equip the woman' and 'create equal opportunity'. While these goals may have limited impact, they are nevertheless positive for some women, e.g. those who receive better job training and/or can take advantage of 'equal opportunities'. Individual policies can also foster a re-valuation of women through the strategies of 'managing diversity and valuing difference', focusing on gender differences as resources for organizations and society (see Section Four on Diversity, particularly the chapters by Omanović and Costea). Benschop and Verloo rather favour structural strategies such as the radical strategy that strives for creating equal outcomes and a 'gender mainstreaming' strategy which, if embraced and implemented, can support a post-equity strategy. A post-equity strategy addresses power processes that produce gender inequalities as part of everyday organizational routines and interactions. It requires collaboration and understanding between researchers and organization members.

Organization change theories and gender theories are used to identify a range of impediments to gender-equality change: the managerialist tendency of planned change, the need for simultaneous short and long-term agendas for change, the issue of resistance, the need to address gender-related emotions and attitudes, the intersectionality of multiple inequalities, and the inclusion and voice of all stakeholders. The authors offer their own genderXchange strategy which, they say, can overcome many impediments to gender equity in organizations that they review here. This strategy addresses both individual and structural levels and shows how they must be organized to produce lasting systemic transformations. They also call for a political, participatory processual approach that includes attention to individual attitudes and emotions that may obstruct gender change projects.

# REFERENCES

Brewis, J., Hampton, M. and Linstead, S. (1997) Unpacking Priscilla: Subjectivity and Identity in the Organization of Gendered Appearance, *Human Relations*, 50(10), 1275–1304.

Butler, J. (2004) *Undoing Gender*. London: Routledge.

Lorber, J (2005) *Breaking the Bowls: Degendering and Feminist Change*. New York: W.W. Norton.

Rosener, J. B. (1990) Ways Women Lead, *Harvard Business Review* (November–December), 119–125.

# 13

## Does Gender Inequality Ever Disappear?*

### Joanne Martin
*Graduate School of Business, Stanford University*

There is a question that is seldom explicitly addressed by feminist researchers: Is there any society, anywhere, any time, where men and women have had equal status? Two feminist anthropologists, Rosaldo and Lamphere (1974) dared to try and answer this question. They surveyed the Harvard Area Files, which summarized a considerable subset of all the anthropological studies ever conducted, and then they supplemented this sample with a review of contemporary studies not included in the Area Files. They found that all societies studied were male dominated. Whether the men were the hunters or the gatherers, whether Western industrialized culture had made inroads into the society or if it had been left relatively isolated, no matter what tasks assignments men held, they had greater status, prestige, and material resources than women. There was no refuge for Amazonian superwomen; no matriarchies were found. Rosaldo and Lamphere's results held no matter when or where the studies were conducted, no matter whether a study's authors were male or female. The question these anthropologists asked was a centrally important one, and the results are sobering.

In this chapter I want to ask the same question of contemporary organizational settings: Are there any nations or types of organization, anywhere, where men and women are actually equal? To reframe this question less dichotomously (equal versus unequal): Do some kinds of nations and organizations have significantly less gender inequality? If so, why? Or is gender inequality pervasive, simply changing its form – reduced in one arena but exacerbated in another (e.g. Ridgeway, 1997)?

### OVERVIEW OF A FOUR-PART CHAPTER

Because in some countries, policies, laws, and practices regarding gender are primarily determined at the national rather than the organizational level of analysis, I

---

*I would like to thank Emma Jeanes and Patricia Yancey-Martin for helpful suggestions regarding this chapter.

will begin by reviewing studies of national differences in gender inequality. Next, I will move to the organizational level of analysis. Using a typology of organizations that are supposedly more or less gender-equal, I will examine the data to see if any of these types are safe havens for women and men seeking gender equality. Finally, I will conclude by outlining several innovative research projects that could tell us what an organization might look like, if it were actually gender equal.

## Body Counts versus a Process of Gendering

To avoid confusion, we will need some definitional specificity and theoretical grounding for this discussion. Gender inequality lies, tacitly or explicitly, at the heart of almost all gender research. Rhode (2002) has usefully distinguished two contradictory aspects of gender advocacy: sometimes advocates call for gender equality (as in equal pay for equal work) and sometimes they call for recognition and accommodation of gender differences (as in pregnancy policies). In this chapter, we will repeatedly find it useful to follow this lead, and distinguish studies of gender differences (often related to studies of sex segregation) from studies of the prevalence of gender inequalities such as unequal pay or educational attainment.

Social science theory, notably in Europe and particularly in feminist theory, has taken a discursive turn, creating a backlash against 'body-counting' research (i.e. Alvesson and Due Billings, 2002; Britton, 2000) that assumes a dichotomous distinction between pre-existing, biologically distinct categories of man and woman. Many gender inequality studies, both qualitative and quantitative, implicitly or explicitly take this kind of dichotomous approach. In contrast, more recent gender research is likely to conceptualize gender as socially constructed – a process of 'gendering,' that is socially enacted, shaped by discourse (for example, in policy statements or conversation), and therefore less determined by biology and more able to be changed (e.g. Martin, 1990; West and Zimmerman, 1987). This social construction approach enables the researcher to see gender as a complex continuum, with many different ways of enacting masculinity and femininity. Bacchi (2001: 117) summarizes the advantages of this approach: 'We recommend talking about gender as a verb or gerund (gendering), to shift attention from the idea that gender is a characteristic of a person to understanding gendering as an attributional process. That is, "differences" do not inhere in people; rather, they are attributions assigned to people through political meaning-making practices.'

One problem with the gendering approach is that it makes it difficult (but not impossible) to offer credible assessments of whether inequality is increasing or decreasing in comparative or chronological terms. Whether one prefers quantitative or qualitative methods, a central goal of much feminist gender research is to find ways to reduce inequality. If we cannot credibly make the case that one approach or policy is more effective than another in reducing inequality, the persuasive impact of our research is damaged. Especially when addressing skeptical audiences, many researchers use quantitative measures of inequality, assuming these audiences will find numerical evidence more credible and less reflective of subjective biases of various kinds. Although this may just be an illusion of objectivity, it does have a self-perpetuating effect, whereby many studies of inequality use 'body-counting' measures of numbers disaggregated by sex. This chapter will draw on numerical and categorical studies of gender inequality as well as studies that take a social constructivist approach to the process of gendering. The results of the two kinds of studies complement each other and help us to understand why gender inequality is so persistent.

Given the breadth of the question this chapter addresses, a few carefully selected references will be discussed in some depth; a full review of the relevant literature on gender inequality will not be attempted, as this is such a broad topic.

## GENDER INEQUALITY AT THE NATIONAL LEVEL OF ANALYSIS

Gender studies often identify the nations where data were collected, but they seldom attempt to contextualize their data by discussing whether those particular countries are settings where some kinds of gender inequality are particularly acute or relatively modest. Because the magnitude of gender inequality differs enormously across kinds of gender inequality and across national boundaries, it is important to situate the national source of one's data in some kind of systematically comparative international context. This does not mean that all studies must collect and analyze international comparative data, but it does mean that gender research would be strengthened if we discussed at least whether a given nation was atypical or average in the magnitude of the kinds of gender inequality being observed.

### Types of national gender systems

Are there countries where gender inequality has been significantly reduced? If so, why? To address these questions without going through long lists of countries one by one, we need some categories that group together countries that have similar magnitudes of gender inequality or similar gender policies. The best classification I have found for this purpose is offered by Rantalaiho (1997), who distinguishes three types of national gender systems:

A *market-liberal model* that has minimal public funding to support parenthood. These countries look primarily to organizations for voluntary, often innovative gender policies (e.g. United States, United Kingdom, and Canada);

A *conservative marriage/family model* that supports women as wives and mothers through public funding (e.g. Germany, Austria, Switzerland, Netherlands, Italy, France, and Belgium); and

A *Nordic model* that has considerable public funded support for male and female parenthood, based on a social-democratic welfare system (e.g. Sweden, Denmark, Norway, and Finland).

### Which nations, and which types of nations, are most equal?

Rantalaiho's tri-partite classification system has the important disadvantage that she uses it to categorize primarily Western industrialized countries. Within this limitation, this system can be applied to international studies of gender inequality to ask which countries have the least gender inequality, and why. Every few years the United Nations (UN) does a careful international study of gender inequality, seeking measures that are comparable across national boundaries. This is the best international data set I can find, but the ways these have been presented and analyzed in the UN Reports (1996; 2000; 2005) have been much criticized. Problems include the ways the analyses dealt with such factors as the proportion of women in each national labor force, differences in the ways each nation classified occupations, and various statistical complexities in the measurement of inequalities. In a thorough and well argued re-analysis of the UN data, Blackburn, Jarmon, and Brooks (2000) argue that it is essential to distinguish three types of gender inequality: *Gender-related development*, a measure which favors the Western industrialized countries, includes gender inequality in life expectancy at birth, educational attainment, and standard of living as measured by GDP per capita. A second measure of inequality reflects *gender empowerment* and it includes the extent of female representation in parliament, the proportion of senior (not top) jobs held by women, and the degree to which income for comparable jobs approaches gender equality. The third, and conceptually quite distinct, measure assesses the degree of *occupational sex segregation*, controlling for the proportion of the labor force who are female and the number of occupations in the nation. It is essential to separate occupational sex segregation from these other two types of inequality because they are conceptually distinct and sometimes negatively correlated.

When these types of inequality are separated, and Rantalaiho's classification of countries is used, the following results are found:

Nations using the market-liberal model tend to be male dominated, specifically, very (US and Canada) or moderately (UK) unequal on the first two kinds of inequality (gender-related development and gender empowerment), with moderate (US and Canada) or high (UK) levels of occupational sex segregation.

Nations using the conservative marriage-family model tend to be male dominated, with moderately high levels of the first two kinds of inequality, and moderately low levels of occupational sex segregation.

Nations using the Nordic model have, comparatively, the smallest gender inequality, with women more equal than elsewhere in gender-related development and gender empowerment. This does not mean, even on these dimensions, that gender inequality has disappeared in the Nordic countries; it is simply less than in other nations. Although the Nordic model countries have the least gender inequality on these two dimensions, they have unusually large magnitudes of occupational sex segregation (e.g. Blackburn et al., 2000) – only Bahrain and Kuwait have more sex-segregated work forces.

## Looking at the Nordic model in more depth

It is interesting to speculate why the Nordic model produces this juxtaposition of less gender inequality and more occupational sex segregation. Common explanations for gender inequality in other countries include: fewer women than men work and fewer women than men work full-time; women invest less effort in their work, and are more likely to take career breaks ('opt out') because of family responsibilities; women are generally less educated than men; and women are less likely to organize to protect their interests (e.g. join unions). None of these explanations works well in Nordic countries.

For example, in Finland, Rantalaiho (1997) finds that a large majority of women work and an even higher proportion of mothers with children under the age of three (over 80%) are employed. Ninety percent of the Finnish women who work, work full-time. Finnish women are, on average, better educated than Finnish men. Women in Finland are more likely than men to belong to unions. In spite of these distinctive attainments, Finnish women are not equal to Finnish men. Ninety to 99% of public and private top leadership positions in Finland are held by men. Women earn 75% of what men earn. Although these sources of inequality are generally of greater magnitude in other countries, they remain a problem in Finland as well. The primary reason for these Finnish inequalities is occupational sex segregation. In Finland, women tend to work in 'caring' jobs, such as education, nursing, elder care, and office work. Men tend to work in repair, technical services, transportation, traffic, and construction. In accord with Bielby and Baron's (1986) study of occupational sex segregation in California, when one looks closely at Finnish jobs that are apparently gender mixed (40–60% female), such as journalism, tasks and career paths are gendered, with women in less prestigious, less well paid positions with few if any well established career paths to top leadership positions in these fields.

This raises the question of why Finnish women (and Nordic women more generally) 'choose' caring occupations. Is this a voluntary, freely chosen preference, or are women somehow funneled into these jobs with few equally viable alternatives? Evolutionary scholars would claim that such jobs reflect nurturance preferences that are biologically determined and unchangeable (e.g. Fogel and Melson, 1986). There are other equally plausible explanations. In many Nordic countries, students choose or are funneled into vocational tracks at an early age, often when they are on the verge of puberty – a time in life when gender identities are being formed and responsiveness to peer pressure is great. It may be more socially acceptable for girls to go into caring jobs in Nordic countries. Additionally, caring jobs may also be preferred by mature women, because in Nordic countries there is greater government control of pay equity and greater support for families in the public sector, where most caring jobs are located.

Occupational sex segregation is the Achilles heel of Nordic claims to greater gender equality; there are no easy answers coming from the Nordic model. Nevertheless, the distinction among three types of national gender systems will prove useful as we turn our attention from the national level of analysis to the organizational level. Policies which shape gender relations are generated primarily at the governmental (federal) level of analysis in the nations that adhere to the Nordic and conservative marriage/family models. In nations that adhere to the market-liberal model (US, UK, and Canada) relatively few gender policies (for example, about equal pay for equal work, day care, or parenting support) are generated at the governmental level, and those that are, are irregularly enforced; not surprisingly, in these market-liberal countries the initiation and innovation of gender policy is de facto left to the organizational level of analysis (Pearce, 2001), where fiscal demands may take precedence over gender concerns for justice and equity. This may account for the dearth of English-language studies of gender policy at the governmental level of analysis, and the plethora of English language organizational level studies, in the market-liberal nations (e.g. Ring et al., 2005). Clearly, a more multi-lingual review of the relevant literature would be helpful, to see if these same patterns of research are found, especially in countries utilizing the conservative, marriage-family model.

## GENDER INEQUALITY AT THE ORGANIZATIONAL LEVEL OF ANALYSIS

Contemporary studies of gender in organizations conceptualize organizations as places where gender, race, ethnicity, and class intersect. These demographic categories are generally theorized as: (1) systems that intertwine (Acker, 1992) or (2) policy-related discourses that are sometimes enacted as organizational practices (Acker, in press; Butler, 2004) or (3) cultural manifestations (Aaltio-Marjosola and Mills, 2002; Halford and Leonard, 2001; Alvesson and Due Billing, 1992), including various ways of enacting masculinities and femininities at work (Knights and McCabe, 2001; Collinson and Hearn, 1994). These three theoretical approaches go beyond counting bodies in the various intersecting demographic categories, to include discourse and behavior as means of shaping enacted forms of gender – gendering as a process rather than a dichotomy. This is an important theoretical advance, but two caveats must be acknowledged. First, organizational gender studies may theorize about this demographic nexus, but in practice they often do not include systematic empirical analysis of race, ethnicity, and class. And second, the discursive turn sometimes fails to acknowledge the importance of material issues such as embodiment in organizational contexts (for example, in relation to pregnancy policies). With these two caveats, we can proceed to review the relevant organizational literature. First, however, one more theoretical distinction is useful.

As in the discussion of national differences in the magnitudes of different kinds of inequality, it is helpful to have a way of grouping organizations that permits us to summarize relevant research without going through a long list of organizational studies, one by one. One obviously relevant way to approach this problem is to classify organizations by whether they are:

*Male dominated* (relatively few women employees, mostly clustered near the bottom of the hierarchy).

*Female dominated* (relatively few male employees, with a substantial proportion of females at the top). Do such organizations provide women with a desirable haven?

*Mixed gender* (40–60% female overall) In gender mixed organizations, does gender inequality disappear?

In essence, this typology classifies organizations studied by counting the sex of people employed, but as we shall see, the approaches these studies take go far beyond body counting. Below I review research on each of these three types of organizations, describing a few sample studies, summarizing common research results for each type of organization, and then critically, and hopefully evenhandedly, discussing the disadvantages of having this kind of gender mix in an organization.

## Sample studies of male dominated organizations

Most organizations are male dominated and so, not surprisingly, there are hundreds of studies of such organizations. For example, Poggio (2000) contrasts four organizational contexts, showing: overt hostility towards women in the construction industry; women as second class citizens, as banking jobs tipped from being male positions to being female positions; more subtle forms of resistance when diversity hiring was mandated in European-based multinational companies; and less unequal gender relations in the technology industry. Czarniawska and Sevon (2008) used archival materials (diaries, letters, biographies, etc.) to document the struggles of several of the first women to become full professors in European universities. Many of these women were not born in the country where they were ultimately employed, as if foreign birth made gender-deviant behavior more acceptable. This dual-cultural grounding created unique and difficult adjustments by each of these women. Dellinger (2002) wrote a funny and insightful cultural portrait of sexualized gender norms at two magazines: one a male dominated organization that focused on heterosexual pornography (the other, to be discussed in the next section of this chapter, was a feminist publication produced by a female dominated organization). Yancey-Martin (1996) documents the ways contemporary male academics in male dominated universities enact competing forms of masculinity, describing various self-aggrandizing patterns of behavior that will be easily recognizable by many readers of this volume.

## Results of studies of male dominated organizations

Even in this small number of studies cited, it is clear that a wide range of historical periods, small and large organizations, and a variety of industries can be found in studies of male dominated organizations. What is surprising, in light of this variation, is that the results of these studies are so congruent: competitive forms of masculinity are frequently observed; aggressive arguments, threats, and hardball negotiations are commonplace; self-promotion is expected; women's contributions are ignored or devalued; stereotyping of both sexes is evident; and loyalty is rewarded over competence (Marshall, 1984; Kerfoot and Knights, 1993; Collinson and Hearn, 1994). Women in male jobs generally expect meritocratic rewards which they often do not receive. Instead, their performance evaluations are disproportionately inaccurate when subjective measures are used. Women tend to be socially less integrated in predominantly male groups; they feel less able to be 'authentically' themselves at work, are on average paid less and promoted more slowly than comparable men, in contexts where they are outnumbered. In Martin and Meyerson's (1998) study of a large technology corporation, all of the top female executives encountered these problems. Each woman blamed herself for what she saw as a personally unique set of problems, rather than asking whether the corporation was at least partially responsible for these commonly experienced difficulties. Women in lower status, traditionally female jobs (such as Pringle's secretaries (1989) and Kanter's clerical workers (1977)), also experience low pay and slower promotions. These women are expected to enact traditional gender relations, and not surprisingly, sexual harassment is a common concern.

## Disadvantages of male dominated organizations

Beyond the results discussed above, there are several less obvious disadvantages to male dominated organizations. Not all men are comfortable with competitive masculinity, yet other ways of enacting masculinity are often not valued in male dominated organizations, resulting in a loss of talent, skills, and productivity (Knights and McCabe, 2001; Collinson and Hearn, 1994). Women in male dominated organizations, especially when they enter traditionally male jobs, are more likely than comparable males to quit after the company has invested in their training. This is costly to the organization, usually demoralizing for the women involved, and frustrating for the men who tried 'to make it work' (Federal Glass Ceiling Commission, 1995). In limited labor markets, where well educated and highly experienced employees are relatively scarce (such as Australia), this lack of retention of talented women is an acute problem (Baxter and Wright, 2000). Finally, in addition to the business/fiscal impact of male domination, there is the question of whether intentionally or unintentionally giving preference to men is ethical.

## Sample studies of female dominated organizations

Although many organizations have a majority of female employees, a female dominated organization must by definition have a substantial proportion of women in the top ranks as well as many female managers. Female dominated organizations are relatively rare, and so too are studies of such organizations. In a comprehensive review of available studies at the time, Ferree and Yancey-Martin (1995) found that most female dominated organizations were small and in the non-profit sector. Those firms that were for-profit tended to be entrepreneurial companies focused on delivery of products or services to mostly female customers. For example, the feminist magazine studied by Dellinger (2002) was a female dominated organization. Tom (1995) studied a feminist bank in New York City, with two classes of employees: female, white, middle-class professional managers and female tellers of mixed race and lower class backgrounds, who had been on welfare and were unused to full-time employment. This combination not surprisingly exacerbated class and race conflicts between these two groups of women. Martin, Knopoff, and Beckman (1998) studied one of the largest, for-profit women dominated companies: The Body Shop, a UK based cosmetics company. At this company, most of the employees were women, and an unusual 85% of the managers were women. However, even at this bastion of female employment, only 17% of the top executives and Board members were female. The question here is: Do these companies offer a haven for women?

## Results of studies of female dominated organizations

Although studies of female dominated companies are not as plentiful as studies of male dominated companies, the results again are congruent, in the following ways. The cultures of female dominated companies tended to require unusually high levels of personal self-disclosure. Close personal relationships among employees often developed and were sometimes expected. There was a lack of personal/family/work–life separation, as calls from children interrupted meetings and advice about parenting and elder care was shared. These organizations often developed rituals centered around eating together, and leisure activities often had a traditionally female tone. For example, employees at Ariel, an equestrian boot manufacturer, watched television soap operas at lunch. There was a competition for the cutest tea cozy[1] at The Body Shop. Attempts to reduce hierarchy through skills cross-training, job rotation, leadership rotation, and decision by consensus were often observed.

## Disadvantages of female dominated organizations

A 'female culture' of personal closeness, self-disclosure, and family-sensitivity is not to everyone's taste – male or female (Martin et al., 1998). It is also time consuming – not a positive direct influence on productivity – although some would argue it has an indirectly positive effect on performance by improving morale and ease of work-related communication. Egalitarian practices, such as cross-training, job rotation, and consensual decision-making are also time consuming, often inefficient, and not always helpful, for example in improving the quality of decisions. These egalitarian practices were often met with resistance (Ferree and Martin, 1995; Tom, 1995). As the study of the New York Bank revealed, not all females want egalitarian treatment or professional advancement. These facts complicate the enactment of feminist goals which are often, but not always, a tacit or explicit part of the strategy of female dominated organizations.

It is difficult to grow female dominated organizations – to attract enough motivated women. For example, The Body Shop headquarters is in the south of England; it quickly became evident that, even in this relatively well educated market, most of the large number of women employed (and employable) were relatively traditional in their ideas about gender. It should not be news that many working women are not feminists, whether self- or behaviorally defined. Ferree and Martin (1995) studied explicitly feminist, female dominated organizations that arose during the second wave of feminism. In part because of recruitment and retention problems, these kinds of female dominated organizations tended to be rare, small, in the non-profit sector, and relatively short-lived. Having tried to follow up female dominated organizations since then, my informal sense is that non-profits, such as rape crisis centers have survived and even proliferated, but that for-profit female dominated organizations tend to be relatively rare, small, and short-lived. Systematic studies of the reasons for such a poor organizational survival rate would be quite useful. Finally, beyond the business/fiscal difficulties caused by a 'female culture,' egalitarian

---

[1] A tea cozy is a covering for a tea pot, designed to keep tea warm.

work practices, a limited labor market, and the financial difficulties any small organization encounters, one more question deserves consideration: is giving preference to women just?

## Sample studies of gender mixed organizations

Increasingly, male dominated organizations are transforming themselves into gender mixed organizations. However, this is an unstable category, as often a mixed organization, like a gender-balanced occupation, will tip to become male dominated again. This process of gendered organizational development, with moments of apparent gender balance, can be seen in Mills' historical studies of the Canadian airline industry (see Aaltio and Mills, 2002), where pilots, flight attendants, clerical workers, and mechanics offered different kinds of career opportunities. Kondo (1990), a Japanese-American anthropologist, has done a wonderfully complex study of a small food production company in Japan, where age, gender, and class intersect in fascinating ways. Although this company would be classified as gender mixed, jobs were gender segregated, with unusually explicit gender norms for different age groups. Hochschild (1997) has studied a large US-based multinational manufacturing company, where time-obsessed employees fight an endless battle to meet the needs of their families while working full-time. Each of these companies includes, at some of the time period(s) covered by the study, roughly equal numbers of men and women although, as described below, the genders differed in their access to power.

## Results of studies of gender mixed organizations

The results of studies of mixed gender organizations have some commonalities, although the circumstances of each company are unique. There is usually considerable occupational sex segregation in mixed gender organizations. Women generally have limited promotion opportunities. They are generally clustered at the bottom of these hierarchies, where there are glass ceilings (limits to career advancement), concrete walls (once assigned to a job track it is especially difficult for women to move laterally or to gain cross-functional experience), and sticky floors, especially for minorities who sometimes find promotion opportunities completely blocked (Federal Glass Ceiling Commission, 1995; Padavic and Reskin, 2002; Collins, 2004; cf., Baxter and Wright, 2000). Higher level positions in mixed gender organizations tend to be held by men and at the very top, female executives and Board members are very rare.

Women tend to cluster in certain functional areas, like human resources, and particular jobs, like clerical work. Ostensibly gender-balanced jobs are rare and often include special limited tracks or assignments for women (e.g. Bielby and Baron's Lathe Operators I and II (1986)). Gender-balanced jobs often tip, becoming predominantly single gender, and consequently garner lowered prestige and lower pay, as happened for example to bank tellers and clerical workers (Strober, 1984), and, perhaps some day, Professors of Organizational Behavior and of Psychology.

## Disadvantages of gender mixed organizations

The bottom line, then, is that ostensibly mixed gender organizations are, in effect, male dominated at the top, with considerable occupational sex segregation at other levels. Thus, mixed gender organizations have many of the same problems as male dominated organizations, although perhaps in a less acute form. Less aggressive and competitive forms of masculinity are devalued, resulting in a loss of male talent, skills, and productivity (Connell, 1995; Collinson and Hearn, 1994). Women in jobs usually held by men are likely to quit after investment in their training, a result that is generally demoralizing and costly to the organization. In limited labor markets, where well educated and experienced talent is scarce, exclusion or failure to retain talented employees is especially costly.

Women in a mixed gender organization are most often employed in 'pink velvet ghettos,' jobs that are primarily held by females (Padavic and Reskin, 2002). Within jobs and functions filled mostly by women, there will be the same disadvantages as were observed in female dominated organizations. A 'female culture' of personal closeness, sensitivity to family needs, and considerable self-disclosure will not be to everyone's taste. Job rotation and especially leadership rotation will cause inefficiencies; consensual decision-making will be time consuming and not always helpful. And finally, beyond any issue of business/fiscal efficiency, there is the question: Is sex segregation just?

## SUMMARY: GENDER INEQUALITY EVERYWHERE

As the anthropologists found in 1974, none of the studies discussed here offer a vision of a gender equal organizational context. On the national level, the market-liberal, conservative marriage/family, and Nordic models all produced extensive gender inequality, both in terms of gender-related development (such as life expectancy at birth, educational attainment, and income) and gender empowerment (such as the number of women in top leadership positions). Furthermore, in Nordic countries where these two types of gender inequality were lessened, occupational sex segregation was greater than any other nation except Bahrain and Kuwait. These are sobering results that gender researchers need to pay attention to.

These results should affect choice of future research topics. This review has relied on English language studies. Would similar conclusions be drawn from a multi-language review? Overall, systematic comparative international studies, and in depth qualitative studies published in languages other than the language of the people studied, would enrich our understanding of gender relations cross-nationally. More country-specific, in depth studies of race, class, ethnicity, and religion – as these interact with gender – are much needed because the meanings and consequences of these categories change across national boundaries, in part because of differences between advanced industrialized and less economically developed nations, particularly those with colonial histories.

Generally speaking, organizational gender researchers have done a better job at documenting inequality than studying how organizational leaders can build a more gender equal work environment. Specifically, we know now what gender inequalities we are likely to see in a male dominated organization. Once again, more attention to racial, ethnic, and class differences among women and among men in these kinds of organizations would be helpful, but another study of a male dominated organization would probably be more of a replication than an original contribution to understanding. Although studies of female dominated organizations are less prevalent, future studies of this kind of organization would probably be more of a replication of existing understandings, unless there is reason to expect that a particular female dominated organization would produce results different from those described above. Similar observations could be made concerning studies of future mixed gender organizations. So if we shouldn't do more of the same, what kinds of future research projects would be most productive?

## WHAT WOULD A GENDER EQUAL WORK ENVIRONMENT LOOK LIKE?

I think it would be more innovative and more helpful to ask: What would a gender equal organization look like? To what extent would it recognize, and be comfortable with, gender differences? There is an inherent conservatism in empirical research (Martin, 1992), that we need to take into account when addressing a research question like this; empirical researchers have to collect data on what is, not what might be. However, we can seek out the unusual outlier, the special organization where a unique degree or extent of gender equality has been achieved, and ask: How have they done it here? What works, and what seems dysfunctional? Of course there are dangers in generalizing from an atypical case study, but here the goal would not be generalization, but rather to study an exemplar of another way of organizing. Studies of gender-related change go beyond the documentation of gender inequality (e.g. Ely and Meyerson, 2001; Meyerson and Kolb, 2000). Many are designed to help guide interested organizations to a more equal future, offering a viable, proven model for how to get there (e.g. Fletcher and Bailyn, 1996; Kanter and Roessner, 2003). Below are at least three innovative ways to approach the study of gender-related change in organizations.

## DEGENDERING ORGANIZATIONS: ANDROGYNY AT WORK

Imagine a photograph of a glass door of a large office building. In front, stand the company's two co-directors, a man and a woman. Each is young, casually dressed in beige slacks, a long sleeved dress shirt, and flat slip-on shoes. It's hard to tell, at first, who the man is and who the woman is. A similar picture might be found in a Swedish technology magazine, where a set of several prize-winning executives stand or sit casually at a conference table. Most of the executives like to wear black. Several of the men have longish hair, and none look intimidating or unapproachable. If you look closely, you can see that one of these executives is a woman. Her hair is pulled back from her face, with no jewelry visible. Like some of her male colleagues, she is wearing a black turtle neck. She is sitting at the table, resting her head on her arms so her lower body is concealed by the table. This she looks at first glance like a he.

The physical androgyny in these imaginary photographs might echo a kind of cultural androgyny; in organizations where these people work, traditionally gendered patterns of behavior, ways of being a man or a woman, might be rarely seen. Instead, both men and women might behave in ways not easily associated with one gender rather than another (Lorber, 2005). This form of androgyny at work might well reduce the sexual tensions that Hearn and Parkin (1987) found so ubiquitous in organizations, and it might alleviate sexual harassment at work. Such androgyny is apparently common in some Nordic organizations. Rantalaiho (1997: 21) described it this way: 'a rather uneroticized working life . . . with a relative lack of "femininity" and erotic signals.' (Note that 'erotic' here is associated with femininity, not masculinity.)

Let us return to the two imaginary photographs of androgyny: the two, similarly dressed co-directors or the group of prize-winning executives. These men and women might have egalitarian relationships with each other, or the women might tacitly be being pressured to adopt masculine norms, creating an apparent absence of difference due to a male-centered homogeneity, raising questions of whether the women felt able to be 'authentically' themselves. Women as well as men can enact forms of masculinity (Connell, 1995) – even some hegemonically dominant forms of masculinity. For example, Connell's (2008) concept of 'transnational business masculinities,' which entail comfort with entrepreneurialism and self-promotion, could well be enacted by some female as well as male executives in multinational corporations. A study of an androgynous organization would need to look at all levels of the organizational hierarchy. It is an open question, whether androgyny at the leadership level translates into company-wide androgyny beyond the executive ranks, or whether we have yet another example of a familiar type of organization: male dominated, female dominated, or mixed gender with considerable occupational sex segregation. It is also an open question whether forms of androgyny are disproportionately found in multinational organizations in industrially developed countries, or if they are more widespread.

If a relatively androgynous organization could be found, it would be interesting to study: Do these organizations tend to hire relatively androgynous people? Do longer term employees (using Butler's (2004) ideas about performativity as a means of undoing gender) become apparently physically or culturally more androgynous? Do they like working in such an atmosphere? What happens to someone who prefers more traditionally gendered appearance or behavior – is there room for deviance and what form does it take? What works well and what dysfunctions are observed, in an androgynous organization? What environmental factors or product/service focus enable such androgyny to thrive?

## INSTRUMENTAL USE OF CONVENTIONAL SEXUAL STEREOTYPES

Another way to approach gender equality is to retain or even encourage the use of traditional gendered behavior patterns. Consider for example photographs of Andrea Jung, the Chief Executive Officer of the Avon cosmetics company. She appears generally in a short, tight skirt, with bright red lipstick, shiny well-coiffed hair, and glittering jewelry. She is always extremely well groomed, in a traditionally feminine manner. Here again, to study an organization that encourages the display of traditionally feminine and traditionally masculine patterns of behavior, we would need to go beneath the dress and décor, to study enacted practices as well as policies, and thoughts and values as well as behavior – at all levels of the hierarchy, not just the top.

Gherardi (1995) describes what we might find if we were to study an organization that fostered conventionally gendered behavior. She argues that women in such a setting could and should demand equality in some arenas, like comparable pay for comparable work, fair and equal promotion possibilities, and clear recognition of competence. However, because these forms of on-the-job equality would upset the traditional gender order, Gherardi argues that women could and should restore men's comfort level by developing friendly relationships that include joking, flirtation (without necessarily following through with sexual availability), dressing attractively, etc. This is an interesting set of ideas, and it is possible that this form of traditionally gendered behavior might work better in some contexts (Gherardi is Italian) than others. For example, in the US, flirtation might be taken as a sexual invitation, and refusal might create resentment as a 'sexual tease.' Some women might take offense at the suggestion that would be expected to joke and flirt with men they don't find attractive. On the other hand, an organization that accommodates traditional gendered behavior in this way might be a kind of organization where many people would be both comfortable and productive. This is the kind of approach to 'equality' that is seldom studied by market-liberal feminists and therefore, there is all the more reason to explore it.

## BREAKING TRADITIONAL SEXUAL STEREOTYPES

For this third approach to equality, imagine a very dirty, smiling, strong oil rig worker. His face is smeared with grease and he looks like he is enjoying talking with a very good friend. Ely and Meyerson (in press) studied oil rig workers, again in an atypical organizational setting. Oil rigs set into the ocean floor miles from the shore are very dangerous places to work. Individual accidents can leave workers seriously injured, drowned, or otherwise dead. Larger scale accidents can blow up an entire rig, potentially killing dozens of workers, losing large amounts of money, polluting the ocean, killing sea life, and ruining the reputation of the sponsoring oil corporation. Given this level of danger, oil rig workers generally have quite a tough guy, macho image. Ely and Meyerson, however, heard of a few oil rigs where, in the interest of increasing safety, there had been a deliberate attempt to build a different kind of culture, where emotions like fear and upset were expressed without inhibition, and where personal closeness and caring were the norm. All this was gender atypical behavior, but the men on the rig adapted to the new norms because when emotions could be expressed rather than suppressed, and close relationships were encouraged, it was easier to get the workers to adhere to safety conscious rules. Work-related accidents on these 'caring culture' oil rigs were rare, and so a gender atypical pattern of behavior became acceptable and macho forms of deviance were severely curtailed.

This is quite an achievement. There are probably dozens of other organizational contexts where, for one reason or another, gender atypical forms of behavior are condoned, even encouraged. Studying these kinds of gendered transformation might open eyes to new ways of reaching gender equality, in ways our mothers and fathers might never have imagined.

## STUDYING A MORE EQUAL FUTURE

These three approaches to gender equality are quite different from each other, and quite different from the usual kinds of organizational gender study. It is possible that androgynous organizations are not the wave of the future, as so few men and women would be comfortable abandoning more conventional expressions of their genders. However, in some countries and some industries, various forms of androgyny might even now be commonplace. The question, then, would be: Why does androgyny thrive in some contexts and not others?

The expression of more traditional forms of masculinity and femininity, in the second option, might be the most popular of the three options for most people. This traditional approach to gender equality has been understudied. Gherardi's formulation is more subtle than this shorthand label indicates, as she couples claims to work-related equality, for example in pay and recognition, with order-restoring comfort gestures on the part of women on other dimensions. Exploring this option involves challenging feminist (particularly in the market-liberal countries) disdain for flirtation and other modes of soothing male egos, but the fact remains that most people in most countries are more comfortable than feminists are with traditional gender relations. This option deserves exploration, including the question of whether men might be expected to make comparable moves to enhance the comfort levels of their female co-workers.

Finally, the third option – of finding novel ways to enact being a man or being a woman at work – might point the way to finding havens for those men and women who do not feel comfortable in traditionally gendered corporate settings. This third option also might demonstrate ways of approaching those who are used to traditional forms of gendered behavior, and giving them work-related, self-interested reasons for trying new ways of being a man or a woman at work. Here again Butler's ideas of playfulness, parody, and performativity (2004) might suggest powerful ways of undoing gender inequalities in unanticipated ways. This third option might be the most practical of the three, in that it entails change in small steps, one job or one site at a time: small wins (Meyerson and Kolb, 2000).

No doubt, these three approaches to equality are only scratching the surface of what is possible. If gender researchers as a group were to turn our attention away from documenting inequality, and if we were to investigate instead what novel forms of organizational gender equality are possible, we might point the way to a more equal future. Surely, this is, at this point, more helpful than observing familiar inequalities endlessly reproduce themselves in new forms. Maybe someday, with this kind of innovative gender research, we would see some forms of gender inequality simply disappear.

# REFERENCES

Aaltio, I., and Mills, A. (eds) (2002) *Gender, Identity, and the Culture of Organizations*. New York: Routledge.

Acker, J. (1992) 'Gendering Organizational Theory' in A. Mills and P. Tancred (eds), *Gendering Organizational Analysis*. London: Sage.

Acker, J. (in press) 'Theorizing Class, Race, and Gender in Organizations' in E. Jeanes, D.Knights, and P. Yancey-Martin (eds), *Gender, Work, and Organization Handbook*. Oxford: Blackwells,

Alvesson, M., and Due Billing, Y. (1992) *Understanding Gender and Organization*. London: Sage.

Alvesson, M., and Due Billing, Y. (2002) 'Beyond Body Counting: A Discussion of the Social Construction of Gender at Work' in I. Aaltio and A. Mills (eds), *Gender, Identity, and the Culture of Organizations*. New York: Routledge.

Bacchi, C. (2001) 'Beyond "Multiple Subjectivities"' in P. Nursey-Brady and C. Bacchi (eds), *Left Directions: Is There a Third Way?* Perth: University of Western Australia Press.

Baxter, J., and Wright, E. (2000) The Glass Ceiling Hypothesis: A Comparative Study of the United States, Sweden, and Australia, *Gender and Society*, 14(2) 275–294.

Bielby, W., and Baron, J. (1986) Men and Women at Work: Sex Segregation and Statistical Discrimination, *American Journal of Sociology*, 91(1) 759–799.

Blackburn, R., Jarmon, J., and Brooks, B. (2000) The Puzzle of Gender Segregation and Inequality: A Cross-national Analysis, *European Sociological Review*, 16(2) 119–135.

Britton, D. (2000) The Epistemology of the Gendered Organization, *Gender & Society*, 14(3) 418–434.

Butler, J. (2004) *Undoing Gender*. London: Routledge.

Collins, P. (2004) *Black Sexual Politics: African Americans, Gender, and the New Racism*. New York: Routledge,.

Collinson, D., and Hearn, J. (1994) Naming Men as Men: Implications for Work, Organization, and Management, *Gender, Work and Organization*, 1(1) 2–22.

Connell, R. (1995) *Masculinities*. Cambridge, UK: Polity Press.

Connell, R. (2008) A Thousand Miles from Kindness: Men, Masculinities, and Modern Institutions, *Men's Studies Press*, 16, 237–253.

Czarniawska, B., and Sevon, G. (2008) The Thin Edge of the Wedge: Foreign Women Professors as Double Strangers in Academia, *Gender, Work and Organization*, 15(3) 235–287.

Dellinger, K. (2002) Wearing Gender and Sexuality 'On your Sleeve': Dress Norms and the Importance of Occupational and Organizational Culture at Work, *Gender Issues*, Winter, 3–25.

Ely, R., and Meyerson, D. (2001) 'Theories of Gender in Organizations: A New Approach to Organizational Analysis and Change' in B. Staw and R. Sutton (eds), *Research in Organizational Behavior*. Greenwich, CT: JAI Press, 103–151.

Ely, R., and Meyerson, D. (in press) Unmasking Manly Men: The Organizational Reconstruction of Men's Identity, *Administrative Science Quarterly*.

Federal Glass Ceiling Commission (1995) *Good for Business: Making Full Use of the Nation's Human Capital*. Washington, DC: Government Printing Office.

Ferree, M., and Yancey-Martin, P. (1995) *Feminist Organizations*. Philadelphia, PA: Temple University Press.

Fletcher, J., and Bailyn, L. (1996) 'Challenging the Last Boundary: Reconnecting Work and Family' in M. Arthur and D. Rousseau (eds), *The Boundaryless Career*. Oxford: Oxford University Press.

Fogel, A., and Melson, G. (eds) (1986) *Origins of Nurturance: Developmental, Biological, and Cultural Perspectives on Caregiving*. Princeton, NJ: Erlbaum.

Gherardi, S. (1995) *Gender, Symbolism, and Organizational Cultures.* London: Sage.

Halford, S., and Leonard, P. (2001) *Gender, Power, and Organizations.* New York: Palgrave.

Hearn, J., and Parkin, P.W. (1987) *Sex at Work.* Brighton, UK: Wheatsheaf.

Hochschild, A. (1997) *The Time Bind: When Work Becomes Home and Home Becomes Work.* New York: Metropolitan Books.

Kanter, R. (1977) *Men and Women of the Corporation.* New York: Basic Books.

Kanter, R., and Roessner, J. (2003) Deloitte & Touche (B): Changing the workplace. Harvard Business School Case 9-300-013. Boston, MA: Harvard Business School Publishing.

Kerfoot, D., and Knights, D. (1993) Management, Masculinity, and Manipulation: From Paternalism to Corporate Strategy in Financial Services in Britain, *Journal of Management Studies,* 30(4) 659–677.

Knights, D., and McCabe, D. (2001) A Different World: Shifting Masculinities in the Transition to Call Centres, *Organization,* 8(4) 619–645.

Kondo, D. (1990) *Crafting Selves: Power, Gender, and Discourses of Identity in a Japanese Workplace.* Chicago: University of Chicago Press.

Lorber, J. (2005) *Breaking the Bowls: Degendering and Feminist Change.* New York: W.W. Norton.

Marshall, J. (1984) *Women Managers: Travellers in a Male World.* Chichester: John Wiley & Sons Ltd.

Martin, J. (1990) Deconstructing Organizational Taboos: The Suppression of Gender Conflict in Organizations, *Organizational Science,* 1, 339–359.

Martin, J. (1992) 'The Inherent Conservatism of Empirical Organizational Research' in R. Stablein and P. Frost (eds), *Doing Exemplary Research.* New York: Sage, 233–239.

Martin, J., and Meyerson, D. (1998) 'Women and Power: Conformity, Resistance, and Disorganized Co-action' in R. Kramer and M. Neale (ds), *Power and Influence in Organizations.* Thousand Oaks, CA: Sage, 311–348.

Martin, J., Knopoff, K., and Beckman, C. (1998) An Alternative to Bureaucratic Impersonality and Emotional Labor: Bounded Emotionality in The Body Shop, *Administrative Science Quarterly,* 2, 115–139.

Meyerson, D., and Kolb, D. (2000) Moving out of the 'Armchair': Developing a Framework to Bridge the Gap between Feminist Theory and Practice, *Organization,* 7, 589–608.

Padavic, I., and Reskin, B. (2002) *Women and Men at Work.* 2nd edn. Thousand Oaks, CA: Pine Forge Press,.

Pearce, J. (2001) *Organization and Management in the Embrace of Government.* Mahwah, NJ: Lawrence Erlbaum Associates,.

Poggio, B. (2000) Between Bytes and Bricks: Gender Cultures in Work Contexts, *Economic and Industrial Democracy,* 21, 381–402.

Pringle, R. (1989) *Secretaries Talk: Sexuality, Power, and Work.* Sydney: Allen and Unwin.

Rantalaiho, L. (1997) 'Contextualising Gender' in L. Rantalaiho and T. Heiskanen (eds), *Gendered Practices in Working Life.* London: MacMillan, 16–35.

Rhode, D. (2002) *The Difference Difference Makes: Women and Leadership.* Stanford, CA: Stanford Law and Politics.

Ridgeway, C. (1997) Interaction and the Conservation of Gender Inequality: Considering Employment, *American Sociological Review,* 63, 218–235.

Ring, P., Bigley, G., D'Aunno, T., and Khanna, T. (2005) Perspectives on how Governments Matter, *Academy of Management Review,* 30(2) 308–320.

Rosaldo, S., and Lamphere, L. (1974) *Women, Culture, and Society.* Stanford, CA: Stanford University Press.

Strober, M. (1984) 'Toward a General Theory of Occupational Sex Segregation: The Case of Public School Teaching' in B. Reskin (ed.), *Sex Segregation in the Workplace: Trends, Explanations, Remedies.* Washington, DC: National Academy Press, 144–156.

Tom, A. (1995) 'Children of our culture? Class, power and learning in a feminist bank' in M. Ferree and P. Yancey-Martin (eds), *Feminist Organizations*. Philadelphia, PA: Temple University Press, 165–179.

United Nations (1996, 2000, 2005) *Human Development Report*, Oxford: Oxford University Press.

West, C., and Zimmerman, D. (1987) Doing Gender, *Gender & Society*, 1, 125–151.

Yancey-Martin, P. (1996) 'Gendering and Evaluating Dynamics: Men, Masculinities, and Managements' in D. Collinson and J. Hearn (eds), *Men as Managers, Managers as Men: Critical Perspectives on Men, Masculinities, and Management*. London: Sage.

# 14

# Practicing Gender Neutrality in Organizations

PÄIVI KORVAJÄRVI
*University of Tampere*

## INTRODUCTION

The aim of this chapter is to rethink the tensions between the simultaneous culture of denial and acceptance of the significance of gender at work, and reflect such tensions in a framework of feminist theorizations on the current developments in capitalism. The argument for the simultaneous ignorance and approval of gender matters is based on empirical work conducted in Finland. Finland is usually found to be representative of the Nordic countries, which are renowned for their social democratic welfare systems (Esping-Andersen, 1999). The overwhelming majority of the Finnish labor force works in the service sector (Pyöriä, 2005: 35) with the economy based on the advanced use of information and communication technology – developing itself as a leading information society as well as preserving the main structures of the welfare state (Castells and Himanen, 2002: 156).

Nonetheless, Finland is not a high-tech welfare wonderland. On the contrary, during the first few years of the twenty-first century significant cuts in the services provided by the welfare state have been made and a strong trend toward outsourcing welfare services has been observed. In addition, the rapid growth of knowledge work, which is partly based on information and communication technology, has come to an end (Pyöriä, 2005: 288). It has been estimated that the changes underway are leading to deeper social divisions and inequalities in society (ibid.). Still, the Nordic labor markets are dominated by a discourse of gender equality and equal opportunities, even though everyday work practices belie this assumption (Haavind and Magnusson, 2005; Lister 2009). The background to this contradictory picture is partly rooted in persistent occupational segregation. Although occupational gender segregation has slightly decreased in the last fifty years, it is still striking in Finland and one of the steepest in the European Union (Lister, 2009). As has been suggested by Gherardi (1995: 15), occupational segregation may simultaneously contribute to

an increase in hierarchical differences between women and men and to the protection of women's and men's own activities within their 'own' areas. Thus segregation
may also dampen the prospect of open competition and conflict between women
and men.

Yet there remains a continuous tension between the silent agreement on gender
equality and the everyday practices of employees in work organizations. On the
one hand, employees tend to conceive of gender issues as culturally non-existent
problems at the workplace level. On the other hand, employees commonly identify
existing or even increasing gender conflicts at the societal level, such as the wage gap
(Rantalaiho and Heiskanen, 1997). Accordingly, the perceived practices of equality
at the level of the society at large and everyday life intertwine in contradictory ways.
This situation serves as a good context for exploring gender neutrality. The focus
of this chapter is on gendered work organizations engaged in service work, which
crucially represent the tendencies of the new economy with its intensive emphasis
on the requirements of communication at work.

In the following sections, I first provide an overview of the relevant conceptualizations which are useful in exploring the tendencies of neutralizing gender matters.
Special attention is paid to the possible ways of analyzing the culture of gender neutrality, which includes the denial of the significance of gender and sexuality in work.
The chapter thus begins with a discussion of practicing gender and related research
approaches and goes on to explore the notions of emotional labor, aesthetic labor,
and gender as cultural work, which I find crucial in a gendered analysis of the current changes in service work. Furthermore, drawing on empirical findings from
Finland, I present examples which imply simultaneous acceptance and denial as
ways of practicing gender in work. Finally, the chapter concludes with suggestions
for future research.


## GENDER VIEWS ON THE NEW ECONOMY: MAPPING THE FIELD

Thinking about gender as either absent or present in work means that gender is
defined as an activity in the workplace. Consequently, the relevant conceptualizations with which to grasp the phenomena of denying and recognizing gender in work
are based on understandings of gender-as-performance, such as the interactional
and cultural approaches to studying gender in society. I explore these approaches
through two dynamics which intertwine. The first approach has its starting point in
gender dynamics (West and Zimmerman, 1987; Acker, 1990; 1992; Gherardi, 1994;
Gherardi and Poggio, 2007; Martin, 2001; 2003; 2006; Rantalaiho and Heiskanen
1997) and the second in the dynamics of the economy (Hochschild, 1983/2003;
McDowell, 1997; Witz et al., 2003; Warhust and Nickson, 2009; Adkins, 2005; Lewis
and Simpson, 2007). The gender-driven approaches can be further divided into interactional approaches, processual or practical approaches, and cultural approaches of
doing gender. Each one emphasizes slightly different aspects of gender. However, all
approaches share the view that gender is an activity, not a characteristic of people.

The interactional approach serves as a background to the processual and
practical approaches. The starting point here is that gender is done in everyday

interaction in which it is routinely maintained and reproduced, as suggested by West and Zimmerman (1987) and Fenstermaker and West (2002). Thinking of gender as interaction based on ethnomethodology provided a path-breaking approach to conceiving gender in work. Drawing on Fenstermaker and West (2002: 42–44), it is possible to describe doing gender as an elastic rather than a strict concept. Its core idea is that gender is, as the authors write, 'an ongoing accomplishment' which means that 'we must locate its emergence in *social situations*' (ibid.: 42, italics in original). The interactional approach is not only limited to immediate social/ communicative situations but also applies to broader levels of society; according to the authors, it is about 'how situated social action contributes to the reproduction of social structure' (ibid.: 43). Thus activities that take place in particular social situations contribute to the maintenance and creation of social structures, such as occupational gender segregation.

The approach of 'doing gender' has provided a footing for the further development of gender as the activities of people. A powerful example of this is conceiving of gender as processes and practices (Acker, 1990; 1992), which I find fruitful since the approach looks for gender issues within and beyond observable interaction patterns. Gender-as-process includes the production of divisions between women and men as well as symbols and images which create femininities and masculinities and transform their conventional contents. It also includes interaction between women and men, and the internal mental work in which people look for appropriate ways of doing gender in the different contexts of work (Acker, 1992). Thus the concrete doing of gender includes patterns of thought, symbols, and images connected to women and femininities as well as to men and masculinities in various interactional contexts.

Acker's conceptualization has inspired empirical analyses based on observations and interviews on gender in work, particularly in Finland (Kantola, 2008; Husu, 2001; Korvajärvi, 2002; Rantalaiho and Heiskanen, 1997). The analyses based on interviews and texts reveal ways of both hiding gender and creating gender difference in work (Rantalaiho and Heiskanen, 1997). However, other interesting observations have been made which examine ways in which gender is embedded in the official definitions of the categories of statistical classifications (Gastelaars, 2002; Kinnunen, 1997), the (gendered) meaning of productivity in labor policy (Lehto, 1996), and efforts to define the comparable worth of work (Acker, 1989).

A slightly different view is suggested by Silvia Gherardi (1994), who looks at the gender dynamics located within social interactions and culture. She suggests that gender is not only done but thought. Accordingly, in interaction – in discussions, cooperation, negotiations, gossip, and humor between people – gender-related issues are based on what people use as resources in their thoughts. Moreover, their thoughts include culturally shared meanings which people in general recognize in society. The social orders as well as work cultures are also intertwined with the symbols and images that shape people's thoughts and interaction. Gherardi (ibid.) has stressed the significance of the symbolic order and the metaphorical aspects of gender in the analysis of gender in work. She has studied gender in organizations by asking both female and male employees to describe in interviews how women have entered male dominated work organizations. The analysis reveals the continuous mobility in the practice of hiding and emphasizing gender difference (Gherardi and Poggio, 2007).

Patricia Yancey Martin (2001; 2003; 2006) makes a distinction between gendering practices and practicing gender. She argues that gendering practices serve the discourses that are available as resources for people when they talk or think about gender, whereas practicing gender includes the concrete activities that people do at work. Particularly, practicing gender centers on situations, events, and patterns of thought and activities in which gender is usually done unreflectively in fluid episodes. Yancey Martin does not emphasize symbolic orders, culture, or metaphors in the same ways as Gherardi, yet she creates short stories and vignettes based on her interviews and observations. Interestingly, her main argument is that the dominant way of practicing gender in work is non-reflective. At the same time, however, non-reflective ways of practicing gender are collectively and routinely understandable in work organizations. Thus gendering practices and practicing gender are mutually reinforcing.

The interactional, processual, and cultural approaches have their roots in the same theorizations. The authors use as their resources both the conceptualizations of interaction and cultural sociology (Goffman, 1959; Bourdieu, 1980/1990) and a variety of feminist theorizations on discourses and identities (Connell, 1987; Butler, 1990; Kondo, 1990). The interactional, processual, and cultural approaches share the view that theoretical contributions need to be based on rich empirical work and the focus is on what happens every day in work organizations: in the discourses, identities, and understandings around work. The starting point of the approaches comprises the questions, narratives, and problems of gender. Gender and its fluidity, mobility, and elusiveness are the crucial common denominator for these approaches. Scholars like Acker, Gherardi, Yancey Martin are thus indebted to West and Zimmerman, and retain a focus on gender dynamics.

In contrast, I introduce here starting points that draw on the changing economy and consist of a variety of views which do not have as strong a common footing as the gender-driven views. At the same time, the roots of the economy-based approach are in sociological understandings of change in work and economy, working conditions, and the emerging requirements of reflecting gender and identities in work. Consequently, rather than gender, their common denominator is change in the economy and its impact on everyday work. My argument is that, from the perspective of the economy-dynamic, the most relevant approaches to gender matters are the conceptualizations of emotional labor, aesthetic labor, and the cultural feminization of work.

The concept of emotional labor focuses on the ways in which commercialization and markets force employees to manipulate their own and others' selves (Hochschild, 1983/2003). The core idea of emotional labor is the transmutation of emotions for commercial purposes in performance-based work cultures. The goal of emotional labor is to create, according to Hochschild, 'a proper state of mind in others' (ibid.: 7). The discussion on emotional labor has been continuous and heated (Abiala, 1999; Bolton and Boyd, 2003; Witz et al., 2003; Lewis and Simpson, 2007; Meanwell, Wolfe, and Hallett, 2008; Payne, 2009). Drawing on the interactional tradition in sociology, for example Goffman, Darwin, and Freud (see Hochschild,

1983/2003: 211–232), the concept of emotional labor has provided a path-breaking view in understanding emotions as employee and management resources in work. Managing emotions includes activities, expressions, and performances of gender that include and represent femininities and masculinities in the context of, or according to, actual situations (McDowell, 1997: 198). This is close to what Acker (1992) has called a process of internal mental work. However, Acker describes more individually self-managed situations, whereas the management of emotions refers to the activities inspired and forced by management and customers or clients.

The concept of aesthetic labor operates in a critical relationship to emotional labor, but lays stress on the significance of physical appearances and styles in service work (Witz et al., 2003). More broadly, aesthetic labor consists of management's activities to mobilize corporeality as a capacity in work. In the same way as the concept of emotional labor, aesthetic labor includes the idea of the commercialization and commodification of human activities in work (Warhurst and Nickson, 2009; Adkins, 2001). However, the particularity of aesthetic labor lies in its emphasis on the commodification of the body and corporeality at work (Warhurst and Nickson, 2009).

The approach of emphasizing the cultural feminization of work is based on the theorization of the crucial changes in the current economy caused by the penetration of knowledge-intensive services (Adkins, 2001, 2005; Gray 2003; Jokinen, 2005). Accordingly, management and clients increasingly define the content of work in interaction with their customers and subcontractors. Appropriate skills, in using language, communication, the management of emotions, styles, and performances, and the creation of trust relations, are demanded of the employees. These skills are suggested to be laden with femininities (Adkins, 2001). It has even been argued that the process of restructuring labor means the cultural feminization of the current economy (Adkins, 2005). In these processes, the employees use and are expected to use gender and sexuality as their aesthetic and stylistic resources with the aim of convincing and attracting customers (Korvajärvi, 2009).

It has been suggested that, with this line of development, women's positions and women's futures would improve in the labor market (McDowell, 1997: 207). Furthermore, it has been put forward that this kind of cultural feminization of work could be a sign of the deconstruction of the stereotypical divide between women and men in working life (ibid.). However, it is not self-evident that appreciating feminine skills will increase the esteem of work done by women. Rather, it has been shown that women's feminine performances at work are perceived as natural and taken for granted (Rantalaiho and Heiskanen, 1997). Whilst men's performances of femininity, or use of emotions, may be highly appreciated, women's masculine performances at work typically have negative consequences for women (McDowell, 1997: 137–157; Lewis and Simpson, 2007; Brannan, 2005). The denial of performances of femininity by women and the celebration of performances of femininity by men leads to the possibility that gender and sexuality may be an emerging resource in work, however, not for women (Adkins, 2001).

In sum, the views starting from gender, on the one hand, and from the economy, on the other hand, differ from each other in several ways. The view stressing gender-dynamics focuses mostly on various routine and non-reflective ways of doing gender at work, whereas the view stressing the requirements of the new economy aims to analyze various ways of doing gender in activities which both management and customers mobilize the employees to do – where the doing of gender is a deliberate strategy. The gender-driven views concentrate much on culturally shared activities that take place in the social communities of work. The economy-driven views focus on processes to which the employees need to adapt. Both gender- and economy-driven views emphasize gender as a dynamic action in work. They emphasize the analysis both in discourses, i.e. in gendering practices (Yancey Martin, 2003; 2006), and in concrete activities, i.e. in practicing gender (ibid.).

These approaches argue for the significance of gendered symbols, thought models, and assumptions which lie in the background of the visible activities. The approaches which grow from the changes in work and economy stress the commodification of the activities required of the employees. Emotional labor, aesthetic labor, and the ideas of cultural feminization presuppose both consciously aimed and internally adopted practices and performances in which gender and sexuality are embedded. Aesthetic labor and gender as cultural feminization also bring in the significance of the body and bodily activities in work.

With these understandings in mind, I now turn to the example of service work in Finland. Specifically, I analyze the particular constructions of gender and its practice in the current knowledge economy. These include the aim of neutralizing the significance of gendering practices that serve to create an unreflective gender harmony in Finnish society.

## NEUTRALIZING FEMININITY IN ORGANIZATIONS?

Gender neutrality is regarded as silence on gender issues, meaning that gender and sexuality are obscured in organizations (Acker, 1990; Korvajärvi, 2002). Furthermore, gender neutrality is connected to the belief that society has achieved full gender equality, as is often thought in Finland (Heiskanen and Rantalaiho, 1997: 196; Ronkainen, 2001). The term 'gender neutrality' is closely connected to interpretations of empirical findings (Korvajärvi, 2002). However gender neutrality as a concept is under-theorized. It is suggested that gender neutrality is a non-gendered approach including the idea that gender has no impact on work or on the activities of employees (Hanmer and Hearn, 1999). From this point of view, gender neutrality can be conceived of as a sign of undoing gender in such a way that gender does not structure work organizations or people's activities in work. Here, however, I argue that gender neutrality is a way of doing gender which masks gender conflicts in work. Further, I propose that it is a dominant way of doing gender in some countries, such as Finland. It is mostly a non-reflective way of practicing gender which maintains gender neutrality as a way of creating and sustaining harmony in work organizations.

The interviews, observations and other ethnographic fieldwork on which this discussion is based were conducted in two phases. The first phase, from 1986–1996 involved a variety of research sites: an insurance company, a metal factory, a local bank branch, a chemical factory, an employment agency, a regional hospital, a unit in a social welfare office, and an inland revenue office. Four of the case study organizations (the insurance company, metal factory, employment agency, and the unit in a social welfare office) have been analyzed in detail (Korvajärvi, 1998). In the second phase, case studies based on research and fieldwork along similar lines were conducted in four call centres, the first between 1998–2002, the second between 1999–2005, and the other two in 2005–2006 (Korvajärvi, 2004; 2009; Koivunen, 2006).

The research results from Finland show that the content of everyday interaction in service work has dramatically changed during the last twenty years (Korvajärvi, 1998, 2004, 2009). In the 1980s, service work in the case study organizations, according to the service workers, was imbued with friendly, helpful service and empathetic relationships with the customers and clients. It was the customer or client to whose questions or demands the employee had to adapt. The aim was to find a solution which satisfied the wishes of the customer or client. Thus the employee was in a subordinate relationship to the customer. In the 1990s, the situation gradually changed. Instead of following the customer in the interaction, it became more and more important to 'do business' – to make deals with the customer in the private sector, and to require the customer to help her/himself instead of expecting services from authorities in the public sector.

As a result of this shift, the leading figure in the customer–employee communication became the employee. However, she or he was not an autonomous subject in this situation. Instead, the targets and aims set by the management and administrative bodies forced the employees to direct their interaction and negotiations with the customers accordingly. Similar changes have taken place in Britain (Warhust and Nickson, 2007) due to strong pressures toward a market orientation in public and private services. This has led to a contradictory situation of simultaneous efficiency and personal orientation to the customers, which are both defined by the management. This has been called customer-oriented bureaucracy (Korczynski, 2009).

New partners, such as customers and client organizations, are also involved in shaping the interaction. This is particularly evident in call centers where other firms and organizations outsource their tasks (Korvajärvi, 2004; 2009). The client organizations make the guidelines and scripts for customer service representatives, and may define in what kinds of voices their products or services need to be marketed and sold. In customer satisfaction surveys, the customers give their opinions on from whom and in what kinds of voices they wish to receive services on different occasions and in specific matters. The management takes into account the wishes and views that the customers express on the ways in which the work is to be organized. Gendered discourses are embedded in the wishes and hopes of both the clients and the customers (ibid.).

Thus the substance of the service or the product and a kind of general opinion direct the ways in which gender is embedded in interaction. For example, the employees' experience was that customers like to listen to technology-related advice in a manly voice concerning, among other things, the use of the internet or mobile phones. In particular, the employees' experience was that older women (over 60 years) liked to listen to a low manly voice. Selling insurance policies was found to be the task of a more mature person. The marketing and selling of women's magazines or leisure magazines related to women's activities (e.g. knitting) was self-evidently found to be a woman's task in the call centers. Drawing on the customers' and clients' opinions produced a stereotypical and segregated division between women's and men's jobs. At the same time, it made gender a routine issue related to the content of the services (Koivunen, 2006).

The employees and customer service representatives are taught to internalize and mobilize the ways of interaction to be used in different customer situations. Emotional labor and aesthetic labor, through changing the ways of using the voice, its tone and speed, according to the (assumed) expectations of the female and male customers, are the tools and styles which the employees use in order to fulfill the various demands placed upon them. Many of the current requirements at work relate to the 'proper' acting and performing of behaviors appropriate to situations. An experienced customer service representative described her work in a call centre in 2005:

> The most important thing is that you listen to the customers, what they say, and you know to ask the right question at the right moment . . . [. . .] You have to somehow find the kind of contact that the customer and I are on the same wavelength, so if the customer starts listening, she/he soon starts to think that this offer would be fine for her/him.

At the same time, a supervisor described the work content of the customer service representatives in the same call center:

> The job is really more about having a chat with the customer than trying to press them into buying services and products.

Furthermore, the voice on the phone was said to be important, as a manager in a call center put it:

> A smiling voice, a joyful voice, a captivating voice are all of great interest. What we don't want is a desultory, passive and dumb voice or a voice in which you can't hear the employee smiling. Smiling is extremely important.

The employees' crucial contribution is to produce images and impressions that present the firms, products, and services in a pleasant and attractive light to the customers. However it is these chatty, cheerful, attentive voices that are associated with feminine skills (Adkins, 2001), suggesting a gendered, rather than neutral, practice.

The new demands of conscious acting such as using one's voice, dressing properly or using gestures in face-to-face situations stress interactive and bodily elements at work. They also bring in gender issues. However, drawing on the second phase analysis, it is also apparent that the evidence supports the view that challenges the arguments of feminization *for* women. Lisa Adkins (2001: 691) warns that women rarely get good positions in the new economy, even if the performances of gender are used as a resource of knowing and using skills at work. This is a paradoxical argument. However, her point is that there is on the one hand a tendency to naturalize and ignore women's performances, both feminine and masculine ones, and, on the other, to recognize and appreciate men's performances whether they are feminine or masculine ones. According to Adkins (ibid.), this means that women and women's activities are separated from, or unable to benefit from, the feminization of work.

I argue that the process of neglecting the gendered meaning of what women are doing is a current trend in Finnish service sector work. Drawing on the second phase follow-up analysis, several ways of understanding the gendering of work entail hiding gender or making gender irrelevant. However, at the same time, there are contradictory trends in conceiving gender. It is the view that gender does not matter in one's own workplace that was the primary way in which gender was negated in the case study organizations. The segregation of women's and men's spheres of activities and the viewing of this situation as natural, or self-evidently reasonable in work assisted in reproducing and maintaining the invisibility of gender as an 'issue.' This appears reflected at a national level. According to representative nationwide statistical surveys in Finland, women, but also the majority of men, recognize gender inequality in terms of the wage gap and lack of career opportunities. However, when the inequalities were discussed in the interviews, the usual phrase was that the wage gap or inequality in career chances did not concern them at their own workplace. Instead, the female and male employees interviewed said that the problems exist on the level of the society at large. Accordingly, from their point of view, adequate legislation was the solution to these problems. It was found that there was nothing to be done at the workplace level (Korvajärvi, 2002). This culturally embedded line of thinking was to locate the social situations at hand as distinct from the social (societal) structures, which were kept at a distance .

Exceptions to the logic of distancing gender were the women who had personal experiences of discrimination, particularly as regards promotions. They were usually educated women in middle managerial positions who found that even when they were well qualified, a younger, less experienced, man had been promoted instead of them. The other exception was women who think that career prospects are dependent on individual decisions. They have chosen not to aim for a promotion or to apply for an upper position on the hierarchical ladder because they did not want a job which includes management and leadership. Having found themselves deemed unsuitable for leadership tasks in various subtle ways, they no longer contemplate it as an opportunity and have thus reduced the issue of gender equality to the appearance of individual aims and desires (Korvajärvi, 2002).

The issue is not only one of neglecting gender. On the contrary, there were certain views expressed in the interviews that aimed strongly at belittling women's activities in work. An example of this is the view observed in the studies that women's social communities at work are 'envious.' The view of women's workplaces as envious social communities with a negative social atmosphere was common to all the case study organizations. At the same time, those women who talked about this 'fact' said that this was not true at their own workplace – they told stories about other female dominated and quarrelsome workplaces (Korvajärvi, 2002).

## Reflections, and Implications for Future Research

The phenomenon of distancing gender as a way of doing gender is not limited to Finland. Interestingly enough, the empirical evidence from public-sector work-sites in New South Wales shows very similar patterns (Connell, 2006). In Connell's research, too, the sense of gender problems being located elsewhere was a common mode of thought. According to her study, the cultural distance of gender issues was intertwined with neo-liberal views. Such views disguise structural and cultural gender patterns and address gender issues as the freedom to choose for individuals, who are not conceived as women or men.

Moreover, the analysis of narratives on gender in Italy also brings in similar types of processes (Gherardi and Poggio, 2007). Particularly striking was the silencing of masculinities in discursive practices by connecting gender issues only to women, thus normalizing the masculine side in organizations. In addition, as was also the case in Finland, in men's views gender was naturalized into motherhood and its assumed consequences, for which only women were thought to be responsible. Moreover, the discursive practice conceived of women as maintaining and reproducing an envious social collective of work – as also happened in the Finnish case.

To conclude, the complexity of gender dynamics in work organizations was tied to changes in work requirements which were being pushed through management-set targets. From the point of view of gender-driven approaches the crucial issue in the Finnish case is the shared but unreflective conceiving of gender as a distant matter. In contrast to this, economy-driven targets require individual gendered performances which are deliberated in interaction with customers. Gender-driven approaches focus the analysis on the shared culture among the employees in an organization, whereas economy-driven approaches, the emotional and aesthetic labor, and cultural feminization of work, address the creation of the desired 'proper' relationships between the organizations, employees, and customers or clients. Both the unreflective gender-driven and reflective economy-driven ways of doing gender undervalue the significance of women's activities irrespective of their feminine or masculine contents. Thus gender dynamics and the dynamics of economic changes feed into one another. Accordingly, in my view both gender- and economy-driven approaches are invaluable and inseparable. The analyses of changing gendering practices as shared understandings, and of changing requirements of practicing gender as activities of people, need to be understood as intertwining.

The practices of both gender and economy result in concrete forms in local cultural conditions and situations. Thus in future research it is worth engaging in international and comparative research on such issues and forming communities of practice to analyze the various localities and their differences and similarities. Further, the considerations here are based on empirical evidence which focuses on white and (more or less) middle-class employees in an advanced market economy, in the context of an established welfare society. In the future, the economies of the Global North will be increasingly dependent on a more diverse workforce, with an immigrant labor.

The challenge is to analyze and reconsider how the cultural denial of gender, in particular women, in everyday work and the acceptance of gender divisions at the societal level are shaped in the complex situation of transnational everyday work. The crucial challenge for future analysis is to look for the complexity of doing femininities, masculinities, and ethnicities in work. Will feminine aspects of gender become even more hidden in work, and in this sense neutral, while other aspects become more prominent? Further analysis of the contradictions between denying and perceiving gender needs conceptual reworking. It is crucial to analyze how the dynamics between gender and economy address both discourses and practices which simultaneously make gender hidden and visible in work.

## ACKNOWLEDGEMENTS

My thanks go to M.A. Laura Tohka for language checking. Further I highly appreciate the excellent comments and corrections of Joan Löfgren PhD. The writing of the chapter has been supported by the Academy of Finland, project 112 5476.

## REFERENCES

Abiala, K. (1999) Customer Orientation and Sales Situations: Variations in Interactive Service Work, *Acta Sociologica*, 42(3) 208–222.

Acker, J. (1989) *Comparable Worth: Gender, Class and Pay Equity*. Philadelphia: Temple University Press.

Acker, J. (1990) Hierarchies, Jobs and Bodies: A Theory of Gendered Organizations, *Gender & Society*, 4(2) 139–158.

Acker, J. (1992) 'Gendering Organizational Theory' in A. Mills and P. Tancred (eds), *Gendering Organizational Analysis*. Thousand Oaks, CA: Sage, 248–260.

Adkins, L. (2001) Cultural Feminization: 'Money, Sex and Power' for Women, *Signs*, 26(3) 669–695.

Adkins, L. (2005) The New Economy, Property and Personhood, *Theory, Culture & Society*, 22(1) 111–130.

Bolton, S.C., and Boyd, C. (2003) Trolley Dolly or Skilled Emotion Manager? Moving from Hochschild's Managed Heart, *Work, Employment and Society*, 17(2) 289–308.

Bourdieu, P. (1980/1990) *The Logic of Practice*. Stanford: Stanford University Press.

Brannan, M. (2005) Once More with Feeling: Ethnographic Reflections on the Mediation of Tensions in a Small Team of Call Centre Workers, *Gender, Work and Organization*, 12(5) 420–439.

Butler, J. (1990) *Gender Trouble: Feminism and Subversion of Identity*. New York: Routledge.

Castells, M., and Himanen, P. (2002) *The Information Society and the Welfare State. The Finnish Model*. Oxford: Oxford University Press.

Connell, R. (1987) *Gender and Power*. Stanford: Stanford University Press.

Connell, R. (2006) The Experience of Gender Change in Public Sector Organizations, *Gender, Work and Organization*, 13(5) 435–451.

Esping-Andersen, G. (1999) *Social Foundations of Postindustrial Economies*. Oxford: Oxford University Press.

Fenstermaker, S., and West, C. (eds) (2002) *Doing Gender, Doing Difference. Inequality, Power and Institutional Change*. New York: Routledge.

Gastelaars, M. (2002) 'How do Statistical Aggregates Work? About the Individual and Organizational Effects of Gender Classifications' in B. Czarniawska and H. Höpfl (eds),

*Casting the Other. The Maintenance and Production of Inequalities in Work Organizations.* London: Routledge, 7–22.

Gherardi, S. (1994) The Gender we Do, the Gender we Think, the Gender we Do in Everyday Organizational Lives, *Human Relations,* 47(6) 591–609.

Gherardi, S., and Poggio, B. (2007) *Gendertelling in Organizations. Narratives from Male-dominated Environments.* Copenhagen: Liber & Copenhagen Business School Press.

Goffman, E. (1959) *The Presentation of Everyday Life.* Garden City, New York: Doubleday.

Gray, A. (2003) Enterprising Femininity. New Modes of Work and Subjectivity, *European Journal of Cultural Studies,* 6(4) 489–506.

Haavind, H., and Magnusson, E. (2005) The Nordic Countries – Welfare Paradises for Women and Children? *Feminism & Psychology,* 15(2) 227–235.

Hanmer, J., and Hearn, J. (1999) 'Gender and Welfare Research' in F. Williams, J. Popay, and A. Oakley (eds), *Welfare Research: A Critical Review.* London: UCL Press, 106–130.

Hochschild, A.R. (1983/2003) *Managed Heart. Commercialization of Human Feeling.* Berkeley, CA: University of California Press.

Husu, L. (2001) *Sexism, Support and Survival in Academia: Academic Women and Hidden Discrimination in Finland.* Helsinki: Department of Social Psychology, University of Helsinki.

Jokinen, E. (2005) *Aikuisen arki.* Helsinki: Gaudeamus.

Kantola, J. (2008) Why do all the Women Disappear? Gendering Processes in a Political Science Department, *Gender, Work & Organization,* 15(2) 202–225.

Kinnunen, M. (1997) 'Making Gender with Classifications' in L. Rantalaiho and T. Heiskanen (eds), *Gendered Practices in Working Life.* London: Macmillan, 37–51.

Koivunen, T. (2006) .Asiakastyön ruumiillisuus yhteyskeskuksissa, *Työelämän tutkimus – Arbetslivsforskning,* 4(1) 1–11.

Kondo, D. (1990) *Crafting Selves: Identity, Work and Gender in a Japanese Factory.* Berkeley, CA: University of California Press.

Korvajärvi, P. (1998) *Gender Dynamics in White-collar Work Organizations.* Tampere: University of Tampere.

Korvajärvi, P. (2002) 'Gender-neutral Gender and Denial of Difference' in B. Czarniawska and H. Höpfl (eds), *Casting the Other. The Maintenance and Production of Inequalities in Work Organizations.* London: Routledge, 119–137.

Korvajärvi, P. (2004) 'Women and Technological Pleasure at Work?' in T. Heiskanen and J. Hearn (eds), *Information Society and the Workplace. Spaces, Boundaries and Agency.* London: Routledge, 125–142.

Korvajärvi, P. (2009) Attracting Customers through Practicing Gender in Call-centre Work, *Work Organisation, Labour and Globalisation,* 3(1) 131–143.

Korczynski, M. (2009) 'Understanding the Contradictory Lived Experience of Service Work. The Customer-oriented Bureaucracy' in M. Korczynski and L. Macdonald (eds), *Service Pork. Critical perspectives.* New York and London: Routledge, 73–90.

Lehto, A.-M. (1996) 'Tuottavuus- ja joustavuuspuheiden sukupuoli' in M. Kinnunen and P. Korvajärvi (eds), *Työelämän sukupuolistavat käytännöt.* Tampere: Vastapaino, , 71–87,

Lewis, P., and Simpson, R. (2007) 'Gender and Emotions: Introduction' in P. Lewis and R. Simpson (eds), *Gendering Emotions in Organizations.* Basingstoke: Palgrave Macmillan, 1–15.

Lister, R. (2009) A Nordic Nirvana? Gender, Citizenship, and Social Justice in the Nordic Welfare States, *Social Politics: International Studies in Gender, State and Society,* 16(2) 242–278.

McDowell, L. (1997) *Capital Culture.* Oxford: Blackwell.

Meanwell, E., Wolfe, J., and Hollett, T. (2008) Old Paths and New Directions: Studying Emotions in the Workplace, *Sociology Compass,* 2(2) 1–23.

Payne, J. (2009) Emotional Labour and Skill: A Reappraisal, *Gender, Work and Organization*, 16(3) 348–367.

Pyöriä, P. (2005) 'Introduction: Why Finland?' in P. Pyöriä, H. Melin, and R. Blom (eds), *Knowledge Workers in the Information Society*, Tampere: Tampere University Press, 21–55.

Rantalaiho, L., and Heiskanen, T. (eds) (1997) *Gendered Practices in Working Life*. London: Macmillan.

Ronkainen, S. (2001) Gendered Violence and Genderless Gender. A Finnish Perspective, *Kvinder, køn & forskning*, 10(2) 45–57.

Warhurst, C., and Nickson, D. (2007) A New Labour Aristocracy? Aesthetic Labour and Routine Interactive Service, *Work, Employment and Society*, 21(4) 785–798.

Warhurst, C., and Nickson, D. (2009) Who's Got the Look? Emotional, Aesthetic and Sexualized Labour in Interactive Services, *Gender, Work and Organization*, 16(3) 385–404.

West, C., and Zimmerman, D. (1987) Doing Gender, *Gender & Society*, 1(2) 125–151.

Witz, A., Warhurst, C., and Nickson, D. (2003) The Labour of Aesthetics and the Aesthetics of Organization, *Organization*, 10(1) 33–54.

Yancey Martin, P. (2001) Mobilizing Masculinities: Women's Experiences of Men at Work, *Organization*, 8(4) 587–618.

Yancey Martin, P. (2003) 'Said and Done' versus 'Saying and Doing'. Gendering Practices, Practicing Gender at Work, *Gender & Society*, 17(3) 342–366.

Yancey Martin, P. (2006) Practicing Gender at Work: Further Thoughts on Reflexivity, *Gender, Work and Organization*, 13(3) 254–276.

# 15

# Women Professionals' Gender Strategies: Negotiating Gendered Organizational Barriers

SHARON R. BIRD AND LAURA A. RHOTON
*Iowa State University, Ames, Iowa, USA*

Gender equity and gender mainstreaming efforts in countries around the world have drawn tremendous attention to the gendered structural barriers and interpersonal biases that women confront in their efforts to advance and attain positions of leadership and authority in different types of work organizations. Women remain the primary instigators, agitators, and leaders of concrete efforts to diminish institutionalized gender barriers and subtle gender biases (e.g. National Academy of Sciences, *Beyond Bias and Barriers Report* 2007). Understanding how women professionals view and try to address gender barriers and biases in professional work organizations is crucial.

In this chapter, we review research on the personal gender strategies that women professionals in male dominated professional work organizations develop and use in their efforts to attain career success. We offer select comparisons with women's gender strategies in other types of work organizations to demonstrate some of the unique aspects of women's careers in professional work organizations. We are especially interested in how women professionals' uses of various *gender strategies* affect their *collective efforts* to promote fairness in the distribution of opportunities and rewards in male dominated work organizations. What kinds of gendered barriers exist in professional work organizations? What are gender strategies? What do previous studies suggest about how women professionals in professional work organizations develop and use gender strategies? How successful are these strategies in enabling women to attain professional goals? And how might differences among women professionals in the kinds of gender strategies they pursue affect their

*This work was supported in part by a grant from the National Science Foundation (SBE 0600399). The authors thank Carol Heaverlo, Chrisy Moutsatsos, the participants of the Iowa State University Women's Studies Brown Bag series, and Emma Jeanes for their input and suggestions. Address all correspondence to Sharon R. Bird, Department of Sociology, Iowa State University, Ames, IA 50010, USA.

abilities to work together to illuminate and address institutionalized gender barriers and subtle gender biases (Ely, 1994; Kvande, 1999)?


## GENDERED BARRIERS AND PROFESSIONAL WORK ORGANIZATIONS

Professional work organizations are 'professional bureaucracies' comprised of a high degree of decentralization, highly educated and autonomous organizational members, and participation of professionals in both the core operations and the administration of the organization (Mintzberg, 1979; Mintzberg, 1980). Though the nature of professional organizations has changed over the past few decades, they remain distinct from other types of work organizations in important ways (Bate, 2000; Green, 2003). Professional bureaucracies such as law firms, hospitals, engineering firms and universities rely heavily on organizational members' uses of specialized knowledge gained via years of training to perform vital organizational functions. Organizational members belong to occupationally specific professional associations, each of which establishes its own standards for evaluating work (Eveline, 2004; Martin, 1994; Mintzberg, 1979).

Professional organizations commonly exist within highly institutionalized environments. In these environments, the organization of work, decision-making processes, and performance evaluation practices are commonly taken for granted as the only rational or 'right' way of organizing (Kark and Waismel-Manor, 2005; Meyer and Rowan, 1977; Meyerson and Tompkins, 2007). For this reason, many organizational arrangements and practices persist not because they are the most organizationally efficient, but rather because they are consistent with long-standing traditions and ways of doing things (Ely and Meyerson, 2000; Mumby and Putnam, 1992). Among the organizational arrangements that persist are work hours for professionals that are largely incompatible with family involvement, decision-making processes that reward complicity with hegemonic practices of masculinity, promotion structures that are more conducive to the advancement of men than women professionals, and information networks that marginalize historically underrepresented groups, including women and people of color (Acker, 1990; Ely and Meyerson, 2000; Hearn and Parkin, 1983; Martin, 2003).

Power-holders in top decision-making positions in professional organizations often are highly invested in preserving existing organizational structures and practices because they view them as crucial to organizational success *and* because they benefit personally from them (Mumby and Putnam, 1992). The process by which individuals are promoted into upper level administrative roles within these organizations typically requires adherence to existing 'organizational logics,' or the 'institutionalized understandings and beliefs' that 'reinforce dominant understandings' of how work processes *ought* to be arranged, how personnel *ought* to be managed, and how performances *ought* to be rewarded (Meyerson and Tompkins, 2007: 308). This is true for the many men who advance into positions of power as well as for the few women who do. Over time, personal adherence to 'organizational logics' often reduces the extent to which individual decision-makers are able to imagine alternative ways of organizing (p. 308). Thus, even as a few women move into upper organizational ranks, the structures that reproduce gendered barriers remain entrenched.

The work that professionals do in professional organizations is evaluated in terms of standards established by the profession (e.g. National and State Bar associations, medical associations) as well as by procedures established by the employing organization. Because the performance standards of the profession are sometimes inconsistent with organizational goals, professionals often must figure out how to navigate conflicting expectations. Professional codes of ethics, for example, might suggest that medical researchers adhere to practices that make it more difficult to obtain funding for their research. Navigating these discrepancies successfully requires access to relevant information networks. Women and people of color, on average, however, have less access to these networks than white men in male dominated professional work organizations (Chen, 1999; Dellinger and Williams, 2002; Ely, 1994; Pierce, 1995).

The relatively decentralized decision-making structures of professional organizations, coupled with shifting organizational and occupational performance criteria, increases the likelihood that organizational leaders' subjective assessments will enter into important personnel decisions. Decisions about whom to hire, promotions and other rewards may all be influenced (often unintentionally) by decision-makers' subjective assessments (Hearn and Parkin, 1983; Kanter, 1977; Martin and Collinson, 2002; Ridgeway, 1997). When key decision-makers in professional organizations are white men, for example, who place a premium on the gender practices with which they feel most comfortable personally, and on personal preferences regarding the evaluation of current and potential organizational members, the result is high levels of homophily within the most powerful organizational positions (Baron and Pfeffer, 1994; Collinson and Hearn, 1994; Davey, 2008; Ibarra, 1992; Martin, 1996).

Professional organizations that are already dominated by men and in which the very definition of 'professionalism' is typically equated with organization- and occupation-specific imperatives of hegemonic masculinity pose many unique challenges for the women professionals who pursue careers in them (Collinson and Hearn, 1994; Kerfoot and Knights, 1998; Kvande, 1999; Martin, 1996, 2001). Though most women professionals bring the necessary credentials to their work in male dominated professional organizations, organizational structures, cultures and practices often are not as conducive to women's success as they are men's success (Bleijenbergh, Blonk, Schulte, and van Engen, 2008; Czarniawska, 2008; Gherardi and Poggio, 2001; Katila and Merilainen, 1999; Meyerson and Tompkins, 2007; Pierce, 1995).

## Gender strategies

The concept of gender strategies emerged out of social constructionist perspectives of gender. These views assume that gender is comprised of *socially constructed* meanings about how people should act, feel, and express themselves as girls/women or as boys/men (see also Chapter 1 in this volume by J. Martin on social construction approaches). Constructionist views assume that gender meanings inform the personal practices of individuals, become an integral part of social norms and collective practices, and inform the very manner in which societies are organized (Butler, 1990; Connell, 1987; Lorber, 1994; Martin, 2004; West and Zimmerman, 1987;

Young, 1990). A *gender strategy* is a gendered 'plan of action' for organizing personal practices. Gender strategies are shaped by personal beliefs about how women *as women* and men *as men* ought to act in social life (i.e. personal gender ideology) and by the structural constraints and opportunities available for acting according to her or his personal beliefs. Women and men use gender strategies to help reconcile their personal gender ideologies with their actual circumstances. The effectiveness of personal gender strategies is shaped by the personal *resources* and *opportunities* at one's disposal for taking up particular gendered courses of action (Hochschild, 1989; Messerschmidt, 2000; Swidler, 1986). Gender strategies differ from one woman (or man) to the next (Greener, 2007; Henson and Rogers, 2001; Lindsay, 2008; Webber and Williams, 2008).

The concept of a 'gender strategy,' when applied specifically to the experiences of women in paid employment and their career aspirations, suggests that if a woman believes that she is entitled *as a woman* to every opportunity that similarly situated men have to succeed in their careers (i.e. an equal opportunity ideology), then any persistent barrier that she experiences (to the extent that she perceives it as a barrier) is likely to prompt a personal need to reconcile the gap between her current circumstances and the opportunities that she believes she ought to have. Most women who are professionals in male dominated professions, as a result of the extensive time and educational investments that they have already made, will have developed a strong sense of themselves as equally capable and qualified as men. This does not mean, however, that the male dominated organizations within which these women professionals most commonly work accommodate women's career aspirations to the same extent as men's career aspirations. Reconciling gaps between career ideologies and career opportunities in the workplace therefore requires developing gender strategies.

## WOMEN PROFESSIONALS' GENDER STRATEGIES

Women professionals in male dominated professional work organizations develop a variety of personal gender strategies. This is true, for example, of attorneys in law firms, among women scientists in universities, and engineers in engineering companies (e.g. Ely, 1994; Kvande, 1999; Fletcher, 1999; Miller, 2002; Ong, 2005; Pierce, 1995). Though the extant literature on this topic is still fairly new, studies reveal important patterns regarding women professionals' gender strategies. These patterns have implications for women's efforts to reduce institutionalized gender barriers and subtle gender biases. Our review of the literature reveals six primary themes. These are outlined below. We note also, where appropriate, similarities and differences between the gender strategies of women professionals in professional work organizations and those of women who work in other types of work organizations.

### *Aligning with white, hegemonic practices of masculinity*

Women professionals' gender strategies vary in the extent to which they align with the hegemonic practices of masculinity. Hegemonic practices of masculinity are built into organizations and support institutionalized arrangements and belief systems (Hearn and Parkin, 1983; Martin and Collinson, 2002). These practices, arrangements, and belief systems are taken for granted by many, if not most, organizational members.

Recent studies show that many women professionals who work in male dominated professional organizations adopt gender strategies that involve aligning with hegemonic practices of masculinity. Miller, for instance, uses the example of a woman geologist working primarily with male engineers to demonstrate this strategy. 'I consciously decided that the way to approach management was to be like a man, to just come in and [. . .] say, "this is the way it is and we should drill here",' explained the geologist (Miller 2004: 63). Kvande (1999) notes, similarly, that women engineers often use a 'one-of-the-boys' strategy in efforts to gain the respect of male colleagues and to enhance career opportunities in male dominated organizations. Ranson (2005) and Powell, Bagilhole, and Dainty (2009) add that women engineers often seek to prove that they are worthy of men engineers' respect by consciously acting in accordance with hegemonically masculine standards of success.

Aligning personal practices and expectations with hegemonic practices of masculinity has multiple consequences for women. Because the range of behaviors and models for presenting oneself as professional is so narrow for women, many are squeezed out of competition for advancement, not because they lack the qualifications or ambition necessary to succeed, but because the professional practices in which they engage are interpreted and framed by others as less appropriate for women. Women who align their personal practices with hegemonic practices of masculinity may gain greater legitimacy and access to promotions, higher salaries, and somewhat more respect from colleagues and clients but rarely become insiders to men's networks and decision-making processes (Ong, 2005; Pierce, 1995). As Ranson (2005) explains, women who align their own practices with masculinist practices of 'professionalism' are not typically accepted by men as 'one of the boys.' And to the extent that women's alignments with practices of masculinity are interpreted by others on the job as 'unfeminine,' the women who engage in them risk being marginalized and often feel compelled to assure their colleagues and clients that they are appropriately feminine (Britton, 2003; Gherardi and Poggio, 2001; Martin and Meyerson, 1997; Miller, 2004; Pini, 2005; Rhoton, 2009).

Women professionals' attempts to increase personal legitimacy and influence by aligning personal actions with hegemonic masculinity practices are further complicated by racialized constructions of the 'ideal' professional (Chen, 1999; Cheng, 1996; Ong, 2005). Because 'whiteness' in the United States (and in many other Western nations) is constructed as normative and 'standard,' and cultural images (and related practices) of professionals are often of white males, women of color often have an even more difficult time than white women in being accepted and respected as professionals (Beoku-Betts, 2005; Jackson, 2004; Ong, 2005; Turner, 2002). Stereotypes that suggest that women of color, especially Latina and Black women, are lazy or less intelligent, for example, leave many women of color in professional organizations in the untenable position of trying to disprove negative race, ethnic, and gender stereotypes while also trying to advance their careers. Ong (2005) explains, for example, that some women of color in academic science employ strategies that involve aligning personally with behaviors that are often considered to be positively characteristic of black women when invoked in the workplace but that are also associated strongly with practices of hegemonic masculinity – practices such as speaking in a commanding voice and acting assertively.[1]

Women who work in settings other than male dominated professional organizations may also employ gender strategies of alignment with hegemonic masculinity. Gherardi and Poggio (2001), for example, describe women who are television editors who argue that in order to succeed in their chosen career fields, 'you have to give up female identity [. . .] you become just like men' (2001: 254). Britton (1999) explains similarly that women prison guards align with hegemonic practices of masculinity in their efforts to succeed in their work in a men's prison.

## Aligning with conventional practices of femininity

Women's gender strategies vary also in the extent to which they align with practices commonly thought to be 'appropriately feminine.' Few practices that signify appropriate or socially valued 'femininity' are viewed as 'professional' or yield the same opportunities and rewards as hegemonic practices of masculinity in male dominated professional work organizations (Bird, forthcoming; Katila and Merilainen 1999; cf. Pini 2005). Gherardi and Poggio (2001: 255) use the example of a woman engineer to demonstrate this strategy. The woman explained that she would

> . . . try to feign ignorance, asking for an opinion, trying to make the other person feel superior, so that [she could] get better treatment, because if you as a woman enter a male work setting and you're an analyst and you begin to make comments, they cut you out.

Dryburgh (1999) explains that many women engineers begin using the 'alignment-with-femininity' strategy well before they begin their professional careers. As engineering students and interns, women use these strategies to demonstrate to others that they are 'team players.' Some women, for example, play into men engineers' acts of benevolent sexism. Dryburgh cites one woman who explained that she believed that she benefited from being treated by men engineers as 'like a daughter' (1999: 676). Greener (2007) reports that women National Health Service managers either 'mother' clinicians or engage in 'flirting' with clinicians in order to garner support for the management's agenda. Other women participate in heterosexual banter with men, assuming the role of a sexual object, in efforts to be viewed as 'one of the team' (Dryburgh, 1999).

As these examples suggest, in professional work organizations, practices associated with 'appropriate' femininity – including deference, cooperation and dependence – are commonly cast in relation to practices of masculinity as demonstrations

---

[1] These women may also pay a heavy psychological price when enacting such strategies (Ong, 2005).

of weakness. Practices of femininity, when performed by women in professional work settings, are targets of men's ridicule or framed as affirmation of men's benevolent or chivalrous sexism (Dellinger, 2004; Miller, 2002; Miller, 2004; Pierce, 1995; Quinn, 2002). Women who conform to these femininity practices may benefit professionally in the short term by gaining the tolerance of male colleagues, but in the long term can undermine their own (and women's collective) legitimacy and efforts to advance in the organization (Ely, 1995; Gherardi and Poggio, 2001; Meyers, 2004; Miller, 2004; Powell et al., 2009).

Practices commonly associated with femininity, such as collaboration, may also be interpreted differently when employed by *men* instead of women in male dominated professional organizations. Women scientists in universities, for example, who frequently collaborate with colleagues are evaluated less positively than men who collaborate. Men who collaborate are viewed as leaders, whereas women who collaborate are more often viewed as followers (Steinpreis, Anders, and Ritzke, 1999). Many women professionals therefore avoid practices usually thought to exemplify femininity – not because these practices are uniformly devalued, but rather because they are devalued only when women enact them (Ely, 1994; Eveline and Booth, 2004; Jorgenson, 2002; Kvande, 1999).

Research shows that organizational policies and cultures, along with other factors, including the proportion of women in high level decision-making roles, also may shape the extent to which women construct and use gender strategies that align with conventional practices of femininity. Policies that support work–life balance, having colleagues who play active roles in family members' lives, and having a critical mass of women in top leadership positions help enable women professionals to employ gender strategies that involve 'doing femininity' in professional work organizations as a way to succeed without being stigmatized or marginalized (Blair-Loy and Wharton, 2002; Bleijenbergh, Blonk, Schulte, and van Engen, 2008; Boulis and Jacobs, 2008; Ely, 1995). In the absence of such policies and women in top organizational leadership roles, however, women professionals who align themselves with stereotypical femininity, whether by choice or circumstance, often become discouraged and find ways to divest themselves of their career responsibilities and invest more of their time and effort into activities outside the workplace (Kvande, 1999; Stone and Lovejoy, 2004; Valian, 1999; Weight and Solomon, 2008).

Many studies show that women who work in organizations other than male dominated professional organizations also develop gender strategies that involve aligning with stereotypical notions of femininity. Many female dominated work organizations and jobs within organizations, in fact, require job holders to conform to practices stereotypically associated with femininity. Table-serving in family and fast-food restaurants and clerical work in service organizations, for example, are jobs that commonly require the enactment of practices including deference and nurturing (Erickson, 2004; Leidner, 1993; Tibbals, 2009), though men in these jobs develop strategies that allow them to engage in stereotypical masculinity as a way to distance themselves from practices of traditional femininity (Britton, 1999; Dellinger, 2004; Erickson, 2004; Henson and Rogers, 2001; Leidner, 1993; Mirchandani, 2005; Williams, 1995).

## *Claiming gender neutrality*

Studies also indicate that women professionals in male dominated professional organizations adopt gender strategies that involve a variety of 'gender neutrality' claims. 'Gender neutrality' claims include (a) casting oneself or one's actions as gender-neutral, (b) rejecting others' attempts to frame one's actions as 'gendered', and (c) supporting the idea that that organizational structures, cultures and practices are gender-neutral (Dryburgh, 1999; Korvajarvi, 2009; Kvande, 1999; McIlwee and Robinson, 1992; Miller, 2004; Pierce, 1995; Smithson and Stokoe, 2005). Claiming gender neutrality in individual practices, as Dryburgh (1999), Jorgenson (2002: 368), and Rhoton (2009) explain, is one of the many ways in which women professionals seek to demonstrate to their male colleagues that women view men as colleagues and teammates, and not as discriminators. Women professionals may also use overt vocalizations of 'gender neutrality' (in individual practices) in efforts to encourage male colleagues to act in non-sexist ways (Dryburgh, 1999; Jorgenson, 2002).

Casting oneself or one's actions as gender-neutral is an aspect of women professionals' gender strategies that takes many forms. Jorgenson (2002), for example, explains that some women engineers try to cast themselves in gender-neutral terms by saying that their career motivations are primarily a matter of personal intellectual aptitude, not as a matter of being female or male. Miller (2004: 65) cites a variation on this same theme when quoting a woman geologist in a male dominated engineering company who says 'I actually don't think much about being female and doing my job this way because I'm female. I just kind of think of myself as being a person.'

Women professionals in professional organizations may also claim gender neutrality by rejecting *others'* claims that gender influences women's work as professionals. Miller (2004: 65) cites many examples of this strategy. As one woman engineer explained, 'They asked me if I knew any woman engineers, and I was a bit snarky and said, "well, I know lots of mechanical engineers, and civil engineers, and chemical engineers, every kind of engineer, but I don't know a single solitary person who has a degree in woman engineering."'

A somewhat different take on gender neutrality claims occurs when women professionals cast the structures, cultures, or practices of their organizations as gender-neutral. Miller (2004) quotes women engineers and geologists whose training has led them to internalize the belief that because the science that constitutes their work is completely 'objective,' so, too, are the rules by which one succeeds within their professions and their organizations. Ong (2005) explains, similarly, that women physicists commonly embrace the notion that science is 'cultureless,' and thus 'context-free.' Meyerson and Tompkins (2007) add that in academia many women (and men) professionals view the promotion structure of tenure as gender-neutral because beliefs about the necessity of the tenure system are so fully institutionalized. Ranson (2005: 160) explains, moreover, that claims of organizational gender neutrality may come in the form of women distancing themselves from insinuations that workplace policies favor one sex over another, and rejecting claims that male colleagues' practices are ever sexist or discriminatory towards women. Women professionals do this, for instance, by stating their opposition to affirmative action programs and ignoring men colleagues' sexist remarks (Ranson, 2005; McIlwee and Robinson, 1992).

As many studies show, however, most women who claim gender-neutrality are confronted with countless contradictions to their stated views on this issue (Dryburgh, 1999; Miller, 2002; Ranson, 2005; Smithson and Stokoe, 2005). Many women professionals nonetheless maintain their stated views by framing contradictions as unusual (non-systemic) exceptions to an otherwise gender-neutral work environment (Jorgenson, 2002; Ranson, 2005; McIlwee and Robinson, 1992). Others develop alternative gender strategies. Women who, for example, find it impossible to reconcile contradictions between their responsibilities as a professional and their responsibilities as a parent are more apt to 'see' gendered systemic barriers and are thus more likely to de-individualize their experiences (Kvande, 1999; Meyerson and Tompkins, 2007). These women are more likely, as will be discussed momentarily, to develop gender strategies aimed at either challenging existing organizational structures, practices, and cultures, or, in some cases, to leave the organization (Kvande, 1999; Williams, 2000).

## *Framing (overtly) gender-based policies, practices and programs as 'political'*

Often related to women professionals' claims of 'gender neutrality' are their claims that overtly gender-based policies, programs, and practices are inappropriately 'political.' Many women professionals reject policies such as affirmative action and programs oriented towards empowering women (e.g. The Society of Women Engineers), for example, labeling them as negatively 'political.' These policies and programs, according to these women, do a disservice to women because they force organizations to use criteria other than employees' credentials when making decisions about hiring, salaries, and promotions and because they set women apart from men rather than helping women to assimilate into the networks and cultures of their organizations (Dryburgh, 1999; Jorgenson, 2002; Kvande, 1999; Miller, 2004).

Many studies (Jorgenson, 2002; Kvande, 1999; Miller, 2004; Ranson, 2005) offer examples of women engineers who reject affirmative action programs – claiming that such programs enable male colleagues to discount the qualifications and credibility of women and people of color as truly qualified. Affirmative action programs may also undermine the self-confidence of women professionals (and professionals who are people of color) who are left wondering whether they were hired because they are women or because they were the most qualified person for the job. Jorgenson (2002: 369) quotes a woman engineer who explains, 'I was a member of the Society of Women Engineers [sic] in college. However, my belief is that the goal of the organization should be not to be in existence anymore.' The same author quotes another woman engineer who says, 'As much as I enjoy supporting other women and mentoring and so forth, I don't understand why you have a society that's gender based.'

Interestingly, women professionals' efforts to distance themselves from gender-based policies and programs (and the people who support them), though framed by the women themselves as efforts to avoid 'politics,' are in fact political in their consequences. By supporting the belief that professional work organizations and their members are gender-neutral, these women, often unknowingly, help to legitimize the status quo (Meyerson and Tompkins, 2007), and thus may undercut the efforts of women professionals who might seek to deconstruct actual gender barriers.

Unlike the many women who distance themselves from gender-based policies and programs, many other women professionals *embrace* gender-based programs as necessary and beneficial because they can 'see' the systemic barriers that hinder women's advancement, and thus participate enthusiastically in women's professional organizations. These are women who recognize gender issues as political, but do not distance themselves from the 'politics.' Kvande (1999) explains that women professionals who view their personal gender strategies as necessarily political often have a history of feminist engagement and consciousness (Hammers, 2009). Many factors influence the extent to which women professionals view personal gender strategies as *positively* 'political.' Access to mentors who embrace feminist ideals and exposure to feminist principles via women's studies programs in colleges and universities, for example, affect the extent to which women professionals frame personal gender strategies as positively political. Political consciousness about gender strategies may be more apt to result from women's personal experiences of running into gendered organizational barriers or having to deal with colleagues who engage in masculinist exclusionary practices (Kvande, 1999; Martin, 2001; Ong, 2005; Pierce, 1995).

## *Using multiple gender strategies*

Women professionals often experiment with and use multiple strategies throughout their careers. Women who are just starting their professional careers, because they have yet to encounter gendered practices that might lead to their exclusion or gendered policies that might disproportionately disadvantage women, for example, are more apt to believe that the proverbial 'playing field' is equal for everyone. Their gender strategies often reflect this belief. These women are less apt to view their organizations as gendered, or to view their own or others' practices as contributing to gender inequalities.

Many studies show, for example, that young women professionals, especially those who have no children, are more likely than more experienced women professionals and those who are mothers to employ strategies that involve aligning with hegemonic practices of masculinity (see also Gherardi and Poggi, 2001; Guillaume and Pochic, 2009; Kvande, 1999; Miller, 2004; Ong, 2005; Ranson, 2005). These women often believe that because they are just as qualified and capable as men professionals, they need only to engage in the kinds of practices that the organization values most highly in order to succeed – i.e. practices that are consistent with hegemonic ideals of masculinity. Many of the women professionals who employ this strategy in the early stages of their careers, however, often find that over time this strategy becomes untenable. As noted, few women professionals who align themselves with practices of masculinity are (by their own accounts and by the accounts of men) fully accepted or treated as 'one of the boys' by men colleagues (Martin, 2001; Miller, 2004; Ong, 2005; Pierce, 1995; Quinn, 2002). Many women who begin their careers by trying to become 'one of the boys' thus eventually realize that this strategy will further their careers only to the extent that those in power within the organization are willing to accept and reward it. This realization leads many women professionals to re-evaluate their gender strategies (Guillaume and Pochic, 2009; Jorgenson, 2002; Ranson, 2005).

Other factors contribute to women professionals' uses of different gender strategies as well. Life circumstances, such as becoming pregnant, adopting a child, or caring for a parent with a prolonged illness lead many women professionals to rethink the 'one-of-the-boys' strategy (Guillaume and Pochio, 2009; Jorgenson, 2002). Though some woman professionals are able to rely on a co-parent, other family members, friends, or hired caregivers to help manage family responsibilities, and do their best to maintain their status as 'conceptual men' in their workplace, many other women come to view the costs of aligning with practices of masculinity as too high (Ranson, 2005). Long work hours, extensive business travel, and maintaining a singular focus on work are all expectations that conflict with pregnancy, infant care, and raising young children.

Women professionals who initially employ gender strategies that involve aligning with conventional femininity practices may also come to realize the limitations of their strategies. Women who employ such strategies, for example, are often taken less seriously by their colleagues, viewed as followers rather than leaders, and find that they have to work much harder than equally qualified men in order to be appropriately recognized and rewarded for their work (Martin and Meyerson, 1997; Valian, 1999). Many of these women, like many women who align personal practices with hegemonic practices of masculinity, come to view the psychological costs of their strategies as too high. It is not surprising, therefore, that many women professionals eventually decide that their best option is to embrace a gender strategy that involves lowering personal career aspirations in order to distance themselves from what they view as unjust circumstances or to invest more time in their families (Boulis and Jacobs, 2008; Gherardi and Poggio, 2001; Kvande, 1999; Miller, 2004; Stone and Lovejoy, 2004; Williams, 2000). As discussed further in the next section, still other women professionals, upon realizing the limitations of their initial gender strategies reformulate their strategies in ways that challenge the organizational and interactional barriers they confront (e.g. Gherardi and Poggio, 2001; Kvande, 1999).

## Challenging gendered organizations

As our review thus far suggests, the forces that determine the degree to which women professionals engage in gender strategies that comply with gendered organizational structures, practices, and cultures are multiple, complex, and intertwined. For some women, conforming to existing organizational arrangements and dominant expectations for organizational members is viewed, at least temporarily, as personally beneficial. Women who employ a 'one-of-the-boys' strategy (Kvande, 1999; Gherardi and Poggio, 2001), for example, by their very presence as women in male dominated organizations and professions, may help to chip away at gender dichotomies that equate rationality and professionalism with the practices of white men. But because these women define themselves and are commonly defined by others as exceptions to a more general pattern, they do little to unsettle the organizational structures that render most women's lives less conducive to success in professional organizations than most men's lives (Acker, 2000; Bird, forthcoming; Kvande, 1999; Martin, 2003; Meyerson and Tompkins, 2007; Miller, 2004; Rhoton, 2009; cf. Ong, 2005).

Aligning with practices of hegemonic masculinity is not, however, the only gender strategy that involves being complicit with existing organizational arrangements. Women who embrace conventional practices of femininity, for example, and who also believe that existing work arrangements and criteria for success in professional organizations are all necessary and unavoidable may rationalize that it is incumbent upon each professional to decide the extent to which they want to invest in their careers versus their families. From this view, professional organizations are *necessarily* structured in ways that enable people who are less encumbered by family responsibilities to succeed (Kvande, 1999; Miller, 2004). Women who align with conventional practices of femininity are thus less likely to challenge organizational structures than they are to adapt to them.

Still other women professionals may comply with existing organizational structures, practices, and cultures not because they have benefited from doing so or because they feel that existing organizational arrangements serve necessary functions, but because they feel they have no other option (Blair-Loy and Wharton, 2002; Guillaume and Pochic, 2009; Stone and Lovejoy, 2004). The woman who tries to become 'one of the boys' and fails, for example, or who believes that organizational arrangements have less to do with organizational efficiency than with maintaining the advantages of those in positions of power may not have the resources or opportunities to effectively challenge the status quo or to seek alternative forms of employment.

Gender strategies that involve *challenging* gendered professional organizations, our review suggests, are less common than those involving a high degree of complicity with existing organizational arrangements. Women professionals' positions within organizational hierarchies, credibility as professionals, and embeddedness in networks of organizational decision-makers all affect the likelihood of pursuing organizational change efforts and of being effective in these efforts (Cohn, 1987; Meyerson and Tompkins, 2007). Women (and men) professionals who have the most decision-making power tend also to be the ones who benefit most from current organizational arrangements and logics. Women (and men) professionals who have the least decision-making power tend also to be those who would have the most to gain from altering existing organizational arrangements and logics. This presents a dilemma in that those with the most power to effect change are the least likely to pursue it (Gramsci, 1971; Lukes, 1974).

'Tempered radicals' (Meyerson and Scully, 1995) or 'organizational catalysts' (Sturm, 2006) are women who bring critical consciousness about organizational structures and practices and awareness about alternative models for organizing equitable work processes and policies into decision-making processes via the organizational roles that they play. Meyerson and Fletcher (2000) argue that when these women act as leaders in producing gradual changes in organizational structures and practices, they create 'small wins' (Weick, 1974), which can result in significant changes over time. In some cases, key organizational leaders may even recognize that the long-term benefits of adopting the kinds of changes that 'tempered radicals' suggest are worth their investment because the long-term benefits of such changes outweigh the projected costs associated with not making them. Many have cited recent organizational efforts to offer 'flexible career' opportunities that attempt to make professionals' investments in careers and family life more compatible as examples of how cumulative 'small wins' can lead to more significant organizational changes (Greenhaus, Collins, and Shaw, 2003).

## FUTURE OUTLOOK

How do women professionals' gender strategies affect their abilities to work together to illuminate and address institutionalized gender barriers and subtle gender biases? While some researchers argue that 'tempered radicals' and 'organizational catalysts' are able to mobilize like-minds in ways that fundamentally alter work organizations, others suggest that these efforts lead only to marginal gains for underrepresented groups (Meyerson and Tompkins, 2007). Acker (2000; 2006) contends that these 'small wins' are simply not enough. Even when 'tempered radicals' or 'organizational catalysts' hold positions of leadership in professional organizations and succeed in mobilizing efforts that lead to new policies and work arrangements, they rarely succeed in creating significant shifts because other high level decision-makers fail to take up the cause. Thus, explain Guinier and Minow (2007), achieving organizational changes that diminish systemic gender barriers requires that reformers develop and utilize 'networks of relationships' among large numbers of (eager) organizational change agents who are willing to question and change ongoing organizational operations in ways that reduce institutionalized mechanisms of bias and exclusion.

Our review suggests, furthermore, that building the kinds of networks that Guinier and Minow (2007) and others (e.g. Meyerson and Tompkins, 2007) describe, at least within male dominated professional work organizations, will require acknowledging that not all women (or men) embrace the same gender strategies, and that differences among women may hinder their efforts to work together. Creating networks that include multiple women as organizational change agents will likely require building a foundation of mutual understanding between network members. Acknowledging difference between women in the gender strategies that they pursue will help to enhance communication and trust, and in turn enable women professionals to work across their differences to develop and support more viable strategies for systemic change.

Developing these networks of change agents, explains Guinier and Minow (2007), will also increase the likelihood that 'top down' organizational policies aimed at reducing gendered organizational barriers to equality will have their intended effect. Previous research shows, for example, that utilization of newly codified 'family friendly' organizational policies, including part-time professional positions and time off from work following the birth or adoption of a child, will be under-utilized unless the cultures and practices of organization (or departments within organizations) also support employees' use of such policies (Blair-Loy and Wharton, 2002). As Guinier and Minow (2007: 271) explain, generating and supporting deep organizational change requires that reformers pay close attention to 'what connects individuals to their settings, what influences a sense of membership, and what directs and redirects the practices of power. Institutional change does not merely require good rules, but also a culture that endorses the values behind the rules, and attitudes and incentives that sustain rather than rebuff processes of change.'

Studies also show that few of the contemporary organizational programs aimed at reducing inequalities between women and men, or between people of color and white people, involve proactive measures and goals to which higher level administrators in professional organizations are held accountable (Kalev, Dobbin, and Kelly, 2006; Kelly and Dobbin, 1998). Unlike some previous equality efforts targeted at work organizations, like affirmative action in the United States, more recent equality initiatives (commonly referenced as 'diversity' programs) are not supported by large-scale social movements that operate independently of work organizations or by legislation that mandates proactive organizational efforts. These conditions, coupled with the tendency for high level decision-makers in professional organizations to surround themselves with others who accept current organizational arrangements and to marginalize those who do not, suggest that even if women professionals develop and implement gender strategies that involve challenging gendered organizations, their prospects for mobilizing large numbers of like-minded women (or men) and creating deep organizational changes are slim. We should not, however, simply dismiss all prospects for women professionals to work together to effect deep organizational change. Over the past decade, efforts have been made on the part of 'quasi-public organizations' (grand-funding agencies; Sturm, 2006) to enable women professionals in some organizations, in this case, US universities, to implement experimental programs aimed at transforming organizational structures, practices, and cultures. The 'quasi-public organizations' supporting these efforts are funding agencies, like the National Science Foundation in the US, that provide large, multi-year grants (e.g. 'ADVANCE grants') to universities to support organizational transformation efforts aimed at increasing the recruitment, retention, and promotion of women and people of color. Because continued funding requires demonstrating progress toward the overarching goals of the grants, the 'quasi-public organizations' incorporate a level of *accountability* that is missing from most organizational diversity- enhancement programs. These grant-funded programs also provide a legitimate space for women whose gender strategies involve challenging gendered organizations to mobilize other like-minded women (and men). Though these experimental programs are still quite new, evaluations of them are hopeful (Dobbin and Kalev, 2007; Meyerson and Tompkins, 2007; Sturm, 2006). Creating the conditions necessary for women to become more aligned in their strategies may be possible under these and elated programs that leverage the influence of 'quasi-public organizations' to create a form of external accountability to equality goals that professional organizations would not otherwise be compelled to proactively pursue (Meyerson and Tompkins, 2007; Sturm, 2006).

# REFERENCES

Acker, Joan (1990) Hierarchies, Jobs, Bodies: A Theory of Gendered Organizations, *Gender & Society*, 4, 139–158.

Acker, Joan (2000) Gendered Contradictions in Organizational Equity Projects, *Organization*, 7, 625–632.

Acker, Joan (2006) Inequality Regimes: Gender, Class and Race in Organizations, *Gender & Society*, 20, 441–464.

Baron, James N., and Pfeffer, Jeffrey (1994) The Social Psychology of Organizations and Inequality, *Social Psychology Quarterly*, 57, 190–209.

Bate, Paul (2000) Changing the Culture of a Hospital: From Hierarchy to Networked Community, *Public Administration*, 78, 485–512.

Beoku-Betts, Josephine (2005) 'African Women Pursuing Graduate Studies in the Sciences: Racism, Gender Bias and Third World Marginality' in Jill. M. Bystydzienski and Sharon R. Bird (eds), *Removing Barriers: Women in Academic Science, Engineering, Technology and Mathematics*. Bloomington, IN: University of Indiana Press

Bird, Sharon R. (forthcoming) Unsettling Universities' Incongruous, Gendered Bureaucratic Structures: A Case Study Approach, *Gender, Work and Organization*.

Blair-Loy, Mary, and Wharton, Amy S. (2002) Employees' Use of Work-Family Policies and the Workplace Social Context, *Social Forces*, 80, 813–845.

Bleijenbergh, Inge, Blonk, Eelke, Schulte, Lodewijk, and van Engen, Marloes (2008) 'Explaining Women's Careers at a Dutch University: Model Building as a Method for Knowledge Elicitation in Gender Analysis' in *Conference of the System Dynamics Society*. Athens, Greece: System Dynamics Society.

Boulis, Ann K., and Jacobs, Jerry A. (2008) *The Changing Face of Medicine: Women Doctors and the Evolution of Health Care in America*. Ithaca, NY: Cornell University Press.

Britton, Dana M. (1999) Cat Fights and Gang Fights: Preference for Work in a Male Dominated Organization, *Sociological Quarterly*, 40, 455–474.

Britton, Dana M. (2003) 'Engendering the Prison' in *At Work in the Iron Cage*. New York: New York University.

Butler, Judith (1990) *Gender Trouble*. New York: Routledge.

Chen, Anthony S. (1999) Lives at the Center of the Periphery, Lives at the Periphery of the Center: Chinese American Masculinities and Bargaining with Hegemony, *Gender & Society*, 13, 584–607.

Cheng, Cliff (1996) '"We choose not to compete': The 'merit' discourse in the selection process, and Asian and Asian American men and their masculinity." in *Masculinities in organizations*, edited by C. Cheng. Thousand Oaks, CA: Sage.

Cohn, Carol (1987) Sex and Death in the Rational World of Defense Intellectuals, *Signs*, 687, 703–718.

Collinson, David L., and Hearn, Jeff (1994) Naming Men as Men: Implications for Work, Organization, and Management, *Gender, Work and Organization*, 1, 2–22.

Connell, R.W. (1987) *Gender and Power: Society, The Person and Sexual Politics*. Stanford, CA: Stanford University Press.

Czarniawska, Barbara (2008) *A Theory of Organizing*. Cheltenham, UK: Edward Elgar.

Davey, Kate Makenzie (2008) Women's Accounts of Organizational Politics as a Gendering Process, *Gender, Work and Organization*, 15, 650–671.

Dellinger, Kirsten (2004) Masculinities in 'Safe' and 'Embattled' Organizations: Accounting for Pornographic and Feminist Magazines, *Gender & Society*, 18, 545–566.

Dellinger, Kirsten, and Williams, Christine L. (2002) The Locker Room and the Dorm Room: Workplace Norms and the Boundaries of Sexual Harassment in Magazine Editing. *Social Problems*, 49, 242–257.

Dobbin, Frank, and Kalev, Alexandra (2007) The Architecture of Inclusion: Evidence from Corporate Diversity Programs. *Harvard Journal of Law & Gender*, 30, 279–301.

Dryburgh, Heather (1999) Work Hard, Play Hard: Women and Professionalization in Engineering – Adapting to the Culture, *Gender & Society*, 13, 664–682.

Ely, Robin J. (1994) The Effects of Organizational Demographics and Social Identity on Relationships among Professional Women, *Administrative Science Quarterly*, 39, 1287–1302.

Ely, Robin J. (1995) The Power of Demography: Women's Social Constructions of Gender Identity at Work, *Academy of Management Review*, 38, 589–634.

Ely, Robin J., and Meyerson Debra E. (2000) Theories of Gender in Organizations: A New Approach to Organizational Analysis and Change, *Research in Organizational Behavior*, 22, 103–151.

Erickson, Karla (2004) "To Invest or Detach? Coping Strategies and Workplace Culture in Service Work." *Symbolic Interaction*, 27, 549–572.

Eveline, Joan (2004) *Ivory Basement Leadership*. Crawley, Western Australia: University of Western Australia Press.

Eveline, Joan, and Booth, Michael (2004) 'Don't Write about It': Writing 'The Other' for the Ivory Basement, *Journal of Organizational Change Management*, 17, 243–255.

Fletcher, Joyce K. (1999) *Disappearing Acts: Gender, Power and Relational Practice at Work*. Cambridge, MA: MIT Press.

Gherardi, Sylvia, and Poggio, Barbara (2001) Creating and Recreating Gender Order in Organizations, *Journal of World Business*, 36, 245–259.

Gramsci, Antonio (1971) *Selections from the Prison Notebooks of Antonio Gramsci (Translated by Q. Hoare and G. N. Smith)*. New York: International.

Green, Roger (2003) Markets, Management, and 'Reengineering' Higher Education, *The ANNALS of the American Academy of Political and Social Science*, 585, 196–210.

Greener, Ian (2007) The Politics of Gender in the NHS: Impression Management and 'Getting Things Done', *Gender, Work and Organization*, 14, 281–299.

Greenhaus, J.H., Collins, K.M. and Shaw, J.D. (2003) The Relation between Work-Family Balance and Quality of Life, *Journal of Vocational Behavior*, 63, 510–531.

Guillaume, Cicile, and Pochic, Sophie (2009) What Would You Sacrifice? Access to Top Management and the Work–Life Balance, *Gender, Work and Organization*, 16, 14–36.

Guinier, Lani, and Minow, Martha (2007) Preface to Responses: Dynamism, Not Just Diversity, *Harvard Journal of Law and Gender*, 30, 269–277.

Hammers, Corie (2009) 'But I Love Men': How Young Women Leverage Heteronormativity to Negotiate Feminist Stigma, in *American Sociological Association Annual Meetings*. San Francisco, CA.

Hearn, Jeff, and Parkin, Wendy (1983) Gender and Organisations: A Selective Review and a Critique of a Neglected Area, *Organization Studies*, 4, 219–242.

Henson, Kevin D., and Krasas Rogers, Jackie (2001) 'Why Marcia You've Changed!' Male Clerical Temporary Workers Doing Masculinity in Feminized Occupation, *Gender & Society*, 15, 218–238.

Hochschild, Arlie (1989) *The Second Shift*. New York: Viking-Penguin.

Ibarra, Herminia (1992) Homophily and Differential Returns: Sex Differences in Network Structure and Access in an Advertising Firm, *Administrative Science Quarterly*, 37, 422–447.

Jackson, Judy (2004) "The Story is Not in the Numbers: Academic Socialization and Diversifying the Faculty." *National Women's Studies Association Journal*, 16, 172–185.

Jorgenson, Jane (2002) Engineering Selves: Negotiating Gender and Identity in Technical Work, *Management Communication Quarterly*, 15, 350–380.

Kalev, Alexandra, Dobbin, Frank, and Kelly, Erin (2006) Best Practices or Best Guesses? Assessing the Efficacy of Corporate Affirmative Action and Diversity Practices, *American Sociological Review*, 71, 589–617.

Kanter, Rosabeth Moss (1977) *Men and Women of the Corporation*. New York: Basic.

Kark, Ronit, and Waismel-Manor, Roni (2005) Organizational Citizenship Behavior: What's Gender Got to Do With It? *Organization*, 12, 889–917.

Katila, Saija, and Merilainen, Susan (1999) A Serious Researcher or Just Another Nice Girl? Doing Gender in a Male-Dominated Scientific Community, *Gender, Work and Organization*, 6, 163–173.

Kelly, Erin, and Dobbin, Frank (1998) How Affirmative Action Became Diversity Management: Employer Response to Antidiscrimination Law, 1961–1996, *American Behavioral Scientist*, 41, 960–985.

Kerfoot, Deborah, and Knights, David (1998) Managing Masculinity in Contemporary Organizational Life: A Managerial Project, *Organization*, 5, 7–26.

Korvajarvi, Paivi (2009) 'Practicing Gender Neutrality in Organizations' in D. Knights, E. Jeannes, and P. Y. Martin (eds), *Handbook of Gender, Work and Organization.*

Kvande, Elin (1999) 'In the Belly of the Beast': Constructing Femininities in Engineering Organizations, *European Journal of Women's Studies*, 6, 305–328.

Leidner, Robin (1993) *Fast Food, Fast Talk: Service Work and the Routinization of Everyday Life.* Berkeley, CA: University of California Press.

Lorber, Judith (1994) *Paradoxes of Gender.* New Haven, CT: Yale University Press.

Lukes, Steven (1974) *Power: A Radical View.* London: Macmillan.

Martin, Joanne (1994) The Organization of Exclusion: Institutionalization of Sex Inequality: Gendered Faculty Jobs and Gendered Knowledge in Organization Theory and Research, *Organization*, 1, 401–432.

Martin, Joanne, and Meyerson, Debra (1997) 'Women and Power: Conformity, Resistance, and Disorganized Co-Action' in R. Kramer and R. Neale (eds), *Social Influence in Organzations.* Newbury Park, CA: Sage Publications.

Martin, Patricia Yancey (1996) 'Men, Masculinities and Managements: Gendering and Evaluating Dynamics' in D.L. Collinson and J. Hearn (eds), *Men as Managers, Managers as Men: Critical Perspectives on Masculinity.* London: Sage, 186–209.

Martin, Patricia Yancey (2001) 'Mobilizing Masculinities': Women's Experiences of Men at Work, *Organization*, 8, 587–618.

Martin, Patricia Yancey (2003) 'Said and Done' vs. 'Saying and Doing'-Gendered Practices/ Practicing Gender, *Gender & Society*, 17, 342–366.

Martin, Patricia Yancey (2004) Gender as Social Institution, *Social Forces*, 82, 1249–1273.

Martin, Patricia Yancey, and Collinson, David L. (2002) 'Over the Pond and Across the Water': Developing the Field of Gendered Organizations, *Gender, Work and Organization*, 9, 245–265.

McIlwee, J.S., and Robinson, J.G. (1992) *Women in Engineering: Gender, Power, and Workplace Culture.* Albany: State University of New York Press.

Messerschmidt, James W. (2000) *Nine Lives: Adolescent Masculinities, the Body and Violence.* Boulder, CO: Westview.

Meyer, John W., and Rowan, Brian (1977) Institutionalized Organizations: Formal Structure as Myth and Ceremony, *American Journal of Sociology*, 83, 340–363.

Meyers, Kristen (2004) "Ladies First: Race, Class and the Contradictions of a Powerful Femininity." *Sociological Spectrum*, 24.

Meyerson, Debra E., and Scully, Maureen A. (1995) Tempered Radicalism and the Politics of Ambivalence and Change, *Organization Science*, 6, 585–600.

Meyerson, Debra and Joyce K. Fletcher (2000) "A Modest Manifesto for Shattering the Glass Ceiling." *Harvard Business Review* January–February:126–136.

Meyerson, Debra, and Tompkins, Megan (2007) Tempered Radicals as Institutional Change Agents: The Case of Advancing Gender Equity at the University of Michigan, *Harvard Journal of Law & Gender*, 30, 303–322.

Miller, Gloria E. (2002) The Frontier, Entrepreneurialism, and Engineers: Women Coping with a Web of Masculinities in an Organizational Culture, *Culture and Organization*, 8, 145–160.

Miller, Gloria E. (2004) Frontier Masculinity in the Oil Industry: The Experience of Women Engineers, *Gender, Work and Organization*, 11, 47–73.

Mintzberg, H. (1979) *The Structuring of Organizations.* Englewood Cliffs, NJ: Prentice Hall.

Mintzberg, Henry (1980) Structure in 5's: A Synthesis of the Research on Organization Design, *Management Science*, 26, 322–341.

Mirchandani, Kiran (2005) "Gender Eclipsed? Racial Hierarchies in Transnational Call Center Work." *Social Justice*, 32, 105–119.

Mumby, Dennis. K., and Putnam, Linda L. (1992) The Politics of Emotion: A Feminist Reading of Bounded Rationality, *Academy of Management Review*, 17, 465–486.

National Academy of Sciences (2007) "Beyond Biases and Barriers." National Academy of Sciences, Washington DC.

Ong, Maria (2005) Body Projects of Young Women of Color in Physics: Intersections of Gender, Race and Science, *Social Problems*, 52, 593–617.

Pierce, Jennifer L. (1995) *Gender Trials: Emotional Lives in Contemporary Law Firms*. Berkeley, CA: University of California Press.

Pini, Barbara (2005) The Third Sex: Women Leaders in Australian Agriculture, *Gender, Work and Organization*, 12, 73–88.

Powell, Abigail, Barbara Bagihole, and Andrew Dainty (2009) "How Women Engineers Do and Undo Gender: Consequences for Gender Equality." *Gender, Work and Organization*, 16, 411–428.

Quinn, Beth A. (2002) Sexual Harassment and Masculinity: The Power and Meaning of 'Girl Watching', *Gender & Society*, 16, 386–402.

Ranson, Gillian (2005) No Longer 'One of the Boys': Negotiations with Motherhood, as Prospect or Reality, among Women in Engineering, *The Canadian Review of Sociology and Anthropology*, 42, 145–166.

Rhoton, Laura A. (2009) Practicing Gender or Practicing Science? Gender Practices of Women Scientists. Doctoral Thesis, Department of Sociology, Iowa State University, Ames, Iowa, United States.

Ridgeway, Cecilia L. (1997) Interaction and the Conservation of Gender Inequality: Considering Employment, *American Sociological Review*, 62, 218–235.

Smithson, Janet, and. Stokoe, Elizabeth H. (2005) Discourses of Work-Life Balance: Negotiating 'Genderblind' Terms in Organizations, *Gender, Work and Organization*, 12, 147–168.

Steinpreis, Rhea E., Anders, Katie A., and Ritzke, Dawn (1999) The Impact of Gender on the Review of the Curricula Vitae of Job Applicants and Tenure Candidates: A National Empirical Study, *Sex Roles*, 41, 509–528.

Stone, Pamela, and Lovejoy, Meg (2004) Fast-Track Women and the 'Choice' to Stay Home, *The ANNALS of the American Academy of Political and Social Science*, 596, 62–83.

Sturm, Susan (2006) The Architecture of Inclusion: Advancing Workplace Equity in Higher Education, *Harvard Journal of Law & Gender*, 29, 247–334.

Tibbals, Chauntelle Anne (2007) "Doing Gender as Resistance: Waitresses and Servers in Comtemporary Table Service." *Journal of Contemporary Ethnography*, 36, 731–751.

Turner, Caroline Sotello Viernes (2002) "Women of Color in Academe: Living with Multiple Marginality." *The Journal of Higher Education*, 73, 74–93.

Valian, Virginia (1999) *Why So Slow*. Cambridge: MIT Press.

Webber, Gretchen, and Williams, Christine L. (2008) Mothers in 'Good' and 'Bad' Part-time Jobs: Different Problems, Same Results, *Gender & Society*, 22, 752–777.

Weick, Karl E. (1994) Small Wins: Redefining the Scale of Social Problems, *American Psychologist*, 39, 40–49.

Weight, Jill M., and Richards Solomon, Catherine (2008) Work-family Management among Low-wage Service Workers and Assistant Professors in the USA: A Comparative Intersectional Analysis, *Gender, Work and Organization*, 15, 621–649.

West, Candice, and Zimmerman, Don H. (1987) Doing Gender, *Gender & Society*, 1, 125–151.

Williams, Christine L (1995) *Still a Man's World*. Berkeley, CA: University of California Press.

Williams, Joan (2000) *Unbending Gender: Why Family and Work Conflict and What to Do about it*. New York: Oxford University Press.

Young, Iris Marion (1990) *Justice and the Politics of Difference*. Princeton, NJ: Princeton University Press.

# 16

## Gender and Work: A Technofeminist Analysis

JUDY WAJCMAN
*London School of Economics and Political Science*

The purpose of this chapter is to locate current discussions about women's position in science, engineering, and technology in the wider context of feminist debates on gender and technology. Indeed, these debates developed largely in response to the long-standing marginalization of women from technically-oriented organizations and professions, such as engineering. So it is not surprising that early feminist analyses of technology tended to have a pessimist tone. Technology was seen as a defining feature of masculinity, perpetuating and producing occupational segregation by sex in organizations.

Since then, ground breaking developments in digitalization and biotechnologies have led many contemporary feminists to surmise that the traditional link between technology and male privilege is finally being severed. This chimes with theories of the 'information society' or 'knowledge economy', that argue that the old hierarchies are disintegrating and being replaced by less rigid and more flexible networks. Globalization gurus like Manuel Castells give prominence to the intensity, extensity, and velocity of global flows, interactions, and networks embracing all social domains. For these writers, such changes herald an exciting new post-traditional network society.

The Internet is the central emblem of these changes for both cybergurus and cyberfeminists. The idea that the Internet can transform conventional gender roles, altering the relationship between the body and the self via a machine, is a popular theme in recent postmodern feminism. The optimistic register of such feminisms resonates with a new generation of women who live in a world of greater sex equality. That a strong current of seventies feminism sought to reject technology as malevolent is now seen as fanciful. Indeed, early concerns about women being left out of the communications revolution, victims of the digital divide, have been eclipsed by a recognition that the gender gap in ownership and access to information and communication technologies (ICTs) is fast disappearing.

How, then, do we account for the fact that women are still underrepresented in science, engineering, and technology (SET) occupations? Is there something about the gendered culture of technology and organizations that makes it hard for women to pursue careers in these fields? This chapter will first provide some background on the current position of women in these sectors. I will then outline early feminist debates that conceptualized technology and technical expertise as closely identified with masculinity. Thirdly, contemporary cyberfeminist theory will be evaluated, particularly the claim that digital technologies are inherently liberating for women. A critical weakness of this literature is its leaning towards technological determinism, which I address in the final section. This section will argue that in order to fully understand the position of women in SET careers, we need to understand the gendered character of technoscience itself.

## The Brain Drain in Science, Engineering, and Technology

Let me begin by briefly presenting some evidence about the gender imbalance in technoscience. Current surveys of women in SET show that women have made significant strides in these sectors, despite the well-known challenges and barriers that girls face in the educational system and the wider culture (Bebbington, 2000). In the private sector in the US, for example, 41% of highly qualified scientists, engineers, and technologists on the lower rungs of corporate career ladders are women (Hewlett et al., 2008). Young women are gaining ground and excelling in SET fields such as the biological sciences and chemistry, where 46% and 31% of PhDs respectively are now awarded to women. With the important exception of computer science (where the trend lines are down), women are also making some headway in engineering and physics, although from a much lower base. While these figures are grounds for optimism, Hewlett et al.'s (2008: i) company survey also revealed that, over time, approximately half (52%) of highly qualified females working for SET companies quit their jobs, 'driven out by hostile work environments and extreme job pressures'. In sum, the report stresses that while many young women start out keen and committed to careers in SET, the mass exodus of women results in very few making it to the top.

A recent report by the European Commission (2008) on women in the ICT sector paints an even less rosy picture. Although the trend across tertiary education level shows a general increase in the number of highly educated females, in computing, engineering. and engineering trades, female graduates are significantly outnumbered by male graduates. In the EU (27 countries) in 2004, 78% of computer science graduates were male as opposed to 22% for females. While there are variations in these numbers both within Europe and across other countries, a consistent gender gap emerges. Only in the life sciences do women PhDs outnumber men. A valuable aspect of this report is that it also presents data on the under-representation of women on scientific boards, in senior managerial positions in both academia and high technology knowledge-intensive services and manufacturing, and in research and development in the business enterprise sector. Thus it documents a gender imbalance in the main activities that are shaping, creating, and managing new knowledge, processes, methods, and systems: 'women are under represented in *decision making positions* where science and technology strategies are set, ICT policies are developed, and the agenda for the future is determined' (2008: 6) In other words, women are still largely inhabiting a world designed and built by men.

Documenting and explaining women's limited access to scientific and technical institutions and careers has been a major concern of the women's movement since its inception (Rossiter, 1982). From the early 1970s, biographical studies of great women scientists served as a useful corrective to mainstream histories of science in demonstrating that women have in fact made important contributions to scientific endeavour. The biographies of Rosalind Franklin (1975) and Barbara McClintock (1983) are probably the best known examples. Recovering the history of women's achievements became an integral part of feminist scholarship in a wide range of disciplines. However, as the extent and intransigent quality of women's exclusion from science became more apparent, the approach gradually shifted from looking at exceptional women to examining the general patterns of women's participation.

Many studies have identified the structural barriers to women's participation, looking at sex discrimination in employment and the kind of socialization and education that girls receive which have channelled them away from studying mathematics and science (Francis, 2000; Long and Fox, 1995). Schooling, youth cultures, the family, and the mass media all transmit meanings and values that identify masculinity with machines and technological competence. Sex stereotyping in schools is a key factor, particularly the processes by which girls and boys are channelled into different subjects in secondary and tertiary education, and the link between education and the segregated labour market (Crompton, 1997; Glover and Campling, 2000). Explaining the under-representation of women in science education, laboratories and scientific publications, much research highlights the construction and character of femininity encouraged by our culture (Kelan, 2007; Lohan and Faulkner, 2004).

The problem of women's marginalization is intensified by the masculinity of organizations, in particular, managerial culture (Kvande, 1999; Smith-Doerr, 2004). To pursue a successful career in the new information technology sector requires navigation of multiple male cultures associated not only with scientific and technological work, but also with managerial positions. A central argument of this Handbook is that gender relations are integral to the structure and practices of organizations and this is fundamental to understanding how men define and dominate organizations. Gendered processes operate on many institutional levels, from the open and explicit to more discrete forms that are submerged in organizational decisions, even those that appear to have nothing to do with gender. They include the way men's influence is embedded in rules and procedures, in formal job definitions, and in functional roles as well as in everyday interactions. Through such cultural representations and meanings, people build their understandings of the gendered structure of work and opportunities. Indeed, organizations are one area in which widely disseminated images and practices of gender are continuously invented and reproduced (Acker, 1990; Wajcman, 1998).

The long-hours culture embedded in the role of a senior manager is a particular barrier as the high-echelon SET jobs are more extreme than even the management norm. Women in science, engineering, and technology are more likely than women in other sectors to be coping with 100-hour work weeks, dealing with 24/7 customer demands and working across multiple time zones (Hewlett et al., 2008: 31). In my own research on senior managers in multinational companies in high-technology sectors, I found that a high proportion of successful women are not parents, in sharp contrast to their male counterparts (Wajcman, 1998). In addition, the evidence of ubiquitous sexual harassment in this sector suggests a hostile masculine culture that makes it unsurprising that so many women leave the sector (Hewlett et al., 2008). Such issues, especially those in relation to work–life balance, are increasingly recognized as major factors impeding women's full participation in scientific and technical employment and careers. This is familiar terrain. Perhaps less well known is feminist scholars' long engagement with the gender relations of technoscience itself, and it is to this that I now turn.

## Machinery of Masculinity

Much early feminist politics was of a liberal cast, demanding equal access for women within existing power structures, including technoscience. It was based on an empiricist view of science and technology as fundamentally (gender) neutral. Sexism and androcentrism were therefore understood as social biases capable of correction by stricter adherence to the methodological norms of scientific inquiry. The problem was framed in terms of the uses and abuses to which science and technology have been put by men (Rossiter, 1982).

Given the intransigence of gender segregation, however, it is not surprising that much second-wave feminism adopted a pessimistic tone in relation to the gender-technology relationship. From the outset, the microelectronic revolution was seen as having a negative impact on women's work, and this led to a pronounced anti-technology stance. There were fears that computerization of office work, for example, would lead to deskilling, with jobs fragmented into routine and standardized tasks subject to the control of the machine. Influenced by Marxist analyses of science and technological change, feminist researchers revealed how the capitalist division of labour intersected with sexual divisions (Cockburn, 1983).

Indeed, by the 1980s, feminist criticisms of science had, in Sandra Harding's (1986) words, evolved from asking the 'woman question' in science to asking the more radical 'science question' in feminism. Rather than asking how women could be more equitably treated within and by science, they asked how a science apparently so deeply involved in distinctively masculine projects can possibly be used for emancipatory ends. Western science was characterized as a masculine project of reason and objectivity, with women relegated to nature rather than culture. Rejecting scientific knowledge as patriarchal knowledge, there were calls for the development of a new science based on women's values. In a parallel move, socialist and radical feminist analyses of technology shifted beyond the approach of 'women and technology' to examine the very processes by which technology is developed and used, as well as those by which gender is constituted (Cowan, 1983; Rothschild, 1983; Wajcman, 1991). In other words, feminists were exploring the gendered character of artefacts themselves.

A crucial historical perspective was brought to bear on the analysis of men's monopoly of technology. Extensive research on manufacturing and engineering demonstrated that women's exclusion from technology was as a consequence of the male domination of skilled trades that developed during the industrial revolution (Bradley, 1989; Milkman, 1987). Craft workers, typically seen as the defenders of working-class interests in disputes over technical change, resisted the entry of women to skilled technical jobs in order to protect their own conditions. Historians of engineering similarly showed that it was only during the late nineteenth century that mechanical and civil engineering came to define technology as the province of men. Technical expertise became the defining feature of this white, male, middle-class profession, and femininity was reinterpreted as incompatible with technological pursuits (Oldenziel, 1999). Industrial technology from its origins thus reflected men's designs, and became a defining feature of masculinity.

Much second-wave feminism, then, saw masculinity as embedded in the machinery itself, highlighting the role of technology as a key source of male power (Wajcman, 1991). The problem was not only men's monopoly of technology, but also the way gender is embedded in technology itself. Technology was seen as socially shaped, but shaped by men to the exclusion of women. While this literature did reflect an understanding of the historical variability and plurality of the categories of 'women' and 'technology', it was nevertheless pessimistic about the possibilities of redesigning technologies for gender equality. The proclivity of technological developments to entrench gender hierarchies was emphasized rather than the prospects they afford for change. In short, not enough attention was paid to women's agency. And it is precisely this rather negative register that provoked a reaction from a new generation of feminist scholars.

Reflecting more general trends in social theory, feminists have become increasingly uneasy with the negative cast of the debates about technology and society. They warmed to information, communication, and biotechnologies as being fundamentally transformative, unlike previous technologies. Theories of the global, networked, knowledge society see these technologies as revolutionary in their impact, providing the basis for a new information age (Castells, 1996; 2001; Harvey, 1989). Cyberfeminists have been particularly influenced by these ideas and, more generally, the 'cultural turn' in social theory (Braidotti, 2003; Kember, 2003). The virtuality of cyberspace and the Internet is seen as ending the embodied basis for sex difference and facilitating a multiplicity of innovative subjectivities.

Certainly, the proliferation of mobile phones, the Internet, and cyber cafes are providing new opportunities and outlets for women, particularly those in highly industrialized countries who are better placed to take advantage of these technologies. While the early adopters of the Internet were overwhelmingly men, data from the USA shows no gender difference in Internet use (NTIA, 2008). In Europe too, the Internet use habits of men and women are similar, age being a much more significant dimension of the digital divide (European Commission, 2008). China, a country where Internet take-up is relatively recent, shows how rapidly change can occur. Over an eight-year period from 1997, the proportion of Internet users who were female rose from 12% to 39% (CNNIC, 2005). Certainly in the Western world, already there seems to be no gender gap whatsoever in relation to ownership of or access to the mobile phone. Especially among younger people, new media communication technologies are not culturally coded as either masculine or feminine. Technologies appear to be losing their masculine hue.

## CYBERFEMINISM

Contemporary feminist approaches, then, are much more positive about the possibilities of ICTs to empower women and transform gender relations (Kemp and Squires, 1998; Kirkup et al., 2000). Indeed, many postmodern cyberfeminists enthusiastically embrace Web-based technologies. A common argument in this literature is that the virtuality of cyberspace and the Internet spell the end of the embodied basis for sex difference. According to a leading exponent of this approach, Sadie Plant (1998), digital technologies facilitate the blurring of boundaries between humans and machines, and male and female, enabling their users to choose their disguises and assume alternative identities. Industrial technology may have had a patriarchal character, but digital technologies, based on brain rather than brawn, on networks rather than hierarchy, herald a new relationship between women and machines. In the wireless world, traditional hierarchies are replaced by horizontal, diffuse, flexible networks, which have more affinity with women's culture and ways of being than men's. Cyberfeminists claim that the Internet provides the technological basis for a new form of society that is potentially liberating for women.

For Plant, technological innovations have been pivotal in the fundamental shift in power from men to women that occurred in Western cultures in the 1990s, the genderquake. Old expectations, stereotypes, senses of identity, and securities have been challenged as women gained unprecedented economic opportunities, technical skills, and cultural powers. Automation has reduced the importance of muscular strength and hormonal energies and replaced them with demands for speed, intelligence, and transferable, interpersonal, and communication skills (Plant, 1998: 37–38). This has been accompanied by the feminization of the workforce that favours independence, flexibility, and adaptability. While men are ill prepared for a postmodern future, women are seen as ideally suited to the new technoculture (Kelan, 2010).

The idea that the Internet can transform conventional gender roles, altering the relationship between the body and the self via a machine, is a popular theme in postmodernism. The message is that young women in particular are colonizing cyberspace where, like gravity, gender inequality is suspended. In cyberspace, all physical, bodily cues are removed from communication. As a result, our interactions are fundamentally different because they are not subject to judgements based on sex, age, race, voice, accent, or appearance. In *Life on the Screen*, Turkle (1995) enthuses about the potential for people to 'express multiple and often unexplored aspects of the self, to play with their identity and to try out new ones . . . the obese can be slender, the beautiful plain, the "nerdy" sophisticated'. It is the increasingly interactive and creative nature of computing technology that now enables millions of people to live a significant segment of their lives in virtual reality, such as *Second Life* (an online virtual world with over two million registrations). Moreover, it is in this computer-mediated world that people can experience a new sense of self that is decentred, multiple, and fluid. In this respect, Turkle argues, the Internet is the material expression of the philosophy of postmodernism.

The most influential feminist commentator writing in this vein is Donna Haraway (1985; 1997). She too argues that we should embrace the positive potential of technoscience, and is sharply critical of those who reject technology. Famously, she prefers to be a 'cyborg' – a hybrid of organism and machine parts – rather than an ecofeminist 'goddess'. She notes the great power of science and technology to create new meanings and new entities, to make new worlds. She positively revels in the very difficulty of predicting what technology's effects will be and warns against any purist rejection of the 'unnatural' hybrid entities produced by biotechnology. Genetic engineering, reproductive technology, and the advent of virtual reality are all seen as fundamentally challenging traditional notions of gender identity.

For postmodern feminists then, the collapse of these oppressive binaries – nature/culture, animal/man, human/machine, subject/object – is liberating. The cyborg creature – a human-machine amalgam – fundamentally redefines what it is to be human and thus can potentially exist in a world without gender categories. Cyberfeminism sees these technologies as dissolving the sex/gender nexus in the hybridization of the lived body and machines. As such, they mark a new relationship between women and technology.

Such developments in feminist scholarship have stimulated important insights into the gender relations of technology, and are a refreshing antidote to the technophobia that characterizes much earlier feminist thought. Importantly, they stress women's agency and capacity for empowerment, treating ICTs as flexible and open to new meanings and uses. However, there is a tendency in this postmodern writing on gender and technology to fetishize the new. For example, Haraway's piercing analysis of the interconnections between capitalism, patriarchy, and technoscience sits uneasily with her belief in the emancipatory potential of advanced technologies. At times, her enthusiasm for the cyborg figure appears dangerously close to endorsing cyberfeminism's embrace of all technological innovations *per se*. A sharp divide is made between cutting-edge technologies and existing technologies. Such a discourse of radical discontinuity has echoes of technological determinism – albeit of a celebratory rather than pessimistic kind.

As I noted earlier, such claims about the transformative effects of digital technologies are not confined to postmodern feminist scholarship. They abound in mainstream millennial reflections, whether it be theories of globalization, risk, or the 'network society'. In many ways, cyberfeminism closely resembles the more popular cybergurus, but with a feminist inflection.

Take, for example, Manuel Castells (1996; 2001), who argues that the revolution in information technology is dramatically changing the character of capitalism. In the 'informational mode of development', labour and capital, the central variables of the industrial society, are replaced by information and knowledge. In the resulting 'Network Society' the compression of space and time made possible by the new communication technology alters the speed and scope of decisions. Organizations can decentralize and disperse, with high level decision-making remaining in 'world cities' while lower level operations, linked to the centre by communication networks, can take place virtually anywhere. Information is the key ingredient of social organization, and flows of messages and images between networks constitute the basic thread of social structure (1996: 477). For Castells, the information age, organized around 'the space of flows and timeless time', marks a whole new epoch in the human experience.

This idea, that we are entering a new form of market capitalism rooted in technological invention and innovation, is widespread. Whatever the term used, such theories share an emphasis on intangibles, such as creativity and knowledge, being the core of capitalism, replacing raw materials and factory labour. It is commonly assumed that in the new world of work, old patterns of social inequalities, like class, race, and gender will no longer play a role. In the words of Nicholas Negroponte, former Head of the iconic MIT Media Laboratory: '[B]eing digital is different . . . in the digital world, previously impossible solutions become viable' (1995: 231).

## TECHNOFEMINISM: COMBINING FEMINIST AND TECHNOLOGY STUDIES

All these writers play the card of discontinuity and shower us with promises of freedom, empowerment, and wealth. Such claims about the revolutionary impact of new technologies on society are hardly novel, yet they are still seductive, and appear to render pointless our knowledge of the present and past (Robins and Webster, 2002). Previous periods of major technological innovation were also characterized by hyperbolic claims about the societal transformation that would follow. Furthermore, the egalitarian image of creative knowledge work is belied by numerous empirical studies of the increasing polarization of jobs in the new economy (Edwards and Wajcman, 2005). As I noted above, these industries are still characterized by a hierarchal sexual division of SET skills and expertise.

However, this is not to imply that we simply have new information technologies, but the same old social relations, values, and goals. The issue of gender and IT is *not the same* as it was in the late 1970s. Computers are very different from what they used to be when feminists first began to study gender and computing. Likewise, men and women are changing their practices and entering new relationships with each other and their environment, and masculinity and femininity are now understood to be unstable constructions, dynamic rather than static. So, for example, while the Internet is necessarily producing new forms of connectivity and sociality, it is important to stress that the social arrangements in which they are embedded are also changing. We can only understand the widespread discussion about the possibilities in cyberspace of experiencing multiple, fluid, innovative, gender-bending subjectivities, in the context of the transformation in women's lives, and in gender relations, over the twentieth century. In other words, it is important to credit feminism with many of the social and political transformations that are usually attributed to technoscience.

Digital technologies, then, are not inherently patriarchal or unambiguously liberating, but are shaped by the social circumstances within which they are designed and used. Indeed, the social studies of science and technology (STS) has been challenging this type of 'technological determinism' since at least the 1970s (for an introduction to STS, see Hackett et al., 2008). Social scientists increasingly recognize that technological innovation is itself shaped by the social circumstances within which it takes place. Objects and artefacts are no longer seen as separate from society, but as part of the social fabric that holds society together; they are never merely technical or social. Within what is widely known as the social shaping or constructivist approach, we now understand technology as a socio-technical product – a seamless web or network combining artefacts, people, organizations, cultural meanings, and knowledge (Bijker, Hughes, and Pinch, 1987; Law and Hassard, 1999; MacKenzie and Wajcman, 1999). The idea that technological artefacts are socially shaped, not just in their usage, but also with respect to their design and technical content is no longer controversial.

Within mainstream STS, however, the ways in which technological objects may shape and be shaped by the operation of gender interests or identities has not been a central focus. Whilst innovations are seen as sociotechnical networks, it has been largely incumbent on feminists to demonstrate that gender relations inform these networks. After all, if 'technology is society made durable' (Latour, 1991: 103), then gender power relations will influence the process of technological change, which in turn configures gender relations. Women's systematic absence from the sites of observable conflict over the direction of technological developments is therefore as indicative of the mobilization of gender interests as is the presence of other actors. Empirical research on everything from the microwave oven (Cockburn and Ormrod, 1993), the telephone (Martin, 1991) and the contraceptive Pill (Oudshoorn, 1994) to robotics and software agents (Suchman, 2007) has clearly demonstrated that the marginalization of women from the technological community has a profound influence on the design, technical content, and use of artefacts.

A social constructivist framework is now widely adopted by feminist STS scholars (Berg, 1996; Faulkner, 2001; Lie, 2003). In common with my own technofeminist theory, it conceives of technology as both a source and consequence of gender relations (Wajcman, 2004). In other words, gender relations can be thought of as materialized in technology, and masculinity and femininity in turn acquire their meaning and character through their enrolment and embeddedness in working machines. In this way, the culture of masculinity is embedded in the technology itself. Such a mutual shaping approach recognizes that the gendering of technology affects the entire life trajectory of an artefact. Indeed, feminist research has been at the forefront of more general moves within STS to deconstruct the designer/user divide, and that between production and consumption, emphasizing the connectedness of all phases of technological development. The gendering of technologies can then be understood as not only shaped in design, but also shaped or reconfigured at the multiple points of consumption and use.

The capacity of women users to produce new, advantageous readings of artefacts is, however, dependent on their broader economic and social circumstances. For example, a young woman in the West may experience her silver mobile phone as a liberating extension of her body. For her working mother, it may be both a tool to keep track of her daughter and a means whereby her employer keeps track of her. For women working as traders in Bangladesh, the mobile phone provides the means to run businesses selling communication services to other women. And for women in China working in factories that mass-produce phones, they provide employment. There is enormous variability in gendering by place, nationality, class, race, ethnicity, sexuality, and generation and thus women's experience of technologies will be diverse.

This point is particularly crucial as much feminist politics in relation to technology is still largely limited to agency in relation to use rather than innovation at the point of design. STS scholarship increasingly recognizes that the social meanings of technology are contingently stabilized and contestable, that the fate of a technology depends on the social context and cannot simply be read off fixed sets of power arrangements. The 'domestication' framework, in particular, has sensitized researchers to some of the complex processes at work in incorporating technologies into everyday life (Haddon, 2004). In line with social shaping principles, domestication foregrounds user agency in the way people continuously interpret, appropriate, and use artefacts in their everyday lives. Given that the concept of gender itself is now understood as a performance (Butler, 1990), both technology and gender can be conceptualized as products of a moving relational process, emerging from collective and individual acts of interpretation. Feminist theorists are now acutely aware of the contradictory effects of technology on women, and that the same artefact can have different meanings for different groups of women. The result is more nuanced research that captures the increasingly complex intertwining of gender and technoscience as an ongoing process of mutual shaping over time and across multiple sites.

## Conclusion

This chapter has argued that the gendered culture of technology accounts for women's limited success in science, engineering, and technology, and their enduring under-representation in these fields. The gendering of organizational practices, in particular those related to managerial culture, are compounded by the gender relations of technoscience itself.

Technology is, then, both a source and a consequence of gender relations. In the process of defining what SET is, how it should be used, what SET skills are, or in other words what 'counts' as valuable knowledge and expertise, gender functions as a cultural category in 'sorting things out' (Lie, 2003). In this process of negotiating boundaries, gender is a marker that still functions to sort out high-tech from low-tech or no-tech. In other words, gender is constitutive for what is recognized as technology, and gendered identities and discourses are produced simultaneously with technologies. The fact that technology, culture, and gender relations are so interwoven helps to explain why this link has proved so durable.

We have seen how feminist theories of gender and technology have developed over the last few decades, oscillating between pessimism and optimism. At times these arguments have tended towards the technological determinism found in wider debates. However, the intellectual exploration at the intersection of feminist scholarship and STS has enriched both fields immeasurably. Both foreground the way that people and artefacts co-evolve: that technologies are not the inevitable result of the application of scientific and technological knowledge. Feminist STS or technofeminism has demonstrated that gender relations are also integral to this sociotechnical process. We can then understand the ways in which women's identities, needs, and priorities are configured together with digital technologies.

Getting more women into science, engineering, and technology is not only an equal employment opportunity issue, but also an issue of how the world we live in is designed, and for whom. We cannot rely on new technologies to achieve the social changes we seek. If women are to participate fully in the information age, we need to continue to challenge the conception of femininity as incompatible with techno-logical pursuits. This entails not simply embracing technological innovations but actively shaping them. It also requires a new model of work and life, where women and men are equally represented in all jobs, including the top jobs, of the digital economy.

## REFERENCES

Acker, J. (1990) Hierarchies, Jobs, Bodies: A Theory of Gendered Organizations, *Gender & Society*, 4, 139–158.

Bebbington, D. (2000) Women in Science, Engineering and Technology: A Review of the Issues, *Higher Education Quarterly*, 56(4) 360–375.

Berg, A. (1996) *Digital Feminism*. Norwegian University of Science and Technology, Trondheim.

Bijker, W., Hughes, T., and Pinch, T. (eds) (1987) *The Social Construction of Technological Systems*. Cambridge MA: MIT Press.

Bradley, H. (1989) *Men's Work, Women's Work*. Cambridge: Polity Press.

Braidotti, R. (2003) 'Cyberfeminism with a Difference' in M. Peters, M. Olssen, and C. Lankshear (eds), *Futures of Critical Theory*. Rowan and Littlefield, 239–259.

Butler, J. (1990) *Gender Trouble: Feminism and the Subversion of Identity*. London and New York: Routledge.

Castells, M. (1996) *The Rise of the Network* Society. Oxford: Blackwell.

Castells, M. (2001) *The Internet Galaxy*. Oxford: Oxford University Press.

CNNIC (China Internet Network Information Centre) (2005) 14th Survey Report.

Cockburn, C. (1983) *Brothers: Male Dominance and Technological Change*. London: Pluto Press.

Cockburn, C., and Ormrod, S. (1993) *Gender and Technology in the Making*. London: Sage.

Cowan, R. (1983) *More Work for Mother: The Ironies of Household Technology from the Open Hearth to the Microwave*. New York: Basic Books.

Crompton, R. (1997) *Women and Work in Modern Britain*. Oxford: Oxford University Press.

Edwards, P., and Wajcman, J. (2005) *The Politics of Working Life*. Oxford: Oxford University Press.

European Commission: Information Society and Media (2008) *Women in ICT*. Directorate General.

Faulker, W. (2001) The Technology Question in Feminism: A View from Feminist Technology Studies, *Women's Studies International Forum*, 24(1) 79–95.

Francis, B. (2000) *Boys, Girls, and Achievement: Addressing the Classroom Issues*. London: Routledge.

Glover, J., and Campling, J. (2000) *Women and Scientific Employment*. London: St Martin's Press.

Hackett, E., Amsterdamska, O., Lynch, M., and Wajcman, J. (eds) (2008) *The Handbook of Science and Technology Studies: Third Edition*. Cambridge, MA: M.I.T. Press.

Haddon, L. (2004) *Information and Communication Technologies in Everyday Life*. Oxford: Berg.

Haraway, D. (1985) A Manifesto for Cyborgs: Science, Technology, and Socialist Feminism in the 1980's, *Socialist Review* 80, 65–108.

Haraway, D. (1997) *Modest_Witness@Second_Millennium. FemaleMan?_Meets_Oncomouse?* . New York: Routledge.

Harding, S. (1996) *The Science Question in Feminism.* New York: Cornell University Press.

Harvey, D. (1989) *The Condition of Postmodernity.* Oxford: Blackwell.

Hewlett, S., Luce, C., Servon, L., Sherbin, L., Shiller, P., Sosnovich, E., and Sumberg, K. (2008) *The Athena Factor: Reversing the Brain Drain in Science, Engineering, and Technology.* Harvard Business Review Research Report no. 10094.

Kelan, E. (2007) Tools and Toys: Communicating Gendered Positions Towards Technology, *Information, Communication & Society,* 10(3) 357–382.

Kelan, E. (2009) *Performing Gender at Work,* London: Palgrave Macmillan.

Keller, E. Fox (1983) *A Feeling for the Organism: The Life and Work of Barbara McClintock.* San Francisco, CA: Freeman.

Kember, S. (2003) *Cyberfeminism and Artificial Life.* London and New York: Routledge.

Kemp, S., and Squires, J. (eds) (1998) *Feminisms: An Oxford Reader.* Oxford: Oxford University Press.

Kirkup, G., Janes, L., Woodward, K., and Hovenden, F. (2000) *The Gendered Cyborg: A Reader.* London: Routledge.

Kvande, E. (1999) In the Belly of the Beast: Constructing Femininities in Engineering Organizations, *The European Journal of Women's Studies,* 6, 305–328.

Latour, B. (1991) 'Technology is Society made Durable' in J. Law (ed.), *A Sociology of Monsters: Essays on Power, Technology and Domination.* London: Routledge, 103–131.

Law, J. and Hassard, J. (eds) (1999) *Actor Network Theory and After.* Oxford: Blackwell.

Lerman, N.E., Oldenziel, R., and Mohun, A.P. (eds) (2003) *Gender and Technology: A Reader.* Baltimore: John Hopkins University Press.

Lie, M. (ed) (2003) *He, She and IT Revisited: New Perspectives on Gender and the Information Society.* Oslo: Gyldendal Akademisk.

Lohan, M., and Faulkner, W. (2004) Masculinities and Technologies: Some Introductory Remarks, *Men and Masculinities,* 6, 319–329.

Long, Scott, J., and Fox, Frank, M. (1995) Scientific Careers: Universalism and Particularism, *Annual Review of Sociology,* 21, 45–71.

MacKenzie, D., and Wajcman, J. (eds) (1999) *The Social Shaping of Technology: Second edition.* Milton Keynes: Open University Press.

Martin, M. (1991) *'Hello Central?': Gender, Technology, and the Culture in the Formation of Telephone Systems.* Montreal: McGill-Queen's University Press.

Milkman, R. (1987) *Gender at Work: The Dynamics of Job Segregation during World War II.* Urbana: University of Illinois Press.

Negroponte, N. (1995) *Being Digital.* London: Hodder & Stoughton.

NTIA (2008) *Network Nation: Broadband in America 2007.* US Department of Commerce: Washington, DC.

Oldenziel, R. (1999) *Making Technology Masculine: Men, Women and Modern Machines in America.* Amsterdam: Amsterdam University Press.

Oudshoorn, N. (1994) *Beyond the Natural Body: An Archaeology of Sex Hormones.* London: Routledge.

Plant, S. (1998) *Zeros and Ones: Digital Women + the New Technoculture.* London: Fourth Estate.

Robins, K., and Webster, F. (2002) Prospects of a Virtual Culture, *Science as Culture,* 11(2) 235–256.

Rossiter, M. (1982) *Women Scientists in America: Struggles and Strategies to 1940.* Baltimore: The Johns Hopkins University Press.

Rothschild, J. (ed.) (1983) *Machina Ex Dea: Feminist Perspectives on Technology.* New York: Pergamon Press.

Smith-Doerr, L. (2004) *Women's Work; Gender Equality vs. Hierarchy in the Life Sciences.* Boulder, CO: Lynne Rienner Publishers.

Suchman, L. (2007) *Human-Machine Reconfigurations: Plans and Situated Actions.* 2nd edn. Cambridge: Cambridge University Press.

Turkle, S. (1995) *Life on the Screen: Identity in the Age of the Internet.* New York: Simon and Schuster.

Wajcman, J. (1991) *Feminism Confronts Technology.* Cambridge: Polity Press.

Wajcman, J. (1998) *Managing Like a Man: Women and Men in Corporate Management.* Cambridge: Polity Press.

Wajcman, J. (2004) *TechnoFeminism.* Cambridge: Polity Press.

# 17

# Gender Change, Organizational Change, and Gender Equality Strategies[1]

## YVONNE BENSCHOP AND MIEKE VERLOO
### *Radboud University Nijmegen, The Netherlands*

## INTRODUCTION

Change is at the heart of gender studies and the field of gender, work, and organization is no exception to that. Since second-wave feminism provided the impetus to question women's and men's positions in society, an ever increasing flow of research has problematized the gendered division of labor and made a plea for gender equality. A quest for change is thus more or less central to the field. Despite many initiatives aimed at changing organizations into gender-balanced or gender-equitable workplaces, change is slow at best. Only from a historical perspective, when one looks back a few decades, does it become clear that changes toward equality have indeed occurred, at various levels (welfare states, organizations, and the attitudes of people).

Work by Mills (2006) on gender in the airline industry illustrates that gender change does occur. In the twenty-first century, direct discrimination by sex and sexual harassment are forbidden by law, at least in many Western countries. Virtually all occupations are now formally open to women as well as men, although the first women to enter certain masculine occupations still make headline news. Nonetheless, a depressing amount of evidence on asymmetries between the sexes persists in economic, cultural, and political domains (Fraser, 2009).

Studies of gender inequality in paid work and organizations offer insightful descriptions of patterns of gender inequality. A good example is documented in a *leaky pipeline* analysis that goes beyond description of the absence of women in top positions to diagnose how organizations systematically lose women on their way to the top (Osborn, Rees, Bosch, Hermann, Hilden, and Mason, 2000; Pell, 1996; Van den Brink, 2009). While knowledge about gender inequalities has grown, we

[1] The authors are immensely grateful to Pat Martin for her numerous enthusiastic comments, fruitful suggestions, and superb editing.

know less about how to change inequalities, particularly about the actual practices of change that are most effective. Scholarly research tends to focus on the description, analysis, or deconstruction of the *status quo* (depending on the theoretical preferences of the author) while it remains disconnected from actual initiatives of gender transformations. Although many scholars simultaneously engage in putting their thoughts into practice in consultancy and organizational change projects, we perceive a gap between scholarship and these knowledge-based advocacy activities. From our experience as critics and designers of gender equality policies, we understand that policy-making and the academy are different worlds. The results of applied research conducted at the behest of third parties often do not find their way into academic debates. And complex theoretical notions often fail to work well in practical settings. Gender equality policies are developed in a context where theory is thin and actions are based on the common sense of practitioners fuelled by a mix of political fashions, self-acclaimed best practices, scholarly work, time constraints, and the urge to show visible success.

This chapter provides an overview of attempts developed over many years to facilitate change in organizations and societies toward greater gender equality. It discusses the aims and content of strategies and interventions and assesses their performance in practice on both discursive and material levels. To do so, we invoke insights from political science, organization studies, and gender studies. We analyze the strategies for gender change on two dimensions: from the individual to the structural level and from a narrow to a (more) wide-ranging scope. We also identify gaps in knowledge that hinder the impact of interventions aimed at enhancing gender equality. The chapter then turns to organization change theories and gender theories to examine key impediments to gender-related change: the challenges of planning gender-related change, efforts oriented to incremental change, resistance to gender equality, the issue of intersectionality, and the need for voice. We end by identifying a new approach to gender change in organizations that sets out to cope with these impediments, which we call the genderXchange strategy.

## An Overview of the Quest for Organizational Change Toward Gender Equality

Strategies for gender equality are characterized by a process of continuous innovation. From the birth of gender equality policies in the 1970s, policy-makers and academics who follow these policies critically have sought to identify the ideal content and ideal form of change strategies (see, for example, Bacchi, 1996; Jenson, 2008; Liff and Cameron, 1997; and Nentwich, 2006). Ongoing theoretical debates and problematic constructs also characterize the history of this effort (Squires, 2007; Walby, 2005), which limits knowledge about how to effectively combat gender inequalities.

Two debates have had an impact on the strategies for gender change: (a) sameness–difference and (b) structure–agency. The debate on sameness and difference focuses on the question of whether women are the same as or different from men. The debate on structure and agency pertains to the question of whether social inequality is the effect of societal structures or the effect of individual actions. Rooted in old controversies in social theories between voluntaristic and deterministic paradigms, gender scholars debate how individual or collective actors are able to escape structures that are theoretically conceived as the unintentional but inescapable result of human activity. Applied to organizational change goals, this means that gender equality strategies primarily target individuals *or* structures and only rarely transcend this dichotomy.

The classical difference argument is that women *essentially* differ from men in nearly every meaningful respect – biologically, intellectually, emotionally, and behaviorally. These differences result in an undervaluing of the feminine in organizations (among other contexts) which, in fact, should be valued positively. According to this argument, women have a special contribution to make to work and organizations because their different experiences, values, characteristics, behavior, feelings, and thoughts provide them with qualifications that are much needed in organizations and that men often fail to offer. Fletcher (1999), for instance, speaks of women's relational skills and ability to connect to others in contrast to men's deficits in these respects.

The perspective of sameness, on the other hand, is that any differences between the genders are caused by patterns of discrimination and prejudice against women versus privilege and favoritism toward men. The basic argument is that no essential gender differences exist in abilities, qualifications, or work orientations that can account for occupational segregation, wage gaps (Padavic and Reskin, 2002), and other deficits regularly experienced by women at work. Failing to use the full potential of women employees is practically inefficient, economically unwise, and a formidable waste of talent. In its focus on the similarities of women and men, the sameness perspective tends to overlook differences between women that are based on social identity categories, including ethnicity, age, and social class and their intersections. Heated debates about equality and diversity do not prevent these notions from being used to underpin strategies for change that have developed over the years in various disciplines (Jewson and Mason, 1986; Kirton and Greene, 2005; Rees, 1998; Walby, 2005).

## A TWO-DIMENSIONAL COMPARISON

Although parallel developments in different disciplines can be confusing, on the issue of gender equality policies and feminist interventions, the similarities exceed the differences. Indeed, the similarities are striking. Our review of strategies for gender change is inspired by Jewson and Mason's work on equality policies (1986), which contrasts liberal and radical equality policies, and by the work of Kirton and Greene (2005) who add managing diversity and gender mainstreaming to the mix. Additionally, we review the four feminist intervention strategies for change that are noted by Meyerson and Kolb (2000). We review these approaches to gender change in order to compare them on two dimensions. As noted earlier, the first is the classic individual–structure distinction and the second pertains to the scope of the changes that are envisioned, that is, consisting of inclusion, re-valuation or transformation.

TABLE 17.1: A two-dimensional model of strategies for gender change.

|            | *Inclusion* | *Re-valuation* | *Transformation* |
|------------|-------------|----------------|------------------|
| Individual | LIBERAL Equip the woman Create equal opportunity | MANAGING DIVERSITY Value difference | |
| Structural | RADICAL Create equal opportunity | | GENDER MAINSTREAMING Post-equity |

**Individual/inclusion.** At this level, strategies are focused on individual women maximizing their potential to survive and thrive in organizations and societies (see Table 17.1). A *liberal equality* strategy (Jewson and Mason, 1986) stresses the need for equal opportunities for all individuals and insists on formal equal treatment for all, regardless of social categories such as gender, ethnicity, social class, and age. This strategy sees inequality between men and women in organizations as the core problem and the solution to the problem is an improvement in the position of women.

The strategy of '*equip the woman*,' identified by Meyerson and Kolb (2000), also assumes a liberal vision of work organizations. In particular, it rests on the assumptions that jobs are acquired through merit alone and that women and men have equal opportunity to acquire and succeed in all jobs. Change is geared towards improving the qualifications of women so they are better equipped to compete with men. The kinds of exemplary measures that have the potential to produce this result include management development and mentoring and/or training programs that will teach women critical skills and rules of the game (that men, presumably, already know).

In individual strategies like these, the agency of individuals is at the center of the remedy. It is primarily women who are targeted, who must be 'tinkered' with (Rees, 1998), so they can become more productive and successful workplace participants. Men also could be 'equipped' with new capacities and skills to enable them to function better in gender equal organizations (and societies) but men are not typically targeted. In brief, these interventions target only one-half of the players and not the game, thus explaining why individual inclusion strategies have produced little concrete change. If equality means that women and men should get equal opportunities to become ideal workers for their organizations, this is at best a meager form of gender equality. This version of organizations is exposed by Nancy Fraser (2009) as reflecting an unsavory liaison between second-wave feminism and neoliberal capitalism that thrives on the principle of flexible labor participation and low wages for women.

And yet, many laws, rules, and regulations that were developed in response to the call for equal opportunities have had a positive impact on organizations in challenging direct discrimination based on a worker's sex. Equal pay and fair employment procedures for recruitment and promotion may not be realized yet but thanks to equal opportunity strategies of the individual/inclusion type, they are recognized as worth striving for. Likewise, the call for equal opportunities and special programs for women have helped to increase the number of women in top organizational positions. In the US, for example, mentoring appears to be more fruitful for black women while networking has proved more effective for white women (Castilla, 2005; Kalev, Dobbin, and Kelly, 2006: 604). While neither strategy has improved the lot of all women, research evidence suggests that each can be effective, at least for some women and to a degree.

**Individual/re-evaluation.** A second set of strategies focused on the individual stresses the need to re-evaluate the notion of sameness and difference. These strategies celebrate gender differences, seeing them as a resource for organizations and for society. Gender inequality is viewed implicitly as a result of failing to value the capacities and life experiences of women while valorizing those of men. (What exactly constitutes 'feminine' or 'masculine' capacities is rarely addressed in these strategies.) A *value difference* strategy calls for acknowledging the special contributions of feminine styles and qualities such as listening, collaborating, and communicating in organizations (Fletcher, 1998). The aim is to change the hierarchical order in organizations that *values the masculine over the feminine* (see Martin (1993) on how feminine and feminist management strategies differ). The strategy builds on feminist standpoint theory (Harding, 2004) which produces knowledge based on the actualities of women's everyday lives and uses that knowledge politically to question the practices of powerful institutions. Our position is that a call to revaluate the feminine unaccompanied by a corrective revaluing of the masculine is doomed to failure. As Fletcher's research (1999) on engineers in the Xerox Corporation showed, men routinely failed to view their women colleagues' 'feminine contributions' as real work.

*Managing diversity*, a strategy that emphasizes each individual's unique contribution to an organization, similarly values employee diversity. Gender diversity, the somewhat awkward term for gender differences in this model, is recognized as an important diversity dimension along with cultural and other forms of diversity. In this framework, everyone is diverse – not only women, minorities, the elderly, or handicapped. Even men are diverse. Furthermore, differences are positive. Heterogeneity is valuable and can be utilized to enhance an organization's effectiveness. Within a managing diversity strategy, gender equality is a means to the business goal of maximizing profits. However, measures associated with actually assessing the effectiveness of this strategy are mostly intangible. Mission statements about the value of an inclusive organization culture are popular but how one is achieved is far from clear (Kunda, 1992).

Individual re-valuation strategies differ from individual inclusion strategies in demanding a revaluation of classic femininity, but they similarly disregard organizational and societal structures as the causes and conditions for including women (the first approach) or re-evaluating difference. Both of these strategies fail to address gender inequalities. A business case rationale inspires a 'happy diversity' discourse (Hoobler, 2005) that accentuates the sameness of individuals rather than a positive valuation of their differences. Reliance on business case goals again plays a tune consistent with neoliberal capitalism. An emphasis on individual contributions prevents understanding of the processes of power, privilege, and subordination. Even when managing diversity makes difference a positive issue, often it reinforces stereotypes and fails to challenge the fact that women and minorities remain in subordinate positions. This is exemplified in diversity training programs that teach participants about communal women and agentic men (Rudman and Glick, 1999). Nevertheless, individual revaluation strategies have fostered a discourse about the special contribution to organizations that women and minorities can make. A study of the Dutch police force (Boogaard and Roggeband, 2010) shows how this discourse can be used to illuminate the contributions of police women to the core work of police departments when their relational skills help de-escalate tense situations.

To no one's surprise, we do not find strategies that focused on the individual level calling for transformation of the organization or society. The absence of strategies to 'equip' men for more gender equal workplaces and societies and the focus on 'classic femininity' (re)installs traditional gender categories without challenging the unequal power relations between them. This absence prohibits a *transformative* approach and thus prevents realization of true gender equality.

**Structural/inclusion.** A structural strategy that aims for including women, the *radical equality* strategy, focuses attention on a 'reset' of opportunity structures for women that resembles the liberal structural strategy of *creating more opportunities*. The *radical equality* strategy does not stop at fostering equality of opportunity for women but makes equality of outcomes a central goal (Kirton and Greene, 2005). This strategy has an eye for the systematic discrimination of social groups and for stereotypes and prejudices that prevent recognition of the merits of those groups. This strategy utilizes measures geared towards positive discrimination, for example, by applying quotas and preferential treatment to realize desired equality outcomes. The label of 'radical' expresses that this is a contested model. It requires direct interventions – aimed at a just division of advantages for women and men – that are often perceived as unfair (Bacchi, 1996).

In many countries and under European law, measures such as quotas are outlawed because they are presumably discriminatory against men. Nevertheless, direct interventions including quotas have proved to be effective at placing gender equality change on the political agenda and at actually producing positive change. Quotas for women in politics have spread to more than 100 countries around the globe (Krook, 2008). Quotas that target the representation of women on the boards of governing bodies have been implemented in several Nordic countries and quotas in Norway have also spread to the private sector (Tienari, Holgersson, Merilainen, and Hook, 2009). Quota laws have been also found to be just mildly effective in increasing women's presence (Htun and Jones, 2002). That quotas have been widely implemented despite resistance shows that women have gained in political power (Dahlerup, 2006).

A *create equal opportunity* strategy acknowledges the existence of structural barriers, sees organization structures as the key problem, and wants to change the sloped playing-field into a level playing-field. This strategy addresses biased recruitment, biased promotion, and biased evaluation procedures (Martin, 1996). Typical examples of measures are transparent recruitment practices, flexible work arrangements, and alternative career paths. These interventions have contributed to the quality of working life for both men and women and have had an impact on the numerical representation of women in organizations. However, a focus on structure alone can lead to alternative career paths and/or time issues for women [the so-called mommy tracks, (Benschop and Doorewaard, 1998)] that are restricted by and bound to gendered social norms. Removing structural barriers without addressing underlying cultural norms related to gender, work, and organization lowers the odds of this strategy for creating positive gender change (Mescher, Benschop, and Doorewaard, 2010).

A usual criticism of structural inclusion approaches is that they are too weak to abolish gender inequality. However, this criticism stops short of considering what would happen to an organization (or society) if all women were fully included. Would gendered norms and stereotypes still exist? Would gender remain a structuring principle if women were structurally included in all realms of society? Perhaps the problem with this approach is that it often involves women's 'structural inclusion' in only one domain, that is, the economy. But perhaps full inclusion in one domain can provide a tipping point for producing change in other domains (Walby, 2009). Women's full inclusion across the economy, civil society, and polity could perhaps bring about true transformation, thus blurring the distinction between inclusion and transformation.

A structural revaluation strategy is not de facto a strategy for true gender change. There are no empirical examples of what Squires calls a strategy of reversal (Squires, 2007), a strategy of turning societies or organizations upside down by organizing them according to feminine values. Some examples exist of feminist organizations that take issue with traditional hierarchies and capitalist masculinist ways of organizing (Iannello, 1992) but they have not been applied to broader strategies for gender change.

**Structural/transformation.** Last but not least, we address structural transformation strategies that are represented to be 'ideal' and 'transformative' in the sense that they address and try to change gender as a structure.

*Gender mainstreaming* is a structural transformation strategy that aims to transform organizational processes and practices by eliminating gender biases from existing routines. It involves regular organizational actors in the transformation process (Council of Europe, 1998). This strategy introduces new responsibilities for policy-makers who are on the 'inside' and who try to identify and change the routines and fossilized norms that (re)produce gender inequality (Eisenstein, 1996). To be successful, they must call on and cooperate with gender experts to confront and challenge policies that foster gender inequality at work. Gender mainstreaming thus mobilizes many people to engage in changing gender relations in different areas in organizations (Stratigaki, 2005). Many scholars and activists agree that gender mainstreaming is potentially a transformative strategy (Verloo, 2005).

However, the social dynamics required for this strategy to be effective asks feminists and policy-makers to cooperate to the point that 'gender' and 'the mainstream' agree to common problem definitions. This practice entails processes of stretching and bending problem definitions and compromises to cope with resistance and compromise, actions that can (and at times do) undermine the transformative potential of gender mainstreaming (Benschop and Verloo, 2006; Lombardo, Meier, and Verloo, 2008). This resonates with the 'dual agenda' challenge noted by Ely and Meyerson (2000) in the context of the post-equity strategy (see below). A key critique of gender mainstreaming concerns the inadequate economic, political, and bureaucratic support that prevents structural transformation success. McGauran (2009) points to bureaucratic characteristics that foster an integrationist, but not transformative, implementation of gender mainstreaming. Gender mainstreaming lacks a clear and concise methodology for achieving its goals. Also, policies and practices routinely diverge in ways that prevent or discourage genuine change (Eveline, Bacchi, and Binns, 2009). Regarding the methods for accomplishing gender mainstreaming, technocratic tools such as gender impact assessment and gender budgeting techniques outnumber the participatory tools needed for feminist groups and marginalized women's voices heard to be heard (Walby, 2005; Verloo, 2005) Gender mainstreaming is critiqued also because it fails to address feminist theories of intersectionality and privileges the category of gender over other social categories such as ethnicity or class. Sometimes, a shift to diversity mainstreaming is propagated (Hankivsky, 2005) in regard to intersectionality but this term is contested because it is associated with individualizing and apolitical tendencies (Eveline, Bacchi, and Binns, 2009) that fail to produce gender equality.

*Post equity.* Ely and Meyerson (2000) propose another structural transformation strategy. The 'post equity' strategy sees gender as an axis of power and core organizing principle that shapes social structures, knowledge, and identities. Their work addresses challenges to the ongoing social construction of gender at work. The central problem, as viewed in this strategy, is the processes that produce gender inequalities as part of everyday organizational routines and interactions (Acker, 1992). The strategy advocates action-research projects that apply a specific form of critique focused on how gender inequalities are detrimental to organizational performance, followed by experiments that interrupt gendering processes while improving work effectiveness, and concluded by narratives about the experiments and their successes (Ely and Meyerson, 2000). Change depends not on the action of one actor but on fruitful collaboration between researchers and organization members who understand and accept a feminist critique and interventions that stem from that critique. Ely and Meyerson (2000) note how a *dual agenda of gender equality and business success* is difficult to maintain because of the dominance of business issues over gender issues. Yet a dual agenda focus may foster a seductive discursive strategy that aligns to good effect with a managerial discourse about organizational performance (Benschop and Verloo, 2006). And yet, the risk of 'losing gender' to business issues is real, especially when targeted organizational routines serve the interests of those in power.

The *post equity* and *gender mainstreaming* strategies share some similarities, among them their theoretical promise but problematical chances for implementation. Both lack a deep theoretical understanding of how change can happen without violently disrupting society or how *revolution without a revolution* can come about. They recognize a need to transcend the individual level (sometimes to the extent of overlooking this level altogether) but are poorly developed when it comes to assigning duties to particular actors, the best ways to initiate change, the most promising sequencing of change, specification of smaller and bigger steps, and a way to take intersecting inequalities into account. All too often, they call for changing everything everywhere by everyone.

**Discussion.** Upon reviewing a range of strategies, we now note some absences and tensions in recommended methods for producing gender equality change. First, most strategies are not informed by social theories of change that could help articulate how change in gender relations can be realized. Second, while gender change in practice entails an eclectic amalgam of strategies, in theoretical work the strategies are mostly discussed as if they do not and cannot co-exist. The sad result is that this obscures reflection on the potential effect of combinations of strategies in terms of transforming organizations to foster gender equality. Exceptions include Dickens' (1999) plea for a tripod of business case, legal, and social regulation strategies as a sounder basis for equality action and Booth and Bennett's (2002) plea for a three-legged stool where equal rights, positive action, and gender mainstreaming are pursued at once. Third, feminist academics express a preference for structural transformation but they also present it in their critiques as 'mission impossible.' Their transformative approaches are unattractive to policy-makers and practitioners because they are bereft of practical instruments and strong in 'scary radicalism,' thus prompting fear and resistance. Fourth, intersectionality is, as a rule, present only in watered-down individual strategy solutions and thus women members of disadvantaged groups and also most men see little that relates to their welfare. Finally, the voice of marginalized groups is hard to find in the various change strategies. We explore these issues further in the next section.

## GENDER CHANGE AND ORGANIZATION CHANGE?

Most organizational change theories that speak to changes in gender equality pay a great deal of attention to obstacles hindering change and portray genuine change as complex, difficult, and problematical (Greenwood and Hinings, 2006). Three themes are relevant to gender change: (a) the possibility of planned change, (b) the likelihood of revolutionary (or fundamental) change that will turn an organization in a new direction, and (c) resistance to organizational change. As useful as organization change theory might be, gender blindness lowers its utility and keeps key issues of gender change of the agenda. Intersectionality and voice for marginalized groups are such key issues that have a profound impact on gender change as well.

The issue of *planned and unplanned change* is critical to an understanding of gender equality strategies in organizations. Our review of diverse models aimed at producing positive gender change underscores that point. Organizational change is complex and unforeseen consequences are bound to happen (Burke, 2002). This point is no different relative to gender than to culture or anything else. Connell (2006) questions whether the processes of gender change can be intentionally steered, that is, whether an agenda of transformation can be successfully implemented. And yet, a strong belief exists in the field of gender, work, and organization that systematic, planned change is needed to produce organizational transformations toward greater gender equality. The US ADVANCE program is an example of a planned comprehensive change program (Bilimoria, Joy, and Liang, 2008). The goals of planned change easily devolve into managerialism, however, because a mechanistic understanding of change (Sturdy and Grey, 2003) prompts development of detailed regulations, controls, and monitoring. Managerialism elevates control and regulation as the sole factors leading to effective and successful change. In declaring content and understanding irrelevant, managerialism fosters 'doing the paper instead of doing the deed' (Ahmed, 2007), creating additional bureaucracy instead of meaningful change. It also lures feminist change agents into considering themselves as saviors of the organization, clearly a belief beyond reality (Parker, 2002).

Regarding *revolutionary versus incremental change*, the gender mainstreaming and post-equity strategies seek to transform organizations via revolutionary change whereas other strategies focus on an incremental or more evolutionary process. Indeed, most of the latter strategies frame organizational changes as continuous, small improvements rather than as strong disruptions reflecting revolution. Cockburn (1989) speaks of the short and long agenda for change, recognizing a need for both incremental and radical gender change in organizations. Meyerson and Fletcher (2000), in contrast, advocate for incremental gender changes that they call 'small wins.' First, they state that the nature of gender inequality in organizations calls for incremental changes because direct gender discrimination has been adequately dealt with and remaining gender inequalities are intertwined with everyday work practices.

A second reason to prefer small changes over big ones is the issue of *resistance to change*. A small wins strategy is 'a way to chip away barriers that hold women back without sparking the kind of sound and fury that scares people into resistance' (Meyerson and Fletcher, 2000: 128). Resistance to change is typically strong when an organization's cultural norms, beliefs, attitudes, and values are the target of change efforts. This is certainly the case with projects that target the gender bias in organizational routines (Benschop and Verloo, 2006). It is thus unsurprising that studies of gender change report extensive resistance. Resistance comes in many forms and shapes. Examples include men who resist women's entry into previously masculine domains, challenges to the authority of women managers, denying problems with gender in the organization (Connell, 2006; Martin, 2006), requests for research or training in order to avoid action, and attempts to escape involvement in gender change efforts (Benschop and Verloo, 2006).

In the organizational change literature, a direct approach to changing organization cultures is not advised because this approach triggers strong resistance and emotions. Rather, some scholars urge change agents to start with *behavioral change* in hopes they will trigger favorable *changes in attitudes* and values (Burke, 2002). A similar plea is made in the gender mainstreaming literature with Stark (1998) advocating the *organization of obligations* because that approach is more effective than trying to change attitudes. In our experience, Stark's claim fails to hold. Feminist change agents should not assume that organizing behavioral changes will ensure gender equality (Benschop and Verloo, 2006: 30). We have seen too many implementation problems with this approach, partly due to its ignoring gender blindness and gender biased attitudes.

*Intersectionality* is a key concept in gender studies programs and literature (McCall, 2005; Phoenix, 2006; Verloo, 2006). Social categories such as gender, race, class, and sexuality are framed as inextricably interconnected in the production of social inclusion and exclusion (Crenshaw, 1997). However, as Holvino (2010) notes, intersectionality is not well acknowledged by organization studies and/or organization change scholars. A disproportionate amount of attention is paid to glass ceilings and work–life balance, which are biased (even if unintentionally) toward white, middle-class, heterosexual women. Without question, such women are the most likely beneficiaries of glass ceiling projects, part-time work arrangements, flexible leave policies, and teleworking projects. These kinds of change projects target the classic nuclear family rather than lone mothers. They also fail to focus on the concerns of working-class women, ethnic/racial minority women, and/or lesbians. Gender change projects in organizations need urgently to address the implications of race, gender, class, ethnicity, sexuality, and nation when discussing equality and fairness in organizations (Holvino, 2010).

The issue of *voice* is a long-time feminist issue that refers to the structural involvement of women in agenda-setting and decision-making. It draws attention to a 'woman's point of view' (or feminist standpoint) and urges its inclusion when deciding on which changes to pursue. While workers' representation is important relative to an organizational change agenda, the voices of women have been channeled to trade unions and work councils where support for gender equality and diversity has been lacking. The equality project within trade unions is far from completed (Kirton and Greene, 2005) and workplace democracy remains a utopian goal. Yet, the inclusion of voices that articulate and defend (intersectional) feminist positions is a necessity if gender equality is to be achieved in organizations. One way to strengthen the voice of women in agenda-setting and decision-making is through creating gender equality infrastructures such as equality/diversity departments, taskforces, and coordinators. The potential of such units or officials to realize gender change is high but it also depends on their authority to make things happen (Benschop and Verloo, 2002; Kalev et al., 2006). Furthermore, the ability and commitment to ally with women's and other groups and experts are required.

## A Forward Looking Strategy: genderXchange

Further development of strategies for gender equality in organization change theory and gender theory are urgently needed. What currently appears as the more promising approaches – gender mainstreaming and post equity – nevertheless inadequately address many impediments to change. Among those impediments are: the managerialist tendency of planned change, the need for simultaneous short and long-term agendas for change, the issue of resistance, the need to address gender-related emotions and attitudes, the intersectionality of multiple inequalities, and the inclusion and voice of all stakeholders, not only particular categories of women.

We end the chapter with an outline of a new approach to accommodate many of these issues. We propose a *genderXchange strategy* that takes a political approach to change and frames change as a socially accomplished, dynamic, and contextual process with many actors and interests at play. In the process, ample time should be dedicated to establishing constructive relations between gender equality experts and organization change agents and addressing individual attitudes and emotions that may obstruct gender change projects. The strategy requires activists to address both the individual and structural levels in order to organize needed systemic transformations. It requires development of a flexible planned change process with many feedback loops to deal with unforeseen developments that will occur during transformation. The planning process needs to be as democratic and participatory as possible to include the voices of all who are affected by gender change and to avoid the pitfalls of managerialism.

Active involvement of all affected parties should lower the odds of resistance, an effect that will be facilitated by having both short and long-term agendas. As for content, the approach must deal with intersectionality by developing a complex project that goes beyond gender equality alone. In organization studies, debates about intersectionality are recent and organization scholars can learn about them from feminist theories and political science. A genderXchange project can produce *transversal politics* (Squires, 2007; Yuval-Davis, 2006) that recognize the need for dialogue between different standpoints, organize an encompassing commitment to a broad equality project, and differentiate between positioning, identity, and values so participants can negotiate a common political position from which to initiate and support genuine change.

# REFERENCES

Acker, J. (1992) 'Gendering Organizational Theory' in A.J. Mills and P. Tancred, *Gendering Organizational Analysis*. Newbury Park: Sage, 248–260.

Ahmed, S. (2007) 'You End up Doing the Document Rather than Doing the Doing': Diversity, Race Equality and the Politics of Documentation, *Ethnic and Racial Studies*, 30(4) 590–609.

Bacchi, C. (1996) *The Politics of Affirmative Action*. London: Sage.

Benschop, Y., and Doorewaard, H. (1998) Covered by Equality: The Gender Subtext of Organizations, *Organization Studies*, 19(5) 787–805.

Benschop, Y., and Verloo, M. (2002) Shifting Responsibilities: The Position of Equality Agencies in Gender Mainstreaming, *International Management*, 7(1) 93–101.

Benschop, Y., and Verloo, M. (2006) Sisyphus' Sisters: Can Gender Mainstreaming Escape the Genderedness of Organizations? *Journal of Gender Studies*, 15(1) 19–33.

Bilimoria, D., Joy, S., and Liang, X.F. (2008) Breaking Barriers and Creating Inclusiveness: Lessons of Organizational Transformation to Advance Women Faculty in Academic Science and Engineering, *Human Resource Management*, 47(3) 423–441.

Boogaard, B., and Roggeband, C. (2010) Paradoxes of Intersectionality: Theorizing Inequality in the Dutch Police Force through Structure and Agency, *Organization*, 17(1) 53–75.

Booth, C., and Bennett, C. (2002) Gender Mainstreaming in the European Union – Towards a New Conception and Practice of Equal Opportunities? *European Journal of Womens Studies*, 9(4) 430–446.

Burke, W.W. (2002) *Organization Change*. Thousand Oaks, CA: Sage.

Castilla, E.J. (2005) Social Networks and Employee Performance in a Call Center 1, *American Journal of Sociology*, 110(5) 1243–1283.

Cockburn, C. (1989) Equality: the Long and Short Agenda, *Industrial Relations Journal*, Autumn, 213–225.

Connell, R. (2006) The Experience of Gender Change in Public Sector Organizations, *Gender Work and Organization*, 13(5) 435–452.

Council of Europe (1998) Gender Mainstreaming. Conceptual Framework, Methodology and Presentation of Good Practices. Strasbourg: Council of Europe.

Crenshaw, K. (1997) 'Intersectionality and Identity Politics: Learning from Violence Against Women of Colour' in M.L. Shanley and U. Narayan, *Reconstructing Political Theory*. Oxford: Polity Press.

Dahlerup, D. (2006) *Women, Quotas and Politics*: Routledge.

Dickens, L. (1999) Beyond the Business Case: A Three Pronged Approach to Equality Action, *Human Resource Management Journal*, 9(1) 9–19.

Eisenstein, H. (1996) *Inside Agitators: Australian Femocrats and the State*: Temple University Press.

Ely, R.J., and Meyerson, D.E. (2000) Advancing Gender Equity in Organizations: The Challenge and Importance of Maintaining a Gender Narrative, *Organization*, 7(4) 589–608.

Eveline, J., Bacchi, C., and Binns, J. (2009) Gender Mainstreaming versus Diversity Mainstreaming: Methodology as Emancipatory Politics, *Gender Work and Organization*, 16(2) 198–216.

Fletcher, J.K. (1999) *Disappearing Acts: Gender, Power and Relational Practice at Work*. Cambridge: MIT Press.

Fraser, N. (2009) Feminism, Capitalism and the Cunning of History, *New Left Review*, 56, 97–+.

Greenwood, R., and Hinings, C.R. (2006) 'Radical Organizational Change' in S. Clegg, . C.Hardy, T, Lawrence, and W. Nord, *The Sage Handbook of Organzation Studies*. London: Sage.

Hankivsky, O. (2005) Gender vs. Diversity Mainstreaming: A Preliminary Examination of the Role and Transformative Potential of Feminist Theory, *Canadian Journal of Political Science-Revue Canadienne De Science Politique*, 38(4) 977–1001.

Harding, S. (ed.) (2004) *The Feminist Standpoint Reader*. New York: Routledge.

Holvino, E. (2010) Intersections: The Simultaneity of Race, Gender and Class in Organization Studies, *Gender, Work & Organization*, 17, 248–277.

Hoobler, J.M. (2005) Lip Service to Multiculturalism – Docile Bodies of the Modern Organization, *Journal of Management Inquiry*, 14(1) 49–56.

Htun, M.N., and Jones, M.P. (2002) 'Engendering the Right to Participate in Decision-making: Electoral Quotas and Women's Leadership in Latin America' in *Gender and the Politics of Rights and Democracy in Latin America*. New York: Palgrave, 32–56.

Iannello, K. (1992) *Decisions without Hierarchy: Feminist Interventions in Organization Theory and Practice*. London: Routledge.

Jenson, J. (2008) Writing Women Out, Folding Gender in The European Union 'Modernises' Social Policy, *Social Politics*, 15(2) 131–153.

Jewson, N., and Mason, D. (1986) The Theory and Practice of Equality Policies: Liberal and Radical Approaches, *The Sociological Review*, 34(2) 307–334.

Kalev, A., Dobbin, F., and Kelly, E. (2006) Best Practices or Best Guesses? Assessing the Efficacy of Corporate Affirmative Action and Diversity Policies, *American Sociological Review*, 71(4) 589–617.

Kirton, G., and Greene, A. (2005) *The Dynamics of Managing Diversity*. Oxford: Elsevier Butterword-Heinemann.

Krook, M.L. (2008) Quota Laws for Women in Politics: Implications for Feminist Practice, *Social Politics*, 15(3) 345–368.

Kunda, G. (1992) *Engineering Culture*. Philadelphia, PA: Temple University Press.

Liff, S., and Cameron, I. (1997) Changing Equality Cultures to Move Beyond 'Women's Problems', *Gender, Work & Organization*, 4(1) 35–46.

Lombardo, E., Meier, P., and Verloo, M. (2008) *The Discursive Politics of Gender Equality. Stretching, Bending and Policy-making*, London: Routledge.

Martin, P.Y. (1993) 'Feminist Practice in Organizations: Implications for Management' in E. Fagenson, *Women in Management: Issues, Trends and Problems*. Newbury Park: Sage, 274–296.

Martin, P.Y. (1996) 'Gendering and Evaluating Dynamics: Men, Masculinities, and Managements' in D. Collinson and J. Hearn, *Men as Managers, Managers as Men: Critical Perspectives on Men, Masculinities and Management*. London: Sage, 186–209.

Martin, P.Y. (2006) Practising Gender at Work: Further Thoughts on Reflexivity, *Gender, Work and Organization*, 13(3) 254–276.

McCall, L. (2005) The Complexity of Intersectionality, *Signs*, 30(3) 1771–1800.

McGauran, A.M. (2009) Gender Mainstreaming and the Public Policy Implementation Process: Round Pegs in Square Holes? *Policy &Politics*, 37(2) 215–233.

Mescher, S., Benschop, Y., and Doorewaard, H. (2010) Representations of Work-Life Balance Support, *Human Relations*, 63(1) 21–39.

Meyerson, D.E., and Fletcher, J.K. (2000) A Modest Manifesto for Shattering the Class Ceiling, *Harvard Business Review*, 78(1) 126–+.

Meyerson, D.E., and Kolb, D.M. (2000) Moving out of the 'Armchair': Developing a Framework to Bridge the Gap between Feminist Theory and Practice, *Organization*, 7(4) 553–571.

Mills, A.J. (2006) *Sex, Strategy and the Stratosphere*. New York: Palgrave Macmillan.

Nentwich, J.C. (2006) Changing Gender: The Discursive Construction of Equal Opportunities, *Gender Work and Organization*, 13(6) 499–521.

Osborn, M., Rees, T., Bosch, M., Hermann, C., Hilden, J., and Mason, J. (2000) *Science Policies in the European Union: Promoting Excellence through Mainstreaming Gender Equality*. Brussels: European Commission.

Padavic, I., and Reskin, B.F. (2002) *Women and Men at Work*. Thousand Oaks, CA: Pine Forge Press.

Parker, M. (2002) *Against Management: Organization in the Age of Managerialism*. Cambridge: Polity

Pell, A.N. (1996) Fixing the Leaky Pipeline: Women Scientists in Academia, *Journal of Animal Science*, 74(11) 2843–2848.

Phoenix, A. (2006) Intersectionality, *European Journal of Womens Studies*, 13(3) 187–192.

Rees, T. (1998) Equal Opportunities and Social Policy: Issues of Gender, Race and Disability, *Work Employment and Society*, 12(4) 793–794.

Rudman, L.A., and Glick, P. (1999) Feminized Management and Backlash toward Agentic Women: The Hidden Costs to Women of a Kinder, Gentler Image of Middle Managers, *Journal of Personality and Social Psychology*, 77(5) 1004–1010.

Squires, J. (2007) *The New Politics of Gender Equality*. Basingstoke: Palgrave.

Stark, A. (1998) 'Developments in Mainstreaming Sex Equality in Europe' in M. Vieill, *Sex Equality in the Public Sector. Report of a Joint Equal Opportunities Commission and European Commission Conference*. London: Equal Opportunities Commission.

Stratigaki, M. (2005) Gender Mainstreaming vs Positive Action – An Ongoing Conflict in EU Gender Equality Policy, *European Journal of Womens Studies*, 12(2) 165–186.

Sturdy, A., and Grey, C. (2003) Beneath and beyond Organizational Change Management: Exploring Alternatives, *Organization*, 10(4) 651–662.

Tienari, J., Holgersson, C., Merilainen, S., and Hook, P. (2009) Gender, Management and Market Discourse: The Case of Gender Quotas in the Swedish and Finnish Media, *Gender Work and Organization*, 16(4) 501–521.

Van den Brink, M. (2009) *Behind the Scenes of Science: Gender Practices in the Recruitment and Selection of Professors in the Netherlands*. Nijmegen: Doctoral thesis.

Verloo, M. (2005) Displacement and Empowerment: Reflections on the Concept and Practice of the Council of Europe Approach to Gender Mainstreaming and Gender Equality, *Social Politics*, 12(3) 344–365.

Verloo, M. (2006) Multiple Inequalities, Intersectionality and the European Union, *European Journal of Womens Studies*, 13(3) 211–228.

Walby, S. (2005) Gender Mainstreaming: Productive Tensions in Theory and Practice, *Social Politics*, 12(3) 321–343.

Walby, S. (2009) *Globalization and Inequalities: Complexities and Contested Modernities*. London: Sage.

Yuval-Davis, N. (2006) Intersectionality and Feminist Politics, *European Journal of Womens Studies*, 13(3) 193–209.

# Section Four

## DIVERSITY IN/AND MANAGEMENT AND ORGANIZATIONS

### EDITORIAL INTRODUCTION

Many discussions of diversity in the management/organization literature focus on fairness and equality. A typical rationale asserts that a *more diverse organization is a fairer organization*. If decision-makers will use 'objective qualifications' *rather than* categorical distinctions such as gender, ethnicity, race, sexual orientation, religion, and so on when making decisions, they will create a more just organization when making decisions (cf. Kalev, Dobbins, and Kelly, 2006). Claims about fairness and justice are regularly made about gender diversity since women's educational qualifications often equal or exceed those of men (as does their work experience) while they remain dramatically underrepresented in the higher ranks of management.[1] Interpretations of this condition allege that women have been discriminated against due to their gender and diversity requires the presence of more women in powerful positions.

Diversity is discussed also in relation to creativity and innovation with the implication that diversity improves organizational performance, *if managed properly* (cf. Bassett-Jones, 2005). Bassett-Jones (2005) says organizations that operate in a 'high-commitment context' can 'either seek to harness diversity in order to promote creativity and innovation or they can ignore the diversity dimension . . . If they are successful in embracing diversity, then organizational agility, founded upon creativity and innovation, can ensue' (p. 169). This approach to diversity in management/organization circles focuses more on corporate benefits – profits, creativity, innovation – than fairness (see Omanović, this volume). Also, this literature focuses more on

---

[1] In the US, according to a 2010 survey of 500 companies, 15.2% of all company directors were women. This compares with 12.2% in the UK (although the UK Equal Opportunities Commission says 10% of directors of UK FTSE 100 firms are women (http://news.bbc.co.uk/1/hi/business/6428513.stm). The percentage for Norway is 44, for Sweden 21.9, and for Finland, 16.8. The mean for North America is 14.1% versus a mean for Europe of 9.7%. Asia and the Gulf countries are particularly low, with fewer than 2.0% each.

cultural, ethnic, and racial diversity than on diversity associated with gender, sexual orientation, age, ablebodiedness, or religion (see Table 1, below).

Despite the concept's popularity, scholars define diversity in varying ways and some fail to define it at all. What is diversity? What makes any organization diverse? Kalev, Dobbins, and Kelly (2006) suggest that diversity is the presumed solution

TABLE 1: Number of refereed journal articles indexed by ISI Web of Science, January 2010.

| Diversity 'search' terms used | In ISI Social Science Journals | In ISI Social Science + Humanities Journals |
|---|---|---|
| Cultural diversity | 3584 | 3998 |
| Ethnic diversity | 1865 | 1960 |
| National diversity | 1777 | 1878 |
| Gender diversity | 1526 | 1563 |
| Diversity and gender | 1526 | 1563 |
| Diversity and women | 1508 | 1582 |
| Diversity and race | 1230 | 1262 |
| Diversity and age | 1168 | 1236 |
| Age diversity | 1168 | 1236 |
| Racial diversity | 1047 | 1071 |
| Diversity and ethnicity | 799 | 821 |
| Diversity and men | 643 | 660 |
| Sexual diversity | 554 | 575 |
| Religious diversity | 550 | 766 |
| Diversity and religion | 358 | 436 |
| Diversity and nation | 348 | 388 |
| Diversity and sexuality | 138 | 145 |
| Sexual orientation diversity | 141 | 141 |
| Diversity and sexual orientation | 141 | 141 |
| Diversity and transgender | 35 | 35 |
| Diversity and lesbians | 72 | 72 |
| Diversity and homosexuality | 56 | 58 |
| Diversity and gays | 14 | 14 |
| Diversity and organizations | 1113 | 1123 |
| Diversity and management | 2490 | 2515 |
| Managing gender diversity | 46 | 46 |
| Managing ethnic diversity | 51 | 51 |
| Managing racial diversity | 28 | 28 |
| Managing sexual diversity | 11 | 11 |
| Organizations and gender diversity | 173 | 175 |
| Organizations and ethnic diversity | 99 | 100 |
| Organizations and racial diversity | 83 | 83 |
| Organizations and sexual diversity | 22 | 22 |

to 'gender and racial segregation' in organizations (p. 590), implying that segregation indicates a lack of diversity (segregation implicitly means that women and racial/ethnic minorities are excluded from senior management jobs and/or are crowded into lower status or lower skilled jobs). Bassett-Jones (2005: 169–170), in contrast, offers a broader definition; diversity is '. . . a range of differences in ethnicity/nationality, gender, function, ability, language, religion, lifestyle or tenure.' Diversity means more than 'demography,' he says; it takes into account cultural and intellectual capacity differences. Bassett-Jones emphasizes the latter point to assert that more than demographic variation is required for diversity to help companies perform better.

The varying views of diversity in organizations and management are suggested by data in Table 1, showing the frequency with which particular phrases have been used in social science literature (based on the Thompson Web of Science ISI system that indexes refereed articles in a database containing thousands of journals from around the world). The top of Table 1 shows that cultural diversity followed by ethnic and national diversity have been studied most, with gender diversity close behind (for more on ethnic diversity, see Calás and Smircich, this volume). To see if the wording affects the results, the phrases 'gender diversity' and 'diversity and gender' were inserted to provide comparisons. In most cases, little difference was found although 'diversity and race' (N = 1230 articles) was used more often than 'racial diversity' was (N = 1047) and, for whatever reasons, 'ethnic diversity' (N = 1865) was studied far more than 'diversity and ethnicity' (N = 799).

Moving down Table 1, we see that 'diversity and women' (N = 1508) has been studied more than 'diversity and men' (N = 643), supporting claims that women's situation at work is frequently framed as a diversity issue. Gender, ethnicity, race, and age diversity are popular, although cultural diversity tops them all. In comparison, religious diversity receives little attention. Table 1 shows that 'diversity and management' is a more popular concept (N = 2490) than is 'diversity and organizations,' with the latter showing less than half as many sources (N = 1113). Evidence on *managing in relation to gender, ethnic, racial, and sexuality diversity*, shows relatively few sources, however, with 51 for gender diversity and 11 for sexual diversity. Also, articles on *organizations and gender diversity* show up (173) more than *managing gender diversity* does (46) and more articles use the phrase 'organizations and ethnic diversity,' 'organizations and racial diversity,' and 'organizations and sexual diversity' than use *managing* in relation to these labels.

In a recent study of 'best practices' related to diversity initiatives at work, Kalev, Dobbins, and Kelly (2006) found that some management strategies are superior to others in terms of increasing the proportion of women and minority members in an organization's 'management ranks.' They looked at six US 'common diversity programs' which included '. . . affirmative action plans, diversity committees and task forces, diversity managers, diversity training, diversity evaluations for managers, networking programs, and mentoring programs' (2006: 590). Based on data obtained from 708 US companies, they found that *diversity training* failed to contribute to an increase in the representation of women and race/ethnic minorities in management whereas *having a commission or oversight body* to *monitor* the goal of increasing diversity did. The following summary notes that organizations with more positive results were those that 'established responsibility' for achieving diversity.

> We find a clear pattern in the data. Structures establishing responsibility (affirmative action plans, diversity committees, and diversity staff positions) are followed by significant increases in managerial diversity [by which they meant that the management cadre was more diverse on gender and/or race/ethnicity]. Programs that target managerial stereotyping through education and feedback (diversity training and diversity evaluations) are not followed by increases in diversity. Programs that address social isolation among women and minorities (networking and mentoring programs) are followed by modest changes. The effects of these initiatives vary across groups, with white women benefiting most, followed by black women. Black men benefit least. We also find that responsibility structures make training, performance evaluations, networking, and mentoring programs more effective. Federal affirmative action requirements, which typically lead to assignment of responsibility for compliance, also catalyze certain programs. (Kalev, Dobbins, and Kelly, 2006: 590)

Three papers in this section address diversity, although only one discusses the content of diversity at work – in this case, sexuality/ies. The chapter by Jeff Hearn overviews issues associated with sexuality in work, organization, and management and, in contrast, Vedran Omanović and Bogdan Costea focus on the philosophical underpinnings of the 'diversity push' in management and organizations. If those assumptions are laid bare, they suggest, organization and gender scholars (and others interested in categorical distinctions) will become more reflexive about their role in shaping research and action agendas. Omanović contends that researchers play an active role in forming and prioritizing particular diversity ideas and interests in management and organization studies and, by extension, in the world of work. Applying this reasoning, all three chapters challenge readers to question and take responsibility for the ideas and interests that their research implies.

## OVERVIEW OF CHAPTERS

Jeff Hearn, in a chapter titled 'Sexualities, Work, Organizations, and Managements,' reviews theory and research over 20 years on sexualities, gender, and work in relation to organizations and management. Hearn did path-breaking work on the topic in the 1980s and since then has pushed the envelope by addressing violence in organizations (Hearn and Parkin, 2002). While calling for more research on sexualities, Hearn opposes (a) equating sexualities with sexual orientation and (b) creating a separate field of sexuality and organizations, instead favoring critical attention to how gender and sexualities are intertwined. Organizations are '*sexualed*' in many ways, Hearn says, by which he means that a diverse range of meanings connected with sexuality and sexualities are evident both within and beyond workplaces. Framing organizations as sexualed reminds us that so-called private domain issues such as women's unpaid labour and responsibilities for the home affect workplace arrangements and dynamics.[2]

Hearn's chapter reviews empirical studies, policy developments, and theoretical and conceptual issues.

*Empirical studies.* Empirical work on sexualities in organizations is presented in four categories: Sexual harassment (including mobbing), heterosexual experiences and relationships, gay/lesbian experiences and relationships in organizations, and organizational and occupational case studies that focus on sexuality's links to appointment processes, reinforcement of gender power and authority relations, managerial controls, and shopfloor dynamics. Debates about definitions and assumptions in each realm are reviewed along with classic and current research studies. Case studies are particularly useful, Hearn contends, when they focus on the interconnections of sexuality and power in organizations, especially men's power over women but also men's relations with each other. Sexuality is used to reinforce managerial power (and to resist it) and it is highly relevant in the conduct of organizational activities such as teamwork, counseling, supervision, and mentoring, even among men.

*Policy developments.* Areas of policy development noted in the chapter include sexual harassment and respect for gay, lesbian, bisexual, transgender, transsexual, and intersex people and sexualities at work. Campaigns and other political interventions regarding such issues began in the 1970s and 1980s and while progress is far from complete, some has been made in work and organization settings.

*Theoretical and conceptual progress.* Hearn credits Gibson Burrell's 1984 paper on 'sex and organizational analysis' with the kick-off of attention to sexuality in/and organizations and subsequent years have produced many critical assessments of the presence and dynamics of sexuality at work. Organization sexuality differs from 'sex work in organizations,' Hearn says, urging attention to embodiment, particularly the uses organizations make of sexuality and bodies (see Embodiment Section, this volume).

*Information and communication technologies.* Finally, Hearn explores the role of information and communication technologies (ICTs) in organizations relative to their ability to organize sexuality – including the practice of new forms of sexuality such as techno-sex, high-tech sex, non-connection sex, mobile phone sex, internet dating, consensual sex between strangers, email sex, cybersex, cyberaffairs, virtual sex, and multimedia interactive sex. He also addresses the surveillance potential of ICTs and wonders how globalization forces related to these dynamics will change both the workplace in relation to sexuality and also conceptions of work itself.

The chapter by Vedran Omanović, 'Diversity in Organizations: A Critical Examination of Assumptions about Diversity and Organizations in Twenty-first Century Management Literature,' identifies the philosophical underpinnings of

---

[2] Mescher, Benschop, and Doorewaard (2010) find, for instance, that corporations view benefits in support of 'work–life' balance as a privilege, not a right, thus indicating to employees not to expect them. It is also likely that this view communicates that work–life balance supports are for women (by focusing initiatives on the needs of the encumbered worker, such as mothers), thus making women a 'special case' rather than a 'generic' (or ideal, as in free of family care obligations) worker.

research on diversity in management literature during the first decade of the twenty-first century. Each of four philosophical perspectives reflects unique assumptions about what diversity is and what organizations are like. To find empirical articles, Omanović searched two databases – Business Source Premier and Sage Journals Online – with the key words of Managing Diversity, Diversity in Organizations, Diversity and its Management. His chapter summarizes the results of his analysis in a table showing key features of four philosophical stances.

*Positivist.* Diversity research from a positivist approach takes the organization for granted and reflects an 'objectivist,' managerialist, and ahistorical view of organizational change. Typically, it sees diversity as a business goal, claiming the organization is more effective, profitable, or productive if it is more diverse. Positivist studies often use quantitative methods such as surveys, experiments, scenarios, and questionnaires to collect data and they tend to represent organizations as neutral sites in regard to gender, race/ethnicity, age, sexual orientation, and other such distinctions. While few studies confirm the positive effects of diversity, this perspective remains predominant, particularly in the US.

*Interpretative.* Researchers in this perspective frame organizations as socially constructed. Many of them focus on how organizations 'do diversity' by asking how organization members create 'shared meanings' about diversity at work. Interpretavists explore the meanings managers and other organizational members create about diversity. Committed to a phenomenological perspective, scholars working within this frame use qualitative methods and often focus on quality of work life issues.

*(Critical) Discursive.* Scholars employing a discursive frame view diversity as socially constructed by means of discourse that is expressed in talk and texts, although discourse is unstable and constantly under construction. Omanović differentiates simple discourse analysis (DA) from critical discourse analysis (CDA) in noting that the latter employs a Foucauldian focus on power, including how some discourses are used to control others. Scholars working in this perspective employ qualitative methods to study conversations and analyze policy manuals and other similar documents.

*Critical-dialectic.* The fourth frame views diversity and organizations as reflecting a dialectical social-historical process that is actively constructed by parties involved in the production of particular contexts. This approach is historical and focuses on process and contexts, seeing organizations as a part of the social world that is always in a state of becoming and that depends on the interests and ideas of people in power. Besides summarizing the perspectives, Omanović addresses the limits and advantages of each and urges scholars to take account of how context, history, and politics shape discussions of diversity. He also calls for a more reflexive stance regarding how researchers' assumptions affect their own work and academic discourse generally.

A third chapter, by Bodgan Costea, ('Diversity, Uniqueness, and Images of Human Resourcefulness,') explores how recent scholarship on diversity relates to subjectivities, including the valorization of the self and individual achievement in Western cultures. Costea argues that *diversity management* is the apotheosis of a recent tradition in which gender, sexuality, and race are seen as key identities in the cultural project of realizing individual uniqueness and potential. A focus on managing diversity is part of a development within human resource management and, more generally, modern culture where the cult of the individual and realization of human potential reign supreme. Far from contradicting the gender, sexuality, and race agenda, managerial discourses and practices over the past three decades are in perfect harmony with it, largely because they reflect and reinforce a culture of promoting the self in its 'unique' individuality, creative resourcefulness, and knowledge.

Diversity management may occupy the space involuntarily vacated by discourses of equal opportunity but, for Costea, this development represents a significant conceptual mutation which, while incorporating an equality agenda, creates new categories that 'address the whole of human subjectivity as an emancipatory project.' Diversity management is thus seen to have affinities with popular culture where individual performance is celebrated in talent and reality TV shows, sporting events, popular music, and other media. Costea's approach is 'indirect' relative to gender in that he sees gender as just one of many aspects of human resource management where the prime object of managerial focus is subjectivity and/or the development of human potential. His approach is based on the variety of cultural functionalism of Blumenberg where the concepts and discourses that prevail at any point in time – in this case equal opportunity, diversity, and self-realization – are cultural responses to deeply felt anxieties of the age, such as discrimination, inequality, and exploitation.

But why change from a managerial focus on equality or equal opportunity to one on diversity? Costea sees the shift as a conceptual mutation whereby diversity encompasses earlier concerns with equal opportunity and yet addresses the whole of human subjectivity and its emancipation from oppressed identities. Whereas an equal opportunity discourse concentrates on society's negative fault lines and/or historical failures, diversity management integrates an equality agenda with a less confrontational discourse directed at the self as the object of affirmation and emancipation. By means of a conceptual extension, diversity management incorporates all aspects of human life rather than just the negative constraints of discrimination. Costea concludes that while the unique individual is one of the most successful transformations of modern managerialism (in integrating cultural anxieties around emancipation with managing subjectivity at work), it ultimately glosses over the fundamental existential void upon which it is constructed. The real crisis of society is that the search for identity is a self-defeating project grounded on a sense of emptiness that fuels insecurity which forever chases its tail in pursuit of a fulfilled life.

## REFERENCES

Bassett-Jones, Nigel (2005) The Paradox of Diversity Management, Creativity, and Innovation. *Creativity and Innovation Management*, 14(2) 169–175.

Hearn, J., and Parkin, W. (2001) *Gender, Sexuality and Violence in Organizations: the Unspoken Forces of Organization Violations*. London and Thousand Oaks, CA: Sage.

Kalev, Alexandra, Dobbin, Frank, and Kelly, Erin (2006) Best Practices or Best Guesses? Assessing the Efficacy of Corporate Affirmative Action and Diversity Policies, *American Sociological Review*, 72 August, 589–617.

Mescher, Samula, Benschop, Yvonne, and Doorewaard, Hans (2010) Representations of Work–Life Balance Support, *Human Relations*, 61(1) 21–39.

# 18

# Sexualities, Work, Organizations, and Managements: Empirical, Policy, and Theoretical Challenges

JEFF HEARN

*Linköping University, Sweden; University of Huddersfield, UK;*
*Hanken School of Economics, Finland*

## INTRODUCTION

Sexuality, work, organization, management – which is the odd one out? In considering this question, it is important not to see sexuality as a separate or autonomous phenomenon. Rather, sexualities exist and persist in relations with other social phenomena, social experiences, and social inequalities – around gender, class, ethnicity, racialization, embodiment, and multiple intersectionalities. This means addressing intersectionalities, especially between age, class, disability, ethnicity, gender, generation, 'race', religion, and violence, in analyzing organizations and sexuality. Thus my broad approach might be summarized in terms of the political economies of sexualities, and shifts from intersectionalities towards transsectionalities: the 'transformulation' of social, in this context sexual, categories, rather than just their mutual constitution and interrelations (Hearn, 2008b).

Within the field of studies that has come to be known as 'gender, work and organizations', the question of sexuality has figured perhaps more strongly than might have been expected. Why this should be is difficult to explain, but it would seem to reflect an historical convergence of empirical, policy, political, theoretical, technological, spatial, and indeed personal concerns among its proponents. I will return to some of these various connections, but suffice to say at this point that rather than seeing one arena as the 'true cause' of the rise in research interest in 'sexuality, work and organizations', these various concerns feed into and off each other (Hearn, 2008a). At the same time, somewhat paradoxically, there is a still frequent tendency, certainly for mainstream and often for supposedly critical scholars, to ignore sexuality in their analyses.

This chapter examines how the question of sexualities is relevant to all the issues raised in the Handbook. In this, work, and indeed many organizations and managements, can be understood as 'sexualed', i.e. having meaning in relation to sexuality, rather than necessarily specifically sexualized (Hearn and Parkin, 1987/1995). This understanding of the sexualing of organizations is for several reasons, not least that sexual arrangements in the private domains provide the base infrastructure, principally through women's unpaid labour, for public domain organizations.

A key challenge for research and policy development is how to increase the focus on sexuality whilst not creating a paradigm or object of analysis that is separated off from gender. While organizational analysis focusing on sexuality is often neglected and needs to be more fully developed, this is not to be understood in any way that is competitive with research on 'gender, work, and organizations'. The field of sexuality and organizations does not constitute a separate paradigm. Similarly, to argue that organizations are sexualed is not to say that sexuality is a separate or the predominant social division in particular organizations.

## OVERVIEW

The recognition of sexuality in research studies as a central feature of work, organization(s), and management is relatively recent, and has developed particularly since the late 1970s. It has been prompted by a range of disciplinary and theoretical positions, and a number of phases can be recognized in studies on sexuality in organizations. Foremost of these influences and phases has been second-wave feminism and the range of different feminisms then and since. These have highlighted concerns with women's control over their bodies and sexuality, and critiques of sexualization in and of organizations, and sexist uses of sexuality, in corporate advertising and organizational displays, and indeed more directly in corporate 'entertainment' (Allison, 1994). The politics of sexuality at work and in organizations needs to be placed in the context of the full range of women's demands for political autonomy. A second and sometimes related force for change has been the modern lesbian, gay, and queer movements. A third stimulus has come from poststructuralism, postcolonialism, and intersectionality theory. The growth of interest in social studies of the body has provided a further impetus to research in this area. The most profound impact of all such moves has been in de-naturalizing sexuality, especially heterosexuality, and essentialized views of sexuality. With at least some versions of queer theory, the problematizing process has also been carried over into the very category of 'homosexuality', so that people are *not* seen as essentially gay or lesbian.

The term 'sexuality' or 'sexualities' is used here broadly. It refers to the social experience, social expression, or social relations of physical, bodily desires, by and for others or for oneself. Others may be the same or different sex/gender[1] or of indeterminate sex/gender (Hearn and Parkin, 1987/1995). Sexual practices vary from fantasy to mild flirtation to sexual acts, of many kinds. Sexuality can be closely connected with intimacy, power, sometimes violence and violation (Hearn and

---

[1] I am using the joint term 'sex/gender' so as not to prioritize one over the other, to recognize their complex interplays, and to acknowledge the extensive debate on the social construction of sex.

Parkin, 2001). The term, sexuality, in organizations and more generally in society, is now often used in the plural – sexualities. This is partly to emphasize that there are many different forms of sexuality, including narcissistic, lesbian, gay, bisexual, transgender, transsexual, transitioning, intersexual, and heterosexual practices and preferences. It also reflects the idea that sexualities are not fixed, but may be subject to change and development over the life course.

There are many theoretical approaches to sexuality. Some basic distinctions may be drawn between those based in: biological essentialist approaches; sexuality as the outcome of sex/gender roles; sexuality as social (class-like) categories within patriarchies; and sexuality as discursive constructions of power (Burrell and Hearn, 1989). In addition, there is growing research interest in the intersections of humans, technologies, and machines, on one hand, and of humans, nature, and animals, on the other – and thus consequent implications for sexualities.

Gender and sexuality are intimately, indeed definitionally, connected and inter-related with each other. Gender occurs *along with* sexuality, and vice versa. It is rather difficult to conceive of gender and sexuality without the other: 'without a concept of gender there could be, quite simply, no concept of homo- or hetero- sexuality' (Sedgwick, 1991: 31). Sexuality can be understood as both a foundation of gender (MacKinnon, 1982) and a focused specific aspect of gender relations. As Catharine MacKinnon (1989: 113), suggests: 'Sexuality, then, is a form of power. Gender, as socially constructed, embodies it, not the reverse. Women and men are divided by gender, made into the sexes as we know them, by the social requirements of its domi-nant form, heterosexuality, which institutionalizes male sexual dominance and female sexual submission. If this is true, sexuality is the linchpin of gender inequality.'

The development of the field of sexuality, work, organizations, and manage-ment can be traced through a number of key foci. These all have clear and direct implications for understandings of gender, work, and organizations. Three main approaches are outlined: empirical studies, policy development, and theoretical and conceptual reviews. These are followed by more specific attention to the use of information and communication technologies and their relevance for sexualities in work, organizations, and management.

## EMPIRICAL STUDIES

### Sexual harassment

In the early and mid-1970s journalistic and political interventions named repeated, unwanted sexual behaviour as *sexual harassment.*[2] An early book on the topic was Lin Farley's *Sexual Shakedown: The Sexual Harassment of Women on the Job* pub-lished in 1978. In this pioneering work, Farley tells how, whilst teaching in the US on women and work, she realized that she and her women students had all had the

---

[2] It should be noted that some scholars differentiate specifically between sexual harassment and gender harassment (see Martin et al., 2002). These two forms of harassment remain dif-ficult to disentangle according to many legal systems.

experience in common of having left a job or study because they had been made 'too uncomfortable' by the behaviour of a man. In subsequent years, there followed general social research analyses, detailed examinations of legal cases, and sexual-social surveys (for example, Gutek, 1985; Fitzgerald, 1988), establishing the pervasiveness of sexual harassment, mainly of women by men, although other permutations of harassment cases have been documented. Interestingly, in some surveys higher levels of harassment were reported by women in occupations and organizations that were then 'non-traditional' for women, such as the law or journalism, compared with those that were 'traditional' for women, such as nursing or bar work (Gutek and Morasch, 1982). At that time at least, in the latter case harassment may have been normalized, seen as part of what was to be expected the job.

Since the late 1970s and early 1980s, analyses of sexual harassment have placed it within a broad framework of gendered power relations. MacKinnon (1979) defined sexual harassment in terms of its link to the power of men's heterosexuality: sexual harassment refers to the unwanted imposition of sexual requirements in the context of a relationship of unequal power. Power, especially men's power and domination over women, that appears to be derived from or based in one social sphere may carry over to the enactment of deprivations in another: when put together, the cumulative sanction is especially powerful. Indeed some detailed studies show that women who are harassed have little or no effective recourse or redress, whatever their reactions (Collinson and Collinson, 1996). Accordingly, sexual harassment, and moreover reactions thereto, can be understood as an aspect of male domination (Gruber and Morgan, 2005).

There is a proliferation of discourses on and approaches to sexual harassment – organizational, managerial, policy, trade union, feminist, quantitative, and so on. High levels of harassment have been reported in surveys worldwide. The dominant discourse is still that of an isolated harasser harassing an isolated victim, with the harassing experience dominantly constructed as intermittent harassing rather than ongoing over time (Hearn and Parkin, 2001). The harassed person, usually a woman, is not generally constructed as *identifying* as a victim/survivor of harassment, unlike the victims/survivors of some other crimes. There is often a stigma to being subjected to this kind of behaviour that is sometimes couched in questions such as, 'Did she encourage him?' Such constructions tend to inhibit the formation of collectivities of survivors, as well as the coalescence of groups of protesters. In short, sexual harassment is still seen most often as an individual rather than workplace problem.

While it has been argued that all women experience sexual harassment (Wise and Stanley, 1987), there is some evidence of same-sex harassment as well, and other sexualized harassments are recognized, including ethnic and racial harassments. For this reason some commentators prefer more generalized concepts, such as personal harassment or 'mobbing'. Such distinctions – by social division, discourse, language – become especially important when considering harassment in a comparative or transnational perspective (Haavio-Mannila, 1994; Timmerman and Bajema, 1999; Hearn and Parkin, 2001). In some European countries 'mobbing', constructed as, though not necessarily, gender-neutral, is a stronger focus than sexual harassment (cf. Hearn and Parkin, 2001; Zippel, 2006).

## Heterosexual experiences and relationships in organizations

Second, many empirical studies of *heterosexual relationships* and sexual liaisons in organizations and management have been produced (for example, Horn and Horn, 1982; Kakabadse and Kakabadse, 2004). In most organizations, heterosexual practices, cultures, and ideologies predominate. An early study by Quinn (1977) on 'romantic relationships in organizations' used third party reports about relationships they knew of or had observed. He concluded that men tended to be in higher, more powerful positions than women who were involved in such relationships and men tended to suffer less adverse consequences once ended, for example, in terms of moving or losing a job, within or from the organization. Though some early studies were not particularly critical, they can be understood in the context of the growing attempts to develop explicit social theorizing on heterosexuality. Even with extensive gender segregation of jobs, many organizations provide plenty of opportunities for heterosexual flirting, interactions, and intimate relationships (Pringle, 1988; Hearn and Parkin, 1987/1995). There have been many studies since that show that workplaces, including educational settings, are a major site for initiation of heterosexual sexual or sexual-social relationships.

## Lesbians' and gay men's experiences and relationships in organizations

Third, another empirical strand developed from the 1970s and 1980s on *lesbians' and gay men's experiences* in organizations, particularly of discrimination and violation. Many early studies were linked to campaigns or other political interventions. Recent studies have examined wider experiences of lesbians and gay men at work, including business (Woods and Lucas, 1993), public sector (Humphry, 2000), police (Burke, 1993), military (Cammermeyer, 1994; Hall, 1995), and community (Oerton, 1996a; 1996b) organizations. An especially recommended collection is that edited by Jukka Lehtonen and Kati Mustola (2004), *'Straight people don't tell, do they . . .?' Negotiating the Boundaries of Sexuality and Gender at Work*. This last study reports on the experiences of lesbian, gay, bisexual, transsexual, and transvestite people in and around workplaces.

Most organizations and managements embrace dominant heterosexual norms, ideologies, ethics, and practices, for example, in constructions of men managers' reliance on wives in traditional marriage (Hearn et al., 2008; Raeburn, this volume). On the other hand, the UK Gay and Lesbian Census conducted by ID Research in 2001 found that while 15% of lesbians and gay men in the workplace who responded believe their sexuality has hindered their job prospects, a surprisingly large number, indeed 43%, had managerial jobs, although these figures are probably not representative. A 2005 UK survey of readers of the magazines *Diva* and *Gay Times* by Out Now Consulting (2005) found that only 52% of gay men and 51% of lesbians reported that they can be completely honest about their sexuality with work colleagues. At the same time, the gay men responding earned on average almost £9400 (€10 540) more than the national average for men, and the lesbians about £6000 (€6730) more than the national average for women. These figures should be treated with caution, as the data were provided by volunteers rather than results from a random survey. Indeed in a more comprehensive US analysis, using national census and other data, Lee Badgett (2001) rejects the idea that lesbians and gay men are more affluent than heterosexuals. In this, she considers the complex interplay of income and standard of living of gay men and lesbians with such factors as financial and family decisions, workplace discrimination, and denial of health care benefits to partners and children.

## Organizational and occupational case studies

Fourth, there have been *detailed case studies* of specific organizations on how sexuality links to appointment processes, reinforcement of gender power and authority relations, managerial controls, and shopfloor dynamics. Some of these studies use case study evidence on sexuality in total institutions. For example, prisons often try to control, sometimes even forbid, sexual relations, and yet they also create possibilities for different sexualities and sexual violences (for example, Wooden and Parker, 1982; Jenness et al., 2010). These may provide more accentuated sexual dynamics compared with more mainstream workplaces (Hearn and Parkin, 1987/1995), to either enforce or resist dominant organizational power regimes (Cavandish, 1982; Collinson, 1992).

In several case studies Cynthia Cockburn (1983, 1991) has examined how men, both men managers and workers, maintain and reproduce power over women in workplaces, including by sexual domination alongside domination of jobs in the labour market. Rosemary Pringle's (1988) analysis of boss–secretary relations reports the pervasiveness of gender and sexual power in management and organizations, including 'paired' practices of 'compulsory heterosexuality', 'family roles', master-slave relationships, and sadomasochism. Drawing on poststructuralist theory, she charted how gender/sexual power relations operate in multiple directions and may be understood more fully through psychodynamic, unconscious, and fantasy processes. Such boss–secretary relationships could, at that time at least, be seen as the paradigm case of sexual/gender relations between men and women in organizations. A developing area is the place of sexuality in service organizations, where there is close worker–customer contact. An example of this approach is Lisa Adkins' (1995) study of the tourism, leisure, and catering industries in which she examines overlaps between sexuality and the labour market in constituting gender inequality. Women may be hired, or not, on the grounds of their sexualized appearance and behaviour rather than the transferability of their more obviously functional skills in the labour market.

Despite their links, empirical and conceptual distinctions can usefully be made between sexuality and gender dynamics in organizations, for example, in terms of the presence/absence of managers, professionals, and other organizational members of different genders and with different sexualities. In Sarah Rutherford's (1999) study of an airline company, the presence of gay men in some organizational divisions appeared to co-exist with the reduction of heterosexual harassment. Albert Mills' (2006) documentary case study of the airline industry focused on historical changes in the use of sexuality by management in the construction of women air cabin staff. This shows how discriminatory practices in the hiring and treatment of female employees were explicitly sexualized in the 1950s and 1960s, as part of the social construction of heterosexuality and homosexuality, prior to the onset of gender equity policies and discourses in the 1970s.

Case studies such as these emphasize the interconnections of sexuality and power in organizations, especially men's power over women, but also in relation to each other. Sexuality can be used to reinforce managerial power or to resist it. It is highly relevant in the conduct of such organizational activities as teamwork, counselling, supervision, and mentoring (Morgan and Davidson, 2008). Some studies recognize the homosexual or homosocial subtext (Wood, 1987), including homosociality and homosocial desire (Roper, 1996) in men's relations with each other, for example, in (homo)sexualized forms of men's emulation of each other or men's horseplay between men identifying as heterosexual (Collinson, 1992; Dorsey, 1994). This may involve avowedly heterosexual men engaging in what might be interpreted as 'homosexual' displays and even sexual assaults, such as grabbing other men's genitals or attacking bottoms with brooms or other work tools (Hearn, 1985).

## Policy Development

Another important aspect of the field has been the development of policy, whether at the local, organizational, national, or supranational level. The European Union (EU) is a case in point. The EU Rome Treaty 1957 Article 119 (now Article 141) introduced policy on Equal Pay that was initially to be implemented by 1962. The EU Amsterdam Treaty 1997 Article 2 added 'equality between men and women' to the list of general principles to be promoted by the EC. This primary legislation was supplemented in 2002 by Directive 2002/73/EC, according to which all employers should take measures to end all forms of gender discrimination, particularly sexual harassment. This directive also distinguished sexual harassment related to sex, and harassment of a sexual nature.

Within the frame of policy intervention, the basis of sexual harassment is usually sexual – that is, with sexuality as a medium – but not necessarily so. Talking about 'the sexual' may suggest that harassment feeds the explicit sexual desire of the harasser. However, this is not always so, as, for example, when a group of heterosexual men tease a heterosexual man that he is gay. This was one aspect of the scenario in the landmark *Oncale v Sundowner Offshore Services, Inc.* (96-568) case in the US. According to the Supreme Court '(o)n several occasions, Oncale was forcibly subjected to sex-related, humiliating actions against him by Lyons, Pippen and Johnson in the presence of the rest of the crew. Pippen and Lyons also physically assaulted Oncale in a sexual manner, and Lyons threatened him with rape' (http://www.law.cornell.edu/supct/html/96-568.ZO.html). The *Oncale* case was eventually settled 'out of court'. Once the US Supreme Court said he could sue, the company decided to give in and pay him an undisclosed amount of money. The importance of the case was that it extended sexual harassment to activities men can do to each other, even if they are heterosexual. Sexuality may be used, but not necessarily for explicit sexual desire.

Thus it is difficult to identify a comprehensive list of behaviours that could unequivocally be termed sexual harassment. However, it is possible to describe the sorts of behaviour usually seen as harassment, including physical conduct such as touching, pinching, physical actions which intimidate or embarrass (leering, whistling, suggestive gestures), physical sexual advances, and assault; verbal conduct such as statements which are experienced as insults, jokes of a derogatory nature, threatening or obscene language, verbal sexual advances; and offensive materials which are seen to degrade or offend such as pornographic pictures, badges, or graffiti. A key issue in both the study of and policy development on sexual harassment is how the behaviour is *perceived and received* by the individual; in some perspectives it is harassment if it felt to be so by the recipient. The European Commission's Code of Practice 1991 noted that it is for each individual to determine what behaviour is acceptable and what is offensive. The unwanted nature of the conduct distinguishes sexual harassment from friendly behaviour which is welcome and mutual.

Legal definitions of sexual harassment in the US include 'quid pro quo' stipulations ('You sleep with me or I'll fire you or not give you a raise!') and the presence of a 'chilly climate' (creation of a harassing climate at work that prevents the worker from doing his/her job effectively). These could be interpreted not as based in individual perception as such, but rather the perception of the target will have to be plausible for the courts to uphold it. For example, if men firefighters show pornographic films all day and the women feel harassed as a result, this is apt to stand up in court as constituting a chilly climate that interferes with work. Disapproval of the 'quid pro quo' standard is widespread, so it is very solid. But views on the chilly climate are much more diverse, and difficult to prove in court.

Sexual harassment can have wide-ranging consequences, ranging from feelings of shame and humiliation, to loss of confidence, becoming physically or mentally ill, loss of work through illness, and leaving jobs. On the other hand, Jo Brewis (2001) has argued that some policy and other discourses of/on sexual harassment can unwittingly reproduce gender power relations more generally, and even the object of their gaze. A counter-view that is more positive towards reformist progress is provided by Karen Ashcraft and Dennis Mumby (2004).

Another important area of policy development concerns respect for gay, lesbian, bisexual, transgender, transsexual, and intersex people and sexualities at work. As with sexual harassment, campaigns and other political interventions began in the 1970s and 1980s. Now, in some organizations, and even with continuing discriminations, LGBTI (lesbian, gay, bisexual, transgender, intersexual) sexualities are apparent and visible. These changes are themselves the product of other organizations, specifically social movement organizations and organizing in civil society (Davis, 2009). A recent progressive example of organizational policy is the 'Ally' project in the University of Western Australia (Skene at al., 2008) which aims, through leadership, training and policy, to produce sexually inclusive organizations for LGBTI people and sexualities. Moves toward more inclusive sexualities may well continue, if slowly, even with the rise of religious fundamentalisms and neo-conservativisms, and in so doing continue to problematize (hetero)sexual normativity.

## THEORETICAL AND CONCEPTUAL REVIEWS

There have also been general reviews of the place and impact of sexuality in organizations. One early example was Gibson Burrell's (1984) article, 'Sex and Organizational Analysis', that outlined how rationalistic organizations in practice and also organizational theory are oppositional to and subjugating of sexuality. *'Sex' at 'Work,'* by Hearn and Parkin (1987/1995) was a comprehensive study of sexuality and organizations, showing how organizational goals and beneficiaries relate to sexuality in many ways, including sexploitation (for example, in pornography, prostitution, and the sex trade), sexual service organizations (for example, sex therapy), mutual sexual organizations (for example, lesbian and gay telephone lines), and subordinated sexual organizations (where members' sexual interests appear subordinated to what are represented as 'non-sexual' organizational tasks). It outlined various ways in which organizations construct sexuality, sexuality constructs organizations, and organizations and sexuality occur simultaneously, hence the notion of 'organization sexuality'. This phenomenon occurs in varied ways, such as the social organization of movement and proximity within workplaces; patterns of feelings and emotions; the construction of ideology and consciousness; and the use of sexual language and imagery. The concepts of sexual work/labour, the selling of sexual work/labour, and sexual labour power also are developed in the book. These processes are perhaps most obvious in the retail, advertising, tourism, and leisure industries but they also exist elsewhere in more subtle forms, for example, in selling, marketing, and event organizing.

These issues were explored further in *The Sexuality of Organization* (Hearn et al., 1989) where our contributors framed sexuality as a key element for constructing organizational processes, not just something for analysis as 'the organization of sexuality'. Sexual processes and organizational processes are intimately connected in the general structuring of organizations and the details of everyday social interaction. This perspective was extended by Brewis and colleagues (Brewis and Grey, 1994; Brewis and Linstead, 2000) in terms of the eroticizing of organization(s), for example, in arguing for the relevance of practices, experiences, and dynamics in the sex trade for understanding mainstream organizations (cf. Pateman, 1988).

The concept of 'sexual work' is useful in organizational analysis (Hearn and sexualized Parkin, 1987/1995; also Bland et al., 1978). Rather than 'work' being framed as something that can then separately be sexualized, a closer relationship between work and sexuality is possible, challenging the very definitions of both sexuality and work. In some contexts, sexuality is the work. Organizations are arenas for sexual labour just as they are for emotional labour and manual/physical labour. The notion of sexual work is distinct from the specific term 'sex work', as sometimes used to characterize pornography, prostitution, and the sex trade, and often seeking to place those activities into a normalized framework of employment (Brewis and Linstead, 2000). There are a wide range of forms of interrelations of and connections between sexuality and kinds of work/labour. Linked to these debates is that more generally around the status of 'the economic', capitalism and capitalist economic relations, in the construction of sexuality and sexual harassment. 'Organization sexuality' is not a specific product of capitalist labour processes, though they are relevant (Hearn and Parkin, 1987, 1995). A recent framework outlined by Warhurst and Nickson (2009) sees sexualized labour as a more specific extension of, emotional labour and aesthetic labour. In turn, sexualized labour can be passively sanctioned or accepted by management or actively encouraged and prescribed by management, as for example in some bar work (Loe, 1996).

A focus on sexuality has also prompted concern with violence in and around organizations (Hearn and Parkin, 2001). The link between gender, sexuality, and violence in organizations encompasses sexual harassment, sexual violence, and sexual abuse.

And, yet, in studies of sexualities and organizations, the relations of sex, sexuality, and violence are relatively neglected. A related and growing area is that of embodiment at work, prompted by studies on the social construction of the body. Sexuality constitutes one of many effects of the body. The deployment of the body including sexuality varies according to different kinds of work and organization (Wolkowitz, 2006). Healthcare, social care, and therapy organizations are sites where intimate bodywork may be performed, and where relevant codes of conduct around sexuality are used or needed. More specifically in terms of bodies at work, there is a developing strand of research on transsexual bodies at work, and what workers go through there when they change genders (Namaste, 2000; Schilt, 2006; Schilt and Connell, 2007; Schilt and Wiswall, 2008).

## THE CASE OF INFORMATION AND COMMUNICATION TECHNOLOGIES

A recent key area concerns socio-technological issues and organizations, including the interrelation of sexualities and sexual violences with information and communication technologies (ICTs) and the dynamics of 'globalization'. We live in a period of historical transformation of sexuality, sexual violence, and the sex trade (including pornography, prostitution, and trafficking), including recently developed yet powerful information and communication technologies (ICTs). Clearly, pornography and other sex trade products are produced by organizations, both large 'mainstream' publishing and video corporations and small-scale enterprises.

Interplays of virtualities and surveillances, along with changes around (cyber)sexualities at a distance and non-direct physical contact mediated by 'new' technologies, constitute major historical changes with profoundly contradictory implications. These are likely to bring new forms of transnationalization, trans(n ational)patriarchies, imperialism, and neo-colonialism. Virtual imperialist/neo-colonialist exploitation may flourish alongside and supportive of direct non-virtual imperialisms/neo-colonialisms, for example, by using ICTs to facilitate global sex trade (Pyle and Ward, 2003; Hearn, 2006; 2008b). They also bring work changes and policy challenges in organizations, such as rules for organizational members' online access to sex websites and/or pornography. This section outlines how ICTs intersect with sexualities and considers the implications of ICTs for consumers, users, and sexualities in/and organizations.

ICTs create vast possibilities to organize sexuality and for the practice and experience of new forms of sexuality, including techno-sex, high-tech sex, non-connection sex, mobile phone sex, internet dating, consensual sex between strangers, email sex, cybersex, cyberaffairs, virtual sex, multimedia interactive sex, and so on (Hearn, 2006). Virtual communities and organizations of sexual interest, for and against particular sexualities, appear to offer trustworthy, organized arenas for support. Yet familiarity with the Web can be deceptive. ICTs and the worldwide web (WWW) offer an apparent 'home' for sexual communities yet they are also sites for diffusion of disembodied sexual capitalism, sexual consumer cultures, and sexual pleasures (Bernstein, 2001). MySpace.com, the networking site and blog community widely used by young people to meet virtually, was bought from Intermix Media by Rupert Murdoch's NewsCorp. What begin as self-help social-sexual communities can become pay-to-use capitalist enterprises, as part of wider global capitalism.

The impact of ICTs increases potential for creating various global/local sexualized cultures in organizations and elsewhere and a more general pornographizing of sex and social life generally. ICTs have historically transformed prostitution and (re)constituted the sex trade by supplying encyclopaedic information online (Hearn and Parkin, 2001; Hughes, 2002). Live videoconferencing using advanced technology on the WWW, with live audio and video communication capable of being transmitted over the Internet from video recorder to computer and back again. This way of organizing can involve buying live sex shows, in which men can direct the show in some cases, with real-time communication possible. Pornographers have been leaders in developing Internet privacy and secure payment services. Viewers can interact with DVD movies similarly to video games, giving users, usually men, a more active role. As modes of exchange, production and communication become more disembodied possibilities for the reproduction of sexual texts increases – accessible on millions of PC screens worldwide through photo- and video-sharing. The 'real' and the 'representational' converge and sexual commodification proceeds apace. In the conduct of sexuality and sexual violence in these cybercontexts, there is little separation of sexual information, sexual advertising, production of sexual material, and sexual consumption and experience (Hearn, 2006).

ICTs provide many possibilities for meeting sexual partners or for sexual identity exploration. Also, specialized technological organizations produce possibilities for new cyber(org)sexualities that include fostering sexually-coded devices that allow people to seek others with presumably compatible sexualities. Such technologizations can be external to the body skin in a 'blackberry' or similar device or implanted under the skin. Possibilities are growing for many-to-many 'social software' and 'new sexual affordances' for mutual identification (as with matchmaker systems combining virtual community, collaborative filtering, and web-to-cellphone technology, so people can know who in their physical vicinity shares certain affinities and willingness to be contacted) (Wellman, 2001). These represent new intersections of organizations and sexualities.

ICTs are not merely media for sexualities but they increasingly organize and are constitutive of them. Sexuality can be constructed in the context of disembodied social institutions, including the state and corporations. ICTs offer organizational possibilities for new forms of sexualities whereby people, individually or in groups, display their sexualities, including the 'whole' of their sexual lives. Webcams, mobile phones, and reality shows provide new possibilities for practice, identity, and image-making, through 'revealing', not avoiding surveillance (Koskela, 2004), and new forms of sexuality with 'the disappearance of disappearance', the unattainabilty of privacy (Haggerty and Ericson, 2000). All 'privacy' is now potentially public and thus organized (Hearn, 1992).

One aspect of ICTs is surveillance. While many ICTs are experienced and represented as giving individuals access to 'more information', they also provide means for corporate entities to access information 'about us'. Google and similar organizations hold masses of information on people's personal preferences, including sexual preferences, through their virtual inquiries and searches. Such compilations, sexual and otherwise, are part of 'surveillant assemblages', compositions of online data referring to surveilled lives. They are producing and likely to further produce new forms of the body and commodifications of the self, whereby flesh and sexualities are reduced to 'data doubles' (Haggerty and Ericson, 2000), the paralleling of lives, including sexual lives, in the realms of data. To put this simply, the implications of these socio-technical changes for sexualities and work are very difficult to chart and predict, in the light of amazingly powerful and increasing available ICTs.

## Conclusions and Future Research

Work, managements, and organizations more generally can be understood as structured, gendered, and sexualed (re)productions, for both those who work there and for analysts. Organizations can be understood as structured, gendered/sexualed, sexually-encoded (re)productions, for both organizational members and organizational analysts. Sexuality is a material aspect of the reproduction of patriarchies and patriarchal relations. The social (re)production of sexuality is a major, but not of course the only, element in the formation of the gendered body. Contemporary social change exerts effects on what sexuality *is*, as with the impacts of ICTs. Political economies of sexualities are likely to be reformulated. In particular, global technological, financial, environmental and other changes are likely to have major effects in sexualities at work and organizations in some parts of the world (Hearn, 2010).

Analyses of work, organizations, management, and sexuality raise many theoretical issues, including relations of material, bodily experiences, and oppressions around sexuality and discursive constructions of sexuality. Critical interrogation of sexualities can lead to more general consideration of the relevance of the visual and the haptic for knowledge of social reality, for example, the epistemological significance of touch, looks and appearance(s), and interpretations of people through the sexuality of clothing and body displays, such as breast implants and tattoos.

In addition, future researchers on gender, sexuality, work, organizations, and management face several fundamental challenges. First, sexuality categories may become defined in more complex ways. Some limited blurring of sexual categories, such as the homo/hetero binary (Brickell, 2006), and growth of bi-curious and other changing sexual practices in turn have implications for organization sexualities. These include public discourses and organizational sexual practices that may drift in quite opposite directions regarding sexual power and organizational inequalities (Burr and Hearn, 2008). Second, sexual practices can suggest interesting metaphorical organizational practices, such as sexual sado-masochism being paralleled by symbiotic sadistic exploitative management and masochistic docile workers.

Another potential research area is the impact of the ageing of organizational workers, members, and users, in relation to sexualities. Age-conscious naming and claiming of ageing sexualities, including intersections of ageing, disabilities, and illness, are likely to increase in and around organizations. Ageing sexualities may challenge (hetero)sexual normativity, by subverting or problematizing taken-for-granted youthful sexualities. Crip theory (McRuer, 2006), combining disability theory and queer theory, provides a fertile base for researching intersections of work, organizations, disability, sexuality, ageing, and dying. A final issue is the likely increased problematization of biological sex 'itself', including definitions and understandings of 'female'/'male' and their presumed natural 'givenness'. These and related issues are ripe material for future researchers on work, organizations, and management.

## ACKNOWLEDGEMENTS

I would like to thank again Wendy Parkin for our friendly collaboration on these issues since 1978, and Patricia Yancey Martin for helpful detailed suggestions on an earlier version of this chapter.

## REFERENCES

Adkins, L. (1995) *Gendered Work: Sexuality, Family and the Labour Market.* Buckingham: Open University Press.

Allison, A. (1994) *Nightwork: Sexuality, Pleasure and Corporate Masculinity in a Tokyo Hostess Club.* Chicago: University of Chicago Press.

Ashcraft, K., and Mumby, D. (2004) *Reworking Gender: A Feminist Communicology of Organization.* Thousand Oaks, CA: Sage.

Badgett, M.V.L. (2001) *Money, Myths, and Change: The Economic Lives of Lesbians and Gay Men.* Chicago: Chicago University Press.

Bernstein, E. (2001) The Meaning of the Purchase: Desire, Demand and the Commerce of Sex, *Ethnography,* 2(3) 389–420.

Bland, L., Brunsdon, C., Hobson, D. and Winship, J. (1978) 'Women "Inside" and "Outside" the Relations of Production' in Women's Studies Group, Centre for Contemporary Cultural Studies, University of Birmingham (eds), *Women Take Issue.* London: Hutchinson, 35–78.

Brewis, J. (2001) Foucault, Politics and Organizations: (Re)-constructing Sexual Harassment, *Gender, Work and Organization,* 8(1) 37–60.

Brewis, J., and Grey, C. (1994) Re-eroticizing the Organization: An Exegesis and Critique, *Gender, Work and Organization,* 1(2) 67–82.

Brewis, J., and Linstead, S. (2000) *Sex, Work and Sex Work: Eroticizing Organization.* London: Routledge.

Brickell, C. (2006) Sexology, the Homo/Hetero Binary, and the Complexities of Male Sexual History, *Sexualities,* 9(4) 423–447.

Burke, M.E. (1993) *Coming Out of the Blue: British Police Officers Talk about their Lives in 'The Job' as Lesbians, Gays and Bisexuals.* London and New York: Cassell.

Burr, V., and Hearn, J. (eds) (2008) *Sex, Violence and The Body: The Erotics of Wounding.* Houndmills and New York: Palgrave Macmillan.

Burrell, G. (1984) Sex and Organizational Analysis, *Organization Studies*, 5(2) 97–118.

Burrell, G. and Hearn, J. (1989) 'The Sexuality of Organization' in J. Hearn, D. Sheppard, P. Tancred-Sheriff, and G. Burrell (eds), *The Sexuality of Organization.* London: Sage, 1–28.

Cammermeyer, M. (1994) *Serving in Silence.* Harmondsworth: Penguin.

Cavandish, R. (1982) *Women on the Line.* London: Routledge and Kegan Paul.

Cockburn, C.K. (1983) *Brothers: Male Dominance and Technological Change.* London: Pluto.

Cockburn, C.K. (1991) *In the Way of Women: Men's Resistance to Sex Equality in Organizations.* Basingstoke: Macmillan.

Collinson, D.L. (1992) *Managing the Shopfloor. Subjectivity, Masculinity and Workplace Culture.* Berlin: de Gruyter.

Collinson, M., and Collinson, D.L. (1996) 'It's only Dick': the Sexual Harassment of Women Managers in Insurance Sales, *Work, Employment and Society*, 10(1) 29–56.

Davis, G. (2009) Mobilization Strategies and Gender Awareness: An Analysis of Intersex Social Movement Organizations. Unpublished manuscript, Department of Sociology, University of Illinois at Chicago.

Dorsey, D. (1994) *The Force.* New York: Ballantine.

Farley, L. (1978 *Sexual Shakedown: The Sexual Harassment of Women on the Job.* London: Melbourn House.

Fitzgerald, L.F. (1988) The Incidence and Dimensions of Sexual Harassment in Academia and the Workplace. *Journal of Vocational Behavior*, 32(2) 152–175.

Gruber, J., and Morgan, P. (eds) (2005) *In the Company of Men: Sexual Harassment and Male Domination.* Boston: Northeastern University Press.

Gutek, B.A. (1985) *Sex and the Workplace: Impact of Sexual Behavior and Harassment on Women, Men and Organizations.* San Francisco: Jossey-Bass.

Gutek, B.A., and Morasch, B. (1982) Sex Ratios, Sex-role Spillover and Sexual Harassment of Women at Work, *Journal of Social Issues*, 38(4) 55–74.

Haavio-Mannila, E. (1994) 'Erotic Relations at Work' in M. Alestalo, E. Allardt, A. Rychard, and W. Wesolowski (eds), *The Transformation of Europe.* Warsaw: IFIS, 293–315.

Haggerty, K.D., and Ericson, R.V. (2000) The Surveillant Assemblage, *British Journal of Sociology*, 51(4) 605–622.

Hall, E. (1995) *We Can't Even March Straight.* London: Vintage.

Hearn, J. (1985) 'Men's Sexuality at Work' in A. Metcalf and M. Humphries (eds), *The Sexuality of Men.* London: Pluto, 110–128.

Hearn, J. (1992) *Men in the Public Eye.* London: Routledge.

Hearn, J. (2006) The Implications of Information and Communication Technologies for Sexualities and Sexualised Violences: Contradictions of Sexual Citizenships, *Political Geography*, 25(8) 944–963.

Hearn, J. (2008a) The Personal is Work is Political is Theoretical: Continuities and Discontinuities in (Pro)Feminism, Women's Studies, Men and my Selves. *NORA: Nordic Journal of Feminist and Gender Research*, 16(4) 241–256.

Hearn, J. (2008b) Sexualities Future, Present, Past . . . Towards Transsectionalities, *Sexualities: Studies in Culture and Society*, 11(1) 37–46.

Hearn, J. (2010) 'Global/Transnational Gender/Sexual Scenarios' in A.G. Jónasdóttir, V. Bryson and K.B. Jones (eds), *Sexuality, Gender and Power: Intersectional and Transnational Perspectives.* New York: Routledge, 209–226.

Hearn, J., Jyrkinen, M., Piekkari, R., and Oinonen, E. (2008) 'Women Home and Away': Transnational Managerial Work and Gender Relations, *The Journal of Business Ethics*, 83(1) 41–54.

Hearn, J., and Parkin, W. (1987/1995) *'Sex' at 'Work': The Power and Paradox of Organization Sexuality.* Hemel Hempstead: Prentice Hall/Harvester Wheatsheaf; New York; St Martin's.

Hearn, J., and Parkin, W. (2001) *Gender, Sexuality and Violence in Organizations: The Unspoken Forces of Organization Violations.* London and Thousand Oaks, CA: Sage.

Hearn, J., Sheppard, D., Tancred-Sheriff, P., and Burrell, G. (eds) (1989) *The Sexuality of Organization.* London and Newbury Park, CA: Sage.

Horn, P.D and Horn, J.C. (1982) *Sex in the Office: Power and Passion in the Workplace.* Reading, MA: Addison-Wesley.

Hughes, D. (2002) The Use of New Communication and Information Technologies for the Sexual Exploitation of Women and Children, *Hastings Women's Law Journal,* 13(1) 127–146.

Humphrey, J. (2000) Organizing Sexualities, Organization Inequalities: Lesbians and Gay Men in Public Service Occupations, *Gender, Work and Organization,* 6(3) 134–151.

ID Research (2001) *Gay and Lesbian Census.* London: ID Research.

Jenness, V., Maxson, C.L., Sumner, J.M., and Matsuda, K.N. (2010) Accomplishing the Difficult, but not Impossible: Collecting Self-report Data on Inmate-on-inmate Sexual Assault in Prison, *Criminal Justice Policy Review,* 21(1). In Press.

Kakabadse, A., and Kakabadse, N. (2004) *Intimacy: International Survey of the Sex Lives of People at Work.* New York: Palgrave.

Koskela, H. (2004) Webcams, TV Shows and Mobile Phones: Empowering exhibitionism. *Surveillance and Society,* 2(2) 199–215. Available at: http://www.surveillance-and-society. org/articles2(2)/webcams.pdf.

Lehtonen, J., and Mustola, K. (eds) (2004) *'Straight people don't tell, do they . . .?' Negotiating the Boundaries of Sexuality and Gender at Work.* Helsinki: Ministry of Labour. Available at: http://www.esr.fi.

Loe, M. (1996) Working for Men at the Intersection of Power, Gender and Sexuality, *Sociological Inquiry,* 66(4) 399–421.

MacKinnon, C.A. (1979) *The Sexual Harassment of Working Women.* New Haven, CT: Yale University Press.

MacKinnon, C.A. (1982) Feminism, Marxism, Method and the State: An Agenda for Theory, *Signs,* 7(3) 515–544.

MacKinnon, C.A. (1989) *Toward a Feminist Theory of the State.* Cambridge, Mass.: Harvard University Press.

McRuer, R. (2006) *Crip Theory: Cultural Signs of Queerness and Disability.* New York: New York University Press.

Martin, P.Y., Reynolds, J., and Keith, S. (2002) Gender Bias and Feminist Consciousness among Judges and Attorneys: A Standpoint Theory Analysis, *Signs,* 27(3) 665–701.

Mills, A.J. (2006) *Sex, Strategy and the Stratosphere: Airlines and the Gendering of Organizational Culture.* Houndmills and New York: Palgrave Macmillan.

Morgan, L.M. and Davidson, (2008) Sexual Dynamics in Mentoring Relationships – A Critical Review, *British Journal of Management,* 19(S1) S120–S129.

Namaste, V. (2000) *Invisible Lives: The Erasure of Transsexual and Transgendered People.* Chicago: University of Chicago Press.

Oerton, S. (1996a) *Beyond Hierarchy: Gender, Sexuality and the Social Economy.* London: Taylor and Francis.

Oerton, S. (1996b) Sexualizing the Organization, Lesbianizing the Women: Gender, Sexuality and Flat Organizations, *Gender, Work and Organization,* 3(1) 289–297.

Out Now Consulting Gay Times and Diva Readers Surveys (2005) www.OutNowconsulting. com Also see: *Gay at Home But Not at Work.* New study – UK gays unable to reveal sexuality at work.

http://www.gaywork.com/page.cfm?Sectionid=5&typeofsite=storydetail&ID=269&storyset=yes

Pateman, C. (1988) *The Sexual Contract*. Cambridge: Polity.

Pringle, R. (1988) *Secretaries Talk: Sexuality, Power and Work*. London: Verso.

Pyle, J.L., and Ward, K.B. (2003) Recasting our Understanding of Gender and Work during Global Restructuring, *International Sociology*, 18(3) 461–489.

Quinn, R.E. (1977) Coping with Cupid: The Formation, Management and Impact of Romantic Relationships in Organizations, *Administrative Science Quarterly*, 22(1) 30–45.

Roper, M. (1996) ' "Seduction and Succession": Circuits of Homosocial Desire in Management' in D.L. Collinson and J. Hearn (eds), *Men as Managers, Managers as Men: Critical Perspectives on Men, Masculinities and Managements*. London: Sage, 210–226.

Rutherford, S. (1999) Organisational Cultures, Patriarchal Closure and Women Managers. Doctoral thesis. Bristol: University of Bristol.

Schilt, K. (2006) 'Just one of the Guys?: How Transmen Make Gender Visible in the Workplace, *Gender and Society*, 20(4) 465–490.

Schilt, K., and Connell, C. (2007) Do Gender Transitions Make Gender Trouble? *Gender, Work, and Organization*, 14(6) 596–618.

Schilt, K., and Wiswall, M. (2008) Before and After: Gender Transitions, Human Capital, and Workplace Experiences. *The B.E. Journal of Economic Analysis and Policy* 8(1), Article 39. 26 pp. http://www.econ.nyu.edu/user/wiswall/research/schilt_wiswall_transsexual.pdf.

Sedgwick, E.K. (1991) *The Epistemology of the Closet*. Berkeley, CA: University of California Press.

Skene, J., Hagan, J., de Vries, J., and Goody, A. (2008) *The ALLY Network at the University of Western Australia: The Early Years*. Perth: The University of Western Australia.

Timmerman, G., and Bajema, C. (1999) Sexual Harassment in Northwest Europe, *The European Journal of Women's Studies*, 6(4) 419–439.

Warhurst, C., and Nickson, D. (2009) Who's Got the Look? Emotional, Aesthetic and Sexualized Labour in Interactive Services, *Gender, Work and Organization*, 16(3) 385–404.

Wellman, B. (2001) Physical Space and Cyberspace: The Rise of Personalized Networking, *International Journal of Urban and Regional Research*, 25(2) 227–252.

Wise, S., and Stanley, L. (1987) *Georgie Porgie: Sexual Harassment in Everyday Life*. London: Pandora.

Wolkowitz, C. (2006) *Bodies at Work*. London: Sage.

Wood, R. (1987) '*Raging Bull*: The Homosexual Subtext in Film' in M. Kaufman (ed.), *Beyond Patriarchy: Essays by Men on Power, Pleasure and Change*. Toronto: Oxford University Press, 266–276.

Wooden, W.S., and. Parker, J. (1982) *Men Behind Bars: Sexual Exploitation in Prison*. New York: Plenum Press.

Woods, J.D., and Lucas, J.H. (1993) *The Corporate Closet: the Professional Lives of Gay Men in America*. New York: Free Press.

Zippel, K.S. (2006) *The Politics of Sexual Harassment: A Comparative Study of the United States, the European Union, and Germany*. Cambridge: Cambridge University Press.

# 19

## Diversity in Organizations: A Critical Examination of Assumptions about Diversity and Organizations in Twenty-first Century Management Literature

VEDRAN OMANOVIĆ, PhD
*The School of Business, Economics and Law
at The University of Gothenburg, Sweden*

### BACKGROUND

Several scholars claim that diversity management first emerged in the US in the early 1990s (e.g. Nkomo and Cox, 1996; Pringle and Scowcroft, 1996; Lynch, 1997; Prasad and Mills, 1997; Kelly and Dobbin, 1998; Ivancevich and Gilbert, 2000; Lorbiecki and Jack, 2000; Lorbiecki, 2001; Ashkanasy et al., 2002; Zanoni and Janssens, 2004; Janssens and Zanoni, 2005; Omanović, 2006, 2009). The US movement against racial discrimination of the 1960s is often cited as the cause of the subsequent focus on diversity in the workplace (e.g. Thomas, 1990; Ashkanasy et al., 2002; Omanović, 2009). This movement challenged occupational segregation in US companies and organizations and led to their adoption of affirmative action programs that promoted equal employment opportunity.

The main proponents of workplace diversity in the US are/were human resource managers, workplace consultants, and Equal Employment Opportunity (EEO) and Affirmative Action (AA) specialists. In response to the dramatic curtailment of the administrative enforcement of workplace diversity by unsympathetic national administrations, EEO/AA specialists replaced legal arguments for EEO/AA programmes with efficiency arguments aimed at managing diversity (Kelly and Dobbin, 1998; Omanović, 2009).

Thus managing diversity in the US changed from 'redressing past and present factors that tend systematically to advantage or disadvantage individuals based on group identities like gender and racio-ethnicity' (Cox, 1994: 250) to an economic and demographic imperative that sees diversity as an asset that is instrumental in organizational success. As Thomas (1990) emphasizes, in his argument for a business-oriented view of diversity, managing diversity is a way to obtain from a heterogeneous workforce the same productivity, commitment, quality, and profit that companies obtain from a homogeneous workforce. This view is still widely held, especially in the US.

However, no strong empirical evidence supports the view that well-managed diversity results in improved organizational effectiveness and profitability (e.g., Kochan et al., 2003; Shoobridge, 2006). The research reports conflicting findings (Christian et al., 2006).

Despite strong and robust networks (especially in the US) that try to universalize and objectify the business argument for diversity, several management researchers have complemented earlier ideas of diversity by offering alternative perspectives. In discussing 'diversity', they do not address organizational effectiveness and profitability and/or diversity management. Rather, they focus on the meanings or idea(s) that people have of diversity and/or differences and how people do (or manage) diversity. Still others focus on ideas about and interests in diversity that are favoured to the exclusion of others.

## CHAPTER PURPOSE

By focusing on journal articles published in the twenty-first century, this chapter asks *how diversity is being represented in the management and organization literature*. In answering this question, I examine researchers' assumptions about what diversity is, or can be, and examine the process by which they reach their assumptions about what diverse organizations are, or can be. Using examples of diversity interpretations in the literature, I show how researchers position diversity in organizations differently and ask different questions and/or design research projects differently. I identify and examine four philosophical traditions in the literature: *the positivist, the interpretative, the (critical) discursive*, and *the critical-dialectic* (see Table 19.1). In Table 19.1, I review the following issues in each tradition: (a) views of diversity, (b) views of organizations, (c) implications for research, (d) relevant questions, (e) favoured theoretical frames, (f) favoured methods, and (g) possible results and implications for organizations. By examining each perspective in terms of these issues, readers can gain a sense of the range of ways that diversity is framed in recent management and organization literature.

Aside from providing readers with an overview of diversity literature, an argument of the chapter is that we, as researchers, play an active role (given certain societal conditions) in forming and prioritizing diversity ideas and interests. In that sense, research is never neutral or objective because the desire for neutrality or objectivity is also a kind of historically developed construction.

## SEARCH METHODS

As noted, my focus is on twenty-first century journal diversity articles although some earlier articles are reviewed to provide historical contextualization. Only articles that

TABLE 19.1  A Summary of Multiple Views of Diversity in Organizations Traditions

| Content and Issues | Positivist | Interpretative | (Critical) discursive | Critical-dialectic |
|---|---|---|---|---|
| View of diversity | Demographic categories of diversity as independent, universal and ahistorical variables. No symbiotic relationships among categories. | Socially constructed phenomena through social activities, such as words, symbols and behaviours. | Socially constructed phenomena. Diversity is viewed as organizational and social discourse expressed in talk and/or texts. | A dialectic, social-historical process, actively constructed by particular parties involved in its production in specific context(s). |
| View of organizations | Regulatory view. Organizations as race-ethnicity-nationality-gender-age neutral, established to maintain social order. | Socially constructed systems of shared meanings. | (DA) Socially constructed and reproduced institutions by different communicative activities. (CDA) Multi-sided, contradictory and unstable. | Socially constructed and a process- history- and context-oriented view. The organization as a part of the social world, always in a state of becoming and dependent on the interests and ideas of people in power. |
| Implications for research | Objective approach focusing on the status quo; science results in objective knowledge generalization. | Subjective approach focusing on present processes of interaction, reaffirmation, change and understanding (shared meanings) of events and actors (without influencing them). | (DA) Subjective approach focusing on language use as expressed in talk and/or texts. (CDA) Focuses on regulatory, controlling, historically-constructed and unequal regimes of knowledge. | Subjective approach focusing on processes by which diversity ideas and interests, contradictions and praxes are produced and maintained in specific social/organizational/historical contexts. Focus on revealing and demystifying dominant |

TABLE 19.1 (continued)

| Content and Issues | Positivist | Interpretative | (Critical) discursive | Critical-dialectic |
|---|---|---|---|---|
| | | | | ideas and interests, which are viewed as preliminary and choices exist between (historical) alternatives. |
| Relevant questions | What are the effects of workforce ethnic, race, gender, and/or sexual orientation diversity on financial performance? Also, questions related to attitudes, behaviours, values, performances and leadership preferences/perceptions/commitments/styles related to diversity are of interest. | How do organization members 'do diversity'? or How do they 'do diversity' by managing diversity? Also, questions related to understandings by managers and other organizational participants on the meanings/interpretations of diversity management/cultural diversity/workplace diversity/workplace fairness; experiences of ethnic minority women in white, Western organizations. | How are orderly patterns of diversity constructed and discursively controlled? How are minority employees discursively controlled? How is resistance to management of diversity expressed as text, discursive practice, and social practice? How does power operate using the language of diversity? | How and why do organizations and their employees socially produce diversity? Which diversity ideas and interests are favoured in the production of diversity? Are there alternative ways of producing diversity, and if so, why are they suppressed? |
| Favoured theoretical frames | A psychological approach, applying social psychological theories such as social identity theory and social categorization theory. | Hermeneutics, Phenomenology. | Neo-institutionalism; rhetoric, linguistic. Also, a post-structuralist viewpoint primarily based on the work of Foucault. | A dialectical view of organization analysis, (developed and applied by Benson); the critical perspective (of the Frankfurt School). |

| | | | | |
|---|---|---|---|---|
| *Favoured methods* | Objective and mostly quantitative methodologies, (e.g. surveys, questionnaires, scenarios, and experiments). Larger sampling numbers. Hypothesis testing research. | Qualitative approaches inspired by (conventional) ethnography, including empirical data, such as interviews, non-participant/participant observations and archival material. Smaller sampling numbers without a priori assumptions (of representativeness). | Qualitative approaches using conversations, or/and interview records and/or written linguistic expressions such as personnel policies, scholarly and practitioner-oriented books, journal articles, and Internet sites. | Conventional/Critical ethnography using various empirical data such as archival research, in-depth interviews and detailed participant observations. |
| *Possible results and implications for organizations* | Orderly patterns, control and expertise (e.g. counting patterns of leaders' attitudes, behaviours, commitments, and styles). Measurements of the effects of diversity on firm performance. | Commitment and quality work life (e.g. promotion and implementation of diversity as a learning process).. | Deepened and varied understanding and problematizations. Alternative understandings aimed at changing managerial diversity discourse. | Participation and change. Conditions created for organizational changes that support the interests of the diverse participants rather than those of management. |

are empirically based and relate to organizations and organizing were selected. I used two databases for this search: Business Source Premier and Sage Journals Online. The most common key words of my search were: Managing Diversity, Diversity in Organizations, Diversity and its Management.[1] The results discussed below reflect my interpretation of the primary theoretical foci of the sources I found.

## The positivist tradition – diversity as variables and resources, instrumental in organizational success

Researchers in the positivist tradition (a historically dominant management discourse) are described variously in the literature. Alvesson and Deetz (2000) describe this tradition as including methodological determinists, functionalists, normative researchers, including law and variable analytic theorists. Many of these theorists take a social psychological approach and use concepts such as social identity, social categorizations, and/or decision-making. The social identity concept predicts, for instance how diversity affects organizational participants' attitudes, behaviour, and/or performance. A basic argument for the decision-making concept is that diverse workforces can have positive impacts on performance, including, for instance goal achievement, satisfaction, problem-solving, and creativity. The social categorization concept is more sceptical. Its focus is largely on measuring the effects of diversity on the financial performance of organizations.

In many management and organization studies, inspired by the positivist tradition, diversity has normative connotations with regard to the distribution of certain, typically demographic, organization characteristics such as race-ethnicity (e.g. Gilbert and Stead, 1999; Mollica, 2003; Kidder et al., 2004; Roberson and Park, 2007; McKay, 2008) and gender (e.g. Gilbert and Stead, 1999). These researchers are concerned with 'deep-level diversity' (Harrison et al., 1998) or with psychological attributes (e.g. Ng, 2008) such as attitudes, behaviours, values, performances, and leadership characteristics (e.g. Kirby and Richard, 2000). Alternatively, they focus on individuals and/or groups (often managers) in their study of reputation (Roberson and Park, 2007), reactions (e.g., Mollica, 2003), sexual orientation (Johnston and Malina, 2008; Ng, 2008), personal values and belief systems (Smith et al., 2004), diversity climate and inclusion (Härtel, 2004; Roberson, 2006; McKay, 2008), organizational attractiveness (Smith et al., 2004), success (Gilbert and Stead, 1999), and status (Harris et al., 1996).

Researchers in the positivist tradition collect 'objective' data, often using survey methods (e.g. questionnaires, scenarios, and experiments). Some researchers combine survey methods with 'qualitative research' methods, such as interviews and/or secondary data and observations (e.g. Härtel, 2004; Roberson, 2006; Sub and Kleiner, 2007). Roberson (2006) provides an example of how a researcher in the

[1] My search was not focused at any particular categories/aspects that usually relates to 'diversity' (such as ethnicity, race, gender, age, sexual orientation, disability and the like). That's probably one of the possible reasons why some of these aspects are far more prevalent in my search in relation to organizations than are other aspects (e.g. gender diversity).

positivist tradition collects data. In her study of organizations aimed at identifying patterns of diversity and inclusion, using prior research and an email survey consisting of open-ended questions addressed to human resource or diversity officers at 51 large, publicly traded companies, Roberson defines diversity and inclusion and differentiates between the diverse and the inclusive organization. She constructs an instrument to measure how well the attributes she identified support diversity and inclusion. Finally, using a 9-point Likert Scale, she asks 186 respondents to rate how each attribute describes the diverse organization and the inclusive organization. This research is managerialist in its assumptions and its goal is to secure knowledge about diversity that assists management in improving organizational performance.

Other researchers use an hypothesis-testing approach where the focus is on grouping the organization's functions around goal orientation and maintenance (e.g. Watson et al., 1993; Harrison et al., 1998; Gilbert and Stead, 1999; Richard, 2000; Mollica, 2003; Kidder et al., 2004; Roberson and Park, 2007; Johnston and Malina, 2008). Diversity is objectified as, for instance cultural, racial, surface-level, and deep-level diversity, and then transformed into measurable operational variables. The most common operational variables are white and minority/black; heterogeneous and homogeneous groups; female and male; and sexual orientation.

A commonality among these studies is that most are situated in the US although there are exceptions such as the research by Härtel (2004) in Australia and Sub and Kleiner (2007) in Germany.[2] Authors typically neglect the geographical and historical context of their research (e.g. Mollica, 2003; Watson et al., 1993; McKay, 2008). In minimizing the importance of location, diversity is thus viewed as existing in a decontextualised and ahistorical space, and diversity management is assumed to have universal application.

Researchers in a positivist tradition favour the business-oriented view of promoting diversity in organizations. In taking this perspective, they often relate diversity to individual, group, and/or organizational performance (Watson et al., 1993; Robinson and Dechant, 1997; Hambrick et al., 1998; Harrison et al., 1998) or propose different strategies for managing human resource diversity (e.g., Watson et al., 1993; Robinson and Dechant, 1997; Richard, 2000; Kearney and Gebert, 2006). For instance, Watson et al. (1993) note the effect of a high degree of cultural diversity on group interaction and group problem-solving. In their focus on multinational diversity and group performance, Hambrick et al. (1998) claim that effects of diversity depend on whether the group's task is primarily creative, computational, or coordinative.

There is strong evidence in recent management literature (largely from the US) of this business-oriented interest in diversity (e.g. Richard, 2000; Thomas, 2004; Roberson and Park, 2007; Johnston and Malina, 2008). For instance, taking inspiration from the resource-based view of the firm, Johnston and Malina examine the relationship between a firm's market value and its management of gender diversity. Roberson and Park (2007) examine the links between diversity reputation/

---

[2] Sub and Kleiner partly contextualize diversity management by describing how the diversity management discussion in Germany has developed in recent years. Unlike the US, the starting point for diversity management in Germany was the discussion of equal employment opportunities for men and women.

leader racial diversity and firm performance. Using upper-echelon theory[3] as their starting-point, Roberson and Parker argue that diversity reputation (defined as the stakeholders' perceptions of an organization's ability to create diverse work environments) and leaders' racial diversity (defined as the representation of ethnic minorities in top management) are related to firm performance.

Thus, an underlying assumption in these studies is that diversity is a resource, an asset necessary for organizational and financial success (e.g. Gilbert and Stead, 1999). Such business interests are typically perceived as in everyone's best interests. In these studies, diversity is examined as if it is an 'objective' phenomenon independent of managers' and researchers' interests in managing it or promoting it as an object to be managed. Race, gender, age, and sexual orientation(s) are treated as independent, ahistorical variables with no symbiotic relationships between them.

Organization researchers in the positivist tradition treat organizations as existing entities, which are made for instrumental ends, most often increasing profitability, or securing a desired position in the market. These primary goals are usually related to other social goals (such as promoting diversity). Such researchers therefore are often concerned with managerial problems and the organizational life of executives (e.g. managing workforce diversity or focusing on leaderships attributes) and research questions often stem from practical problems.

The positivist tradition is useful for identifying patterns that facilitate the measurement(s) of the financial effects of different aspects of diversity. However, like many other approaches, it has a limited outlook. This tradition does not, for instance, explain the origins of and motives for patterns of diversity, thus it neglects the wider political, societal, and 'meaning' contexts. Also, several management-inspired studies assume that managers have a crucial influence in managing diversity. In other words, the management role (often lionized) is taken for granted while the role of other participants is simply to meet management goals.

*Other Perspectives* Since the late 1990s, diversity researchers have employed interpretative, discursive, and critical approaches to their work, although this research remains somewhat marginalized in the literature, especially compared to research in positivist traditions. By developing alternative logics and frames for diversity studies, researchers established some independence from contextual situations (diversity in organizations and/or in countries with significant immigration) and began adding original content to the research.

In the following sections I discuss contributions from organization researchers who focus on 'diversity in organizations' by using interpretative, (critical) discursive, and critical-dialectic traditions.

## *The interpretative tradition – diversity as socially constructed*

Interpretativists study diversity as socially constructed or as the product of social activities (West and Fenstermarker, 1995) and have focused on a variety of issues.

---

[3] According to upper echelon theory, a firm's leaders have a critical impact on firm performance given the significant organization decisions they make (Roberson and Parker, 2007).

Hermon's (1996) study, for instance, examines the perspectives of both employees and senior managers in a US organization in order to determine if communication generated by advisory panels[4] results in a shared understanding of and commitment to diversity. Hermon's assumption is that individuals create and shape their own reality through communication. That study thus tries to *understand* and *capture* the opinions of the company's diverse workforce involved in panel discussions.

In several studies, researchers focus on managing diversity in organizations (Gilbert and Ivancevich, 2000), including its various meanings (Omanović, 2002; Foster, 2005; Foster and Harris, 2005; Subeliani and Tsogas, 2005).

For instance, operational managers' *interpretations* and *understandings* of the *meaning(s)* of the concept of diversity management and its practical applications in British retailing is the focus of Foster and Harris's study (2005) while Subeliani and Tsogas (2005) examine diversity management practices at one of the major banks in The Netherlands (Rabobank). These authors contrast theoretical *premises* of the concept of managing diversity with the bank's diversity management practices and the bank's managers and employees' *understandings* and reasons for these practices. Their findings show, among other things, that diversity management was used to attract ethnic customers to the bank rather than to advance the quality of working life and career prospects of ethnic minority employees. Boxenbaum (2006) examines how a group of Danish business actors *translate* the American practice of diversity management to a Danish setting. This ethnographic study shows that actors' *interpretations* are strongly based on their individual preferences as well as on pragmatic choices (i.e. available funding) and the local context.

It may seem that researchers in the positivist tradition and the interpretative tradition study the same phenomena. For example, in Dameron and Joffre's (2007) interpretative study, the focus is also on the *impact* of diversity management, as in the positivist tradition inspired studies. Yet the fundamental conceptions of research methodology differ between the two. On the one hand, the important issue for some positivist researchers is the *measurement* of the *effects* of diversity on organizational performance whereas many researchers in the interpretative tradition aim to *understand the meaning(s)* of diversity. When the latter study diversity, they also study other concepts such as sense-making (e.g. how people make sense of the business case for diversity (e.g. Omanović, 2002), managing (cultural) diversity (e.g. Foster, 2005; Foster and Harris, 2005; Subeliani and Tsogas, 2005), ethnic minority women's experiences of stereotypes and views on how they are perceived in predominantly white Western organizations (Kamenou and Fearfull, 2006), understanding teamwork across national and organizational cultures (Gibson and Zellmer-Bruhn, 2001), or identifying shared understandings (Hermon, 1996). In short, interpretative researchers are concerned with 'how' questions. And they produce studies that are both descriptive and empirical.

Additionally, the interpretative tradition, unlike the positivist tradition, treats orderly patterns of diversity as constructed arrangements with latent possibilities that can be transformed. Interpretative researchers believe that diversity is

---

[4] The advisory panels represented diverse groups of employees including African-Americans, Hispanics, and women.

socially constructed through the words, symbols, relationships, and behaviours of organization members. Diversity, in this tradition, is regarded as a negotiated and constructed process. Researchers in the interpretative tradition study processes that underlie diversity management initiatives in organizations by focusing on symbolic actions by which diversity and its management are created/translated, maintained, and changed (e.g. Barry and Bateman, 1996; Gilbert and Ivancevich, 2000; Omanović, 2002). Some research questions in this perspective are: How do organizational members 'do diversity'? (e.g. Omanović, 2002) and How do organizational members 'do diversity' by managing diversity? (e.g. Gilbert and Ivancevich, 2000; Subeliani and Tsogas, 2005).

Organization researchers working in the interpretative tradition do not conceive of the existence of organizations in any specific way because their understanding is that the social world is a continuous process of reaffirmation and change. Organization participants, using language and various activities, construct the idea(s) of the organization. Thus organizations from interpretativists' point of view are understood as socially constructed systems of shared meanings. Unlike researchers in the positivist tradition, most interpretative researchers are interested in documenting the processes of organizational reality construction and experiences of an organization's members in these processes. To study processes, these researchers usually use qualitative approaches (which might be inspired by conventional ethnography) and use different types of empirical material such as interviews (e.g. 'semi-structured', 'in-depth', and/or 'open-ended') and/or nonparticipant/participant observations and archival material. The sampling in interpretative studies generally requires fewer informants and, unlike positivist-inspired studies, makes no claims to representativeness.

Finally, by studying the societal and organizational contexts of diversity, interpretative studies contribute valuable insights into how we understand the complexity of contextual situations where diversity constructions occur. However, while studying diversity and its management as socially constructed phenomena, researchers in this tradition often have a taken-for-granted and static view of the contextual factors (e.g. Dameron and Joffre, 2007 and Foster, 2005) since they are often presented as stable and unchangeable or as facts (see also Boxenbaum, 2006)[5]. Such studies lack sensitivity to the dynamics of change in the context of society and to interactions with other local discourses (organizations, workgroups, individuals). Thus the role of societal and organizational contexts in shaping the constructions of diversity in organizations and vice versa is largely marginalized or ignored.

### *The (critical) discursive tradition(s) – diversity and its management as (organizational) discourse*

Around the turn of this century, organizational researchers began studying diversity as organizational discourse (Litvin, 1997; 2000; 2006; Dick and Cassell, 2002;

---

[5] For instance, in Boxenbaum's study, the democratic decision-making in Denmark (equity among people and their opinions) is uncritically presented by making the assumption that this ethos permeates all aspects of Danish society.

Kirby and Harter, 2002; Zanoni and Janssens, 2004; 2007; Kamp and Hagedorn-Rasmussen, 2004; Jack and Lorbiecki, 2007; Poster, 2008). By discursively analysing diversity and its management – viewing it as a form of social text or a discursive and/or social practice(s) – these researchers analysed the use of language in talk and/or texts.

In one of the first organization studies of diversity inspired by discourse analysis, Litvin (1997) analyses how US organizational behaviour textbooks construct diversity as the essence of a group, drawing upon biology and natural social categories. Litvin explores the organizational consequences of the adoption of such essentialist assumptions about diversity. In a later study, Litvin (2000) extends her earlier analysis to the production of cultural-ideological control in the meanings constructed for diversity and its management in the US. Unlike the positivist and interpretative traditions, Litvin's conceptualization[6] of diversity management is a cultural formation, an ongoing product in interaction and co-production in historical, economic, and social contexts. Litvin shows how the dominant meanings of diversity and managing diversity are discursively constructed and how diversity is taken for granted and naturalized as something that is 'new'. She challenges such constructions by illustrating and claiming that the US workforce has always been diverse. Rather than viewing the current 'problem' of diversity as the result of American workforces becoming more ethnically diverse, Litvin seeks motives and arguments for diversity in the context of the US in the continuing history of power relations and imbalances among racial and other social identity groups.

Other organization researchers inspired by discursive analysis have also examined the discourse of diversity management and its translation: societal and organizational contexts in Denmark (Kamp and Hagedorn-Rasmussen, 2004); resistance to diversity initiatives in dominant and subordinate groups in a UK police force (Dick and Cassell, 2002); national identity and organizational globalization in diversity management initiatives in three British organizations (Jack and Lorbiecki, 2007); the creation and control of orderly patterns of diversity in Belgium (Zanoni and Janssens, 2004); the control of minority employees and active participation by employees in control activities in Belgium (Zanoni and Janssens, 2007). In all of these studies, researchers deepen and vary the problems raised by research inspired by both the positivist and interpretative traditions.

In most research using this framework, diversity and management discourse are studied as social texts which are, for instance, regulatory and controlling (Jack and Lorbiecki, 2007) or they focus on historically constructed regimes of knowledge (Dick and Cassell, 2002) that privilege certain managerial and economic interests (e.g. Kirby and Harter, 2002; Litvin, 2006). For instance, while Jack and Lorbiecki (2007) study the discourse of diversity management, the use of language is not the main subject of their study. They give empirical illustrations of how language provides rules that favour certain aspects of diversity (e.g. 'those who are British') while at the same time watering down others aspects of diversity (e.g. those who 'do not have the "right" background', such as immigrants from China, North Korea, Iran,

---

[6] Influenced, apart from discourse analyses, by critical management studies.

and Iraq). This study provides a good example of a constructivist nature of a managing diversity discourse that has regulatory and controlling characteristics.

Independent of other aspects of diversity, the use of language is central in discursive studies because it is assumed that diversity and its management, as well as different social relationships, are constructed and reproduced by different communicative activities. Therefore, from the discursive viewpoint, identification and knowledge of these activities is important for understanding resistance to diversity initiatives (Dick and Cassell, 2002), in changing existing diversity discourses (Kamp and Hagedorn-Rasmussen, 2004), and in providing alternative understandings of the business case for diversity (Litvin, 2006).

Organization researchers in discursive analysis make particular assumptions about organizations. They view organizations as social systems of shared meanings that are constructed by different forms of communicative activities, inside and outside organizations. By studying different aspects of communicative activities, practices, and structures, researchers collect empirical material that describes how diversity is presented in everyday language. In order to study these aspects of diversity in organizations, researchers usually study conversations and/or interview records (based on 'semi-structured', 'in-depth', and/or 'open-ended' interviews) as well as written, linguistic expressions (such as personnel policies, scholarly and practitioner-oriented books, journal articles, and Internet sites).

In a more critical variant of discursive analysis (CDA), which is, in a few of the studies discussed in this section, primarily based on Foucault's middle or 'genealogical' period (see Knights, 2002), researchers view diversity management initiatives as an example of an organizational discourse that acts as a panoptic structure in working life (Jack and Lorbiecki, 2007) and/or as a way of reproducing or resisting specific relations of power (Dick and Cassell, 2002).

In the CDA, based on an integrative Foucauldian theoretical frame that explicitly incorporates the archaeological and ethical periods in Foucault's work (ibid.), organizations arise, exist, and change because of their power relationships and ideological systems of knowledge. Unlike simple discourse analysis (DA) research, CDA-inspired research views the organization in its socio-cultural, institutional, and political contexts rather than simply as a language activity reflecting different organizational activities, practices, and structures. For these reasons, the view in a Foucauldian-inspired version of CDA allows the study of diversity and organizations as multi-sided, contradictory, and unstable. The focus of analysis in future CDA-inspired studies on diversity in organizations will need to be more explicit on the examination of the relationship(s) between discourse and (disciplinary) power and, as Knights (2002) suggests, on knowledge/truth and subjectivity/ethics (see also Alvesson and Deetz, 2000).

### The critical-dialectic tradition – diversity and its management as a critical-dialectical social-historical process

In several recent conceptual studies on diversity in organizations, researchers have called for more processual research based on intensive case studies of micro politics (Pringle, Konrad, and Prasad, 2006) and longitudinal data (Proudford and Nkomo,

2006) that captures the process dynamic of the workplace (Prasad, 2006) and relationships of power among groups at both macro and micro levels (Di Thomaso et al., 2007). These recent calls for alternative perspectives on diversity, and the critical turn appearing in several empirical, discursive-inspired studies on diversity increase the possibilities for studying diversity in organizations differently.

Influenced by the critical-dialectic view,[7] Omanović (2008) expands, for instance, on critical-interpretative discursive research by showing how the organization of diversity production at a large, manufacturing company in Sweden both prioritizes some ideas on diversity and ignores or marginalizes others. His study focuses on the psychic and social *process* of reality that influences the process(es) of diversity and its management and controls organizational participants. Omanović shows how this process of favouring and marginalizing occurs in the contradictions he discovers in the diversity process, such as opening the door to diversity by using an economic rhetoric that creates expectations of better conditions versus closing the door to diversity by removing some potential conflicting aspects such as unemployment, discrimination, and segregation in Swedish society.

In another study, also influenced by the critical-dialectic view, Omanović (2009) shows that diversity and its management in the US and Sweden are dialectically produced by different parties via a substructural network of relationships. It also reveals how different environments and actors are tightly or loosely linked. The promotion of diversity in different environments (e.g. in literature, organizations, companies and societies, and by policies and programmes) causes conflicts in established s tructures, generates contradictions, and leads to a search for alternative social arrangements and praxes.

In order to examine diversity as *a critical-dialectical social-historical process*, these studies use a methodology inspired by ethnography. This methodology incorporates some elements of a critical orientation in ethnography, such as the focus on diversity in terms of injustices (e.g. discrimination and marginalization) and domination (e.g. particular sectional interests related to diversity). The components of data collection are derived from archival research, in-depth (ethnographic) interviews, and detailed participant observations.

Some interesting research questions in this tradition are: How and why do organizations and their employees produce diversity? Which ideas and interests related to diversity are favoured/marginalized in the process of diversity production? Are there alternative ways to produce diversity, and if so, why are they suppressed? (e.g. Omanović, 2008; 2009).

Similar to the interpretative and discursive perspectives, the critical-dialectical perspective from dialectical organizational analysis (developed by Benson, 1977) views organizations as a part of the social world and always in a state of becoming.

---

[7] Dialectical analysis has its roots in Hegel and Marx (e.g. Marcuse, 1983). A Marxian view of dialectic analysis that is developed and applied by Benson (1977) to organizational analysis (see also, Lourenco and Glidewell, 1975) focuses upon the transformation through which one set of arrangements gives way to another (Benson, 1977). The dialectic is seen as a sequence, where the parties are related as thesis and antithesis and resolve into the form of synthesis (Lourenco and Glidewell, 1975).

A dialectical view also emphasizes, as some critical discursive studies do, that the social production of social reality depends upon the power of various participants, that is, their ability to control the direction of events. Powerful actors can design the organization as an instrument in the service of specific purposes, adjust its directions and/or motivate its participants with certain ends in view (Benson, 1977: 8).

Both in the critical discursive and the critical-dialectic perspectives, researchers problematize the dominant economic interests in diversity that prevail in the studies inspired by the positivist tradition. They argue that this way of studying diversity limits ideas about tensions that exist around this phenomenon such as those related to social welfare, equality, unemployment, poverty, segregation, and discrimination against various minority/disadvantaged groups. The marginalization and suppression of such uncomfortable areas in the management literature enforce the idea that this 'business', 'economic', and 'effectiveness' way of studying diversity is superior and cannot be changed significantly. In that view, the 'objective order of things' – such as economic laws, the marketplace and the like – is an impediment to change.

Unlike the approach(es) used in the CDA-inspired studies, the critical-dialectic approach involves simultaneously all four aspects of the dialectical analysis (social construction, context, contradiction, and praxis). Thus, the focus of analysis is the social processes by which organizational arrangements are produced and maintained as well as the contradictory notion of organizations and their praxes. By studying (contradictory) actions and praxes, researchers identify mechanisms that mediate between contradictions and (eventual) organizational changes. From this perspective, the organization is viewed as a product of past acts of social production and its future direction depends upon the interests and ideas of people in power who can channel the production and maintenance of social formations.

## Summary

This chapter has reviewed the theoretical conceptualizations of diversity by addressing the following question: How is diversity represented in the management and organization literature during the first decade of the twenty-first century? The chapter identifies and reviews four research traditions that address this question. Because of differences between traditions, it is not possible to present a definitive summary statement of researchers' views on diversity in organizations. However, within the four traditions, some points of commonality exist.

As this review reveals, diversity is not a single or simple concept (e.g. the business case for diversity, or managing diversity). Diversity reflects many different ideas and interests that may affect our view of what diversity is or can or should be. Diversity is, in other words, actively constructed. By constructing diversity, researchers directly and indirectly make constructions of what organizations are or might be. In that sense, research is never neutral or objective because the desire for neutrality and objectivity is also a kind of historically developed construction.

Thus, as researchers, we play an active role in the social production of ideas about and interests in diversity, recognizing or ignoring, for instance, contextual influences and the conflicting and contradictory character in diversity social production.

Additional fieldwork in the study of diversity production is needed to allow researchers to contextualize their publications and research projects. The research focus should be on such questions as What motivates us to undertake this research? Why do we choose certain theoretical and methodological perspectives? Are there alternative ways of studying the production of diversity? How may alternatives help establish a critical social consciousness able to penetrate existing ideological (business-oriented) views of diversity? How can different assumptions reveal the effects of power and robust networks that positivists have created, especially in the US literature?

In addition to incorporating the historical character of diversity in future fieldwork research on *diversity production*, it is important to recognize the political nature of all empirical material. In this way, researchers, organizational participants, and others may eventually create ways of presenting the new and various ideas on diversity, which in turn can eventually lead to new and emancipating organizational praxes.

## ACKNOWLEDGEMENTS

For his comments and suggestions, I wish to thank David Knights. Conversations with Marta Calás and Linda Smircich and their suggestions and critique in an earlier stage of working on this manuscript also helped my thinking. Finally, I am grateful to the Swedish Council for Working Life and Social Research and to the Research Foundations (Jan Wallander, Tom Hedelius, and Tore Browaldh) for their support of my research.

## REFERENCES

Alvesson, M., and Deetz, S. (2000). *Doing Critical Management Research*. London: Sage Publications..

Ashkanasy, N., Härtel, C., and Daus, C. (2002) Diversity and Emotion: The New Frontiers in Organizational Behaviour Research, *Journal of Management*, 28(3) 307–338.

Barry, B., and Bateman, T.S. (1996. A Social Trap: Analysis of the Management of Diversity, *Academy of Management Review*, 21(3) 757–790.

Benson, J.K. (1977) Organizations: A Dialectical View, *Administrative Science Quarterly*, 22(1) 1–21.

Boxenbaum, E. (2006) Lost in Translation: The Making of Danish Diversity Management, *American Behavioral Scientist*, 49(7) 939–948

Christian, J., Porter L.W., and Moffitt G. (2006) Workplace Diversity and Group Relations: An Overview, *Group Process and Intergroup Relations*, 9(4) 459–466.

Cox, T. (1994) *Cultural Diversity in Organizations: Theory, Research and Practice*. San Francisco: Berret–Koehler Publishers.

Dameron, S., and Joffre, O. (2007) The Good and the Bad: The Impact of Diversity Management on Co-operative Relationships, *International Journal of Human Resource Management*, 18(11) 2037–2056.

Dick, P., and Cassell, C. (2002) Barriers to Managing Diversity in a UK Constabulary: The Role of Discourse, *Journal of Management Studies*, 39(7).

Di Thomaso, N., Post, C., and Parks-Yancy, R. (2007) Workforce Diversity and Inequality: Power, Status, and Numbers., *The Annual Review of Sociology*, 33, 473–501.

Foster, C. (2005) Implementing Diversity Management in Retailing: Exploring the Role of Organisational Context., *International Review of Retail, Distribution and Consumer Research*, 15(4) 471–487.

Foster, C., and Harris, L. (2005) Easy to Say, Difficult to Do: Diversity Management in Retail, *Human Resource Management Journal*, 15(3) 4–17.

Gibson, C.B., and Zellmer-Bruhn, M.E. (2001) Metaphors and Meaning: An Intercultural Analysis of the Concept of Teamwork, *Administrative Science Quarterly*, 46, 274–303.

Gilbert, J.A., and Ivancevich, J.M. (2000) Valuing Diversity: A tale of Two Organizations, *Academy of Management Executive*, 14(1).

Gilbert, J.A., and Stead, B.A. (1999) Stigmatization Revisited: Does Diversity Management Make a Difference in Applicant Success? *Group and Organization Management*, 24(2) 239–256.

Hambrick, D.C., Davison, S.C., Snell, S.A., and Snow, C.C. (1998) When Groups Consist of Multiple Nationalities: Towards a New Understanding of the Implications, *Organization Studies*, 19(2) 181–205.

Harris, E.W., Tanner, J.R., and Knouse, S.B. (1996) Employment of Recent University Business Graduates: Do Age, Gender, and Minority Status Make a Difference? *Journal of Employment Counselling*, 33.

Harrison, D.A., Price, K.H., and Bell, M.P. (1998) Beyond Relational Demography: Time and the Effects of Surface-and Deep-Level Diversity on Work Group Cohesion, *Academy of Management Journal*, 41(1).

Hermon, M.V. (1996) Building a Shared Understanding and Commitment to Managing Diversity, *The Journal of Business Communication*, 33(4) 427–442.

Härtel, C.E.J. (2004) Towards a Multicultural World: Identifying Work Systems, Practices and Employee Attitudes that Embrace Diversity, *Australian Journal of Management*, 29(2).

Ivancevich, J.M., and Gilbert, J.A. (2000) Diversity Management Time for a New Approach, *Public Personnel Management*, 29(1).

Jack, G., and Lorbiecki, A. (2007) National Identity, Globalization and the Discursive Construction of Organizational Identity, *British Journal of Management*, 18, S79–S94.

Janssens, M., and Zanoni, P. (2005) Many Diversities for Many Services: Theorizing Diversity (Management) in Service Companies, *Human Relations*, 58(3) 311–334.

Johnston, D., and Malina, M.A. (2008) Managing Sexual Orientation Diversity: The Impact on Firm Value, *Group Organization Management*, 33(5) 602–625.

Kamenou, N., Watt, H., and Fearfull, A. (2006) Ethnic Minority Women: A Lost Voice in HRM, *Human Resource Management Journal*, 16(2) 154–172.

Kamp, A., and Hagedorn-Rasmussen, P. (2004) Diversity Management in a Danish Context: Towards a Multicultural or Segregated Working Life? *Economic and Industrial Democracy*, 25(4) 525–554.

Kearney, E., and Gebert, D. (2006) Does More Diversity Lead to More Innovativeness? An Examination of the Critical Role of Leadership. Paper presented at IFSAM VIIIth World Congress, September 28–30, 2006, Berlin, Germany.

Kelly, E., and Dobbin, F. (1998) How Affirmative Action Become Diversity Management, *American Behavioral Scientist*, 41(7) 960–984.

Kidder, D.L., Lankau, M.J., Chrobot-Mason, D., Kelly, A., Mollica, K.A., and Friedman, R.A. (2004) Backlash Toward Diversity Initiatives: Examining the Impact of Diversity Program Justification, Personal and Group Outcomes, *The International Journal of Conflict of Management*, 15(1) 77–102.

Kirby, E.L., and Harter, L.M. (2002) Speaking the Language of the Bottom-Line: The Metaphor of 'Managing Diversity', *Journal of Business Communication*, 40(1) 28–49.

Kirby, S.L., and Richard, O.C. (2000) Impact of Marketing Work-Place Diversity on Employee Job Involvement and Organizational Commitment, *The Journal of Social Psychology*, 140(3) 367–377.

Knights, D. (2002) Writing Organizational Analysis into Foucault. *Organization*, 9(4) 575–593.

Kochan, T., Bezrukova K., Ely R,, Jackson S., Joshi A., Jehn K., Leonard J., Levine D., and Thomas D. (2003) The Effects of Diversity on Business Performance: Report of the Diversity Research Network, *Human Resource Management*, 42(1) 3–21.

Litvin, D. (1997). 'The Discourse of Diversity: From Biology to Management.' *Organization* 4(2): 187–209.

Litvin, D. (2000). *Defamiliarizing Diversity*. Amherst, MA: Isenberg School of Management. (An unpublished doctoral dissertation).

Litvin, D. (2006). 'Diversity – Making Space for a Better Case.' In *Handbook of Workplace Diversity* (A.M, Konrad, P. Prasad and J. K. Pringle, Eds.). Thousand Oaks, CA: SAGE Publications Inc.

Lorbiecki, A. (2001). 'Changing Views on Diversity Management – The Rise of the Learning Perspective and the Need to Recognize Social and Political Contradictions.' *Management Learning*, 32(3) 345–361.

Lorbiecki, A., and Jack, G. (2000). 'Critical Turns in the Evolution of Diversity Management.' *British Journal of Management*, 11 (Special Issue) S17–S31.

Lourenco, S.V. and Glidewell J.C. (1975). A Dialectical Analysis of Organizational Conflict. Administrative Science Quarterly 20: 489–508.

Lynch, F.R. (1997). *The Diversity Machine. The Drive to Change the 'White Male Workplace'*. New York: The Free Press.

Marcuse H. (1983). *Um i revolucija*. Veselin Masleša – Svjetlost, Sarajevo. (Reason and Revolution).

McKay, P. F. (2008). 'Mean Racial-Ethnic Differences in Employee Sales Performance: The Moderating Role of Diversity Climate.' *Personnel Psychology* 61: 349–374.

Mollica, K.A. (2003). 'The Influence of Diversity Context on White Men's and Racial Minorities' Reactions to Disproportionate Group Harm.' *The Journal of Social Psychology* 143(4): 415–431.

Ng, E. S.W. (2008). 'Why Organizations Choose to Manage Diversity? Toward a Leadership-Based Theoretical Framework.' *Human Resource Development Review* 7(58).

Nkomo, S.M. and Cox, Jr, T. (1996). 'Diverse Identities in Organizations' in S. Clegg and C. Hardy (eds), *The Handbook of Organization Studies*. Thousand Oaks, CA: Sage Publications.

Omanović, V. (2002). Constructing the business case for diversity. Paper presented at 'Meeting Ourselves and Others – Perspectives in Diversity Research and Diversity Practices'. Göteborg, Sweden, 29–31 August 2002.

Omanović, V. (2006). *A Production of Diversity: Appearances, Ideas, Interests, Actions, Contradictions and Praxis*. Göteborg, Sweden: BAS Publishing.

Omanović, V. (2008). 'Opening and closing the door for diversity: A dialectical analysis of the process of (social) production of diversity in a large manufacturing company'. Paper presented at EURAM 2008, 14–17 May 2008, Ljubljana and Bled, Slovenia. Track: 'Diversities Influencing HRM'.

Omanović, V. (2009) Diversity and its Management as a Dialectical Process: Encountering Sweden and the U.S., *Scandinavian Journal of Management*, 25(4) 363–373.

Poster, W. (2008) Filtering Diversity: A Global Corporation Struggles With Race, Class, and Gender in Employment Policy, *American Behavioral Scientist*, 52(3) 307–341.

Prasad, A. (2006) 'The Jewel in the Crown: Postcolonial Theory and Workforce Diversity' in A.M. Konrad, P. Prasad, and J.K. Pringle (eds), *Handbook of Workplace Diversity*.,Thousand Oaks, CA: Sage.

Prasad, P. and Mills, A.J. (1997) 'From Showcase to Shadow – Understanding the Dilemmas of Managing Workplace Diversity' in P. Prasad, A. Mills, M. Elmes and A. Prasad (eds), *Managing the Organizational Melting Pot – Dilemmas of Workplace Diversity.* Thousand Oaks, CA: Sage Publications.

Pringle J.K., Konrad, A.M., and Prasad, P. (2006) 'Conclusion – Reflections and Future Directions' in A.M. Konrad, P. Prasad, and J.K. Pringle (eds), *Handbook of Workplace Diversity.* Thousand Oaks, CA: Sage Publications Inc.

Pringle, J., and Scowcroft, J. (1996) Managing Diversity: Meaning and Practice in New Zealand Organizations, *Asia Pacific Journal of Human Resources,* 34(2) 28–43.

Proudford, K.L., and Nkomo, S. (2006) 'Race and Ethnicity in Organizations' in A.M. Konrad, P. Prasad, and J.K. Pringle (eds), *Handbook of Workplace Diversity.* Thousand Oaks, CA: Sage.

Richard, O.C. (2000) Racial Diversity, Business Strategy, and Firm Performance: A Resource-Based View, *Academy of Management Journal,* 43(2) 164–177.

Roberson, Q. (2006) Disentangling the Meanings of Diversity and Inclusion in Organizations, *Group and Organization Management,* 31(2) 212–236.

Roberson, Q.M., and Park, H.J. (2007) Examining the Link Between Diversity and Firm Performance: The Effects of Diversity Reputation and Leader Racial Diversity. *Group and Organization Management,* 32(5) 548–568.

Robinson, G., and Dechant, K. (1997) Building the Business Case. *Academy of Management Executive,* 11(3) 21–31.

Shoobridge, G.E. (2006) Multi-Ethnic Workforce and Business Performance: Review and Synthesis of the Empirical Literature, *Human Resource Development Review,* 5(1), March, 92–137.

Smith W.J., Wokutch, R.E., Harrington, K.V., and Dennis, B.S. (2004) Organizational Attractiveness and Corporate Social Orientation: Do Our Values Influence Our Preference for Affirmative Action and Managing Diversity? *Business and Society,* 43(1) 69–96.

Sub[ce1], S., and Kleiner, M. (2007) Diversity Management in Germany: Dissemination and Design of the Concept, *International Journal of Human Resource Management:* 1934–1953.

Subeliani, D., and Tsogas, D. (2005) Managing Diversity in the Netherlands: A Case Study of Rabobank, *International Journal of Human Resource Management,* 16(5) 831–851.

Thomas, A.D. (2004) *Diversity as Strategy.* Boston: Harvard Business School (EBSCOhost).

Thomas, R.R., Jr (1990) From Affirmative Action to Affirming Diversity, *Harvard Business Review,* 68 107–117.

Watson, W.E., Kumar, K., and Michaelsen, L.K. (1993) Cultural Diversity's Impact on Interaction Process and Performance: Comparing Homogeneous and Diverse Task Groups, *Academy of Management Journal,* 36(3) 590–602.

West, C. and Fenstermaker, S. (1995) Doing Difference, *Gender and Society,* 9(1) 8–37.

Zanoni, P., and Janssens, M. (2004) Deconstructing Difference: The Rhetoric of Human Resource Managers' Diversity Discourses, *Organization Studies,* 25(1) 55–74.

Zanoni, P., and Janssens, M. (2007) Minority Employees Engaging with (Diversity) Management: An Analysis of Control, Agency, and Micro-emancipation, *Journal of Management Studies,* 44(8) 1371–1397.

# 20

# Diversity, Uniqueness, and Images of Human Resourcefulness

Bogdan Costea
*Lancaster University*

## Introduction

This chapter aims to broaden the horizon of inquiry into the relationship between gender (as a core contemporary point of debate) and work from a slightly indirect perspective (what 'indirect' means will be explained in the first section). I will seek to explore the way in which managerialism operates with various dimensions of what appears to make humans 'unique' (such as gender, race, religion, ethnicity, sexuality, and so on) *and* the imperatives of productive work as they have come to be conceived over the last three decades. The chronological overlap between the great emancipatory movements of the twentieth century, their translation into managerial terms such as 'Diversity Management', and the rise of a specific managerial vocabulary (crystallised most palpably under the label 'Human Resource Management') is not, I will argue, coincidental. My point is that a student of management and organisations who wants to understand how work is seen in relation to gender needs to develop a way of grasping the cultural affinities between different elements on the managerial agenda such as: gender (as a key dimension of identity), the relatively recent exaltation of workforce diversity, and what has come to count as human resourcefulness at a time when everybody is exhorted to be 'unique' in terms of 'talent', 'creativity', 'knowledge', etc. – in other words, to be 'individual', self-directed, entrepreneurial, ready to take initiative.

It becomes essential in this line of argumentation to be sensitive to the wider cultural relationships between management and the social imaginaries of popular culture. None of these managerial desiderata are confined to work itself or have even been invented by managerialism; rather they are central to the self-understanding of pop culture in general and such motifs circulate more widely than any other at this particular historical stage. To mention just an immediate example, all the dominant (more or less) reality TV programmes today (*X Factor, American Idol, Britain's Got Talent* and all the other 'talent' shows, as well as *Survivor* or *Big Brother*, followed by the much more interesting recent formats of series such as *Paris Hilton's British or*

*American Best Friend*) have in common the invitation to express individual unique-ness. Pop culture stands for one essential value (amongst others): the affirmation of unique 'individuality' in its self-expressive mode over and against all other potential counter-values centred on self-renunciation in the name of a value outside the 'self' (be it traditional community, nature, or divinity). An important explanatory note needs however to be added at this precise point: the 'self' at stake in popular culture is far from being a solitary, a-social 'self'. Hence, the comment about its central-ity could be easily interpreted as missing a key constituent in the popular cultural process. The fact that this 'self' is very much bound to its social mirrors (various groupings more or less stable) in a narcissistic manner (cf. Lasch 1979), that it is fundamentally 'other-directed' (to use Riesman's effective and prescient category from his 1950 analysis), is something that this argument wants to highlight rather than ignore. In other words, the self-centredness of the 'pop-self' is not one of soli-tude or withdrawal, this is not a 'Romantic' self, but rather one that is essentially performative, one that does not exist outside its own daily performance – this is the 'show off' self of ceaseless searches for public visibility. The sociality of performance in front of ephemeral peer groupings is not however to be confused with the social-ity of traditional community in a Durkheimian sense; rather we are surrounded by what Mestrovic called (following Durkheim and Riesman) a 'post-emotional' crea-ture in a 'post-emotional society' (Mestrovic, 1997).

In brief, what I will try to show is that the managerial idiom of the last three decades is ingeniously attuned to – rather than contradicting – the agenda that lies behind the affirmation of gender, race, or sexuality as key points in the poli-tics of identity. The relationships between diversity management and HRM are far more complex and profound than they are usually credited with. Put simply, the historical level at which this depth of affinity can be located is no more and no less than the fundamental question of modernity itself: the self-assertion of the human subject as the ground of contemporary culture. If we read diversity man-agement and HRM in this key (i.e. as securing a language in which individuality and autonomy are safeguarded) then a new perspective on the power and subtlety of managerialism emerges. And it is this perspective that appears useful in a Handbook dedicated to three of the pivotal components of the process of self-assertion in recent modernity: work, organisations, and gender. It may well be easy to claim to see the failures of all managerial attempts to allow the emancipation of the human subject in its fullness; it is all too easy to interpret all such attempts as covers for capitalism's always deceitful purposes, but it is simply not accurate to overlook the cultural legitimacy and success of these attempts in capturing the social imaginaries characterising Western and global modernity in the last thirty years or so.

## APPROACH

In order to make clearer how this chapter works, it is important to explain here why, in the very first phrase, I used the word 'indirect' regarding the topic of gender. What this is meant to indicate is that in this chapter I am not seeking to approach the topic of gender in itself: I am not asking questions about gender as such – what it might be, how important it is or not, how relevant to understanding work or organisations, and other similar direct problematisations. Rather, I am asking how gender, alongside other elements of the equal opportunities and diversity agenda, plays a role in another set of themes central to the managerial vocabulary today – in the themes that show how subjectivity has become the pivotal object of management over the last three decades or so. I am interested, more precisely, in the expansion and intensification of a particular segment of the managerial vocabulary (of which gender is one part – namely, *Diversity Management*) and its crucial relationships with another, even more crucial segment: *Human Resource Management*. Furthermore, I am interested in the affinities between these themes in managerialism and their wider circulation in popular culture today in order to reflect on how the former functions as part of the latter.

This manner of thinking has a series of consequences. First, it is important to establish what archive has to be considered in relation to the object of inquiry. As stated above, the object of this investigation is managerial *vocabulary* – the way in which management constitutes its discursive territory by elaborating and interlinking various concepts and themes. Hence the sources used here will be *textual*. Management 'texts' come in a broad variety: managerial and non-managerial literature: academic, corporate, or consultancy-oriented; mass media of all types, written or oral, referring to work and non-work; political and legal discourses and practices – as well as others. What they have in common is that they represent the *public spheres* in which managerial discourses are constituted and in which the motifs of diversity circulate and are attached to various social and cultural processes at work. What becomes obvious from this list is that the notion of 'text' is therefore taken in its broadest sense. What constitutes 'text' about diversity, or gender, or work, or identity needs to be seen in as extensive a sense as possible if the nuances of these themes in our culture are to be seized from the viewpoint of the open-minded cultural analyst. In other words, I am actually including in the notion of 'text' more than just the 'written word' preserved somehow. I am including attention to *context* (the occasion or circumstances in which texts or utterances are produced), as well as to '*supra-text*' or the *genre* of a text (is it an academic textbook or handbook, a business magazine article or a blog, a newspaper or a TV item, is it a political speech or a party programme, etc.?). In interpreting managerial discourses it is quite important to pay attention to all such details if we are to appreciate the ways in which certain motifs circulate and echo throughout what Foucault would call managerialism's 'discursive formation' (1972: 31–39). What Foucault's elaborate notion advocates is attention to what is generally captured by the term *inter-textuality* – i.e. the ways in which various occurrences of key notions are linked to each other, reinforce or nuance each other.

Yet by opening up the investigation to this broadest of empirical perspectives, am I not ruling out from the start the possibility to cover the field? Depicted in this way, the empirical domain that I have put before this argument seems endless. The only possible approach is through a reduction of the field to certain representative samples. I will be selecting certain examples with which to illustrate the hypotheses put forward above regarding managerialism and diversity. The plausibility of these illustrations will then be a matter of interpretation on behalf of the reader.

The second important aspect of this investigation which needs a brief explanation is why it is important to take into account the level of detail I am pointing at. The answer is that this chapter is based on a precise variety of cultural functionalism for which Hans Blumenberg's work (1983; 1985; 1987a) is the foundation. Put briefly, the general position of cultural functionalism is that there is nothing in culture that does not have a function, that is not in other words a sense-making device, and that does not have some organic relationship with other aspects of that culture (one good reference for this interpretation of culture is the Encyclopaedia Britannica, http://www.britannica.com/EBchecked/topic/146165/cultural-anthropology/38791/Functionalism-and-structuralism, accessed 14 September 2009). The sense in which Blumenberg's work is a variety of cultural functionalism is specific though. In his view, various central concepts and discourses in a particular society, at a particular historical juncture, have the function of addressing some of the fundamental questions around which that society's main anxieties are revolving (see, for instance, Blumenberg, 1983: 465). In the case of this chapter, I interpret the proliferation of vocabularies of equality, diversity, emancipation, self-expression, self-realisation, and so on, as exemplifying the central positions from which, at this point in historical time, modern man and woman (at a global level) understand their very condition. Hence, Blumenberg would argue, it is important to analyse and understand the ways in which such concepts function as legitimate cultural responses to questions that mark our age (such as discrimination, inequality, suppression of free expression, exploitation, etc.). Elizabeth Brient characterised Blumenberg's cultural functionalism very well as 'dialogical functionalism' (2002: 27–39).

What Blumenberg has to offer in addition is also a way of explaining the movement and replacement of cultural concepts in time. For instance, I will try to show below why it is important to understand the success of 'diversity management' as a conceptual replacement for what used to be called 'equal opportunities' – arguably, 'diversity' opens up a very different horizon of self-understanding than 'equality' because it is capable of evoking something more about who we think we are than equality (which remains a mere premise of freedom but is not freedom itself). Blumenberg calls this struggle for cultural legitimacy between various concepts 'reoccupation of positions' – new ways of framing what is important emerge because existing ones have become unsatisfactory, exhausted (Blumenberg, 1983: 457–482; 1985: 183; 1987b). New concepts take the horizons of interpretation beyond the perceived limits of the old ones.

DIVERSITY VERSUS EQUALITY: USURPATION OR REOCCUPATION?

Blumenberg's historical approach allows me to ask this question: has diversity management simply usurped the agenda of equal opportunities and turned it cunningly into yet another mechanism of exploitation? Or has diversity management – as a new managerial idiom – achieved a different kind of move, a reoccupation of the position of equal opportunities by way of a very significant conceptual mutation?

As analysts (e.g. Kandola and Fullerton, 2001 or Kirton and Green, 2005) tend to situate it, diversity management became an established feature of the management agenda in all types of organisation from around the late 1980s onwards. Its consolidation over the 1990s took the usual forms of the institutionalisation of a new vocabulary: there appeared business textbooks, corporate literature and new systems of practices, accrediting professional associations (such as the Chartered Institute for Personnel Development in the UK, or the Society for HRM in the USA), NGOs (such as the Work Foundation), and management consultancy services. The amount of literature devoted to diversity management is daunting; a very brief list of examples could include: Dickens and Dickens (1991), Roosevelt Thomas et al. (1992, 1999), Adler and Izraeli (1994), Cox (1994), Henderson (1994), Baytos (1995), Golembiewski (1995), Stitch (1998), Fernandez and Davis (1998), Sonnenschein and Bell (1999), Thomas, Gabbros, and Scott (1999), Zemke et al. (2000), Kandola and Fullerton (2001), and Kirton and Greene (2005). Prestigious publishing houses included in their series (such as the *Cambridge Companion to Management*) whole volumes dedicated to the topic (Cambridge's is entitled *Diversity at Work*, edited by Brief, 2008).

In one way or another, something strange seemed to happen in the struggle against various forms of discrimination at work: old and well-established traditions of fight against oppression, injustice, and unequal chances (both from liberal and radical camps – see Jewson and Mason's important paper of 1986) were assaulted and replaced by a strident newcomer with claims not simply to the equality agenda itself, but also to its capacity to add completely new kinds of categories able to address the whole of human subjectivity as an emancipatory goal – diversity management. Moreover, this new way of speaking forcefully redrew traditional lines in the struggle for equality and reallocated the main roles: the 'oppressed' no longer initiated the struggle and claimed the issues; rather managerialism seemed to become the prime guardian and conceptual agent of emancipation in the wake of the legislator's (the state's) extensive interventions.

One of the most direct ways to illustrate what was at stake in this conceptual reoccupation is the title of a famous academic intervention from 1992: Roosevelt Thomas' *Beyond Race and Gender: Unleashing the Power of Your Total Work Force By Managing Diversity*. This title outlines very clearly the conceptual clash in which the discourses of equal opportunities and diversity management were engaged. Except that the idea that this was a 'clash' was one-sided: it was only the defenders of equality as a struggle against oppression that saw it in this light. For diversity management, the equality agenda was not something to be discarded but rather integrated and extended in ways in which only a *non-confrontational* perspective on work and management could outline.

This is where it becomes crucially important to understand why the very concepts of this encounter made it so easily possible for diversity to replace equality whilst keeping hold of the latter's categories at the same time. The terms 'diversity' and 'management' have certain key properties which enable them to overcome some of the limitations of the earlier movements aiming to ensure 'equal opportunities' for all in society and work. *Equal opportunities* implied a prior crisis (of inequality) and an associated acceptance of guilt by institutions for that crisis. What the agenda of equal opportunities pointed to was a series of historical failures to see the human subject of modern civilisation in the proper light of equal access to freedom. Whilst the hard political, social, and cultural struggles for the emancipation of slaves, women, races, or minorities did achieve serious results over the nineteenth and twentieth centuries, the ultimate cultural logic of emancipation characterising modernity – the ideal of self-realisation through self-assertion (Dupré, 1993) – remained difficult to reconcile with these irreducibly collective causes. The ultimate horizon of liberation from the shackles of discrimination was (and is) the modern 'Self' – and this category has always puzzled both liberals and radicals, right and left. It is however the 'Self' who is the central addressee and underlying principle of emancipation. For the 'Self', equality remains the key political and cultural premise – but only a premise. The equality agenda could not 'exhaust' the implications of the twin questions: What is the emancipated self to become? How is it to achieve it?

The space opened up by substantive emancipatory policies towards the end of the twentieth century was indeed welcomed – politicians and corporations, public and private organisations became obliged to safeguard equality as premise of personal freedom and dignity. But the opening required a content, a name for the new horizon of self-realisation at work. And indeed it is precisely into this opening that 'diversity management' steps with its capacity to provide conceptually a legitimate managerial vocabulary that fills the need to give meaning to a new sense of what work might mean: self-affirmation, rather than self-renunciation.

As Roosevelt Thomas' title shows, the content added to the mix is extremely nuanced culturally and needs to be seriously addressed if diversity management is to be understood properly: the use of the word 'total' is quite crucial. It appears as a totalising, controlling move in line with what was usually assumed that management would always do. Yet the 'unleashing of power' that lies within the total identity of the subject at work is a much more subtle move, one in which control over work is actually conceptually redistributed between management and 'workers'.[1] 'Managing diversity, however, is seen as being the concern of all employees, especially managers, within an organisation', argue Kandola and Fullerton (2001: 10, authors of the HR manager's 'manual' for diversity management under the aegis of the UK's *Chartered Institute for Personnel Development*). This is a new relationship: diversity management authors claim its increased ethical legitimacy because diversity liberates individuality from constraining practices.

The sense of 'total' is, I think, to be read in a different key altogether: 'total' indicates a new set of possibilities for conceiving of the human subject at work, a set that would include aspects of subjectivity that were previously either ignored, or even seen as nuisances. Traditional lines of engagement are expanded to *individual subjectivity in general* as a domain of concern for diversity management: 'First, managing diversity is not just about concentrating on issues of discrimination, but about ensuring that all people maximise their potential and their contribution to the organisation' (Kandola and Fullerton, 2001: 9). A good illustration of this extension of understanding is SHRM's definition of diversity:

> At SHRM, we define diversity as the collective mixture of differences and similarities that includes for example, individual and organizational characteristics, values, beliefs,

---

[1] Of course, managers are also workers and it turned out that the new vocabularies of performativity were applied just the same, if not more intensely, to the managerial corps.

experiences, backgrounds, preferences, and behaviors. (source: http://www.shrm. org/Communities/VolunteerResources/Documents/Diversity_CLA_Definitions_of_ Diversity_Inclusion.ppt, accessed September 2009)

The image that accompanies it is even more revealing [Figure 20.1]:

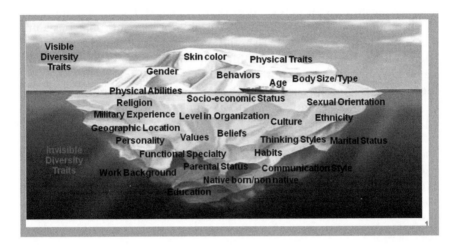

FIGURE 20.1

This version of the well-known iceberg allegory conveys quite clearly what I meant above by the conceptual extension that diversity delivers in comparison to equality, but also the very conscious presentation of diversity *as* an extension. This image aims to mark, with the 'visible'–'invisible' boundary, the superiority of the diversity agenda not just in quantity, but also in the quality of its gestures: these attributes are more or less a depiction of what the US-based Society of Human Resource Management sees as the 'human' in the syntagm 'HRM'. Moreover, this human subject has a particular condition in contrast to the collective subject depicted by gender, race, age, etc.: this is the total individual subject, the *person* treated as *unique*. One of the statements from the CIPD in the UK makes this link clear:

What is diversity?

   People are not alike. Everyone is different. Diversity therefore consists of visible and non-visible factors, which include personal characteristics such as background, culture, personality and work-style in addition to the characteristics that are protected under discrimination legislation in terms of race, disability, gender, religion and belief, sexual orientation and age. Harnessing these differences will create a productive environment in which everybody feels valued, their talents are fully utilised and organisational goals are met.

   CIPD defines diversity as valuing everyone as an individual – valuing people as employees, customers and clients. (retrieved from: http://www.cipd.co.uk/subjects/ dvsequl/general/divover.htm?IsSrchRes=1, May 2009)

This radical reconfiguration of the equality agenda is a major departure whose import will be treated in the next section.

## UNIQUENESS AND THE LIMITS OF HUMAN RESOURCEFULNESS

What does it mean to treat people at work as *unique*, to have a whole conceptual system set up by the HRM profession to deal with the human subject as a unique, unrepeatable entity, for whom work should represent a stage in which that uniqueness should be expressed? How does this view of management's task fare by comparison to F.W. Taylor's view of humans as a homogenised and indifferent factor of production working mindlessly through a set of prescribed operations?

The latter part of the twentieth century becomes representative of a new kind of conceptualisation of the human subject in managerialism. And in this sense, diversity management is attuned to the rest of the body of ideas and images that now populate the managerial domain. In this new language, the idea of uniqueness is not marginal or simply confined to diversity management. It is, in fact, omnipresent. What do I mean? An interesting example comes from Camelot Group's *Diversity Statement* which defines it in terms of uniqueness:

> What is diversity?
> Diversity is valuing everyone as an individual, whether they are an employee, a customer or client, or another stakeholder. Diversity therefore values the qualities, skills and attributes that different people bring to their jobs and to the resolution of problems and business opportunities. It ensures that all individuals maximise their potential and contribution to the organisation. (retrieved from: http://www.camelotgroup. co.uk/crreport2008/files/Policies/IVP23813Diversity_Policy.doc, May 2009)

As I have argued elsewhere (Costea, Crump, and Amiridis, 2007, 2008), the last three decades have been characterised by a turn to the self in management ideas and practices: the main logic and main object of management has become the mobilisation of the human *subject* of work. This cultural economy has the following logic: economic performance has become dependent upon human subjects intensifying their contribution as *whole selves* at work (treated more extensively in Costea, Crump, and Amiridis, 2008). The various voices of managerialism (managers, consultants, academics, media, and popular culture) have produced almost incessantly (since the 1980s) discursive motifs which capture this logic. The list of such tropes is long, dynamic, and unfolding: it started, at first hopefully and fitfully, with 'culture', 'commitment', 'empowerment', 'change', and so on. But then the success of these moves created confidence and the proliferation of such vocabularies has become the staple diet of managerialism: performativity, organisational learning, self-development, HRM, HRD, knowledge work, creativity, innovation, talent, wellness – and so on and on. Overall, managerialism is an invitation to think about work as a site of self-expression, of fulfilment of one's unique potentialities; it links uniqueness with performativity, creativity, learning, innovation, personal well-being, commitment, and participation.

But managerialism does not operate in a cultural vacuum; quite the contrary, uniqueness in the more usual category of individuality ('I am an individual') is *the* mantra of pop culture. No credible proposition in the current cultural context can be made without recourse to individuality. Let me give a very brief but very relevant example of what I mean. This year, Cancer Research UK's awareness campaign about skin cancer ran under the title 'Skindividual' and adopted a 'Glastonbury' approach:

What's it all about?

There's no denying it: your skin is a massive part of what makes you YOU. So your 'skin-dividuality' is something to be proud of and to protect – particularly in the summer.

To make the point, SunSmart – Cancer Research UK's skin cancer awareness campaign – has created the prize of a lifetime open to all those who prize their skin.

The charity will be putting on a free, all-star gig with Ladyhawke, Bombay Bicycle Club and New Young Pony Club – exclusively for one winner and their social network. But the twist is, there's only one ticket and only one way to win. To get your hands on that golden ticket, the winner has to invite more mates than anyone else. The biggest guest list wins. (retrieved from: http://skindiv.com/about.aspx, September 2009)

Under the banner of 'unique individuality', pop culture forces all sorts of dis-courses to seek shelter. Our fascination with our own individuality runs so deep as to even run counter to vital interests (such as the hope that actually our bodies are not that unique and a significant common medicine is possible). Uniqueness becomes the leitmotif of the most improbable cultural areas.

Perhaps this explains the explosion in the last decade of similar vocabularies in the labour market. How else could we explain the cultural functionality of exces-sive job advertising, especially in the graduate market? Bloomberg's presentation of career opportunities at entry level from 2008 read:

We recruit exceptional individuals and students to work in areas ranging from Sales to Software Development, Global Data to News. If your ideal employer is an innova-tive, fast paced entrepreneurial business, Bloomberg is the company for you. We draw everyone together in our determination to thrill customers with the service we provide and, in doing so, we have a lot of fun. Join us and you'll be offered unlimited opportu-nities for training and advancement. You'll contribute to our business from your first day and progress as fast as you're able. Our training is comprehensive and combines classroom and self-study sessions with practical on-the-job learning. To find out more, please visit our career development page. We're continually looking for talented people and have start dates throughout the year, so there are usually no deadlines for entry-level roles. (retrieved from: http://about.bloomberg.com/careers/entrylevel.html, October 2008)

What is at stake in this superlative invitation to work? To whom is it addressed and how? In various forms, *uniqueness* has become somehow central to HRM. The aim to mobilise it has a double cultural function: on the one hand, being a 'unique person' is seen as the basis for accessing hitherto untapped performative potential in the form of creativity, learning, commitment, and more recently 'talent'; on the other hand, the invitation to be 'unique' as a self – and to express that uniqueness – is part of the more general vocabularies of self-realisation through work. In other words, both the person and the organisation stand to benefit from distinct managerial attention to 'uniqueness'.

I would suggest that the links between the idiom of excellence, that of talent and 'exceptional' individuals ought to be brought into focus at this point. This is because the more recent references to the 'exceptional' have affinities with the much deeper performative matrix of the 'search for excellence' and 'total quality'. It is in this specific connection that the image of a unique, 'exceptional' individual as an idealised form of human resource links the accent of diversity management upon uniqueness with performativity. Uniqueness is not only something each individual possesses but also something which calls for its own performance, for its own playing out, for its own 'display' on the stage of work. To 'excel' means to surpass oneself and others, to reach ahead of the actual present, to rise perpetually higher for something which lies outside the realm of the immediate. For this 'talent' is required, sought after and rewarded – but 'talent' obliges the individual to its continuous actualisation in an endless sequence of extra-ordinary working days – at least if the discourse produced by managerialism is to be given serious attention (see Figure 20.2).

FIGURE 20.2

The invocation of uniqueness is interesting because of the specific economy it points to: an extra layer of complexity added by the translation of uniqueness into a certain *excess* of human resourcefulness, an extra level of potentialities of the self at work. It is to these always-posited potentialities (creativity, talent, self-actualisation) that managerialism seeks to give new forms and makes it its task to awaken and mobilise them. These categories also facilitate management's intensified traffic with motifs of pop culture, which has become its hallmark in the 1990s and 2000s. The wide-ranging cultural confidence of managerialism at the dawn of the twenty-first century is what gives cause for legitimate interest in the seemingly unstoppable proliferation of these discourses. What is interesting in this kind of governmental discourse is that it centres itself so much on what might be termed 'utopic human-ism' (cf. Knights and Willmott, 2002) that it manages to pre-empt the inevitable and legitimate charge that it is always already on the way to generate as much insecurity and anxiety as it claims to resolve. The 'self' becomes both the *topos* (source) of unending potentialities as well as its own source of shortcomings (its own *dys-topos*, its own 'ugly' reflection in the mirror of the ideal) – but the self remains the *topos* (place, site) of the resolution of this perpetually circular search for perfection through self-actualisation.

Throughout this chapter, I have been trying to draw attention to the links between uniqueness (as part of the family of diversity management discourses), other mana-gerial concepts such as talent, excellence, performativity, and so on (the figure of the 'exceptional individual' currently invoked by managerial vocabularies), and per-formativity as the search to actualise the excess of potentiality which supposedly lies in every individual. How can we understand these connections? Why are managerial concepts overflowing with attention to what human resourcefulness might possess in excess? How can the complexity of this set of concepts of what elsewhere we called 'infinite human resourcefulness' (Costea, Crump, and Amiridis, 2007) be grasped? I think the superficial answer is not sufficient: it would be all too easy to deploy the tra-ditional supposition of an administrative elite conspiring against a paralysed victim class (both corresponding to a simplistically conceived 'one-dimensional', 'totally administered' world). It seems that something more complicated and significant lies beyond the appearance (albeit seductive) that management is once again caught red-handed in its long-standing attempts to find ways of exploiting labour.

## Concluding Remarks

I will conclude therefore by reiterating the succession of ideas in this argument. The starting point of the whole exercise was the question: what becomes of topics such as 'gender' (but not exclusively) in managerial vocabularies? Addressing this issue from the perspective of cultural history, I tried to present diversity management as a new kind of idiom in managerialism that has come to replace equal opportunities because it brings with it a new kind of symbolism of identity significantly differ-ent from that of 'equality'. Diversity, I argued, stands comfortably alongside other attributes of subjectivity such as creativity, talent, etc. mobilised by managerialism since the 1980s, especially through the consolidation and expansion of HRM.

What is important to understand in this historical episode of conceptual reoccupation is that diversity is a genuine metaphorical innovation; that it does, in other words, take the debate about identity at work onto a new terrain where equality cannot easily follow. In other words, diversity management could swallow the equal opportunities agenda (regardless of whether this is considered detrimental to the latter or not), but not the other way around. 'Diversity' resists being dragged back into the logic of 'equality'; it resists substitution by the previous concept because it has opened up a new horizon of affirmation of identity. And this new horizon corresponds firmly to the modern social imaginary: the generally held value of individual human existence as 'unique' in all respects.

'Uniqueness' is not an invention of diversity management; to the contrary, the individualism of diversity management is a key connection between management and contemporary culture. From 'skindividuality' to 'exceptional individuality', our current self-understanding revolves around 'being unique' as its elementary ground. Especially in management terms, the globalisation of this value (which has become so familiar as to go without saying in all parts of the world) is concretely manifest in most of HRM's practices, from recruitment to reward systems. The vocabulary of uniqueness speaks to a global imaginary shared by all those who seek careers in business – they could not even participate in that game without participating in its imaginary.

Arguably, as far as the history of managerial concepts is concerned, the appropriation of uniqueness is one of the most successful transformations operated by managerialism in its integration of emancipatory programmes. Uniqueness gives name to something very seductive: a permanent excess of potentialities the 'self' always already possesses and for which work is an opportunity of realisation. 'Uniqueness' and 'diversity' carry a surplus of meaning over the idea of 'equality', which has given them the upper hand in the overall evolution of managerialism; they revolve around the belief that there is *in actual fact* a 'special person' inside all of us. Moreover, the cultural-political corollary is that there is a personal entitlement to the belief that such a special, unique place is occupied by each and every 'self'. This is the central politics of pop culture and this is why it becomes complicated to offer a critique of managerialism today as an oppressive regime of self-interpretation. In its successful reaching for various motifs of pop culture, managerialism has developed its recent repertoire in such a way that its discourses tempt significantly with the image of an infinite remainder/repository of human resourcefulness that lies hidden in us all and that makes us different, unique, special.

This argument cannot however end at that – diversity management is not a resolution of the human condition. Not at all. It is simply the reiteration of a profound cultural crisis – the fundamental crisis of modern man and woman: the inability to articulate what the human subject is, what identity is as a structure of being – and it is the derecognition of this fundamental emptiness that actually becomes the basis of affirmation of the subject *as if* it was the repository of endless qualities. The struggle of managerialism, and especially of HRM, stems from this far more essential plane; hence, 'managerialism' cannot be simplistically accused of always expressing somebody else's 'interests'. It does in a fundamental sense express what the modern subject is in itself: forever empty, forever a 'project', forever seeking fillers for that emptiness, forever insecure and thus ever more expansive. Because it does not have an ethical core, a character, the 'self' is perpetually expanding the demands for the recognition of its 'lack' as fullness . . . and managerialism delivers an endless set of props in the play.

# REFERENCES

Adler, Nancy J., and Izraeli, Dafna N. (1994) *Competitive Frontiers: Women Managers in a Global Economy.* Oxford: Blackwell.

Baytos, Lawrence M. (1995) *Designing and Implementing Successful Diversity Programs,* Prentice Hall.

Blumenberg, Hans (1983) *The Legitimacy Of The Modern Age.* M.I.T. Press.

Blumenberg, Hans (1985) *Work On Myth.* M.I.T. Press.

Blumenberg, Hans (1987a) *The Genesis of the Copernican World.* M.I.T. Press.

Blumenberg, Hans (1987b) 'An Anthropological Approach to the Contemporary Significance of Rhetoric' in Kenneth Baynes, James Bohman, and Thomas McCarthy (eds), *After Philosophy: End or Transformation?* Cambridge, MA: MIT Press, 429–458.

Brief, A. (2008) *Diversity at Work.* Cambridge: Cambridge University Press.

Brient, Elizabeth (2002) *The Immanence of the Infinite: Hans Blumenberg and the Threshold to Modernity.* Washington, DC: Catholic University of America Press.

Costea, Bogdan, Crump, Norman, and Amiridis, Kostas (2007) Managerialism and 'Infinite Human Resourcefulness': A Commentary upon the 'Therapeutic Habitus', 'Derecognition of Finitude' and the Modern Sense of Self, *Journal for Cultural Research,* 11(3) 245–264

Costea, Bogdan, Crump, Norman and Amiridis, Kostas (2008) Managerialism, the Therapeutic Habitus and the Self in Contemporary Organising, *Human Relations,* 61(5) 661–685.

Cox, Taylor (1994) *Cultural Diversity in Organizations: Theory, Research and Practice.* Berrett-Koehler Publishers.

Dickens, Floyd, and Dickens, Jacqueline B. (1991) *The Black Manager: Making It in the Corporate World.,* AMACOM.

Dupre, Louis (1993) *Passage to Modernity: An Essay in the Hermeneutics of Nature and Culture.* Yale University Press.

Fernandez, John P. and Davis, Jules (1998) *Race and Rhetoric: The True State of Race and Gender Relations in Corporate America.* McGraw-Hill.

Foucault, Michel (1972) *The Archaeology Of Knowledge.* London: Tavistock Publications.

Golembiewski, Robert T. (1995) *Managing Diversity in Organizations.* University of Alabama Press.

Henderson, George (1994) *Cultural Diversity in the WorkPlace: Issues and Strategies.* Greenwood Publishing Group, Inc.

Jewson, N., and Mason, D. (1986) The Theory and Practice of Equality Policies: Liberal and Radical Approaches, *The Sociological Review,* 34(2) 307–334.

Kandola, R., and Fullerton, J. (2001) *Diversity in Action: Managing the Mosaic.* London: Chartered Institute of Personnel and Development.

Kirton, Gill, and Greene, Anne-Marie (2005) *The Dynamics of Managing Diversity: A Critical Approach.* 2nd edn. Amsterdam: Elsevier.

Knights, D., and Willmott, H. (2002) 'Autonomy as Utopia or Dystopia' in M. Parker (ed.), *Organization and Utopia.* London: Sage.

Lasch, Christopher (1979) *The Culture Of Narcissism: American Life In An Age Of Diminishing Expectations.* New York: Warner Books.

Mestrovic, Stjepan G. (1997) *Postemotional Society.* London: Sage.

Riesman, David. (1950) *The Lonely Crowd: A Study of the Changing American Character.* New Haven: Yale University Press.

Roosevelt, Thomas, R. (1992) *Beyond Race and Gender: Unleashing the Power of Your Total Work Force by Managing Diversity.* AMACOM

Sonnenschien, William, and Bell, Arthur H. (1999) *The Diversity Toolkit: How You Can Build and Benefit from a Diverse Workforce.* Contemporary Books

Stitch, A. (1998) *Breaking the Glass Ceiling: Sexism and Racism in Corporate America The Myths, Realities and the Solutions.* Warwick: Warwick Publishers.

Thomas, David A., Gabbros, John J., and Tap Scott, Don (1999) *Breaking Through: The Making of Minority Executives in Corporate America.* Boston: Harvard Business School.

Thrift[ce1], N. (1997) 'The Rise of Soft Capitalism', *Cultural Values,* 1: 29–57.

Zemke, Ron, Raines, Claire, and Filipczak, Bob (2000) *Generations at Work: Managing the Clash of Veterans, Boomers, Xers, and Nexters in your Workplace.* AMACOM.

# Section Five

## GLOBALIZATION AND GENDER IN/AND MANAGEMENT AND ORGANIZATIONS

### EDITORIAL INTRODUCTION

**Globalization.** What does globalization mean? A great many things (see Calás and Smircich, this volume). In recent decades, journalists and scholars have exposed the devastating effects of colonial exploitation of vulnerable parts of the planet by various super powers. Colonial forces often controlled and exploited indigenous peoples and their resources and, upon departure, left behind language, cultural, political and economic practices, and other influences that negatively affected the lives of the occupied peoples. A burgeoning international trade made it possible for material goods and practices to 'migrate' from one culture to another, fostering a global form of homogenization in, for example, music, ideas, activities, and economic practices. Labor migration, particularly in Europe in the past half-century (and elsewhere), brought less affluent individuals and families to work in more affluent nations where, often, they were (and are) treated as 'visitors,' more than as bona fide citizens with guaranteed rights and privileges.

In recent years, multinational corporations have assumed ever more influence on global relations and dynamics. They regularly avoid the constraints of national boundaries by operating in multiple nations and shifting from site to site to avoid taxes and regulation. One might argue, as some have done, that multinational corporations are more powerful than any but a few national states. Recent actions in the world of finance reflect a system of global capitalism that no one is 'in charge of' but that affects everyone, not always advantageously. Finance capitalism, according to some commentators, is one of the more destructive features of current economic practices. Obscure financial instruments such as derivatives and the ability of large banks to make risky loans and then 'hedge' against their possible failure have placed both private and public resources at risk.

Global politics have flourished since the Second World War. Transnational organizations such as the World Bank, International Monetary Fund, International Labor

Organization, North Atlantic Treaty Organization, United Nations, European Union, and G7, among others, exercise extensive influence on nation-states and also on the media and other forces as well. (Both Woodward and Casey, in this Section, address the role of transnational organizations relative to gender equality.) These organizations have created a 'global society' that, economically and in other respects, is characterized by increasing levels of interdependence. Events and conditions in one part of the world quickly affect other parts, as the 'Great Recession' of 2009–2010 did. Global wars, e.g. those led by the US against Iraq and Afghanistan, and joined by personnel from many world regions, have brought together people from many nations and regions to use their combined force to occupy and/or control. Many poor African nations torn by internal strife have representatives of other nations on site (e.g. in the form of the military) to help restore order and avoid destructive conflicts.

The rapid industrialization of China (and to a lesser extent India) is exacerbating concerns about climate change. Multinational meetings about climate change to discuss goals and options are now held at frequent intervals (one held in Denmark in 2009 was attended by representatives of 140+ nations). Concerns about clean air and water and the potentially devastating effects of pollution combined with global warming continue to bring national and international leaders together to consider alternatives. Even poverty and the AIDS and 'Swine' flu epidemics are global phenomena, hardly limited to a single nation or world region. The 2010 earthquake in Haiti and the financial straits of Greece, Ireland, Portugal, and Spain have sent shudders up the collective spine of the developed world. Additionally, there were the tragedies associated with global corporate violations by, for example, Union Carbide in Bhopal India in 1984 (resulting in thousands of deaths due to gas poisoning) and Coca Cola's use of water in India that left small farmers unable to water their crops. Furthermore, recent efforts by some religious groups to promote a world vision where religious leaders rule have taken on a global character.

Results like these indicate that globalization is complex and many-faceted. Lest we sound too pessimistic, we hasten to add that not all aspects of globalization are negative. Improvements in medicine and public hygiene have contributed to better health in many nations. At the same time, however, drug companies often deprive poorer subjects in the developing world of medical cures because of high prices and their demand for profits. The ability to engage in transcontinental travel adds to the education and pleasures of people who can afford to do it. Yet through tourism, it also exports the dominant Western (particularly US) culture globally and has the effect of adding to the problems of global warming. Extensive use of telephones and the Internet enable easy contact among friends, family, and associates in diverse world regions. Radio, television, and films have increased the rate at which awareness of fashions, music, and ideas circles the globe.

And, yet, Barbara Czarniawska (2002) cautions, things that 'migrate' do not assume identical form upon arrival at their destination (cf. Connell, 2007). Locals often 'do their own thing' with global phenomena and transform them into something other than what their creators or initiators envisioned. Czarniawska calls local transformations of global influences a process of *glocalization*, recognizing that phenomena from elsewhere are regularly altered according to local cultures and customs. This dynamic no doubt characterizes principles of organizational change that feminists have used to initiate and support gender equality. Chapters by Woodward, Casey, and Sasson-Levy in this Section show that the diffusion of gender equality practices is both uneven and uncertain.

All chapters in this Section question the effects of globalization on gender equality, offering grounds for both celebration and concern. On the good news side, analyses by Woodward and Casey of transnational organizations' support of gender equality initiatives in recent years are heartening. While progress is uneven, multiple transnational bodies have stepped up to support formal policies and practices for women's fair treatment. Sasson-Levy, in contrast, paints a less positive picture. While formal policies on women's participation in military organizations worldwide have become more inclusive, women are still marginalized and denigrated, leaving the military institution's 'extreme masculinism' intact. Sasson-Levy is also pessimistic about the likelihood that this situation will improve substantially in future years.

Calás and Smircich point out limitations in the management/organization research regarding global transnationalism that prevent the realization that transnational flows permeate organizational life. They borrow the conceptualizations of 'transmigrants' and 'transnational social fields' from transnational migration studies to reposition examples of organizational literature and highlight what they are missing. Everyone is now a 'transmigrant' of sorts, they argue, that is, actors whose daily lives depend on interconnections across international borders and whose identities are articulated in relationship to more than one nation-state. Through participating in work assignments in other nations and through traveling, using telephones, Internet/email, and other such means to span the globe, everyone is creating new negotiated spaces that transgress the nation-state, which they call 'transnational social fields.' Through our actions as editors of this Handbook, for example, we help to create a transnational social field with complex 'back and forth' dynamics between our respective localities of origin and academic specialties, genders, and race/ethnicities. Hopefully, our efforts will contribute to changed ways of thinking about gender, work, and organization and about who the important actors in these contexts are. Because transmigration processes are fundamentally gendered/sexualized, racialized, ethnicized, and classed, transmigrants do more than adjust to 'new locales,' they also change them and create new spaces for action in their 'back and forth.' Calás and Smircich challenge scholars to pay attention to these spaces, attending to the multiplicity of actors that create and populate them beyond the elite, (mostly) white, and (mostly) men who appear as the 'cosmopolitan' or 'local' actors in the transnational management/organization literature.

Chapters in this Section thus conclude that global gender equality is far from assured (see also, J. Martin, this volume). Current global economic processes threaten to undermine progress and the unfettered dominance of forms of capitalism that devalue women's work and 'chains of care' is a critical concern. As a result, efforts to institute alternative economic systems will be difficult. Additionally, power relations in the new media and the ability of religious fundamentalists to get across messages about gender (particularly women's inferior status) challenge progress on gender equality both in organizations and in national and international realms. We now summarize the chapters. The first two focus on transnational organizations that have promoted gender equality around the globe.

Alison Woodward ('International Organizations and the Organization of Gender') reports on four major transnational intergovernmental organizations (IGOs) that have acted since the 1970s to promote gender equality. She focuses on two issues: (1) the extent to which intergovernmental accords forged through international agreements improved women's work conditions globally (with the chapter documenting how they were achieved); and (2) the extent to which international organizations practice what they preach, including how they have dealt internally with gender inequality and multinational diversity, issues that IGOs routinely face.

IGOs that were targeted by women's movements around the globe responded by supporting a range of gender equality initiatives. Marshalling evidence from two primary sources – international gender scholars who have consulted for these organizations and international relations specialists who have documented the impact of international organizations on national policies (including the methods of policy-making employed) – Woodward shows how IGOs fostered improvements in women's status nationally and internationally and attempted to improve gender equality in their own ranks. Treaties and agreements reached in the United Nations, International Labor Organization, Council of Europe, European Union, and World Bank helped to forge goals and norms aimed at improving women's status.

The international process, reflecting interaction between states and gender activists at national and international levels, led to three key developments. IGOs became important standard setters in promulgating laws and collecting comparative statistics on the position of women; IGOs redefined issues in ways that focused on women's contributions to the economy and highlighted the problem of violence against women; and IGOs helped bring women into contact with each other and created institutions to support them. Woodward concludes that the United Nations' family of organizations has been more successful than most at promoting women's welfare, although all of the above-named organizations have produced progress on gender equality, and she is cautiously optimistic about the transformative role IGOs can play in future to improve women's status around the globe.

Catherine Casey ('Toward Gender Equality in European Union Labour Markets: Achievements and Contemporary Challenges') reviews the actions of the European Union (EU) on gender equality policies and enforcement for three decades (1975–2008). She shows that they enacted many action programs and legislative initiatives aimed at fostering gender equality across all industry and occupational sectors in EU member states. Major EU milestones toward gender equality included the use of 'hard law' such as European Council Directives and also 'soft law' which is enacted through an Open Method of Coordination (OMC), especially through the European Employment Strategy. Casey demonstrates that the single most important piece of legislation – the 1975 Directive on equal pay – was quickly followed by the 1976 Directive calling for equal access to employment and the 1978 Directive promoting equal treatment in social security and pension schemes.

Casey emphasizes the development of the European Employment Strategy (EES) which has been operative since the late 1990s. The EES adopted an explicit strategy for mainstreaming gender in order to make gender equality prominent in all aspects of employment policies and practices. EES initiatives linked gender equality in employment with wider social goals such as social justice and women's full societal equality and citizenship participation, efforts that have gained attention and admiration worldwide. While progress had been made, especially in regard to women's labour market participation, Casey worries that the EU's current emphasis on liberalized economic policies for reform and growth may undermine past gains and prevent further progress. She regrets the EU's policy emphasis, since 2005, on competitive economic development and liberalized employment strategies which may undermine efforts to achieve gender equality goals.

A further challenge to advancing gender equality arises from the recent expansion of the European Union. Until the mid-2000s, the EU had 15 member states but by 2007, the total was 27. Casey is concerned that cultural, social, and employment customs and gender regimes in some newer EU states may impede EU-wide progress, although the EU's 'road map for equality between women and men 2006–2010' (European Commission 2006) proposes to 'accelerate progress toward real equality.' Gender equality is still on the EU's agenda but commitment to this goal in many member states appears to be weak. Under these conditions, Casey says, it is unclear if the Open Method of Coordination which uses 'soft' rather than 'hard' methods of achieving gender equality will produce concrete results and hoped-for progress.

Orna Sasson-Levy ('The Military in a Globalized Environment: Perpetuating an 'Extremely Gendered' Organization') reviews the impact of global processes on military gender regimes and assesses their success in generating gender equality. Focusing on military organizations and cultures in the late twentieth and early twenty-first centuries, she reports on women's entry into the military in varied ranks and positions. She argues that the global shift in the past decade away from *mass armies* toward *professional militaries*, together with decisions made by national and transnational courts, have resulted in dramatic changes in the gender structures of Western militaries. Nonetheless, despite many changes, the militaries' fundamental gender regimes, cultures, and identities have remained resistant to women's unfettered participation.

The gender regimes of western militaries are shaped globally by decisions of transnational courts and also the imitation of larger militaries by smaller ones. Critical decisions by such transnational organizations as the European Union Court of Justice and the North Atlantic Treaty Alliance (NATO) have affected many nations' military policies and practices. For instance, a lawsuit by a German woman in 2000 (over the right to work in a combat unit) prompted the European Court of Justice (ECJ) to order all EU states to have gender-equal policies in their military organizations. In response, Germany eliminated its policy forbidding women's service in certain roles and, by 2009, Denmark, Belgium, the Czech Republic, Norway, Luxemburg, and Spain also placed no restrictions on women's participation. And yet, women constitute only small minorities within most military organizations and they are regularly excluded from higher ranks, combat positions, and submarines. Israel is one of a few nations that conscript women, although many considerations can excuse women from serving (pregnancy, religiosity, and more). Worldwide, military women continue to be assigned to *feminine* jobs such as secretary, nurse, or counselor. Also, men's sexism in the form of sexual harassment and sexual assault are ongoing, even as governments decry and forbid such behavior (see also Hope, this volume).

Due to these conditions, Sasson-Levy depicts the military as an 'extremely-gendered institution.' Extreme masculinity and masculinism are so ingrained, she says, that legal and social pressures for change cannot alter them very much. The equation of masculinity/masculinism and men with the 'military' has the effect of marginalizing and denigrating women. It appears that 'gender integration,' meaning the entrance of women into men's exclusive (military) domain, constitutes a threat to hegemonic definitions of masculinity and to men's control over weapons, policies, and violent force. Military organizations' informal culture and interactions thus enforce gender distinctions that undergird men's dominance and foster their resistance to women's full participation. While early proponents of a 'new' globalized military said it would be better for all, including women, research fails to confirm this claim.

Marta Calás and Linda Smircich ('In the Back and Forth of Transmigration: Rethinking Organization Studies in a Transnational Key') argue that transnational relations under contemporary conditions of globalization are based on mobility across time and space, not only crossing boundaries between established places but also creating new spaces and relationships. Notions of 'home' and 'not home' are no longer appropriate for understanding what is going on. Thus, they extend the concepts of *transmigration* and *transnational social fields* as contemporary transnational processes which attend to the potential formation of new hierarchical relations in these spaces and, concurrently, to the formation of new relevant actors within them.

Calás and Smircich ask: Who are the relevant actors in a transnational organizational world so conceived? Where are they found? They argue that a shift in perspectives within organization studies, including recognizing the formation of new historical actors, may be needed before these questions can be answered. They ask us to rethink ourselves as transmigrants who are involved with transnational flows of all kinds – people, money, ideas, images – so we can see how we link our world of origin with our world of arrival and help create transnational spaces which are, at once, comprised of emerging and negotiated gendered/sexual, racialized/ethnicized and classed identities and relationships. Guided by theoretical perspectives from transnational migration studies and transnational feminism, they posit that transnational spaces are not equivalent to nations or contained by national boundaries but are formed in transnational mobilizations linking and re-linking social relations across borders, between those who move and those who stay. Thus, it is no longer possible to differentiate among local, national, transnational, and global connections.

To illustrate their observations, Calás and Smircich assess organizational research which, in their view, conceals transmigration processes as well as actors within these processes. Repositioning the actors in these literatures as transmigrants who act within and between gendered/ethnic/classed social fields, they examine examples in three areas: (1) transnational entrepreneurs; (2) diversity; and (3) new modes of expatriation. They show that transnational entrepreneurs, often discussed as 'born-global,' are explained as a homogeneous group that reaches out transnationally to gain competitive advantage. This depiction fails to note variations among them that result from their gender, ethnic transnational networks, and social location in the countries where they operate. By contrast, transnational migration studies have documented all this, and could provide better explanations.

On *diversity*, they note that the literature often focuses on the *adjustments* of ethnic migrants to their host-country's conditions while failing to explore migrants' ongoing relations to their home countries, that is, they fail to consider them as transmigrants. As a result, the literature homogenizes these populations as 'ethnic transplants,' shedding more light on the host country than on the transnational processes and relationships the immigrants may be enabling. Regarding the third area, they maintain that the literature on *new modes of expatriation* ignores what happens in transnational spaces – that is, in transnational social fields, where many gendered and classed processes are at play. These processes are enacted by actors who disappear or are glossed over by such notions as 'family issues' and local practices in countries of origin that reduce women's participation in transnational activities. The literature also fails to note the appearance of new actors, e.g. 'nannies,' who emerge as part of the requirements of elite transnational mobilizations.

At the end, Calás and Smircich emphasize that opening space for conceptualizing all organizational activities as occurring within transnational social fields will mitigate the dominance of managerial elites as organizational actors, a dominance that is supported by the ideological principles of neoliberalism. Meanwhile, when conceptualized as transnational actors, populations of all kinds are given voice in these activities. Research in transnational social fields will provide organization theory with ways to articulate the centrality of gender/sexuality/race/ethnicity/class relations in invisibly sustaining modalities of neoliberal globalization. And, more importantly, it can provide ways to address the complicity of organization theorizing in the co-construction and exploitation of gender/sexuality/race/ethnicity/class relations worldwide.

## References

Connell, R.W. (2007) *Southern Theory: The Globalization of Knowledge in Social Science.* Cambridge and Boston: Polity Press.

Czarniawska, Barbara (2002) *A Tale of Three Cities or the Glocalization of City Management.* Oxford: Oxford University Press.

# 21

# International Organizations and the Organization of Gender

ALISON E. WOODWARD

*Institute for European Studies, Vrije Universiteit Brussel*

The global order is a gendered order where organizations and individuals operate at multiple levels to shape our lives. The economy, polity, and civil society are increasingly organized beyond the boundaries of the nation-state by international and transnational organizations ranging from Coca Cola and the European Union (EU) to Greenpeace. Raewyn Connell (2008) argues that such organizations should be examined because they are both the product of gender relations and the producer of gender effects through multilevel and complex interactions. Connell's call for a gendered analysis of the multiplex of global institutions is only beginning to be followed (Hearn, 2004; Rai and Waylen, 2008). There is some attention to gender in multinational enterprises, but the powerful international political organizations often escape the gendered lens.

It is particularly worthwhile to concentrate on intergovernmental organizations (IGOs). As associations of countries, they act as supra-states to shape norms and produce policies that constrain and form markets, define peace and security, and proclaim universal values of human rights. Virtually no area of life escapes being monitored and regulated by one or another IGO. We should address them in gendered terms 'if we want . . . to prevent war and genocide, to slow down global warming, to pursue social justice or even to make a small increase in public understanding of what is going on' (Connell, 2008: 238). IGOs occupy a special place in any discussion of gender and organizations because they have played a crucial role in deciding the rules of the economy, changing the place of women in employment, and cajoling governments and organizations to confront the role of gender in their operations and policies.

IGOs are both a target and a tool. They are a target for protest against injustice, violence, and inequalities and for policy demands for improvement. They can be a tool that works oppressively (as in the International Monetary Fund and World Bank's restructuring plans (Harcourt, 2005)) or they may provide instruments for emancipation and autonomy and the norms for a gender-friendly state (Borchorst and Siim, 2008; Bergqvist et al., 1999). Finally they can serve as a fascinating object for organizational study because of their special characteristics of multinationality, their international civil servants, and their bureaucratic heritage.

This chapter examines the role of intergovernmental organizations as *organizations* acting to promote gender equality and producing gender orders internally and externally. After defining the unique features of intergovernmental organizations, it reflects on how contributions from gender and organization research help illuminate IGOs as producers and reproducers of gendered orders. It also discusses the role IGOs have played in organizing other organizations. International accords on gender equality have been important for work conditions and organization globally by promulgating standards and promoting women's rights while working for improvement of women's status. IGOs frequently lack sanctioning power but they have normative power. Thus their own behavior needs to be exemplary in order to embody the principles they promote. The chapter concludes by sketching the extent to which IGOs have practiced what they preach and developed new ways to promote gender justice in situations of multinational diversity. These organizations *as organizations* provide important examples of the role of gender at work and its interaction with other forms of identity including national identity. While much of what we know about gender and organizations is relevant to IGOs, much comparative research waits to be done on these important transnational actors.

## INTERNATIONAL ORGANIZATIONS – DEFINITIONS AND PERSPECTIVES

International organizations can be divided into two types, those formed by governments and those formed by private initiative (Reinalda, 2009; Rittberger and Zangl, 2006; Karns and Mingst, 2004). *Intergovernmental organizations* (IGOs) aim to achieve goals shared by the member governments. *Non-governmental organizations* (NGOs) aim to achieve the goals of their founders or their members. Business or economic organizations dominate those formed by private initiative. The most well-known and studied are trans- and multinational enterprises, (multinational corporations or MNCs) since business and finance make up the lion's share of internationally organized activity. Although international non-governmental civil society organizations (INGOs) such as the women's movement have an important voice in shaping international norms, the focus in this chapter is primarily on IGOs.

IGOs are created by treaties signed by states and include three or more members. Their organizational design aims to achieve goals set out in charters or covenants subscribed to by the member governments (Archer, 2001). IGOs tend to be coordinated by a secretariat structured in an extremely formal and hierarchical manner. These secretariats and their departments and divisions carry out the tasks assigned to them by national member states. Staff members are usually international civil servants recruited in a highly regulated fashion, often including competitive examinations (Udom, 2003). In contrast to many MNCs where the management team may be composed of people from different nationalities while the local level workers usually share nationality, IGOs frequently require national diversity at all levels of organization. Paradoxically this multinational personnel is expected to leave their passport at the door and be bound by the principles of internationalism and universalism.

These broad characteristics cover a variety of organizations ranging from the globally dominant UN family to small regulatory agencies with one staff member. Depending on the strictness of definition, there are from around 250 to more than several thousand IGOs in the world (Reinalda, 2009). IGOs have grown exponentially since the founding of the UN in 1945 (Karns and Mingst, 2004) although growth slowed in the 1990s (Pevehouse et al., 2004). Recent IGO growth has been primarily among regional organizations such as the EU (McGrew, 2000: 141) or emanations from other IGOs. As Barkin says, IGOs are not only expanding, but reproducing (Barkin, 2006: 36).

The major IGOs were set up at a time when formal bureaucracy and scientific management were considered the most efficient and fair way to administrate. The UN and the EU began in the 1950s before there was a whiff of human resource management, let alone the idea that a public administration could be 'managed.' The organizational form of the UN with its dominant position has been the model for other IGOs; although the EU also attempted to imitate the best features of the top civil services of the founding members (Page, 1997; Stevens and Stevens, 2007).

IGOs have influence in part through their socialization role as teachers and communicators and in part because they can claim legitimacy. In fact, being bureaucratic organizations *per se* invests them with rational-legal authority. IGOs' ability to reach their goals is related to the extent 'to which they are recognized as experts in a given issue area and the extent to which they are considered impartial' (Joachim et al., 2008: 11). Barnett and Finnemore underline the fact that 'international organizations are not only established by states to solve problems and pursue collective interests but also to help define these problems and pursuits' (2004: 31). Supra-state organizations have created arenas and 'most intergovernmental organizations have encouraged NGOs and transnational movements to participate directly or indirectly in their deliberations as a way to legitimate their authority or acquire much needed expertise' (McGrew, 2000: 147). The areas of human and women's rights show how social groups lobby to push their specific definitions (Keck and Sikkik, 1998). Through the back and forth of international conferences, the UN Decade for Women, and UN Women's World Conferences, the women's movement gradually moved from being outside the process to being influential in shaping the debate. Dorsey claims that 'few movements have ever had such success in using the resources, forums, legitimacy and agencies of the UN to advance their strategies' (Dorsey, 2005: 436) but it is a two-way street.

IGOs need an image of fairness to achieve goals. Yet it is the very rational and legal arrangements of the bureaucracy which IGOs borrowed from the national civil services which provide a key element of the gender critique of IGOs and the hate–love relation that gender equality advocates have with it. The international civil service (ICS) shares some characteristics with public bureaucracy, such as recruitment on competence and merit through formal and transparent procedures, hierarchical structure and promotion practices and the pledge of neutrality in service of the public good. However, the ICS also has unique features. It needs to be a 'representational' bureaucracy in terms of geography while also asking staff to deny their national identities inside the organization. Udom notes that from the beginning of the twentieth century the international civil service mentioned 'men and women' (due to lobbying by women to put an article in the League of Nations Covenant in 1919: Reinalda, 1997: 205). He acknowledges that gender balance has not been achieved, although he does not analyze how elements in the principles for the international service may in their supposed neutrality produce gender bias.

## IGOs and Gender

Both their organizational form and mission link public bureaucracies inextricably with gender relations and gender politics. What makes them particularly important is their potential power to maintain the status quo or promote change. While there is little extensive investigation of the gendered operation of IGOs, a number of approaches within gender and organization research are applicable. As bureaucracies, the literature on feminism and bureaucracy is relevant. Studies that investigate how organizations produce and reproduce masculinities, femininities, and gender (in)equalities also have great relevance. Finally work on states as actors and targets for gender politics helps to explain when the international state has nonetheless been gender-friendly.

### Public bureaucracies: gender neutrality or men's rules?

Most formal organizations 'were set up by men, for men and run by men's rules' (Ely and Meyerson, 2000: 23). The feminist critique of bureaucracies as privileging men and being based on a man's body and life is fundamental to the analysis of gender in organizations (Acker, 1990; Martin and Knopoff, 1999). In radical feminist analysis, the apparatus of the state and its forms were seen as major actors in the oppression of women because they shored up patriarchy (MacKinnon, 1989). The most obvious reflection of organizations as male bastions is the predominance of men in powerful positions. For organizations purporting to be agents of democracy, they look undemocratic when it comes to gender (Paxton, 2008). Women's presence in politics is important (Phillips, 1995). The demand for more women in decision-making, bolstered by the critical mass theory (Kanter, 1977; and Celis, 2008, for a review) became widespread and was first directed at electoral politics. To be democratic, women needed to be descriptively present. The same demand was placed on public bureaucracies where women were absent, although the argument that bureaucracies needed to be 'descriptively representative' was controversial due to beliefs about the requirements of 'neutrality.'

If women's representation in the upper levels of civil service systems in most democratic countries is low, in international bureaucracies it is lower. Since top functions in national bureaucracies and diplomatic corps often have few women, women's chances of a high status international career are limited. Compounding the factors that inhibit the rise of women generally are issues similar to those affecting women in international management, including stereotyping and problems in terms of work/family, dual careers, and trailing spouse issues.

Besides low representation of women, state bureaucracies were criticized because of the nature of bureaucracy itself. As seen above, the bureaucratic and 'bias-neutral' structure of IGOs is important for their legitimacy. Research on gender and public bureaucracies showed that rules were far from gender-neutral. Seen through a gender lens, every rule, from function description and job requirement to merit promotion and hierarchical organization, can produce gender inequality. Ferguson (1984), studying American social welfare agencies, framed bureaucracies as incapable of achieving feminist goals. A cornerstone of the state bureaucratic model is 'neutral recruitment and promotion' based on merit but research since the 1980s has demonstrated that few actual rules are gender-neutral and that bureaucratic criteria actually favor men and men's lives (Burton, 1987). Examinations demonstrated the masculine bias of supposedly 'neutral' rules of bureaucracy, set up to put neutral round pegs into round holes (Martin and Knopoff, 1997). Witz and Savage (1992), Halford (1992), and Halford and Leonard (2001), deconstructed the features of Weberean bureaucracy, demonstrating step by step how supposedly neutral and rational logic is shot through with androcentric assumptions which make gender equity difficult to achieve. Joan Acker's (1990; 1992; 2006) path-breaking work identifies organizations as sites where gender is reproduced in both public and private organizations. The implication was that bureaucracies may have to be abolished for gender parity to be achieved (cf. Britton, 2000: 422) although calls for more feminist theory on this continue (Bearfield, 2009).

For such reasons, many women's movement actors do not trust the state or its organizations. Hester Eisenstein (1995; 1996) analyzes the complexities of bureaucrats' relations with the state by exposing the reasons for an outsider strategy and noting the paradoxical possibilities to work within the structure for positive change (she labels 'inside feminists' as femocrats). Other analyses of public organizations suggest that the relation between feminist goals and gender and bureaucratic organization are not black and white (Billing, 1994). Franzway et al. (1989) argued that public organizations bring forth a variety of masculinities and femininities and thus offer the potential to use this variety to foster positive change.

## Hegemonic masculinities

Organizations are not only people and rules but they are also practices and processes. Theories about how femininities and masculinities are produced in IGOs are also highly relevant to understanding the international organization of gender. Field work in international organizations such as the EU (Woodward, 1996) suggests that multinational interactions often produce masculinities that exclude or otherwise fail to help women. The military, the primary tool of the classic modern state, produces a narrowly defined version of men and masculinities (Enloe, 1989; 2007; Morgan, 1994) and tends to cast women in a 'less than full citizen' role (Sasson-Levy, this volume). But the state in international relations is also an important producer of manliness to the extent that one can talk about dominant forms of masculinity (Hooper, 2001).

Masculinities are produced in organizations, between men and over the heads of women, as Martin's observations suggest (2001; 2003). Christine Beasley (2008) shows the interlocks between multiple sites of the gender production using Connell's argument that local, regional, and global hegemonic masculinities co-exist. These intersect in the interactions and interdependencies of governmental entities in IGOs which in turn produce and/or regulate aspects of a global gender order (Connell, 2005). In the case of IGOs, the production of masculinities and femininities occurs in interaction with various national gender models. Staffs are recruited from the bureaucracies of national governments, and structures are copied from one organization to another (DiMaggio and Powell, 1983). The traditions of international diplomacy and the subject matter of conflict, war, and peace have been male terrains until recently and the kinds of masculinities that this history has produced are highly relevant for understanding how IGOs are gendered in ways that fail to help women.

## *Public bureaucracies, states, and IGOs: tools for gender equity?*

Although international state systems are sites for the promotion and production of masculine hegemony they are also contested. Research on the gendered state was motivated in part by a desire to examine the potential of the state to improve gender equality. The state can be a tool for change thanks to its need to respond to democratic demands (Eisenstein, 1996), but to be legitimate, the state needs to be exemplary.

Given that women are underrepresented in decision-making, and given the strident critique of the state by feminists, *using government as a tool* was not a self-evident strategy. Yet even though civil society movements of the 1970s and 1980s were highly critical of the state, there was nonetheless a liaison between women inside and outside many state organizations (Sawer, 1990; Reinelt, 1995), At all levels of the policy process there were interactions between politicians, women's movement activists, and civil servants with feminist agendas (femocrats) in formalized consultations (Outshoorn, 1997) combined formalized and informal interactions (Snyder, 2006) or informal feminine governance structures – the so-called Velvet Triangles of women-identified-women inside and outside of the state (Woodward, 2004). Pressures and coalitions of actors at the international and national level led to the constitution of women's policy machineries in governments dedicated to improving the status of women, as well as soft and hard measures to advance gender equality. The development of national organs promoting an improvement of the status of women cannot be understood outside the architecture of the international system of IGOs (Reinalda, 1997: 204).

## INTERNATIONAL ORGANIZATIONS ORGANIZING GENDER

Even if the international system can hardly be seen as fully gender-friendly, it has been targeted by women as a place to obtain help in equality struggles. The normative and sometimes binding actions of IGOs have definitely improved the lives of women in working life and society (Meyer and Prügl, 1999; Hawkesworth, 2006;

Pietilä and Vickers, 1996; Rai, 2003). IGOs have been major players in the struggle for gender equality and the creation of a global women's movement (Desai, 2006; Ferree and Tripp, 2006). Through their reporting mechanisms and global conferences, IGOs have made women visible by demanding disaggregated statistics. They have exposed government positions, created networks and equality architecture (such as women's policy machineries), and designed new tools such as gender mainstreaming and budgeting while driving forward agreements that have resulted in legislation at regional and national levels.

In three ways, IGOs have also positively affected other organizations. First IGOs are important as *standard setters*. Although some member states may be ahead of IGOs, the identification of standards can inspire others to improve. In the last 50 years, the IGO system (particularly the UN family) has forged common ambitions for gender equity. We can identify achievements in terms of standards such as equal treatment (leading to measurement as equal pay for work of equal value) and non-discrimination, both of which are fundamental for women's empowerment. In setting standards, IGOs have also been active in a second way – by reconceptualizing *problems* and *launching new agendas* that could not be seen without new concepts or a radical revisioning of old concepts (Verloo and Lombardo, 2007). IGOs as normative gender entrepreneurs have transformed definitions of human rights and politics. While these definitions may be contested (Bacchi, 1999), they have moved the goal posts globally for how women and men are treated. For instance, in looking at development, the unpaid work of women is now included. The transformation of the definition of 'human' rights to include gender (that is, woman's rights *are* human rights) opened the door to seeing the gendered aspects of violence in war.

Finally, a third set of impacts on gender equity entails creating and supporting *actors and institutions*. The process of discussing and drafting policy through the system of UN world conferences (Stienstra, 1994) and the inclusion of women in conferences on the environment, human rights, and population (Chen, 1995; 1996) can be credited with helping establish a transnational women's movement (Dorsey, 2005). IGO activity through conference preparation and consultation requirements has provided meeting places for women and others to share ideas. Member states are affected by this process as well. The formal requirements of transposing, implementing, and evaluating policy have forced member states to create and charge formal organizations while attending to women's issues and women's policy machinery.

### Standard setting and three stages of equality policy

International standard setting about gender has been a matter of very slow change often described in variations of three stages (Squires, 2007; Rees, 1998; Reinalda, 1997; Hoskyns, 1996; Mazur, 2002; Walby, 2005). First came the demand for formal recognition of equal rights and equal treatment, reflecting the aims of liberal feminists. Recognition of the inherent problems in non-discrimination led to a second phase of policies for equal opportunities, affirmative action, and a space for women's specific needs. The third stage included a horizontal approach of addressing the production of gendered inequalities in all parts of the policy process using gender mainstreaming.

(i) Prime examples of equal treatment legal frames important to gender in organizations are the long-standing ILO accord on equal pay for work of equal value (Discrimination (Employment and Occupation) Convention 1958 (No. 111), Equal Remuneration Convention 1951 (No. 100), Workers with Family Responsibilities Convention 1981 (No. 156), and the Maternity Protection Convention 2000 (No. 183)). This also made its way into the Treaty of Rome of the European Union in 1957 which ultimately resulted in European Union's Equal Treatment Directives in the 1970s. Every firm that does business with the EU, companies involved in a country that is part of the WTO, and workers of the world are affected by the norms enshrined in these treaties.

(ii) The second strategy goes beyond equal treatment. It is aimed at eliminating discrimination and reaching equal outcomes. It can be seen as a product of second wave feminism and the first UN World Conference on Women (1975) which resulted in the United Nations Convention for the Elimination of Discrimination against Women (CEDAW, 1979).

While the ratification and implementation of CEDAW seems to be an endless task, there are concrete results in the fight against discrimination. In 1993, Marta Calás and Linda Smirich began an article imagining a situation where employment advertisements would specifically address both women and men, people of color, the disabled, sexual minorities, of all faiths, and said that this was a utopian dream. Today, such advertisements are reality in much of the EU thanks to international treaties including non-discrimination laws that have been transposed into national laws as well. The need to measure equal opportunities led to the creation of monitoring bodies specifically for women, while the lack of progress has generated adoption of various affirmative action plans.

(iii) The third phase launched a redefinition of the problem by focusing on the social construction of sex and gender. The Beijing Platform for Action (1995) considered all areas of society and mandated the mainstreaming of a gender equality perspective in all policy areas. Even though it was an intergovernmental agreement focusing on the policy-making process, the gender mainstreaming approach calls for examining all areas of organizational activity and contributes to the production of gender equity. It was not only applied to IGOs but also to trade unions and many workplaces.

## Redefinitions

Snyder (2006) notes that there is often an underestimation of the role of IGOs in shaping the context of legal rights for women. Women's distinctive needs and experiences were formerly excluded when international law and its remedies were developed. 'Gender pressure' led to a redefinition of basic concepts such as 'Human Rights' that now explicitly includes Woman's Rights (Johnstone, 2006). The idea of development was initially 'woman-free,' but women were gradually included. Thanks to the understanding of the concept of gender, today both women and men are implicated. These understandings have become widespread thanks to the arenas that have been fought for and infiltrated via international interaction (Joachim, 2003; 2007).

Examples of redefinition include recognition that violence has a gendered face. The Vienna UN Conference on human rights in 1993 put violence against women on the global agenda (Peters and Wolper, 1995). In December 1993, The United Nations adopted the Declaration on the Elimination of Violence Against Women and, with that step, the international community acknowledged its global dimensions. The victory of seeing rape in war *not* as collateral damage but as *war crime* against women (International Tribunal in The Hague, 2001 and UN resolution 1820 voted in 2008 (Harvey, 2008)) is a vital instance of redefinition. Zippel's (2006) study of how reconceptualizations of sexual harassment as violence, as a health issue, and/or as discrimination led to increased protections for women workers also offers an example of how international fora provide platforms for creating and strategically shifting problem definitions to advance gender justice. Seeing sexual harassment not only as violence but as an infringement on one's freedom to earn a living changes how we see the world. The IGO level provided alternative venues for voices that were not heard at the national level and the back and forth process between national, regional, and supranational levels helped spread new ideas about the sources of gender inequality, including how to recognize and challenge it. One fundamental achievement was a redefinition at the global level of economic development to include women's roles in the evaluation of development aid and, more broadly, to consider how a gender perspective affects the conceptualization of gender mainstreaming (United Nations Office of the Special Advisor on Gender Issues and the Advancement of Women, 2001). Gender was also addressed in analyzing global progress and the Millennium Goals linking women to the elimination of poverty and hunger. While gender is not everywhere in public policy, the new millennium is substantially different for women, in part thanks to changes promoted by IGOs and diffused to their member states (Gray et al., 2006; Hawkesworth, 2006).

## Actors and institutions

A particular dynamic in the redefinition process above was the addition of new voices that coincided with the addition of many new member states to the UN system leading to the breakthrough of the women's movement globally. The strong growth of the global women's movement '. . . was in large part made possible by coopting the UN as its unlikely godmother, using the power of its blessing to influence the policies and programs of major global and national institutions and to build new institutions' (Snyder, 2006: 45). Thanks to IGOs, women became informed about their government's official stance and more knowledgeable. The hate–love relationship between feminist critics and the state developed into a sort of symbiosis after the 1970s as the state increasingly became an effective weapon to advance women's status. Participation in governmental processes and lobbying led to a professionalization of women's movements so that they became less 'movement' and more 'organization' than before, producing what we today call transnational social movement organizations (Smith, 1999).

A second element that helps assure the longevity of gender justice efforts is the proliferation of the policy machinery inside and around governments in the form of administrations, consulting, and advisory bodies. A 1995 volume edited by Stetson and Mazur called the phenomenon 'State Feminism' which continued to spread, even if a replication (Kantola and Outshoorn, 2008) indicates some stagnation today. A study by True and Mintrom (2001) of 157 countries after Beijing note the unprecedented diffusion of new bureaucratic entities and procedures to deal with women's issues. In less than three decades, virtually all countries had responded to pressures to earmark an architecture for gender, even though, as Squires notes, suspicion among some about the 'bureaucratization of feminism' remains (2007: 33). To feed the policy machinery and measure progress and processes, information about women, from their health to their presence in decision-making, has proliferated. Today, we have far more refined international indicators of the status of women (UN Gender and Empowerment Index, Human Development Index), providing powerful tools to use in arguing for improvements.

## GENDERING INTERGOVERNMENTAL ORGANIZATIONS

The challenges for IGOs are not only about promulgating policy to others, but also about their own shop. IGOs were forced into self-reflection thanks to feminist challenges. An analysis of the gender record of IGOs must be twofold: including first the internal gender order and second the activities of the organization. What is the progress on improving the number and situation of women members of international organizations and what impact has the discussion on gender mainstreaming had on IGOs' policy-making?

### Advancement of women inside IGOs

The UN has always been rhetorically sensitive to the issue of the representation of women in its own ranks. A commitment to gender equality is underwritten by the Universal Charter of Human Rights from 1948 in one of the first paragraphs (ILO, 2008: 2). Multiple subsequent declarations on eliminating discrimination and conventions that mandate policies to promote gender equality exist. Other IGOs are also committed on paper to gender equality. The International Civil Service Commission (ICSC) began issuing recommendations on gender balance in 1985. The EU set up an inter-service board of union representatives and employers to collect statistics about women's employment and conditions (COPEC – Comité paritaire pour l'égalité des chances) in the late1970s and the EU Commission (see Casey, this volume) dates its formal equal opportunities personnel policy from 1988.

From the 1970s onward, the UN General Assembly produced proclamations supporting equal opportunities for women in the UN system. It explicitly recognized the need for gender balance in staffing in resolution 2715 (XXV, 1970) calling for appropriate action to ensure equal opportunities to qualified women in senior and other professional positions. Beginning in 1976, the UN Chief Executives Board for Coordination across the United Nations system reported gender disaggregated data annually for all organizations of the United Nations common system (UN Office of the Special Advisor on Gender Issues, 2007/2009: 16). The UN consistently set high targets for the representation of women at all levels of the system without managing to reach them. The run up to the Beijing conference of 1995 seems to have been crucial for consolidating efforts around representation (Friedman, 2003). While the UN General Assembly in 1986 set a target of 30% women to be reached by 2000, in 1995 this goal was moved to 50% for the year 2000 in line with the goals of the Beijing Platform for Action of parity in decision-making. Unfortunately, reality has led to the General Assembly's move away from a specific target date to the phrase to be achieved 'in the very near future' (adopted in 2004; UN Office of the Special Advisor on Gender Issues, 2007/2009: 23) Experts called in to analyze the situation concluded in 2007 that:

> [t]he United Nations is one of the world's foremost norm-setting bodies. To truly promote gender equality around the world, the Organization must first abide by the high standards it has set. As the statistics demonstrate, the United Nations has not yet attained its goal of 50/50 gender balance at all levels. (UN Office of the Special Advisor on Gender Issues, 2007/2009: 43)

Frustration over the relative lack of progress in improving representation and the gender climate in IGOs drips from the report. It notes that the efforts and recommendations to improve the situation have been going on for more than three decades while the target remains unmet.

The same naming and shaming setting of standards that is employed to bring their member states to perform better in policy issues is being used within the IGO community regarding gender equity. Table 21.1, published in the European Commission 4th Action Programme for Equal Opportunities, shows wide variation in the percentage of women in management functions, with the EU occupying a relatively poor position. The worst situation is in organizations devoted to hard science such as the Atomic Energy Commission.

Most of the surveyed UN organizations (UN Office of the Special Advisor on Gender Issues, 2007/2009) documented efforts to change to increase the percentage of women in upper positions. However, efforts to improve the representation of women throughout the organization and flexible policies such as the possibility of working part-time or being able to take sabbaticals and 'care leave' are not necessarily accepted with open arms. Although the majority of UN organizations (UN Office of the Special Advisor on Gender Issues, 2007/2009: 22–23) as well as EU organizations have adopted such policies, a survey of European Commission officials, a very large international bureaucracy, revealed that people thought their career progress would be harmed if they took advantage of family-friendly measures. Additionally there is a significant gap between men and women in the perception of the role of personal networks in promotion and the extent to which women have equal opportunities to get ahead (Research voor Beleid, 2007).

Recent self-analyses by the ILO (2008), EU (2004), and UN system (2008a, 2008b) reveal a failure to appreciate how family social networks relevant for child care, or geographic distance from aging parents may interfere with women's careers.

TABLE 21.1 Representation of women in the workforce for selected agencies as of 31 December (data generated 11 June 2003) (A newer version of this table may be available).

| | | Summary Total Professional Workforce[1] | | Detail: % Women | |
|---|---|---|---|---|---|
| | | %Women | #Women | Management[3] | Professionals excluding Management[4] |
| 1 | UNFPA[2] | 46,5% | 79 | 41,7% | 56,4% |
| 2 | UNESCO[5] | 46,0% | 443 | 28,6% | 54,6% |
| 3 | UNICEF | 45,5% | 842 | 36,1% | 49,4% |
| 4 | UNAIDS | 41,1% | 69 | 30,0% | 57,4% |
| 5 | UNHCR | 40,9% | 661 | 23,1% | 44,0% |
| 6 | WFP[6] | 40,8% | 410 | 30,6% | 44,2% |
| 7 | World Bank Group | 40,0% | 2 307 | 23,2% | 46,3% |
| 8 | UNDP | 39,0% | 577 | 33,0% | 42,6% |
| 9 | International Fund for Agricultural Development | 38,5% | 92 | 22,0% | 40,0% |
| 10 | Inter-American Development Bank | 36,6% | 479 | 14,7% | 41,0% |
| 11 | ILO[7] | 36,3% | 255 | 24,4% | 50,6% |
| 12 | UN | 35,6% | 1 905 | 30,2% | 37,1% |
| 13 | European Bank for Reconstruction & Development | 34,1% | 215 | N/A | |
| 14 | World Health Organisation | 32,7% | 461 | 24,8% | 42,2% |
| 15 | IMF | 31,2% | 598 | 15,2% | 34,8% |
| 16 | European Commission | 29,5% | 2 824 | 15,4% | 32,1% |
| 17 | Organisation for Security & Cooperation in Europe | 29,3% | 415 | 9,0% | 30,0% |
| 18 | OECD | 29,2% | 248 | 13,0% | 33,0% |
| 19 | Europesn Investment Bank | 27,5% | 189 | 10,4% | 33,2% |
| 20 | ADB | 27,5% | 217 | 6,2% | 31,0% |
| 21 | European Space Agency | 26,9% | 359 | 14,9% | 34,5% |
| 22 | WMO | 23,7% | 28 | 15,0% | 25,5% |
| 23 | UNIDO | 22,5% | 56 | 13,0% | 29,0% |
| 24 | International Atomic Energy Agency | 18,4% | 184 | 9,4% | 22,0% |

1 Internationally recruited staff (excludes staff with appointments of less than 12 months); with input from ORIGIN fact sheets.

2 UNFPA core staff only.

3 For agencies in UN common system, management consists of P.5 and above; UNICEF management also includes representatives at all levels – P.4–D.2.

4 For agencies in UN common system, consists of staff in P.1–P.4.

5 Figures for UNESCO from 1 April 2003.

6 ALDs included only in total number of women in professional workforce, e.g. column 1 and 2 (breakdown by grade and sex not available).

7 Funded by regular budget (this excludes 293 staff on technical cooperation in professional and higher categories).

*Source:* EUROPEAN COMMISSION DG ADMIN (2004) *Fourth Action Programme for equal opportunities for women and men at the European Commission 2004–2008.* p. 16

Issues around stereotypes, multinational sexism, and male bonding are also not dealt with directly. The situation for women who work in international public sector organizations and the roadblocks for representation of women at all levels of the organization, share significant commonalities with women in international corporate management (Adler, 2002; 2006). Roadblocks for women in international management such as the immobile male spouse, concerns about elder and child care, and cross-national societal stereotypes and prejudices also confront women in IGOs. Although research demonstrates that women diplomats and civil servants are equally as ambitious as men and are as willing to move, stereotypes about women still impede their progress. Additional hurdles for women in public service are the link between the masculine world of diplomacy (Neuman, 2008) to military and security issues, underlining the assumption that it is a man's world (Elias, 2008). It is as tough (and perhaps tougher) for a woman to rise to the top of an international organization as it is to become a CEO of a corporation.

The International Civil Service Commission and a group of experts examined the UN system in late 2007 and 2008 and found a spotty and uncoordinated picture of gender equity initiatives. In one survey by the UN, only 30% of the organizations in the system had a score card to measure their progress on required gender equality plans (United Nations, 2008a: 15). The monitoring of career progression, including results and accountability, is missing. While agencies are required to report on their progress, poor results have no consequences for management if they fail to do so. Accountability, which has been an essential feature in successful gender equality operations in the private sector, is missing in the UN family. As a result, much remains at the level of 'ringing declarations.'

## Gender mainstreaming

Finding comparative evidence on the second aspect of gendering international organizations, viz, the extent to which the organizations attempt to carry out gender mainstreaming in their activities, is difficult. *Gender mainstreaming* (GM) as a strategy was launched by the UN in Beijing. Governments and other actors were asked to promote an active policy of mainstreaming a gender perspective in all policies and programs (see Casey, this volume). The majority of IGOs developed, often in collaboration, their own operationalization of gender mainstreaming (Verloo, 2005; Rees, 1998; True, 2003). The EU in particular made an early commitment to it, in 1996, thus earning positive reviews from, among others, Hafner-Burton and Pollack in 2002. A GM approach aims at transforming the policy process and attempts to do this horizontally using persuasion and socialization. Today Hafner-Burton and Pollack (2009) and Woodward (2008) are more pessimistic. Nearly 15 years after the UN conference that launched the gender mainstreaming strategy, only limited evidence shows gender activity as having spread successfully beyond the offices that were already concerned with it, such as the Directorate General working on Employment, Social Affairs and Equal Opportunities. Only 27% of the 41 EU services studied by Hafner-Burton and Pollack mention women or gender in relation to their policies in their annual reports. Incorporating a gender perspective in agriculture or foreign affairs requires strong incentives, they argue.

So far, little research compares IGOs in terms of producing gender-sensitive policy as envisioned by the gender mainstreaming strategy. One of the few studies, by Hafner-Burton and Pollack (2002), compared the implementation of gender mainstreaming in the World Bank, the United Nations Development Program (UNDP), the Organization for Security and Cooperation in Europe, and the EU. They underline the effects of organizational, structural, and environmental characteristics on the way gender mainstreaming is applied. Weaver (2008) argues that gender mainstreaming is at its most effective when officials have a sufficient period to internalize a gender perspective. Hafner-Burton and Pollack (2009) on the other hand argue that hard incentives are necessary for real action and chalk up the gradual improvement in women's representation in EU management to the hard incentives in Equal Opportunity policies. Gender mainstreaming shows little progress, and this is due to lack of force.

While the concept of gender mainstreaming came out of a process steered by IGOs, it seems that it is very hard to apply the principle to their own activities and begin to use all their policies and not just social policy to pursue gender equality.

## FURTHER RESEARCH

It is unfortunate that more research on IGOs in relation to gender has not been done. Apart from reports prepared by the institutions themselves, there is a shortage of studies of intergovernmental organizations as places of work and as organizations, even though such settings offer a 'natural laboratory' of national diversity. Qualitative case studies examining the production of gender relations and gendered policies and the dynamic intersections of nation and gender at different levels of organizations are urgently needed. The lack of scholarly efforts to illuminate not only the UN system but other intergovernmental and non-governmental international bodies is striking. A number of paths for further research could prove useful.

We need more comparative work along the lines of Hafner-Burton and Pollack's 2002 study on the progress of IGOs toward transforming their organizations by bringing their practices in line with a gender mainstreaming approach. Is it the case that only administrations directly connected with gender issues succeed in questioning and improving their policies relative to gender equity? While IGOs help set the rules for operation of private business, business organizations may provide good practices for the world of public service to emulate. Since genuine gender equity is essential for achieving believability when trying to convince recalcitrant countries to improve the situations of their own women, IGOs need to become better students. We need studies of the impact of having proportionally more women in IGO/INGO bureaucracies. Substantial research exists on the impact of having more women in electoral politics but only minimal information is available on the impact of more women in bureaucracies, let alone in international organizations. Some studies of public servants (Keiser et al, 2002: 562; Dolan, 2004) indicate that diversity of people in public bureaucracies has positive effects for both clients and policies. We need more and better studies that look into changes that different equality initiatives have had on the gendered nature of IGOs and their effects on their members, their target audiences, and society.

## CONCLUSIONS

IGOs have accomplished much by setting standards related to gender equity and providing stimulus for women's fight for gender justice. In terms of accomplishing goals of representation and the integration of women across all activities, they have done some work but they need to do more in order to live up to the standards they set for others. Despite a long-standing official commitment to gender equality, many IGOs are far from gender-friendly workplaces according to their own reporting. Even agencies such as UNESCO have made relatively minimal progress in addressing gender concerns. Reports produced by internal and external experts show as many failures as successes for more than 30 years after the first UN decade for women. The processes of gender production in relation to ameliorative policies and the politics of implementation are under-researched. Also, questions about how the forms of masculinity that are favored in international diplomacy and the civil service impact on the interests of women in a world increasingly affected by global governance need investigation. International organizations play a critical role in global governance and their role in producing gender inequality and potential for advancing an equality agenda needs to be spotlighted and subjected to intensive review.

## REFERENCES

Acker, J. (1990) Hierarchies, Bodies and Jobs: A Gendered Theory of Organizations, *Gender and Society* 4 (2) 139–158.

Acker, J. (1992) 'Gendering Organizational Theory' in A.J. Mill and P. Tancred (eds), *Gendering Organizational Analysis*. Newbury Park: Sage, 248–260.

Acker, J. (2006) *Class Questions, Feminist Answers.* Lanham and Boulder: Rowman and Littlefield.

Adler, N. J. (2002) Global Managers: No Longer Men Alone, *International Journal of Human Resource Management* 13 (5) 743–60.

Adler, N. J. (2006) 'One World: Women Leading and Managing Worldwide' in D. Bilimoria and S. K. Piderit (eds), *Handbook on Women in Business and Management.* Cheltenham: Edward Elgar Publishing, 330–356.

Archer, C. (2001) *International Organizations,* London, Routledge.

Bacchi, C. L. (1999) *Women, Policy and Politics.* London: Sage Publications.

Barkin, J. S. (2006) *International Organizations: Theories and Institutions.* New York: Palgrave Macmillan.

Barnett, M. and Finnemore, M. (2004) *Rules for the World: International Organizations in Global Politics.* Ithaca: Cornell University Press.

Bearfield, D. A. (2009) Equity at the Intersection: Public Administration and the Study of Gender, *Public Administration Review* 69 (3) 383–86.

Beasley, C. (2008) Rethinking Hegemonic Masculinity in a Globalizing World, *Men and Masculinities* 11(1) 86–103.

Bergqvist, C., Borchorst, A., Christensen, A.-D., Ramstedt-Silén, V., Raaum, N. C., and Styrkádóttir, A. (eds) (1999) *Equal Democracies? Gender and Politics in the Nordic Countries.* Oslo: Scandinavian University Press.

Billing, Y. D. (1994) Gender and Bureaucracies: A Critique of Ferguson's 'The Feminist Case against Bureaucracy', *Gender, Work and Organization* 1(4) 179–193.

Borchorst, A., and Siim, B. (2008) Woman-friendly Policies and State Feminism: Theorizing Scandinavian Gender Equality, *Feminist Theory* 9 (2) 207–224.

Britton, D. M. (2000) The Epistemology of the Gendered Organization, *Gender and Society* 14(3) 418–434.

Burton, C. (1987) Merit and Gender: Organisations and the Mobilisation of Masculine Bias, *Australian Journal of Social Issues* 22 (2), 424–435.

Càlas, M., and Smircich, L. (1993) Dangerous Liaisons: The 'Feminine-in-Management' Meets Globalization, *Business Horizons* 36 (2) 164–180.

Celis, K. (2008) 'Representation' in G. Goetz and A. Mazur (eds), *Politics, Gender and Concepts: Theory and Methodology*. Cambridge: Cambridge University Press, 71–93.

Chen, M. A. (1995) Engendering World Conferences: The International Women's Movement and the United Nations, *Third World Quarterly* 16(3) 477–493.

Chen, M. A. (1996) 'Engendering World Conferences: The International Women's Movement and the UN' in T. G. Weiss and L. Gordenker (eds), *NGOs, the UN, and Global Governance*. Boulder: Lynne Rienner, 139–158.

Connell, R. (2008) A Thousand Miles from Kind: Men, Masculinities and Modern Institutions, *The Journal of Men's Studies* 16(3) 237–252.

Connell, R. (2005) 'Globalization, Imperialism and Masculinities' in M. S. Kimmel, J. Hearn and R. W. Connell (eds), *Handbook of Studies on Men and Masculinities*. London: Sage, 71–89.

Desai, M. (2006) 'From Autonomy to Solidarity: Transnational Feminist Struggles' in K. Davis, M. Evans and J. Lorber (eds), *Handbook of Gender and Women's Studies*. London: Sage, 459–470.

DiMaggio, P. and Powell, W. (1983) The Iron Cage Revisited: Institutional Isomorphism and Collective Rationality in Organizational Fields, *American Sociological Review* 48 (April) 147–160.

Dolan, J. (2004) Gender Equity: Illusion or Reality for Women in the Federal Executive Service? *Public Administration Review* 64(3) 299–308.

Dorsey, E. (2005) 'The Global Women's Movement: Articulating a New Vision of Global Governance' in P. F. Diehl (ed.), *The Politics of Global Governance*. Boulder, Co.: Lynne Rienner, 415–442.

Eisenstein, H. (1995) 'The Australian Femocrat Experiment: A Feminist Case for Bureaucracy' in M.M. Ferree and P. Y. Martin (eds), *Feminist Organizations Harvest of the New Woman's Movement*. Philadelphia: Temple University Press, 69–83.

Eisenstein, H. (1996) *Inside Agitators: Australian Femocrats and the State*. Philadelphia: Temple University Press.

Elias, J. (2008) Introduction – Hegemonic Masculinities in International Politics, *Men And Masculinities* 10 (4) 383–88.

Ely, R. J., and Meyerson, D. E. (2000) 'Theories of Gender in Organizations: A New Approach to Organizational Analysis and Change' in B. Staw and R. Sutton (eds), *Research in Organizational Behaviour* Vol. 22. Elsevier Science & Technology Books, 105–153.

Enloe, C. (1989) *Bananas, Beaches and Bases: Making Feminist Sense of International Politics*. London: Pandora Press.

Enloe, C. (2007) *Globalization and Militarism; Feminists Make the Link*. Boston: Rowman and Littlefield Publishers.

European Commission Directorate General Administration. (2004) *Fourth Action Programme for Equal Opportunities for Women and Men at the European Commission 2004–2008*. Brussels: DG ADMIN.

Ferguson, K. (1984) *The Feminist Case Against Bureaucracy*. Philadelphia: Temple University Press.

Ferree, M. M., and Tripp, A. M. (eds) (2006) *Global Feminism: Transnational Women's Activism, Organizing and Human Rights*. New York: New York University Press.

Franzway, S., Court, D., and Connell, R. (1989) *Staking a Claim: Feminism, Bureaucracy and the State*. Cambridge: Polity Press.

Friedman, E. J. (2003) Gendering the Agenda: The Impact of the Transnational Women's Rights Movement at the UN Conferences of the 1990s, *Women's Studies International Forum* 26 (4) 313–331.

Gray, M. M., Kittilson, M. C., and Sandholtz, W. (2006) Women and Globalization: A Study of 180 Countries, 1975–2000, *International Organization* 60 (2) 293–333.

Hafner-Burton, E. M. and Pollack, M.A. (2002) Mainstreaming Gender in Global Governance, *European Journal Of International Relations* 8 (3) 339–373.

Hafner-Burton, E. M., and Pollack, M. A. (2009) Mainstreaming Gender in the European Union: Getting the Incentives Right, *Comparative European Politics* 7(1) 114–138.

Halford, S. (1992) 'Feminist Change in a Patriarchal Organisation: The Experience of Women's Initiatives in Local Government and Implications for Feminist Perspectives on State Institutions' in M. Savage and A. Witz (eds) *Gender and Bureaucracy (Sociological Review Monographs, volume 40)*. Oxford: Blackwell.

Halford, S. and Leonard, P. (2001) *Gender, Power and Organization*. London: Palgrave.

Harcourt, W. (2005) *Report on the NCDO-SID-WIDE International Workshop on the Millennium Development Goals, Gender Equality and Human Security*, The Royal Tropical Institute, Amsterdam, The Netherlands, 18 May 2005. Amsterdam, NCDO and SID and WIDE.

Harvey, H. (2008) A Triumph for Women at the UN, *The Guardian*, 25 June.

Hawkesworth, M. (2006) *Globalization and Feminist Activism*. Lanham, MD.: Rowman and Littlefield.

Hearn, J. (2004) Tracking the 'Transnational': Studying Transnational Organizations and Managements and the Management of Cohesion, *Culture and Organization* 10(4) 273–290.

Hooper, C. (2001) *Manly States, Masculinities, International Relations and Gender Politics*. New York: Columbia University Press.

Hoskyns, C. (1996) *Integrating Gender: Women, Law and Politics in the European Union*. London: Verso.

International Labour Organization (ILO) (2008) *ILO Action Plan for Gender Equality 2008–2009*. Geneva: International Labour Office.

Joachim, J. (2003) Framing Issues and Seizing Opportunities: The United Nations and Women's Rights, *International Studies Quarterly* 47(2) 247–274.

Joachim, J. (2007) *Agenda-Setting, the UN and NGOs: Gender Violence and Reproductive Rights*. Washington DC: Georgetown University Press.

Joachim, J., Reinalda, B. and Verbeek, B. (2008) *International Organizations and Implementation: Enforcers, Managers or Authorities*. London: Routledge.

Johnstone, R. L. (2006) Feminist Influences on the United Nations Human Rights Treaty Bodies, *Human Rights Quarterly* 28 (1) 148–85.

Kanter, R. M. (1977) *Men and Women of the Corporation*. New York: Basic Books.

Kantola, J., and Outshoorn, J. (eds) (2008) *Changing State Feminism*. Basingstoke: Macmillan.

Karns, M. P., and Mingst, K. A. (2004) *International Organizations: The Politics and Processes of Global Governance*. Boulder, Co: Lynne Rienner.

Keck, M., and Sikkink, K. (1998) *Activists Beyond Borders: Advocacy Networks in International Politics*. Ithaca, N.Y.: Cornell University Press.

Keiser, L., Willens, V., Meier, K., and Holland, K. (2002) Lipstick and Logorithms: Gender, Institutional Context and Representative Bureaucracy, *American Political Science Review* 96(3) 553–564.

MacKinnon, C. (1989) *Toward a Feminist Theory of the State*. Cambridge Mass: Harvard University Press.

Martin, J. and Knopoff, K. (1999) 'The Gendered Implications of Apparently Gender-Neutral Organizational Theory: Re-reading Weber' in A. Larson and E. Freeman (eds), Ruffin Lecture Series (volume III): *Business Ethics and Women's Studies*. Oxford: Oxford University Press, 30–49.

Martin, P. Y. (2001) Mobilizing Masculinities': Women's Experiences of Men at Work, *Organization* 8 (4) 587–618.

Martin, P. Y. (2003) 'Said and Done' vs. 'Saying and Doing': Gendering Practices, Practicing Gender at Work, *Gender and Society* 17 (3) 342–366.

Mazur, A. (2002) *Theorizing Feminist Policy*. Oxford: Oxford University Press.

McGrew, A. (2000) 'Power Shift from National Government to Global Government' in D. Held (ed.), *A Globalizing World? Culture, Economics and Politics*. London: Routledge/Open University Press, 127–169.

Meyer, M. K and Prügl, E. (eds) (1999) *Gender Politics in Global Governance*. Oxford: Rowman and Littlefield.

Morgan, D. (1994) 'Theater of War. Combat, the Military, and Masculinities' in M. Kaufman and H. Brod (eds), *Theorizing Masculinities*. Thousand Oaks, CA: Sage, 165–182.

Neumann, I. B. (2008) The Body of the Diplomat, *European Journal Of International Relations* 14 (4) 671–95.

Outshoorn, J. (1997) 'Incorporating Feminism: The Women's Policy Networks in the Netherlands' in F. Gardiner (ed.), *Sex Equality Policy in Western Europe*. London: Routledge, 109–127.

Page, E. C. (1997) *People Who Run Europe*. Oxford: Clarendon.

Paxton, P. (2008) 'Gendering Democracy' in G. Goetz and A. Mazur (eds), *Politics, Gender and Concepts: Theory and Methodology*. Cambridge: Cambridge University Press, 47–70.

Peters, J. and Wolper, A. (eds) (1995) *Women's Rights, Human Rights: International Feminist Perspectives*. London: Routledge.

Pevehouse, J., Nordstrom, T. and Warnke, K. (2004) The Correlates of War 2 international governmental organizations data version 2.0, *Conflict Management and Peace Science* 21(2) 101–119.

Phillips, A. (1995) *The Politics of Presence: The Political Representation of Gender, Ethnicity and Race*. Oxford: Oxford University Press.

Pietilä, H. and Vickers, J. (1996) Making Women Matter: The Role of the United Nations. London: Zed.

Pollack, M., and Hafner-Burton, E. (2000) Mainstreaming Gender in the European Union. *Journal of European Public Policy* 7(3) 432–457.

Rai, S. (ed.)(2003) *Mainstreaming Gender, Democratising the State? International Mechanisms for the Advancement of Women*. Manchester: Manchester University Press.

Rai, S., and Waylen, G. (eds) (2008) *Global Governance: Feminist Perspectives*. Basingstoke: Palgrave.

Reinalda, B. (1997) 'Deus ex Machina or the Interplay between National and International Policy Making: A Critical Analysis of Women in the European Union' in F. Gardiner (ed.), *Sex Equality Policy in Europe*. London: Routledge, 197–215.

Reinalda, B. (2009) *Routledge History Of International Organizations: From 1815 To The Present Day*. London: Routledge.

Rees, T. (1998) *Mainstreaming Equality in the European Union*. London: Routledge.

Research voor Beleid. (2007) *Comparative Study on the Career Development of Male and Female AD Officials: Final Report. Financed by DG Admin of the European Commission, Project Number B3216*. Leiden: Research voor Beleid, http://ec.europa.eu/civil_service/docs/comparative_study_en.pdf [consulted November 15, 2010].

Reinelt, C. (1995) 'Moving onto the Terrain of the State: The Battered Women's Movement and the Politics of Engagement' in M. M. Ferree and P.Y. Martin (eds), *Feminist Organization: Harvest of the New Women's Movement*. Philadelphia, PA., Temple University Press, 84–104.

Rittberger, V., and Zangl, B. (2006) *International Organization: Polity, Politics and Policies.* Houndsmill, Basingstoke: Palgrave/Macmillan.

Sawer, M. (1990) *Sisters in Suits: Women and Public Policy in Australia.* Sydney: Allen and Unwin.

Smith, J. (1999) 'Transnational Organizations' in *Encyclopedia of Violence, Peace, Conflict* (Vol. 3). San Diego: Academic Press, 591–602 .

Snyder, M. (2006) 'Unlikely Godmother: The UN and the Global Women's Movement' in M. M. Ferree and A. M. Tripp (eds), *Global Feminism: Transnational Women's Activism, Organizing and Human Rights.* New York: New York University Press, 24–50.

Squires, J. (2007) *The New Politics of Gender Equality.* Houndsmill, Basingstoke, Hampshire: Palgrave-Macmillan.

Stetson, D. M., and Mazur, A. (eds) (1995) *Comparative State Feminism.* Thousand Oaks: Sage Publications.

Stevens, A. and Stevens, H. (2007) *Brussels Bureaucrats? The Administration of the European Union.* Houndsmill, Basingstoke, Hampshire: Palgrave Macmillan.

Stienstra, D. (1994) *Women's Movements and International Organizations.* New York: St. Martin's Press.

True, J. (2003) Mainstreaming Gender in Global Public Policy, *International Feminist Journal of Politics* 5(3) 368–396.

True, J., and Mintrom, M. (2001) Transnational Networks and Policy Diffusion: The Case of Gender Mainstreaming, *International Studies Quarterly* 45(1) 27–57.

Udom, U. E. (2003) The International Civil Service: Historical Development and Potential for the 21st Century, *Public Personnel Management* 32 (1) 99–124.

United Nations (2008a) 'Improvement of the Status of Women in the United Nations System. Report of the Secretary- General, A/63/364', *Sixty-third Session Item 59 (a) of Provisional Agenda.* New York, United Nations.

United Nations (2008b) 'Report of the International Civil Service Commission for 2008', *General Assembly Official Records Sixty-third Session, Supplement no. 30.* New York: United Nations.

United Nations Office of the Special Advisor on Gender Issues and the Advancement of Women (2001) *Fact Sheet: Gender Mainstreaming: Strategy for Promoting Gender Equality.* New York, United Nations.

United Nations Office of the Special Advisor on Gender Issues and the Advancement of Women (2007/2009) *Report of the Expert Group Meeting on Measures to Accelerate the Improvement in the Status of Women in the United Nations System.* New York: United Nations.

Verloo, M. and Lombardo, E. (2007) 'Contested Gender Equality and Policy Variety in Europe: Introducing a Critical Frame Approach' in M. Verloo (ed.), *Multiple Meanings of Gender Equality: A Critical Frame Analysis of Gender Policies in Europe.* Budapest: Central European University Press, 21–50.

Verloo, M. (2005) Displacement and Empowerment: Reflections on the Concept and Practice of the Council of Europe Approach to Gender Mainstreaming and Gender Equality, *Social Politics* 12 (3) 344–65.

Walby, S. (2005) Gender Mainstreaming: Productive Tensions in Theory and Practice, *Social Politics* 12 (3) 1–25.

Weaver, C. (2008) The Strategic Construction of the World Bank's Gender and Development Agenda. Paper presented at the International Studies Association Annual Meeting, 25 March, San Francisco, CA.

Witz, A. and M. Savage (1992) 'The gender of organizations' in M. Savage and A. Witz (eds), *Gender and Bureaucracy.* Oxford: Basil Blackwell, 3–62.

Woodward, A. (1996) 'Multi-National Masculinities and European Bureaucracy' in D. Collinson and J. Hearn (eds), *Men as Managers, Managers as Men.* London: Sage, 167–185.

Woodward, A. (2004) 'Building Velvet Triangles: Gender and Ínformal Governance' in T. Christiansen and S. Piattoni (eds), *Informal Governance and the European Union*. London: Edward Elgar 76–93.

Woodward, A. (2008) Too Late for Mainstreaming: The View from Brussels, *European Social Policy* 18 (3) 289–302.

Zippel, K. S. (2006) *The Politics of Sexual Harassment*. Cambridge: Cambridge University Press.

# 22

# Toward Gender Equality in European Union Labour Markets

## *Achievements and Contemporary Challenges*

CATHERINE CASEY
*University of Leicester, UK*

### INTRODUCTION

Over the last three or four decades many efforts at national and supranational policy levels have sought to improve gender equality in the working lives of women and
men (see J. Martin, this volume). Prominent among these efforts have been those
of the policy institutions of the European Union (EU) which have initiated action
programmes along with legislative measures to improve gender equality across a full
spectrum of industry and occupational sectors and across all member states of the
European Union. Many important developments toward advancing gender equality
have resulted. In particular, the European Employment Strategy since its inception
in the late 1990s has explicitly adopted a strategy for mainstreaming gender (defined
below) in order to raise gender equality issues to a central prominence in employment policies and practices and to advance their achievement. These policy efforts,
which link gender equality in employment with wider social aspirations toward full
gender equality, social justice, and social citizenship participation in society more
broadly, have gained attention and influence in other parts of the world.

The adoption of European Union and national member state policies and regulations toward achieving gender equalities in the labour market has achieved
significant increases in rates of employment participation, expanded education
and training participation, and wider opportunities for occupational and professional participation for women. These accomplishments are well recognized and
welcome. Yet, even as they are in themselves scarcely a full complement of gender equalities, these accomplishments are notably uneven, incomplete, and precarious. The significant and persistent gender inequalities that remain evident in
labour market dynamics, in organizational practices, and in everyday workplace

life demand further critical and policy attention. Key among these are: persistent gaps between women and men in rates of employment participation (EGGE, 2009; Fagan and Burchell, 2002; Plantenga and Remery, 2006; Shire, 2007) in pay and benefits (Aisenbrey and Brückner, 2008; Gustafsson and Menders, 2000; Rubery et al., 2006), in occupational or workplace representation (Charles and Grusky, 2004; Rubery et al., 1999; Lopez-Claros and Zahidi, 2005) in opportunities for education and training (European Commission, 2006; Walby, 2007; Webster, 2004; 2007), and in participation in management and governance of organizations in all sectors of the labour market (Burke and Davidson, 2004; Casey, 2009; Rubery et al., 2003). Gender equality in the world of work and employment is a pivotal underlay of the broader social policy objective of gender equality across all dimensions of social relationships. Therefore, the fragility of the accomplishments of equal rights, equal opportunity, and equal treatment of women and men in employment in the European Union remains of significant social concern.

These concerns, moreover, are intensified with the recent enlargement of the European Union to comprise 27 member states. The EU's 2004 and 2007 expansions include the membership of 12 Central, Eastern and Southern European countries. The gender inequalities that had persisted in the 15 EU member states[1] prior to enlargement are at risk of exacerbation as the enlarged European Union experiences increased diversity of gender regimes and patterns of labour market participation and as central policy-making institutions struggle with multiple problems of enlargement.

Research efforts to analyze factors of the persistent gender gaps and to develop measures aimed at their redress raise questions of current policy directions in the European Union. Some analysts scrutinize the European Union's gender mainstreaming policies and find much to criticize. For some, the European Union's current emphasis on economic policies for reform and growth produces problematic gender effects. The principal aim of this chapter is to review and appraise key achievements toward gender equality in European Union labour markets and to point to main areas of concern in current research. The policy adoption of gender mainstreaming – which is understood as the incorporation of gender equality perspectives in all policies at all levels of their development and implementation[2] – has been a particular feature of European Union employment policy. It warrants close attention in this chapter. In a final section I draw attention to features of current European Union economic policy and contemporary labour market dynamics that

---

[1] What is today known as the European Union has developed, since the signing of the Treaty of Rome in 1957 by six countries to form the European Economic Community, through processes of expansion and a series of treaties. The Maastricht Treaty in 1993 formally established the European Union, at that time comprised of 12 member states. Three more countries joined in 1995 with no further expansion until 2004. The EU-15 is the chief reference point for research data on EU gender equality policies and outcomes into the 2000s.

[2] There are various definitions of gender mainstreaming in the literature. For the purposes of this discussion the definition of the Council of Europe1998 (document EG-S-MS (1998) 2) is used. Gender mainstreaming is defined as: 'the (re)organisation, improvement, development and evaluation of policy processes, so that a gender equality perspective is incorporated in all policies at all levels and at all stages, by the actors normally involved in policy-making'.

may generate friction and obstruction in progress toward gender equality. These features pose challenges to further policy development and to practical action for gender equalities in concrete workplaces.

## Gender Equality Policy in European Union Labour Markets: Key Developments

An extensive literature has developed over recent decades on gender issues in the world of work and employment, and in organizations and management. Women's participation in the world of paid work in the advanced economies rapidly accelerated in the latter decades of the twentieth century. Their participation brought a range of new effects and demands on the labour market and on workplaces. Policymakers at national, and supranational, levels variously turned to address these issues. Among the earliest concerns were those regarding equal pay for women and men working in jobs of equal skill and productivity. As women collectively demanded recognition of inequalities in regard to rates of pay and participation in education and skills training other issues arising from workplace experiences emerged. These latter issues, which involve gender and sexuality discrimination and inequality in other dimensions of workplace life and organizational practices, and that include sexual harassment (Zippel, 2006), family care responsibilities (Pascall and Lewis, 2004; Perrons et al., 2006), and management and organizational structures (Wajcman, 1998) continue to attract much research and have effected some institutional changes. Nonetheless, the problem of equal pay remains salient. Despite the issue of equal pay having been included at the outset of the European Union's establishment in 1957, under Article 119 of the Treaty of Rome, and gaining successive legislative commitments, the successful accomplishment of equal pay for equal work in all member states of the European Union is still awaited (EGGE, 2009).

In the decades since the 1970s there has been much policy activity concerned with progressing gender equality. It is important to note that the development of EU policy on gender has come about as a piecemeal, untidy affair. That course of development reflects the varying political prominence and fortunes of gender concerns alongside other EU level policy debates, notably market integration and intricate constitutional debates regarding supranational EU institutions and their relationship with national level jurisdictions of member states. Nonetheless, amid the extensive documentation of policy and case law in the area of gender policy, we can usefully identify some key events of law and employment policy that have exercised significant effect. These are Directives of the Council of the European Union[3] and the European Employment Strategy.

---

[3] The Council of the European Union, also known just as the European Council, is the principal decision-making body of the EU. It is comprised of national members from each member state. It is a supranational body which means that national member states may share or concede sovereign powers to its higher authority. It passes laws usually jointly with the European Parliament. Directives are legislative acts binding on all member states, although with provision for national timeframes and procedures in their achievement.

## Council of the European Union Directives

A number of key legislative acts, known as Directives, of the Council of the European Union frame the current context and warrant discussion. These are:

- 1975 Directive on equal pay (Directive 75/117/EEC);
- 1976 Directive on equal treatment in access to employment (Directive 76/207/EEC);
- 1978 Directive on equal treatment in social security and pension schemes (Directive 86/378/EEC);
- 1996 Directive on parental leave (Directive 96/34/EC);
- 1997 Directive on equal treatment in part-time work (Directive 97/81/EC);
- 2002 Directive on discrimination and sexual harassment at work (Directive 2002/73/EC).

Political campaigns for equal pay, which won increased popular support in the 1960s and 1970s, were forged by coalitions of working women, trade unions, and political representatives including the European Women's Lobby through earlier decades of the twentieth century.[4] These efforts (for which more detailed discussion can be found, for instance, in Lenz, 2007; Woodward, 2004; and Zippel, 2006) gained successful legislative recognition in different national contexts and at the European Union level in the 1970s and 1980s. Importantly, the legislative act of the Council of the European Economic Community through its Directive on Equal Pay (Directive 75/117/EEC[5]) sought to implement the principle of equal pay for men and women. The 1975 Directive stated that: ' "the principle of equal pay", means, for the same work or for work to which equal value is attributed, the elimination of all discrimination on grounds of sex with regard to all aspects and conditions of remuneration'. It was followed in 1976 by legislation that sought to extend the provisions on equal pay to equal treatment of men and women in the 'principle of equal treatment' (Directive 76/207/EEC). The latter directive sought to implement equal treatment in regard to access to employment, vocational training, promotion, and working conditions. By the 1980s, directives were in place that sought further implementation of the principal of equal treatment in areas of social security and pension schemes (Directive 86/378/EEC). The following decade saw provisions for parental leave (Directive 96/34/EC), for equal treatment in part-time work (Directive 97/81/EC), and for proscribing discrimination and sexual harassment at work (Directive 2002/73/EC). Amendments to these key directives appear in numerous subsequent directives, for example, efforts to encourage implementation of what the Council refers to as 'the principle of equal opportunities and equal treatment

---

[4] Note, for instance, Beatrice Webb's influential book: *Wages of Men and Women – Should they be Equal?* published in 1919 (London: Fabian Society) as exemplary among the early twentieth century efforts to raise gender equality issues in wider industrial and political circles.

[5] References to 'EEC' refer to European Economic Communities that preceded the establishment of the European Union (EU) in 1993. 'EES' refers to the European Employment Strategy, 'EC' refers to European Council, and 'CEC' refers to the Commission of the European Communities (also known as the European Commission).

of men and women in matters of employment and occupation' are expressed in Council Directive 2006/54/EC.

The Directive on equal pay has, for many analysts, been the most significant, certainly the most urgent, in the advancement of gender equality in employment. But each of these key directives has made a particular contribution to the advance of gender equality. The importance, for instance, of the directive on Part-Time Work (97/81/EC) legislated in 1997 must also be underlined. That directive sought 'the elimination of discrimination against part-time workers and to assist the development of opportunities for part-time working on a basis acceptable to employers and workers'.[6] It provided part-time workers (on a *pro rata* basis) the same contractual entitlements as full-time employees with the same employer. Those entitlements include, for example, benefits and bonus schemes, membership of occupational pension schemes, and opportunities for training and promotion. As the vast majority of part-time workers in any country are women, the Part-time directive has had a significant effect in encouraging women's labour market participation and for advancing gender equality in regard to that measure. The directive required member states to implement national level policies to ensure that part-time employees are not treated less favourably than comparable full-time employees. Importantly, the directive makes no exemption for small employers in whose enterprises many women are employed on part-time or flexible contracts. However, as the definition of what constitutes part-time work varies across member states (Rubery et al., 1999), the directive framework makes provision for each member state to devise its national policy on equality of part-time work according to national context.

## The European Employment Strategy (EES)

In addition to these key legislative directives, two further achievements at the supranational European Union level are significant. Each indicates efforts to consolidate the gains of equality regulation and endorse continuing EU commitment to advancing gender equality. The European Union Treaty of Amsterdam in 1997 (effective 1999) and the launch of the European Employment Strategy (EES) in 1998 respectively brought gender equality into mainstream concern in EU institutions. Notwithstanding the directives on the principles of gender equality, concrete advances toward achieving it were slow. The Amsterdam Treaty integrated gender equality and gender mainstreaming principally through its explicit mainstreaming of employment policy. That is, gender equality was mainstreamed, not as a discrete policy objective, but through its recognition in employment policy.

The mainstreaming of employment policy – as the omnibus for gender mainstreaming – refers to the explicit emphasis on jobs and growth and active labour market participation being brought into all areas of social and economic policy, rather than treated as a separate domain with particular concerns. In the course of that generalized emphasis, gender equality in employment extends to wider areas of social activity. The European Employment Strategy (EES) similarly sought

---

[6] Council Directive 97/81/EC of December 1997 on part-time work, [1997] OJ L014, 20/01/1998 P. 0009–0014.

to integrate gender equality principles as core objectives for the EU's employment policy. But importantly, the EES differed from the binding legislative regulations of the EU Treaties and of European Council Directives in its adoption of a new mode of governance. This new mode of governance, formally termed the Open Method of Coordination (OMC), is characterized by 'soft regulation' that is practised as an accompanying form of governance to 'hard' legislation in EU institutions ('soft' and 'hard' regulation are explained below). The formal instruments of Treaty provisions and Council Directives had advanced recognition of gender equality in employment but the Open Method of Coordination brought additional measures and methods to the pursuit of gender equality objectives across the various national state members of the EU, as discussed below.

The intention of the European Employment Strategy was to require that gender equality objectives be pursued through the mainstreaming of gender into all aspects of employment policy and through the workings of the OMC. The EES (European Commission, 1999) designed a strategy around a structure of 'four pillars'. These were, as listed by the EC, employability, entrepreneurship, adaptability, and equal opportunities. The first of the pillars, employability, aims to facilitate access to the labour market, ability to gain training and skills, and removal of barriers of age, disability, and mobility. Entrepreneurship aims to promote new businesses and encourage the growth of small and medium enterprises. The third pillar, adaptability, refers to flexibility in organization of work and working patterns, and adaptability of regulation and trainings systems to new conditions of technology and innovation. The fourth pillar of equality of opportunities refers to fostering equality of opportunities for education, training, employment, and the removal of disadvantage on the basis of their sex, race, language, religion, economic, or family situation.

The establishment of equality of opportunity for women in the world of work as one of the four pillars marked a significant step in EU policy. The 'Equal Opportunities pillar' promoted the reduction of gender gaps, the mainstreaming of gender equality, the reconciliation of work and family life, and facilitating reintegration into labour market work, for instance, after child-raising priorities at home were met. Yet, responsibility for implementing the equal opportunities pillar, as the other three pillars, lay with the member states. Therefore, member states adopted various approaches to implementing the four pillars – a variety that included differential weightings of importance and priority to the pillars. This variation in national level response affected the pace and quality of the developments toward gender equality in the labour market. While national variation is an expected, and accommodated, response to EU level policy, it is simultaneously a key factor in limiting the reach of EU level policy aspirations for gender equality. It is precisely these tensions which the OMC is intended to lubricate.

The OMC method of non-binding arrangements is based on agreement of shared broad policy objectives by EU member states. It is a method that recognizes national differences in labour market policies and in models of welfare and it leaves to member states decisions in regard to implementing at the national level goals agreed at supranational level. The emphasis in the OMC is on a subordination of formal methods (such as laws and rulings which incur legal consequences in their breach) in preference for collective methods such as coordination and reaching a negotiated consensus. The material difference between these methods is that formal methods are legally binding and 'soft' methods or collective negotiation and consensus incur no legal consequence of sanction. Collective methods rely on political participation, partnerships, networks, bench-marking, peer review, and development of knowledge-sharing rather than legal enforcement. Yet, the nature of these multi-level processes, their networks and diverse forms and actors, and their iterative style and general untidiness can make the OMC, as a policy strategy, difficult to evaluate according to conventional measures. It is difficult to attribute causality for national policy changes to the OMC whereas hard law is generally more accountable and enforceable. Nonetheless, the OMC has come to be applied to a wide range of policy areas in addition to work and employment.

Feminist analysts have found much to debate over the OMC's[7] effectiveness for gender mainstreaming aimed at equality. Beveridge and Velluti (2008) argue that the intricate relationship of the OMC and gender mainstreaming is such that it is not possible to draw a clear distinction between their processes. In other words, gender mainstreaming is of necessity a process of soft regulation, of 'buy in' through informal education and learning, negotiation and sharing. For many feminists and activists formed in the women's movement political campaigns, the OMC has found much resonance. Certainly, gender equality activists in the decades prior to the Amsterdam Treaty and the EES launch in the late 1990s were well practised in deploying strategies that were later recognized as the 'open method'. Feminist activists' efforts won a consensus that helped to regularize gender mainstreaming across all EU policy actions and the adoption of legislative acts using the OMC method. Zippel (2006) reports that informal networks of feminists developed transnational expertise in lobbying and advising emerging EU institutions in the 1980s and 1990s on gender issues, prior to the more formal establishment of the OMC. Those activist networks succeeded in placing key gender issues such as sexual harassment in the workplace on the EU agenda. They influenced the formulation of gender equality policies and, moreover, influenced the adoption of the OMC itself as a mode of governance.

The supranational institutions of the EU, with their deliberate efforts to develop and utilize transnational expertise in policy-making, created policy innovations and pressures on national state members to address issues that otherwise might have languished at national levels. Zippel points out that the OMC has enabled success, for example, in regard to combating sexual harassment, where earlier efforts to gain binding legislation at EU level to eradicate sexual harassment had failed. The wide national variation in recognizing sexual harassment as a problem proved too great a barrier to feminist efforts to gain sufficient support in the formal law-making institutions at the EU level. Instead, the laborious process of slowly winning consensus through transnational discussion and coordination eventually enabled soft law measures (guidelines) to be adopted at EU level and the subsequent adoption by member states of formal legislation for their national contexts. Those measures in

[7] An extensive discussion of the OMC in regard to gender equality is found, for instance, in Beveridge and Velluti (2008), Hafner-Burton and Pollock (2000), Mazey (2002), Rubery (2005), and Woodward (2004).

turn further led to EU level legislation. The European Council Directive 2002/73/EC and its recast statement as the Council Directive 2006/54/EC on equality between men and women in employment are key examples of legislation enacted *subsequent* to soft law and peer-pressure effects among member states. Furthermore, Sifft (2003: 150) argues that in the British case successive governments have insisted on national sovereign rights in devising social and gender policy, yet 'no other woman's movement has so effectively used the EU as a means to circumvent the reluctance of its national government'. In short, two important dynamics appear to be effective means toward advancing gender equality: those of the interactive processes of hard law and the soft law of the OMC; and those of the dialectical relationships between EU level policy-making and national level adoption, implementation, and feedback.

The EES, as the principal example of the OMC, encouraged the development of National Action Plans on a range of employment issues and goals. Following European Commission guidelines, the idea of the national action plans was that national member states develop specific strategies toward *inter alia* gender mainstreaming objectives. They included the concrete improvement of equality of opportunity and treatment (refer to 'principle of equal treatment' (Directive 76/207/EEC)) and greater participation of women in employment. The EES, as an iterative process, continues to undergo changes. The 2003 revision of the EES replaced the four pillars arrangement by three main objectives and ten 'priorities for action'. Gender equality in employment objectives remained included in the ten priorities but many critics argued that gender equality had lost its prominence (Rubery, 2005). In 2005, a mid-term review of the European Union's Lisbon Agenda was undertaken. That review was a significant turning point in the EES. The re-launched Lisbon Agenda places much greater emphasis on jobs and growth and commitment to efforts to streamline broad economic policy.

In place of national action plans are National Reform Programmes intended to place greater emphasis on economic growth and employment participation targets for the adult population. Gender issues remain included as policy objects in the emphasis on equal opportunities, targets for childcare provisions, targets for women's employment participation, and reconciliation of work and private life, but none of the revised Employment Guidelines 2005–2008 (Council of the European Union, 2005) makes specific reference to gender in its title. The failure to explicitly promote gender equality in the revised Employment Guidelines gives rise to much concern. The salient concern is that this omission may indicate a reduction and marginalization of gender equality concerns.

## CURRENT CONCERNS: OUTCOMES AND PROBLEMS

For many researchers, the European Employment Strategy (EES) and its Open Method of Communication (OMC) especially until 2005, effectively and positively mainstreamed gender equality and enabled greater integration of equal opportunities in the European employment framework. Goetschy (2001), Rubery et al. (2003), and EGGE (2009) writing across the decade, recognize an increase in female employment rates and a reduction in the pay gap at aggregate EU levels. Other researchers argue that advancements in gender equality in regard to expanded childcare provisions and efforts to reconcile work and family life across the EU were made (Beveridge and Velluti, 2008; Perrons, 2005). Rubery and colleagues (Rubery et al., 2003: 429) offer concrete examples of gender mainstreaming successes, including the OMC's success at effecting national policies and legislation. They note a law in France adopted in 2001 in response to EES objectives that 'requires the social partners to engage in equality bargaining'. *Equality bargaining* refers to the inclusion in collective bargaining negotiations between unions and employers on gendered related behaviours, duties, needs, and concerns. In a second example, Rubery and colleagues cite the Swedish Equal Opportunity Act that requires employers to publish wage data by gender and annually review their pay structures and practices from a gender equality perspective. These are noteworthy developments, even as researchers also point out that these developments are markedly uneven across member states.

From the evidence and research discussions it is reasonable to conclude that the EES and the OMC have achieved notable advancement of gender equality in EU labour markets. The European Union's commitment to gender equality in employment at the policy level is consistently demonstrated – even if concrete achievements remain slow. Nonetheless, research evidence also reveals persistent gaps across most dimensions of employment equality. The European Commission's own expert consultants report that equal pay remains elusive and is highly variable across the EU member states; they also report that while participation rates have increased, there is no evidence of their likelihood of meeting the target of 60% female participation in the labour market by 2010 (EGGE, 2009). Moreover, researchers report that patterns of gender segregation in employment remain salient. Gender segregation is observed both horizontally and vertically (often popularly termed the 'glass ceiling') across wide sectors of the labour market, including in high-tech industries (Webster, 2007). Researchers find, too, much variation across member states, and across industry sectors, in the implementation of gender equality policies and recognition of the demands of integration of gender equality in employment with gender equality in other social policies. Rubery and colleagues (Rubery et al., 2006), upon scrutinizing the EU's National Reform Programmes that superseded the National Action Plans, reported that the loss of specific gender equality guidelines at the supranational EU level has resulted in a reduction of attention to gender equality in national reports and in national employment data. The loss of gender-specific guidelines may prove especially problematic for advancing gender equality as the recent European Union enlargement adds further variation to the national and regional variations in labour markets and models of welfare under the former EU-15, as well as more challenges to EU policy-makers' aspirations for gender equality.

The effects of gender regimes in underpinning the assumptions on gender relations in employment participation and duties of care in home/family and private life remain crucial in explaining both national variations in advancement toward gender equality and in demonstrating the limits of EU level policy. These gender regimes are typically under-addressed in, or outside the reach of, economically-oriented employment policy. Policy models for gender equality in employment through high levels of labour market participation may be accompanied by extreme domestic inequality. Women bear the brunt of that inequality while at the same time being urged to increase their labour market participation (Aybars, 2008; Pascall and Lewis, 2004; O'Connor, 2008). O'Connor (2008: 95), for instance, in focusing on the powerful role of gender regimes, contends that '[t]aking the EU as a whole, with the exception of considerably increased gender equality in labour market participation and some improvement in childcare provision, there has been no marked positive movement in other indicators of labour market gender equality'.

Researchers raise concerns for the future of gender equality objectives in EU employment policy. For Fagan and colleagues (2006) the revised EES, and the omission of specific reference to gender in the key Employment Guidelines, risk subordinating the gender equality objective to economic reform objectives. Rubery and colleagues (2003) share that concern and question how long gender equality will remain an explicit component of EU policy agenda. They point out, as does Zippel (2006), that the new emphasis on equality and non-discrimination in regard to other dimensions such as race, sexual orientation, and age may place gender equality concerns in competition with these interests. There is a risk that the policy move to mainstream equality issues for disadvantaged groups occurs at the expense of gender, despite the latter affecting all citizens and being irreducible to minority interests.

Yet others raise questions about mainstreaming strategy itself. For Stratigaki (2005), mainstreaming of gender may foster important disadvantages over the longer term. In this perspective, mainstreaming has led to a 'policy softening and institutional weakening' at EU level that lets member states neglect positive action toward gender equality goals. Gender mainstreaming has been used to sideline positive action for women and to undermine the enlargement of the scope of gender equality in EU policy. In short, Stratigaki argues that the strategy of gender mainstreaming has failed to affect core policy areas, especially macro-economic policy as indicated in the new *Broad Economic Guidelines* announced in the revised Lisbon Agenda. Lombardo and Meier (2006), in a similar vein, argue that gender mainstreaming as a concept has become an 'open signifier that can be filled with both feminist and non-feminist content'. The authors claim that the widening of the concept of mainstreaming to include equality demands of other disadvantaged sectors, such as people with disabilities or particular religious requirements, renders mainstreaming gender-neutral. That is, conceptual diversification limits the effectiveness of mainstreaming for advancing gender equality. They argue that gender mainstreaming allows policy framing to position women as the 'problem' and requires no demands on men to change their conventional behaviour. Child and elder care and work–family life balance, for instance, continue to be framed as women's issues. They regret the marginalization of expressly feminist politics that can inform policy discourse and the lack of integration of gender equality across wider social and economic policies and arenas.

Sarrano Pascual (2008: 172) further elaborates the latter point. She argues that persisting gender norms and assumptions in much policy formulation enables 'male-streamed perspectives' to remain hegemonic. In these perspectives it is women's behaviour, especially in regard to work and employment, that is interpreted as problematic and women are implicitly asked to change. Too often, policies are guided by stereotyped conceptions of gender that do not challenge prevailing patri-archal gender regimes. Gender equality policy must go much further. It must make visible, and contest, the unquestioned norm of male-streamed perspectives and the merits of gender mainstreaming must be acknowledged (Sarrano Pascual, 2008). Gender mainstreaming, she contends, 'entails a paradigm shift in thinking and act-ing compared to previous policies designed to achieve gender equality . . . Gender mainstreaming requires intervention aimed at combating the causes rather than the symptoms of gender inequality' (2008: 170). Its potential to radically transform the asymmetrical power relations requires a change of emphasis so that policy proc-esses, not women, are the primary objects of change. And it requires that the way gender is reasoned needs to be questioned.

Zippel's (2006) extensive study of sexual harassment demonstrates that despite advances in combating sexual harassment in workplaces, complacency and inatten-tion to its concerns are now prevalent. Evidence shows that it is currently regarded as 'uncool' for women to complain about male-normed sexualized behaviours in the workplace. Although workers are formally protected by EU law from sexual har-assment, it appears that in some workplaces the existence of that formal protection can enable the matter to be relegated as unimportant or its elimination assumed to be accomplished. In addition, Zippel finds that sexual harassment dynamics in Germany are increasingly framed in a gender-neutral manner that may radically disregard the particularities of women's subjectivities in workplaces.

Some researchers note that gender equality has always been primarily a socio-cul-tural concern rather than a matter relevant to economic productivity, efficiency and growth. The socio-cultural concern of gender equality ineluctably exists in tension with economic objectives and appears readily subject to the fortunes of the latter. Even in the 1970s and 1980s when popular movements for gender equality were typ-ically motivated by principles of social justice and equality of citizenship for women and men as a social right, the economic objectives of expanding and integrating the European Common Market provided much of the impetus for EU legislation in regard to the expansion of women's labour market participation (Beveridge and Nott, 2002; Mazey, 2002). Women's labour power was useful to economic growth but its equality of value was an open question. It was only in 2003 that the European Court of Justice formally recognized the twin objectives of the equal pay principle as being both an economic and a social objective of the European Union. Acceptance of those twin objectives, however, does not guarantee their equality of pursuit across economic and social policies.

That point is important. It reminds us not only of a need for caution in regard to attributing much success to the EES and gender mainstreaming policies. It also draws attention to tensions and contestations between economic and social aspira-tions that continue to affect gender equality in the world of work and employment. A heightened emphasis on economic objectives in the re-launch of the European Union's Lisbon Strategy in 2005 and the diminished salience of the socio-cultural objectives of gender equality in the revised EES subsumed under the Broad Economic Policy Guidelines are cause for concern. The particular successes of the EES toward gender equality and the promotion of participatory democracy through the EES's open method of governance are rightly acknowledged. But these achievements are shadowed by significant and persistent inequalities between the genders. For many national polities, it seems that a level of gender inequality is passively tolerated. A European Commission publication (*Group of Experts on Gender, Social Inclusion and Employment*, 2008) claims that many EU nations have failed to implement the principle of gender mainstreaming that has been agreed to at the European Union level. This failure indicates weak commitment at national levels, the low prioritizing of gender, and complacency in regard to earlier advances in gender equality. However, the EU's European Commission launched in 2006 a 'Road Map for Equality between Women and Men 2006–2010' (European Commission, 2006), an effort that seeks to 'accelerate progress toward real equality'.

This expression of renewed commitment to advancing gender equality in view of the evidence for persistent inequalities and the admission of weaknesses in policy commitment and implementation at national member state levels is welcome. Its success will require, however, much closer attention to other key factors in current EU policy, particularly economic policy. The revised Lisbon Agenda with its primary emphasis on labour market participation, jobs and growth, and its adoption of a programme of economic liberalization may actively undermine advances in gender equality in employment. It may also contradict the expressed commitment to the 'road map to gender equality'. Most especially, the priority of emphasis on women's labour market participation in order to boost national and EU levels of productivity and growth risks an aggressive economistic subordination of socio-cultural objectives of gender equality and social justice across very many measures of public and private life (Casey, 2007). Without attention to wider gender equality issues, including normative conceptualizations of gender and expectations of gendered behaviour and 'male-streamed' norms in organizational and workplace behaviour, the accomplishment of gender equality at work will remain elusive.

A further point must be made. The elevation of economic growth and competitiveness has been accompanied by a liberalization of employer action. Privileged employer action, currently assumed as favourable to job growth, is enabling significant alterations to employment relations at the EU level. These changes include, for instance, greater flexibility in contractual arrangements which incur a range of effects on the social organization of work, including an increase in temporary, insecure, and low-productivity jobs (Gold, 2009). At the same time, EU economic and employment policy targets a considerable increase in the female labour market participation rate. Labour market activation policy expressly encourages women to find a job – any job will do – and to comply with employer-favoured flexibilities, poorer quality conditions, and acceptance of individualized employment contracts. The growth in women's employment over the last two decades has included women's significant participation in atypical and precarious jobs and their concomitant vulnerability to other effects of deregulated employment relations such as poor protection and poor employer accountability (Fagan and Burchell, 2002). The new, liberalized, employer arrangements make employer obligations, under hard or soft law, difficult to enforce or even measure in respect to equal pay or equal opportunities or freedom from sexual harassment. The liberalized revision of the Lisbon Agenda in 2005, notwithstanding subsequent policy efforts in the European Commission's

2006 'Road Map to Gender Equality', may effectively obstruct genuine advance of gender equality across a full spectrum of demands in European labour markets.

## CONCLUSION

Research continues on exposing and analysing the obstructions and frictions that despite policy accord subvert gender equality and integration. In reviewing the recent debates and policy developments on gender equality in European Union labour markets, this chapter shows that there is little doubt that many forms of gender inequality persist. The current situation appears to be one in which serious advancement toward full and secure gender equality across the European Union is running at a low gear, if not entirely stalled. There is an evident risk of stabilization at current unequal but improved levels of achievement on some key dimensions. There is a risk of marginalization of gender equality on the basis of both complacency in regard to what has been achieved thus far and in terms of a reduction of visibility of, and commitment to, gender equality that now competes with other equality pressures. As the debates indicate, concern over the continuing viability of gender mainstreaming in employment policy in respect to producing improvements is mounting.

For some analysts, improved policy evaluation methods and stronger pressure on member states to converge toward commonly defined goals and the explicit monitoring of processes may forge some progress. The development of gender-sensitive statistics and audits can produce visible increases in awareness of gender inequalities and prompt national level efforts to improve. But these measures are necessarily limited and entail further risk of favouring the reporting of more measurable features, such as labour market participation rates. A raft of other gendered features and behaviours are omitted from attention and measure. Crucially, the current dynamics in European Union labour markets that are fuelled by the liberalized reforms of the re-launched Lisbon Strategy and the new Broad Economic Policy Guidelines exhibit features that engender a subversion of socio-cultural aspects of gender equality. Liberalization, flexibilization, and de-collectivization of employment relations occur at the same time as EU employment policy favours labour market activation. Gender mainstreaming in employment has become reduced simply to getting women into jobs. The removal of barriers to women's participation in employment in regard, for instance, to child care and access to education and training, have been promoted in employment policies as significant features of gender mainstreaming. Yet their promotion requires little or no alteration in the behaviour of men. Furthermore, the absence of demand on employing organizations in regard to pressures on workers for production intensification, long work hours, mobility, and insecurity, reveal the weakened conception and scope of gender mainstreaming. The rendering of gender mainstreaming as a problem of women's behaviour and its reduction to activation in service of economic policy objectives poses an immense challenge to critical feminist analysts and activists.

Despite the promise, and evident success, of gender mainstreaming, its fate under the liberalized economic climate at supranational EU level may be that of an ineluctable weakening and containment. The wider socio-cultural aspects of gender equality in relations between women and men that play out in economic and workplace relationships are currently at risk of being marginalized from public view and public policy address. Responsibility for achieving gender equality risks being de-collectivized and dispersed to individual workers and their employers, and to individual women and men in their private lives. In view of that possibility, efforts to revitalize and radicalize gender mainstreaming at all levels of economic and social policy development are more pressing than ever.

## REFERENCES

Aisenbrey, S., and Brückner, H. (2008) Occupational Aspirations and the Gender Gap in Wages, *European Sociological Review*, 24(5) 633–649.

Aybars, A. (2008) 'The European Employment Strategy and the Europeanization of Gender Equality in Employment' in F. Beveridge and S. Velluti, S. (eds), 2008, *Gender and the Open Method of Coordination: Perspectives on Law, Governance and Equality in the EU*, Surrey: Ashgate, 55–76.

Beveridge, F., and Nott, S. (2002) Mainstreaming: A Case for Optimism and Cynicism, *Feminist Legal Studies*, 10, 299.

Beveridge, F., and Velluti, S. (eds) (2008) *Gender and the Open Method of Coordination: Perspectives on Law, Governance and Equality in the EU*, Surrey: Ashgate.

Burke, R., and Davidson M. (eds) (2004) *Women in Management Worldwide: Facts, Figures and Analysis*, Aldershot: Ashgate.

Casey, C. (2007) 'Workers of Europe: Citizens or Resources in European Policies for a Knowledge Economy?' in M. Kuhn (ed.), *Who is the European – a New Global Player?* Berlin: Peter Lang, 181–197.

Casey, C. (2009) Organizations, Workers and Learning, *Citizenship Studies*, 13(2) 171–186.

Charles, M., and Grusky, D. (2004) *Occupational Ghettos: The Worldwide Segregation of Women and Men*. Stanford: Stanford University Press.

Council of European Union (2005) Guidelines for the Employment Policies of the Member States, *Official Journal of the European Union*, Luxembourg: Office for Official Publications of the European Communities.European Commission, 2008, *Gender Mainstreaming of Employment Policies: a comparative review of 30 countries*, Luxembourg: Office for Official Publications of the European Communities.

European Commission (1999) *European Employment Strategy*, Luxembourg: Office for Official Publications of the European Communities.

European Commission (2005) *Working Together for Growth and Jobs: A new start for the Lisbon Strategy*, COM(2005/24). Brussels: CEC.

European Commission (2006) *Road Map for Equality between Women and Men 2006–2010*. COM(2006/92). Luxembourg: Office for Official Publications of the European Communities.

European Commission (2008) *Gender Mainstreaming of Employment Policies: A Comparative Review of 30 Countries*. Luxembourg: Office for Official Publications of the European Communities.

EGGE (European Network of Experts on Employment and Gender Equality) (2009) *The National Reform Programmes 2008 and the Gender Aspects of the European Employment Strategy*. Brussels: European Commission.

Fagan, C., and Burchell, B. (2002) *Gender, Jobs and Working Conditions in the European Union.* Luxembourg: European Foundation for the Improvement of Living and Working Conditions.

Goetschy J. (2001) The European Employment Strategy from Amsterdam to Stockholm: Has it Reached its Cruising Speed? *Industrial Relations Journal,* 32(5) 401–418.

Gold, M. (ed.) (2009) *Employment Policy in the European Union.* Basingstoke, UK: Palgrave Macmillan.

Gustafsson, S., and Menlders, D. (eds) (2000) *Gender and the Labour Market: Econometric Evidence of Obstacles to Achieving Gender Equality.* London: Macmillan.

Hafner-Burton, E., and Pollock, M. 2000, Mainstreaming Gender in the European Union, *Journal of European Public Policy,* 7(3) 432–456.

Lenz, I. (2007) 'Varieties of Gender Regimes and Regulating Gender Equality at Work in Global Context' in S. Walby, H. Gottfried, K. Gottschall, and M. Osawa (eds), *Gendering the Knowledge Economy.* Basingstoke UK: Palgrave Macmillan.

Lombardo, E., and Meier, P. (2006) Gender Mainstreaming in the EU Incorporating a Feminist Reading? *European Journal of Women's Studies,* 13(2) 151–166.

Lopez-Claros, A., and Zahidi, S. (2005) *Women's Empowerment: Measuring the Global Gender Gap.* Geneva: World Economic Forum.

Mazey, S. (2002) Gender Mainstreaming Strategies in the EU: Delivering on an Agenda? *Journal of Feminist Legal Studies,* 10, 227–240.

O'Connor, J. (2008) 'The OMC and the EES: Broadening the Possibilities for Gender Equality?' in F. Beveridge and S. Velluti (eds), *Gender and the Open Method of Coordination: Perspectives on Law, Governance and Equality in the EU.* Surrey: Ashgate, 77–102.

Pascall, G., and Lewis, J. (2004) Emerging Gender Regimes and Policies for Gender Equality in a Wider Europe, *Journal of Social Policy,* 33(3) 373–394.

Perrons, D. (2005) Gender Mainstreaming and Gender Equality in the New (Market) Economy: An Analysis of Contradictions, *Social Politics: International Studies in Gender, State and Society,* 12(3) 389–411.

Perrons, D., Fagan, C., McDowell, L., Ray, K., and Ward, K. (eds) (2006) *Gender Divisions in Working Time: Changing Patterns of Work, Care and Public Policy in Europe and North America.* Cheltenham, UK: Edward Elgar.

Plantenga, J., and Remery, C. (2006) *The Gender Pay Gap: Origins and Policy Responses.* Luxembourg: European Commission.

Pollack, M., and Hafner-Burton, E. 2000, 'Mainstreaming Gender in the European Union', *Journal of European Public Policy,* 7 (3):432-456.

Rubery, J. (2005) 'Gender Mainstreaming and the OMC: Is the Open Method too Open for Gender Equality Policy?' in J. Zeitlin and P. Pochet (eds), *The Open Method of Coordination in Action: The European Employment and Social Inclusion Strategies.* Brussels: PIE-Peter Lang.

Rubery, J., Grimshaw, D., Fagan, C., Figueiredo, H., and Smith, M. (2003) Gender Equality Still on the Agenda – but for How Long? *Industrial Relations Journal,* 34(5) 477–497.

Rubery, J., Grimshaw, D., Smith, D., and Donnelly, R. (2006) *The National Reform Programme 2006 and the Gender Aspects of the European Employment Strategy – Final Report,* Equality Unit of the European Commission.

Rubery, J., Smith, M., and Fagan, C. (1999) *Women's Employment in Europe,* London: Routledge.

Serrano Pascual, A. (2008) 'Is the OMC a Provider of Political Tools to Promote Gender Mainstreaming? in F. Beveridge, F. and S. Velluti (eds), *Gender and the Open Method of Coordination: Perspectives on Law, Governance and Equality in the EU.* Surrey: Ashgate.

Shire, K. 'Gender and the Conceptualization of the Knowledge Economy in Comparison' in S. Walby, H,.Gottfried, K. Gottschall, and M. Osawa (eds), *Gendering the Knowledge Economy.* Basingstoke UK: Palgrave Macmillan.

Sifft, S. (2003) 'Pushing for Europeanisation: How British Feminists link with the EU to Promote Parental Rights' in U. Liebert (ed.), *Gendering Europeanisation*. Brussels: Peter Lang.

Stratigaki, M. (2005) Gender Mainstreaming vs Positive Action: An Ongoing Conflict in EU Gender Equality Policy, *European Journal of Women's Studies*, 12(2) 165–186.

Wajcman, J. (1998) *Managing like a Man: Women and Men in Corporate Management*. PA, USA: University of Pennsylvania Press.

Walby, S., Gottfried, H., Gottschall, K., and Osawa, M. (eds) (2007) *Gendering the Knowledge Economy*. Basingstoke UK: Palgrave Macmillan.

Webb, B. (1919) *Wages of Men and Women – Should they be Equal?* London: Fabian Society.

Webster, J. (2004) Digitising Inequality: The Cul-de-sac of Women's Work in European Services, *New Technology, Work and Employment*, 19, 160–176.

Webster, J. (2007) Changing European Gender Relations: Gender Equality Policy concerning Employment and the Labour Market, Report to European Commission, EUR23163.

Woodward, A. (2004) 'Building Velvet Triangles: Gender and Informal Governance' in S. Piattoni and T. Christiansen (eds), *Informal Governance and the European Union*. London: Edward Elgar.

Zippel, K. (2006) *The Politics of Sexual Harassment*. Cambridge, UK: Cambridge University Press.

# 23

# The Military in a Globalized Environment: Perpetuating an 'Extremely Gendered' Organization

ORNA SASSON-LEVY
*Bar-Ilan University, Israel*

In March 2009, the Israel daily newspaper *Haaretz* published an article describing T-shirts designed by soldiers of the Israeli military to celebrate the conclusion of training courses. One of the T-shirts in the article featured the image of a pregnant Palestinian woman with a bull's-eye superimposed on her belly, above a slogan reading, in English, '1 shot, 2 kills.' Another T-shirt depicted a vulture sexually penetrating Hamas Prime Minister Ismail Haniyeh (Blau, 2009). These vulgar T-shirts reflect the construction of a violent armed masculinity, which links together militarism, nationalistic chauvinism, and sexism. The drawings dehumanize Palestinians and legitimize violent attacks on civilians. Interestingly, on the same weekend that the article was published, testimonies were published in other Israeli media outlets of several soldiers who took part in the war in Gaza confirming the excessive use of force on the civilian population.

One 'promise' of globalization was that the spread of a global economy and global networks would bring about the end of wars (Russett and Oneal, 2001). The story above paints a different picture: Although the nature of wars has changed from the conventional wars of the twentieth century to low-intensity armed conflicts and the 'war on terror' of the twenty-first century, violent armed conflicts continue to shape the lives of millions of people, especially in the Middle East, Africa, and Asia. Moreover, scholars argue that, at times, globalization actually depends on militarization and even serves to enhance militarization and can thus be the source of further violent conflicts (Enloe, 2007: 6).

National armed conflicts strengthen traditional perceptions of masculinity and femininity that glorify men as warriors and portray women as victims in need of manly protection (Enloe, 1988). Indeed, research on globalization, gender and militarism concentrates on women and girls as the main victims of wars. These studies focus on the lives of women as refugees and victims of rape or sexual assault, on the dramatic increase in domestic violence in war zones, and on the growing numbers of women trafficked out of war zones and forced to become laborers and sex workers[1] (see Rehn and Sirleaf, 2002). Paradoxically, the perspective that sees women mostly as victims redirects our attention to militaries' gender regimes. What is the significance of the advent of women combat soldiers when women are the main victims of wars and military affairs? Can women warriors break the essentialist gendered perceptions that the military perpetuates? And how do globalization processes affect militaries' gender structures?

This chapter reviews the impact of global processes on military gender regimes and assesses their success in generating change in these regimes. The global shift in the past decade away from 'mass armies'[2] toward professional militaries, together with decisions made by national and transnational courts, have resulted in dramatic changes in the gender structures of Western militaries. The rate of women's participation in Western militaries is growing and women are being integrated into more military positions than ever before. Nonetheless, research often shows that despite the dynamic changes, the militaries' fundamental gender regimes, cultures, and identities have not altered. Therefore, I suggest that conceptualizing the military as an 'extremely-gendered institution' can help us to better understand the gender implications of the military organization.

First, I discuss the military as a gendered organization. In the second section, I review the impact of dynamic globalization processes on these gendered structures and address the failure to create a profound cultural change in the military.[3] I conclude by proposing the concept of the 'extremely-gendered institution' which I believe can be used to enhance understanding of how military organizations are gendered in structure, ideology, and practice.

## THE MILITARY AS A GENDERED ORGANIZATION

The military, as Cynthia Enloe (1988: 10) phrases it, is not 'just another patriarchal institution.' Rather, it is the institution most closely identified with the state, its ideologies, and its policies. At the same time, it is also closely bound-up with essentialist and hierarchal conceptions of gender, and in particular with concepts of men and masculinities. These conditions are true within both liberal and republican discourses of citizenship. According to liberal discourse, military service is perceived as part of the male citizen's minimal obligations to the state, in exchange for which the citizen receives equal civic, political, and social rights (Pateman, 1989). Republican discourse defines citizenship according to the individual's active contribution to the 'common good' (Shafir, 1998), which is often articulated in 'security' terms.

---

[1] Reports point to sexual violence in the ongoing hostilities in Algeria, Myanmar, Southern Sudan, and Uganda. Ninety-four percent of displaced households surveyed in Sierra Leone had experienced sexual assault, including rape, torture, and sexual slavery. At least 250 000 women were raped during the 1994 genocide in Rwanda.

[2] The 'mass army' is based on universal compulsory recruitment (draft) while the professional military is based on paid soldiers, known also as 'all volunteer forces.'

[3] The review relates mostly to NATO countries and Israel, because it is almost impossible to obtain up-to-date data on non-Western militaries.

Thus, republican discourse sees military service as equivalent to 'good citizenship' which serves to delineate the boundaries of the political collective (Burk, 1995). Therefore, military gender regimes have political significance. As long as only men were enlisted into the military, or only men could serve as warriors, only men could be perceived as fully legitimate or 'good' citizens. Women, who were barred from expressing their commitment to the state through 'performance on the battlefield,' were not recognized as men's counterparts in the ultimate obligation to the state (Pateman, 1989: 11) and were therefore not entitled to the same rights and privileges. Thus, the gendered organization of the military also shapes hierarchal and gendered conceptions of citizenship (Sasson-Levy, 2003), which persist today in many societies around the globe.

The theory of gendered organizations argues that gender is not something imported into organizations; rather, it is an integral part of organizational processes (Acker, 1990). The gendering of organizations occurs at several levels: structural (policies, divisions of labor, formal or informal practices), cultural (pervasive images, symbols and ideologies about femininity and masculinity), and interactional (which includes both individual identity and interpersonal relations), in which 'doing gender' is often performed (Martin, 1992; Britton, 2003). The three levels – structure, culture, and agency – can be separated only for analytical purposes. In reality, they interact continuously and operate simultaneously. It is their concurrence that produces and reproduces the 'gender regime' (Connell, 1987) of occupations and of the entire military organization.

An organizational analysis of the military reveals that it maintains strict gender differentiations that uphold identification with and valorization of masculinity (Tallberg, 2009). For most of the twentieth century, gendered distinctions and hierarchies were preserved through various segregation mechanisms: men were conscripted while women served as volunteers and/or in separate women's corps; women's rate of participation in the military was limited; and women were relegated to specific 'feminine' roles and excluded from combat roles. Training frameworks (basic training, officers' training, professional courses) were segregated. These structural and organizational differences limited the range of occupations and ranks to which women could be posted and constituted a formidable barrier to women's advancement (Cohen, 1997). Military promotion depended on combat service and as long as women were barred from combat roles, their advancement in the military was formally restricted. Hence, the militaries' ceiling on women's promotion was made of cement, not glass.

Many examples confirm this strictly segregated organization until the end of the twentieth century. Throughout the three decades following the Second World War, many European states did not enlist women at all, among them Finland, Hungary, Poland, Spain, Portugal, Belgium, and Turkey. In France, the UK, Denmark, and Holland, women served in women's corps, and were posted to a few traditional feminine jobs, usually serving as nurses, secretaries, and administrators (Carrieras, 2006). Greece's Hellenic Armed Forces began formally enlisting women in 1946 but women served only in the Army Nursing Corps.[4] The German military (the

[4] http://www.nato.int/ims/2007/win/pdf/greece-2007.pdf.

Bundeswhr) began allowing women to enlist in 1975 but their participation was initially restricted to the medical service and military bands. In the late 1990s, female soldiers made up about 1.2% of all German service personnel (Kummel, 2002a). In the American military, the women's corps, which was established in May 1942, was perceived as a corps specializing in office skills (Meyer, 1996). Until the early 1970s, the US military maintained a 2% quota for women soldiers, 91% of whom served in clerical positions (Binkin, 1984).

Even in Israel, which is the only Western state to conscript both women and men, the military maintained a strict gendered structure from 1948 to 1995 (Izraeli, 1997). Women, who comprise 34% of the military,[5] are easily exempted from military service on the grounds of marriage, pregnancy, or religious beliefs and are drafted for shorter terms than are men. In the past, all women served in the women's corps, and most of them were assigned traditional feminized jobs (secretaries or teachers: Sasson-Levy 2003). Women cannot be promoted above the rank of brigadier-general but, in practice, the glass ceiling is five ranks below the top, at the rank of lieutenant-colonel.

On a cultural level, researchers argue that hegemonic definitions of the military often conflate with hegemonic masculine culture, which is based upon the exclusion and sometimes oppression of women (Carreiras, 2006; Enloe, 2007; Connell, 1995). This deeply masculinist culture allows men, and sometimes even encourages them, to behave in aggressive and chauvinistic ways that are not acceptable in civilian society (Sasson-Levy, 2003). The language used by soldiers, the pinup pictures in military offices, the (abovementioned) T-shirts that soldiers designed, and the songs soldiers sing during marches frequently convey chauvinistic content that denigrates women or portrays them as sexual objects. Together with the military's gender division of labor, this culture creates and preserves dichotomous, hierarchical, and essentialist conceptions of femininity and masculinity. As I elaborate later, these perceptions superimpose a narrow range of gender identities that are available to individuals within the organization. However, during the last two decades, globalization processes have served as catalysts for change and development in gender relations in many militaries around the world, especially in Western militaries.

## GLOBALIZING GENDERED DYNAMICS

Given the impact of globalization as a driving force in international relations (Beck, 2000), it is unsurprising that globalization has become increasingly central in shaping military organizations, including their social structure in general, and their gender structure in particular. Over the past 20 years, militaries' gender regimes have been shaped by globalization processes through three interrelated mechanisms: (a) the convergence of Western militaries on a 'post-Fordist' model which leads to the abolishment of mandatory conscription; (b) the imposition of gender mainstreaming policies by supranational courts or international organizations; and (c) an ongoing process of diffusion and dissemination of a dominant military model.

[5] Yohalan (Advisor to the chief of the general staff on women issues) (2009). Working year 2008: women's service (Hebrew). See: http://www.aka.idf.il/SIP_STORAGE/files/5/63635.pdf

## Military organizational convergence

Contemporary research indicates that most Western armed forces tend to imitate the current structure of the American military and converge on a structure that has been termed 'post-Fordist' (King, 2006). Chief amongst the characteristics of the post-Fordist military model is the abolition of conscription and an increasing reliance on paid recruits ('volunteers').[6] Even though several European nations still maintain some form of conscription, the era of mass militaries based on compulsory service had generally ended by the turn of the twenty-first century[7] (Haltiner, 1998). The termination of conscription also marked the beginning of an increase in rates of women's participation and the integration of women into positions previously considered masculine (Haltiner, 1998).

One obvious reason for this development is that most countries faced a shortage of manpower after making the shift to professional militaries. The decline in the armies' recruitment rates and legitimacy made it necessary for them to turn to populations that had not been enlisted in the past. This has made the armies more inclusive in terms of gender, race, ethnicity, and class, and as a result they now recruit more women (Iskra et al., 2002; Moskos, 1993; Segal, 1995, Dandeker and Segal, 1996). Moreover, the shift to a professional army expresses a liberal discourse of citizenship, which places an emphasis on human rights and equal opportunities for women. Thus, the less a professional military relies on conscription, and the more this pattern develops, the more women will be found serving in it (Haltiner, 1998; Carreiras, 2006). For example, while women constituted 7.5% of the French armed forces in 1995, their participation rate increased after the abolishment of conscription in 2002 and in 2008 stood at 14.2%.[8] In Holland, the phasing out of conscription in 1996 opened up all military positions and military academies to women but women still make up only about 9% of service personnel.[9] The American military faced a manpower shortage after changing to a volunteer army in 1973. Pressures generated by the contraction in human resources coincided with women's movements pressures for equal rights (Katzenstein, 1998) and brought about the integration of women into military academies (West Point, USAFA, USMA) as early as 1976. Today, women's rate of participation in the US Army is relatively high: women comprise about 14% of the entire armed forces, with higher participation rates in the Air Force (19.6%) and lower rates in the Marines (6.7%).[10]

[6] The other three characteristics of the 'post-Fordist' model are: outsourcing, the centralization of command into joint unified headquarters, and a preference for network warfare.

[7] Karl Haltiner (1998) argues that the dichotomous view of compulsory recruitment versus professional armies is misleading. Instead, there is a continuum of different models, with armies based entirely on compulsory recruitment (Israel) at one end, and armies with no compulsory enlistment at the other (United States, Britain, Canada, Australia). In between these, there are different models of militaries that combine conscription and professional military in different proportions (Turkey, Denmark, Sweden, Germany). While most European states imposed compulsory conscription until 1991, since then they have been significantly reducing or eliminating entirely the proportion of conscripted soldiers in their militaries.

[8] See: http://www.nato.int/ims/2008/win/reports/france-2008.pdf.

[9] See: http://www.nato.int/ims/2008/win/reports/netherlands-2008.pdf.

[10] See: US Department of Defense, Defense Manpower Data Center. Data compiled by the Women Research and Education Institute, January 2008.

In South Africa, the dismantlement of the apartheid regime (1994) also marked the end of mandatory conscription. The South African military was forced to implement full gender equality as part of its affirmative action program to correct past gender and racial imbalances within its ranks (Heinecken, 2002). Currently, the South African military has one of the world's largest proportions of women in service: the SANDF consists of 21% women of whom 61% are black. Ten percent of the personnel currently deployed in Burundi, DRC, and Darfur are women but the majority serve in support and health mustering roles.[11]

A second significant reason for the increase in women's enlistment is the change in the nature of warfare. Contemporary war-making does not involve, as in the past, confrontations between two large armies that deploy roughly equivalent amounts of power. By and large, today's armed forces are deployed in situations of guerilla conflicts, unconventional threats, peace-keeping operations, and the policing of civilian populations. The advancements in civilian communications and information technologies have brought about a fundamental change in the way these wars are fought (Cohen, 1996). Modern warfare, known as the 'revolution in military affairs' (RMA), is characterized by new combat strategies that emphasize hi-tech 'intelligent weapons,' remote-controlled technological combat, expanded intelligence gathering and computing, compact and flexible military units, and network warfare (King, 2006; Cohen, 1996). Since occupations involving computers, electronics and intelligence, which constitute the core of the new warfare, are now no less important than physical combat positions, militaries demand a more educated workforce. In many countries young women are completing high school and college at higher rates than young men and militaries have become especially active in recruiting more women (Enloe, 2007: 85). To conclude, changes in the military's missions and the nature of warfare on the one hand, and the organizational convergence of an 'all-volunteer force' on the other, have facilitated an increase in the rates of women's participation in the military and have opened a variety of military occupations to women.

## (b) Externally Imposed Change by Transnational Courts and Organizations

The struggle of women's organizations and military women for better integration into the military has often been met with resentment, resistance, and flat-out refusal from the military's senior command and sometimes from soldiers themselves (Winslow and Dunn, 2002). At times, a profound change in women's status in the military was achieved only by means of external pressure exerted by global institutions and the rulings of transnational courts.[12]

---

[11] Major General N. Memela-Motumi (Chief Director Transformation Management South African National Defense Force) (2009). SANDF's Approach to Integrate a Gender Dimension in Pursuit of the Defense Mandate. See: http://www.nato.int/issues/women_nato/meeting-records/2009/presentation/Memela-MotumiNATO%20CONFERENCE%20PAPER.pdf.

[12] For a similar argument see Acker (2006) who notes that successful change efforts in organizations' gender regimes appear to combine social movement and legislative support outside the organization. In addition, successful efforts often involve coercion and/or threat of loss. Both affirmative action and pay equity campaigns have these characteristics.

An early example was the UN resolution regarding discrimination against women in the late 1970s. In the Royal Netherlands Armed Forces, the integration policy for women (1979) derived its inspiration from the UN 'Committee on Elimination of all Forms of Discrimination against Women' (CEDAW). The new policy ordered that female personnel could be assigned to the various arms and branches of the three services and the separate female corps was disbanded in 1982.[13]

The increased integration of women into Western armed forces was accelerated by a series of supranational developments. The cap placed by the German military (the Bundeswehr) on women's enlistment was repealed in response to a ruling handed down by the European Court of Justice (ECJ) in the case of Tanja Kriel, an electrician who applied for voluntary service in a combat support function. When her application was declined by the military, she turned to the court, arguing that this bar constituted direct discrimination against women. On January 11, 2000, the European Court of Justice (Case C-285/98) ruled that the European Union's resolution that men and women should be treated equally in the labor market in terms of their access, training, promotion, and terms of employment overruled national level legislation, such as, and in particular, German law. The meaning of this precedent was that the armed forces of all EU countries had to (and most of them did) implement gender egalitarian recruitment policies and grant women access to all military positions[14] (Kummel, 2002b). Following the decision in the *Kreil* case, the Bundeswehr started recruiting women for combat roles (Harries-Jenkins, 2002). Since January 2005, The Act on Equal Opportunities for Female and Male Military Personnel of the Bundeswehr has been in force. According to this law, female military personnel must be considered as underrepresented if their proportion in the statutory areas in all careers (except for medical service careers) is less than 15% and less than 50% in the medical service careers. The target of 15% for most of the military careers is constitutionally justified because these careers have only been open to women since 2001. Women constitute 7.6% of all temporary career volunteers and career soldiers of the Bundeswehr.[15]

Further to the ruling in the *Kreil* case, today there are no formal restrictions on women's service in the militaries of Denmark, Belgium, the Czech Republic, Norway, Luxemburg, and Spain (Carreiras, 2006). However, many informal barriers that exclude or marginalize women in the military continue to confront women, as I show later.

A third global decision of importance is UN Security Council resolution 1325 of October 2000, which addressed the unique implications of warfare on the lives of women and girls. The resolution acknowledged the importance of assimilating a gendered approach in peace-making and conflict resolution, as well as the importance of the role women play in these processes.[16] Based on resolution 1325, the

---

[13] National Report from the Netherlands for the Committee on Women in NATO Forces, The Hague, May 2008. See: http://www.nato.int/ims/2008/win/pdf/netherlands-2008.pdf.

[14] See the website of the European Court of Justice: http://curia.europea.eu/en/transit-page.htm.

[15] http://www.nato.int/ims/2008/win/reports/germany-2008.pdf.

[16] See: http://daccessdds.un.org/doc/UNDOC/GEN/N00/720/18/PDF/N0072018.pdf?OpenElement.

Belgian government passed a law in January 2007, ensuring gender mainstreaming of all government policies. The minister of defense, the chief of defense staff, and three women's organizations signed a charter guaranteeing that equality for men and women and the implementation of UNSCR 1325 would be permanent goals of the Belgian Armed Forces. Women, who represent 8.29% of the total strength of the Belgian military, are currently deployed in various peace-keeping operations in the Balkans, Afghanistan, Africa, and Lebanon.[17] The Netherlands' government has also adopted UN resolution 1325 and a policy of gender mainstreaming. A 'Gender Ambassador' was appointed at the second highest level in the Dutch defense organization in 2002 and a gender policy was put into place with clear objectives, such as having a target of women as 30% of new recruits.[18] The changes implemented by the Belgian and Dutch militaries attest to the interconnected influence of various global mechanisms – in this case UN resolutions and ECJ court rulings – and show how these mechanisms work together to accelerate women's integration into the military.

## Mutual influence

The third change mechanism is reciprocal influence and emulation among militaries worldwide, known in the literature as 'military isomorphism.' Neo-institutional theory argues that organizations become similar to one another through three processes: (1) coercive isomorphism that stems from political influence and the problem of legitimacy, (2) mimetic isomorphism resulting from imitation in response to uncertainty regarding technology, goals or the environment, and (3) normative isomorphism associated with professionalization (Dimaggio and Powell, 1983). Militaries' isomorphism is often explained as both mimetic and normative, meaning that small militaries emulate the world's dominant militaries in order to overcome uncertainties and gain legitimacy and status[19] (Demchak, 2003; Farrell, 2005).

Militaries evince considerable interest in each other. Service personnel study their colleagues whom they get to know through joint exercises or joint warfare, in alliances and coalitions, through multinational military cooperation, or through exchange visits (Farrell, 2005). International diffusion and homogenization effects influence local militaries through joint operations and mutual visits (Kummel, 2002b). Women in militaries have also developed global awareness and created their own international networks. They meet on joint peace-keeping operations when they travel for special training courses or gather at conferences and compare positions and options available to women back home (Enloe, 2007: 65). Increasing modes of communication across national borders, which is the essence of globalization, enhance the influence that militaries have on one another.

[17] Belgian National Report, 2008. See: http://www.nato.int/ims/2008/win/reports/belgium-2008.pdf.

[18] National Report from the Netherlands for the Committee on Women in NATO Forces, The Hague, May 2008. See: http://www.nato.int/ims/2008/win/pdf/netherlands-2008.pdf.

[19] For other explanations of military diffusion and emulation see Goldman (2006). For a critical view of the neo-institutional explanation of military isomorphism see Pretorius (2008).

A good example of reciprocal learning is the annual conference of the Committee on Women in the NATO Forces, which was formally established in 1976 and given permanent status as part of the international military staff at NATO headquarters in 2000 (Carreiras, 2006). In this conference, delegates from each NATO country present the current status of women in their military. NATO's gender mainstreaming approach affected militaries not only through external pressure but also through mimetic and normative isomorphism dynamics.

I emphasize the point of reciprocal influence because in some countries, changes in the military's structure were directly influenced by an examination of the situation elsewhere. The case of the Israeli military demonstrates this point. In Israel, the senior command, The Advisor to the Chief of Staff on Women's Issues, national-Zionist rabbis (inside and outside the military) who often object to gender integration in the military, and civilian women's organizations, all carefully study gender relations in foreign militaries and cite these findings to justify the inclusion or exclusion of women from service. Even though Israel did not abolish mandatory conscription and is not directly affected by ECJ rulings, the status of women in the Israeli military has undergone significant changes over the past decade. The turning point occurred in 1995, when the Israel Supreme Court ruled in the case of *Alice Miller v the Ministry of Defense* that the IDF must open the prestigious pilots' training course to women.[20] Following that ruling, the military realized that it would be legally barred from maintaining strict gender segregation and opened up a few select combat posts to women (border patrol, anti-aircraft, naval commando, artillery, and light infantry). The Women's Corps was dismantled in 2000, certain training courses – from basic training to officers' training – have been gender integrated, and, also, in 2000, the military began to monitor sexual harassment (Sasson-Levy and Amram-Katz, 2007). These changes were clearly prompted by the Israeli Supreme Court ruling; however, reforms in other Western militaries also provided the inspiration for the change.[21]

Without doubt, globalization processes have contributed to the changing nature of military gender regimes and an acceptance of women into the armed forces has become a global, transcultural development (Kummel, 2002b).

## THE MILITARY AS AN EXTREMELY-GENDERED INSTITUTION

In the previous section, I credited globalization processes with changing and improving the status of women in Western militaries. However, even though the changes

[20] *Alice Miller v Minister of Defense,* High Court of Justice 4541/94, 49(4), Supreme Court Reports 94 (1995) (in Hebrew).

[21] The effect of foreign militaries on the changes in women's status in the Israeli military is evident in the Supreme Court decision in the case of *Alice Miller v Minister of Defense.* Two of the five judges that presided in this case mentioned that their decision was based on a careful study of the Canadian SWINTER (service women in non-traditional environment and roles) trial reports, the *Faulkner v Jones* case on the issues of gender integration of the Citadel, and on the Report to the USA president: Women in Combat 1992. In particular, they examined the history of women in aviation in Russia, Australia, and the USA through books such as Ebbert and Hall (1993), Holm (1982), and more.

are impressive, I posit that the status of women in the military is still symbolized by several gaps. One is the gap between men and women in the armed forces; a second is between formal policies and actual policies; and a third is between the legal status and social status of women soldiers. These gaps are apparent in the organizing principles of the military gender regime and in the gendered culture and gendered identities that are formed in the military.

I start with the formal structural aspects. Some countries opened their militaries to women only in the late 1990s (Brazil, Argentina, Austria, Italy), and in many countries, women still do not serve at all or constitute less than 2% of all military personnel (Zimbabwe, Turkey, Poland). In some countries, men are conscripted while women serve as volunteers only (Finland, Germany). Even in Western militaries that have witnessed a notable increase in representation levels, the percentages point to tokenism, with women representing less than 15% of the military population[22] (Kanter, 1977; Carreiras, 2006: 100).

Despite the integration of women into combat roles, in 2000 more than 70% of all women soldiers of the NATO armed forces were concentrated in support and medical functions (Carreiras, 2006: 105), a figure that indicates that women are overrepresented in traditional feminine areas. In most of today's militaries, women are not allowed to serve in the submarine corps, armored divisions, paratroops, infantry, and in elite units (Britain, France, United States, Portugal, Israel, and more).

In Israel, while 88% of all military occupations are accessible to women, in practice women serve in only 67% of them. Other discrepancies are even more glaring: women comprise only 3% of the IDF's combat forces and only 4.4% of its colonels (15 women serve today as colonels and three women are brigadier-generals)[23]. The cement ceiling on women's promotion still exists in the Israeli military, as well as in most other militaries. This accounts for a pattern of 'limited inclusion' that re-affirms women's marginalization (Sasson-Levy, 2003). In the words of the Advisor to the Chief of Staff on Women's Issues, women's status in the Israeli military can be termed as 'exclusive inclusion,' meaning that their inclusion is partial and curtailed.

Another major issue for women soldiers in all volunteer forces is the difficulty of reconciling family life with military employment (Carrieras, 2006), a difficulty that accounts for women's lower rate of retention in the military.[24] In Britain, for example, in spite of generous maternity leave policies, women find the military

---

[22] Rosabeth Moss Kanter (1977) argued that people who constitute a minority at the workplace (less than 15%) suffer from the consequences of tokenism: heightened visibility, social isolation, and gender stereotyping. Her claim was confirmed in reports of women in the military, in prisons, in the police and more. Yoder (1991) argued that Kanter's structural explanation focused on proportional imbalances only and missed the importance of gender *per se*. According to Yoder, the gender of the token affects the status of the token. Women suffer from tokenism both because they are a numerical minority, and because they deviate from gendered (masculine) norms and expectations. When men constitute the minority they do not suffer the same negative effects of the token. Rather, tokenism can provide men an advantage and lead to promotion (cf. Martin, 1985).

[23] Yohalan (Advisor to the Chief of the General Staff on Women Issues), 2009: Working year 2008: women's service (Hebrew). See: http://www.aka.idf.il/SIP_STORAGE/files/5/63635.pdf.

[24] The retention rate of women in the British military is half of the retention rate of men (Reme, 2001).

unfriendly to mothers, mostly because of the belief that service in the Armed Forces is incompatible with flexible working hours (Reme, 2001). As a result, militaries are still far from achieving gender equality on the organizational level.

In addition to formal structural barriers, women are often confronted with non-formal exclusion mechanisms that are more difficult to expose and change. My research on gender integration of officers' training in the Israeli military found that the integration has led to a dual-process of degendering and regendering (Sasson-Levy and Amram-Katz, 2007). *Degendering*[25] was the result of deliberate structural changes. In contrast, *regendering* occurred through more subtle mechanisms, through which organizations actively gender their members, and recreate gender hierarchies (see Martin, 1992). An example of informal dynamics was the combat-related character of the training. Although the integrated course is aimed at non-combatant staff officers, combat-related demands were intensified following gender integration. The result was that physical fitness became a goal in itself. When physical tests are the main rite of passage, they not only reinstate but also 'naturalize' and perpetuate socially constructed distinctions between men and women. Another informal boundary was using 'endurance' as a measure for evaluating cadets. *Endurance* is understood as the ability to withstand physical and mental difficulties without complaint. A male battalion commander explained: '. . . The most important thing is the officer's ability to suffer silently. With girls [sic] this doesn't happen. Very few of the girls can carry out a task and suffer it quietly.' When endurance is evaluated only through physical performance, women are often judged as unsuitable.

Most telling of the phenomenon of regendering were the gendered discourses that were prevalent in the course. We detected three discourses regarding gender integration: (1) 'Everybody wins' – this was the official discourse of the course which claimed that the general level was raised following gender integration because each sex 'brought its own relative advantages.' (2) 'Male cadets lose out' – a very prevalent discourse that argued that men lose out from gender integration because a course that includes women is bound to be less combat-oriented or because men have to work harder to help the women. (3) 'Female cadets lose out,' a much less common discourse which suggested that the course is too physically demanding and out of synch with the demands of the women's prospective positions, or, alternatively, that women take a less active part in the integrated course because 'the boys overshadow them.'

All three discourses emphasize gender differences (positively or negatively), and focus on gender comparisons and thus regender the sphere of relationships and actions, as well as course content and outcomes. In this case, the gendering effect is not planned and orchestrated from above but occurs on a cultural level and is performed via daily interactions (Sasson-Levy and Amram-Katz, 2007). These informal discursive processes are derived from the overbearing hegemony of the masculine combat soldier model in the culture of the course and they also reproduce and maintain the army as a masculine arena.

[25] Degendering, according to Judith Lorber (2005), attacks the structure and process of gender by recognizing that the two genders are not homogeneous groups (as they are intersected by other major social statuses), and by recognizing gender similarities in behavior, thinking, and emotions.

The masculinist model of the military privileges men's body and men's sexuality. Though bureaucratic organizations are supposedly suppressing sexuality in order to protect production and efficiency, research has often shown the persistence and dominance of men's sexuality within organizations (Collinson and Collinson, 1989; Hearn, this volume). This is even truer in the military, where men's sexuality is not only prevalent but is encouraged, and usually linked to organizational power. This is one explanation of the pervasiveness of sexual harassment in the military (Firestone and Harris, 1999) and even more so in military academies (Pershing, 2003). Researchers claim that 'sexual harassment and sexual assault is an epidemic in the U.S. army' (Enloe, 2007: 85). In the summer of 2008, US Congressional hearings on sexual assault in the military revealed that over a quarter of women in the military had been sexually assaulted or raped while on duty. Given the extent of this problem, the US Department of Defense launched a new sexual assault prevention campaign and declared April 2009 as 'sexual assault awareness month.'[26] Clearly, military academies and military bases fail to constitute women-friendly environments.

Likewise, the British Equality and Human Rights Commission exposed that a significant proportion of servicewomen in the British armed forces have experienced some form of sexual harassment.[27] The commission claimed that the prevalence of sexual harassment has a direct impact on the retention of women in the Armed Forces (House of Commons Defence Committee, 2008). Even in Canada, where legislation regarding women in the military is the most progressive in the world, legal integration did not bring about social integration. Women are not fully accepted as equals and often encounter hostility and resistance. This is especially true within the combat forces, the labor intensive support units, and the senior command levels, which hold traditionalist and conservative perceptions and continue to set barriers to further integration (Winslow and Dunn, 2002).

To sum up, informal boundaries and criteria explain why, despite legislation, women are still overrepresented in certain traditional feminine positions and underrepresented in most military occupations and ranks.

## Militarized gender identities

This long list of gaps, barriers, and obstacles facing women in the military demonstrate that despite all the changes, the military remains one of the most ideologically masculinized of all organizations. The construction of feminine difference as inherently problematic permeates army culture from one end to the other (Woodward and Winter, 2006: 58); the gendered difference is perceived as more fundamental and immutable than any other social difference. Integrating women into the military in general and into combat roles in particular seems to pose a threat to the army's collective sense of itself as a masculine institution (Woodward and Winter, 2004: 294).

---

[26] See: http://www.aauw.org/advocacy/laf/lafnetwork/library/SAAMmilitary.cfm and also: http://www.preventsexualassault.army.mil/.

[27] House of Commons Defense Committee, (2008) Memorandum from the Equality and Human Rights Commission. Retrieved on April 1, 2009, from: http://www.publications.parliament.uk/pa/cm200708/cmselect/cmdfence/424/424we10.htm.

Therefore, women are perceived as exceptions and as requiring special accommodations, with the masculine always constituting the standard.

As Cynthia Enloe (2007) argues, women serve military interests only when the military can control where and how they serve. The strict gendered divisions of labor are designed to solve the 'patriarchal challenge' that militaries face: how to enlist women without challenging the image of the military as a masculinity-conferring institution (Tallberg, 2009).

The self-conception of the military as an institution that defines manhood and constructs masculinity imposes a limited repertoire for practicing gender. Patricia Yancey Martin (2003) analyzes the intersection of gender and organizations through the double terms of 'gendering practices,' which embody institutionalized gender distinctions, and 'practicing gender,' in which people constitute gender relations in their ongoing workplace activity. Hence, men and women socially construct each other at work by means of a double-sided interaction of gendering practice and practicing of gender (Martin, 2003: 343)[28].

An exploration of how people practice gender in the military reveals that the military imposes binary perceptions of gender and often forces men and women into performing 'extreme' gender identities. The hegemonic identity in the military, the one that symbolizes the uniqueness of the military and its distinctive character, is the combat soldier, who embodies the epitome of hypermasculinity.[29] This image of the hegemonic man dictates the criteria according to which other identities are judged and evaluated. Both men and women who serve in combat roles are often forced to practice 'hypermasculinity.' For example, gender integration of officers' training has led to 'extremely-gendering' of the entire course and especially to an overdoing of masculinity by its participants. This does not mean that all the cadets took on the image of hegemonic masculinity as their own but that the male cadets often mobilized 'contesting masculinities' through which they distanced or differentiated themselves from others, by demonstrating rank, status, or physical strength superiority (see Martin, 2001: 603). These behaviors, which conflate the military role with doing masculinity, confirm that gender integration poses a threat to the masculinity of the cadets and the course in particular and to the masculinity of the military and warfare in general (Sasson-Levy and Amram Katz, 2007).

In the same way, women soldiers in non-traditional roles are often evaluated according to masculine criteria. These women tend to adopt practices of combat masculinity by imitating behavioral and speech patterns characteristic of the combat soldier, by differentiating themselves from other women and traditional perceptions of femininity, and by trivializing the sexual harassment that they endure[30] (Sasson-Levy, 2003). They attain power by constructing identities that constitute an alternative to the gender dichotomies dictated by the military framework and by deconstructing the link between sex and gender. At the same time, their imitation of the combat soldier's behavior reinforces the identification of masculinity with militarism and reproduces androcentric militaristic thinking (Sasson-Levy, 2003).

---

[28] More on how organizations gender their members proactively see Martin (1992).
[29] On the characteristics of combat masculinity see Sasson-Levy (2008) and Higate (2003).
[30] On why women in the military do not report sexual harassment, see Pershing (2003).

In contrast, Israeli women soldiers serving in secretarial positions are frequently required to perform domestic roles such as office cleaning and food preparing. They are thus required 'to do traditional femininity' (Sasson-Levy, 2007) and are often enraged and feel that their time, energy, and skills are all but wasted in their military service. Since they are called upon to fulfill 'feminine' roles with which most of them do not always identify, they are able to see the military's built-in gender discrimination. They know they are serving as secretaries because they are women. That is, they experience, relatively early in life, outright gender discrimination that they are able to perceive and call by name. Therefore, their experience of military service contradicts the principles of equality and egalitarian citizenship that underlie mandatory recruitment (Sasson-Levy, 2007).

In the US military, the policy of 'don't ask, don't tell' that excludes lesbians and homosexuals from military service (Lehring, 2003) means that women soldiers must be careful not to be perceived as too masculine lest they be considered lesbians and discharged. Women soldiers thus adopt exaggerated feminine identities in order to reassure the military environment that they are not only feminine but also heterosexual. However, if their behavior is overly feminine, they are seen as weak and incapable or are perceived as permissive and 'loose' and treated as sex objects. Women soldiers in the US Army must strike a balance between feminine and masculine practices: they have to appear masculine enough to be judged worthy of participating in military missions but not so masculine as to 'act like' lesbians or be perceived as deviant regarding femininity standards (Herbert, 1998).

In research based on participant observation of the Dutch peace-keeping forces in Bosnia and Kosovo, Liora Sion (2008) reports that the although Dutch military has adopted a gender mainstreaming policy and its troops perform mainly peace-keeping rather than combat operations, it preserves a traditional military gender regime. Training exercises for peace-keeping missions emphasize infantry combat training and the male soldiers find a range of ways to exclude the women who serve with them. Some women respond by adopting a neutral sexual identity – neither masculine nor feminine – while others adopt a conformist feminine identity, signified by obedience, weakness, and flirtatiousness (Sion, 2008).

Thus, although gendered identities in the military are dynamically constructed at the intersection of gender, socioeconomic status, ethnicity, sexuality, and military occupation, they are nonetheless governed by militarized gender regimes that are inflexible, enduring, and powerful. The military allows only for a small range of dichotomous gender identities: in this social atmosphere, women often have no way to win.

## CONCLUSION: THE MILITARY AS AN EXTREMELY GENDERED ORGANIZATION

The evidence summarized here indicates that structural changes have not altered the masculinist cultural model of military organizations. Globalization processes have introduced some change into rigid military gender regimes but these changes have taken place mostly at the margins. The military is obviously not a homogeneous institution (Winslow and Dunn, 2002); but though militaries differ from one society to another, changes in their gender regimes have been minor to date, and the consequences of gender-equality reforms are, in many cases, largely symbolic. On the whole, we can conclude that military organizations resist change in their gender regimes. Accordingly, I propose framing the military as an 'extremely gendered' organization.

The concept of 'extremely gendered' organizations suggests that there are different kinds and levels of gendering and different possibilities for 'degendering' them (Lorber, 2005). In some organizations, the level of gendering is 'low,' making these the most amenable to reform. In others it is 'medium,' meaning that greater effort is required to modify the gender regime. And in yet a third category, it can be 'high,' dictating the need for compensatory affirmative action. In the military, the gender regime is so deeply ingrained that it constitutes an extreme case.

Gender regimes in organizations can be measured on two dimensions: The first is a horizontal comparison of different organizations at a specific point in time based on their level of gendering (as detailed below). The second dimension, which is closely related to the first, consists of a chronological analysis of organizations according to their acceptance of, or resistance to, change in their gender regimes. An exploration of each dimension demonstrates that the military is extremely gendered in both respects.

To analyze the first dimension – gendering across various organizations – I applied Britton's (2003) argument that gendering occurs in three spheres: structure, culture, and agency. The structure of the military, as shown throughout this chapter, is strictly organized by gender. Unlike many other institutions, where gender is an informal and sometimes even illegitimate organizing principle, the military is unique in that its gender policies are public and formal, and constitute one of its major features. Despite the changes brought about by globalization, gender segregation is still the norm. In addition to a rigid structure, gender segregation is maintained through the military culture. The combination of a rigid gendered structure and masculinist culture foster a narrow repertoire of gendered identities for both men and women. Hence, the military is extremely gendered in all three aspects posited by Britton (2003).

On the chronological dimension, which analyzes organizations' capacity for change, I argue that the military is more resistant than other organizations. The gender regimes of many social institutions changed during the twentieth century. Over the past 60 years, an increasing proportion of women have entered the labor force, with attitudes toward the appropriate roles of men and women in the workplace changing accordingly (Coltrane, 2000). Though women still perform most household chores and childcare, time diaries demonstrate that men carry out more such tasks than they once did (Kark and Eagly, 2010). Women's participation in politics has also increased dramatically: In 1890, women did not have the right to vote anywhere in the world; currently, only one country (Saudi Arabia) denies women this right. Women make up almost 50% of the national legislatures in countries such as Sweden and Rwanda (Paxton et al., 2006), while women's parliamentary representation averages 18% worldwide (Inter-Parliamentary Union, 2008). In the economic sector, substantially more men than women occupy positions of authority and decision-making and yet the increased presence of women in managerial roles is remarkable, with one quarter to one half of executive positions in many nations now being filled by women (Kark and Eagly, 2010).

A singular example of a societal institution that has changed dramatically is the field of higher education, which has been relatively favorable to women compared to other spheres (Jacobs, 1996). During the 1950s, the majority of students in Western universities were men. The gender gap in education began to shrink in 1970, and parity was achieved around 1990. By 2000, average women's enrollment was almost 25% higher than that of men's. It is noteworthy that this so-called 'new gender gap,' which has recently been observed in studies of industrialized countries, is evident on a global scale (Schofer and Meyer, 2005). Women comprise the majority of university students in numerous countries, ranging from the US, Canada, France, and Greece to Cuba, Jamaica, and Panama (Jacobs, 1996). In Iran, for example, women are a majority of students in all fields. Educational opportunities for Iranian women in general, and their participation in higher education in particular, have grown exponentially since the 1979 Revolution (Mehran, 2009). The entrance of women into higher education was not an easy process, however, requiring a protracted struggle and, even today, universities are not arenas of gender egalitarianism. Women are often channeled into different fields of study than men and the faculties of most universities are male dominated (Jacobs, 1996). Yet the change that has occurred over two generations is striking, extending its impact beyond the campus as well: the gender composition of lawyers and physicians, for example, has undergone a significant shift.

By contrast, the gender regime of most militaries has not changed to a great extent, despite the efforts at reform discussed in this chapter. The military's gender regime is so firmly entrenched that not even legal or social pressures for change have had much of an effect; in fact, in some respects, it seems that the situation – other than at the margins – is hopeless.

Theoretically, the concept of 'extremely gendered organizations' demands that we identify and explain factors that explain the different possibilities for degendering social organizations. Joan Acker (2006) offers compelling explanations as to organizations' willingness and ability to change. According to Acker, organizations are more prone to change if their inequality regimes: (1) have high visibility; (2) are not perceived as legitimate (or have low legitimacy); (3) are based on poor control mechanisms and therefore carry a low level of compliance; and (4) are situated within a social and political environment that encourages change.

Applying Acker's parameters to the military shows that their inequality regimes are highly visible, but at the same time are perceived as highly legitimate by men (and often women) soldiers, by commanders, and by the public at large (Winslow and Dunn, 2002; Cohn, 2000). The level of control in the military is high: the system is based on a steep hierarchy of command, and soldiers cannot strike or easily appeal for their rights. As for the fourth and final parameter, though the global environment encourages change, local social and political forces often oppose it. This resistance to change is linked to the high level of legitimacy accorded to the military's gender hierarchy. In short, not only is the military highly masculinist but its masculinism enjoys strong cultural legitimacy.

We need to explain then the legitimacy question – how does a discriminatory institution acquire such a high level of legitimacy? To answer this question, I would add to Acker's model other explanatory factors, which are unique to the military. The first is the centrality of the male body in the military organization. Having a masculine body that is healthy, strong, and sturdy is a prerequisite for becoming a combat soldier. The military schema positions the masculine body of the warrior as a universal military ideal (Sasson-Levy, 2007). As military rites of passage are mainly physical they reproduce socially constructed gender differences. These differences are then used to justify and legitimize the original hierarchal social categories.

Interestingly, another field that is based first and foremost on the human body is organized sports. Unlike the military, however, the field of competitive sports has changed dramatically – women now compete in almost all sports, and in many countries women's sports receive funding from the state and/or private companies (though not at levels equal to men's sports). Women's achievements in sport in the last fifty years have been tremendous; however, this remarkable change took place while maintaining strict gender segregation. As a result, women's participation in sports does not constitute a threat either to men's dominance of this field or to the hegemonic dichotomous gender order. Indeed, when women are suspected of being transgender, they create gender chaos, threaten gender segregation, and are quick to be expelled and excluded from competition.[31] Hence, the centrality of the male body in the military does not offer an adequate explanation in and of itself.

Another important factor is the meaning of the military in the hegemonic patriarchal order. The military, as Cynthia Enloe has noted, plays a unique role in the ideological construction of patriarchy due to the major significance of combat in the construction of masculine identities and the justification of masculine superiority (Enloe, 1988: 7; 2000: 36). At the same time, the military is the institution most closely identified with the state, its ideologies, and its policies. The relationship between the military, masculinity, and the state has been portrayed as harmonious and mutually affirming (Enloe, 1988; Pateman, 1989; Nagel, 1998). It is the interplay between these elements that grants men the power of control: control over weapons, control over policies, and control over violent force. Gender integration, meaning the entrance of women into men's exclusive (military) domain, thus constitutes a multi-level threat – to hegemonic definitions of masculinity and to men's control of the areas cited above. A change in the military's gender regime has the potential to bring about changes in the hegemonic gender order, a prospect that generates fear and anxiety – along with efforts to maintain the status quo.

Consequently, we can ask whether genuine change in the military gender order is even possible. And further, is it wise to integrate women into military organizations in the first place? Without invoking feminist arguments for or against women's participation in military organizations (see Feinman, 2000; Peach, 1996; Sasson-Levy, 2003), we should bear in mind that the integration of women into the armed forces supports the image of the military as a modern, progressive, and egalitarian social institution (Enloe, 2007; Woodward and Winter, 2004). This image contributes to the military's legitimacy and social power, and thus may augment local processes of militarization (Tallberg, 2009). On the other hand, abolishing women's military service can harm the economic interests of some women and, in militaristic states such as Israel, might lead to women's exclusion from central decision-making

---

[31] See Levy (2009).

processes and diminish the modest benefits women have gained from military service. Women's military service thus poses a conundrum, the answer to which, I believe, lies not in the military itself but rather in local and global peace processes that will render the military less central and powerful worldwide.

# REFERENCES

Acker, J. (1990) Hierarchies, Jobs, Bodies, a Theory of Gendered Organizations, *Gender and Society*, 4(2) 139–158.

Acker, J. (2006) *Class Questions, Feminist Answers.* Lanham: Rowman and Littlefield Publishers.

Beck, U. (2000) *What is Globalization?* Trans. Patrick Camiller. Cambridge: Polity Press.

Binkin, M. (1984) *America's Volunteer Military – Progress and Prospects.* Washington DC: The Brookings Institute.

Blau, U. (2009) Dead Palestinian babies and bombed mosques – IDF fashion 2009, Ha'aretz, March 20, 2009. http://www.haaretz.com/hasen/spages/1072466.html.

Britton, D. (2003) *At Work in the Iron Cage: the Prison as Gendered Organization.* New York: New York University Press.

Burk, J. (1995) Citizenship Status and Military Service: The Quest for Inclusion by Minorities and Conscientious Objectors, *Armed Forces and Society*, 21(4) 503–529.

Carreiras, H. (2006) *Gender and the Military: Women in the Armed Forces of Western Democracies.* London and New York: Routledge.

Cohen, E. (1996). A Revolution in Warfare. *Foreign Affairs*, 75(2) 37–54.

Cohen, S. (1997) Towards a New Portrait of the (New) Israeli Soldier, *Israeli Affairs*, 3(3 and 4) 77–117.

Cohn, C. (2000) How Can She Claim Equal Rights when She Doesn't Have to Do as Many Push-ups as I Do? The Framing of Men's Opposition to Women's Equality in the Military, *Men and Masculinities*, 3(2) 131–151.

Collinson, M., and Collinson, D.L. (1989) 'Sexuality in the Workplace: The Domination of Men's Sexuality', in G. Burrell, J. Hearn, D. Sheppard and P. Tancred-Sherriff (eds.), *The Sexuality of Organization.* London: Sage.

Connell, R.W. (1987). *Gender and Power: Society, the Person and Sexual Politics.* Stanford, CA: Stanford University Press.

Connell, R.W. (1995) Masculinities. Berkeley: University of California Press.

Dandeker, C., and Segal, M.W. (1996) Gender Integration in Armed Forces: Recent Policy Developments in the United Kingdom, *Armed Forces and Society*, 23(10) 29–47.

Demchak C. (2003) 'Creating the Enemy: Global Diffusion of the information technology-based military model' in E. Goldman and L. Eliason (eds), *The Diffusion of Military Technology and Ideas.* Stanford, CA: Stanford University Press.

DiMaggio, P., and Powell, W. (1983). The Iron Cage Revisited: Institutional Isomorphism and Collective Rationality in Organizational Fields, *American Sociological Review*, 48, 147–160.

Ebbert J., and Hall, M. (1993) *Crossed Currents: Navy Women from WWI to Tailhook.* Washington: Brassey's.

Enloe, C. (1988) *Does Khaki Become You?* London: Pandora.

Enloe C. (2000) *Maneuvers, The International Politics of Militarizing Women's Lives.* Berkeley: University of California Press.

Enloe, C. (2007) *Globalization and Militarism: Feminists Make the Link.* Lanham: Rowman and Littlefield.

Farrell, T. (2005) World Culture and Military Power, *Security Studies*, 14(3) 448–488.

Feinman, I.R. (2000). *Citizenship Rites: Feminist Soldiers and Feminist Antimilitarists*. New York: New York University Press.

Firestone, J.M., and Harris, R. J. (1999) Changes in Patterns of Sexual Harassment in the U.S. Military: A Comparison of the 1988 and 1995 DoD Surveys, *Armed Forces and Society*, 25(4) 613–632.

Goldman E. (2006) Cultural Foundations of Military Diffusion, *Review of International Studies*, 32(1) 69–91.

Haltiner, K.W. (1998) The Definite End of the Mass Army in Western Europe? *Armed Forces and Society*, 25(1) 7–36.

Harries-Jenkins, G. (2002) Women in Extended Roles in the Military: Legal Issues, *Current Sociology*, 50(5) 745–769.

Heinecken, L. (2002) Affirming Gender Equality: The Challenges Facing the South African Armed Forces, *Current Sociology*, 50(5) 715–728.

Herbert, M.S. (1998) *Camouflage isn't Only for Combat*. New York: New York University Press.

Higate, P. (2003) *Military Masculinities: Identities and the State*. Westport, CT: Praeger.

Holm, J. (1982) *Women in the Military: An Unfinished Revolution*. Novato, CA: Presidio Press.

Inter-Parliamentary Union (2008) Women in national parliaments (situation as of July 31, 2008). Retrieved on September 1, 2008 from http://www.ipu.org/wmn-e/world.htm.

Iskra, D., Trainor, S., Leithauser, M., and Segal, M.W. (2002) Women's Participation in Armed Forces Cross Nationally: Expanding Segal's Model, *Current Sociology*, 50(5) 771–797.

Izraeli, D. (1997) Gendering Military Service in the Israeli Defense Forces, *Israel Social Science Research* 12(1) 129–166.

Jacobs, J. (1996) Gender Inequality and Higher Education, *Annual Review of Sociology*, 22, 153–185.

Kanter, R.M. (1977) *Men and Women of the Corporation*. New York: Basic Books.

Kark, R., and Eagly, A. (2010) 'Gender and Leadership: Negotiating the Labyrinth' in J.C. Chrisler and D.R. McCreary (eds), *Handbook of Gender Research in Psychology*. New York: Springer.

Katzenstein, M. Fainsod (1998) *Faithful and Fearless: Moving Feminist Protest inside the Church and the Military*. Princeton: Princeton University Press.

King, A. (2006) The Post-Fordist Military, *Journal of Political and Military Sociology*, 34(2) 359–374.

Kummel, G. (2002a) Complete Access: Women in the Bundeswehr and Male Ambivalence, *Armed Forces and Society*, 28(4) 555–573.

Kummel, G. (2002b) When Boy Meets Girl: The 'Feminization' of the Military, *Current Sociology*, 50(5) 615–639.

Lehring, G. (2003) *Officially Gay: The Political Construction of Sexuality by the U.S. Military*. Philadelphia, PA: Temple University Press.

Levy A. (2009) Either/Or, Sports, Sex and the case of Caster Semenya. *The New Yorker*. November 20, 2009, Pp. 46–59.

Lorber, J. (2005) *Breaking the Bowls: Degendering and Feminist Change*. New York: Norton.

Martin, P.Y. (1985) 'Group Sex Composition in Work Organizations: A Structural-normative Model' in S. Bacharach and R. Mitchell (eds), *Research in the Sociology of Organizations 4*, Greenwich, CT: JAI Press, 311–349.

Martin, P.Y. (1992) 'Gender, Interaction, and Inequality in Organizations' in Cecelia Ridgeway (ed.), *Gender, Interaction, and Inequality*. New York: Springer-Verlag, 208–231.

Martin, P.Y. (2001) 'Mobilizing Masculinities': Women's Experiences of Men at Work, *Organization*, 8(4) 587–618.

Martin, P.Y. (2003) "Said and Done' versus 'Saying and Doing': Gendering Practices, Practicing Gender at Work.' Gender and Society 17, 3, 342–366.

Mehran, Golnar (2009) Doing and Undoing Gender: Female Higher Education in the Islamic Republic of Iran, *International Review of Education*, 55(5/6) 541–559.

Meyer, L. (1996) *Creating GI Jane: Sexuality and Power in the Women's Army Corps during World War II.* New York: Columbia University Press.

Moskos, C. (1993) From Citizens' Army to Social Laboratory, *Wilson Quarterly*, Winter, 83–95.

Nagel, J. (1998) Masculinity and Nationalism: Gender and Sexuality in the Making of Nations, *Ethnic and Racial Studies*, 21(2) 242–270.

Pateman, C. (1989) *The Disorder of Women: Democracy, Feminism, and Political Theory.* Stanford, CA: Stanford University Press.

Paxton P. et al. (2006). The International Women's Movement and Women's Political Representation, 1893–2003, *American Sociological Review*, 71, 898–920.

Peach, L.J. (1996) 'Gender Ideology in the Ethics of Women in Combat' in J.H. Stiehm (ed.), *It's Our Military Too!* Philadelphia: Temple University Press, 156–194.

Pershing, J. (2003) Why Women Don't Report Sexual Harassment: A Case Study of an Elite Military Institution, *Gender Issues*, 21(4) 3–30.

Pretorius J. (2008). The Security Imaginary: Explaining Military Isomorphism, *Security Dialogue*, 39(1) 99–121.

Rehn, E., and Sirleaf, E.J. (2002) Women, War and Peace: The Independent Experts' Assessment on the Impact of Armed Conflict on Women and Women's Role in Peace-building, United Nations Development Fund for Women (UNIFEM).

Reme K. (2001) The Retention of Women in the Armed Forces: The Mothers' Dilemma or Maternal Wall? Joint Services and Staff College, British Armed Forces.

Russett B., and Oneal, John R. (2001) *Triangulating Peace: Democracy, Interdependence, and International Organizations.* New York: Norton.

Sasson-Levy, O. (2002) Constructing Identities at the Margins: Masculinities and Citizenship in the Israeli Army, *The Sociological Quarterly*, 43(3) 353–383.

Sasson-Levy, O. (2003) Feminism and Military Gender Practices: Israeli Women Soldiers in 'Masculine' Roles, *The Sociological Inquiry*, 73(3) 440–465.

Sasson-Levy, O. (2007) Contradictory Consequences of Mandatory Conscription: The Case of Women Secretaries in the Israeli Military, *Gender and Society*, 21(4) 481–507.

Sasson-Levy, O. (2008) Individual Bodies, Collective State Interests: The Case of Israeli Combat Soldiers, *Men and Masculinities*, 10(3) 296–321.

Sasson-Levy, O., and Amram-Katz, S. (2007) Gender Integration in Israeli Officer Training: Degendering and Regendering the Military, *Signs: Journal of Women in Culture and Society*, 33(1) 105–135.

Schofer, E., and Meyer, J. (2005) The World Wide Expansion of Higher Education in the Twentieth Century, *American Sociological Review*, 70, 898–920.

Segal, M.W. (1995) Women's Military Roles Cross National: Past, Present and Future, *Gender and Society*, 9(6) 757–775.

Shafir, G. (1998) *The Citizenship Debate.* Minneapolis: University of Minnesota Press.

Sion, L. (2008) Peacekeeping and the Gender Regime: Dutch Female Peacekeepers in Bosnia and Kosovo, *Journal of Contemporary Ethnography*, 37, 561–585.

Tallberg T. (2009) The Gendered Social Organization of Defence, Ph.D. Dissertation, Hanken School of Economics, Helsinki, Finland.

Winslow, D., and Dunn, J. (2002) Women in the Canadian Forces: Between Legal and Social Integration, *Current Sociology*, 50(5) 641–667.

Woodward, R., and Winter, P. (2004) Discourses of Gender in the Contemporary British Army. *Armed Forces and Society*, 30(2) 279–301.

Woodward, R., and Winter, P. (2006) Gender and the Limits to Diversity in the Contemporary British Army, *Gender, Work and Organization*, 13(1) 45–67.

Yoder, J.D. (1991) Rethinking Tokenism: Looking Beyond Numbers, *Gender and Society*, 5(2) 178–192.

# 24

# In the Back and Forth of Transmigration: Rethinking Organization Studies in a Transnational Key

MARTA B. CALÁS AND LINDA SMIRCICH
*University of Massachusetts at Amherst*

Along with the conditions of globalization, a dominant feature of social life has become the increase of transnational flows of multiple kinds – people, money, ideas, and images – (Appadurai, 1990; 1996; Vertovec, 2009). Within the organization studies literature, however, little attention is paid to the fact that transnational flows and interconnections are manifested in a multidirectional 'back and forth' of people, practices, and the like. Instead transnationalism in this literature refers mostly to transferring practices from one country to another, such as from headquarters to subsidiaries; or to the allocation of labor between 'home' and 'not home' such as with expatriate managers or immigrant workers, and even when offshoring work. In this chapter we suggest that the limited understanding of transnationalism in the organizational literature prevents observing that transnational flows permeate all organizational life whether in big or small organizations, 'local' or 'global.' To this effect, we propose ways for reconsidering organization studies, more generally, in a transnational key.

At its most fundamental, transnational relations under these contemporary conditions are based on mobility across time and space, not only crossing boundaries between established places but also creating new spaces and relationships among them. Some of these relationships are hierarchical, for instance new conditions of subordination for displaced populations (e.g. sourcing of 'nannies' worldwide); but others are transversal, such as when domestic workers organize in transnational labor unions. Thus, a transnational focus of analysis would attend to the potential formation of new hierarchical relations in these spaces but, concurrently, would pay attention to other emerging relationships and, in effect, to the formation of new relevant actors within them. This means that attending, for instance, to transnational alliances of all kinds would not necessarily presuppose historical or cultural conditions of domination and subordination as a starting point (e.g. Ong, 1999). In this sense, postcolonial analyses, in particular, may be sometimes pertinent (e.g. Lee and Park, 2008) but not sufficient for understanding the complex formation of new transnational spaces and ensuing relationships emerging from these at present (Sharpe, 1995; McClintock, 1995).

In developing this line of argument, we draw upon a specific body of transnational theorizing: contemporary transnational migration studies (e.g. Levitt and Jaworsky, 2007). Reviewing basic works, we focus in particular on their conceptualizations of transmigration and transnational social fields. Transmigration, as a core transnational process, focuses on 'immigrants whose daily lives depend on multiple and constant interconnections across international borders and whose public identities are configured in relationship to more than one nation-state' (Glick Schiller, Basch, and Szanton-Blanc, 1995: 48). Transmigrants simultaneously reiterate and transgress the bounded nation, and at the same time foster the formation of transnational social fields – comprised of shifting relationships and networks – which are, in fact, negotiated transnational spaces (e.g. Brah, 2007). Gendered/sexual, racialized/ethnicized, and classed relations are central in constituting these fields (e.g. Hondagneu-Sotelo, 2000; Mahler and Pessar, 2001; 2006), as also noted more generally in studies of gendered processes in globalizing capital (e.g. Acker, 2004; 2006; Connell, 1998; 2005).

Using this theoretical support, we briefly review and illustrate with examples recent literatures in three domains of organization studies: international entrepreneurship, diversity, and expatriation. Each of these literatures contains an 'international' theme but they do not quite represent what we mean by 'transnational.' Through notions of transmigration and the formation of transnational social fields, we reposition them as occupying contiguous spaces in a common field of analysis, which allows articulating what is silenced in each as well as what they share in common. In so doing, we intend to provide a suitable entry point for, eventually, extending these arguments to various other organizational literatures.

Epistemological foundations for our analyses are also supported by transnational feminist scholarship. This work questions how nation-state boundaries become naturalized, noting the artificiality and contingent nature of 'the nation,' as well as its contemporary reproduction in diverse patriarchal 'nationalisms' (e.g., Mendoza, 2002). Boundaries are continuously in process, they argue, rearticulated as well as variously undercut by innumerable types of networks in which people in the world are involved. At the same time, they note the heterogeneity of these networks and question claimed commonalities of 'the global,' such as in 'global sisterhood.' Analyses focus on shifts in boundaries and networks and, in this context, examine interconnections between, for instance, finance, labor, gender, race, and sexuality (e.g. Grewal, 2008; Grewal and Kaplan, 1994; Kaplan and Grewal, 1999; Mohanty, 2003; Spivak, 1999).

Drawing from these perspectives, the kind of organizational theorizing we believe is needed now would start from the gendered/racialized/classed processes of production and consumption worldwide which enable the globalization activities of a myriad of transnational actors (e.g. Grewal, 2005; Mohanty, 1997; 2003; Rofel, 2007). In this context, there is no longer 'local' without 'global' but this is not the same as 1990s popularized notions of 'glocal' – e.g. 'think globally, act locally' – also in studies of globalization (e.g. Robertson, 1992; Hampton and Wellman, 2002). Rather, this requires taking into account concurrently but without conflation 'the global' in 'the local' and 'the local' in 'the global' as transnational relationships – i.e. the constant 'back and forth' of people between places – define the possibilities of a continuously changing world (see e.g. Briggs, McCormick and Way, 2008; Kearney, 1995).

In summary, we posit that transnationalism is the state of the world today and that in this world we all are the transmigrants. Globalization in the neoliberal economics sense is one of the processes producing this situation, but with caveats remarking the variability and heterogeneity of forms of neoliberalism at present (Ong, 2006). At its most fundamental this is a world of mobility and mobilization, of interconnections and networks, but with a 'from' and a 'to' and a 'back again'. Based on these premises, we ask two basic questions: First, who are the relevant actors in a transnational organizational world so conceived? Second, where are they found? A shift in perspectives within organization studies, including recognizing the formation of new historical actors, may be needed before these questions can be answered appropriately.

Yet, we are clear that theoretical analyses of this kind are an early step in rethinking organization studies in the transnational key we are imagining; thus, we forward this chapter as a modest starting point for what we suggest is a needed conversation. At the end, we also consider briefly how these ideas could affect empirical research, including defining the subject/s of research, methodological issues, as well as the position of the researcher and the questions s/he would ask.

## Transmigration and the Creation of Transnational Social Fields

In contrast to traditional notions of immigrants as those who move from one nation-state and settle into another leaving behind their past, transmigrants are the subjects of transnational migration. As stated in the works of Glick-Schiller and colleagues, transnational migration (i.e. transmigration) 'is inextricably linked to the changing conditions of global capitalism and must be analyzed within the context of global relations between capital and labor' (Basch, Glick-Schiller, and Szanton-Blanc, 1994: 22; see also, Glick-Schiller, Basch, and Blanc-Szanton, 1992). In fact, the original adoption of 'transnational' in association with 'migration' – i.e. transmigration – was intended to parallel works on 'transnational corporations' to highlight the contrast between the free movement of capital and the barriers to movement faced by labor (Glick Schiller and Levitt , 2006).

Transmigrants may become incorporated into the country where they reside, and participate in economic and political activities in that country but, concurrently, 'maintain connections, build institutions, conduct transactions, and influence local and national events in the countries from which they emigrated' (Glick-Schiller et al., 1995: 48). Thus, transmigrants are not just migrants moving from one place to another but enablers of other activities, changing the economic, political, and cultural configurations of the various countries involved, and as such questioning assumptions of the bounded nation-state. Importantly, beyond political and economic activities, Glick-Schiller et al. observe the implication of transmigration in class, gender, and race differentiation in relational identity formations between and within each of these countries.

Levitt and Glick Schiller (2004), further problematize the nation-state as privileged territory for understanding social relations by extending the concept of transnational social field to be considered simultaneously with national social fields. These fields are not equivalent to nations or contained by national boundaries but are formed in transnational mobilizations and, for that reason, they offer a powerful way for understanding the continuous processes linking and re-linking social relations across borders between those who move (e.g. transmigrants) and those who stay. Specifically, these authors note how it is no longer possible to differentiate among local, national, transnational, and global connections, for 'near and distant connections penetrate the daily lives of individuals lived within a locale. But within this locale, a person may participate in personal networks or receive ideas and information that connects them to others in a nation-state, across the borders of a nation-state, or globally without ever having migrated' (2004: 1010). They also consider a need for extending these notions beyond the domain of migration, as this is only one among other transnational practices and processes informing transnational social fields, such as 'firms and markets as parts of transnational fields of investment, production, distribution, and exchange' (p. 1029).

Problematizing the boundaries of the nation-state, as transnational feminism also does, is part of inquiry into the relationships between global movements and the continuity of the nation-state, seen as dialogic and often contested and contradictory processes (e.g. Yuval-Davis, Anthias, and Kofman, 2005). Transmigration literatures admit to contemporary accounts of globalization, such as time-space compression through technological connectivity and ease of travel, as well as the circulation of ideas and ideologies, the importance of complex networks, and various processes underpinning new identity formations (e.g. Appadurai, 1990; Castells, 1996; Harvey, 1989; Tomlinson, 1999). In addition, they do not ignore or reject reconceptualizations of the nation and nationalisms such as 'imagined communities' (Anderson, 1983/1991) or 'border thinking' (Grosfoguel, Saldívar, and Maldonado-Torres, 2007; Mignolo, 2000), but take these ideas beyond theoretical analyses to critically zero-in on concrete movements, bodies, places, and displacements, as well as on material outcomes of all these. Their focus is on the agency of transmigrants as builders of social fields.

Altogether, by paying attention to the core formation processes of the transmigrant as residing in the materiality of actual practices and in the consequences of their realization, transnational migration studies concretely show how people and places matter. Interrelationships among gender, race, and class or what is often termed 'intersectionality' (Davis, 2008), are crucial in the constitution of the transmigrant, part and parcel of transmigration activities (e.g. Burton, 2004; Elmhirst, 2000; Grillo, 2007; Levitt and Glick Schiller, 2004; Mahler and Pessar, 2001; 2006; Walton-Roberts and Pratt, 2005). Yet, in this work intersectionality is a social process emerging from concrete practices, ideas, and social relations operating simultaneously in transnational social fields (Levitt and Glick Schiller, 2004). It cannot be seen merely as interplay of pre-established social categories or multiple relational subjectivities. Rather, these ideas have inspired alternative identity conceptualizations in transnational migration such as Anthias' 'translocational positionality' (2002; 2006). Specifically, gender/sexuality/race/ethnicity and class relations are negotiated and reorganized accordingly in one location in reference to another, as well as according to economic and social circumstances in each place.

For instance, a woman's understanding of her gender/race/ethnicity and social status in the location where she lives may well be the opposite of her self-understanding in the location where she came from and to which she may return, as gender, race, ethnicity, and class may not be practiced or be meaningful in the same way in each place. Further, her social positioning as 'migrant' or 'native' is part of transmigrant circulation, which acquires meanings in actions and interactions with others in each and between locations. The same would indeed apply to men. Further, all these variations in gender/sexuality/race/ethnicity and class relations are carried in practices from place to place, informing those places as much as transforming them, and therefore redrawing the boundaries of 'national' understandings about gender, race, and class. In fact, these new understandings are negotiated in transnational social fields.

In summary, the relevant analytical argument here is about the variations of gendered/sexualized/racialized/ethnicized/classed relations constructed simultaneously in transnational social fields – i.e. spaces created and reconfigured in the 'back and forth' of transmigration. These analytical premises recognize the historical but contingent sedimentation of places, institutions, and traditions and make visible what happens thereafter as new actors appear in this 'back and forth'. It is from these perspectives that we examine the organization literatures below.

## WHERE ARE THE TRANSMIGRANTS? EXAMINING THREE ORGANIZATION LITERATURES

Who are the relevant actors in a transnational organizational world? Where are they found? We briefly review international entrepreneurship literature; diversity literature involving the movement of people and/or practices; and international management literature dealing with new modes of expatriation, and rethink them as examples of transmigration. In this rethinking, we claim, all actors are transmigrants and, in their activities, they produce and become subjects of transnational social fields. Yet, in order to bring all this to visibility it is necessary to reposition these literatures. What may be missing in each of them? What else, who else may be there?

### Who is a transnational entrepreneur?

As starting point, this theme brings organizational literature in almost direct engagement with transnational migration literature on the same theme. Contrasting these two literatures allows us to observe a multiplicity of transnational social fields that otherwise may be hidden in the organization literature.

First, in the entrepreneurship literature, international entrepreneurship has been gaining attention but it is usually positioned within the broader international business literature where the focus is on managerial activities and business goals rather than on the social location of the people involved (e.g. Oviatt and McDougall, 1994). The notion of 'born-global', in particular, is now prominent in this literature (e.g. Moen and Servais, 2002). Succinctly, these are small enterprises that shortly after being founded participate in international activities. Typical explanations for their internationalization processes are a search for competitive advantage beyond national borders, facilitated by the globalization of markets and the ease of transportation and communication. However, more recently, some authors have noted the unique importance of cross-border social networks for born-global entrepreneurs, where ethnic and other social ties play a vital role (e.g. Karra and Phillips, 2004; Zhou, Wu, and Luo, 2007).

Meanwhile, in the transnational migration literature, there is a long-standing stream focusing on immigrants' transnational entrepreneurial ventures, usually addressing the implication of ethnic relations in these activities (e.g. Moraswska, 2004; Portes and Guarnizo, 1991). Class location, ethnic resources, and racial status of immigrants in the host society when related to the economic and political importance of their home countries for the host country's interests seem to steer immigrant entrepreneurs' transnational activities along diverse paths. For instance, in New York City, Chinese traders are contributors to global finance and to the expansion of transnational corporations, but Dominican immigrants function as laborers in the city while concurrently creating a network of small businesses in their own country (Moraswska, 2004). Thus, the 'born-global' phenomenon could be refined, the populations involved could be better understood, and better explanations about what facilitates or hinders their activities could be obtained, through analyses such as these – linking ethnicity, race, and class, and structural level processes in transnational social fields – than by traditional managerial explanations.

In contrast to the 'born-global' literature, recent organizational studies focuses on the entrepreneurial activities of immigrants within host countries, highlighting the gender and ethnic social location of these entrepreneurs (e.g. Pio, 2007). For example, the work of Essers et al. (Essers and Benschop, 2007; 2009; Essers, Benschop and Doorewaard, 2010) researched Muslim immigrant women in the Netherlands, acknowledging the importance of diasporic traditions that were maintained but also reframed in the context of local entrepreneurial activities. Yet, they fail to discuss whether these entrepreneurs maintain relationships between host and home countries. Meanwhile, Katila (2010) interviewed primarily male members of Chinese family businesses in Finland, and noted how the extant organizational literature stereotypes them, concealing variations of cultural adaptations to the host country by different generations. Some interviewees indicated that they were considering China as a location for retirement, but there was no follow-up in the interviews regarding how social ties with China would have been maintained in the meantime. In short, potential transnational activities of each group – e.g. Muslim women in the Netherlands; Chinese restaurateurs in Finland – including possible remittances, imports, and travel, do not appear in these studies, nor do the ways gendered ethnic identities may foster or hinder them.

Findings in the transnational migration literature, meanwhile, indicate the importance of the Chinese diaspora for local development in China (e.g. Smart and Hsu,
2004). Others have shown that gender, ethnicity, and class serve to differentiate
immigrants engaged in entrepreneurship across borders, and those who otherwise
limit their activities within the host country. For instance, some studies report that
migrant transnational entrepreneurs are overwhelmingly married men and tend
to be better educated, have higher occupational status in the host countries, and
participate in multiple cross-borders networks (Portes, 2003; Portes, Escobar, and
Radford, 2007). Thus, in the organizational literature, it would be fruitful to investigate how these conditions – which occur in transnational social fields – might play
out in limiting or facilitating transnational activities of women immigrant entrepreneurs and of certain ethnic groups, who otherwise may appear as engaged by choice
only in host country entrepreneurial activities.

In contrasting entrepreneurship organization literatures with transnational migration literature on entrepreneurship, we have highlighted aspects of the latter which
could be easily related to, and therefore integrated with existing organizational topics. However, as we show in the next two sections, the notions of transmigration and
transnational social fields have conceptual value that extends beyond their applica-
bility to the common topic of entrepreneurship. Much more is happening in the
'back' and 'forth' of transmigration.

### Diversity: moving people and moving practices

Within the now extensive literature on diversity in organizations, two themes are
appearing more frequently: the first addresses participation of members from various ethnic backgrounds, often immigrants or refugees, in established organizations
and institutions within host countries; the second is concerned with the transformation of diversity practices as they are implemented in a range of countries. In
principle, these two literatures have little in common other than falling under the
umbrella of 'diversity,' however we see them connected in what they omit, as both
literatures reiterate 'the local' despite the evident transnational elements of their
topics.

Adib and Guerrier (2003) is a frequently cited example within the first theme.
Focusing on four cases based on interviews, their study addressed how gender,
nationality, race, ethnicity, and class intersect and are negotiated to shape the work
identities of women management trainees in hotel reception and chambermaid
work. All interviewees resided in the UK, but one was British and the other three
were immigrants from Jamaica, Israel, and Spain. Two, including the UK national,
trained in the UK and the other two in the US. While articulating clearly the race/
ethnicity and nationality of all interviewees, the significance of the immigrant status
of three interviewees is mostly ignored throughout the study until almost the end,
and only in the context of an incident in the US, a fact that in effect marks the interviewees as otherwise integrated into UK society. Below, we'll come back to this study
and discuss its relevance for our argument.

Meanwhile, most studies within this theme are much less clear in recognizing
specific differentiation between the groups represented in their studies, usually

making distinctions only between immigrants and non-immigrants. This, in effect, homogenizes the immigrants in distinction to the host society while, at the same time, muting their specific relationships with their places of origin (e.g. Boorgaard and Roggeband, 2010; Siebers, 2009). For example, Kalonaityte (2010) studied the incorporation of immigrants into Swedish society via a cultural training program established for these purposes. Supported by postcolonial arguments, the study is critical of the contradictions between diversity and assimilation; however differences among the immigrants involved in these activities are very much effaced while the Swedish context is reiterated throughout the critiques.

Similarly, Tomlinson (2010) considered experiences of women refugees in the UK, originally from various countries, as volunteers in organizations serving as pathways to regular employment. The study focused on contradictions between policies fostering refugees' labor participation and their implementation, in contrast to how the refugees reported the obstacles for obtaining sustained paid employment. The article emphasized the potential 'othering' of these populations by multicultural policies, which might limit their participation more widely in UK society. However, this concern in the study may have also smoothed out important differences between experiences reported by the refugees themselves – depending on their specific origin – and limited understanding of the variety of reasons for their difficulties. These literatures, more generally, share a strong focus on identity formation in organizations, addressing tensions between promoting equality and recognizing differences of diverse non-native populations that, seemingly, are expected to be incorporated into the host society. Paradoxically, the arguments shed more light on the host society than on the non-native populations.

From our perspective, what is missing in this literature is recognition that the immigrant populations may retain their ties and identifications with their home countries while being physically located in the host countries, and accepting or resisting incorporation. They are likely to be members of diverse diasporas and identify themselves in relation to those and others in their countries of origin with whom they may be connected. These networks and interconnections may well be of more relevance for understanding how they act in the host countries than observations obtained only from their places of work. Yet, analyses of this kind would require rethinking these populations as transmigrants, and studying them relationally in the context of activities occurring in transnational social fields between sending and receiving countries (e.g. Morawska, 2004).

One potential example of this type of analysis was prefigured even if not fully addressed in Adib and Guerrier's research already described: One trainee, residing in the UK but originally from Spain, was sexually harassed by a co-worker from Latin America while she trained in the US. In the interview, the trainee explained that it was mostly immigrant women from several countries who were harassed by this same co-worker, and further noted that this may have been because he lacked a visa and therefore he would not harass American women, who could create trouble for him. The interviewee also reported being able to defuse the advances of the co-worker by drawing on their common language (Spanish) and immigrant status, which helped her claim solidarity with him insofar as they both were subjected to similar difficulties in the workplace. In the analyses of these incidents, the research did note the significance of differentiation among immigrants, in this case from Hispanic diaspora populations, and the intercrossing of specific ethnicities and genders. Even so, for us there is more to the dynamics reported by this interviewee and others in the study insofar as the overarching theme is the encounters they report in their movements from place to place. From this perspective, they offer excellent examples of the 'back and forth' of transmigration, and the existence of activities that would only be seen, and be meaningful, if studied as occurring in transnational social fields.

This brings us to another contemporary organizational literature, which studies what happens when diversity practices and programs originally conceived in the US become implemented in various other countries. Recent examples, among others, include Boxenbaum (2006) and Kamp and Hagedorn-Rasmussen (2004), who reflect on the implementation of diversity policy in Denmark; Klarsfeld's (2009) observations regarding the adoption of diversity programs in France as simultaneously voluntary and mandated in contrast to voluntary practices in the US; Omanović's (2009), which focused on the production of diversity programs in an originally Swedish multinational acquired by a US company; and Poster's (2008) case study of a transfer of diversity programs from a US multinational to its subsidiary in India.

Perhaps the most obvious point we can make is that, taken together, all the studies mentioned reflect the appearance of a transnational phenomenon – i.e. the transfer across borders of diversity practices and programs. However, only Poster's addresses this transfer as part of transnational dynamics. The others focus, instead, on the differentiation of these programs from the norm in the US as they arrive to their local 'destinations.' Sometimes these studies note the implication of certain transnational actors in the movement of diversity practices between countries, such as networks of consultants, but, in general, the literature is not attentive to what happens 'across borders'; that is, the transnational social fields that are formed through the networks in which these actors are involved.

Poster's research, meanwhile, is a good representative of what we imagine as studying this topic in a transnational key that recognizes the formation of transnational social fields. For instance, her case includes noting hierarchical relationships between headquarters and subsidiary in the transfer of diversity programs from the US to India. These relationships are mediated, on the one hand, by the North–South locations of these countries in the global political economy and, on the other, by the decentralized organization structure of the multinational, which gives some voice to the subsidiary's local (i.e. Indian) managers. In this context, she notes the deployment of 'global/local' rhetoric by both management sides involved in negotiations to transfer these programs, such that gendered rhetoric dominates the US side despite the fact that employees report ethnic/racial discrimination, while racialized rhetoric dominates in India even when employees report gender discrimination. Concurrently, the author observes that both sides tend to ignore the intersections of gender, race, and class inequalities. In general, the study finds that often it is the interests of the actual managers involved that determine the outcome, as '[d]iversity policy then becomes the symbolic focal point for expressing tensions managers have with these various global and local actors' (2008: 336).

## New modes of expatriation

In this last theme, we move to the context of transnationalism proper where Levitt and Glick-Schiller (2004) have argued that 'firms and markets as parts of transnational fields of investment, production, distribution, and exchange' (p. 1029) are implicated in the formation of gendered, racialized, and classed transnational social fields.

In this context, some of the transnational organizational literature recently has noted the complexity but continuous importance of face-to-face contacts and interactions for globalization. Virtual connections are not enough, in particular, when professional workers and other elite organizational groups are involved (e.g. Beaverstock, 2005; Kennedy, 2005; Nooteboom, 2000). Therefore, new modes of expatriation seem to be emerging. For instance, Jones (2007) posited the necessity of face-to-face interactions at all levels of the organization for daily productive activities in transnational operations. As empirical evidence, Jones interviewed several lawyers working transnationally and among the quotes used for illustration he noted, in a footnote, the masculine pronoun used by one interviewee, a senior partner in a law firm in the UK, when referring to his peers. The footnote explains the masculine pronoun as indication that in the UK there are few women at senior levels in law firms because of 'the high dropout rate of women between the associate and Partner level in the firm' (2007: 238, footnote 6). Nothing else is said as to why such is the case and no other demographics are noted throughout the article. In fact, the data are so gender-neutral that it seems the footnote was needed only because the interviewee violated the researcher's intended gender neutrality for his data. The face-to-face is at the end rendered necessary but unremarkable as a normal practice of transnationalization. From our perspective, however, this account fails to note how the face-to-face produces gendered transmigrants. That is, insofar as the lack of women lawyers from the UK involved in transnational engagements is simply footnoted as due to their 'high dropout rate' in that country, the account naturalizes the transnational face-to-face as mostly a practice of elite men.

Transmigration is also produced in the performance of TNCs ordinary activities traditionally known as 'expatriation.' For example, Millar and Salt (2008) discuss how UK-based TNCs source and manage expertise and mobilize people to various locations in the world within their internal labor markets. The article focuses on highly skilled people in two sectors: aerospace and extractive industries, but it does not report specific demographics regarding who these people are. Yet, there is indeed a class-related argument in that 'managing the mobility of expertise has become a key element in corporate globalization' (p. 27). The rest of the article goes on to research how companies attain these ends, deriving a typology of 'portfolios of mobility' which includes long- and short-term assignments, commuting, rotation, business travel of shorter and longer duration and, lastly, virtual mobility.

A gendered subtext under the guise of 'family issues' is frequently repeated as one of the defining characteristics of these portfolios, but gender is never explicitly mentioned. Family issues serve as a rationale for engaging in one type of mobility versus another when, for instance, family members usually do not accompany the assignee in short-term assignments but are likely to do so in those of a longer term. However, commuting may be a substitute option for career development when someone would prefer not to be in either a long- or short-term assignment for family reasons; as well, business travel may supplement or substitute for these types of assignment under certain personal circumstances such as dual-career families 'where travel can dislocate family life' (2008: 35). In the conclusion, the authors remark that '[c]ompanies allocate human resources as circumstances dictate in ways that resolve constraints and that fit in with the desires and aspirations of their workforce' (p. 46). Who that workforce might be is left unspecified, and thus these explanations are disembodied (see chapters in the Section on Embodiment this volume).

However, Hearn, Jyrkinen, Piekkari, and Oinonen (2008) put some flesh onto this picture by noting the non-gendered character of most IHRM and global management research. Even when gender is addressed it is usually in reference to women as expatriates or as spouses of men expatriates, while men managers are seldom mentioned by gender. They also note that research on work/home balance tends to neglect 'global and transnational matters while research on IHRM neglects work/home relations' (2008: 52). Thus, their research sets out to correct these omissions by connecting three distinct but interlinked arenas in the gendering processes of transnational management: careers; transnational managerial work; and personal, family, and marriage-type relations.

Interviewing men and women, middle managers from seven different Finnish multinationals with high levels of internationalization in their operations, the researchers also note that Finland has a well-developed ideology and politics of gender equality and leads, together with other Nordic countries, in women's empowerment worldwide. The country has a tradition of women working full-time but also has a dual gendered labor market, where recruitment for business management positions, especially for top management, tends to be male.

A high degree of internationalization does not seem to influence negatively the proportion of women managers in Finland; however, the research did find several differences between women's transnational managerial work and that of their male counterparts, as well as differences in their personal circumstances. Most foreign assignments were long-term, however, and all managers, men and women, had to travel on international work assignments about five days per month. All male managers were married and had at least one child. Some women managers were single or divorced, some had no children, and, compared to male managers, on average had less than half the number of children. Men managers took for granted the traditional heterosexual marriage, considering it a 'natural choice' for their wives to stay at home and take care of the children, and mostly saw themselves as sometimes helpers to their wives rather than as adults responsible for everyday life. Meanwhile, for women managers a pressing issue was reconciling work and home life. In many cases, this required additional support such as a nanny or grandparents to take care of children. Some women managers 'ended up commuting between countries to cope with the reality of having a working husband and a family in Finland' (2008: 52).

So, what have we learned from these examples? In principle, it would be possible to say that they represent varieties of expatriation where the face-to-face plays a central role. It would also be possible to say that there has been an increasing attention to the gendering of these activities from the first to the last example. Yet, in our view they share many weaknesses when seen through the lenses of transnational migration studies. Specifically, this literature ignores the 'back and forth' of expatriation and how transnational social fields are created and populated by gendered/sexualized/racialized/ethnicized and classed relations, which change the state of the world where they operate.

For instance, by not recognizing the transnational implications of the 'lack of women' – which remained attached to a 'national situation' – the first example ignores what this may mean in the gendering of transnational law work, or in the gendering of transnational face-to-face work more generally – i.e. who actually goes 'back and forth.' Similarly, by disregarding that 'family issues' are gendered processes occurring in the space of transnational social fields, the second example ignores social reconfigurations happening between the various localities when actual people seek to or fail to mobilize with one another across putative national borders. This also includes the ethnic/racialized and classed processes that occur when companies decide, for instance, 'what nationalities can work on particular projects' (Millar and Salt, 2008: 40), often in negotiations with national governments granting visas or work permits.

In the third example, the authors provide very detailed descriptions of actual people involved in international assignments, and the gendered practices and processes associated with these assignments. They emphasize that 'there are very different social worlds inhabited by senior women and men managers' and that 'transnational processes can make those differences even greater' as 'men in very traditional social worlds may work alongside the few innovative women managers' (Hearn et al., 2008: 52). However, by focusing on the particularities of Finnish men's persistent traditionalism despite the country's record of gender equality – the article misses regarding these activities as gendered practices in transnational social fields. For instance, when commuting for family reasons the act of commuting is a 'back and forth' full of different engagements between self and others. Who commutes to where, and what happens on each side between the commuters and those who stay may change understanding between the ones and the others, perhaps producing more emancipatory gendered practices but also possible emergent patriarchies.

Finally, all our examples share, as well, a focus on managerial and highly skilled positions and practices attuned to 'cosmopolitan' populations (i.e. whose 'family issues' are portrayed?). These arguments are presented as understood from the particulars of managerial positions in dominant European countries (UK and Finland in our examples), intertwined with industries supporting 'national interests' in the case of Millar and Salt's research. Who is not seen here? Various others disappear from view (see e.g. Acker, 2004; Connell, 1998; 2005; Freeman, 2001; Hearn, 2004). For instance, who are the nannies taking care of the children of Finnish women expatriates? Where do they come from?

Several gendering (as well as ethnic, racial, and class) patterns occur, for example, when recruiters for TNCs – or for local companies with whom TNCs contract or make alliances – decide who is best for certain jobs. Recruitment patterns occur in transnational social fields, supported through ideologies carried by employers and their agents as to who constitutes an 'ideal worker' in often standardized and apparently neutral tools of HRM recruitment and selection technologies developed by TNCs and deployed globally (e.g. Yu and Wu, 2009). It is through these that the bodies of men and women, and genders, ethnicities, races, social classes, and so on, become slotted into their 'rightful places' (e.g. Geppert & Williams, 2006; McDowell, 2008). These include purveyors of low wage work in movements of rural populations to manufacturing zones, urban domestic services sometimes servicing expatriates, and many others who enable the 'local' activities of transnational organizations (Mahler and Pessar, 2006).

The mobilizations provoke other transmigration micro-activities such as sending remittances home, which change family relations between those who moved and those who stayed. That is, these activities occur in transnational social fields populated by people whose interconnections and linkages in various national and transnational networks remain silenced when theorizing about TNC operations privileges the market activities of 'the global command elite' (Burton, 2004: 793).

## Transnational social fields as places of research

Much of what we have discussed above may well apply to most people in the world at present, either because one moves or because one is related in various ways to those who do. Further, relationships among organizations within and between nations, including varieties of institutions, public and private, media, and so on, are carriers of these processes. From these perspectives, we all are relationally involved in 'transmigration' activities as a matter of course in everyday life.

If we all are implicated in these processes, as organizational scholars we can open space for conceptualizing all organizational activities as occurring within transnational social fields. At a minimum, this will mitigate the highly valorized distance of the corporate elite supported by abstract ideological principles of neoliberalism – as noted by Burton (2004) – who would no longer be able to deny their implications in the concrete consequences of their actions wherever they occur. As well, populations of all kinds would be given voice in these spaces by, paraphrasing Davis (2001), recognizing the absolute simultaneity and the radical contemporaneity of all groups in contact in the world. At the end, 'transnational' (implying 'between nations') may become a redundant category of analysis insofar as 'the nation' would have become disrupted as a conceptual space. Instead, transnational social fields would be the place for research.

How does one do research in transnational social fields? To this effect, a couple of further questions are in order. First, who are the subjects of the research, insofar as we all are transmigrants? One interesting argument from Doyle's (2009) reflecting on the possibilities for bringing the transnational and the intersubjective together may offer some clues. She starts from a notion of 'tilted subjects' partially informed by Merleau-Ponty's intercorporeality, and ends up with a vision of subjects 'thrown' together 'caught-up-alongside each other, intertwined dialectically with each other by way of a materiality we never quite hold yet always inhabit [. . .] In truth, no "subject" enters the exchange; rather the exchange continually makes the subject – socially encircled intersubject' (pp. 10–11).

What would this imply methodologically? Studies of transmigration, often carried out by anthropologists through ethnographic works, are rich in details highlighting the nature of these activities and engaging their participants directly and reflexively. In this sense, intersubjectivity is no stranger to ethnographic work, and – after postmodernism – it could easily accommodate a socially encircled transmigrant intersubject. Nonetheless, it is important to acknowledge that transnational social fields are wide networks of interconnections beyond locality and, therefore, the question of place is more a question of relational engagements wherever the encounter between research co-participants may be happening.

Thus, addressing methodology as such is perhaps premature, as many other possible methodological approaches would equally serve the purpose, (e.g. latitudinal citizenship (Ong, 2006); multi-sited ethnographies (Marcus, 1995); relational geometries (Yeung, 2002)). Yet, transnational feminist research has also addressed the possible lack of relevance of 'traveling' theoretical frameworks and languages for the populations with whom one does research. There are also difficulties in co-producing relevant knowledge for varieties of populations across geographical and cultural borders within the constraints of academic structures in 'the West' and even within westernized academic institutions in 'the Rest' (e.g. Nagar, 2002; Spivak, 1990).

Perhaps the most significant question for us then is: Research in transnational social fields for what? For us, research in transnational social fields would provide ways to articulate clearly and consistently in organization theory the centrality of gender/ sexuality/race/ethnicity/class relations invisibly sustaining modalities of neoliberal globalization. And, more importantly, it would provide ways to duly note as a matter of course the complicity of organization theorizing and their attendant practices in the co-construction and exploitation of gender/sexuality/race/ethnicity and class relations worldwide. We have not yet fully formulated this engagement; rather we are asking for attention to be paid first to the simultaneity of processes that occur as organizational activities, at their most conventional, disrupt the bounded nation and new social spaces –transnational social fields – are created in those disruptions. Concretely, who are the new historical subjects produced in transmigration if this is the state of the world today? A 'multitude' would not just do (see e.g. Federici, 2008).

## References

Acker, J. (2004) Gender, Capitalism and Globalization, *Critical Sociology*, 30(1) 17–42.

Acker, J. (2006) *Class Questions Feminist Answers*. Lanham: Rowman and Littlefield.

Adib, A., and Guerrier, Y. (2003) The Interlocking of Gender, Nationality, Race, Ethnicity and Class: The Narratives of Women in Hotel Work, *Gender, Work and Organization*, 10(4) 413–432.

Anderson, B. (1983/1991) *Imagined Communities: Reflections on the Origin and Spread of Nationalism*. New York: Verso.

Anthias, F. (2002) Beyond Feminism and Multiculturalism: Locating Difference and the Politics of Location, *Women's Studies International Forum*, 25(3) 275–394.

Anthias, F. (2006) 'Belonging in a Globalizing and Unequal World: Rethinking Translocations' in N. Yuval-Davis, K. Kannabiran, and U. Vieten (eds), *The Situated Politics of Belonging*. London: Sage Publications, 17–31.

Appadurai, A. (1996) *Modernity at Large*. University of Minnesota Press.

Appadurai, A. (1990) Disjuncture and Difference in the Global Cultural Economy, *Public Culture*, 2(2) 1–24.

Basch, L., Glick Schiller, N., and Szanton-Blanc, C. (1994) *Nations Unbound: Transnational Projects and the Deterritorialized Nation-State*. New York: Gordon and Breach.

Beaverstock, J.V. (2005) Transnational Elites in the City: British Highly-skilled Inter-company Transferees in New York City's Financial Districts, *Journal of Ethnic and Migration Studies*, 31(2) 245–268.

Boorgaard, B., and Roggeband, C. (2010) Paradoxes of Intersectionality: Theorizing Inequality in the Dutch Police Force through Structure and Agency, *Organization*, 17(1) 53–75.

Boxenbaum, E. (2006) Lost in Translation: The Making of Danish Diversity Management, *American Behavioral Scientist*, 49(7) 939–948.

Brah, A. (2007) Travels in Negotiations: Difference, Identity, Politics, *Journal of Creative Communications*, 2(1&2) 245–256.

Briggs, L., McCormick, G., and Way, J.T. (2008) Transnationalism: A Category of Analysis, *American Quarterly*, 60(3) 625–648.

Burton, B. (2004) The Transmigration of Rights: Women, Movement and the Grassroots in Latin America and Caribbean Communities, *Development and Change*, 35(4) 773–798.

Castells, M. (1996) *The Rise of the Network Society*. Oxford: Blackwell.

Connell, R.W. (1998) Masculinities and Globalization, *Men and Masculinities*, 1(1) 3–23.

Connell, R.W. (2005) Change among the Gatekeepers: Men, Masculinities, and Gender Equality in the Global Arena, *Signs*, 30(3) 1801–1825.

Davis, K. (2008) Intersectionality as Buzzword. *Feminist Theory*, 9(1) 67–85.

Davis, N.Z. (2001) 'Polarities, Hybridities: What strategies for Decentering?' in G.Warkentin, G. and C. Podruchny (eds), *Decentering the Renaissance: Canada and Europe in a Multi-disciplinary Perspective, 1500–1700*. Toronto: University of Toronto Press, 19–32.

Doyle, L. (2009) Toward a Philosophy of Transnationalism, *Journal of Transnational American Studies*, 1(1) Article 7.

Elmhirst, R. (2000) A Javanese Diaspora? Gender and Identity Politics in Indonesia's Transmigration Resettlement Program, *Women's Studies International Forum*, 23(4) 487–500.

Essers, C., and Benschop, Y. (2007) Enterprising Identities: Female Entrepreneurs of Moroccan and Turkish Origin in the Netherlands, *Organization Studies*, 28(1) 49–69.

Essers, C., and Benschop, Y. (2009) Muslim Businesswomen doing Boundary Work: The Negotiation of Islam and Ethnicity within Entrepreneurial Contexts, *Human Relations*, 62(3) 403–423.

Essers, C., Benschop, Y., and Doorewaard, H. (2010) Female Ethnicity: Understanding Muslim Migrant Businesswomen in the Netherlands, *Gender, Work and Organization*, 17(3) 320–339.

Federici, S. (2008) Precarious Labor: A Feminist Viewpoint. *The Onion*, June 18.

Freeman, Carla (2001) Is Local: Global as Feminine: Masculine? Rethinking the Gender of Globalization, *Signs*, 26(4) 1007–1038.

Geppert, M., and Williams, K. (2006) Global, National and Local Practices in Multinational Corporations: Towards a Sociopolitical Framework, *International Journal of Human Resource Management*, 17(1) 49–69.

Grewal, I. (2005) *Transnational America: Feminism, Diaspora, Neoliberalism*. Durham: Duke University Press.

Grewal, I. (2008) 'The Transnational in Feminist Research: Concept and Approaches' in H. Brabandt, B. Rooss,, and S. Zwingel (eds), *Mehrheit am Rand? Geschlechterverhaeltnisse, globale Ungleichheit und transnationale Loesungsansaetze*. Wiesbaden: VS Verlag, 189–199.

Grewal, I., and Kaplan, C. (1994) *Scattered Hegemonies, Postmodernity and Transnational Feminist Practices*. Minneapolis: University of Minnesota Press.

Glick-Schiller, N., Basch, L., and Blanc-Szanton, C. (1992) *Towards a Transnational Perspective on Migration: Race, Class, Ethnicity and Nationalism Reconsidered*. New York: New York Academy of Sciences.

Glick Schiller, N., Basch, L., and Szanton-Blanc, C. (1995) From Immigrant to Transmigrant: Theorizing Transnational Migration. *Anthropological Quarterly*, 68(1) 48–63.

Glick Schiller, N., and Levitt, P. (2006) Haven't We Heard This Somewhere Before? A Substantive View of Transnational Migration Studies by Way of a Reply to Waldinger and Fitzgerald. Working paper CMD #06-01, 33 pp. *The Center for Migration and Development.* Princeton: Princeton University.

Grillo, R. (2007) Betwixt and Between: Trajectories and Projects of Transmigration, *Journal of Ethnic and Migration Studies*, 33(2) 199–217.

Grosfoguel, R., Saldívar, J.D., and Maldonado-Torres, N. (forthcoming) *Unsettling Postcoloniality: Coloniality, Transmodernity and Border Thinking.* Durham: Duke University Press.

Hampton, K. and Wellman, B. (2002) 'The not so Global Village of Netville' in B. Wellman and C. Haythornthwaite (eds), *The Internet in Everyday Life.* Oxford: Blackwell, 345–371.

Harvey D. (1989) *The Condition of Postmodernity: An Enquiry into the Origins of Cultural Change.* Cambridge, MA: Blackwell.

Hearn, J. (2004) Tracking 'the Transnational': Studying Transnational Organizations and Managements, and the Management of Cohesion, *Culture and Organization*, 10(4) 273–290.

Hearn, J., Jyrkinen, M., Piekkari, R., and Oinonen, E. (2008) 'Women Home and Away': Transnational Managerial Work and Gender Relations, *Journal of Business Ethics*, 83(1) 41–54.

Hondagneu-Sotelo, P. (2000). Feminism and Migration, *Annals of the American Academy of Political and Social Science*, 571, 107–120.

Jones, A. (2007) More than 'Managing across Borders?' the Complex Role of Face-to-face Interaction in Globalizing Law Firms, *Journal of Economic Geography*, 7(3) 223–246.

Kamp, A., and Hagedorn-Rasmussen, P. (2004). Diversity Management in a Danish Context: Towards a Multicultural or Segregated Working Life, *Economic and Industrial Democracy*, 25, 525–554.

Kaplan, C. and Grewal, I. (1999) 'Transnational Feminist Cultural Studies: Beyond the Marxism/ Poststructuralism/Feminism Divides' in C. Kaplan, N. Alarcón, and M. Moallem (eds), *Between Woman and Nation: Nationalisms, Transnational Feminisms and the* State. Durham: Duke University Press, 349–363.

Karra, N., and Phillips, N. (2004) Entrepreneurship Goes Global, *Ivey Business Journal*, November/December, 1–6.

Katila, S. (2010) Negotiating Moral Orders in Chinese Business Families in Finland: Constructing Family, Gender and Ethnicity in a Research Situation, *Gender, Work and Organization*, 17(3) 297–319.

Kearney, M. (1995) The Local and the Global: The Anthropology of Globalization and Transnationalism, *Annual Review of Anthropology*, 24(1) 547–565.

Kennedy, P. (2005) Joining, Constructing and Benefiting from the Global Workplace: Transnational Professionals in the Building-design Industry, *The Sociological Review*, 53(1) 173–197.

Klarsfeld, A. (2009) The Diffusion of Diversity Management: The Case of France, *Scandinavian Journal of Management*, 25(4) 363–373.

Kolonaityte, V. (2010) The Case of Vanishing Borders: Theorizing Diversity Management as Internal Border Control. *Organization*, 17(1) 31–52.

Lee, Y., and Park, K. (2008) Negotiating Hybridity: Transnational Reconstruction of Migrant Subjectivity in Koreatown, Los Angeles, *Journal of Cultural Geography*, 25(3) 245–262.

Levitt, P., and Glick Schiller, N. (2004) Conceptualizing Simultaneity: A Transnational Social Field Perspective on Society. *International Migration Review*, 38(3) 1002–1039.

Levitt, P., and Jaworsky, B.N. (2007) Transnational Migration Studies: Past Developments and Future Trends, *Annual Review of Sociology*, 33, 129–156.

Mahler, S.J. and Pessar, P.R. (2001) Gendered Geographies of Power: Analyzing Gender Across Transnational Spaces, *Identities: Global Studies of Culture and Power,* 7(4) 441–459.

Mahler, S.J., and Pessar, P.R. (2006) Gender Matters: Ethnographers Bring Gender from the Periphery toward the Core of Migration Studies, *International Migration Review,* 40(1) 27–63.

Marcus, G.E. (1995) Ethnography in/of the World System: The Emergence of Multi-sited Ethnography, *Annual Review of Anthropology,* 24, 95–115.

McClintock, A. (1995) 'Introduction: Postcolonialism and the Angel of Progress' in *Imperial Leather: Race, Gender and Sexuality in the Colonial Contest.* New York: Routledge.

McDowell, L. (2008) Thinking Through Work: Complex Inequalities, Constructions of Difference, and Trans-national Migrants, *Progress in Human Geography,* 32(4) 491–507.

Mendoza, B. (2002) Transnational Feminism in Question, *Feminist Theory,* 3(3) 295–314.

Mignolo, W. (2000) *Local Histories/Global Designs: Coloniality, Subaltern Knowledges, and Border Thinking.* Princeton: Princeton University Press.

Millar, J., and Salt, J. (2008) Portfolios of Mobility: The Movement of Expertise in Transnational Corporations in Two Sectors – Aerospace and Extractive Industries, *Global Networks,* 8(1) 25–50.

Moen, O., and Servais, P. (2002). Born Global or Gradual Global? Examining the Export Behavior of Small and Medium-sized Enterprises, *Journal of International Marketing,* 10(3) 49–72.

Mohanty, C.T. (1997) 'Women Workers and Capitalist Scripts: Ideologies of Domination, Common Interests, and the Politics of Solidarity' in M.J. Alexander and C.T. Mohanty (eds), *Feminist Genealogies, Colonial Legacies, Democratic Futures.* New York: Routledge, 3–29.

Mohanty, C.T. (2003) *Feminism Without Borders: Decolonizing Theory, Practicing Solidarity.* Durham: Duke University Press.

Morawska, E. (2004) Immigrant Transnational Entrepreneurs in New York: Three Varieties and their Correlates, *International Journal of Entrepreneurial Behavior and Research,* 10(5) 325–348.

Nagar, R. (2002) Footloose Researchers, 'Traveling' Theories, and the Politics of Transnational Feminist Praxis, *Gender, Place and Culture,* 9(2) 179–186.

Nooteboom, B. (2000) *Learning and Innovation in Organizations and Economies.* Oxford: Oxford University Press.

Omanović, V. (2009) Diversity and its Management as a Dialectic Social-historical Process, *Scandinavian Journal of Management,* 25(4) 352–362.

Ong, A. (1999) *Flexible Citizenship: The Cultural Logics of Transnationality.* Durham: Duke University Press.

Ong, A. (2006) *Neoliberalism as Exception: Mutations in Citizenship and Sovereignty.* Durham: Duke University Press.

Oviatt, B., and McDougall, P. (1994). Toward a Theory of International New Ventures, *Journal of International Business Studies,* 25(1) 45–64.

Pio, E. (2007) Ethnic Minority Migrant Women Entrepreneurs and the Imperial Imprimatur, *Women in Management Review,* 22(8) 631–649.

Portes, A. (2003) Conclusion: Theoretical Convergencies and Empirical Evidence in the Study of Immigrant Transnationalism, *International Migration Review,* 37(3) 874–892.

Portes, A., Escobar, C., and Radford, A.W. (2007) Immigrant Transnational Organizations and Development: A Comparative Study, *International Migration Review,* 41, 242–281.

Portes, A., and Guarnizo, L.E. (1991) 'Tropical Capitalists: U.S.-bound Immigration and Small Enterprise Development in the Dominican Republic' in S. Diaz-Briquets and S. Weintraub (eds), *Migration, Remittances, and Small Business Development, Mexico and Caribbean Basin Countries.* Boulder: Westview Press, 101–131.

Poster, W.R. (2008) Filtering Diversity: A Global Corporation Struggles with Race, Class, and Gender in Employment Policy, *American Behavioral Scientist*, 52(3) 307–341.

Robertson, R. (1992) *Globalization: Social Theory and Global Culture*. London: Sage.

Rofel, L. (2007) *Desiring China: Experiments in Neoliberalism, Sexuality and Public Culture*. Durham: Duke University Press.

Sharpe, J. (1995). Is the United States Postcolonial? Transnationalism, Immigration and Race, *Diaspora*, 4(2) 181–200.

Sievers, H. (2009) Struggles for Recognition: The Politics of Racioethnic Identity among Dutch National Tax Administrators, *Scandinavian Journal of Management*, 25, 73–84.

Smart, A., and Hsu, J.-H. (2004) The Chinese Diaspora, Foreign Investment and Economic development in China, *The Review of International Affairs*, 3(4) 544–566.

Spivak, G.C. (1990) The Problem of Cultural Self-representation. An Interview in S. Harasym (ed.), *The Post-Colonial Critic: Interviews, Strategies, Dialogues*. New York: Routledge.

Spivak, G.C. (1999) *A Critique of Postcolonial Reason: Toward a History of the Vanishing Present*. Cambridge: Harvard University Press.

Tomlinson, F. (2010) Marking Difference and Negotiating Belonging: Refugee Women, Volunteering and Employment, *Gender, Work and Organization*, 17(3) 278–296.

Tomlinson, J. (1999) *Globalization and Culture*. Chicago: University of Chicago Press.

Vertovec, S. (2009) *Transnationalism*. New York: Routledge.

Walton-Roberts, M., and Pratt, G. (2005) Mobile Modernities: A South Asian Family Negotiates Immigration, Gender and Class in Canada, *Gender, Place and Culture*, 12(2) 173–195.

Yeung, H.W.-C. (2002) Towards a Relational Economic Geography: Old Wine in New Bottles? Paper presented at the 98th Annual Meeting of the Association of American Geographers, Los Angeles, March 19–23.

Yu, T., and Wu, N. (2009) A Review of Theories on Transnational Transfer of HR Practice within Multinationals, *International Journal of Business and Management*, 4(5) 121–127.

Yuval-Davis, N., Anthias, F., and Kofman, E. (2005) Secure Borders and Safe Haven and the Gendered Politics of Belonging: Beyond Social Cohesion, *Ethnic and Racial Studies*, 28(3) 513–535.

Zhou, L., Wu, W.-P., and Luo, X. (2007) Internationalization and the Performance of Born-Global SMEs: The Mediating Role of Social Networks, *Journal of International Business Studies*, 38, 673–690.

# Biographies

JOAN ACKER

Joan Acker is Professor Emerita, Department of Sociology, University of Oregon, USA. Her scholarship has focused on class, women and work, gender and organizations, and feminist theory. Her visiting professorships include three years at the Swedish Center for Working Life in Stockholm, Sweden and the Marie Jahoda International Guest Professorship at Bochum University, Bochum, Germany. She has been awarded the American Sociological Association's Career of Distinguished Scholarship Award and the ASA Jessie Bernard Award for feminist scholarship. She is the founding director of the Center for the Study of Women in Society at the University of Oregon, a major feminist center for scholarship on gender and women. Her book, *Class Questions: Feminist Answers*, was published in 2006 by Rowman & Littlefield. A new book, *Stretched Thin: Poor Families, Welfare Work, and Welfare Reform*, coauthored with Sandra Morgen and Jill Weigt, was published in January 2010 by Cornell University Press. 'Inequality Regimes: Gender, Race, and Class in Organizations' published in *Gender & Society* in 2006 is a recent article. Earlier work includes *Doing Comparable Worth: Gender, Class and Pay Equity* (1989) and 'Hierarchies, Jobs, Bodies: A Theory of Gendered Organizations' (*Gender & Society* 1990).

EMMA BELL

Emma Bell is a Senior Lecturer in Organisation Studies at University of Exeter. Prior to this she worked at Universities of Bath, Queen Mary, and Warwick. A substantial aspect of her work at the moment explores the relationship between religion, spirituality and organization. She is also interested in issues relating to management research methods including visual analysis, ethnography, and research ethics and is co-author with Alan Bryman of *Business Research Methods* (2007), published by Oxford University Press. Her research has been published in journals like *Human*

*Relations, Journal of Management Studies,* and *Organization* and she has recently written a book on *Reading Management and Organization in Film* (2008) published by Palgrave Macmillan.

### YVONNE BENSCHOP

Yvonne Benschop is Professor of Organizational Behavior at the Nijmegen School of Management, affiliated with the Institute for Gender Studies at the Radboud University of Nijmegen, The Netherlands. Her main inspirations are feminist organization studies and critical management studies. Current research interests include the role of power and resistance in organizational change and the gender practices in networking and impression management. She is an associate editor of Organization and of Gender, Work and Organization. She is a regular speaker on gender and diversity at work at business conferences, and provides policy advice and contract research for government departments and private organizations.

### SHARON R. BIRD

Sharon R. Bird is Associate Professor of Sociology at Iowa State University. Bird's teaching and research focus primarily on issues of inequality and paid labor. She is currently Co-PI and Research Director of Iowa State University's ADVANCE Institutional Transformation project. ADVANCE is an NSF-funded project focused on the recruitment, retention, and promotion of women in academic science, technology, engineering and mathematics (STEM) fields. In addition to research related to the ADVANCE program, she is also currently conducting research on gendered organizations and the sex gap in small business success. Bird's recent research appears in journals including *Gender, Work & Organization, Teaching Sociology, Gender & Society,* and *Social Psychology Quarterly.*

### JOANNA BREWIS

Joanna Brewis works at the University of Leicester School of Management, UK, where she teaches research methodology, runs the doctoral programme and tries to find time to write about organizing as it pertains to identity, the body, sexuality, consumption, and popular culture. She has an unhealthy preoccupation with US police procedurals, flip-flops, and fridge magnets.

### MARTA B. CALÁS

Marta B. Calás is Professor of Organization Studies and International Management at the University of Massachusetts, Amherst, USA and adjunct faculty at the department of Women, Gender, and Sexuality Studies. Her work pursues the development of critical and socially engaged organization and management studies. Her research, in collaboration with Linda Smircich, applies insights from cultural studies and feminist theorizing to organizational topics such as entrepreneurship, knowledge production, business ethics, globalization, leadership, and work and family. In 2006 Marta and Linda received the Sage Award for scholarly contributions from the Gender, Diversity and Organization division of the Academy of Management. Marta is part of the founding editorial team of *Organization: The critical journal of organization, theory and society* and on the editorial board of *Gender, Work, and Organization*.

## CATHERINE CASEY

Catherine Casey is Professor of Organization and Society at the University of Leicester, United Kingdom. She holds an MA in Politics and Sociology; and a PhD in Sociology and Education from the University of Rochester, New York. Formerly working at the School of Business and Economics at the University of Auckland, New Zealand, she has held visiting fellowships at a number of international institutes and serves in advisory capacities to various policy and research bodies including the European Commission. She is currently Senior Editor of *Organization Studies*. Her research addresses questions in economy and society, with a main focus on education, work, organizations and institutions, labour markets and employment relations, and with a specialist interest in European labour markets. She is author of *Work, Self and Society: After Industrialism* (Routledge) and *Critical Analysis of Organizations: Theory, Practice, Revitalization* (Sage), and numerous scholarly articles published in international forums.

## BOGDAN COSTEA

Bogdan Costea works in the Department of Organization Work and Technology at Lancaster University. He is interested in the cultural and conceptual history of managerialism and its relationship to subjectivity and work in the context of modernity. Recent publications include: The Ethos of Business in H.G. Wells' Novel *The Wife of Sir Isaac Harman* ((2007), *Journal of Management History*, 13(1) 21–32); Managerialism and 'Infinite Human Resourcefulness': A Commentary on the 'Therapeutic Habitus', 'Derecognition of Finitude' and the Modern Sense of Self' ((2007), *Journal for Cultural Research*, 11(3) 245–264); Managerialism, the Therapeutic Habitus and the Self in Contemporary Organising ((2008), *Human Relations*, 61(5) 661–685).

## BARBARA CZARNIAWSKA

Barbara Czarniawska holds a Chair in Management Studies at GRI, School of Business, Economics and Law at University of Gothenburg, Sweden. She takes a feminist and constructionist perspective on organizing, most recently exploring the connections between popular culture and the practice of management, and the organization of the news production. She is interested in methodology, especially in techniques of fieldwork and in the application of narratology to organization studies. Recent books in English: *A Tale of Three Cities* (Oxford University Press, 2002), *Narratives in Social Science Research*, (Sage, 2004), *Actor-Network Theory and Organizing* (edited with Tor Hernes, Liber, 2005), *Global Ideas* (edited with Guje Sevón, Liber, 2005), *Management Education and Humanities* (edited with Pasquale Gagliardi, Edward Elgar, 2006), *Shadowing and Other Techniques of Doing Fieldwork in Modern Societies* (Liber, 2007), *A Theory of Organizing* (Edward Elgar, 2008).

## SILVIA GHERARDI

Silvia Gherardi is Professor of Sociology of Work and Organization at the University of Trento, Italy, where she coordinates the Research Unit on Communication, Organizational Learning, and Aesthetics (www.unitn.it/rucola). Her current interests include the study of learning and knowing in organizations and in relation to technological change. Her interests also span the theme of gender, narratives, safety, and organizational cultures. She has published extensively (20 books and 100 articles), including in top tier international journals such as *Organization, Organization Studies, Human Relations, Journal of Management Studies,* and *Management Learning.*

## JEFF HEARN

Jeff Hearn is Professor in Gender Studies (Critical Studies on Men) Linköping University, Sweden; Professor in Management and Organisation, Hanken School of Economics, Helsinki, Finland; and Professor of Sociology, University of Huddersfield, UK. His books include *'Sex' at 'Work'* (1987/1995), *The Gender of Oppression* (1987), *The Sexuality of Organization* (1989), *Men, Masculinities and Social Theory* (1990), *Men in the Public Eye* (1992), *Men as Managers, Managers as Men* (1996), *The Violences of Men* (1998), *Men, Gender Divisions and Welfare* (1998), *Hard Work in the Academy* (1999), *Gender, Sexuality and Violence in Organizations* (2001), *Information Society and the Workplace* (2004), *Handbook of Studies on Men and Masculinities* (2005), *Men and Masculinities in Europe* (2006), *European Perspectives on Men and Masculinities* (2006); *Sex, Violence and the Body* (2008), *Managers Talk About Gender* (2009), and *Leadership through the Gender Lens* (2010). He is an elected Academician (AcSS) of the Academy of Learned Societies for the Social Sciences (UK). His research interests include: men, gender, sexuality, violence, organisations, management, transnationalisation and postcolonialism.

## ANGELA HOPE

Angela Hope is Adjunct Professor of Religious Studies at the University of the Incarnate Word and in the Theology Department at Saint Mary's University, San Antonio, Texas. She received her Masters in Theological Studies from Boston University School of Theology, and is currently a PhD student at St. Mary's University Sobey School of Business in Halifax, Canada. She is a military police captain in the US Army Reserve and commands the HHC, 321st Civil Affairs Brigade. Her interests are in the body, religious influences in organizations, gender, trauma in the organization, and the military. Angela serves on the editorial board of the journal *Equality, Diversity, and Inclusion* and also is an Associate Editor for the journal *Gender, Work and Organization.*

## HEATHER HÖPFL

Heather Höpfl is Professor of Management at the University of Essex and Head of the Management Group. A psychologist by training but not by inclination, she has worked in a number of different jobs and fields including working on design with a large engineering company in Bristol, as an Economics teacher in a convent grammar school in Liverpool, as tour manager for a touring theatre company and a researcher with ICL,

Logica, and the DHSS. Since the 1990s she worked with British Airways on the design of their safety information system. She is a Visiting Professor at the Humanistic University, Utrecht and European editor of the *Journal of Management, Spirituality and Religion* and publishes widely. Recent publications have been on theorisation and reflection, on hell and damnation, on the sacred heart, and on heroines. She is married to Harro Höpfl and has two sons, George and Max.

### EMMA L JEANES

Emma L Jeanes is a Senior Lecturer at the University of Exeter, and holds visiting positions at Lund University, Sweden and Queensland University of Technology, Australia. Emma is an Associate Editor of *Gender, Work and Organization* and series editor for the *Gender and Organizational Theory* book series, Ashgate Publishing. She has published on gender, and more broadly in organisation theory, and draws on political theory and philosophy to inform her research. Emma recently completed her MA in Political Theory. Dr Jeanes is currently principal investigator on a British Academy funded project exploring the effects of the 'marriage bar' on women's lives.

### KATE KENNY

Kate Kenny is a Lecturer in Political Science and Sociology at the National University of Ireland, Galway. She is a Fellow and visiting Lecturer at Cambridge University's Judge Business School. She is a fellow of the Cambridge European Trust, and held an ESRC Postdoctoral Fellowship from 2007–08. Dr Kenny's research interests include issues of identity and power in contemporary workplaces, and the use of poststructuralist feminist theory to explore these phenomena.

### DAVID KNIGHTS

David Knights works in the Centre for Leadership and Organizational Ethics, Bristol Business School, UWE, BS16 1QY and is a Visiting Professor at Gothenburg School of Business, Economics and Law, Sweden. His latest book is *Introducing Organizational Behaviour and Management* (London: Thomson Cengage, 2005) (with H. Willmott). Latest journal articles are Myopic Rhetorics: Reflecting epistemologically and ethically on the demand for relevance in organizational and management research (2008), *Academy of Management Learning and Education*, December; and Making and Mending your Nets: The Management of Uncertainty in Academic/Practitioner Knowledge Networks (2009) *British Journal of Management*, 20, 125–142 (with C. Alferoff).

### PÄIVI KORVAJÄRVI

Päivi Korvajärvi is Professor of Women's Studies at the School of Humanities and Social Sciences of the University of Tampere, Finland. She has conducted research on gendered transformations in service work. Her work includes numerous ethnographic case studies. Recently her research has focused on call centres. She is interested in emotional and aesthetic work and cultural feminization of work.

## Joanne Martin

Joanne Martin is the Fred H. Merrill Professor of Organizational Behavior, Emerita, at the Graduate School of Business, Stanford University. Martin received a PhD in Social Psychology from Harvard in 1977 and honorary doctorates from Copenhagen Business School in 2001 and the Vrej University in Amsterdam in 2005. She is known for her research on income inequality and perceptions of injustice, and more recently, on conflicts and contradictions within organizational cultures (books include *Cultures in Organizations: Three Perspectives* and *Organizational Culture: Mapping the Terrain*). Her current research focuses on gender in organizations, including subtle barriers to advancement for women and how to structure equity interventions that create long lasting change. Martin has received numerous awards, including the Gordon Allport Intergroup Relations Award from the American Psychological Association in 1988 (for a paper with Thomas Pettigrew on barriers to inclusion for African-Americans); the Distinguished Educator Award from the Academy of Management in 2000 (for doctoral education), the Centennial Medal from the Graduate School of Arts and Sciences, Harvard University, (for research-based contributions to society) in 2002; and the Distinguished Scholar Career Achievement Award from the National Academy of Management, Organization and Management Theory Division, in 2005.

## Patricia Yancey Martin

Patricia Yancey Martin is sociologist and Emerita Professor at Florida State University (Tallahassee, Florida, USA) where she taught, conducted research, and supervised students for many years. She has published numerous articles and books on gender and organizations (including *Feminist Organizations: Harvest of the New Women's Movement* with M.M. Ferree and *Rape Work: Victims, Gender, and Emotions in Organization and Community Context*). She frequently serves as Visiting Professor at US. (e.g. University of Illinois at Chicago) and European universities (recently at Ruhr University in Bochum, Germany; Gothenburg University in Sweden; and Trento University in Italy). Her recent publications concern practicing gender at work (in *Gender, Work and Organization*), the emotions of working with rape cases (in Steve Fineman's book, *The Emotional Organization*), and rape crisis centers as transformative organizations (in Yeheskel Hasenfeld's book *Human Service Organizations*). In 2007, the American Sociological Association gave Martin the Jessie Bernard Award for her work on gender that 'is given in recognition of scholarly work that has enlarged the horizons of sociology to encompass fully the role of women in society.' Martin is widely recognized for her skills in teaching field work in organizations using grounded theory methods.

## Vedran Omanović

Vedran Omanović is a senior lecturer and researcher at the School of Business, Economics and Law, Gothenburg University, Sweden, where he also completed his doctorate. His research and teaching interests have focused on organization change, alternative paradigms, the notions of 'diversity in organizations' and (organizational) emancipating praxis. Recent publications include: Diversity and its Management as a Dialectical Process: Encountering Sweden and the U.S. (2009), *Scandinavian Journal of Management*, 25(4) 352–362; and *A Production of Diversity: Appearances, Ideas, Interests, Actions, Contradictions and Praxis* (Gothenburg, Sweden: BAS Publishing, 2006).

## ALISON PULLEN

Alison Pullen is based at Swansea University, Wales. Alison's research explores the intersections between gender, embodied subjectivity, and ethics as they relate to work and organization. Alison is an Associate Editor of *Gender, Work and Organization*.

## CARL RHODES

Carl Rhodes is Professor of Organization Studies at Swansea University. Carl has written on issues related to ethics in organizations, knowledge, and identity in organizations, and popular culture and organizations. His current research focuses on critically interrogating the narration and representation of organizational experience in practice and culture, with a particular concern with the possibilities for organizational justice, ethics, and responsibility. His recent books include *Bits of Organization* (Liber, 2009, with Alison Pullen) and *Critical Representations of Work and Organization in Popular Culture* (Routledge, 2008, with Robert Westwood).

## LAURA RHOTON

Laura Rhoton is a Post-doctoral research associate with the ADVANCE program at Iowa State University. Her work focuses on the gender practices and gender strategies of women working in the academic sciences.

## ORNA SASSON-LEVY

Orna Sasson-Levy is currently the head of the Department of Sociology and Anthropology, and teaches at the Gender Studies program at Bar Ilan University, Israel. Her research interests are feminist theory, militarism and gender, masculinities, new social movements, and race and ethnicity. She has published in the areas of femininities, masculinities, and military in *The Sociological Quarterly (2002), The Sociological Inquiry (2003)*, *Gender* & Society (2003; 2007) *Identities* (2003), *Signs* (2007), *Men and Masculinities* (2008), and *Sociological Perspectives* (2008). Sasson-Levy is the author of *Identities in Uniform: Masculinities and Femininities in the Israeli Military* (2006, in Hebrew). In her most recent research, Dr Sasson-Levy examines contemporary ethnic perceptions in Israel, with an emphasis on Ashkenaziyut (Jews of European descent).

## AMANDA SINCLAIR

Amanda Sinclair is Foundation Professor of Management (Diversity and Change), Melbourne Business School, The University of Melbourne. Her research and teaching is in leadership, gender and diversity, organisational culture, change and ethics. She is the author of several books including *Doing Leadership Differently* (1998; 2004) *New Faces of Leadership* (2002) and *Leadership for the Disillusioned* (2007). Amanda coaches individuals and senior management teams and, with colleagues, has pioneered new approaches to teaching and researching leadership, incorporating insights from meditative traditions, mindfulness research and her practice as a yoga and meditation teacher.

### Linda Smircich

Linda Smircich is Professor of Organization Studies at the Isenberg School of Management at the University of Massachusetts, Amherst, USA. Her research, in collaboration with Marta Calás, applies insights from cultural studies and feminist theorizing to organizational topics such as entrepreneurship, knowledge production, business ethics, globalization, leadership, and work and family. In 2006, Linda and Marta received the Sage Award for scholarly contributions from the Gender, Diversity and Organization division of the Academy of Management. Linda is part of the founding editorial team of *Organization: The critical journal of organization, theory and society* and on the editorial board of *Gender, Work, and Organization*.

### Torkild Thanem

Torkild Thanem is an Associate Professor at Stockholm University School of Business and has been a visiting scholar at the universities of Stanford, Oregon and Massachusetts-Amherst. Torkild is particularly interested in how embodiment, identity, space, and power are expressed in and around organizations. S/he sometimes, as in the chapter included in this Handbook, tries to explore these issues from a more embodied and personal perspective than is typically done in academic publications. S/he is Associate Editor of *Gender, Work and Organization*, in which s/he has also co-edited a special issue on sexual spaces. Torkild's research has been published in journals such as *Gender, Work and Organization*, *Organization*, and *Organization Studies*.

### Melissa Tyler

Melissa Tyler is a Reader in Management at the University of Essex. Her work on gender and feminist theory, sexuality and the body, and emotional and aesthetic forms of labour has been published in various international journals and edited collections. Recent books include *The Management of Everyday Life* (Palgrave, 2009), co-edited with Philip Hancock. Melissa's current research is an ethnographic study of emotional and aesthetic labour in sex shops in Soho, London.

### Mieke Verloo

Mieke Verloo combines working as Professor of Comparative Politics and Inequality Issues at Radboud University Nijmegen with being the Scientific Director of QUING, a 6th Framework Project, at the IWM in Vienna, see www.quing.eu. She studied sociology and urban planning, and finished her dissertation in policy studies at the Radboud University Nijmegen. Among her recent publications are *The Discursive Politics of Gender Equality. Stretching, Bending and Policy-Making* (Routledge, 2009) (co-edited with E. Lombardo and P. Meier); Dutch Women are Liberated, Migrant Women are a Problem, (2007) *Social Policy and Administration*, 41(3) 271–288, (co-authored with C. Roggeband); Displacement and Empowerment: Reflections on the Council of Europe Approach to Gender Mainstreaming and Gender Equality (2005) *Social Politics*,12(3) 344–366; and Multiple Inequalities, Intersectionality and the European Union (2006) *European Journal of Women's Studies*, 13(3) 211–229.

## Judy Wajcman

Judy Wajcman is Professor of Sociology at the London School of Economics and Political Science. She has held posts in Cambridge, Edinburgh, Manchester, Sydney, Tokyo, Vienna, Warwick and Zurich. Her scholarship has focused on the sociology of work and employment, science and technology studies, sociology of information and communication technologies, gender theory, and organizational analysis. Her books include *Managing Like a Man: Women and Men in Corporate Management, Feminism Confronts Technology, The Social Shaping of Technology, TechnoFeminism*, and *The Politics of Working Life*. Recent articles include: 'Life in the Fast lane? Towards a Sociology of Technology and Time', *British Journal of Sociology*, 59, 2008, 59–77; and 'Families without Borders: Mobile phones, connectedness and work-home divisions', *Sociology* 42, 2008, 635–652. She is currently President of the *Society for the Social Studies of Science*.

## Carol Wolkowitz

Carol Wolkowitz is a Reader in the Sociology Department at the University of Warwick. Her books include *Bodies at Work* (Sage, 2006) and, with others, a *Glossary of Feminist Theory* (Arnold, 2000). She was principal investigator on an ESRC-funded seminar series titled 'Body Work: Critical Issues, Future Agendas' (2007–9) and is co-editing a forthcoming Special Issue of the *Sociology of Health and Illness* on 'Body Work in Health and Social Care'. An article based on her personal reflections is included in a recent Special Issue of *Sociology* taking stock of recent developments in the sociology of work.

## Alison E. Woodward

Alison E. Woodward (PhD University of California, Berkeley) is Research Professor at the Free University of Brussels (VUB) and co-director of RHEA, the Center for Gender Studies and Diversity Research. Since 2008 she has been a Senior Fellow of the Institute for European Studies of the VUB. As professor or senior researcher she has been affiliated with universities in Sweden, Germany, the Netherlands, and the United States. Her research interests are in the field of comparative European Union public policy and organization. Her current research is on European transnational social movements (gender, sexuality, and ethnicity) and public policy. Her latest books are the co-edited volume with M. Franken, A. Cabo, and B. Bagihole, *Teaching Intersectionality: Putting Gender at the Center,* Central European University Press/ University of Stockholm Gender Studies (2009) and *Transforming Gendered Well-Being: The Impact of Social Movements* (with Jean-Michel Bonvin and Mercè Renom, eds) Ashgate (2010). Among recent journal articles is: Too Late for Mainstreaming: The View from Brussels (2008) *European Journal of Social Policy,* 18(3).

# Index